Sustainable Nutrition in a Changing World

Hans Konrad Biesalski · Adam Drewnowski
Johanna T. Dwyer · JJ Strain
Peter Weber · Manfred Eggersdorfer
Editors

Sustainable Nutrition in a Changing World

 Springer

Editors

Hans Konrad Biesalski
Department of Biological Chemistry
 and Nutrition
Universität Hohenheim
Stuttgart
Germany

Adam Drewnowski
Nutritional Sciences
University of Washington
Seattle, WA
USA

Johanna T. Dwyer
Frances Stern Nutrition Center
Tufts Medical School
Boston, MA
USA

JJ Strain
Northern Ireland Centre for Food and Health
University of Ulster
Coleraine, Northern Ireland
UK

Peter Weber
DSM Nutritional Products Europe Ltd.
Kaiseraugst
Switzerland

Manfred Eggersdorfer
DSM Nutritional Products Europe Ltd.
Kaiseraugst
Switzerland

and

Office of Dietary Supplements
National Institutes of Health
Bethesda, MD
USA

Copy-editing and editorial co-ordination by Jonathan Steffen Limited, Cambridge, UK.

ISBN 978-3-319-55940-7   ISBN 978-3-319-55942-1   (eBook)
DOI 10.1007/978-3-319-55942-1

Library of Congress Control Number: 2017935550

Printed on acid-free paper

This Springer imprint is published by Springer Nature
The registered company is Springer International Publishing AG
The registered company address is: Gewerbestrasse 11, 6330 Cham, Switzerland

Contents

Contributors

Regan L. Bailey Department of Nutrition Science, Purdue University, West Lafayette, IN, USA; Office of Dietary Supplements, National Institutes of Health, Bethesda, USA

Hans Konrad Biesalski Nutrition medicine, Department of Biological Chemistry and Nutrition, Food Security Center University Hohenheim, Stuttgart, Germany

France Caillavet ALISS, INRA, Ivry-Sur-Seine, France

Katia Castetbon Ecole de Santé Publique, Université Libre de Bruxelles, Brussels, Belgium

Nicole Darmon Human Nutrition Division, INRA, CIRAD, SupAgro, CIHEAM-IAMM, Montpellier, France

Adam Drewnowski Center for Public Health Nutrition, University of Washington, Seattle, WA, USA

Johanna T. Dwyer Office of Dietary Supplements, National Institutes of Health, Bethesda, MD, USA; The Jean Mayer US Department of Agriculture Human Nutrition Research Center on Aging, The School of Medicine, Friedman School of Nutrition Science and Policy, and the Frances Stern Nutrition Center, Tufts Medical Center, Tufts University, Boston, MA, USA

M. Eggersdorfer DSM Nutritional Products Ltd., R&D Human Nutrition and Health, Basel, Switzerland

Klaus G. Grunert Department of Management, MAPP Centre, Aarhus University, Aarhus C, Denmark

David I. Gustafson ILSI Research Foundation, Washington DC, USA

Leane Hoey Northern Ireland Centre for Food and Health (NICHE), Biomedical Sciences Research Institute, University of Ulster, Coleraine, Northern Ireland, UK

Catherine Hughes Northern Ireland Centre for Food and Health (NICHE), Biomedical Sciences Research Institute, University of Ulster, Coleraine, Northern Ireland, UK

Janet H. Matope Nestlé Research Center, Vers Chez Les Blancs, Switzerland

Helene McNulty Northern Ireland Centre for Food and Health (NICHE), Biomedical Sciences Research Institute, University of Ulster, Coleraine, Northern Ireland, UK

Carl Meißner Klinikum Magdeburg Gemeinnützige GmbH, Klinik Für Allgemein- Und Viszeralchirurgie, Magdeburg, Germany

Alida Melse-Boonstra Division of Human Nutrition, Wageningen University and Research, Wageningen, The Netherlands

M.H. Mohajeri DSM Nutritional Products Ltd., R&D Human Nutrition and Health, Basel, Switzerland

Elke Oestreicher University of Hohenheim, Stuttgart, Germany

Kristina Pentieva Northern Ireland Centre for Food and Health (NICHE), Biomedical Sciences Research Institute, University of Ulster, Coleraine, Northern Ireland, UK

Andreas F.H. Pfeiffer Abteilung für Endokrinologie, Diabetes und Ernährungsmedizin, Charité—Universitätsmedizin Berlin (CBF), Berlin, Germany

Sabine Pfeiffer University of Hohenheim, Stuttgart, Germany

Marc Pignitter Department of Nutritional and Physiological Chemistry, Faculty of Chemistry, University of Vienna, Vienna, Austria

Tobias Ritter Institute for Social Science Research (ISF Munich), Munich, Germany

Jana Rückert-John Fachbereich Oecotrophologie, Hochschule Fulda, Fulda, Germany

Wim H.M. Saris Department of Human Biology, NUTRIM School for Nutrition and Translational Research in Metabolism, Maastricht University Medical Center, Maastricht, The Netherlands

Loni Schweikert DSM Nutritional Products Ltd., Kaiseraugst, Switzerland

Klaus Schümann Research Center for Nutrition and Food Science, Technische Universität München, Freising, Germany

Noel W. Solomons Center for Studies of Sensory Impairment, Aging and Metabolism (CeSSIAM), Guatemala City, Guatemala

Veronika Somoza Department of Nutritional and Physiological Chemistry, Faculty of Chemistry, University of Vienna, Vienna, Austria

Jörg Spieldenner Nestlé Research Center, Vers Chez Les Blancs, Switzerland

JJ Strain Northern Ireland Centre for Food and Health (NICHE), Biomedical Sciences Research Institute, University of Ulster, Coleraine, Northern Ireland, UK

Barbara Troesch DSM Nutritional Products Ltd, Kaiseraugst, Switzerland

Christina Tzogiou Winterthur Institute of Health Economics, Zurich University of Applied Sciences, Winterthur, Switzerland

M.A.J.S. (Tiny) van Boekel Wageningen University, Wageningen, The Netherlands

Christine A.F. von Arnim Neurologische Universitätsklinik Ulm, Ulm, Germany

Mary Ward Northern Ireland Centre for Food and Health (NICHE), Biomedical Sciences Research Institute, University of Ulster, Coleraine, Northern Ireland, UK

Gilbert M. Weber DSM Nutritional Products, Nutrition Innovation Center, Kaiseraugst, Switzerland

Peter Weber DSM Nutritional Products Europe Ltd, Kaiseraugst, Switzerland

Simon Wieser Winterthur Institute of Health Economics, Zurich University of Applied Sciences, Winterthur, Switzerland

Wilhelm Windisch Institute for Animal Nutrition, Technical University of Munich, Freising, Germany

Marcel Wubbolts Royal DSM, Sittard, The Netherlands

Introduction

Our societies and health systems are faced with a growing problem: affluence. In 1958, the economist J.K. Galbraith published a book entitled *The Affluent Society*, which investigated why in the US the public sector remained poor while the private sector was growing richer all the time. This is precisely the situation in today's affluent societies, in which social inequalities are becoming ever more apparent. Increasing social inequalities will inevitably drive up the numbers of people suffering from food insecurity. This trend will be compounded by modern lifestyles, which often lack the traditional characteristics of family life—with no daily shared meals, for instance, and a prevailing lack of knowledge regarding food and how to prepare it. For many time-poor people, fast food is the answer. But it is not necessarily the best answer in nutritional terms, and widespread societal reliance on fast food and processed foods will have serious, long-term health consequences for the world's population.

This book discusses many aspects of food security and ways of overcoming food insecurity. In the 2001 definition of the United Nations Food & Agriculture Organization (FAO), *Food security [is] a situation that exists when all people, at all times, have physical, social and economic access to sufficient, safe and nutritious food that meets their dietary needs and food preferences for an active and healthy life.*[1] To achieve food security in the terms of this definition will be one of the major challenges of our century.

This definition implicitly includes one major aspect of food security not directly mentioned: sustainability. Food security is a situation which guarantees access to food that is not only sufficient in terms of the calories it provides (quantity) but also sufficiently nutritious in terms of the micronutrients it supplies (quality). Both are necessary to meet dietary requirements for a healthy and active life.

---

[1]FAO, 2001, The State of Food Insecurity in the World.

Sustainable Food Security

To understand the concept of sustainable food security, it is first necessary to understand what sustainability means in the context of food security. It is also essential to understand who is at risk of food insecurity and why. Sustainability depends on many factors, including cultural context, food taboos and food trends. Ultimately, however, the major focus of sustainable food security is health. Food security may be defined as the availability of food that provides a nutritious diet, supports health, and helps prevent non-communicable diseases (NCDs). However, most studies dealing with healthy diets and the prevention of NCDs fail to show a significant or scientifically proven effect in the diets investigated. To what extent, for instance, is it possible to transfer the healthy diet of Japanese people to a European context? Would this diet have the same health effects in Europe as in Japan? Or consider the diet of farmers on Crete in the 1950s, termed the Cretan or Mediterranean Diet and based on the Seven Countries study published by Ancel Keys in 1970. Keys' conclusion that the Mediterranean Diet is healthy because of its low levels of saturated fatty acids is no longer tenable. Would the Mediterranean Diet be a healthy diet for the Japanese or the Norwegians?

This is a matter of debate. Moreover, the increasing volume of scientific evidence that the epigenome, driven by the diet during the 1000-day window and in later life too, has a massive impact on our risk of developing an NCD, makes the concept of a 'healthy diet' more and more questionable.

On top of this, changes in lifestyles and workloads, as well as increasing urbanization, will change what we eat and how we eat it. For it is economic access to food that ultimately defines food security and consequently health. How can sustainable diets be guaranteed? Is a specific type of diet or a particular form of dietary diversity healthy and sustainable for everyone? Indeed, how can the concept of a sustainable, healthy diet be defined at all without considering all the factors involved?

This answer is in fact rather simple: *A healthy diet is one which will not make me sick!*

Sustainable and Healthy Nutrition

Disregarding food which is contaminated with chemicals, bacteria or mold, a diet that lacks any key element such as an essential vitamin or mineral may be harmful to health. A sustainable diet that ensures food security must therefore contain all essential nutrients so as to pre-empt dietary deficiencies and the attendant risk of disease.

The book addresses a range of approaches for ensuring sustainable and at least healthy nutrition in a changing world. The big issue is that global economic pressures, exacerbated by climate change, may push agribusiness toward producing more low-cost calories. This may result in most people consuming a diet predominantly based on staples such as corn, soy, rice and further starchy plant resources which provide energy but are poor in micronutrients.

The challenge is not about producing food in sufficient quantities, but rather about producing food of sufficient quality. Three billion people worldwide suffer from malnutrition, and in particular from inadequate dietary supplies of iron, zinc, iodine, and vitamins D and A. Malnutrition during pregnancy has an especially powerful impact on early development. It exerts a massive influence on physical and cognitive development during childhood. The phenotype of malnutrition which is often not visible is stunting. 180 million children worldwide are stunted and will consequently be impaired with respect to their further lives and ability to work and earn a living. And while malnutrition occurs more commonly in low-income countries, it is also an increasing problem in countries with high incomes.

Groups at risk need to be defined, as do the levels of micronutrient density (quality) within the various foods that are required for delivering sustainable food security. In terms of affordability, the relationship between price and dietary quality needs to be controlled, and issues of cultural acceptance must be appropriately managed. Social disparities will be critically linked to the accessibility of food of adequate quality.

To address all these critical components of food security and achieve a sustainable food-based approach, the industry is faced with a variety of challenges.

Challenges for the Food Industry

At a systemic level, interventions should include agro-industry initiatives, from crop modeling to product reformulation, including biofortification with micronutrients. On the individual level, interventions should focus on education and lifestyle. Food choices and the parameters affecting them need to be explored. The diet of today's generation includes special (self-selected) diets (e.g. vegetarian, vegan, superfood) that may have an impact on sustainability, carbon footprint, water resources and so on, but which may also have an impact on the food security of the individual who consumes them.

As defined by the FAO, sustainable diets are: "diets with low environmental impacts which contribute to food and nutrition security and to healthy life for present and future generations. Sustainable diets are protective and respectful of biodiversity and ecosystems, culturally acceptable, accessible, economically fair and affordable; nutritionally adequate, safe and healthy, while optimizing natural and human resources."[2]

Finally, how can we improve nutrition security in line with demographic changes, in particular with differences in socio-economic status and evolutions of

---

[2]FAO, 2010, Sustainable Diets and Biodiversity.

lifestyles? We need an approach whereby all people, regardless of their age and social status, have access to safe and nutritious food. Key stakeholders such as politicians, government agencies, academia, science and the food industry, as well as consumers themselves, have an important role to play here.

Learning from Each Other

We need to put the issues of the developing countries back into a global perspective once more, as the developing and developed worlds are increasingly interconnected and dependent on each other. Indeed, the two worlds can learn from each other. This book seeks to address the opportunities for multi-sector interventions to ensure nutrition security in a changing world.

Hans Konrad Biesalski

Part I
Food and Nutrition Security
(Johanna Dwyer/Adam Drewnowski)

Chapter 1
Overview: Food and Nutrition Security

Johanna T. Dwyer and Adam Drewnowski

Abstract This chapter discusses the human right to food and nutrition security. Sustainable food and nutrition security has four key components: the nutritional quality of foods and diets, their cost, cultural acceptance, and their impact on the environment. Sustainable diets call for foods that are healthy and safe, nutrient-rich, affordable, culturally acceptable, and appealing. The environmental impact of the food supply system must be considered and steps taken to minimize the impact of eating patterns on land, water, and energy use. Nutrient density of processed foods is another matter for concern. Given global economic pressures, the effects of climate change, marketing considerations and other factors, there is a growing trend for the agricultural and food industries to produce foods that are inexpensive sources of calories but have minimal nutritional value. Food and nutrition insecurity and malnutrition are widespread in many low- and middle-income countries (LMIC). They also exist to a lesser extent in some high-income countries (HIC). While the public health focus has been on diet-related non-communicable diseases (NCDs), hidden hunger and dietary deficiency diseases must be identified and managed both in LMIC and in HIC. Effective management of resources by both the public and the private sector will be required to develop a sustainable food supply

J.T. Dwyer (✉)
Office of Dietary Supplements, National Institutes of Health,
6100 Executive Blvd, Bethesda, MD 20892, USA
e-mail: Dwyerj1@od.nih.gov; Jdwyer1@tuftsmedicalcenter.org

J.T. Dwyer
The Jean Mayer US Department of Agriculture Human Nutrition Research Center on Aging,
The School of Medicine, Friedman School of Nutrition Science and Policy, and the Frances
Stern Nutrition Center, Tufts Medical Center, Tufts University, Boston, MA 02111, USA

A. Drewnowski
Center for Public Health Nutrition, University of Washington,
Seattle, WA 98195, USA
e-mail: adrewnow@fredhutch.org

© Springer International Publishing AG 2017
H.K. Biesalski et al. (eds.), *Sustainable Nutrition in a Changing World*,
DOI 10.1007/978-3-319-55942-1_1

and to ensure equitable access to nutrient-rich foods by vulnerable groups. Political will, along with adequate economic and human resources, will be essential to achieve this.

Keywords Dimensions of food and nutrition security · Nutritional quality · Affordability and availability · Cultural acceptability · Environmental impact of the diet · Low- and middle-income countries (LMIC) · High-income countries (HIC)

1.1   State of the Art

The need for a secure food supply has always shaped our lives as human beings. The profound effects of the prehistoric agricultural revolutions on human civilizations and human health are well recognized. Farming, including the farming of cereals and livestock, remains at the center of securing the global food supply. Based on data from the Food and Agricultural Organization (FAO), most food needs of low- and middle-income countries (LMIC) today are still being met by small family farms.

However, the growing urbanization of the world's populations poses new challenges to existing food systems. Isolated from means of food production, urban dwellers depend on a longer food supply chain and on more complex systems of food storage, distribution, and retail. The dramatic changes in the relations between urban populations and food production, processing, transport, sales, and disposal have been amply documented by social historians [22]. But there is a new element to urbanization that cannot be ignored. Some of the most rapidly growing megacities are now located in LMIC, rather than in high-income countries (HIC). The combination of poverty and urbanization can have dire consequences for food security and nutrition worldwide.

This overview discusses the human right to food and food security. The factors that must be considered to achieve food and nutrition security will be reviewed, and the present state of world food and nutrition security briefly outlined. We conclude by listing some challenges that must be addressed to ensure food and nutrition security for the increasingly urban world.

1.2   The Right to Food and Food Security

Foods that provide the energy and essential nutrients that all humans require to live and thrive are the building blocks of healthy diets and sound nutritional status. The International Covenant on Economic, Social and Cultural Rights recognizes the human right to an adequate standard of living, including adequate food, and the right of all human beings to be free from hunger [11].

The concept of food and nutrition security initially emphasized food availability and the need to re-balance unequal food distribution at the national or regional level. This concept has been broadened since then to include adequate access to food by all people at all times so that they can pursue active, healthy lives. In the 1950s, food security referred to concerns about distributing surplus foods. By the 1960s the concept extended to providing sufficient food for development, and then in the 1970s to assuring an adequate food supply for all. Still broader views of food security emerged in the 1980s and 1990s, with a more explicit consideration of population nutritional status. Today, the term food security implies the goal of freedom from hunger and malnutrition for all human beings.

It is important to consider the root causes of food insecurity as well as the significance not only of food availability and carrying capacity but also of the role of existing environmental conditions and health services in overcoming them. All of those components are needed to ensure satisfactory nutritional status for the world's peoples over the long term.

1.3 Domains of Food and Nutrition Security

The four dimensions of food and nutrition security are: nutritional quality; affordability and availability; cultural acceptability; and environmental impact of the diet (Fig. 1.1). All of these must be considered in assessing and planning diets. The key domains of food and nutrition security and some possible useful metrics are discussed elsewhere in this volume.

Fig. 1.1 Domains of food and nutrition security. *Source* Created by Johanna T. Dwyer for this publication

1.3.1   The Nutritional Quality of Foods and Eating Patterns

1.3.1.1   Individual Foods Vary in Energy and Nutrient Content

Human beings do not require individual foods to survive; they require optimal combinations of nutrients. Foods in a nutritious diet vary greatly in their biological composition and in their content of essential nutrients. Individual foods vary in food energy (kilocalories) per gram, in macronutrients (carbohydrate, protein, fat, alcohol) and in micronutrient content (vitamins, minerals, choline, dietary fiber). Foods also contain other non-essential bioactive constituents that may themselves have health effects. Very few foods as found in nature are nutritionally complete, in the sense that they contain all essential nutrients. The exception is breast milk, which suffices for the first few months of life. Human needs are therefore best met by consuming combinations of foods that include a variety of both plant and animal foods.

Plant foods contain many essential nutrients, but lack preformed vitamin A, vitamin B_{12}, vitamin D, and choline. Present in plant foods, but in insufficient quantities, are calcium, iron, zinc, and possibly riboflavin. Some plant foods contain proteins with a profile of amino acids that is well suited to human needs, while others may contain some, but not all, of the essential amino acids. Those foods must be combined with other plant or animal foods in order to fulfill human protein needs. By contrast, animal foods usually contain high-quality protein with the entire complement of amino acids.

Some animal foods, such as milk and milk products, are rich in calcium and riboflavin; meats are rich in iron, calcium and zinc; and eggs are rich in vitamin B_{12} and choline. Animal foods are also protein-rich but poor in dietary fiber. In some countries, certain staple foods such as milk, breads and cereals are fortified with micronutrients that might otherwise be low in the population's diets.

It must be noted that individual foods are neither inherently 'healthy' nor 'unhealthy'. The exception is foods that contain a bioactive substance such as an allergen that may be deemed unhealthy for particular individuals, or toxins that make it unsuitable for all individuals or groups.

1.3.1.2   Dietary Patterns Vary in Energy and in Nutrient Content

Malnutrition is a world-wide problem with considerable social and economic costs. Although undernutrition is still a problem in many regions of the world, leading to classical dietary deficiency diseases, today malnutrition can also result from dietary excesses and imbalances that lead to diet-related non-communicable diseases (NCDs). The burden of chronic disease as measured in disability-adjusted life years (DALYs) due to NCDs is also considerable. The problem is further complicated by the fact that in the same country both under- and over-nutrition can occur at the same time in different groups, and sometimes even in the same individuals.

Determining the health impact of different dietary patterns is a continuing challenge. Inadequacies, imbalances and excesses of nutrients may all adversely affect diet quality and health. Many different dietary—and non-dietary—factors come into play to increase or decrease NCD risks at the population level. It is the totality of intake of nutrients from foods, dietary supplements, and nutrient-containing over-the-counter medications that determines nutrient exposure. It is well known that nutrients and other bioactive constituents in foods interact with each other; the totality of intakes also takes these interactions into account.

Dietary patterns must always be considered in the contexts in which they occur. Social scientists tell us that it is impossible to separate a food from the person who consumes it and that person from the wider society. Chronic non-communicable diseases have multiple causes that can include dietary constituents but also other inherited and environmental factors, and their prevalence is often associated with education, incomes and other aspects of socio-economic status (SES) or social class.

Ecological studies conducted some years ago pointed to cross-cultural differences in eating habits as potential determinants of NCD risk. Unfortunately, in those studies many socio-cultural and environmental factors other than diet also varied across populations. Given their cross-sectional design, such studies lacked strong causal inference for linking the diets to disease. While they were interesting, they were hypothesis-generating, rather than definitive.

Another approach to the study of different dietary patterns and health outcomes has made extensive use of the longitudinal cohort design, whereby baseline diets of a population are linked to morbidity and mortality at some point later in time. However, such observational cohort studies can be confounded by other health-related factors—from smoking through body weight to social class—that exist in the same populations. Given that the many unobserved components of social class are not easily controlled using a linear regression model or other methods of statistical analysis, the potential causal links between specific dietary constituents and NCDs often remain obscure.

Yet another approach to the study of diet and disease has focused on dietary patterns that are identified using various statistical methods such as factor analysis. The intent was to identify those dietary patterns that seemed to be most strongly associated with healthy outcomes. However, the optimal results generated by factor analysis do not necessarily conform to acceptable dietary patterns for people, and thus are not very useful. The most healthful patterns also vary depending on the eating habits of the population that is being studied. What is acceptable to one population may not be so to another.

Taken together, the studies suggest that the consumption of adequate, but not excessive, amounts of energy and nutrient-dense foods, coupled with a physically active life and the maintenance of body weight in the healthy range, leads to lower morbidity and mortality from diet-related disease. Some eating patterns lead to better health outcomes than do others. Identifying optimal eating habits was the basis of the recommendations of the second FAO International Conference on Nutrition in 2014 for altering diets in more healthful directions [21].

1.3.1.3 Food Safety Is an Essential Component of Dietary Quality

Foods must be both nutritious and safe to eat. The definition of food and nutrition security must therefore include food safety considerations. The importance of food safety is well understood when low- and middle-income countries are being considered, but it is often neglected in the context of high-income countries. Yet foodborne illness is a serious problem in both LMIC and HIC, causing considerable morbidity and mortality.

Dietary patterns therefore also vary in the degree to which they fulfill human nutritional needs and avoid food-borne illness. There are thousands of permutations and combinations of foods that can make up healthy dietary patterns if they are available in sufficient amounts to provide the essential nutrients to satisfy human nutrient requirements. 'Healthy' dietary patterns are sufficient in food energy and other nutrients, without being excessive, and are free of food-borne illness.

Some foods and some food systems are more likely to be associated with food-borne illness and spoilage than others. Some foods contain naturally-occurring bioactive constituents that are harmful to human health which may be removed by food processing, and other foods become contaminated with microorganisms or other pathogens during food storage or preparation. Under modern conditions, a food supply that includes safe, processed foods is essential for food and nutrition security [25].

A report of a workshop on food safety at the US National Academy of Sciences (NAS) concluded that the food supply in the USA is abundant and affordable, but that new food safety problems have arisen which must be dealt with if diets are to be wholesome and healthful [9]. Whereas in the past, the food supply provided consumers with minimally processed basic commodities destined for home preparation and cooking, the modern food supply is geared toward processed products that are either ready to eat or else require only minimal preparation in the home. These technological advances have meant that the food system has progressed dramatically from traditional food preservation processes such as salting and curing to today's marketplace, with frozen ready-to-eat meals and take-out foods.

The microbiological and chemical hazards that are now present in the food supply entail new and increasingly serious challenges which cannot be detected using traditional inspection methods. Likewise, distribution systems for foods have changed greatly. Modern systems provide consumers with a wide array of food products with a high degree of safety, but the more diverse food supply of today carries additional risks as well as benefits. The availability of new food choices such as 'minimally processed' vegetable products (for example, pre-bagged and chopped leaf lettuce mixes) presents benefits but also new risks for microbial contamination.

The NAS report also observed that globalization of the food system brings food from all parts of the world into the HIC marketplace, and with it the potential for food-borne infection or other hazards that are not normally found in rich countries. Further, food patterns increasingly prevalent in HIC tend to increase the risk of food-borne illness through heightened consumption of minimally processed fruits and vegetables and reduced consumption of home-prepared meals. A smaller number of food processing and preparation facilities provide food to increasingly larger numbers of consumers, enhancing the extent of harm that can arise from any one incident. Simultaneously, more people have compromised immune systems because of age, illness, or medical treatment.

High-income countries, including the US, now face multiple food safety problems. These include emerging pathogens and the ability to detect them; maintaining adequate inspection and monitoring of the increasing volume of imported foods, especially of fruits and vegetables; maintaining adequate inspection of commercial food services and the increasing number of larger food processing plants; and the growing number of people at high risk of foodborne illnesses [9].

In order to deal with these pressures, food safety systems must be science-based, with a strong emphasis on risk analysis and prevention, and with resources and activities prioritized to address those risks deemed to have the greatest potential impact. Food safety systems should also be based on national food law that is clear, rational, and scientifically based on risk; and they should include comprehensive surveillance and monitoring activities which may serve as a basis for risk analysis [9].

The development of genetically modified foods, irradiated foods, and modified macronutrients are three examples of new products or technologies that require new ways of evaluating the safety of substances added to the food supply. These same concerns appear to apply to many other high- and middle-income countries.

1.3.1.4 The Importance of Food Processing in Modern Food Systems

Processes and technologies that alter the characteristics of foods may have beneficial or detrimental effects on diet quality and health. For example, some foods are enriched or fortified to improve their nutrient composition, while others are altered by biofortification, other biotechnologies or traditional plant breeding to improve their nutritional or other characteristics. However, improper processing can also destroy nutrients and contaminants.

Processed and unprocessed foods can also be contaminated with microorganisms, filth and other toxic substances such as heavy metals, pesticides, drugs, and other contaminants. The probability of these hazards occurring varies from food to food and from one environment to another. Foods, diets and dietary patterns also differ in the extent to which they are influenced for good or ill by other extrinsic factors. Environmental contaminants in a food and foodborne illness can make foods unhealthy. The processing of foods can improve diets by adding fortificants or other constituents so that overall intakes are more adequate, by preserving foods better, decreasing waste, and improving attractiveness and/or decreasing cost. However, inappropriate processing can remove or alter essential nutrients, introduce toxic contaminants, and increase food waste.

Some experts claim that human health cannot be divorced from the health of ecosystems. According to this view, unprocessed or moderately unprocessed food remains the best way to supply ideal nutrition for people at all ages and life stages. Hence, conservation and sustainable use of food biodiversity become an important part of well-being associated with health and the environment [3]. Others argue that while these considerations are important, food safety as well as affordability must also be considered. In that view, processed foods represent an integral component of sustainable food and nutrition security. Limiting population diets exclusively to unprocessed or moderately processed foods will be difficult, if not impossible, to achieve [8]. Such diets may not conform to the sustainability criteria of safe, adequate nutrition at low cost.

1.3.1.5   The Cost and Affordability of Foods and Eating Patterns

Foods vary greatly in their cost and affordability. They differ in their costs of production, transport and storage, and can be perceived as affordable or otherwise by the consumer. Food availability can depend on multiple factors. The foods that are available at any given time and place depend on economics but also on the environment, as well as on human interactions with it and the food system, such as processing, preservation, trade, and culture. In urban environments, reliance on foods that are processed to preserve them on their journey from where they are produced to where they are consumed is necessary [6].

Dietary patterns that vary in their affordability have become reliable indicators of socioeconomic status. The associations between food, health and income have been apparent for over a century, as has the recommendation that such associations be included in developing dietary recommendations [2]. The critical importance of nutrition economics must not be forgotten in developing recommendations for healthy diets in all countries. Even in high-income countries such as the USA, some of the differences in diet quality across population subgroups, often attributed to ethnicity or culture, may be linked to the low cost of empty calories and the higher cost of many nutrient-rich foods. Poverty is one important driver of food choice [4].

1.3.2   Cultural Acceptability of Foods and Eating Patterns

The acceptability of specific foods varies from one person to another as well as across cultures. Culturally acceptable eating patterns vary both within and across populations. The specific sets of traditions and practices associated with eating patterns that have to do with cooking and food preparation are often referred to using the collective term cuisine. The end result is a particular style of eating and drinking that has distinct and identifiable characteristics. Cuisines are often associated with a particular place or region and sometimes with ethnic groups as well. They are heavily influenced by what foods and ingredients are available locally or by trade, religion and history, as well as culinary and food preservation techniques and lifestyles [13].

The world's eating patterns, foodways, and the major regional cuisines are all affected by geographic differences in climate, cooking traditions and cultures. The influences of factors such as climate change and urbanization are introducing modifications, but the eating patterns and cuisines still remain quite distinctive, being closely guarded and beloved aspects of culture that change only very slowly. It is unrealistic to assume that people will change their traditional diets rapidly and voluntarily. Nonetheless, global homogenization is taking place to a considerable degree. Today, regional eating patterns can be based both on traditional cuisines and on more modern adaptations, occasioned by the nutrition transition. In addition to regional cuisines, global cuisines are emerging that are practiced around the world, with their foods served worldwide.

The traditional eating patterns of Africa use locally available vegetables and cereal grains along with fruits and milk and meat products. They vary greatly from region to region. Asian eating patterns also vary greatly by region, ranging from the Central Asian emphasis on mutton and milk products (reflecting nomadic ways of life) to many others. When it comes to food preparation styles, East Asian cuisines include Japanese and many different Chinese cuisines: Szechuan (from Sichuan, with bold flavors using garlic, peppers, peanuts and sesame paste), Cantonese (from Guangdong, which is heavy on seafood), Mandarin (Beijing or Jing cuisine, heavily influenced by Shandong cuisine), Huaiyang cuisine (from Jiangsu, heavy on seafood and fish, and soup), and others such as Zhejiang, Anhui, and Hunan. Southeast Asian cuisines include the use of fish sauces and many herbs and spices, and employ stir-frying as well as boiling and steaming. South Asian foods served in the Indian subcontinent are influenced by Hindu beliefs and use strong spices, ghee, and meats other than beef, with rice, wheat and barley cakes, and beans.

Western Asian and Middle Eastern cuisines include sesame seed paste, lamb, olives, dates, chickpeas and many other vegetables. Pork is not consumed in the cuisines of Moslem countries. The cuisines of Oceania include the native cuisines of the islands and island groups of Oceania, as well as those native to Australia and New Zealand. Regionally grown produce such as sweet potatoes, yams, cassava, and fresh seafood, as well as pork, are common in the island communities.

European eating patterns were exported to the Americas along with the immigrants who colonized those continents, and they build on native cuisines. Their influence can also vary greatly from one region to another: in the United States and Canada, northern European influences are notable, while in South and Central America, southern European and traditional indigenous diets are more common. Meat is more prominent in North America, and larger portions are served. Wheat flour-based bread, pasta, dumplings, pastries and potatoes are the staple starchy foods consumed.

1.3.3   Environmental Impact on Land, Water and Air Quality

A sustainable food system is one that conserves the ecological balance by avoiding undue depletion of natural resources. As we have just seen, there are very large differences in the sustainability of staples and other foods, as well as in the food-ways that are prevalent in different parts of the world. The influences of factors such as climate change and urbanization are effecting transformations in certain eating habits, but eating patterns still remain distinct from place to place, and change only slowly.

Research on climate change in relation to food and nutrition security can be divided into two principal areas. One approach is to examine the likely impact of global warming, water shortages and catastrophic weather events on future agricultural production and the food supply. Future weather may drive future eating habits. The opposite approach is to examine the current eating patterns, and the consumption of animal and plant foods in particular, in relation to the depletion of natural resources and greenhouse gas emissions. Our present eating habits are capable of driving climate change. Considerations of food loss and food waste have also risen to prominence in recent years.

1.4   Links Between Food and Nutrition Security, Nutritional Status, and Health Outcomes in Populations

The multiple dimensions of food and nutrition security can also be conceptualized as categorical, temporal, socio-organizational, managerial, and situation-related [7]. The categorical or explicit dimension is that food availability, accessibility and utilization (human metabolism) are necessary for achieving and maintaining good nutritional status. Food and nutrition security are achieved if food is adequate in terms of quantity, quality, safety, and affordability, and is socio-culturally acceptable to the consumer. However, the food must also be environmentally sustainable in the long term. The temporal dimension is that availability, accessibility and utilization must be maintained in order to achieve and preserve nutritional status. The managerial and situation-related dimensions involve ensuring that all the domains of food and nutrition security are attended to and sustained over time [7]. All of these are essential to achieve the goal of ensuring good nutritional status and beneficial health outcomes in populations.

There is no legal definition of a sustainable food supply, of sustainable food and nutrition security, or of sustainable development. However, popular definitions of these terms do exist, some of which have been codified into the laws of various countries.

1.4.1 USA Case Study

The 1977 and 1990 USA Farm Bills describe sustainable agriculture with respect to food as an integrated system of plant and animal production practices that will, in the long term, satisfy human food needs, enhance environmental quality along with the natural resource base upon which the agricultural economy depends, and make the most efficient use of non-renewable resources and on-farm resources. In addition, the system is expected to integrate, where appropriate, natural biological cycles and controls, to sustain the economic viability of farm operations, and to enhance the quality of life for farmers and society as a whole [15].

The 2009 Committee on 21st Century Systems Agriculture of the US National Academies of Science identified four generally agreed goals that help define sustainable agriculture: *Satisfy human food, feed, and fiber needs and contribute to biofuel needs; Enhance environmental quality and the resource base; Sustain the economic viability of agriculture;* and *Enhance the quality of life for farmers, farm workers and society as a whole.* The report further specified that sustainability would be best evaluated not simply as an end-state but rather as a process that moves farming systems along a trajectory toward greater sustainability vis-à-vis each of the goals [16].

The US Department of Agriculture Consensus Statement of 2011 expressed its commitment to working with partners and stakeholders toward the sustainability of diverse agricultural, forest and mountain range systems. It sought to balance the diverse goals of: *Satisfying human needs; Enhancing environmental quality, the resource base, and ecosystem services; Sustaining the economic viability of agriculture;* and *Enhancing the quality of life for farmers, ranchers, and society as a whole* [24].

1.4.2 International Arena

The groundbreaking Brundtland Report to the UN in 1987 described sustainable development as meeting the needs of the present without compromising the ability of future generations to meet their own needs. It included the concept of 'needs'—in particular, the essential needs of the world's poor, to which overriding priority should be given, and the idea of limitations imposed by the state of technology and social organization on the environment's ability to meet present and future needs [19].

The British Royal Society stated in 2009 that sustainability in the context of agricultural and food production "incorporates four key principles: (1) *persistence*: the capacity to continue to deliver desired outputs over long periods of time (human generations), thus conferring predictability; (2) *resilience*: the capacity to absorb, utilize or even benefit from perturbations (shocks and stresses), and so persist without qualitative changes in structure; (3) *autarchy*: the capacity to deliver desired outputs from inputs and resources (factors of production) acquired from within key system boundaries; and (4) *benevolence*: the capacity to produce desired outputs (food, fiber, fuel, oil) while sustaining the functioning of ecosystem services and not causing depletion of natural capital (e.g. minerals, biodiversity, soil, clean water). A system is unsustainable if it depends on non-renewable inputs, cannot consistently and predictably deliver desired outputs, can only do this by requiring the cultivation of more land, and/or causes adverse and irreversible environmental impacts which threaten critical ecological functions" [23, p. 6].

Foods and food production systems vary in terms of the environmental resources they use. Some are very resource-intensive and stable, while others are not. The environmental burden caused by plants is generally less than that caused by the animal foods that are derived from them. Certain animal foods, such as poultry and eggs, have lower environmental impacts than others, such as beef and pork. The livestock industry in particular contributes greatly to environmental problems in most of the world. However, the very foods with the highest environmental impacts are also often those that are the most preferred—and are also, by some measures, the most nutrient-rich. Dietary recommendations may thus sometimes have either adverse or beneficial environmental impacts. The propensity to spoilage and waste also varies across food groups.

Food systems in high-income countries provide a safe, nutritious and consistent food supply. However, they also place significant strains on land, water, air and other natural resources. This state of affairs has led to attempts to develop dietary recommendations based on nutritional, and also environmental, considerations. However, it has been difficult to identify what the trade-offs should be, due to a lack of agreed definitions of environmental impact and questions concerning whether food prices must also be considered in discussions of sustainability. Other points at issue include the most appropriate metrics for describing greenhouse gas or other emissions; the lack of collaboration between the disciplines involved; the question of whether or not cultural acceptability should be emphasized; and the influence of economics, food processing and waste on food availability and food security [8].

1.5 Dietary Recommendations to Ensure Sustainable Food Security

Several general principles are helpful for developing dietary recommendations.

1.5.1 Food Biodiversity Must Be Preserved

Biodiversity is the cornerstone of human existence as well as a source of human enjoyment. Most food is of plant origin, and the biodiversity of plants is considerable, with approximately 20,000 species and many different cultivars among them being grown for food. Actually the vast majority of the world's food (over 90%) comes from only 20 of the edible plant species. Animals bred for food are raised by feeding plant foods to them, and fish are caught after consuming plants. Preservation of the biodiversity of the earth's 80,000 edible plants helps to protect the larger environment. Plants, bacteria and fungi break down organic matter and fertilize the soil. Wetlands filter pollutants from water. Trees and plants absorb carbon and reduce global warming. Biodiversity may also add to future food and nutrition security. For example, cross-breeding cultivars with their wild counterparts may confer resistance to diseases and increase crop yields. Other species may be exploitable for feeding humans. Efforts to preserve biodiversity and minimize adverse environmental impacts on food production are relevant to food and nutrition security for all these reasons.

1.5.2 Sustainable Dietary Patterns Can Combine Animal and Plant Foods

Combinations of foods regularly selected by humans are often called dietary patterns. Dietary patterns vary in several ways that may also have an impact on food and nutrition security and sustainability. Among myriad possible patterns, there are usually several cuisines that are particularly popular among various regions and cultures. Only a small percentage of the many species of plant and animal foods are staple foods in these cuisines. In terms of food and nutrition security, it is particularly important to ensure that those species that are so essential to traditional cuisines and patterns are preserved and conserved.

Dietary patterns vary in terms of the environmental impacts that result from their production. Diets and dietary patterns also vary in their sustainability, as well as in their propensity to immediate spoilage and waste: some are very stable, others are not. Gustafson discusses these aspects in greater depth in his chapter (Gustafson this volume).

1.5.3 It is Challenging for Diets to be Nutrient-Rich, Safe, Affordable, Culturally Acceptable and Also to Have Low Environmental Impact

Researchers have wrestled for years with the problem of how best to balance the agricultural, environmental, nutritional, health, environmental, socio-economic and cultural issues that must be taken into account in developing sustainable diets [12]. French workers have shown that it is difficult to integrate nutritional quality, affordability, environmental impact and sustainability in culturally appropriate and otherwise acceptable ways [14].

There is much discussion concerning dietary recommendations that might meet both environmental and nutritional goals [8]. Recommendations in some countries, such as the USA, call for increased consumption of fish, but this may be unsustainable from the environmental standpoint. Recommendations in the USA also call for eating less meat, since this is a food that is an important source of carbon emissions. However, meat is a highly preferred food, and there is a great deal of disagreement as to how the emission effects of animal production should be measured. According to some experts, the effects of food choices pale in comparison to the impact of transportation choices or energy production and utilization [10]. Other experts disagree about the specifics and especially the external effects of animal meat production, and about whether reducing US consumption of animal products could even have a significant impact on climate change [18]. They contend that intensification of meat production has other effects as well, including: water contamination from animal waste, especially in drinking water for rural populations; pesticide use for feed production; antibiotic use and resistance; the spread of antibiotic resistance to workers and consumers; and air quality issues associated with animal crowding.

1.6   Food and Nutrition Security and Nutritional Status in the World Today

Both LMIC and HIC can suffer from many different forms of malnutrition. Energy deficits and protein and nutrient deficiencies are more common in LMIC. Deficiency diseases are associated with under nutrition, but increasingly also occasionally with caloric over nutrition, and with NCDs in LMIC. Increasingly, overweight, obesity and type 2 diabetes are being observed in LMIC as well as in epidemic proportions in HIC.

Overweight, obesity and high rates of NCDs have become the norm in many HIC. Formerly associated with affluence, the NCDs in high-income countries have become concentrated among the urban and rural poor. Some individuals in those populations suffer from 'hidden hunger', characterized by an excess of calories and a deficiency of some key nutrients. Cases of malnutrition found in HIC are generally concentrated among groups with lower education and incomes, and in more disadvantaged neighborhoods. The vulnerable groups include minorities and the poor, and can often be traced to specific neighborhoods and geographic locations. In the US, older adults and women from certain minority groups are among the most vulnerable groups.

North America, North Africa and Asia are the most food-secure regions; in Asia, only about 8.4% of the population is food-insecure. In Latin America and the Caribbean region, the percentage of food-insecure people is expected to fall in the short term. Food insecurity is at 28.4% in sub-Saharan Africa, and it is expected to remain at this level in the near future. In the next decade, in the 76 countries under review, the food insecurity situation is expected to increase from 13.4% in 2015 to 15.1% in 2025. The distribution gap is projected to increase over the next decade in Asia and in southern South America [20].

1.6.1 Low- and Middle-Income-Countries (LMIC)

In a recent report on projections of international food security, estimates on food security for 76 countries were predicted to fall by 9%, from 521 million persons in 2014 to 475 in 2015, and the share of the population that was food-insecure in these countries was expected to decrease from 14.8 to 13.4% [20]. The 'distribution gap' (a measure of the intensity of food insecurity) between the amounts of food needed to reach the nutritional target of roughly 2100 calories per person per day was projected to decline by 6%.

1.6.2 High-Income Countries (HIC)

It is often wrongly assumed that affluent, high-income countries are exempt from problems of food and nutrition insecurity. For example, the United States is viewed by the world as a country with plenty of food, yet not all households in the US are food-secure. Although its severity is far less than in many other countries, a proportion of the population experiences food insecurity at some time in any given year because of food deprivation or lack of access to food due to the constraints on their economic resources [17]. Food security, as the term is used in the United States, means access at all times to enough food for an active, healthy life. Food insecurity exists whenever the availability of nutritionally adequate and safe foods or the ability to acquire acceptable foods in socially acceptable ways is limited or uncertain. Food insecurity in the United States refers to the social and economic problem of lack of food due to lack of resource or other constraints—not to voluntary fasting or dieting, or because of illness, or for other reasons. Although lack of economic resources is the most common constraint, food insecurity can also be experienced when food is available and accessible but cannot be used because of physical or other constraints, such as limited physical functioning among the elderly. Food insecurity also has a temporal dimension: frequency and duration are important, because more frequent or extensive periods of food insecurity indicate more serious problems and have graver consequences for nutritional status. Other conceptually separable aspects of food insecurity include the supply of food or its safety or nutritional quality. These additional aspects are already assessed by other elements of the nutrition monitoring system in the USA, and usually also in those of other highly industrialized countries.

Recent data on the percentage of food-insecure US households remained essentially unchanged from 2013 to 2014, although food insecurity had decreased from a high of 14.9% in 2011. Moreover, the percentage of households with food insecurity in the severe range was 5.6%, unchanged over the past few years [5].

1.6.3 The Likely Global Consequences

The current status of sustainable food and nutrition security is precarious at the global level. The current pressures on agricultural and food systems, exacerbated by climate change, include diverse environmental and economic factors related to land, water and energy use. One danger is that economic and other pressures may push the agricultural and food production industries toward producing low-cost foods that provide ample 'empty' calories that supply energy but lack essential micronutrients. When such foods constitute a major part of the global food supply, the result is dietary patterns that are suboptimal from the health standpoint.

It will be critical to develop and promote food systems that supply nutrient-rich foods, while protecting the ecosystem and sparing natural resources. The challenges that exist for managing food and nutrition security today differ from those in years past. Since most highly industrialized, affluent countries today are predominantly urban, they rely increasingly on a global food supply. Low- and middle-income countries are progressively urbanizing and going in the same direction. Many countries are in the midst of a nutrition transition, and are experiencing a rise in non-communicable diseases and obesity [1].

1.6.4 State of the Art of Nutrition Interventions

The Action Plan of the FAO's second International Conference on Nutrition [21] recommended that the following steps should be taken to develop more sustainable food systems:

- Review national policies and investments and integrate nutrition objectives into food and agriculture policy, program design and implementation, so as to enhance nutrition-sensitive agriculture, ensure food security, and enable healthy diets.
- Strengthen local food production and processing, especially by smallholders and family farmers, giving special attention to women's empowerment, while recognizing that efficient and effective trade is key to achieving nutrition objectives.
- Promote the diversification of crops including underutilized traditional crops, increased production of fruits and vegetables, and appropriate production of animal-source products as needed, applying practices of sustainable food production and natural resource management.

- Improve storage, preservation, transport and distribution technologies and infrastructure so as to reduce seasonal food insecurity and food and nutrient loss and waste.
- Establish and strengthen institutions, policies, programs and services to enhance the resilience of the food supply in crisis-prone areas, including areas afflicted by climate change.

Although these recommendations broadly outlined a way forward, specifics regarding how to achieve the stated goals were not provided. The gaps that remain include lack of information on the various domains of food and nutrition security, lack of agreement on metrics, and broader issues.

1.6.5   Gaps in Information

Gaps in information about domains of food and nutrition security remain in many countries. They include the following.

1.6.5.1   Dietary Quality

Although there is no single perfect dietary pattern, evidence suggests that the consumption of adequate food energy and nutrient-dense foods, coupled with a physically active life and the maintenance of body weight in the healthy range, leads to lower incidence of NCDs and decreased mortality from diet-related disease. Some eating patterns are more beneficial than others. Identifying optimal eating patterns was the basis of the second ICN's recommendations in 2014 for altering diets in more healthful ways. Agreed definitions for appropriate nutrient profiles for individual foods and total diets are needed to operationalize these concepts.

Data on dietary quality, food consumption and the prevalence of malnutrition are often especially inadequate in low- and middle-income countries. Surveys are needed to obtain this information before effective interventions can be planned.

In most highly industrialized countries, the nutritional adequacy, quality and safety of the food supply are accurately characterized using population-based health and nutrition examination surveys. Excessive amounts of food energy are usually available, although balance, variety and moderation in dietary patterns may be lacking. List-based surveys are often in place for assessing the intakes of some, but not all, sub-populations recognized as being at particular risk of malnutrition—such as very young infants and children, the handicapped, and those suffering from diseases with profound nutritional implications (e.g. end-stage renal disease). However, for others (e.g. the very old and frail living at home with physical or mental functional deficits, the homeless mentally ill, the poor homebound chronically ill, and migrant workers and refugees, especially those lacking legal status), little is known about their nutritional status. In most high-income countries, systems are in place to identify and track cases of food-borne illness, but other groups, as mentioned above, remain poorly studied.

1.6.5.2 Affordability

In middle- and low-income countries, data on affordability of foods and diets needs to be collected and used to determine whether healthy and culturally acceptable dietary patterns are possible, given the economic circumstances of various sub-groups in the population. In high-income countries, data is available to assess the affordability of individual foods and total diets, but it is often not used. The relationships between dietary quality and dietary costs are increasingly being explored, along with the cultural acceptability of diets. Actions must be taken to make healthful diets affordable and culturally acceptable to all.

1.6.5.3 Prevalence of Malnutrition

Data on the prevalence of malnutrition is often insufficient or unavailable, particularly in low-and middle-income countries, but also in some high-income countries. Population-based surveys of the general population and list-based surveys of nutritionally vulnerable, high-risk groups are needed in all countries to describe the prevalence of adequacy and inadequacy among them. These are especially important in middle- and low-income countries that are experiencing large geographical shifts in populations as well as in food systems.

1.6.5.4 The Environmental Impact and Sustainability of Existing Food Systems

Little information is available on the environmental impact and sustainability of food systems in most low- and middle-income countries. By contrast with the considerable success that has been achieved in devising metrics and measuring some of the above food and nutrition security domains, issues involving the environmental impact and sustainability of food groups and total diets are only beginning to be explored in most high-, middle- and low-income countries. There is a pressing need to devise valid and agreed metrics to measure these factors. Although carbon cost (greenhouse gas emissions) has become the leading indicator, this is not sufficient. Other measures of land, water and energy resources, and also of labor and social resources, may need to be included in sustainability modeling.

1.6.5.5 Gaps in Metrics to Measure Domains of Food and Nutrition Security

There is an urgent need for consensus regarding metrics to measure the various domains of sustainable food and nutrition security. Once these metrics are available, they need to be applied to foods, food systems and total diets. Culturally acceptable and affordable recommendations that will result in diets of high nutritional quality must then be devised, and recommendations about them disseminated. The issue of food waste should also play a key role in discussions of food sustainability.

1.6.6 Failure to Consider Broader Issues

In addition to nutrition-specific issues, concerns that must also be dealt with include how the quest for sustainable dietary patterns intersects with the changing global environment and with factors that involve food production and supply systems. These include depletion of land and water resources, energy needs, pesticides, fertilizers, biotechnologies, food processing, food safety, global tariffs, and trade.

1.7 The Way Forward

1.7.1 Metrics

Sustainable, healthy, culturally acceptable diets, along with measures of their various domains that incorporate all the domains for food and nutrition security, must be developed. Food and nutrition security can be assured and enhanced by the implementation of sound and agreed metrics for measuring the four domains involving food and nutrition security that are highlighted in this chapter. With solid measures in hand, discussions of how best to alter food and nutrition systems to optimize all of the domains can progress.

1.7.1.1 Develop Better Ways to Balance Dietary Quality, Affordability, Acceptability and Sustainability

The trends discussed above underscore the importance of integrating many different domains to achieve food and nutrition security. The ultimate question is how best to reflect concerns about dietary/nutritional quality, dietary affordability, cultural acceptability, environmental impact and greater sustainability in dietary recommendations to governments and consumers, and who should do this. Another difficult task that must be confronted in the future is how best to integrate dietary quality with affordability/accessibility, cultural acceptability, and sustainability.

In the short term, efforts to develop less environmentally impactful and more sustainable methods of producing both plant and animal foods, and of cutting down on waste in production and consumption, need to be given high priority. In the long term, educational and other interventional efforts to change dietary preferences may also stimulate changes in these respects.

1.7.1.2 Prioritize and Optimize the Domains of Food and Nutrition Security

More study is needed on how the various domains of food and nutrition security interact with each other, and how best to prioritize and optimize these interrelationships in culturally acceptable ways.

1.7.1.3 Marshall the Political Will and Resources to Give Food and Nutrition Security High Priority

Solving these problems expeditiously requires not only political will but also economic and human resources that are adequate to the task.

1.8 Summary: Key Messages

- Food and nutrition security has four characteristics: dietary/nutritional quality, affordability, cultural acceptability, and environmental sustainability.
- Diets should increasingly consist of nutritious, affordable, culturally acceptable, safe and healthy processed and unprocessed foods that are high in dietary quality.
- Food and nutrition insecurity and malnutrition are widespread in many low- and middle-income countries. They also exist to much lesser degrees in highly industrialized countries.
- Effective management of resources is required to ensure access to adequate food high in dietary quality that is affordable, culturally acceptable, and sustainable in both LMIC and HIC.
- The ultimate challenge is to develop and sustain food and nutrition systems that are secure and culturally acceptable in LMIC and HIC alike.
- Political will, along with adequate economic and human resources, will be essential to achieve this.

References

1. Aounallah-Skhiri H, Taissac P, El Ati J, Eymard-Duvernay S, Landais E, Achour N, Delpeuch F, Ben Romdhane H, Maire B Nutrition transiton among adolescents of a south-Mediterranean country: dietary patterns, association with socioeconomic factors, overweight and blood pressure. A cross sectional study in Tunisia Nutr J 2011 April 24; 10:38. doi:10.1186/1475-2891-10-38
2. Boyd-Orr J Food Health and Income: Report on a Survey of Adequacy of Diet in Relation to Income New York and London Macmillan and Company Ltd 1936
3. Burlingame, B., and S. Dernini, eds. 2012. *Sustainable diets and biodiversity: Directions and solutions for policy, research and action.* Rome: Food and Agriculture Organization and Bioversity International
4. Case A and Deaton A Rising morbidity and mortality in midlife among white non-Hispanic Americans in the 21st century PNAS 112: (49) doi/10.1073/pnas.1518393112
5. Coleman-Jensen A, Rabbitt MP, Gregory C, and Singh A Household food security in the United States in 2014 Economic Research Service, USDA Washington 2015 (at http://www.ers.usda.gov/publications/err-economic-research-report/err194.aspx
6. Dwyer JT, Fulgoni VL, Clemens RA, Schmidt DB, Freedman MR Is processed a four letter word? The role of processed foods in achieving dietary guidelines and nutrient recommendations Adv Nutr 3: 536–548 2012
7. Gross R, Shoeneberger H, Pfeifer H, Preuss HJA The four dimensions of food and nutrition security: definitions and concepts Food and Nutrition Security: Definitions and Concepts FAO/European Union, Invent (Internationale Weiterbildung und Entwicklung gGmbH. 2000
8. Institute of Medicine, Food Forum Food and Nutrition Board, Roundtable on Diets Food for Healthy People and A Healthy Planet. Sustainable Diets: Food for Healthy People and a Healthy Planet: Workshop Summary Washington DC National Academy Press 2014
9. Institute of Medicine. *Ensuring Safe Food: From Production to Consumption.* "Executive Summary." Washington, DC: The National Academies Press, 1998. doi:10.17226/6163
10. Institute of Medicine. *Sustainable Diets: Food for Healthy People and a Healthy Planet: Workshop Summary.* Ch 2 Defining Relationships: Synergies and Trade-Offs Between Health and Environmental Impacts. Washington, DC: The National Academies Press, 2014. doi:10.17226/18578
11. International Covenant on Economic, Social, and Cultural Rights 1966 http://www.refworld.org accessed April 30, 2016
12. Johnston JL, Fanzo JC and Cogill B Understanding sustainable diets: a descriptive analysis of the determinants and processes that influence diets and their impact on health, food security, and environmental sustainability Adv Nutr 5: 418–429 2014
13. Laudan, Rachel, editor Cuisine and Empire: Cooking in World History. Studies on Food and Culture. University of California Press, Berkeley CA 2013
14. Masset G, Soller LG, Vieux F, Darmon N Identifying sustainable foods: the relationship between environmental impact, and prices of foods representative of the French diet JAND 114: 852–869 2014
15. National Agricultural Research Extension and Teaching Policy Act of 1977 Section 1404(17) of the National Agricultural Research, Extension, and Teaching Policy Act of 1977 (7 U.S.C. 3103(17) and the Food, Agriculture, Conservation, and Trade Act of 1990 (FACTA), Public Law 101–624. Title XVI, Subtitle A, Section 1603, Government Printing Office, Washington, D.C., 1990 NAL Call#KF1692. A31 1990
16. National Research Council. Toward Sustainable Agricultural Systems in the 21st Century. National Academies Press. Washington 2010
17. Panel to Review U.S Department of Agriculture's Measurement of Food Insecurity and Hunger, National Research Council Food Insecurity and Hunger in the United States: An Assessment of the Measure National Academies Press Washington 2006

18. Pelletier, N., and Tyedmers, P. 2010. Forecasting potential global environmental costs of livestock production 2000-2050. *Proceedings of the National Academy of Sciences of the United States of America* 107(43):18371–18374
19. Report of the World Commission on Environment and Development (Chaired by Gro Brundtland), "Our Common Future", Transmitted to the General Assembly as an Annex to document A/42/427 - Development and International Cooperation: Environment, 1987
20. Rosen, S, Meade, B, Murray A International Food Security Assessment, 2015-25, Economic Research Service, US Department of Agriculture Washington Dc June 2015
21. Second International Conference on Nutrition, 19–21 November 2014 Conference Outcome Document: Rome Declaration on Nutrition, Rome, Food and Agricultural Organization of the United Nations 2014
22. Steele, Carolyn Hungry City: How Food Shapes Our Lives Vintage Books London 2013
23. The Royal Society, 2009, Reaping the Benefits: Science and the Sustainable Intensification of Global Agriculture
24. USDA Concensus statement on Sustainability US Department of Agriculture, Washington DC 2011
25. Weaver CM, Dwyer Jt, Fulgoni VL, King JC, Leveille GA, MacDonald R, Ordovas J, Schnackenberg D Processed foods: contributions to nutrition A J Clin Nutr 2014: 99: 1525–42

Chapter 2
Sustainable, Healthy Diets: Models and Measures

Adam Drewnowski

Abstract The definition of sustainable food and nutrition security involves four principal domains. Foods and food patterns need to be nutrient-dense, affordable, culturally acceptable, and sparing of the environment. Each domain has its own metrics. Nutrient density is measured in terms of nutrients in relation to calories. Affordability is measured in terms of calories and nutrients per unit cost. Cultural acceptance can be measured in terms of frequency of consumption by population subgroups. Lifecycle analysis (LCA) of the environmental impact of foods is based on the use of land, water, and energy resources during food production and utilization. Nutrient profiling models separate foods that are energy-dense from those that are nutrient-rich. Global economic pressures, exacerbated by climate change, may push the agro-food industry toward producing more low-cost calories and insufficient nutrients. Social disparities in diet quality may increase not only in low- and middle- income countries (LMIC) but also in the developed world.

Keywords Sustainable food and nutrition security · Sustainable diets · Nutrient density · Nutrient profiling models · Affordability · Cultural acceptance · Lifecycle analysis

2.1 Introduction

The Food and Agriculture Organization (FAO) of the United Nations has defined sustainable diets as nutritionally adequate, economically affordable, culturally acceptable, accessible, healthy, and safe [1] (Table 2.1). The FAO definition also noted that sustainable diets needed to be protective of both natural and human resources and be respectful of ecosystems and biodiversity [1].

A. Drewnowski (✉)
Center for Public Health Nutrition, University of Washington,
305 Raitt Hall #353410, Seattle, WA 98195-3410, USA
e-mail: adamdrew@u.washington.edu

© Springer International Publishing AG 2017   25
H.K. Biesalski et al. (eds.), *Sustainable Nutrition in a Changing World*,
DOI 10.1007/978-3-319-55942-1_2

Table 2.1 Definitions of sustainable diets

FAO 2010
Sustainable diets are those diets with low environmental impacts that contribute to food and nutrition security and to healthy life for present and future generations. Sustainable diets are protective and respectful of biodiversity and ecosystems, culturally acceptable, accessible, economically fair and affordable, nutritionally adequate, safe, and healthy, while optimizing natural and human resources
Foresight 2010
Sustainability implies a state where the needs of the present and local population can be met without diminishing the ability of future generations or populations in other locations to meet their needs or without causing them harm to environment and natural assets
US Farm Bill. U.S. Code Title 7, Section 3103
Sustainable agriculture will in the long term: satisfy human food needs; enhance natural resources and the environment; use non-renewable resources in the most efficient manner; make farming economically viable; enhance the quality of life for farmers and society as a whole

The popular view seems to be that the most sustainable diets are those that are most environmentally friendly, with minimal impact on land, water, and energy resources. The environmental cost of farming and food production has been measured in terms of greenhouse gas emissions (GHGEs) expressed in carbon dioxide equivalents (CO_2e) per kg of food. Such data have been used to support the argument that locally-sourced, plant-based diets were more sustainable than diets that included animal products, mostly dairy and meat [2].

However, the FAO definition of sustainable diets does include nutrient density of the diet, its monetary cost, and likely health outcomes. The diet's impact on the environment is only one aspect of sustainability; its impact on population health is another. These diverse multi-sector criteria demand the development of new metrics to assess the nutrient density, affordability, and acceptability of different diets together with their overall impact on the environment. It may transpire that no single diet or food pattern fits all the criteria; some compromises may need to be made.

For example, studies have already shown that the most nutrient-dense diets were often the least affordable; it was empty calories that were cheap [3]. Studies from France [4] and the United Kingdom [5] have shown that the most nutrient-dense diets were associated with higher, not lower, GHGEs. Further, some affordable healthy foods were not culturally acceptable and were rejected by lower-income groups [6]. There is some question whether diets can be simultaneously low-cost and nutrient-rich, environmentally friendly and culturally acceptable. In published studies, the highest-quality diets were not the most sustainable, whereas the most sustainable diets were not necessarily the healthiest. Indeed, some studies have identified a shocking paradox. By some current metrics, the plant food that was associated with the lowest GHGEs was sugar.

Clearly, diet sustainability metrics need to go beyond carbon footprint and must take the nutritional value of foods and their health impact into account. The concept

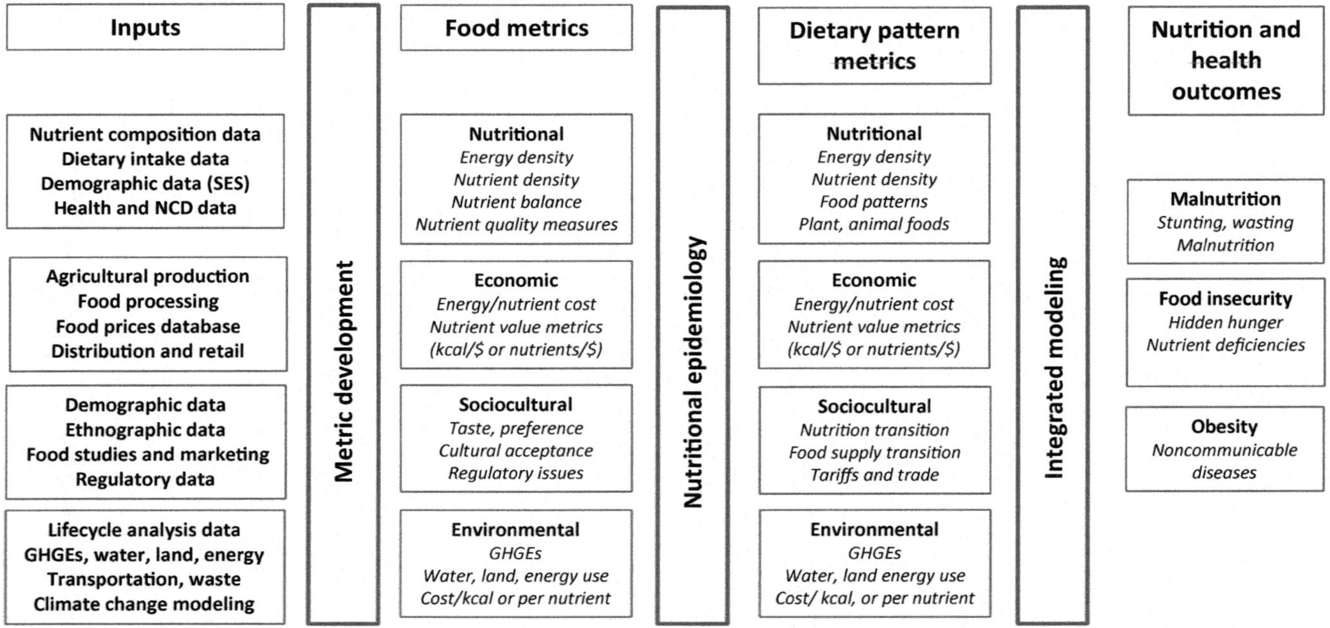

Fig. 2.1 The food and dietary pattern metrics for the four domains of food and nutrition security. *Source* Original figure made for this publication

of sustainable food and nutrition security can be split into four principal domains. The four domains are dietary, economic, sociocultural and environmental. The food and dietary pattern metrics corresponding to each of the domains are indicated in Fig. 2.1 and discussed in detail below.

2.2   The Dietary Dimension

The nutrient density of individual foods can be assessed using a technique known as nutrient profiling [7]. Nutrient profile models assign ratings to individual foods based on their nutrient composition. An alternative approach is to assign foods to categories or classes, based on their overall nutritional value.

The usual goal of nutrient profiling models is to distinguish between foods that are energy-dense and those that are nutrient-rich. Some profiling models are based on calories and on nutrients that are of public health concern only: saturated fat, added (or free) sugars, and sodium that are often consumed to excess in developed countries. Profiling models can also be based on human nutrient requirements, including some shortfall nutrients that are consumed in inadequate amounts. Generally, such nutrients include protein, fiber, and selected vitamins and minerals. Their content in foods is calculated per reference amount: 100 g, 100 kcal, or serving. Balanced nutrient profiling models are based on some combination of nutrients to limit and nutrients to encourage per reference amount.

The Nutrient Rich Foods (NRF) index is a formal metric of nutrient density [8]. The positive nutrients are protein, fiber, vitamins A, C, and E, calcium, iron, potassium and magnesium, whereas nutrients to limit are saturated fat, added sugar, and sodium. The NRF algorithm is the sum of percentage daily values (DVs) for the 9 positive nutrients, minus the sum of %DVs for 3 nutrients to limit, each calculated per 100 kcal and capped at 100% DV. The NRF score has been validated in regression models against the Healthy Eating Index, an independent measure of a healthy diet.

The French SAIN,LIM score [3] is the mean of %DVs for five positive nutrients (protein, fiber, vitamin C, calcium and iron) minus the mean of percent daily values for the three nutrients to limit (saturated fat, added sugar, sodium). Unlike the continuous NRF score, SAIN,LIM assigns foods into one of four categories. The SAIN,LIM model has been validated using linear programming [3].

These nutrient profiling models, designed to capture the nutrient quality of individual foods, have been used for various purposes. In the European Union, nutrient profiling provides the scientific rationale for the potential approval of nutrition and health claims. In the US, proprietary profiling models developed by different supermarkets were expected to nudge consumer purchases toward healthier foods. In the UK, nutrient profile models were used to regulate advertising and marketing to children. Increasingly, the global food industry is using nutrient profile models to reformulate its food product portfolios. Nutrient profiling models provide a valuable metric to assess industry progress toward reducing fat, sugar and sodium in a variety of foods. Importantly, nutrient profiling algorithms developed for use with individual foods can also be adapted to assess the nutrient quality of composite meals and daily food patterns.

There are existing metrics to assess the nutrient quality of the total diet. Measures of diet quality tend to be both food- and nutrient-based. The simplest measures are energy density and mean nutrient adequacy of the diet. Dietary energy density in kcal/g is calculated using solid foods and energy beverages. Mean adequacy ratio (MAR) is the ratio of nutrient intakes relative to the estimated requirements calculated based on national or FAO charts.

Perhaps the best known metric of diet quality is the Healthy Eating Index (HEI) developed to assess compliance with the US Dietary Guidelines for Americans [9]. The HEI is constructed based on 24-h dietary intake data from national surveys such as the National Health and Nutrition Examination Survey (NHANES). The intent of HEI is to monitor the diet quality of the US population with special attention to lower income subgroups. It has also been used to examine the relations between diet quality and health and between diet quality and diet cost.

The HEI was initially created by the US Department of Agriculture Center for Nutrition Policy and Promotion (CNPP) in 1995. It was later revised to reflect the 2005 Dietary Guidelines for Americans, and was updated in 2012 to reflect the most recent 2010 Dietary Guidelines for Americans. Alternative ways of measuring overall diet quality include the Alternative Healthy Eating Index (aHEI); Dietary Approaches to Stop Hypertension (DASH) scores; Mediterranean diet indexes, and other scores. In general, diet quality scores also tracked socioeconomic status: diet quality was higher among the rich than among the poor.

2.3   The Economic Dimension

Food affordability has been calculated in terms of calories or nutrients per unit cost [10]. Metrics of food price per calorie or calories per unit cost are typically deployed to address hunger and calorie deprivation in low- and middle-income countries. Both the FAO and the International Food Policy Research Institute (IFPRI) have used food prices per calorie to evaluate food and agriculture policies in the developing world. The World Bank uses the price of a 2100-kcal basket of reference foods to set the food poverty line. Studies on poverty in rural India calculated the cost of food commodities in rupees per 1000 kcal, showing that cereals and sugar provided calories at far lower cost than did meat, dairy, or vegetables, and fruit.

There has been resistance to applying the same FAO and IFPRI metrics to the US food supply. One view has been that all foods cost the same, such that the use of per calorie pricing is inappropriate. Yet, in the US, higher consumption of added sugars and saturated fats is associated with lower per-calorie diet cost, whereas higher consumption of fiber, vitamin C, potassium, and other nutrients is associated with higher diet cots. Similarly, refined grains, sweets and fats cost less, whereas green leafy vegetables, seafood and whole fruit cost more.

The cost gradient may vary depending on population eating habits, agricultural subsidies, or the use of fortified or supplemented foods. For example, potassium costs might be lower if beans were the principal source of potassium in the US diet as opposed to coffee and French fries. Higher calcium consumption was not associated with higher cost, probably because of the availability of low-cost milk products in the US food supply. Likewise, folate intakes were not associated with higher diet costs, because of fortification—an important point in the nutrition of children and pregnant women.

Studies have also found direct links between HEI scores and per-calorie diet costs. More costly diets were of higher quality, and higher-quality diets did cost more. The observed social gradient in diet quality, noted in both developed and middle-income countries, may be explained in part by food prices and diet costs.

The present affordability metrics for foods and food patterns followed directly from nutrient profiling and diet quality measures. Having a global measure of nutrient density for individual foods and for total diets permitted the subsequent calculations of calories and nutrients per unit cost.

2.4   The Sociocultural Domain

Sustainable food plans need to be socially acceptable as well as affordable and nutritious. In higher-income countries, it is the lower-income groups that have low-quality diets and suffer from higher rates of obesity and non-communicable disease (NCD). One way to link food, health and incomes is through food prices and diet costs.

The search for the affordable nutrient-rich foods was made possible by nutrient profiling and by the new metrics of nutrients per energy and nutrients per unit cost. Based on analyses of nutrient composition and national food prices data, it became clear that some nutrient-rich foods were inexpensive. In the US, the USDA Thrifty Food Plan has featured ground turkey, chickpeas, and condensed or powdered milk. Rice and beans and home-cooked lentil soup have been proposed as staple diets for the US poor. Cost analyses and value metrics for US foods showed that nuts, seeds, legumes, cereals, carrots, potatoes and cabbage offered good nutrition at an affordable cost.

However, many low-cost yet nutritious foods were rejected by the consumer. Their frequency of consumption in the population was close to zero. Assuming that non-consumption equals rejection, the hypothesis was that such foods deviated from the current consumption standards; failed to meet cultural requirements; and could be socially or culturally inappropriate. The custom of the country may have placed such foods outside the accepted social norms. Frequency of consumption of a given food by the total population or its subgroups is one metric of cultural acceptance.

Mathematical optimization models, based on linear programming, have long shown that high-quality diets could be obtained at very low cost. The USDA Thrifty Food Plan (TFP) was intended to be as close as possible to the diets of low-income Americans, while simultaneously meeting both nutritional and cost constraints. The nutrient and food group constraints were based on the DGAs and MyPyramid, respectively, whereas the cost constraint was based on the amount of food assistance. To arrive at the solution, the TFP tolerated up to tenfold deviations from the current eating habits, effectively ignoring the current eating habits of the population.

To highlight the importance of cultural acceptance, a French study [6] used linear programming to develop food plans that met three levels of nutritional requirements and seven levels of increasingly stringent consumption constraints, all at the lowest possible cost. Significant deviations from the existing mainstream French diet were progressively disallowed, so that the final model had little tolerance for any deviation from the French diet. The intent was to estimate the cost of culturally acceptable healthy diets that were also consistent with French cultural expectations and societal norms.

The nationally representative INCA (National Individual Survey of Food Consumption) dietary survey study of 1332 adults provided population estimates of dietary intakes [6]. The lowest-cost food plans that provided adequate calories and met nutrient adequacy standards could be obtained for as little as 1.50 EUR/day. However, meeting nutrition standards at the lowest possible cost led to food plans that provided little variety and were unacceptable. The progressive imposition of consumption constraints based on cultural norms sharply increased costs, without improving nutritional value. In summary, modeled food patterns that were healthy and culturally appropriate were much more expensive than food patterns that were simply healthy. Food plans designed for low-income groups need to be socially acceptable as well as affordable and nutritious.

2.5   The Environmental Domain

One of many metrics of the environmental impact of foods is based on greenhouse gas emissions or GHGEs, otherwise known as carbon footprint or carbon costs. GHGEs (mostly methane gas) are often expressed in grams of CO_2 equivalents per package, can, or bottle of product. Lifecycle Analyses (LCAs) have associated different amounts of GHGEs with agricultural production, food processing, packaging, transport, distribution, and retail. Some LCAs have calculated carbon cost through the post-purchase life of the food product, including preparation, cold storage, disposal, and waste.

The development of environmental impact metrics to calculate carbon cost per calorie or per nutrient was exactly analogous to the development of affordability metrics. In both cases, calories or nutrient density measures were related to the estimates of the monetary or carbon cost. These metrics of nutrient density in relation to environmental cost were developed for individual foods and for total diets.

Some paradoxes were uncovered [5, 6]. In general, healthy diets are supposed to be more environmentally friendly because plant-based foods have lower GHGEs per unit weight than do animal-based foods. However, calculating carbon cost per 2000 kcal diet changes the picture completely, as illustrated by some recent studies.

In a recent study of 1918 French adults, higher-quality diets were defined as those of lower energy density, higher mean nutrient adequacy ratio (MAR), and lower intakes of nutrients to limit [5]. Such diets contained more plant-based foods, fruit and vegetables, and fewer sweets and salted snacks than did lower-quality diets. However, calorie for calorie, higher quality diets were associated with significantly higher GHGEs. Whereas energy-rich sweets and grains had a lower carbon footprint, better diets that were higher in fruits, vegetables, and animal products had a higher carbon footprint. The study concluded that the higher quality diets also had a higher carbon cost.

The question whether healthy diets are also good for the planet would benefit from a more extended debate. Animal food products, meat and dairy, are said to consume land and water resources to excess and to contribute to greenhouse gas emissions more than other foods. On the other hand, transport of out-of-season fresh produce by air has its own very considerable carbon costs.

However, additional indices of environmental impact will be needed. Agricultural production has an impact on soil, water, air, agro-ecosystem biodiversity, wildlife habitats, and landscape. Among the many indicators of sustainable farming are soil quality and soil protection, fertilizer and pesticide use, land conservation, and other aspects of land management. Other measures have included water quality and resources, fertilizer runoff, air pollution, crop modeling, labor and economics.

The US legal definition of sustainable agriculture is based on the 1990 Farm Bill. It is sufficiently broad to encompass the ecological, economic, and social components of sustainable agriculture, referring not only to food production, but also to economic viability, and quality of life. Sustainable farms need to be viable businesses, contributing to the rural economy in terms of employment and incomes. At this time, these new domains have not yet been incorporated into the framework shown in Fig. 2.1.

2.6   Integrated Modeling

Diet quality and health outcomes are very much a part of the ongoing sustainability debate. Global food policies should address the complex interplay between diet quality, monetary costs, and cultural and environmental factors in relation to health. The existing food systems need to assure global food security in the face of population growth and climate change. Sustainable nutrition needs to provide a balance of both calories and nutrients, prevent malnutrition and hidden hunger, and minimize obesity risk [11].

Ongoing research tells us that sugars and grains are generally cheaper per calorie than are some nutrient-rich foods [12]. Cereal and oilseed crops, not meat or dairy, account for most of the calories in the global food supply. Corn, wheat, rice, soy, and sugar cane are all staples that yield inexpensive dietary energy and provide fat, refined carbohydrates, and protein. Climate change will only intensify the pressure to increase the yields of low-cost, energy-dense crops.

Clearly, diet sustainability metrics must go beyond mere carbon footprinting to take the nutritional value of foods into account. Feeding the world in the face of population growth, poverty, and climate change poses new challenges to agro-food industries. Global agriculture is highly vulnerable to the depletion of natural resources, land, water, and energy that may result from global warming. Hidden hunger is one potential consequence as the global food production shifts toward more calories, rather than nutrients.

2.7   Summary: : Key Messages

- Sustainable food and nutrition security involves four principal domains: Foods and food patterns need to be nutrient-dense, affordable, culturally acceptable, and sparing of the environment.
- Each domain has its own metrics. Nutrient density is measured in terms of nutrients in relation to calories. Nutrient profiling models separate foods that are energy-dense from those that are nutrient-rich. Affordability is measured in terms of calories and nutrients per unit cost. Cultural acceptance can be measured in terms of frequency of consumption by population subgroups.
- Lifecycle analysis (LCA) of the environmental impact of foods is based on the use of land, water, and energy resources during food production and utilization.
- Global economic pressures, exacerbated by climate change, may push the agro-food industry toward producing more low-cost calories and insufficient nutrients. Social disparities in diet quality may increase not only in low- and middle- income countries (LMIC) but also in the developed world.

References

1. Burlingame B, Dernini S, eds. Sustainable diets and biodiversity: directions and solutions for policy, research and action. Proceedings of the International Scientific Symposium on Biodiversity and Sustainable Diets: United Against Hunger; 2010 Nov 3–5; Rome, Italy. Rome: FAO; 2012 At: http://www.fao.org/docrep/016/i3004e/i3004e.pdf Accessed 01/31/2015.
2. Scientific Report of the 2015 Dietary Guidelines Advisory Committee. Available at: http://www.health.gov/dietaryguidelines/2015-scientific-report/.

3. Darmon N, Drewnowski A. The contribution of food prices and diet costs to socioeconomic disparities in diet quality and health: A systematic review and analysis. Nutr Rev 2015 (in press).

4. Vieux F, Soler L-G, Touazi D, Darmon N. High nutritional quality is not associated with low greenhouse gas emissions in self-selected diets of French adults. Am J Clin Nutr 2013:97:569–583.

5. Macdiarmid JI. Is a healthy diet an environmentally sustainable diet? Proc Nutr Soc 2013;72:13–20.

6. Maillot M, Darmon N, Drewnowski A. Are the lowest cost healthful food plans culturally and socially acceptable? Public Health Nutrition 2010:13:1178–1185.

7. Drewnowski A. Concept of a nutritious food: toward a nutrient density score. Am J Clin Nutr 2005:82:721–732.

8. Drewnowski A. The Nutrient Rich Foods Index helps to identify healthy, affordable foods. Am J Clin Nutr. 2010; Apr;91(4):1095S–1101S.

9. USDA. Healthy Eating Index 2010 (HEI 2010). Center for Nutrition Policy and Promotion, USDA. 2012. Available online at: http://www.cnpp.usda.gov/healthyeatingindex.htm.

10. Drewnowski A. The cost of US foods as related to their nutritive value. American Journal of Clinical Nutrition 2010; 92: 1181–1188.

11. Masset G, Vieux F, Verger EO, Soler LG, Touazi D, Darmon N. Reducing energy intake and energy density for a sustainable diet: a study based on self-selected diets in French adults. Am J Clin Nutr 2014;99:1460–9.

12. Drewnowski A, Specter SE. Poverty and obesity: diet quality, energy density and energy costs. Am J Clin Nutr. 2004;79(1):6–16.

Chapter 3
Measuring Food Insecurity

Katia Castetbon

Abstract Since the beginning of the 1990s, an extensive literature has existed on the subject of food insecurity, analyzed at various levels: individual, household, sub-population, country, and planet. This chapter reviews studies into food security at the level of the household and of the individual, focusing especially on the question of how to define and measure the complex concept of food insecurity. These studies have led to the development of measurement tools aimed in the first instance at developing countries and in the second at the developed world. They analyze individual social factors such as the characteristics of the members of the household associated with food insecurity, and especially the relevant socio-economic parameters. These partially overlap with the indicators or determinants of poverty.

Keywords Food insecurity · Study · Questionnaire · Measurement tool · Household · Health · Poverty · Developing countries · Developed countries

3.1 Concepts, Definitions and Metrics of Food Insecurity

During the 1970s and 1980s, the concept of 'food security' was highlighted by international organizations in response to various major food crises that occurred around the world, and especially in developing countries. In 1974, the first World Food Conference, which was convened by the United Nations Organization, led to the Universal Declaration on the Eradication of Hunger and Malnutrition, which was ratified by a hundred countries. The "inalienable right to be free from hunger and malnutrition" was proclaimed. The responsibility of the state in this matter was highlighted, especially in terms of agricultural policy and the availability of staple foods. At both country and regional levels, the search for a balance between food

K. Castetbon (✉)
Ecole de Santé Publique, Université Libre de Bruxelles,
Route de Lennik 808 – CP 598, 1070 Brussels, Belgium
e-mail: Katia.Castetbon@ulb.ac.be

© Springer International Publishing AG 2017   35
H.K. Biesalski et al. (eds.), *Sustainable Nutrition in a Changing World*,
DOI 10.1007/978-3-319-55942-1_3

production and food requirements was articulated principally as a macroscopic view of energy requirements.

In 1986, the World Bank extended the concept of food security by defining it as "access by all people at all times to enough food for an active, healthy life" [1]. It thus placed the individual at the center of the definition by specifying the notion of adequate quantity and adequate quality, by emphasizing the importance of security of supply, and by linking these with the individual's state of health. Like those provided by the Food and Agricultural OrganizationOrganization,[1] the United Nations and other institutions during the 1980s and 1990s, this definition high-lighted various issues that could be included in the concept of food insecurity. These ranged from the financial through the material to, of course, the nutritional, in rural and urban contexts alike. In 1996, the World Food Summit[2] also included complementary notions in the definition, such as conditions of access to sufficient food and good sanitary conditions (in terms of microbiology and toxicology): "Food security exists when all people at all times have physical, economic and social access to sufficient, safe, nutritious food to maintain a healthy and active life".

These later definitions, more extensive and multidimensional than the original ones, emphasize the importance of mobilizing various disciplines to assess food insecurity: economists, agronomists, geographers, sociologists, epidemiologists, and so forth, can use all their expertise to understand food security, including the influence of food insecurity on health. Nevertheless, due to the involvement of international non-governmental organizations (NGOs), the focus was still on developing countries.[3] Statistics provided by international NGOs often concentrate on food production and economic access to food, in contexts of structural poverty aggravated by armed conflict and political instability. However, surveys are usually carried out in developing countries at the level of the household and the individual. These surveys use metrics that measure accessibility to main food groups as well as food diversity and dietary intake, and which thus estimate coverage of needs [2, 3].

3.2 Theoretical Studies and Tools for Measuring Food Insecurity

In developed countries, which are generally characterized by food abundance, the possibility of food insecurity, and even hunger, in individuals and households was first considered only in the 1980s and 1990s, principally in the United States. The studies into this subject carried out by Kathy L. Radimer (Cornell University) were absolutely seminal. Radimer and her team were the first to perform a qualitative

---

[1]http://www.fao.org/docrep/x5563E/X5563e00.htm#Contents.
[2]http://www.fao.org/docrep/003/w3613f/w3613f00.htm.
[3]http://www.fao.org/docrep/003/AA039F/aa039f05.htm#TopOfPage.

survey among women on low incomes who described themselves as having experienced hunger or as being at risk of experiencing it [4]. Interviews allowed them to conclude that the experience and perception of hunger were extensive and included various dimensions which varied between individuals and households. These dimensions, both qualitative and quantitative, also had a psychological and social component. For instance, regarding the 'quality' component, the household dimension was identified as "food unsuitable" while it was "inadequate diet" at the individual level [4]. Likewise, the 'social' component was identified as "unacceptable means of food acquisition" in households and as "disrupted eating pattern" in individuals.

Based on these conceptual elements, Radimer et al. developed a questionnaire whose construct validity and reliability were tested in almost 200 women who were the beneficiaries of food and social assistance programs [4]. The innovative nature of this questionnaire stems from the fact that it is based on statements made by the women during the previous qualitative survey to describe hunger in households, individuals and children. The US Department of Agriculture, which was aware of this issue at the time, then proposed, in collaboration with researchers, tools for measurements of food insecurity to regularly provide national statistics.[4] Conceptual definitions were established [5] regarding hunger ("uneasy or painful sensation caused by lack of food") and food security (see above). Food insecurity was defined as "limited or uncertain availability of nutritionally adequate and safe foods or limited or uncertain ability to acquire acceptable foods in socially acceptable ways".

Questionnaires used to measure food insecurity are mostly based on the key principles established by K.L. Radimer [6] in the awareness that hunger was conceived here as the ultimate, but not systematic, consequence of food insecurity, particularly when food insecurity affects children [7]. Statements to which survey participants are asked to respond also show that food insecurity is measured as a process of decision-making and of adaptation to a reduction in income, and also as poor access to, and choice of, foods.

In general, questionnaires include a question (indeed, several questions) on quantitative sufficiency of food—like, for example, in the questionnaire developed for the NHANES III survey in 1988–1994 [8]. However, this aspect on its own is considered insufficient to comprehensively describe the multidimensional concept of food insecurity [9].

Two tools were initially developed specifically to measure 'hunger' at a time when the concept of food insecurity was still not well defined: one, comprising eight questions, was particularly focused on children (*Community Childhood Identification Project*, CCHIP) [10]; the other, which was initially proposed by K.L. Radimer [4], included 10–12 questions, depending on the version used.

---

[4]http://www.ers.usda.gov/topics/food-nutrition-assistance/food-security-in-the-us.aspx.

Finally, more complex questionnaires are used to measure food insecurity with different levels of classification according to the seriousness of the situation, especially in terms of the presence or absence of children in the household. This is the case of the *Food Security Core Module*, FSCM (or *US Household Food Security Survey Module*, HFSS), which includes 18 questions in its complete version (10 questions for households without children) [11] (Table 3.1). A version with just six questions was also validated [12] and used in high-risk groups [13]. However, estimates provided by the short version are less appropriate for distinguishing various levels of seriousness, which is also the case when only two questions are used [14].

Used for national statistics in the US, this questionnaire galvanized the nutrition community on the issue of food insecurity [15, 16]. It should be noted that the questionnaire is principally focused on quantitative aspects of food insecurity, taking little account of other dimensions (such as "unacceptable means of food acquisition"). Compared with other tools, it could encourage underestimation of the prevalence of food insecurity [17].

Other relatively similar tools have been elaborated with a view to being used in an international context, especially for developing countries [18], or adapted to specific populations. The HFSS has been adapted and evaluated for use among adolescents and young adults so as to allow measurement at the level of the individual [19]. For younger children, interviews have to be carried out among the adults of the relevant household, given the sensitivity of the topic [20]. Face-to-face interviews or telephone interviews can influence answers, while the training of investigators and relationships developed with respondents still crucially influence the quality of answers to questions which are hard to ask in any circumstances [21].

This brief review of the general concept of food insecurity and the tools to measure it should not obscure the fact that definitions of food insecurity are still in development, given the multidimensional nature of the subject itself [22] and the complexity of the process of questionnaire validation [23]. Similarly, the deep understanding of what is to be measured, the effects of the conditions of the study in the context of a particularly sensitive subject, the problems of translation in non-Anglophone contexts, and the interpretation of the findings vary from one study to another, and together preclude a simple synthesis of the existing data. Nevertheless, this research topic is expanding, which will produce further findings, and eventually permit a thoroughgoing analysis of the topic of food insecurity.

3.3   Summary: Key Messages

- The concept of 'food security' has been under discussion since the 1970s, and an extensive literature on it has existed since the early 1990s.
- Research into food insecurity has focused primarily on the developing world, but food insecurity also exists in the developed world.

Table 3.1 Excerpts from Food Security Core Module/US Household Food Security Survey Module

Which of these statements best describes the food eaten in your household in the last 12 months: – enough of the kinds of food (I/we) want to eat;—enough, but not always the kinds of food (I/we) want;—sometimes not enough to eat; or,—often not enough to eat? [1] Enough of the kinds of food we want to eat [2] Enough but not always the kinds of food we want [3] Sometimes not enough to eat [4] Often not enough to eat [ ] Don't know or refused Now I'm going to read you several statements that people have made about their food situation. For these statements, please tell me whether the statement was often true, sometimes true, or never true for (you/your household) in the last 12 months—that is, since last (name of current month)
The first statement is "(I/we) worried whether (my/our) food would run out before (I/we) got money to buy more." Was that often true, sometimes true, or never true for (you/your household) in the last 12 months? [1] Often true [2] Sometimes true [3] Never true [ ] Don't know or refused
"The food that (I/we) bought just didn't last, and (I/we) didn't have money to get more." Was that often, sometimes, or never true for (you/your household) in the last 12 months? [1] Often true [2] Sometimes true [3] Never true [ ] Don't know or refused
"(I/we) couldn't afford to eat balanced meals." Was that often, sometimes, or never true for (you/your household) in the last 12 months? [1] Often true [2] Sometimes true [3] Never true [ ] Don't know or refused (continues)

Source Economic Research Service, USDA, 2012
Complete version of the questionnaire is available free of charge on: http://www.ers.usda.gov/topics/food-nutrition-assistance/food-security-in-the-us/survey-tools.aspx#household. Using the complete version is highly recommended

- Questionnaires designed to measure food insecurity most commonly focus on the level of the individual and of the household.
- Questionnaires designed to measure food insecurity have become progressively more sophisticated.
- The definition of 'food insecurity' is still in flux.
- Existing data on food insecurity are too diverse to admit a simple synthesis, but further research will generate findings that will permit a thoroughgoing analysis of the phenomenon.

References

1. WORLD BANK. Poverty and Hunger. Issues and Options for Food Security in Developing Countries. The World Bank, 1986: p. 82.
2. BECQUEY E, MARTIN-PREVEL Y, TRAISSAC P, DEMBELE B, BAMBARA A, et al. The household food insecurity access scale and an index-member dietary diversity score contribute valid and complementary information on household food insecurity in an urban West-African setting. J Nutr 2010, 140: 2233–2240.
3. BECQUEY E, DELPEUCH F, KONATE AM, DELSOL H, LANGE M, et al. Seasonality of the dietary dimension of household food security in urban Burkina Faso. Br J Nutr 2012, 107: 1860–1870.
4. RADIMER KL, OLSON CM, CAMPBELL CC. Development of indicators to assess hunger. J Nutr 1990, 120 (suppl 11): 1544–1548.
5. Anonymous. Core indicators of nutritional state for difficult-to-sample populations. J Nutr 1990, 120 (suppl 11): 1559–1600.
6. RADIMER KL, RADIMER KL. Measurement of household food security in the USA and other industrialised countries. Public Health Nutr 2002, 5: 859–864.
7. COOK JT, FRANK DA. Food security, poverty, and human development in the United States. Ann N Y Acad Sci 2008, 1136: 193–209.
8. ALAIMO K, BRIEFEL RR, FRONGILLO EA, JR., OLSON CM. Food insufficiency exists in the United States: results from the third National Health and Nutrition Examination Survey (NHANES III). Am J Public Health 1998, 88: 419–426.
9. FRONGILLO EA, JR., RAUSCHENBACH BS, OLSON CM, KENDALL A, COLMENARES AG. Questionnaire-based measures are valid for the identification of rural households with hunger and food insecurity. J Nutr 1997, 127: 699–705.
10. KLEINMAN RE, MURPHY JM, LITTLE M, PAGANO M, WEHLER CA, et al. Hunger in children in the United States: potential behavioral and emotional correlates. Pediatrics 1998, 101: E3.
11. CARLSON SJ, ANDREWS MS, BICKEL GW. Measuring food insecurity and hunger in the United States: development of a national benchmark measure and prevalence estimates. J Nutr 1999, 129: 510S–516S.
12. BLUMBERG SJ, BIALOSTOSKY K, HAMILTON WL, BRIEFEL RR. The effectiveness of a short form of the Household Food Security Scale. Am J Public Health 1999, 89: 1231–1234.
13. LEE JS, JOHNSON MA, BROWN A, NORD M. Food security of older adults requesting Older Americans Act Nutrition Program in Georgia can be validly measured using a short form of the U.S. Household Food Security Survey Module. J Nutr 2011, 141: 1362–1368.
14. HAGER ER, QUIGG AM, BLACK MM, COLEMAN SM, HEEREN T, et al. Development and validity of a 2-item screen to identify families at risk for food insecurity. Pediatrics 2010, 126: e26–e32.
15. GUNDERSEN C, KREIDER B, PEPPER J. The economics of food insecurity in the United States. Appl Econ Persp Policy 2011, 33: 281–303.
16. HOLBEN DH. Position of the American Dietetic Association: food insecurity in the United States. J Am Diet Assoc 2010, 110: 1368–1377.
17. DERRICKSON JP, FISHER AG, ANDERSON JE, BROWN AC. An assessment of various household food security measures in Hawaii has implications for national food security research and monitoring. J Nutr 2001, 131: 749–757.
18. COATES J, FRONGILLO EA, ROGERS BL, WEBB P, WILDE PE, et al. Commonalities in the experience of household food insecurity across cultures: what are measures missing? J Nutr 2006, 136: 1438S–1448S.
19. CONNELL CL, NORD M, LOFTON KL, YADRICK K. Food security of older children can be assessed using a standardized survey instrument. J Nutr 2004, 134: 2566–2572.
20. NORD M, HOPWOOD H. Recent advances provide improved tools for measuring children's food security. J Nutr 2007a, 137: 533–536.

21. NORD M, HOPWOOD H. Does interview mode matter for food security measurement? Telephone versus in-person interviews in the Current Population Survey Food Security Supplement. Public Health Nutr 2007b, 10: 1474–1480.

22. WEBB P, COATES J, FRONGILLO EA, ROGERS BL, SWINDALE A, et coll. Measuring household food insecurity: why it's so important and yet so difficult to do. J Nutr 2006, 136: 1404S–1408S.

23. FRONGILLO EA, JR. Validation of measures of food insecurity and hunger. J Nutr 1999, 129: 506S–509S.

Chapter 4
Modeling Sustainable Nutrition Security

David I. Gustafson

Abstract Sustainability considerations should be an integral component of food security assessments. Nourishing the expected global population of nine billion in the face of fast diminishing land and water resources and looming climate change has tremendous economic, environmental, and social implications. Furthermore, whereas much past work on food security had focused on feeding the world through more staple crop calories, the current emphasis is on nourishing the global population through the provision of a more nutrient-rich diet. Hence the focus on micronutrient deficiencies (so-called 'hidden hunger'), dietary diversity, and the nutrient density of the food supply—all critical components of overall nutritional status. To aid future assessments of 'sustainable nutrition security', we need a new methodology and some novel assessment metrics and tools. Seven metrics are proposed, each based on a combination of multiple indicators, for use in characterizing sustainable nutrition outcomes of food systems: (1) nutrient adequacy of foods and diets; (2) ecosystem stability; (3) food affordability and availability; (4) sociocultural wellbeing; (5) food safety; (6) resilience; and (7) waste and loss reduction. Each of the metrics comprises multiple indicators that are combined to derive an overall score (0–100). The metrics can be combined with simulation models and then deployed by decision-makers and investors to set meaningful goals, track progress, and evaluate the potential impact of targeted food system interventions. The goal is to improve food system sustainability and resilience and to improve human nutrition and health outcomes.

Keywords Food systems · Nutrition security · Modeling methodology · Metrics · Sustainability outcomes · Dietary quality outcomes

D.I. Gustafson (✉)
ILSI Research Foundation, Washington DC, USA
e-mail: dgustafson@ilsi.org; dr.dave@real-whirlwind.com

© Springer International Publishing AG 2017   43
H.K. Biesalski et al. (eds.), *Sustainable Nutrition in a Changing World*,
DOI 10.1007/978-3-319-55942-1_4

4.1 Introduction

The world's food systems are under escalating pressure to deliver nutritious and sustainably-produced food in the face of multiple threats, including human population growth, rapid urbanization, dwindling resources, and degraded ecosystems [1]. About 1 billion people lack sufficient food [2] and about 2 billion people suffer from a number of micronutrient deficiencies [3]. Paradoxically, more than 2 billion adults are overweight [4], of whom 500 million are obese [5]. These stark challenges to food systems and nutrition security cast an even more ominous shadow when they are considered in the context of intensifying extreme weather and climate change. The fifth assessment report from the United Nations Intergovernmental Panel on Climate Change (IPCC) highlighted the effects of changes in climate and water availability on crop yields, the resulting spikes and volatility in food prices and likely food shortages [6]. The US Third National Climate Assessment report detailed additional food security threats through effects on food processing, storage, transportation, and retailing [7]. To this was added a special report, prompted by recent extreme weather events, such as drought, wildfire, storms and flooding [8]. General public concern around food sustainability issues is growing.

Adapting food systems to global warming and water shortages is a daunting challenge. In currently dry regions, drought frequency will likely increase [6]. On-going climate change means that all areas are likely to suffer more frequent episodes of severe drought, with potentially devastating impacts on food security [9]. Although there is still much uncertainty in climate model predictions [10], a number of identified geographically-specific 'hotspots' are likely to be most affected [11]. The most vulnerable regions are those where water supply is highly variable, including both severe water scarcity [12, 13] and flooding risk [14]. Crop irrigation will become an ever more essential adaptation strategy [15]. However, there are many important food production regions where irrigation will not be viable in the long term, due to depletion of aquifers and reduced glacier- and snow-melt [16].

The overall net effect of climate on crop yields, commodity prices, and food availability is assessed through the use of so-called 'integrated models,' [17–19], capable of linking climate [20], crop [21], and economic [22] models. The science of integrated modeling, which has advanced rapidly in recent years, is now being increasingly used to assess alternative adaptation and mitigation scenarios and to test potential interventions in local, regional and global food systems. However, the underlying models being used in these assessments are often based on insufficient data. Further, model assumptions have not always been fully tested across different food systems that are critical to food and nutrition security. As a result, estimates can vary widely. Yield reductions due to climate change of more than 25% have been predicted for important grain crops [21]. These impacts on crop yields translate into effects on prices, land use conversion, and total food production. Net impacts on global food prices through year 2050 are estimated through the integrated models to range from negligible to price increases of more than 60% [22].

Agricultural innovations have played a role in adapting to climate change by boosting production, keeping food costs down, and thereby improving food security [23]. Sustainable intensification can help to close yield-gaps, defined as the difference between observed and theoretical crop yields. It can also contribute to climate mitigation, by significantly reducing the carbon footprint of food production. For instance, reducing global maize yield-gaps to the levels achieved in the US would produce an additional 335 MMT of maize grain [24]. Countries such as the US are also generally achieving higher levels of eco-efficiency, as measured by per-unit of production greenhouse gas emissions and the utilization of land, water, and energy [25]. These same countries are seeing their eco-efficiency levels increase more quickly than is the case in countries not pursuing a sustainable intensification strategy. During the first decade of the 21st century, high-intensification countries saw eco-efficiency increases in four major row crops: canola (26%), cotton (23%), maize (17%), and soybeans (18%). In stark contrast, low-intensification countries had no change in eco-efficiency during this same ten-year period [25].

The principal challenge to food systems is to integrate the 'productionist' supply side with the evolving food demand, made more complex by the nutrition transition. Our research center (CIMSANS, the Center for Integrated Modeling of Sustainable Agriculture and Nutrition Security) recently assembled a broad array of diverse private- and public-sector scientists with expertise across the different parts of the overall food system to discuss these issues: experts in agriculture, nutrition, sustainability, and modeling [26]. They described a vision to produce a comprehensive, globally integrated modeling methodology to describe how nutrients are produced, processed and consumed–in order to determine the fundamental role that food systems play in providing for 'sustainable nutrition security' (SNS). Several of these same researchers subsequently published a set of seven food system metrics for use in the assessment of SNS [27]. The primary purpose of this chapter is to describe these seven metrics and show how they may be used to assess SNS.

However, before proceeding further, it is important to distinguish between food security and nutrition security. Food security has been defined by the Food and Agriculture Organization (FAO) as the state or condition wherein:

> All people, at all times, have physical, economic and social access to sufficient, safe, and nutritious food to meet their dietary needs and food preferences for an active and healthy life [28].

Nutrition security is a much broader concept, as underscored by a recent Lancet series [29]. These two elements are brought together in the prevailing definition of food and nutrition security (FNS):

> All people at all times have physical, social and economic access to food, which is safe and consumed in sufficient quantity and quality to meet their dietary needs and food preferences, and is supported by an environment of adequate sanitation, health services and care, allowing for a healthy and active life [30].

The concept of FNS has now been extended to sustainable nutrition security (SNS) by adding the traditional dimensions of sustainability: economic, environmental, and social. Evaluating and eventually enhancing SNS requires the establishment of science-based and decision-relevant metrics that make it possible to categorize and compare different assessment and intervention scenarios [31]. Rather than considering food production only, an overall 'food systems' approach includes the food consumption side and the various strategies involving the food value chain and consumer behavior that are also potential targets for modification [32, 33].

4.2 Metrics for Characterizing Sustainable Nutrition Security

An initial set of SNS metrics was developed as part of a consensus report by a number of nutrition, climate change, food system, and economic experts representing a range of public and private institutions [26]. The present metrics can help to assess progress toward the Sustainable Development Goals (SDGs). Composite metrics can be composed of multiple indicators using a variety of algorithms. Indicators can be defined as quantitative or qualitative factors that capture system changes following an intervention in a simple and reliable manner. Indicators, in turn, are derived from multiple variables, with data collected through modeling or direct field observations.

The metrics, and their component indicators, were further refined at the ILSI RF workshop by a broad set of stakeholders from government, academia, and industry [34]. The seven chosen metrics were: (1) nutrient adequacy of foods and diets; (2) ecosystem stability; (3) food affordability and availability; (4) sociocultural wellbeing; (5) resilience; (6) food safety; and (7) waste and loss reduction [27]. These metrics were selected due to their importance as measures of the overall food system and its impact on human health, as well as its influence on social, economic and environmental sustainability. A key guiding principle in the development of the metrics was to avoid needless creation of new metrics or indicators when suitable ones already existed in the literature or in the community of practice. Another guiding principle was that the metrics should be based upon open data. Accordingly, literature reviews were conducted for each of the seven metrics to identify valid and reliable open data related to each metric and to develop appropriate indicators. After thorough evaluation, descriptions of individual metrics were sent to a range of topical experts for further review. The metrics were then given a final review by a larger, broad group of stakeholders from academia, governmental agencies, and the private sector (see Acknowledgements).

Each of the metrics and indicators was scored from 0 to 100, with higher values desirable. Various systems have been proposed for weighting indicators. However, based on stakeholder feedback, it was decided to apply equal weighting to indicators. Developing a method for quantifying each indicator on a scale of 0–100 was a challenge. In certain cases, a third party had already published an indicator scaled in this manner. Those were directly used as indicators. In other cases, the indicator itself was defined as a percentage, readily convertible to a 0–100 scale. Other indicators had a finite range of possible values, and could be scaled by simply applying a constant multiplicative factor. More challenging, however, were indicators which did not have a bounded range of possible values, such as Greenhouse Gas Emissions (GHGs) or Land Use. In these cases, a logarithmic equation was used to derive a 0–100 score [see 27]. The equation has a series of desirable characteristics. It has a score of 100 for the hypothetical case of no emissions/use, a score of 50 for median performance (e.g. during a specified baseline year), it asymptotically approaches a score of 0 as emissions/use increase, and it generates a normal distribution of scores if the underlying data are log-normally distributed (as is typically the case).

4.2.1 Nutrient Adequacy of Foods, Diets and the Food Supply

A literature review and consultation with a series of nutrition experts resulted in the selection of the following five Food's Nutrient Adequacy indicators: Non-Staple Food Energy, Shannon Diversity, Modified Functional Attribute Diversity, Nutrient Density Score, and Population Share with Adequate Nutrients. One potentially relevant indicator has been developed—the Healthy Eating Index [35]; however, this indicator is specific to the United States, having been developed to measure compliance with that country's Dietary Guidelines. It is also worth noting that these particular indicators focus on the adequacy of national food system nutrient levels to meet dietary requirements for essential nutrients, and therefore do not specifically address over-consumption at unhealthful levels or other nonlinear effects. The first four of the chosen indicators refer to food availability for an average consumer in the country of interest, and the fifth refers to the percentage of the population with dietary intake of specified food nutrients above certain thresholds. As such, the last indicator requires the collection of actual dietary data at the individual level, as well as estimates of inter-individual variation in dietary intake. All five of these indicators have recently appeared in the literature, and there are data available at the country level [36–38].

4.2.2 Ecosystem Stability

A food system cannot be considered sustainable unless its underlying resource base is sustained and it has neutral or positive impacts on important ecosystem services. These overall impacts are characterized using the Ecosystem Stability metric, with an indicator that quantifies the current status of ecosystems (Ecosystem Status) [39], together with a group of indicators based on the notion of eco-efficiency—with higher scores for food systems that have lower per capita environmental impacts.

Robust quantitative approaches for describing the environmental impact of agricultural production systems (pre-farm gate) have been developed [40, 41], but system boundaries for the analysis must be significantly expanded to include post-farm gate activities in order to quantify the overall impact of the food system on the environment. An example of such an approach using Life Cycle Assessment (LCA) modeling for a number of particular foods was recently reported by a multi-partner collaborative effort, the World Food LCA Database [42]. Based on current global data availability and previous LCA modeling work [25], four eco-efficiency indicators are specified: GHG Emissions, Net Freshwater Withdrawals, Non-Renewable Energy Use, and Land Use, all on a per capita basis. When applied at the national level, these indicators refer to all food system activities that take place within that country's borders, except for the GHG emissions and non-renewable energy use associated with movement (though not the production) of exported food, which are both allocated to the ultimate importing country.

All eco-efficiency metrics should be calculated using the accepted principles of LCA as specified in an appropriate International Organization for Standardization (ISO) standard, such as ISO 14040 [43]. As explained in the ISO standards, indirect effects and other forms of so-called 'consequential' LCA (comparing current realities to hypothetical counterfactuals) can be used if properly documented. However, for the sake of simplicity, the definitions and example calculations provided in this chapter use the more traditional form of LCA, known as 'attributional' LCA. This approach considers only the actual emissions and use of resources that can be attributed to current activities—rather than, for instance, comparing them to the water use that would occur in a re-forested farm field, or such factors as indirect land use change.

4.2.3 Food Affordability and Availability

Taste, cost, convenience, and cultural norms are the primary factors driving consumer food choices. Socioeconomic status and ease of access to foods also affect the type and nutrient quality of food purchases. These choices directly impact nutrition and sustainability outcomes, and the degree to which consumers have the capacity to make such choices is directly related to factors such as disposable income and food availability. At the national scale, additional measures of food access include the prevalence of poverty and the degree of income inequality. Four indicators are adopted: Food Affordability, Food Availability, Poverty Index, and Income Equality. The first three of these factors are reported annually as part of the Global Food Security Index (GFSI) [44]. The GFSI reporting system includes a spreadsheet providing country-level scores (0–100) for 109 countries for the years

2012–2015. This format is directly applicable to the methodology described herein and so no further adjustment is needed.

An additional economic metric that has been suggested by certain stakeholders is a measure of the economic health of the various players in the food system value chain. There are compelling arguments for doing so, as it is clear that these players, who are especially but not exclusively food producers, must remain financially viable if the overall food system is to remain sustainable. However, it was not possible to identify a suitable, widely accepted, globally applicable indicator for characterizing the economic health of this sector, so this has been left as a potential future enhancement of the metric methodology.

4.2.4 Sociocultural Wellbeing

Sociocultural wellbeing is essential to sustainable development. Together with environmental and economic considerations, the subject of the two previous metrics, societal factors are widely considered to be the co-equal third 'pillar' of sustainability [45]. Indeed, based on the FAO definition, sustainable diets are those that are nutrient-rich, affordable and culturally acceptable. Taste and culture affect food choices and drive eating habits.

The Sustainability Consortium has used a broad multi-stakeholder process to conduct an extensive 'hot spot' analysis within food supply chains and has identified a number of potential societal issues within commercial supply chains for foods. The list was evaluated to determine which of these factors can be quantified using data currently available at the national scale. This analysis resulted in the selection of the following four 'Sociocultural Wellbeing' indicators: Gender Equity, Extent of Child Labor, Respect for Community Rights, and Animal Health & Welfare.

4.2.5 Resilience

Extreme events, including those related to climate change (droughts, floods, heatwaves), have begun to induce excessive volatility in global food prices [46], causing the United Kingdom, for example, to recently sponsor a special report on the resilience of the global food system [47]. This UK report investigated the immediate impacts and indirect effects (due to a variety of potentially unhelpful national responses) of a multiple breadbasket failure. Such shocks threaten food security and livelihoods in complex ways that challenge conventional approaches to providing humanitarian and development assistance.

Resilience has been defined by the US Agency for International Development (USAID) as the ability of people, households, communities, countries, and systems to mitigate, adapt to, and recover from shocks and stresses in a manner that reduces chronic vulnerability and facilitates inclusive growth. Resilience is also defined as the capacity that ensures adverse stressors and shocks do not have long-lasting negative development consequences [48]. Resilience is difficult to measure, but there has been one comprehensive effort to quantify it at the national level, the ND-GAIN Index [49], one of the two indicators chosen to quantify overall resilience. The other is a measure of diversity in food production, which also helps build resilience by avoiding the potential for catastrophic consequences due to the loss of a sole crop (such as Ireland's historic potato famine of the mid-19th century).

4.2.6 Food Safety

Foods must obviously be free of biological and chemical hazards if they are to safely provide human nutrition. Some of these hazards, particularly harmful microorganisms, are expected to become an increasing concern under climate change, due to the more rapid growth possible with higher humidity and higher temperatures [50]. Potential hazards exist throughout supply chains, and there is extensive monitoring for foodborne disease, as summarized in the Global Burden of Foodborne Illnesses (GBFI) food safety report [51], which serves as one of the two 'Food Safety' indicators. The other indicator comes from the previously cited GFSI report, which contains an independent assessment of country-level efforts to ensure food safety [44].

4.2.7 Waste and Loss Reduction

The FAO estimates that approximately one-third (by weight) of all food produced for human consumption is lost or wasted each year [52]. Pre-consumer losses are relatively more important than post-consumer waste in lower-income countries, whereas post-consumer waste is greatest in higher-income countries. The environmental and economic costs associated with food waste and loss are immense. As noted previously, food systems generate a significant fraction of GHG emissions, are responsible for the majority of net freshwater withdrawals, and negatively impact biodiversity. Further, if decomposition occurs in predominantly anaerobic environments, much of the wasted food generates methane (CH_4), a powerful GHG that adds to the overall environmental burden of the world's food systems.

The proposed metric to quantify Waste and Loss Reduction is to simply express, as a percentage, the portion of the produced food that is not either lost (pre-consumer) or wasted (post-consumer). As noted above, about one-third of all produced food suffers one of these two fates, so the average value of this metric for all countries is a little less than 70. This includes the portion of produced food crops that are not harvested and left in the field. However, inedible or unused portions of food that are intentionally used for other purposes (such as energy generation or to restore soils) should not be counted as waste.

The new 'Food Loss and Waste Protocol' (FLW Protocol) has just been finalized by the World Resources Institute [53], a critical multi-stakeholder effort to develop the global accounting and reporting standard for quantifying food and associated inedible parts removed from the food supply chain. It is intended to enable a wide range of entities—countries, companies, and other organizations—to account for and report in a credible, practical, and internationally consistent manner how much food loss and waste is created and to identify where it occurs, enabling the targeting of efforts to reduce it. It is anticipated that this protocol will provide the most appropriate methodology to follow when attempting to quantify this metric in the future.

4.3   Use of the Metrics for SNS Assessment

Modeling the status of SNS is based on the incorporation of these seven metrics into a novel conceptual modeling framework. Public-private partnerships are being convened by CIMSANS to assemble the resources and expertise needed to implement the framework and conduct such assessments [26]. Through their interactions with each other and additional experts, the partnership members have already identified a number of additional integrated modeling improvements that would be desirable to include in the SNS assessment.

4.3.1   Conceptual Framework

The conceptual framework for what is required in order to characterize SNS is presented schematically in Fig. 4.1.

Current integrated models primarily describe the 'PRODUCERS' box in this figure, whereas the new conceptual framework also captures two new broad categories of food system activities: (1) all of the processes that convert raw agricultural commodities into the types of foods available in the marketplace (labeled 'FOOD CHAIN ACTORS'); and (2) the complex set of factors that combine to determine which and how much of the available foods are actually consumed by individuals (labeled 'CONSUMERS').

The metrics defined in this chapter must be incorporated into an overall food system modeling framework as summarized schematically in Fig. 4.1. The aforementioned partnerships will collaborate with a wide range of other organizations on the development of such tools. Private-sector players in the food value chain have critical information that must be combined with this basic production information. Actual consumption and overall sustainability of the various food types containing these nutrients are then complex functions of consumer preferences (taste,

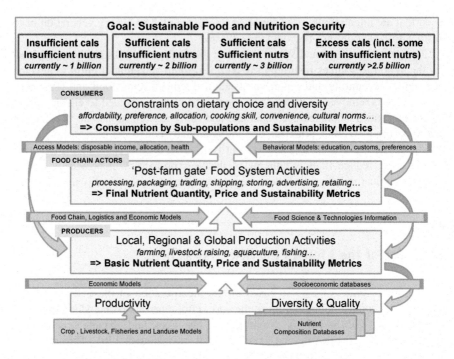

Fig. 4.1 Schematic demonstrating the multiple types of information that must be assembled in order to characterize SNS. Abbreviations: cals, calories; nutrs, nutrients (adapted from [24] and used with permission)

education, culture, food preparation, and waste), and access (disposable income, allocation, and prices). For instance, fruits and vegetables contain certain components (e.g. phytochemicals and other bioactive compounds) that may be critical for good health, which may not be accounted for in nutrient composition databases.

4.3.2   Assessing National Food System Performance

As a first example use of the metrics, they were used to describe the current status of SNS among nine countries for which data were readily available [27]. Projections of future SNS status are of keen interest to many stakeholders, and these metrics are intended to eventually be coupled with the outputs of integrated models such as IMPACT [54]. This will make it possible, for instance, to quantify the effect of climate and water availability changes on future nutrition and sustainability outcomes. One example of this approach already underway involves the calculation of the 'Food's Nutrient Adequacy' metrics from IMPACT model run results (GC Nelson et al., in preparation).

4.3.3   Selection of New Food System Practices

The metrics presented here are ideal for assessing the effectiveness of food system policies and practices intended to improve human nutrition and sustainability outcomes. Such developments are urgently needed in order to build resilience of the global food system to extreme weather under climate change [47]. For instance, greater adoption of Climate-Smart Agriculture (CSA) practices is one set of actions that are needed, including practices that mitigate emissions and build more resilient systems [55]. Modeled values for the seven metrics could be used to assess the relative merits of adopting particular food system policies and practices.

4.3.4   Setting Targets and Monitoring Progress

The metrics can also be used to set targets and monitor progress on the adoption and impact of new food system practices specifically tailored to the needs of particular countries, especially those relevant to attaining the newly adopted SDGs. Food systems have been characterized as complex adaptive systems [56], which means that unintended consequences are possible. For instance, a recommendation to eat more fruits and vegetables may cause additional ground water depletion in drought-stricken areas and have impacts on social systems through increased requirements for immigrant labor. It is therefore essential that whatever metrics are utilized are intrinsically holistic and therefore capable of detecting such nuanced effects. The metrics presented here are specifically intended to do just that, making it possible for policy-makers and investors to set targets on particular areas of current interest (e.g., more nutritious diets), while at the same time having confidence that economic, environmental, and social measures of sustainability are being monitored and potentially improved as well.

4.4   Conclusions

Climate change, extreme weather, and dwindling natural resources represent major challenges for the world's current food systems. Sustainable food systems need to meet accelerating global demand for food in a manner that will meet human nutrition and health needs and comply with environmental constraints. The food system metrics presented here make it possible—for the first time—to holistically and accurately measure food system performance across all relevant domains of interest. The key domains are nutrition, environment, economic, social, resilience, safety, and waste. This new metrics methodology permits a quantification of sustainable nutrition security (SNS)—a potentially useful tool for decision-makers for setting meaningful goals, prioritizing investments, and tracking progress on SDGs.

The seven sustainability metrics can be applied to all countries, regardless of income level. Although the focus of this chapter has been on the application of the metrics at the national scale, some or all of the metrics would also have practical utility at smaller geographic scales, albeit with the requirement for collecting and reporting data of finer spatial resolution. It should also be noted that a lack of data for some countries on some of these indicators could represent a lack of policy monitoring and therefore highlight areas for action.

4.5   Summary: Key Messages

- Sustainability considerations have largely been absent from most food security assessments conducted to date.
- A new methodology has been developed based on the concept of 'sustainable nutrition security.' This novel assessment methodology is intended to remedy both kinds of deficiencies in the previous work by defining seven metrics.
- These metrics are: (1) food's nutrient adequacy; (2) ecosystem stability; (3) food affordability and availability; (4) sociocultural wellbeing; (5) food safety; (6) resilience; and (7) waste and loss reduction.
- These food system metrics make it possible—for the first time—to holistically and accurately measure food system performance across all relevant domains of interest: nutrition, environment, economic, social, resilience, safety, and waste.
- This new methodology allows quantification of sustainable nutrition security (SNS), an approach which can now be deployed by decision-makers and investors to set meaningful goals, track progress on SDGs, and evaluate the potential impact of food system interventions intended to improve both human and planetary health.

Acknowledgements Many scientists contributed to recent research and discussions that served as the underlying basis for this chapter. Space prohibits mentioning all of them, but they include: Tara Acharya, Lindsay Allen, Joanne Arsenault, Steve Betz, Laura Birx, Jessica Bogard, Ken Boote, Marisa Caipo, Joyce Coffee, Janet Collins, Karen Cooper, Brecht Devleesschauwer, Dona Dickinson, Adam Drewnowski, Frank Ewert, Jess Fanzo, John Finley, Martijn Gipmans, Rachel Goldstein, Alona Gutman, Stephen Hall, Paul Hendley, Margaret Henry, Mario Herrero, Mark Howden, John Ingram, Molly Jahn, Sander Janssen, James Jones, Ahmed Kablan, Sue Krebs-Smith, Sascha Lamstein, Marie Latulippe, Ray Layton, Whitney Leet, Uma Lele, Gene Lester, Keith Lividini, Hermann Lotze-Campen, Sarah Lowder, Matt Lyon, John McDermott, Morven McLean, Hans van Meijl, Gerald Nelson, Rosie Newsome, Victor Pinga, Roseline Remans, Malcolm Riley, Kai Robertson, Mark Rosegrant, Anne Roulin, Sherman Robinson, Barbara Schneeman, Bob Scholes, Erin Sexson, Emily Shipman, Nathalie Sinclair, Christy Melhart Slay, Pamela Starke-Reed, Anne Swindale, Sherry Tanumihardjo, Gail Tavill, Allison Thomson, Dominique van der Mensbrugghe, Michael Wach, Richard Waite, Keith Wiebe, and Manfred Zeller. The work of these tremendously gifted scientists, who were all so generous with their time and efforts, is warmly appreciated.

References

1. Freibauer, A., Mathijs, E., Brunori, G., Damianova, Z., Faroult, E., Girona i Gomis, J., O'Brien, L., Treyer, S., 2011. Sustainable food consumption and production in a resource-constrained world, summary findings of the EU SCAR Third Foresight Exercise. EuroChoices 10, 38–43
2. FAO (Food and Agriculture Organization of the United Nations), 2013a. Food Systems for Better Nutrition. Available from: http://www.fao.org/docrep/018/i3300e/i3300e.pdf. Accessed 21 May 2014
3. FAO (Food and Agriculture Organization of the United Nations), 2012. The State of Food Insecurity in the World 2012. Economic growth is necessary but not sufficient to accelerate reduction of hunger and malnutrition. Rome, FAO. Available from: http://www.fao.org/docrep/016/i3027e/i3027e.pdf. Accessed 21 May 2014
4. Ng, M. et al., 2014. Global, regional, and national prevalence of overweight and obesity in children and adults during 1980–2013: a systematic analysis for the Global Burden of Disease Study 2013. The Lancet. Available from: http://dx.doi.org/10.1016/S0140-6736(14)60460-8. Accessed 30 June 2014
5. Keats, S., Wiggins, S., 2014. Future Diets: Implications for Agriculture and Food Prices. ODI Report. Overseas Development Institute, London
6. Field et al. 2014. Climate Change 2014: Impacts, Adaptation, and Vulnerability, Summary for Policymakers, UN IPCC WGII Fifth Assessment Report, Geneva, Switzerland, 44 pp
7. Melilo, J.M.; Richmond, T.C.; Yohe, G.W., Eds. *Highlights of Climate Change Impacts in the United States: The Third National Climate Assessment*; U.S. Global Change Research Program: Washington DC, USA, 2014, pp. 46–47
8. J Buizer, P Fleming, S Hays, K Dow, C Field, D Gustafson, A Luers, R Moss, M Black, G Lough, S Moser, T Richmond, A Waple "Preparing the Nation for Change: Building a Sustained National Climate Assessment Process," US National Climate Assessment and Development Advisory Committee, US Global Change Research Program, Washington, DC, 73 pp. 2013
9. Grayson, M. Agriculture and drought. *Nature* **2013**, *501*, S1
10. Warszawski et al. 2014. The Inter-Sectoral Impact Model Intercomparison Project (ISI-MIP): Project framework, PNAS, 4 March 2014, 111(9):3228–3232
11. Piontek et al. 2014. Multisectoral climate impact hotspots in a warming world, PNAS, 4 March 2014, 111 (9):3233–3238
12. Prudhomme et al. 2014. Hydrological droughts in the 21st century, hotspots and uncertainties from a global multimodel ensemble experiment, PNAS, 4 March 2014, 111(9):3262–3267
13. Schewe et al. 2014. Multimodel assessment of water scarcity under climate change, PNAS, 4 March 2014, 111(9):3245–3250
14. Dankers et al. 2014. First look at changes in flood hazard in the Inter-Sectoral Impact Model Intercomparison Project ensemble, PNAS, 4 March 2014, 111(9):3257–3261
15. Elliott et al. 2014. Constraints and potentials of future irrigation water availability on agricultural production under climate change, PNAS, 4 March 2014, 111(9):3239–3244
16. Haddeland et al. 2014. Global water resources affected by human interventions and climate change, PNAS, 4 March 2014, 111(9):3251–3256
17. Parry, M.L., Rosenzweig, C., Iglesias, A., Livermore, M., Fischer, G., 2004. Effects of climate change on global food production under SRES emissions and socio-economic scenarios. Global Environ. Change 14, 53–67
18. Goulding, K., Jarvis, S., Whitmore, A., 2008. Optimizing nutrient management for farm systems. Phil. Trans. R. Soc. B. 363, 667–680
19. Rosenzweig, C., Jones, J.W., Hatfield, J.L., Ruane, A.C., Boote, K.J., Thorburn, P., Antle, J. M., Nelson, G.C., Porter, C., Janssen, S., Asseng, S., Basso, B., Ewert, F., Wallach, D., Baigorria, G. and Winter, J.M., 2013. The Agricultural Model Intercomparison and

Improvement Project (AgMIP): Protocols and pilot studies. Forest. Agr. Meteorol., 170, 166–182. doi:10.1016/j.agrformet.2012.09.011

20. ES Takle, R Beachy, D Gustafson, GC Nelson, D Mason-D'Croz, and A Palazzo "US Food Security and Climate Change: Agricultural Futures," US. Economics Discussion Papers, No 2013–17, Kiel Institute for the World Economy. http://www.economics-ejournal.org/economics/discussionpapers/2013-17. 2013

21. Rosenzweig et al. 2014. Assessing agricultural risks of climate change in the 21st century in a global gridded crop model intercomparison, PNAS, 4 March 2014, 111(9):3268–3273

22. Nelson et al. 2014. Climate change impacts on agriculture: Economic responses to biophysical shocks, PNAS, 4 March 2014, 111(9):3274–3279

23. Mark W. Rosegrant, Jawoo Koo, Nicola Cenacchi, Claudia Ringler, Richard Robertson, Myles Fisher, Cindy Cox, Karen Garrett, Nicostrato D. Perez, Pascale Sabbagh, Food security in a world of natural resource scarcity : the role of agricultural technologies; International Food Research Policy Institute: Washington DC, USA, 2014, pp. 109–118

24. Gustafson, D.; JW Jones, CH Porter, G Hyman, MD Edgerton, T Gocken, J Shryock, M Doane, K Budreski, C Stone, D Healy, N Ramsey "Climate Adaptation Imperatives: Untapped Global Maize Yield Opportunities," Int. J. Agric. Sustain., DOI 10.1080/14735903.2013.867694 2014

25. Gustafson, D., J Shryock, M Doane, M Matlock, D Zilberman, M Collins, J Fry, S Smith, N Ramsey "Climate Adaptation Imperatives: Global Sustainability Trends and Eco-Efficiency Metrics in Four Major Crops: Canola, Cotton, Maize, and Soybeans," Int. J. Agric. Sustain., DOI: 10.1080/14735903.2013.846017 2013

26. Acharya, T. et al. June 2014. *Assessing Sustainable Nutrition Security: The Role of Food Systems*. ILSI Research Foundation, Center for Integrated Modeling of Sustainable Agriculture and Nutrition Security. Washington, DC, 39 pp. Accessible at: http://bit.ly/ILSIRF_SNS_2014. [Accessed 9 August 2016]

27. Gustafson, D., A. Gutman, W. Leet, A. Drewnowski, J. Fanzo, J. Ingram 2016. Seven Food System Metrics of Sustainable Nutrition Security, Sustainability, 8 (3), 196

28. FAO (Food and Agriculture Organization of the United Nations), 1996. The State of Food and Agriculture. Available from: http://www.fao.org/docrep/003/w1358e/w1358e14.htm#P36_6144. Accessed 21 May 2014

29. Horton, R., Lo, S., 2013. Nutrition: a quintessential sustainable development goal. Lancet 382, 371–372

30. CFS (Committee on World Food Security), 2012. Coming to Terms with Terminology, Food Security Nutrition Security Food Security and Nutrition Food and Nutrition Security. Report of the 39th Session, 15–20 October 2012 Committee on World Food Security Food and Agriculture Organization of the United Nations Rome, Italy

31. Fanzo, J., Cogill, B., Mattei, F., 2012. Metrics of Sustainable Diets and Food Systems. Bioversity International, Rome, Italy

32. Ericksen, P. J., 2008. Conceptualizing food systems for global environmental change research. Global Environ. Change 18, 234–245

33. Ingram J.S.I., 2011. From Food Production to Food Security: Developing Interdisciplinary, Regional-Level Research [thesis]. Wageningen University. Wageningen, The Netherlands. 152 pp. ISBN 978-94-6173-002-2

34. ILSI Research Foundation, 2015. *ILSI Research Foundation Gathers Stakeholder Input on the Ability of our Food Systems to Achieve Long- term Nutrition Security*; ILSI Research Foundation: Washington, DC, USA

35. Guenther, P.M.; Casavale, K.O.; Reedy, J.; Kirkpatrick, S.I.; Hiza, H.A.B.; Kuczynski, K.J.; Kahle, L.L.; Krebs-Smith, S.M. Update of the healthy eating index: HEI-2010. J. Acad. Nutr. Diet. 2013, 113, 569–580

36. Remans, R.; Wood, S.A.; Saha, N.; Anderman, T.L.; Defries, R.S. Measuring nutritional diversity of national food supplies. Glob. Food Secur. 2014, 3, 174–182

37. Arsenault, J.E.; Hijmans, R.J.; Brown, K.H. Improving nutrition security through agriculture: An analytical framework based on national food balance sheets to estimate nutritional adequacy of food supplies. Food Secur. 2015, 7, 693–707

38. Fern, E.B.; Watzke, H.; Barclay, D.V; Roulin, A.; Drewnowski, A. The nutrient balance concept: A new quality metric for composite meals and diets. PLoS ONE 2015, 10, e0130491

39. Hsu, A.; Emerson, J.; Levy, M.; de Sherbinin, A.; Johnson, L.; Malik, O.; Schwartz, J.; Jaiteh, M. The 2014 Environmental Performance Index; Yale Center for Environmental Law and Policy: New Haven, CT, USA, 2014

40. BASF, 2014. *AgBalance: Measuring Agricultural Sustainability*, http://www.agro.basf.com/agr/AP-Internet/en/content/sustainability/measuring_sustainability/agbalance/index [accessed 29 April 2014]

41. Field to Market. Environmental and Socioeconomic Indicators for Measuring Outcomes of on-Farm Agricultural Production in the United States; Field to Market: Washington, DC, 2012

42. Nemecek, T.; Bengoa, X.; Lansche, J.; Mouron, P.; Riedener, E.; Rossi, V.; Humbert, S. Methodological Guidelines for the Life Cycle Inventory of Agricultural Products, Version 3.0; World Food LCA Database: Lausanne and Zurich, Switzerland, 2015

43. International Organization for Standardization (ISO). ISO 14040: 2006—Environmental management—Life Cycle Assessment—Principles and Framework; ISO: Geneva, Switzerland, 2010

44. The Economic Intelligence Unit. Global Food Security Index 2015: An Annual Measure of the State of Global Food Security; The Economic Intelligence Unit: New York, NY, USA, 2015

45. The Sustainability Consortium. Transforming the Consumer Goods Industry to Deliver More Sustainable Consumer Products; The Sustainability Consortium: Fayetteville, AR, USA, 2015

46. World Bank. Responding to Higher and More Volatile World Food Prices; World Bank: Washington, DC, USA, 2012

47. UK Global Food Security Programme. Extreme Weather and Resilience of the Global Food System (2015); Final Project Report from the UK-US Taskforce on Extreme Weather and Global Food System Resilience; UK Global Food Security Programme: London, UK, 2015

48. Federation of Saskatchewan Indian Nations (FSIN). A Common Analytical Model for Resilience Measurement; FSIN: Saskatoon, SK, Canada, 2014

49. Chen, C.; Noble, I.; Hellmann, J.; Coffee, J.; Murillo, M.; Chawla, N. University of Notre Dame Global Adaptation Index Country Index Technical Report; ND-GAIN: South Bend, IN, USA, 2015

50. Miraglia, M.; Marvin, H.J.P.; Kleter, G.A.; Battilani, P.; Brera, C.; Coni, E.; Cubadda, F.; Croci, L.; De Santis, B.; Dekkers, S.; et al. Climate change and food safety: An emerging issue with special focus on Europe. Food Chem. Toxicol. 2009, 47, 1009–1021

51. World Health Organization (WHO). WHO Estimates of the Global Burden of Foodborne Diseases; WHO: Geneva, Switzerland, 2015

52. Food and Agriculture Organization (FAO). Food Wastage Footprints; FAO: Rome, Italy, 2013

53. World Resources Institute Food Loss and Waste Protocol. Available online: http://www.wri.org/our-work/project/global-food-loss-and-waste-measurement-protocol/documents-and-updates#project-tabs (accessed on 8 January 2016)

54. Rosegrant, M.W. International Model for Policy Analysis of Agricultural Commodities and Trade (IMPACT) Model Description; International Food Policy Research Institute (IFPRI): Washington, DC, USA, 2012

55. Food and Agriculture Organization (FAO). Climate-Smart Agriculture Sourcebook; FAO: Rome, Italy, 2013

56. Institute of Medicine (IOM); National Research Council (NRC). A Framework for Assessing Effects of the Food System; IOM: Washington, DC, 2015

Part II
Social Disparities in Food and Nutrition Security (Jana Rückert-John)

Chapter 5
Nutrition Security in Older Adults: Status Quo and Future Development

Christine A.F. von Arnim

Abstract Malnutrition is frequent in older adults on account of a range of physiological, psychological and infrastructural problems. Physiological and psychological problems cannot be circumvented, but the infrastructural aspects of this phenomenon merit closer study. In light of the demographic change occurring worldwide, an increase in the number of malnourished older adults within the global population is to be anticipated. The energy needs of this group decrease with advancing age, but their micronutrient needs remain. Decreased food intake may therefore automatically lead to an inadequate supply of essential micronutrients. Little data currently exists on food security in older adults. The global dimension of the problem of food security in older adults may be overlooked in particular in countries which have plenty of food. Nursing homes present a range of nutritional risks for their residents and exhibit specific problems regarding food insecurity in older adults. Food insecurity and socio-economic issues may have implications not only for immediate nutritional outcomes, but also for age-associated diseases and conditions. Populations at increased risk are therefore in need of specific screening and action plans for food and nutrition assistance. This will be an increasingly tough challenge in the future.

Keywords Malnutrition · Demographic change · Energy needs · Food security · Nursing homes · Socio-economic issues

5.1 State of the Art

Malnutrition is frequent in older adults. It is more common, and is also on the increase, among the older population: in 2004, 16% of those >65 years and 2% of those >85 years were classified as malnourished in the UK [1]. Other studies in

C.A.F. von Arnim (✉)
Neurologische Universitätsklinik Ulm, Ulm, Germany
e-mail: christine.arnim@uni-ulm.de

© Springer International Publishing AG 2017
H.K. Biesalski et al. (eds.), *Sustainable Nutrition in a Changing World*,
DOI 10.1007/978-3-319-55942-1_5

developed countries reported that 15–30% of community dwelling and home-bound older adults have food intake lower than the recommended daily requirements [2]. In a Dutch cohort of geriatric outpatients, prevalence of malnutrition and risk of malnutrition were reported as high as 17% and 58% according to the mini nutritional assessment (MNA) [3]. The problem of malnutrition is even more evident in residents of nursing homes: A longitudinal study in 85-year-old inhabitants of nursing homes in Sweden reported 18% malnutrition by MNA [4]. In a study of institutionalized older adults in Spain, a prevalence of malnutrition and risk of malnutrition of 40% was reported [5]. In a German study in nursing home residents, 60.2% were categorized as malnourished (18.2%) or at risk of malnutrition (42.0%) by MNA [6]. In hospitalized elderly patients, this tendency becomes even more pronounced, with 23–62% reported as suffering from malnutrition [7]. These figures are predicted to rise dramatically between now and 2050, as the older population is increasing worldwide due to demographic changes.

Energy needs decrease with age. The impacts of aging on body composition have an influence on the individual's nutritional needs. The part of total body weight that is accounted for by fat increases by about 50% over time and muscle mass declines, often accompanied by overweight [8]. A decrease in lean body mass due to a loss of skeletal muscle begins on average around the seventh decade. Physical activity and physical energy expenditure decline with aging. Basal metabolic rate declines by about 2% per decade. Energy metabolism also decreases due to a decline in Na^+/K^+-ATPase activity, reduced muscle protein turnover, and possibly also changes in mitochondrial membrane protein permeability. Meal-induced thermogenesis shows a delay to peak, possibly due to a delay in gastric emptying [9]. Thus a lower energy intake is required in older age. However, micronutrient requirements remain, and protein requirements may even be higher than for younger adults, as some studies suggest [10]. This may lead to an inadequate supply of essential micronutrients and proteins in the case of older adults.

There are several reasons why micronutrient levels decrease in older adults:

1. As general food intake is often reduced in older adults due to lower requirements for general energy uptake, the amount of micronutrients in the diet diminishes concomitantly.
2. Impaired absorption and metabolism of certain micronutrients is commonly observed in older adults. The prevalence of atrophic gastritis increases with age, affecting more than 30% of individuals [11] and causing significantly lower absorption of vitamin B_{12}. Age-related decrease of calcium and vitamin D receptor expression in the duodenum has been shown. Furthermore, the synthesis of vitamin D in the skin decreases with age.
3. Olfactory and gustatory functions are reduced. The density of taste buds decreases with age. Changes in taste and smell sensitivity may reduce the pleasure of eating, thereby contributing to a change in eating habits.
4. Multimorbidity and therefore multimedication is common in older adults. This may not only impair appetite, but also have interaction potential regarding the

Table 5.1 Critical nutrients in older adults

Micronutrient	Challenges and problems in older adults
Vitamin B_{12}	Reduces homocysteine. Bioavailability decreases mainly due to atrophic gastritis. Increases risk of cardiovascular diseases and cognitive impairment
Folate	Through its role in reducing elevated homocysteine, closely related to vitamins B_{12} and B_6
Vitamin B_6	Through its role in reducing elevated homocysteine, closely related to vitamin B_{12} and folate
Vitamin B_1	Risk factor: prolonged parental feeding, often underdiagnosed in confused older adults
Calcium	Deficits common in elderly women. Mean intake decreases with age, probably related to general change in diet
Vitamin D	Less sun exposure in older adults. Diminished ability of the skin to build vitamin D and of liver and kidney to hydroxylate vitamin D with age. Increased risk of fracture
Vitamin A	Absorption increases, elimination decreases with age: risk of vitamin A toxicity increases with age
Vitamin C	Smoking increases need
Iron	Women's iron requirements change after the menopause. Deficiencies are mainly seen among hospitalized, institutionalized, or chronically ill older adults
Zinc	Deficiency is common in older adults

uptake and metabolism of micronutrients. Chronic disease can cause increased nutrient turnover.

Several specific micronutrients have been linked to deficiencies in older adults. Key nutrients are listed in Table 5.1.

5.2   Food Security in Older Adults

Older adults tend to show lower levels of food insecurity than younger populations, but estimates of the prevalence of food insecurity among older adults have been increasing in the last decade. Factors that limit the ability of older adults to have access to sufficient food for an active, healthy life are: poor health, disabilities, social isolation and community characteristics (Table 5.2). The growing prevalence of food insecurity in older adults may be overlooked in particular in countries which have plenty of food. According to USDA, in 2008 the prevalence of food insecurity in the United States, as analyzed by specific questionnaires, was 8.1% of households with older adults and 8.8% among older adults living alone [12]. There are still no comprehensive measures to define malnutrition, especially for micronutrient deficits in older persons. The MNA is often applied in research settings, and seems to be a better indicator of malnutrition than body mass index (BMI) alone [13], but is not routinely used in population-based settings.

Table 5.2 Causes of food insecurity and malnutrition in older adults

Medical conditions
Functional limitations and disability, motor capacity
Medication
Poor dentition
Loss of sense of taste, loss of appetite
Perceived abilities, health perception
Food beliefs and attitudes
Poverty
Inability to shop, and to prepare and cook meals
Social isolation, loneliness, loss of partners
Lack of company during meals
Community characteristics (e.g. rural vs. urban, availability of transportation, grocery store, etc.)

Older adults are at high risk of chronic disease conditions, which contribute to functional limitations and disability that can be exacerbated by food insecurity, poor nutritional status, and low physical activity. Causes of food insecurity and malnutrition are listed in Table 5.2. Food insecurity in older adults is associated with low nutrient intakes, increased risk of malnutrition, unhealthy body weight and body size, poorer self-reported health status, anemia, multimorbidity and disability, poorer physical performance, lower cognitive function, anxiety and depression, and decreased quality of life. Food insecurity contributes to the development or exacerbation of diet-related illnesses. It is associated with non-adherence to medications due to cost, increased hypoglycemic episodes, and increased health care utilization [12]. Taken together, food insecurity and malnutrition build a seemingly vicious cycle regarding nutritional and health issues in older adults.

5.3 Socio-Economic and Infrastructural Issues

Many older adults face challenges associated with their environment, their social and financial status, and their level of functional ability. Many older people have been widowed, have had their children move to other geographical areas, are living on a fixed income, and experience disability. Cooking for one may be difficult. There may be financial challenges associated with limited income, living on pensions, or social security. Health care costs can be burdensome, even for someone in relatively good health; in the case of an individual with multiple chronic conditions or acute illness, these costs may be financially disastrous. Disability may lead older adults to become housebound or more dependent on social services that help them meet their basic needs. Transportation may become more difficult for older, physically challenged adults. Obesity is a risk factor for disability, and a sedentary lifestyle is a risk factor for obesity; this is a difficult cycle to avoid, but one that places an additional burden on nutritional intake and status [14].

5.4 Nursing Homes

The risk of obvious malnutrition in older adults living in nursing homes is about twice as high as in older adults living in the community. Institutionalized older adults are a group that typically suffers from a number of medical conditions that are associated either with increased metabolic requirements or with anorexia, with consequently reduced food intake. Energy expenditure is decreased in the setting of a nursing home. Not only poor food intake, but also decreased fluid intake is often observed in institutionalized older adults [15]. Nursing home residents at risk of malnutrition are more often female, in higher need of care, and more dependent during mealtimes. Regarding functional status, cognitive impairment, depression and restricted mobility are typical co-morbid conditions in residents of nursing homes. All nutritional risk markers are consistently associated with functional status [6].

5.5 Consequences

The consequences of malnutrition in older adults are serious. Weight loss is associated with loss of muscle mass, contributing to sarcopenia and frailty [16] and therefore promoting disabilities and loss of independence [17]. The loss of muscle mass as well as the high incidence of osteoporosis, plus associated clinical conditions such as falls and bone fractures, can lead to immobilization and reduced independence. In addition, malnutrition, especially lack of micronutrients, is associated with a broad variety of **increased morbidity** in older persons, including (cardio) vascular diseases, obesity, and metabolic diseases such as diabetes. Increased infections and inflammatory processes can be due to lack of protein and specific micronutrients.

Malnutrition has been associated with cognitive impairment and dementia. Specific nutrient biomarker patterns (NBPs) assessed by blood tests are associated with cognitive function and MRI measures of the brain. Two NBPs are associated with more favorable cognitive outcome: one high in plasma vitamins B (B_1, B_2, B_6, folate and B_{12}), C, D, and E, and another high in plasma marine ω-3 fatty acids. A third pattern characterized by high trans fat is associated with less favorable cognitive function and less brain volume in a study in 104 persons aged 87 +/− 10 years old [18]. Another study using food frequency questionnaires (FFQ) found that DASH-(dietary approach to stop hypertension) and Mediterranean-like dietary patterns are associated with slower rates of cognitive decline in older adults (81.5 +/ −7.1 years) [19].

Current epidemiologic evidence points towards an important role for nutrition not only in the prevention of Alzheimer's disease (AD) but also in the progression of AD (for review, see [20]). Weight loss and malnutrition are indicators of faster progression of AD. When assessing nutritional status not by BMI but by MNA, a baseline lower MNA and a lower cognitive performance were found as predictors of progression. In AD patients, multivariate analysis showed that only the MNA was correlated with rate of decline. Healthy diets may help to attenuate cognitive decline in older adults (for review, see [21]). Adherence to the Mediterranean diet (MeDi) is related to lower risk of AD [22], and also improves subsequent disease course: Higher adherence to the MeDi is associated with lower mortality in AD [23].

A high percentage of elderly nursing home residents in a Danish study suffered from weight loss associated with several potentially modifiable nutritional risk factors such as eating dependency, swallowing problems and enteral nutrition [24]. Malnourished older adults are at risk not only of increased morbidity, but also increased mortality. In the above-mentioned study in Swedish nursing homes, half of the population died after 24 months, with significantly lower survival in the malnourished group [4].

Food insecurity in older adults resulting in malnutrition is a clinically relevant problem that not only increases disease burden, but also has important implications for social and economic factors such as healthcare costs [12] including the quality, expenditures, and utilization of healthcare, and it may also increase demand for individual caregiving costs and national healthcare costs. However, few studies have examined the relationship between food insecurity and the healthcare cost burden in older adults [25]. Food insecurity is associated with cost-related medication non-adherence [26].

Food insecurity in older adults is a complex, multidimensional phenomenon caused not only by financial constraints but also by poor health, physical limitations, lack of social support, and other problems. Therefore food insecurity in older adults does not show a direct relationship to social inequality, as it does in the case of other groups at risk of food insecurity. Food insecurity in this focus group is, rather, related to disease conditions and their implications, and is heightened by the need for institutionalization.

Food insecurity and malnutrition

Food insecurity is associated with poor food and nutrient intake, physical and mental health problems, poor chronic disease management, medication non-adherence, and increased use of healthcare services.

Consequences of **malnutrition** due to food insecurity in older adults include a variety of geriatric conditions and diseases: frailty, sarcopenia, osteoporosis, falls, (cardio) vascular diseases, weight loss (anorexia of aging), but also obesity and diabetes, infections and inflammatory processes, and depression, as well as cognitive impairment and dementia. This leads not only to decreased quality of life, but also increased mortality.

Food insecurity is a persistent, growing, and clinically relevant problem in older adults. However, as an adequate dietary intake has been well recognized as a necessary factor in improving longevity, maintaining good health and quality of life [27], food security in older adults needs to be addressed in light of the demographic changes taking place in society.

As health status and chronic disease conditions are interconnected with food security and malnutrition in older adults in a vicious cycle, an integrated approach with a focus on infrastructural aspects is called for. We also need to define what kind of food patterns and what kind of supply with micronutrients will support longevity with healthy and successful aging. On the other hand, as aging is associated with many chronic disease conditions, we need to learn more about specific needs. Research gaps therefore include identifying specific needs and defining adequate DRAs of older adults in general and also of specific subgroups with specific needs (chronic disease conditions, etc.).

5.6   State of the Art of Intervention

5.6.1   Screening

Early identification of older persons, especially nursing home residents at nutritional risk, is necessary. This should be followed by adequate nutritional support. This can contribute to conservation of muscle function and strength and thereby to maintenance of independence, quality of life, and increased survival. Low BMI, weight loss and low food intake are key factors for diagnosing malnutrition or nutritional risk, but lack sensitivity and specificity. Several screening tools tailored for older adults have been developed. The MNA [13] was published in 1994, and a shorter screening form (MNA-SF) [28] in 2001. These provide healthcare professionals with validated tools to identify older adults at risk of malnutrition and to guide nutritional interventions. The MNA is the most commonly used screening and part of the Comprehensive Geriatric Assessment (CGA), but it is not a mandatory integral part. The CGA is a multidimensional, multidisciplinary diagnostic process used to determine medical, functional, and psychosocial problems and capabilities in a geriatric patient who may be at risk of functional decline. Several studies in Australia showed that it is feasible to include the MNA short form and a nutrition resource kit within routine general practice, identifying one third of obese patients in the at risk-group [29, 30]. However, screening tools are still not routinely used in geriatric practice worldwide.

5.6.2 Food and Nutrition Programs

The next step after identification of individuals at risk is to address the problem adequately. Several programs have therefore been developed, and are already being partially implemented in general practice. Three kinds of program can be distinguished:

1. *General food and nutrition programs for healthy nutrition and aging:* Educational intervention programs have been developed, implemented, and evaluated, and outcomes have been published in senior centers throughout Georgia, US [12]. Websites with specific nutritional advice for older adults have been implemented in many countries. However, there is little data on how effective these measures are, as food insecurity persists, especially in older people. We still need a better understanding of true/unmet needs in older adults, and also of the impact of food assistance programs, to provide adequate program resources and benefits.
2. *Specific programs for persons with specific clinical conditions (e.g. risk of dementia):* Findings from a large, long-term, randomized controlled trial in Finland (FINGER study) suggest that a multi-domain intervention including individualized nutritional advice could improve or maintain cognitive functioning in at-risk older people from the general population [31]. More research into the effectiveness of such measures tailored to specific disease conditions is needed.
3. *Specific programs for populations at risk of malnutrition or in which malnutrition has been identified:* In recent years, several guidelines and standards have been developed to facilitate the translation of scientific knowledge into practice. These guidelines and standards provide recommendations for adequate nutritional care and assistance for the institutionalized older adults based on the scientific state of the art. In Germany, these are the medical Guidelines for Enteral and Parenteral Nutrition in Geriatrics (DGEM/DGG and ESPEN), the DNQP Expert Standard for qualified nurses, the DGE Quality Standards for dietetic personnel, and the interdisciplinary BUKO-QS Standard [32]. The same has been established on a European basis and accepted by the Council of Europe. Other countries have also detailed recommendations, guidelines and standards. Recommendations from different guidelines for nutrition in nursing homes are summarized in Table 5.3. Furthermore, practical local guidelines should be implemented in all geriatric hospital wards and nursing homes in order to improve nutritional care in the daily routine. Important to note is that reasonable nutritional management is not possible without qualified staff in adequate numbers, with enough time to deliver appropriate individual nutritional care [33].

Table 5.3 Recommendations for combatting malnutrition in nursing homes

Care givers should be educated so that they are aware of the factors leading to nutritional problems
A nutrition concept with a structured approach should be implemented
Sensitive screening tools should be used
Acute and chronic illness conditions need to be treated adequately; dental issues need to be solved; and presbyphagia and dysphagia need to be treated
Menus should be planned, and should be adjusted to individual diet requirements
The environment and conditions in nursing homes should be addressed •Eating in company, in a calm and relaxed atmosphere •Allowing adequate time for eating •Adequate preparation of food and support in eating •The adjustment of the texture, taste and consistency of food should be considered in the light of the age and clinical condition of individuals
Help with eating and drinking should be provided when needed
Strategies to increase fluid intake should be implemented, identifying and overcoming individual and institutional barriers to drinking, such as •being worried about not reaching the toilet in time •physical inability to make or to reach drinks •reduced pleasure in drinking; and •reduced social drinking
Guidelines for the use of supplements, enteral or parenteral feeding should be available

5.7 Concepts and Way Forward

Optimal nutritional status throughout the life-span may assist in the preservation of general health, independence and cognitive abilities in old age. Therefore more quantitative and, above all, qualitative knowledge about an optimal diet that supports longevity and successful aging is needed. Recommended Daily Dietary Allowances (RDA) in older adults have been specifically defined for this population, but still more research on optimal recommendations is needed. Studies at the cellular, metabolic and clinical levels are required, along with the translational linking of information from different research settings, in order to better understand the transition from good nutritional health and independence to malnutrition, functional impairment and poor health in older population groups.

Concepts to better understand the extent, nature, and prevention of food insecurity in older adults are needed. We must further explore potential consequences of food insecurity, such as healthcare access, utilization, and cost.

Prospective observational and randomized intervention studies will help define needs at a group level. Documentation of nutritional information in daily routines would enable the uniform collection of data for research. International standards therefore need to be defined and implemented. This will not only bring about improved nutritional status and outcomes, and thus individual benefits for the affected individual, but also economic benefits for both the institution and the healthcare system. Specific concepts and an urgent need for action to combat malnutrition in geriatric populations have been put forward [33].

5.8 Future Development

As people all over the world become older and cognitive impairment is the most common condition causing dependence, maintaining cognitive functions in older adults will be a major challenge in the future. With the FINGER study [31], a multi-domain intervention including diet to prevent disease has been introduced. More studies are needed to determine whether a whole-diet approach embedded in an integrated life-style approach is effective in preserving cognitive function and delaying dementia or other chronic conditions in older adults.

In rodents, caloric restriction increases the life span. However, in humans this has never been shown in a comparable manner. Recent data indicates that increased body weight (BMI 25–35) in older adults is associated with reduced mortality risk [34]. Understanding the differences in the settings and exploring whether caloric restriction or weight management regimes over the lifespan might increase longevity is still an exciting challenge for researchers.

As the population ages worldwide, we need to identify strategies to make healthy food choices available and affordable to older adults with varied socio-economic circumstances in all kinds of geographic locations. Food insecurity is a relatively new field of research, and more data on predictors, definition, consequences, and interventions in older adults are needed [35].

One possible future development may include the enrichment of food and drinks specifically for the general population of older adults. This would involve delivering appropriate levels of fat and proteins, but would also focus on micronutrients.

5.9 A Tough Challenge for the Future

The problems posed by food security and consequent malnutrition in older adults are generally underestimated, and are associated with a number of severe adverse effects on nutritional status, health and quality of life. Inadequate supply with essential micronutrients is associated with cognitive impairment, sarcopenia, frailty and general health condition in older adults. Populations at increased risk (nursing home residents, hospitalized older adults) are in need of specific screening and action plans for food and nutrition assistance. This will be an increasingly tough challenge in the future due to the demographic changes that are occurring worldwide.

5.10   Summary: Key Messages

- Malnutrition is frequent in older adults on account of a range of physiological, psychological and infrastructural problems.
- In light of the demographic change occurring worldwide, an increase in the number of malnourished older adults within the global population is to be anticipated.
- Decreased food intake on the part of older adults may automatically lead to an inadequate supply of essential micronutrients.
- Nursing homes present a range of nutritional risks for their residents and exhibit specific problems regarding food insecurity in older adults.
- Food insecurity and socio-economic issues may have implications not only for immediate nutritional outcomes, but also for age-associated diseases and conditions.
- Populations at increased risk are in need of specific screening and action plans for food and nutrition assistance.

References

1. Ahmed T, Haboubi N. Assessment and management of nutrition in older people and its importance to health. Clinical interventions in aging 2010; 5: 207–216
2. Donini LM, Poggiogalle E, Piredda M et al. Anorexia and eating patterns in the elderly. PloS one 2013; 8: e63539
3. van Bokhorst-de van der Schueren MA, Lonterman-Monasch S, de Vries OJ,2013Prevalence and determinants for malnutrition in geriatric outpatientsClin Nutr32100710113. van Bokhorst-de van der Schueren MA, Lonterman-Monasch S, de Vries OJ et al. Prevalence and determinants for malnutrition in geriatric outpatients. Clin Nutr 2013; 32: 1007–1011
4. Borgstrom Bolmsjo B, Jakobsson U, Molstad S et al. The nutritional situation in Swedish nursing homes—a longitudinal study. Archives of gerontology and geriatrics 2015; 60: 128–133
5. Serrano-Urrea R, Garcia-Meseguer MJ. Malnutrition in an elderly population without cognitive impairment living in nursing homes in Spain: study of prevalence using the Mini Nutritional Assessment test. Gerontology 2013; 59: 490–498
6. Stange I, Poeschl K, Stehle P et al. Screening for malnutrition in nursing home residents: comparison of different risk markers and their association to functional impairment. The journal of nutrition, health & aging 2013; 17: 357–363
7. Morley JE. Anorexia of aging: physiologic and pathologic. The American journal of clinical nutrition 1997; 66: 760–773
8. Elmadfa I, Meyer AL. Body composition, changing physiological functions and nutrient requirements of the elderly. Ann Nutr Metab 2008; 52 Suppl 1: 2–5
9. Wilson MM, Morley JE. Invited review: Aging and energy balance. J Appl Physiol (1985) 2003; 95: 1728–1736
10. Campbell WW, Crim MC, Dallal GE et al. Increased protein requirements in elderly people: new data and retrospective reassessments. The American journal of clinical nutrition 1994; 60: 501–509

11. van Asselt DZ, de Groot LC, van Staveren WA et al. Role of cobalamin intake and atrophic gastritis in mild cobalamin deficiency in older Dutch subjects. The American journal of clinical nutrition 1998; 68: 328–334

12. Lee JS, Fischer JG, Johnson MA. Food insecurity, food and nutrition programs, and aging: experiences from Georgia. Journal of nutrition for the elderly 2010; 29: 116–149

13. Guigoz Y, Vellas BJ. [Malnutrition in the elderly: the Mini Nutritional Assessment (MNA)]. Therapeutische Umschau Revue therapeutique 1997; 54: 345–350

14. Chernoff R. Dietary management for older subjects with obesity. Clinics in geriatric medicine 2005; 21: 725–733, vi

15. Haveman-Nies A, de Groot LC, Van Staveren WA. Fluid intake of elderly Europeans. The journal of nutrition, health & aging 1997; 1: 151–155

16. Bollwein J, Volkert D, Diekmann R et al. Nutritional status according to the mini nutritional assessment (MNA(R)) and frailty in community dwelling older persons: a close relationship. The journal of nutrition, health & aging 2013; 17: 351–356

17. Rolland Y, Czerwinski S, Abellan Van Kan G et al. Sarcopenia: its assessment, etiology, pathogenesis, consequences and future perspectives. The journal of nutrition, health & aging 2008; 12: 433–450

18. Bowman GL, Silbert LC, Howieson D et al. Nutrient biomarker patterns, cognitive function, and MRI measures of brain aging. Neurology 2012; 78: 241–249

19. Tangney CC. DASH and Mediterranean-type Dietary Patterns to Maintain Cognitive Health. Current nutrition reports 2014; 3: 51–61

20. von Arnim CA, Gola U, Biesalski HK. More than the sum of its parts? Nutrition in Alzheimer's disease. Nutrition 2010; 26: 694–700

21. Kuczmarski MF, Allegro D, Stave E. The association of healthful diets and cognitive function: a review. Journal of nutrition in gerontology and geriatrics 2014; 33: 69–90

22. Scarmeas N, Stern Y, Tang MX et al. Mediterranean diet and risk for Alzheimer's disease. Annals of neurology 2006; 59: 912–921

23. Scarmeas N, Luchsinger JA, Mayeux R et al. Mediterranean diet and Alzheimer disease mortality. Neurology 2007; 69: 1084–1093

24. Beck AM. Weight loss, mortality and associated potentially modifiable nutritional risk factors among nursing home residents–a Danish follow-up study. The journal of nutrition, health & aging 2015; 19: 96–101

25. Lee JS, Gundersen C, Cook J et al. Food insecurity and health across the lifespan. Adv Nutr 2012; 3: 744–745

26. Bengle R, Sinnett S, Johnson T et al. Food insecurity is associated with cost-related medication non-adherence in community-dwelling, low-income older adults in Georgia. Journal of nutrition for the elderly 2010; 29: 170–191

27. Bates CJ, Benton D, Biesalski HK et al. Nutrition and aging: a consensus statement. The journal of nutrition, health & aging 2002; 6: 103–116

28. Rubenstein LZ, Harker JO, Salva A et al. Screening for undernutrition in geriatric practice: developing the short-form mini-nutritional assessment (MNA-SF). The journals of gerontology Series A, Biological sciences and medical sciences 2001; 56: M366–372

29. Hamirudin AH, Charlton K, Walton K et al. 'We are all time poor'—is routine nutrition screening of older patients feasible? Australian family physician 2013; 42: 321–326

30. Winter J, Flanagan D, McNaughton SA et al. Nutrition screening of older people in a community general practice, using the MNA-SF. The journal of nutrition, health & aging 2013; 17: 322–325

31. Ngandu T, Lehtisalo J, Solomon A et al. A 2 year multidomain intervention of diet, exercise, cognitive training, and vascular risk monitoring versus control to prevent cognitive decline in at-risk elderly people (FINGER): a randomised controlled trial. Lancet 2015, DOI: 10.1016/S0140-6736(15)60461-5

32. Volkert D. [Nutritional guidelines and standards in geriatrics]. Zeitschrift fur Gerontologie und Geriatrie 2011; 44: 91–96, 99

33. Volkert D. Malnutrition in older adults - urgent need for action: a plea for improving the nutritional situation of older adults. Gerontology 2013; 59: 328–333
34. Kulminski AM, Arbeev KG, Kulminskaya IV et al. Body mass index and nine-year mortality in disabled and nondisabled older U.S. individuals. Journal of the American Geriatrics Society 2008; 56: 105–110
35. Johnson MA, Dwyer JT, Jensen GL et al. Challenges and new opportunities for clinical nutrition interventions in the aged. The Journal of nutrition 2011; 141: 535–541

Chapter 6
Rationale for a Combination of Selected Micronutrients to Improve Cognition and Prevent or Slow Down Age-Related Cognitive Impairment

Hans Konrad Biesalski

Abstract This chapter deals with the question as to whether micronutrients contribute to the maintenance of cognitive function during the aging process. The onset of mild cognitive impairment (MCI) and at least the development of dementia are insidious, and occur years before the loss of cognition becomes apparent. Besides a couple of factors, including genetics and lifestyle, nutrition is claimed as an important factor which interacts with basic pathologies of cognitive decline. In particular, micronutrients (vitamins, trace elements and minerals) can mitigate the risk of cognitive decline, especially in elderly people at risk of deficiencies. Based on epidemiological findings and existing scientific evidence, two major groups of micronutrients will be discussed: homocysteine-lowering vitamins and antioxidants. Cognitive decline, with its early clinical diagnosis mild cognitive impairment (MCI), becomes evident in the age group >60 years. The quality of diet determines survival and health status in free-living elderly people within a European population. High plasma levels of ß-carotene (as a marker for vegetable intake) and α-tocopherol (as a marker for edible plant oils) are especially associated with lower mortality in the elderly (Buijsse et al. 2005). Epidemiological studies demonstrate that with increasing age, the prevalence of nutritional deficiencies increases, in particular deficiencies of antioxidants (ß-carotene, vitamins C, E and selenium and zinc) and B-vitamins (folic acid, B_6, B_{12}). Deficiencies of micronutrients however, may contribute to, or even promote, cognitive impairment. Consequently it is suggested that a straightforward strategy to improve micronutrient status may improve cognition or delay the onset of MCI and Alzheimer dementia (AD).

H.K. Biesalski (✉)
Nutrition medicine, Department of Biological Chemistry and Nutrition,
Food Security Center, University of Hohenheim, Garbenstraße 30, 70593 Stuttgart, Germany
e-mail: biesal@uni-hohenheim.de

© Springer International Publishing AG 2017
H.K. Biesalski et al. (eds.), *Sustainable Nutrition in a Changing World*,
DOI 10.1007/978-3-319-55942-1_6

Keywords Micronutrient status · Nutritional deficiencies · The elderly · Mild cognitive impairment (MCI) · Cognitive decline · Homocysteine-lowering vitamins and antioxidants · Alzheimer's disease · Parkinson's disease

6.1 Micronutrient Intake in the Elderly

The inadequacy of micronutrient supply in the elderly is documented by an increasing number of studies. Recently, a meta-analysis summarized the data from 41 such studies. These show that, depending on the individual micronutrient, between 15 and 90% of elderly people were at risk of deficiency [1]. The risk was calculated for elderly people who were below the estimated average requirement (EAR). Consequently, according to the definition of the EAR, they are at risk of developing a deficiency with clinical consequences if they stay on the intake below EAR. In particular B-vitamin supply is inadequate—a problem which may be harmful for cognition and mood.

6.2 Antioxidants

6.2.1 Importance for Brain Function and Cognition

The brain is considered extremely sensitive to oxidative damage that may occur from reactive oxygen species produced primarily by mitochondria during respiration. The exact amount of ROS produced is around 2% of the total oxygen consumed during respiration, but it may vary depending on several parameters. Some critical components come together in the brain: it is enriched in easily peroxidizable unsaturated fatty acids (20:4 and 22:6), consumes 20% of the total oxygen consumption, and has low antioxidant levels, e.g. 10% of the catalase activity of the liver (Floyd and Carney 1992) and low levels of SOD and GSH (Yoon et al. 2000). Whereas the decrease of endogenous antioxidant enzymes with age cannot really be prevented, exogenous antioxidants may be delivered with the diet or as a supplement to accumulate in the brain. Ascorbic acid seems to be the major-water soluble antioxidant in human brain, at a 15-times higher concentration than in human plasma (Floyd 1999). There is some evidence that oxidative stress contributes to the onset and development of neurodegenerative diseases such as Alzheimer's disease (AD) and Parkinson's disease (PD) (Barenham 2004). Improving the cellular defense against ROS-induced oxidation of neuronal tissue might prevent cognitive impairment and neurodegeneration. In cases of AD, PD and ALS, reduced levels of catalase, super-oxide dismutase and oxidized and reduced glutathione have been documented (Andersen 2004). Deficiencies in antioxidant micronutrients may further contribute to the progression of neurodegenerative diseases and at least cognitive decline with age. At least three prominent changes occur in the brain resulting in cognitive impairment:

- Accumulation of non-essential substances (lipofuscin prominently in cortical neurons), loss of myelin (e.g. in the limbic cortices), and a general shrinkage;
- Reduction in the branching of dendrites and reduction of neurotransmitter availability; and
- Reduction of cerebral blood flow and decline of cerebral blood volume, or at least ischemia.

Accumulation of lipofuscin mainly appears as a result of oxidative stress. The reduction of blood flow may also be a consequence of oxidative modification and, as discussed in the chapter on B-vitamins in this book, the consequence of high homocysteine. With respect to memory, the metabotropic receptors acting via G-proteins are of importance. After binding of a neurotransmitter to that receptor type, the production of a second messenger molecule is induced within the neuron. The induction of the second messenger, travelling in the neuron, results in different cellular reactions. Of greatest importance is the activation of kinases. These enzymes, which can remain active for up to a couple of hours, are involved in long-term changes of the neurons and at least gene expression. The latter may contribute to the formation of novel protein expression and, in some cases, formation of dendrites and new (more or less stable) networks, resulting in a memory. The appearance of a cognitive impairment might be based on a reduced production of neurotransmitters and subsequently reduced activation of kinases. Studies with aging rats revealed that a long-term diet rich in antioxidants can slow down the onset of neuronal degeneration and cognitive impairment (Floyd et al. 1998, 1999). Furthermore, it was shown that the age-related decline in the neuronal process controlled via metabotropic receptors is compensated by a diet rich in antioxidants. The compensation is a result of an improvement of the G-protein on- and off-action (Joseph et al. 1999). Indeed, the animals fed a high antioxidant diet had higher vitamin E levels in the hippocampus compared to the control animals. The hippocampus however, is involved in memory functioning. From the above-described aspects of oxidative stress and its impact on memory, it is suggested that deficiency of antioxidants may contribute to the development of cognitive impairment.

6.2.2   Antioxidant Deficiencies in the Elderly

Age is an important determinant of the serum values of antioxidants, predominantly vitamin E, vitamin C, and ß-carotene [2, 3]. The data from the European SU.VI. MAX trial clearly showed that plasma levels of retinol, tocopherol and ß-carotene decrease with age in 12,741 volunteers aged 35–60 years [3]. Female senior citizens from Germany aged 60–70 years showed inadequate intake and a poor antioxidant status (selenium, vitamin E, vitamin C and ß-carotene) (Wolters et al. 2006). The Iowa Rural Health Study revealed that in 420 individuals aged 79 years or older, 60% had inadequate intake of vitamin E and 25% of vitamin C (Marshall et al. 2001). Interactions of micronutrients with drugs, more frequently consumed by the elderly, increases the problem of antioxidant deficiency [4]. The occurrence of a low antioxidant status is not restricted to a few countries or areas with low socio-economic status: it seems to be a general and unrecognized problem of the aging population. The consequences of a low antioxidant intake are frailty, degenerative diseases, walking disabilities, and higher mortality (Semba et al. 2006, 2007; Michelon 2006). A low intake of antioxidant contributes to a decline in cognition and promotes the development of dementia.

6.2.3   Human Studies

Based on recent published data, the intervention with antioxidants to decrease either the progression or the onset of cognitive impairment is controversial. However, subdividing the studies into short- and long-term interventions, it becomes clear that an interventional approach needs more than one year to be effective. The EVA study evaluated in 980 subjects aged 62–72 years the relationship between the enzymatic system—restricted to copper and zinc superoxide dismutase (Cu/Zn SOD) and the seleno-dependent glutathionperoxidase (GSH-Px)—and decline in cognitive function. Cognitive decline over a four-year period was associated with a lower activity of the GSH-Px and a higher Cu/Zn SOD. Table 6.1 summarizes trials with antioxidants. Five out of six studies which examined the effect of antioxidant supply via food documented statistically significant inverse associations (**). Four out of five observational studies found an inverse relationship between antioxidant intake from supplements (vitamin E, vitamin C) and the risk of AD (*) or cognitive decline (***).

Table 6.1 summarizes the data of prospective and intervention studies with antioxidants.

The above-cited studies clearly show that antioxidants play a preventive role against the development and progression of dementia. Intake of supplements containing antioxidants (vitamins A, C and E, Se and Zn) over a longer period (five years and more) in six studies with more than 800 participants (one with 162) showed prevention of dementia or a benefit to cognitive function. Three studies with a rather low number of participants (<250) were without effect. This shows that, dependent on the statistical power, the effect of antioxidants on cognitive decline becomes evident.

Table 6.1 Data of prospective and intervention studies with antioxidants

Micronutrients	Participants	Duration	Results	Authors
Serum selenium levels	1389 subjects, age 60–71 years (EVA study)	9 years Adjustment for time, sex, education, baseline Se level, cardiovascular risk factors	Decline in Se was associated with cognitive decline as measurement by 4 neuropsychological tests. Probability of cognitive decline increased with the decrease of plasma Se change over time	[6]
Serum β-carotene and ApoE genotype	455 elderly, age ≥ 65 years (MacArthur Studies of Successful Aging)	7 years Adjustment for age, sex, race, baseline SPMSQ score, education, income, smoking status, alcohol consumption, serum CRP and IL6 levels, total and HDL cholesterol level, BMI	The adjusted OR of high β-carotene level for cognitive decline was 0.1 I (95% CI 0 0.02, 0.57) in participants with at least one ApoE4 allele and 0.89 (95% CI 0 0.54, 1.47) among those who were ApoE4 negative	[7]
Supplemental use of antioxidant vitamins	894 subjects with no evidence of dementia (CSHA study), age ≥ 65 years	5 years Adjustment for age, sex, education, sitting diastolic blood pressure, baseline 3MS score, baseline institutional residence	Subjects reporting a combined use of vitamin E and C supplements and/or multivitamin consumption at baseline were significantly less likely to experience significant cognitive decline (adjusted OR 0 0.51; 95% CI 0 0.29, 0.90)	[8]
Food intakes of vitamin E, α-tocopherol equivalents, individual tocopherols	1041 persons clinically evaluated for analysis of AD and 3718 persons for analysis of cognitive change; age ≥ 65 years (CHAP study)	6 years Adjustment for age, sex, race, education, ApoE4 genotype, interaction between ApoE4 and race, time from the determination of disease-free status to the time of clinical evaluation of incident disease, frequency of participation in cognitive activities, intake of saturated fat, trans unsaturated, DHA	162 persons developed AD. Higher intakes of vitamin E (RR = 0.74 per 5 mg/d increase; 95% CI = 0.62, 0.88) and α-tocopherol equivalents (RR = 0.56 per 5 mg/day increase; 95% CI = 0.32, 0.98) were associated with a reduced incidence of AD. A slower rate of cognitive decline was associated with intake of vitamin E and α-/γ-tocopherols equivalents	[9]

(continued)

Table 6.1 (continued)

Micronutrients	Participants	Duration	Results	Authors
Supplemental use of antioxidant vitamins	3227 elderly county residents, age ≥ 65 years (Cache County Study)	3 years Adjustment for age, sex, education, dummy-coded terms for the presence of 1 and 2 ApoE4 alleles, interaction between age and the dummy-coded ApoE4 terms, an indicator term for general health status	104 persons developed AD. Use of vitamin E and C supplements in combination was associated with reduced AD incidence (adjusted HR = 0.36; 95% CI = 0.09, 0.99). No evidence of a protective effect with use of vitamin E or C supplements alone was found	[10]
Midlife dietary intake of antioxidants	2459 Japanese-American men, age 71–93 years (Honolulu-Asia Aging Study)	3 years Adjustment for age, education, physical activity, cardiovascular risk factors, supplemental vitamin intakes, total energy intake, ApoE4 genotype	235 persons developed dementia (102 AD cases, 44 VaD cases, 38 AD cases with contributing cerebrovascular diseases). Intakes of β-carotene, flavonoids, vitamin E, vitamin C were not associated with the risk of dementia or its subtypes	[11]
Intake of antioxidant vitamins	980 elderly subjects initially free of dementia, age ≥ 65 years (WHICAP study)	4 year-adjustment for age, education, sex, ApoE4 status, ethnicity, smoking	242 subjects developed AD in 4023 person-years of follow-up (6 per 100 person-years). Intake of carotenes and vitamin C or vitamin E in supplemental dietary (non-supplemental) form or in both forms was not related to a decreased risk of AD	[12]
Use of supplemental antioxidants	2082 elderly subjects initially free of dementia, age ≥ 65 years (epidemiologic studies of the elderly)	7 years Adjustment for age, sex, race, education, residence, income, BMI,	34.5% experienced cognitive decline during follow-up. Current antioxidant users had a 29% lower	[13]

(continued)

Table 6.1 (continued)

Micronutrients	Participants	Duration	Results	Authors
(vitamins A, C, E plus Se or Zn)		smoking history, alcohol consumption, health status index	risk of experience cognitive decline (adjusted RR = 0.71; 95% CI = 0.49, 1.01)	
Use of supplements containing vitamins C and E	14,968 women, age 70–79 years (Nurses' Health Study)	15 years. Adjustment for age at interview, education, history of diabetes, hypertension and heart disease; multivitamin use, anti-depressant use, HRT, BMI, aspirin use, smoking, mental-health index, energy-fatigue index	33% of women currently used both specific vitamin E and C supplements. Long-term current of vitamin E with vitamin C supplements had better global scores than non-users. There was a trend for increasingly higher mean scores with increasing duration of use. These associations were strongest among women with low dietary intakes of α-tocopherol	[14]
Intake of antioxidant nutrients, vitamin E, vitamin C, β-carotene	815 residents free of AD at baseline, age $\geq$ 65 years (CHAP study)	3.9 years. Adjustment for age, education, sex, race, ApoE4 genotype, length of follow-up	Increasing vitamin E intake from food was associated with decreased risk of developing AD: RR from lowest to highest quintile of intake were 1.00, 0.71 (95% CI = 0.24, 2.07), 0.62 (95% CI = 0.26, 1.45), 0.71 (95% CI = 0.27, 1.88) and 0.30 (95% CI = 0.10, 0.92) (p for trend = 0.5). The protective effect of vitamin E was observed only among persons who were ApoE4 negative. Adjustment for other baseline	[15]

(continued)

Table 6.1 (continued)

Micronutrients	Participants	Duration	Results	Authors
			dietary factors reduces the protective association. Intake of vitamin C, β-carotene, vitamin E from supplements was not significantly associated with risk of AD	
Randomized clinical trial	6377 women 65 years or older participated in an sub-study of cognitive function of the Women's Health Study (WHS). WHS is a randomized, double-blind, placebo-controlled trial of vitamin E supplementation (600 IU on alternate days)	Supplementation period: 1992 and 1995. The sub-study was initiated 5.6 years after randomization and was conducted for 4 years	There were no differences in global score between the vitamin E and placebo groups 5.6 years and 9.6 years after randomization. Mean cognitive change over time was also similar in the vitamin E group compared with the placebo group for the global score. The RR of substantial decline in the global score in the vitamin E group compared with placebo was 0.92 (95% CI = 0.77, 1.10)	[16]
Randomized clinical trial	769 subjects with a MCI were randomly assigned to receive daily either vitamin E (2000 IU) or donepezil (10 mg) or placebo	3 years	212 subjects developed AD. There were no significant differences in the probability of progression to AD in the vitamin E compared to domepezil or placebo groups during the 3 years of treatment. No significant differences emerged among ApoE4 carriers between the vitamin E and placebo groups	[17]

(continued)

Table 6.1 (continued)

Micronutrients	Participants	Duration	Results	Authors
Randomized clinical trial	341 patients with AD of moderate severity were randomly assigned to receive either the selective monoamine oxidase inhibitor selegiline (10 mg/day), or α-tocopherol (vitamin E, 2000 IU/day) or both selegiline and α-tocopherol or placebo	2 years	As compared with the placebo group (440 days), there were significant delays in the time to primary outcome for the patients treated with selegiline (median time, 655 days; $p = 0.012$), α-tocopherol (670 days, $p = 0.001$) or combination therapy (585 days, $p = 0.049$) after adjustment an baseline MMSE score	[18]
Randomized clinical trial	220 healthy free living women aged 60–91. 111 in the suppl. group 150 mg ascorbic acid, 50 mg Mg, 36 mg a-tocopherol, 9 mg ß-carotene, 60 μg Selenium and further water sol. vitamins	6 months	No effect on cognitive performance. The 6-month period, however, seems too short (claimed by the authors)	Wolters et al. (2005)
Randomized clinical trial	910 men > 65 years divided in two groups: supplemented with multivitamin. (50–210% of RDA) (456) and placebo (454)	12 months	Evidence for a beneficial effect in two subgroups: benefit on verbal fluency tests in supplemented participants >75 and in those with increased risk of nutritional deficiencies	McNeill et al. (2007)

The clinical trials showed controversial results. In the Kang trial, there was an 8% reduction in the decline of the global score. The Peterson trial seems to be without effects of antioxidants on cognitive decline or AD development. However, nearly one third of all patients developed AD within three years. Based on a couple of epidemiological and observational studies, the development of AD in patients with MCI is around 5% per year and not more than 10%, as is the case in that study. This difference might be due to an increased number of early AD patients in the MCI group at the beginning of the trial. Antioxidants however, have nil or only a very moderate impact in cases of existing AD.

6.3 Homocysteine-Lowering Vitamins

6.3.1 Importance of B-Vitamins for Cognition

B-vitamins (B_6, B_{12}, folic acid) are involved in the methylation of homocysteine (Hcy). Low intake, higher demand or polymorphism of enzymes (MTHFR; GCPII) results in hyperhomocysteinemia. Hcy is a non-protein-forming sulfhydryl-containing amino acid. Because Hcy is highly cytotoxic, the i.c. concentration is kept low by catabolism and by a cellular export mechanism into plasma. Consequently, a high plasma concentration documents a high cellular Hcy formation. A couple of diseases are discussed as related to high homocysteine levels, such as arteriosclerosis, myocardial infarction, stroke, and peripheral vascular disease, as well as Parkinson's disease and Alzheimer- and vascular-dementia (***). Epidemiological studies show an increase of Hcy with increasing age and a negative correlation with cognitive function. Differing pathomechanisms are discussed as responsible for the effect of Hcy on brain structure and function, such as direct toxicity on dopaminergic neurons (Imamura et al. 2007), or on the vascular endothelium (**). High Hcy or low folate or B_{12} show an influence on cellular redox status, including up-regulation of redox-sensitive transcription factors (NFkB, AP-1), thus promoting calcium influx, amyloid and tau protein accumulation, apoptosis and neuronal death (***). Under conditions of hyperhomocysteinemia, neural cells are exposed to the neurotoxic activity of Hcy. The consequences are a disturbed metabolism of excitatory neurotransmitters (e.g. glutamate), which causes excitotoxic effects associated with increased ROS formation and at least oxidative damage of neuronal tissues (**). This excitotoxic effect of Hcy is assumed to be realized via NMDA receptors (Sachdev 2005). Indeed, Streck and coworker (2003) demonstrated significant increased lipid peroxidation in rat hippocampus following Hcy treatment. The involvement of oxidative stress in the pathogenesis of dementia has been frequently shown in in vitro and in vivo experiments (**). Oxidative stress activates gene expression of a couple of components related to apoptosis and at least neuronal degeneration, such as caspase 3- and 6-dependent activation of apoptotic pathways (Anantharam et al. 2007). Oxidative stress induces apoptotic cell death in dopaminergic-derived N27 cell line and, to a lesser extent, in GABAergic striatum derived and hippocampal cell lines (Anantharam et al. 2007). Cell death was mediated via caspase 3-dependent pathways. The active proteases caspase 3/6 cleave tau proteins at specific sites, generating toxic tau fragments or enhancing the aggregation properties of these microtubule-associated proteins (Park and Ferreira 2005). Caspase 6, a potent cleaving protease of the tau protein (Guo et al. 2004), has been detected in neurofibrillary tangles of humans with MCI, and it is concluded that the activity of caspase 6 precedes the clinical and pathological diagnosis of AD (Albrecht et al. 2007). The interactions of hyperhomocysteinemia, oxidative stress and caspase activation may explain the beneficial effect of lowering Hcy and antioxidative treatment on cognitive impairment (McCaddon 2015; de Lau et al. [5]).

6.3.2   Deficiencies of B-Vitamins in the Elderly

Elderly people with low circulating folate or vitamin B_{12} have higher fasting total homocysteine concentrations. Supplementation with B-vitamins results in normalization of elevated Hcy plasma levels. Data from NHANES III, including 3563 male and 4523 female participants, clearly showed that high homocysteine concentrations were significantly associated with low serum vitamin (folate, B_{12}) concentrations (Selhub 2011). With increasing age, Hcy increases in plasma, mainly due to a low folate intake. Sixty-six percent of the participants (747) aged 67–96 years had a folate intake below the recommended 400 µg, and 16.7% were below 200 µg. Data from the German nutrition survey show that 60% of the population (aged 18–79 years) has an intake of folate below 75% of the recommendation. Low folate and B_{12} intake is a general problem in the elderly and critically contributes to cognitive decline and arteriosclerosis.

6.3.3   Human Studies

Studies estimating intake of foods rich in B-vitamins revealed a clear-cut inverse relationship between the highest intake of fruit and vegetables and fish consumption and cognitive decline in the elderly (Table 6.2).

Table 6.2 Nutrition and prevention of cognitive decline: data from prospective studies on food groups and dietary patterns

Micronutrients	Participants	Duration	Results	Authors
Dietary consumption of fruit, vegetables and fish	3632 elderly (Cache County study on memory, health and aging)	7 years Adjustment for age, gender, education	Participants in the highest quintile of "fruit and vegetables" intake had average score 0.94 points higher than those in the lowest quintile ($p = 0.01$). Participants consuming >1 serving of fish per week had averages 3MS scores 0.81 points that those not consuming fish ($p = 0.008$). Participants with high intakes of both "fruit and vegetables" and fish had averages 3MS scores 1.50 higher than those of the low intakes especially among ApoE4 non-carriers	[19]
Dietary consumption of fruit, vegetables and fish	8085 initially non-demented subjects, age ≥ 65 years (3C study)	4 years Adjustment for age, sex, race, education, center, income, marital status	Similar patterns were found with the risk of AD. 282 subjects developed dementia (including 183 AD). Daily consumption of fruits and vegetables were associated with a reduced risk of all causes dementia ($RR = 0.70$, 95% CI: 0.52, 0.94; $p = 0.02$). Fish consumption (at least once per week) was associated with a reduced risk of dementia only in ApoE4 non carriers ($RR = 0.60$, 95% CI: 0.41, 0.89; $p = 0.01$)	[20]
Fruit and vegetable consumption	3718 participants, age ≥ 65 years (CHAP study)	6 years Adjustment for age, sex, race, education	Compared with the rate of cognitive decline among persons in the lowest quintile of vegetable intake, the rate for persons in the fourth quintile was slower by 0.019 SU/year ($p = 0.01$) and by 0.018 SU/year ($p = 0.02$) in the fifth quintile ($p = 0.02$). Fruit consumption was not associated with cognitive change	[21]

(continued)

Table 6.2 (continued)

Micronutrients	Participants	Duration	Results	Authors
Fruit and vegetable juice consumption	1836 Japanese Americans free of dementia, age ≥ 65 years (Kame project)	9 years Adjustment for age, dietary intake of vitamin C, vitamin E and β-carotene	The HR for AD was 0.24 (95% CI = 0.09, 0.61) for subjects who drank juices at least 3 times per week versus those who drank juices less often than once per week (p for trend <0.1). This inverse association was more pronounced among ApoE4 carriers. No association were found for dietary intake of vitamins E, C or β-carotene or tea consumption	[22]
Mediterranean diet	2258 community-based non-demented individuals (WHICAP study); mean age, 77.2 ± 6.6 years	4 ± 3 years (range: 0.2–13.9) Adjustment for cohort, age, sex, ethnicity, education, ApoE genotype, caloric intake, smoking, comorbidity index, BMI	262 persons developed incident AD. High adherence to the MeDi* was Associated with lower risk for AD (HR: 0.91; 95% CI: 0.83, 0.98; p = 0.0015). Compared with subjects in the lowest MeDi tertile, subjects in the middle MeDi tertile had an HR of 0.85 (95% CI: 0.63, 1.16) and those of the highest tertile had an HR of 0.60 (95% CI: 0.42, 0.87) (p for trend = 0.007) *Mediterranean diet	[23]

Table 6.3 Trials with B-vitamins and cognitive impairment

Micronutrients	Participants	Duration	Results	Authors
Intake of folate and vitamins B_6 and B_{12}	965 persons 65 years or older without dementia at baseline (WHICAP-study)	6.1 ± 3.3 years, Adjustment for age, sex, education, ethic group, Apoe4, vitamins B_6 and B_{12} levels, cardiovascular risk factors	192 m persons developed incident AD. The highest quartile of total folate intake was related to lower risk of AD (HR = 0.5, 95% CI = 0.3, 0.9; p = .02 for trend)	Luchsinger et al. (2007)
Dietary intakes of folate, B_{12}, B_6	1041 residents initially free of AD; ≥ 65 years (CHAP study)	3.9 years, Adjustment for age, sex, race, education, cognitive activities, ApoE4, dietary intake of vitamin E, total niacin	162 persons developed incident AD. No association between quintiles of folate intake or of vitamin B_{12} intake was found with the risk of developing AD. Intake of vitamin B_6 was not associated with incident AD after control for dietary intakes of vitamin E and total niacin	[24]
tHcy and related vitamin plasma concentrations	499 high-functioning community-dwelling persons; age 70–79 years (MacArthur studies of successful aging)	7 years, Adjustment for age, sex, education, baseline cognitive function, baseline physical function, smoking, homocysteine and vitamin levels	Subjects in the lowest quartile of folate had a 1.6-fold increased risk of 7-year cognitive decline (95% CI: 1.01, 2.31; $p = 0.04$)	[25]

(continued)

Table 6.3 (continued)

Micronutrients	Participants	Duration	Results	Authors
Dietary intakes of folate and vitamin B_{12}	3718 residents initially free of AD, $\geq$ 65 years (CHAP study)	6 years, Adjustment for age, sex, education, race, vitamin E, vitamin C	The rate of cognition decline among persons in the top fifth of total folate intake (median, 742 μg/day) was more than twice that of those of the lowest fifth of intake (median, 186 μg/day). Similar patterns were found, with high folate intake from food and with folate vitamin supplementation of more than 400 μg/day. High total B_{12} intake was associated with slower cognitive decline only among the oldest participants	[26]
Total intake (diet plus supplements) of antioxidant vitamins (E, C, carotenoids) and B vitamins (folate, B_{12}, B_6)	579 non demented elderly volunteers, age 49–93 years (Baltimore longitudinal study of aging)	9.3 years, Adjustment for age, gender, education, caloric intake	57 persons developed incident AD. Higher intake of folate (RR = 0.1; 95% CI: 0.22, 0.76), vitamin E (RR = 0.56; 95% CI: 0.30, 1.06) and vitamin B_6 (RR = 0.41; 95% CI: 0.20, 0.84) were associated individually with decreased risk of AD. When the 3 vitamins were analyzed together, only total intake of folate at or above the DRI (RR = 0.45; 95% CI: 0.21, 0.97) was associated with a significantly decreased risk of AD. No association was found with total intake of vitamin B_{12}, vitamin C or carotenoids	[27]

(continued)

Table 6.3 (continued)

Micronutrients	Participants	Duration	Results	Authors
Serum concentration of homocysteine, vitamin B_{12} or folic acid	599 subjects; 85 years of age (Leiden 85-Plus study)	4 years, Adjustment for sex and education level	There were no significant associations of serum concentrations of Hcy, vitamin N_{12} or folic acid with rate of cognitive decline (battery of cognitive tests: MMSE, Stroop test, a letter digit coding test, a word recall test)	[28]
Plasma tHcy, folate, vitamin B_{12}, vitamin B_6 and dietary B vitamin intakes	321 aging men, age 50–85 years (veterans affairs normative aging study)	3 years, Adjustment for baseline cognitive measures, age, education, smoking, alcohol intake, BMI, diabetes, systolic blood pressure, time of second measure relative to folic acid fortification, time interval between the 2 cognitive measures, serum creatinine (for plasma) or total energy intake (for diet)	Decline in constructional praxis (special copying) was significantly associated with plasma tHcy, folate, vitamin B_6, vitamin B_{12} and with the dietary intake of each vitamin. Dietary folate was also protective against a decline in verbal fluency. A high homocysteine concentration was associated with a decline in recall memory	[29]

(continued)

Table 6.3 (continued)

Micronutrients	Participants	Duration	Results	Authors
High plasma tHcy concentration	816 subjects initially free of dementia, mean age 74 years (Conselic Study of Brain Aging)	4 years, Adjustment for age, sex, education, ApoE genotype, vascular risk factors, serum concentrations of folate and vitamin B_{12}	112 persons developed dementia (including 70 cases of AD). In the subjects with hyperhomocysteinemia (Hcy >15 μmol/l); HR was 2.08 (95% CI: 1.31, 3.30; $p = 0.002$) for dementia and 2.11 (95% CI: 1.19, 3.76; $p = 0.011$) for AD. Low folate concentrations ($\leq$11.8 nmol/l) were independently associated with an increased risk of both dementia (1.87; 95% CI: 1.21, 2.89; $p = 0.005$) and AD (1.98; 95% CI: 1.15, 3.40; $p = 0.014$). No significant relation was found with vitamin B_{12}	[30]
High Hcy levels	909 elderly subjects, age 77.2 ± 6.3 years (WHICAP study)	1.5 years, Adjustment for age, sex, education, ApoE4	109 persons developed AD (Incidence: 3206 person-years): Adjusted HR of AD for the highest quartile of Hcy was 1.4 (95% CI: 0.8, 2.4; p for trend = 0.31). High Hcy levels were not related to a decline in memory scores over time. Age was a significant confounder in all the analyses	[31]
Serum tHcy concentration	144 subjects, age 30–80 years	6 years, Adjustment for age, sex, education	No correlation was observed between serum Hcy, vitamin B_{12} and folic acid concentrations, and performance at any of the time-points	[32]

(continued)

Table 6.3 (continued)

Micronutrients	Participants	Duration	Results	Authors
Plasma tHcy level	1092 subjects without dementia; mean age: 76 years (Framingham study)	8 years, Adjustment for age, sex, education, ApoE genotype, plasma vitamin levels, vascular risk factors	111 persons developed dementia (including 83 cases of AD). The RR of dementia was 1.4 (95% CI: 1.1, 1.9) for each increase of 1 SD in the log-transformed Hcy value at baseline or 8 years earlier. The RR of AD was 1.8 (95% CI: 1.3, 2.5) per increase of 1 SD at baseline and 1.6 (95% CI: 1.2, 2.1) per increase of 1 SDD eight years before baseline. The risk of AD nearly doubled with plasma tHcy level greater than 14 μmol/l	[33]
Serum level of vitamin B_{12} and folate	370 non-demented persons, age ≥ 75 years (Kungsholmen Projet)	3 years, Adjustment for age, sex, education	Persons with low levels of B_{12} (≤150 pmol/l) or folate (≤10 nmol/l) had twice the risk of developing AD (RR = 2.1, 95% CI: 1.2, 3.5) compared with people with normal levels of these vitamins. Similar relative risk was found for subjects with both vitamins at low levels and for low levels of B_{12} or folate respectively defined as ≤250 pmol/l or ≤12 nmol/l	[34]

Despite the fact that pure nutrition studies have certain limitations, the data show that a diet rich in phytochemicals and water-soluble vitamins may protect against accelerated cognitive decline. Furthermore, fish intake was inversely correlated with cognitive decline. This preventive effect might be attributed to either n-3 fatty acids and/or vitamin D—essential nutrients that are both present mainly in fish. The data from the nutrition studies show that a mixed diet, rich in antioxidants (fruits, vegetables), which also contains edible oil (vitamin E), meat as a source for selenium and optimum bioavailable folate, and at least B_{12} (Mediterranean diet) does indeed prevent the progression of MCI.

To further elucidate whether single micronutrients are responsible for the preventive effect, studies are carried out which measure either biomarkers of intake of selected micronutrients or else plasma levels of these micronutrients.

Table 6.3 summarizes trials with either dietary or supplemental intake of B-vitamins and cognitive impairment.

High dietary intake of folate and other B-vitamins was associated with a lower rate of cognition decline and at least incidence of AD in nine out of 12 studies. No study showed any negative effect. Plasma levels of homocysteine are correlated with an increased risk of AD or increased cognitive decline in four out of five studies. One study with 1033 participants documented an inverse relationship between plasma folate and cognition and performance independent of Hcy concentration (de Lau et al.) [5]. Taken together, a sufficient intake of Hcy-lowering vitamins results in a decreased decline of cognitive function and a decreased risk of AD.

To further elucidate the role of Hcy-lowering vitamins, clinical intervention studies were carried out (Table 6.4).

Intervention studies reveal conflicting results. This may in part be due to differences in treatment time, dosage and at least study population. Nevertheless, the WHICAP study shows that persons with MCI indeed may benefit from a long-term treatment with Hcy-lowering vitamins. Based on the pathomechanisms discussed above, it seems important to treat patients with MCI with a combination of Hcy-lowering vitamins and antioxidants. Studies combining these micronutrients are at present not available. However, prospective studies estimating the effect of nutrition containing Hcy-lowering and anti-oxidative vitamins do exist (Table 6.4).

6.4 Summary: Key Messages

- Micronutrients support the maintenance of cognitive function during aging.
- Besides genetics and lifestyle, nutrition is claimed as an important factor which interacts with basic pathologies of cognitive decline.
- Vitamins, trace elements and minerals can mitigate the risk of cognitive decline, especially in elderly people at risk of deficiencies.

Table 6.4 Nutrition and prevention of cognitive decline: data from prospective studies and randomized clinical trials on homocysteine-related B vitamins

Micronutrients	Participants	Duration	Results	Authors
Plasma folate	1033 non-demented participants aged 60–90y. Cognition test, psychomotor test and memory. Rotterdam scan study		Higher plasma folate concentrations are associated with better global cognitive function and better performance on tests of psychomotor speed, regardless of homocysteine concentration	[5]
Intake of folate and vitamins B$_6$ and B$_{12}$	965 persons 65 years or older without dementia at baseline (WHICAP study)	6.1 ± 3.3 years, Adjustment for age, sex, education, ethic group, Apoe4, vitamins B$_6$ and B$_{12}$ levels, cardiovascular risk factors	192 m persons developed incident AD. The highest quartile of total folate intake was related to lower risk of AD (HR = 0.5, 95% CI = 0.3, 0.9; p = 0.02 for trend)	[35]
Intervention	276 healthy participants, ≥ 65 years with plasma homocysteine concentrations of at least 13 μmol/l, randomly assigned to receive a daily supplement containing folate (1000 μg), vitamin B$_{12}$ (500 μg) and vitamin B$_6$ (10 mg)	2 years treatment	Plasma homocysteine concentration was 4.36 μmol/l lower in the vitamin group than in the placebo group during follow-up. There were no significant difference between the vitamin and placebo groups in cognition test scores	[36]

(continued)

Table 6.4 (continued)

Micronutrients	Participants	Duration	Results	Authors
Intervention	149 people at high risk of dementia were randomized to receive either low dose aspirin (81 mg) or placebo; and folic acid (2 mg) plus vitamin B_{12} (1 mg) or placebo; and vitamin E (500 mg) plus (C (200 mg) or placebo	12-week treatment	B vitamins lowered plasma Hcy concentration by 30%. No effect of treatment on cognitive function was detected	Vital trial collaborative group 2003 [37]
Intervention	211 healthy younger, middle-aged, and older women, who took either 750 µg folate, 15 µg vitamin B_{12}, 75 mg vitamin B_6 or placebo daily	1-month treatment	Supplementation had a significant positive effect on some measures of memory performance only and no effect on mood. Dietary intake status was associated with speed of processing, recall and recognition, and verbal ability	[38]
Intervention	30 patients with abnormal cognitive decline and folate level below 3 ng/ml randomly assigned to receive folic acid and supplementation	2-month treatment	Patients treated showed a significant improvement of both memory and attention efficiency when compared with placebo group. The intensity of memory improvement was positively correlated with initial severity of folate deficiency. The severity of initial cognitive decline was unrelated to the degree of folate deficiency	[39]

Epidemiological studies demonstrate that with increasing age, the prevalence of nutritional deficiencies increases, in particular deficiencies of antioxidants and B-vitamins.

• Micronutrient deficiencies may contribute to, or even promote, cognitive impairment.

• A strategy to improve micronutrient status may help improve cognition or delay the onset of MCI and at least Alzheimer dementia (AD).

References

1. ter Borg S., Verlaan S., Hemsworth J et al Micronutrient intakes and potential inadequacies of community dwelling older adults: a systematic review. BJN 2015; 113:1195–1206

2. Galan P, Viteri FE, Bertrais S, Czernichow S, Faure H, Arnaud J, Ruffieux D, Chenal S, Arnault N, Favier A, Roussel AM, Hercberg S. Serum concentrations of beta-carotene, vitamins C and E, zinc and selenium are influenced by sex, age, diet, smoking status, alcohol consumption and corpulence in a general French adult population. Eur J Clin Nutr. 2005 ;59 (10):1181–90.

3. Faure H, Preziosi P, Roussel AM, Bertrais S, Galan P, Hercberg S, Favier A. Factors influencing blood concentration of retinol, alpha-tocopherol, vitamin C, and beta-carotene in the French participants of the SU.VI.MAX trial. Eur J Clin Nutr. 2006 Jun;60(6):706–17. Epub 2006 Jan 4

4. Johnson KA, Bernard MA, Funderburg K. Vitamin nutrition in older adults. Clin Geriatr Med. 2002 ;18(4):773–99. Review.

5. de Lau LM, Refsum H, Smith AD, Johnston C, Breteler MM. Plasma folate concentration and cognitive performance: Rotterdam Scan Study. Am J Clin Nutr. 2007 Sep;86(3):728–34

6. Akbaraly T, Hininger-Favier I, Carrière I, Arnaud J, Gouriet V, Roussel AM, Berr C. Plasma selenium over time and cognitive decline in the elderly. Epidemiology 2007; 18: 52–58

7. Hu P, Bretsky P, Crimmins EM, Gurainik JM, Reuben DB, Seeman'TE. Association between serum beta-carotene levels and decline of cognitive function in highfunctioning older persons with or without apolipoprotein E4 alleles: MacArthur Studies of Successful Aging. J Gerontol Med Sci 2006; 61A, 6: 616–620

8. Maxwell CJ, Hicks MS, Hogan DE, Basran J, Ebly EM. Supplemental use of antioxidant vitamins and subsequent risk of cognitive decline and dementia. Dement Geriatr Cogn Disord 2005; 20: 45–51

9. Morris MC, Evans DA, Tangney CC, Bienias JL, Wilson RS, Aggarwal NT et al. Relation of the tocopherol forms to incident Alzheimer disease and to cognitive change. Am J Clin Nutr 2005; 81: 508–514

10. Zandi PP, Anthony JC, Khachaturian AS, Stone SV, Gustafson D, Tschanz JT et al. Reduced risk of Alzheimer's disease in users of antioxidant vitamin supplements: the Cache County Study. Arch Neurol 2004; 61: 82–88

11. Laurin D, Masaki KH, Foley DJ, White LR, Launer IJ. Midlife dietary intake of antioxidants and risk of late-life incident dementia: The Honolulu-Asia Aging Study. Am J Epidemiol 2004; 159: 959–967

12. Luchsinger JA, Tang MX, Shea S, Mayeux R. Antioxidant vitamin intake and risk of Alzheimer's disease. Arch Neurol 2003; 60: 203–208

13. Gray SL, Hanlon JT, Landerman LR, Artz M, Schmader KE, Fillenbaum GG. Is antioxidant use prospective of cognitive function in the community-dwelling elderly? Am J Geriatr Pharmacother 2003; 1: 3–10

14. Grodstein F, Chen J, Willet WC. High-dose antioxidant supplements and cognitive function in community-dwelling elderly women. Am J Clin Nutr 2003; 77: 975–984
15. Morris MC, Evans DA, Bienias JL, Tangney CC, Bennett DA, Aggarwal N et al. Dietary intake of antioxidant nutrients and the risk of incidence Alzheimer's disease in a biracial community study. JAMA 2002; 287: 3230–3237
16. Kang JH, Cook N, Manson J, Buring JE, Grodstein F. A randomised trial of vitamin E supplementation and cognitive function in women. Arch Int Med 2006; 166: 2462–2468
17. Petersen RC, Thomas RG, Grundmen M, Bennett D, Doody R, Ferris S et al. Vitamin E and donepezil for for the treatment of mild cognitive impairment. N Engl J Med 2005; 352: 2379–2388
18. Sano M, Ernesto C, Thomas RG, Klauber MR, Schafer K, Grundman M et al. A controlled trial of selegiline, alpha-tocopherol, or both as treatment for Alzheimer's disease. The Alzheimer's Disease Cooperative Study. N Engl J Med 1997; 336: 1216–1222
19. Wengreen H, Munger R, Zandi P et al. Prospective study of fruit, vegetable and fish in dementia and cognitive function in the Cache County Study on memory, health and aging. J Nutr Health Aging 2006; 10: 209 (Abstract)
20. Raffaitin C, Letenneur L, Dartigue JF, Alperovitch A, Barberger-Gateau P. Consommation d'aliments riches en antioxydants ou en acides gras et risque de démence chez les sujets de la cohorte des 3 Cité. 6èrnes Journées Francophone de Nutrition, Nice, France, 29 nov – 1er déc 2006. Nutrition et Métabolisme 2006; 20 suppl 2 : 894 (Abtract)
21. Morris MC, Evans DA, Tangney CC, Bienias JL, Wilson RS. Associations of vegetable and fruit consumption with age-related cognitive change. Neurology 2006; 67: 1370–1376
22. Dai Q, Borenstein AR, Wu Y, Jackson JC, Larson EB. Fruit and vegetable juices and Alzheimer's disease: the Kame project. Am J Med 2006; 119: 751–759
23. Scarmeas N, Stern Y, Tang MX, Mayeux R, Luchsinger JA. Mediterranean diet and risk for Alzheimer's disease. Ann Neurol 2006; 59: 912–921
24. Morris MC, Evans DA, Schneider JA, Tangney CC, Bienias JL, Aggarwal NT. Dietary folate and vitamins B12 and B6 not associated with incident Alzheimer's disease. J Alzheimers Dis 2006; 9: 435–443
25. Kado D, Karlamangla AS, Huang MH et al. Homocysteine versus the vitamins folate, B6, and B12 as predictors of cognitive function and decline in older high-functioning adults: MacArthur Studies of Successful Aging. Am J Med 2005; 118: 161–167
26. Morris MC, Evans DA, Bienias JL et al. Dietary folate and vitamin B12 intake and cognitive decline among community-dwelling older persons. Arch Neurol 2005; 62: 641–645
27. Corrada MM, Kawas CH, Hallfrisch J, Muller D, Brookmeyer R. Reduced risk of Alzheimer's disease with high folate intake: the Baltimore Longitudinal Study of Aging. Alzheimers Dement 2005; 11–18
28. Mooijaar SP, Gussekloo J, Frolich M et al. Homocysteine, vitamin B-12, and folic acid and the risk of cognitive decline in old age: the Leider 85-Plus study. Am J Nutr 2005; 82: 866–871
29. Tucker KL, Qiao N, Scott T, Rosenberg I, Spiro A III. High homocyteine and low B vitamins predict cognitive decline in aging men: the Veterans Affairs Normative Aging Study. Am J Clin Nutr 2005; 82: 627–635
30. Ravaglia G, Forti P, Maioli F et al. Homocysteine and folate as risk factors fpr dementia and Alzheimer's disease. Am J Clin Nutr 2005; 82: 636–643
31. Luchsinger JA, Tang MX, Shea S, Miller J, Grren R, Mayeux R. Plasma homocysteine levels and risk of Alzheimer's disease. Neurology 2004; 62: 1972–1976
32. Teunissen CE, Blom AH, van Boxtel MPJ et al. Homocysteine: a marker for cognitive performance? A longitudinal follow-up study. J Nutr Health Aging 2003; 7: 155–159
33. Seshardi S, Beiser A, Selhub J, Jacques PF et al. Plasma homocysteine as a risk factor dementia and Alzheimer's disease. N Engl J Med 2003; 346: 476–483
34. Wang HX, Wahlin A, Basun H, Fastbom J, Winblad B, Fratiglioni L. Vitamin B (12) and folate in relation to the development of Alzheimer's disease. Neurology 2001; 56: 1188–1194

35. Luchsinger JA, Tang MX, Miller J, Green R, Mayeux R. Relation of higher folate intake to lower risk of Alzheimer's disease in the elderly. Arch Neuro, 2007; 64: 86–92
36. McMahon JA, Green TJ, Skeaff CM, Knight RC, Mann JI, Williams SM. A controlled trial of homocyteine lowering and cognitive performance. N Engl J Med 2006; 354: 2764–2772
37. Clarke R, Harrison G, Richards S, Vital Trial Collaborative Group. Effect of vitamins and aspirin on markers of platelet activation, oxidative stress and homocysteine in people at high risk of dementia. J Intern Med 2003; 254: 67–75
38. Bryan J, Calvaresi E, Hughes D. Short-term folate, vitamin B-12 or vitamin B-6 supplemetation slightly affects memory performance but not mood in women of various ages. J Nutr 2002; 132: 1345–1356
39. Fioravanti M, Ferrario E, Massaia M, Cappa G, Rivolta G, Grossi E et al. Low folate levels in the cognitive decline of elderly patients and efficacy of folate as a treatment for improving memory deficits. Arch Gerontol Geriatr 1997; 26: 1–13

Chapter 7
Food Insecurity and Poverty in Germany

Sabine Pfeiffer, Tobias Ritter and Elke Oestreicher

Abstract As Germany is considered the most powerful economy in the European Union, one would not expect food insecurity to be a German problem. However, rising social inequality means that food insecurity is an increasingly serious problem in the Global North and in otherwise stable European economies. The predominant responses to food insecurity on the part of the German political and social welfare systems can be characterized by delegation and denial of the problem and by a tendency to stigmatize the poor. Food surveys conducted in Germany exclude from their focus key at-risk groups and suggest that unsatisfactory nutrition is merely a self-inflicted problem caused by unhealthy eating patterns. However, a differentiated look at the data points to a more problematic constellation for Germany. For example, in Germany, 46.6% cannot afford a drink or meal with others at least once a month—a very high percentage compared to the rates of the EU27 (28.8%), Greece (18.5%), and the UK (18.2%). Food insecurity could be an intermittent reality for some 7% of Germany's population. The number of food banks in Germany increased from 480 in 2005 to 916 in 2013, and 60,000 volunteers currently serve food to 1.5 million so-called 'regular customers'. These numbers alone could be interpreted as evidence of food insecurity in Germany. Understanding individual day-to-day coping strategies of at-risk population groups

This article was made possible by the research framework of the third 'Reporting on Socioeconomic Development in Germany—soeb' (www.soeb.de/en/), funded by the German Federal Ministry of Education and Research.

S. Pfeiffer (✉) · E. Oestreicher
University of Hohenheim, Wollgrasweg 23 (550D), 70599 Stuttgart, Germany
e-mail: soziologie@uni-hohenheim.de

E. Oestreicher
e-mail: soziologie@uni-hohenheim.de

T. Ritter
Institute for Social Science Research (ISF Munich), Jakob-Klar-Straße 9,
80796 Munich, Germany
e-mail: tobias.ritter@isf-muenchen.de

will help with the development of social policy strategies to minimize food insecurity not only in Germany but also throughout Europe—provided policy-makers care sufficiently about this issue.

Keywords Food insecurity · Food poverty · Nutritional poverty · Germany · Low-income household · Necessities of life · Nutritional consumption patterns · Food bank

7.1 Food Insecurity in Germany?

The EU crisis that started in 2007 and still seems to be ongoing is complex and multidimensional, involving a banking crisis, a sovereign debt crisis and a macroeconomic crisis [16]. As Germany is considered the most powerful economy in the European Union and the assumed winner of the crisis [6], one would not expect food insecurity to be a German problem. Beyond the complexity of the crisis and the German ability to cope with it, however, public discourse has it that the most severe economic effects of the crisis hit not only fragile national economies but also low-income households all over Europe. And while German GDP per capita has been growing faster than in the EU-15 on average (ibid: 348), income inequality has risen sharply since 2000 [9]. The German Gini Coefficient (disposable income, post taxes and transfers) made a considerable jump between 1999 (0.259) and its all-time high of 0.297 in 2005, before retreating back somewhat to 0.286 in 2010. Thus the German Gini is better than UK value (0.341 in 2010); current German inequality levels, which were similar to those found in some Nordic countries in the 1980s, are very close to the OECD average (ibid).

Unlike rising inequality, in Germany food insecurity seems to be far less of a societal topic than in the UK, which could partly be the result of a more drastic reality that is hard to ignore, considering the 54% increase in food banks in the UK from 2012 to 2013 alone [2]. While Church and welfare organizations are highlighting the problem in the UK [18] and the press is reacting (for example, *The Guardian* started a Food Poverty news section in 2011, and has published more than 180 posts on the topic since then), in Germany food poverty has not yet had the same impact on public discourse, despite the Food Bank monitoring study receiving increasing recognition.

Food poverty in what we consider affluent societies seems to be a contradiction in terms. However, hunger has always been caused by poverty and inequality, not scarcity [5: 595]. With rising inequality, food insecurity—meaning the "inability to acquire or eat an adequate quality or sufficient quantity of food in socially acceptable ways (or the uncertainty of being able to do so)" [3]—is an increasingly serious problem in the Global North and in otherwise stable European economies. Food poverty in the heart of Europe is not an inevitable and short-term consequence of the last economic crisis, but follows certain changes to the social security system, particularly a more punitive sanctions regime [2]. In Germany and the UK alike, the state widely ignores the issue, delegating it to charitable solutions [1, 15]; individual coping strategies at the household level are therefore inevitable.

7.2 State of the Art: Food Insecurity and Poverty in Germany

On the basis of a range of evidence drawn from different sources of quantitative data, in 2011 we tried to prove that there is nutritional poverty in Germany, and in particular that social welfare recipients are widely excluded from eating out [11]. Since then, the situation has intensified. Physiological hunger and hunger for social inclusion by eating out are a reality in contemporary German society. And still, the predominant responses of the German political and social welfare systems can be characterized by delegation and denial of the problem and by a tendency to stigmatize the poor. We now provide some basic information on the state of food-related research in Germany.

As in 2011, we again face the situation of scientific and public obliviousness to the reality of food insecurity in Germany. According to the German food survey (*Nationale Verzehrstudie* [NVS]), one in five people are classified as obese, and excess weight is unequally distributed along the social scale [7]. However, this study was only carried out twice: first in the 1980s (NVS I) and a second time between 2005 and 2007 (NVS II). The scientific and public debate on eating patterns in Germany is dominated by obesity rather than food poverty. Whereas surveys on nutrition in Great Britain (National Food Survey, NFS) do take poorer population strata into consideration, or even over-represent them, the German NVS excluded population groups at a higher risk of nutritional poverty from the study. For example, migrants, homeless people or elderly people are underrepresented [11]. The importance of integrating these groups is indicated, as including these population groups permits more detailed insights into risks of nutritional poverty such as food availability, utilization and accessibility [17]. The German food surveys distort food insecurity because of these missing but particularly affected population groups and therefore implicitly indicate that unsatisfactory nutrition in Germany is merely a self-inflicted problem caused by unhealthy eating patterns such as excessive consumption of alcohol, fat, sugar and nicotine [7]. While nutritional poverty in the UK is discussed in the light of food security, and therefore the focus lies on relevant structures, food availability, food accessibility, subjective utilization and general conditions [11], food surveys in Germany are as granular in nutritional details as they are biased according to social stratification effects.

Despite the lack of thorough food-related research in Germany, there are some indicators that point to the rising problem of food insecurity in Germany. One indicator for deciding whether we face food insecurity in Germany is the few items that point to nutrition-related topics in surveys regularly conducted by the Federal

Statistical Office. In 2011, [11, 12] based on SOEP[1] we estimated that 1% of the population or 800,000 people in Germany were spending less than EUR 99 per month of their household expenditures on food, and were likely to live in nutritional poverty and experience hunger at least from time to time. This may also hold true for an estimated 300,000 homeless people. As we also pointed out in 2011, food insecurity could be an intermittent reality for some of the 7% of the population—more than 5 million people—who have a monthly nutritional spend of EUR 100–199. Again based on the SOEP dataset, spending on food evidently differs according to employment: In 2011 German employed households spent EUR 362 a month on food, beverages and tobacco (13.7% of monthly private consumption expenditures) while unemployed households were only able to spend EUR 205 or 19.2% of their consumption expenses. The differences are much more evident if one compares expenditures for hotels and restaurants—for German employed households spent EUR 147 per month (5.6% of consumption spending), while unemployed households' equivalent expenses total a meager EUR 21 a month, or 2% of their overall expenditure [15].

Unfortunately we do not have a research project in Germany that could be compared to the Poverty and Social Exclusion in the UK Project, which is based on the 'necessities of life' approach, aiming for a consensual measure of relative poverty, using the majority opinion to determine the set of items and activities which are regarded as necessities [4]. However, as there were no significant distinctions to be found between Scotland and the rest of the UK (ibid), we assume German public opinion to be similar regarding what is seen as necessary, and to what extent. The analysis for the UK contains several items that refer to nutrition and food consumption in a narrower sense. As such, 91% see two meals a day as necessary for adults, and 93% consider three meals a day essential for children. Fresh fruit and vegetables every day are seen as a necessity of life for adults by 83% and for children by 96%. And while meat, fish or an equivalent every other day are considered necessary for adults by 76% and for children by 90%, a roast joint or equivalent is only seen as indispensable for adults by 36% (ibid: 328–329).

As nutrition and food security are considered essentials of life, we will now look into some data on both nutritional and social aspects by comparing consumption data from the SILC/Eurostat survey for Germany, the EU27, the UK and Greece. We choose to compare Germany's figures with those from the UK and Greece, because Germany and Greece are at opposite ends of the European scale for almost all social and economic indicators, while the UK is mostly found somewhere in the middle. For example, the 2012 unemployment rate in Greece is the worst in Europe at 24.5%, Germany's was the best with 5.5%, while the UK lay in between with 8.1% (see [10]). This is also true for the share of "yes" responses to the question "Have there been times in the past 12 months when you did not have enough money to buy food that you or your family needed?" For Greece, the number jumped from under 10% in 2006–07 to around 18% in 2012, while there was a

---

[1]German Socio-Economic Panel http://www.diw.de/soep.

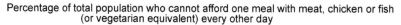

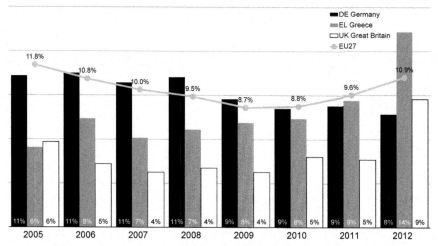

Fig. 7.1 Data by SILC/Eurostat 2013; graphics by authors. For original graphics and data see [12], reprinted with permission by Cambridge University Press

considerable decline in Germany from around 7% to under 5% and a moderate decline from 10% to around 8% in the UK (ibid: 28).

The data only shed light on nutritional behavior in terms of the ability to afford one meal with meat, chicken or fish (or a vegetarian equivalent) every other day (or at least once a day for children). Data (see Fig. 7.1) compared for the EU27, Germany, UK and Greece show a moderate decline in the percentage of the total population; for Germany the amount who could not afford the stated meal every other day dropped from 11% in 2005 to 8.2% in 2012. At first sight, nutritional poverty seems not to be an increasing problem—that is, if German public and political opinion take 8.2% as an acceptable figure—especially as the UK, Greece and EU27 show far higher percentages and instead faced a skyrocketing increase from 2011 to 2012 alone.

However, a differentiated look at the data points to a more problematic constellation for Germany. Figure 7.2 shows that 27% of Germans with an income below 60% of the Medium Equivalized Income (MEI) cannot afford one proper meal every other day—a figure that is without question considerably better than Greece's 42.2%, but higher than the European average of 23.5% and way higher than UK's 11.4%. Even the percentage that cannot afford a proper meal although their income is above 60% of MEI is higher at 5.4% in Germany than in the UK, where 3.6% of the non-poor cannot afford a square meal every other day. Even if they cannot afford one for the adults every now and then, poor households evidently try hard to provide a substantial meal at least once a day for their children, as indicated by the overall lower percentages on the right side of Fig. 7.2 for the

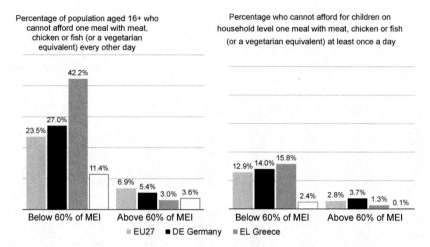

Fig. 7.2 Data for 2011 by SILC/Eurostat; Percentage for below/above Medium Equivalised Income; graphics by authors. For original graphics and data see [12], reprinted with permission by Cambridge University Press

answer "cannot afford". Germany, with 14% (below 60% of MEI) and 3.7% (above 60% of MEI) respectively, shows higher rates than those in the EU27 (12.9%), and considerably higher ones than the UK's 2.4%, but Germany almost catches up with the 15.8% of crisis-stricken Greece.

The aforementioned PSE study [4] also asked about nutrition-related necessities of life that point more to the social core of food consumption and to food-related activities supporting social inclusion. Most of these activities were only explored with reference to adults: to dine out once a month is seen as essential by 25%, going out socially once a fortnight by 34%, and going out for a drink once a fortnight by 17%. Two more items were investigated for adults and children alike: 80% consider celebrations on special occasions as essential for adults and 91% for children; having friends or family round once a month is seen as a necessity for adults by 46%, and 49% see having friends round once a fortnight as essential for kids (ibid: 328–329).

As we previously highlighted [11], being able to afford meals at home is just one side of nutritional poverty. What we have coined *alimentary participation* (ibid)—experiencing the social function of food in public and together with others—has become crucial in a modern and individualized consumer society. We do not learn anything about eating out occasions in the SILC/Eurostat dataset. However, there are some hints, as there is one question aimed at how many can or cannot afford a get-together with friends or family for a drink/meal at least once a month (or for children: invitations to play and eat with friends from time to time).

Again, Fig. 7.3 shows alarmingly high percentages for Germany, especially for those with an income that falls below 60% of MEI: in Germany, 46.6% cannot afford a drink or meal with others at least once a month—a very high percentage

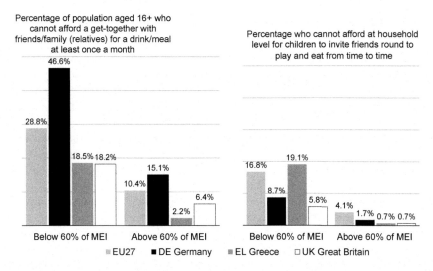

Fig. 7.3 Data for 2011 by SILC/Eurostat; Percentage for below/above Medium Equivalised Income; graphics by authors. For original graphics and data see [12], reprinted with permission by Cambridge University Press

compared to the rates of the EU27 (28.8%), Greece (18.5), and the UK (18.2%). Even for the population with an income above 60% of MEI, Germany shows higher percentages of people who cannot afford to drink and/or eat in company. Despite the cultural differences surrounding the social importance of shared meals or drinking in company all over Europe, and the fact that Germany might be less sociable in this respect, the explicit distance between Germany and the reference countries within the population below 60% of MEI hints at substantial problems of inequality in Germany, not mere cultural distinctions. The percentage that cannot afford children's invitations is considerably lower than for adults and in Germany lower than the EU27 average (16.8%) and the 19.1% of Greece, but with 8.7% below and 1.7% above 60% of MEI the percentages in Germany are higher than in the UK (5.8 and 0.7%).

These actual figures—superficial as they are compared to the social complexities of nutritional patterns, poverty consumption and alimentary participation, and despite the relative success of Germany's economy in coping with the crisis—again prove what we shed light on in 2011 (Pfeiffer et al.): There are people in our midst who are experiencing occasional hunger and are stricken by food insecurity. As delegation, denial, and stigmatization are still the predominant societal strategies for tackling food insecurity in Germany, the affected individuals are required to find their own solutions in their daily lives. The next section will offer a qualitative insight into this side of the problem.

7.3   Consequences: Coping with Nutritional Scarcity

In the underlying qualitative longitudinal study [11], a socio-economic well-balanced sample of initially 106 welfare recipients as defined by Social Code II were repeatedly interviewed over a period of five years, using biographical in-depth interviews [14]. The transcribed material consists of 453 qualitative interviews, of which 81 cases were interviewed over all four waves. The analysis followed the methodology of qualitative content analyses [8], identifying a variety of interacting conditions that shape the ways in which the interviewees are coping with restricted nutritional situations: *"objective" factors* such as accessibility of food banks and other infrastructural features of food supply, facilities for food storing and cooking; *"subjective" factors* such as the overall attitude to food and eating, e.g. lifestyle, indulgence or modest eating, eating culture and health awareness, shopping patterns and use of food banks, capabilities of household and money management including cooking skills; *"medical" factors* e.g. illnesses that require special diets; and finally *factors of "sociality"*, such as caring for others or being cared for, the range and intensity of family and social networks in general, and the time structure of eating.

The way these conditions are entwined with each other was further elaborated: In a dialectical and dynamic form of ongoing biographical transformation and sedimentation, they are both the reason for, and the result of, individual representations of coping types to be described along *three analytical dimensions*: nutrition and alimentary experiences; biographical acquisition of eating habits; and overall food-related capabilities. By following the introduced analytical steps, we identified a broad range of eight individual coping types:

- *Against the odds.* People coping actively with the situation; pragmatic and not shameful use of food banks; making the best of it.
- *Children first.* Subjective feeling of severe restriction of food supply, but trying hard to provide their own children with good and healthy food.
- *Abandonment of quantity or quality.* Coping with financial restrictions for food by lowering the quality and/or quantity of food, even if accompanied by the fatalistic anticipation of serious risks caused by chronic diseases (e.g. diabetes).
- *Surfing the ups and downs.* Due to different financial situations during the month, this type changes the nutrition and strategies of food supply, simulating normality in the beginning and spiraling downward over the course of the month.
- *Embracing nutrition for sense and structure.* For this type, activities such as cooking, eating, and the management of food supplies provide not only practical solutions to the restricted nutritional situation but sense and time structure, too.
- *Enforcing networks.* In order to maintain the food supply, this type depends on social networks: Parents, children and friends are visited to improve the nutritional situation.
- *Risky food financing.* Enhancing the food supply in potentially risky ways such as exploiting their own body (e.g. blood donations) or illegal work.

7.4   Concepts and Way Forward

Denial and stigmatization of hunger and nutritional poverty in Germany are the predominant ways of dealing with food insecurity and poverty in German society and government. The third and actually unique concept in the domain of social policy is delegating the problem to food banks (mostly organized by the *Bundesverband Deutsche Tafeln e.V.*—German Federal Association of Food Bank Initiatives), founded 1993 and mushrooming throughout Germany ever since. Although Germany does not face an abrupt rise in food bank consumption like the UK [2], the increase has accelerated since 2005, the year the Social Code II was introduced, from 480 to 916 food banks in 2013.[2] Currently 60,000 volunteers serve food to 1.5 million so-called 'regular customers'. These numbers alone could be interpreted as evidence for food insecurity in Germany, although the regional distribution of food banks does not always match the socio-economic distribution of demand (ibid). Without acknowledging food poverty as a topical and real problem in Germany and by simply delegating the problem from the realm of social policy to 'sweet charity' [13] with all its contradictions and immanent problems, there is currently no governmental concept for addressing food poverty in Germany.

7.5   Future Development

Denial, stigmatization and delegation of food poverty as an objective problem in Germany are closely interrelated and mutually reinforce each other. If they continue to prevail, they might contribute to an increase in nutritional poverty and hunger. Here, social sciences have a role to play in challenging the current orthodoxy. The best way to do so is to orient its methods and concepts to the realization that alimentary deprivation can also become an existential problem for many people in German society. As social transfers are more often part of consolidation plans reacting to the last crisis than other areas of public spending [10], and therefore spending cuts are more likely to hurt the poor (ibid: 53), food insecurity will remain a problem.

7.6   Conclusion

We have provided some current quantitative data on food insecurity in Germany and contrasted these with qualitative results on nutritional coping strategies. In conclusion, for all coping types one thing seems to hold true: As long as people have to rely on social benefits, they are very likely to suffer from rigid constraints

---

[2]http://www.tafel.de/die-tafeln/zahlen-fakten.html.

concerning alimentary participation, amounting even to exclusion. Alimentary participation in modern consumer societies is a complex problem for the poor, and it leads to a daily experience of exclusion which no individual coping strategy can satisfactorily offset. The results collated shed a first light on nutritional consumption patterns in unemployed German households; we will extend our research into the complex interrelations between food choice and other aspects of poverty consumerism. Understanding individual day-to-day coping strategies will help with the development of social policy strategies to minimize food insecurity not only in Germany but also throughout Europe—provided policy-makers care sufficiently about this issue.

7.7   Summary: Key Messages

- Rising social inequality means that food insecurity is an increasingly serious problem in the Global North, and Germany is no exception, despite its economic power.
- The predominant responses to food insecurity on the part of the German political and social welfare systems can be characterized by delegation and denial of the problem and by a tendency to stigmatize the poor. Food surveys conducted in Germany exclude from their focus key at-risk groups and as a consequence suggest that unsatisfactory nutrition is merely a self-inflicted problem caused by unhealthy eating patterns.
- A differentiated look at the data points to a more problematic constellation for Germany.
- Food insecurity could be an intermittent reality for some 7% of the country's population.
- The number of food banks in Germany increased from 480 in 2005 to 916 in 2013, and 60,000 volunteers currently serve food to 1.5 million so-called 'regular customers'.
- Understanding individual day-to-day coping strategies will help with the development of social policy strategies to minimize food insecurity not only in Germany but also throughout Europe—provided policy-makers care sufficiently about this issue.

References

1. Caraher, M. and Dowler, E. (2014) "Food for Poorer People: Conventional and Alternative' Transgressions", in: M. Goodman, and C. Sage (Eds.), Food Transgressions: Making Sense of Contemporary Food Politics. Farnham, Surrey: Ashgate, 227–246.
2. Cooper, N., Purcell, S., and Jackson, R. (2014) *Below the Breadline. The Relentless Rise of Food Poverty in Britain*. Manchester, Oxford, Salisbury: Church Action on Poverty, Oxfam, Trussel Trust.

3. Dowler, E. and O'Connor, D. (2012) 'Rights based approaches to addressing food poverty and food insecurity in Ireland and UK'. *Social Science & Medicine*, 74, 44–51.
4. Gannon, M. and Bailey, N. (2014) 'Attitudes to the Necessities of Life': Would an Independent Scotland Set a Different Poverty Standard to the Rest of the UK?', *Social Policy and Society*, 13, 321–336.
5. Holt-Giménez, E., Shattuck, A., Altieri, M., Herren, H. and Gliessman, S. (2012) 'We Already Grow Enough Food for 10 Billion People …and Still Can't End Hunger'. *Journal of Sustainable Agriculture*, 36, 595–598.
6. Kaitila, V. (2014) 'Transnational Income Convergence and National Income Disparity: Europe, 1960–2012'. *Journal of Economic Integration*, 29, 343–371.
7. Max Rubner-Institut (2008) Nationale Verzehrstudie II – Ergebnisbericht, Teil 2, Karlsruhe: Bundesforschungsinstitut für Ernährung und Lebensmittel.
8. Mayring, P. (2000). 'Qualitative Content Analysis'. *Forum Qualitative Sozialforschung/Forum: Qualitative Social Research*, 2, Art. 20. http://nbn-resolving.de/urn:nbn:de:0114-fqs0002204.
9. OECD (2011). Divided We Stand: Why Inequality Keeps Rising. Country Note Germany. http://www.oecd.org/germany/49177659.pdf.
10. OECD (2014). Society at a Glance. OECD Social Indicators. OECD Publishing. http://dx.doi.org/10.1787/soc_glance-2014-en.
11. Pfeiffer, S., Ritter, T. and Hirseland, A. (2011) 'Hunger and nutritional poverty in Germany: quantitative and qualitative empirical insights', *Critical Public Health*, 1–12.
12. Pfeiffer, S., Ritter, T. and Oestreicher, E. (2015) 'Food Insecurity in German households: Qualitative and Quantitative Data on Coping, Poverty Consumerism and Alimentary Participation', Social Policy and Society: 1–13.
13. Poppendieck, J. (1999) Sweet Charity? Emergency Food and the End of Entitlementood insecurity in Ireland and UK. New York, London: Penguin House.
14. Rosenthal, G. (2004) 'Biographical Research', in C. Seale, G. Giampieto, J. F. Gubrium and D. Silverman (eds)., Qualitative Research Practice, London: Sage, 48–64.
15. Statistisches Bundesamt (2013). Datenreport 2013: Ein Sozialbericht für die Bundesrepublik Deutschland. Destatis: Wiesbaden.
16. Tosun, J.; Wetzel, A. and Zapryanova, G. (2014). 'The EU in Crisis: Advancing the Debate'. *Journal of European Integration*, 36, 195–211.
17. Withbeck, L., Xiaojin, Ch. and Johnson, K. (2006). 'Food insecurity among homeless and runaway adolescents', *Public Health Nutrition*, 9, 47–52.
18. Webster, A. (2014). 999 Food. Emergency Food Aid in the Thames Valley. A Snapshot. Oxford: Department of Mission Church of England.

Chapter 8
Meat Consumption and Sustainability: How Might It Be Possible to Change the Behavior of Consumers?

Jana Rückert-John

Abstract Current patterns of meat production and consumption have multiple negative consequences from a sustainability perspective. Nutrition and sustainability are closely linked, and meat production and consumption are widely recognized as environmentally harmful. The widespread adoption of healthy nutritional habits could lead to a more sustainable nutrition system, but this requires not only structural changes within the food system itself but also substantial behavioral change on the part of consumers. This chapter inquires why such a change is so hard to achieve. It examines the debate on the repercussions of meat production and consumption for human health and the environment; discusses meat consumption within the context of nutritional practices; and introduces possible ways of changing the nutritional practices of consumers. It argues that only by understanding the nature of meat-based diets and their associated dietary practices will it be possible to bring about significant change in people's dietary habits.

Keywords Meat production · Meat consumption · Meat-based diet · Nutritional practices · Dietary practices · Health · Environment · Consumer · Change

8.1 Introduction

Nutrition and sustainability are closely linked. Food production and processing, supply and demand, consumer preferences and consumption patterns, and, last but not least, the management of food-waste-induced climate change are only a few of many critical environmental issues in which nutrition and sustainability interact. Other key factors include biodiversity, as well as the use of oil, water and land resources.

J. Rückert-John (✉)
Fachbereich Oecotrophologie, Hochschule Fulda,
Leipziger Str. 123, 36037 Fulda, Germany
e-mail: jana.rueckert-john@he.hs-fulda.de

© Springer International Publishing AG 2017   111
H.K. Biesalski et al. (eds.), *Sustainable Nutrition in a Changing World*,
DOI 10.1007/978-3-319-55942-1_8

Meat production and consumption are widely recognized as environmentally harmful. In terms of sustainable development, meat consumption has not only ecological consequences, but also economic, social and, above all, health repercussions. The consumer also plays a central role here, for healthier nutritional habits could lead to a more sustainable nutrition system. This means, first and foremost, less meat in the diet, as well as more responsible behavior on the part of consumers.

It is often thought that such a change must be predicated on a rational approach to consumption. For example, it is often conjectured that a greater understanding of human health and the ecological consequences of meat consumption will lead to modifications in people's nutritional practices. However, many studies in the fields of nutrition and sustainability show that theoretical knowledge is only one factor influencing the formation of daily practices. This is especially true of decisions made regarding alternative practices (such as, for example, eating proportionately less meat and more vegetables). Despite awareness of the harmful effects of a diet with a high meat content, unhealthy and unsustainable behaviors are widely observed among consumers. It is therefore pertinent to ask why a reduction in meat consumption is so hard to achieve.

The following takes a closer look at the debate on the repercussions of meat production and consumption for human health and the environment. The next section discusses meat consumption from a social science perspective within the context of nutritional practices. The last part introduces possible ways of changing the nutritional practices of consumers.

8.2 The Ecological and Health Consequences of Meat Consumption

8.2.1 Status Quo and Prognosis for Meat Consumption

According to the calculations of the United Nations Food and Agriculture Organization (FAO), more than 300 million tons of meat were consumed in 2012. The global average per capita consumption lay at 42.5 kg per year. Though a considerable consumption gap remains between poor and wealthy countries, it is quickly closing. The FAO states that in 2006 the average resident of a developing country consumed 30.7 kg of meat. By 2012, this had risen to 32.7 kg—an increase of almost 7%. Although meat consumption in industrial countries sank from 81 to 79 kg per capita within the same period, it remains high. In Germany alone, 58 million pigs, 630 million chickens and 3.2 million cows are slaughtered annually. Germany now slaughters more pigs annually than any other country in Europe. By contrast, more than 660 million pigs are slaughtered each year in China. However, it must be noted that in Germany meat consumption for 2012 averaged about 2 kg less per resident [1]. Nonetheless, at roughly 60 kg per person, meat consumption in Germany remains considerably above the global average of 42.5 kg.

The increased demand for meat is attributable to population growth, higher income, and changes in eating habits [2]. The FAO estimates that global meat production will almost double from 229 million tons in 1999–2001 to 465 million tons by 2050. This estimate is based on a projected worldwide population of 9.1 billion people by 2050 [2].

8.2.2   The Ecological Repercussions of Meat Consumption

In the debate on sustainable nutrition, the issues most often discussed are the enormous ecological and health impacts associated with meat production. A central theme here is the effect of meat production on the earth's climate. All along the food chain, agricultural production, food processing, food marketing and food retailing generate considerable greenhouse gas (GHG) emissions. In 2006, the European Commission calculated that 20–30% of all GHG emissions in the European Union (EU) are caused by the production, supply and consumption of foodstuffs [3, 4]. For Germany, Fritsche et al. [5] put GHG emissions attributable to food production and consumption at 16%. However, in a study that consolidated several other studies, Nieberg [6] estimated these values at 14–22%. Here almost 70% of the direct GHG emissions can be traced back to products of animal origin. By contrast, only about one third of these emissions are attributed to plant-based products. Throughout their food chain, Germany's 81 million residents produce c. 164 million tons of CO_2 equivalents directly through their nutrition. Almost 67 million tons of this total is attributed to meat consumption alone, while only a tenth is traceable to fruit and vegetable consumption.

In addition, livestock farming is linked to increasing water resource problems. A growing population, as well changes in lifestyles and consumption patterns, translates into a higher demand for water. This, in turn, means that more pressure is placed on natural resources and ecological systems. According to the UNESCO water report, global demand for water will increase by 55% from 2014 to 2050 [7]. Accounting for 70% of total water extraction, the agricultural sector is a major water user. Animal husbandry represents 80% of global water usage, and 7% of this is needed for feed production. Calculations from the German Federal Statistical Office put the virtual water usage in Germany per ton of beef at 16,000 m^3. For pork, this figure is 4,000 m^3. By comparison, plant products use considerably less water per kilo: wheat (1,300 L), tomatoes (184 L) and bananas (859 L) [8]. Water consumption is not considered the only problem here; there is also the problem of the water pollution that goes along with animal husbandry. This leads to eutrophication, dead zones in coastal areas, increasing health problems, and resistance to antibiotics [2].

Not only are enormous amounts of water used for meat production; a large portion of arable farm land is also utilized for this purpose. Worldwide agricultural production requires a surface area of about five billion hectares. Of this total, 3.9 billion hectares are used for livestock farming, and ultimately for producing food products of animal origin. Assuming that global demand for meat continues to increase, so too will the need for agricultural land, and the competition for these surface areas. For meat consumption in Germany at today's levels, almost 19 million hectares are needed. This exceeds Germany's available arable acreage. In terms of arable land per person, it is estimated that in less than 20 years, 2,000 m^2 of agricultural surface area per person will be available [9, 10]. Current meat consumption in Germany, which requires 2,900 m^2 per person, already exceeds available amounts projected for the future. This problem of land usage does not concern Germany alone, but rather all of Europe; land usage for the production of meat is often shifted onto other countries on other continents, such as South America. Between 2008 and 2010, this included on average more than 30 million hectares that the EU occupied 'virtually'. This equates to the combined surface areas of Hungary, Portugal, Denmark and the Netherlands. Germany's portion of this 'virtual land usage' is about seven million hectares. This is roughly the size of the Federal State of Bavaria [11]. Animal feedstuff is largely responsible for this virtual land usage outside the EU. For soy and soy product imports alone, Germany uses some 2.5 million hectares of net virtual land surface, especially in Brazil and Argentina. To this end, rain forests are lost, soils are saturated with pesticides, and foodstuff prices rise, all on account of increased competition for agrarian surfaces.

8.2.3   The Health Consequences of High Meat Consumption

Meat is consumed on a daily basis in many countries. Indeed, in Germany and other industrial countries, meat is consumed in high quantities [12, 13]. Based on recommendations from the DGE (the German Society for Nutrition), as well as other international organizations such as the World Cancer Research Fund (WCRF), too much meat is consumed in Germany and in Europe in general. In 2008, a national consumption study came to the conclusion that the average adult in Germany consumes more than 120 g of meat daily [14]. By contrast, the DGE recommends a daily average of only 64 g per person [15], with the WCRF recommending 71 g daily for adults [16]. This means that Germans eat twice the amount of meat recommended by nutritional experts.

From the nutritional standpoint, meat is considered an important part of a balanced diet for humans. At the same time, high meat consumption is considered by the DGE and WCRF to be linked with health risks. These risks stem from the high intake of animal fat (especially saturated fats) that accompanies a diet high in meat, as well as the way the meat is prepared. Red meat and meat manufacturing processes such as smoking, pickling and salting are considered particularly problematic [12, 14]. Among the nutrition-related diseases linked with high meat consumption are cardiovascular diseases (such as coronary heart disease or stroke), oncological diseases (such as colon cancer), and type 2 diabetes. In the debate on nutritional physiology, however, it is stressed that the cause of these diseases cannot be reduced to high meat consumption alone. Thus, renouncing meat does not necessarily lower a person's risk of cancer [12].

8.2.4 Factory Farming

Meat production today is typically carried out by means of factory farming, which puts places severe strains on the welfare of the livestock. Factory farming generally means crowded housing conditions for animals: examples of standard values here are 2,500 fattening pigs, 750 sows, 600 cows or 40,000 chickens per operation. In recent years, the number of individual farm operations in Germany has decreased while their respective size has increased. This is primarily due to technological advances that encourage the production of more animals with fewer personnel. In addition, economic pressures play a substantial role: meat and products of animal origin are often sold at cheap prices.

For the animals, factory farming means that along with crowded living quarters, they are forced to produce unnaturally high outputs and achieve maximum weight in the shortest time possible. Overcrowded and cramped living negatively influences their social behavior and generates stress and frustration. To avoid injuring each other, these animals must undergo surgical procedures (e.g. the dehorning of cattle and the removal of piglets' curly tails). Illness is another common consequence of factory farming. Especially widespread are cardiovascular problems, bone deformations due to excessively rapid weight gain, ulcers, and behavioral disorders. These illnesses require medical intervention and treatment. Here the massive use of antibiotics is particularly problematic. For example, a broiler chicken has an average lifespan of 32 days, and during that time will be treated 2–3 times with antibiotics.

8.2.5 Reduced Meat Consumption as a Possible Solution

The difficulties discussed in the following debate on sustainable nutrition are not comprehensive. Rather, this paper aims to illustrate from various social perspectives the obvious problems linked with meat production and higher meat consumption. These problems, which denote an unsustainable nutrition system, are the starting-point in the debate. By this means, the foundation may be laid for societal change in the direction of more sustainable nutrition.

In Germany, the onus is often placed on consumers to 'vote with their shopping baskets' and choose to consume more responsibly. General recommendations tend to concentrate on reducing the consumption of meat [17]. Consumers are advised to follow the recommendations from the DGE. According to the DGE, Germans should eat 75% more vegetables and 44% less meat [15]. Converting to the recommended diet would reduce the surface footprint per person by about 230 m^2

[17]. This method of resolution, however, presupposes a conscious and rational change in the individual's nutritional habits. Such a change cannot simply be assumed in the context of what is in actuality a demanding process. This approach underestimates or ignores the fact that meat is a substantial component of ancient nutritional practices. Meat consumption is structurally enabled by economic and political arrangements in the context of modernization. It is becoming increasingly widespread, and is grounded in a symbolic meaning handed down through the generations. The meaning of meat is firmly anchored in western nutritional culture. Thus the question must be confronted: precisely why is it so hard to get away from meat and change dietary habits?

8.3   Meat in the Context of Nutritional Practices

To answer this question, it is helpful to understand the carnivorously inclined diet as a dietary habit which is finds its expression in certain nutritional practices. Social practices are generally understood as routines and familiar actions (e.g. shopping or washing dishes) that become apparent habits (e.g. the preparation of certain dishes and meals). The distinctive feature of practices lies in the fact that they can be reflected upon at greater length. This is because the elements of actions (motive, norms, values, behaviors, structures) are condensed within them. Practices in life are adopted primarily through socialization and stand the test of time by their ordinary and easy implementation. Since practices are oriented around collective values and norms, they generate concrete actions [18]. In this manner, they can guarantee individual capacity for action and security [19, 20]. For carnivorous diets, as well as for every other practice, there are four different elements (see [19, 21]): (1) functional elements or material arrangements such as technology, tools or infrastructure (e.g. slaughterhouses, meat production and supply); (2) motivationally effective elements such as social meanings communicated via values, motives and orientations (e.g. symbols of meat: strength and virility); (3) performative elements, such as physical or linguistic actions existing as skills (e.g. ways of preparing meat); and (4), social settings which offer meat (e.g. company catering, family, school).

8.3.1   The Symbolic Meaning of Meat

The following examines the symbolic meaning of meat as a significant element of a meat-based diet. Even today, meat remains a symbol of power and dominion. Meat stands for domination over nature [22], and embodies ideas of control, strength and virility. This stems from necessity, which links the consumption of meat to the act of killing and shedding blood. The force used to acquire the meat from another living creature is unavoidable. In the process of civilization, this force is engineered and its procedures are hidden from the public. Tucked away in the wings of society, the realities of the meat supply are increasingly marginalized in human consciousness. Meat has become symbolic of a victorious triumph over nature [23]. However, due to its inseparable link with death, meat is not only the most highly valued food; it is also the food whose consumption provokes the most fear. The enjoyment of meat is bound up with many taboos and regulations: the most explicit dietary taboos concern meat [23].

Because of this symbolic meaning, meat is a socially differentiating characteristic that has experienced various manifestations in human history. A substantial and increasingly topical differentiation category is gender. The gender connotations of meat as 'masculine' are often traced back to prehistoric developments. One popular approach of cultural anthropological research assumes that the transition from tribal hunting to deer stalking caused the evolution of gender roles [24].

In this way, hunting for meat increasingly became an exclusively male activity, while female gender roles revolved around reproductive functions and depended on the success of the men's hunting. Thereby the male hunters won control and the power of distribution, and meat became the food of men. There are, however, doubts about this interpretation of a pre-Neolithic gender-specific division of labor [25, 26].[1] It is more likely that the earliest established farms helped form such a division of labor, which eventually found a corresponding expression in nutritional practices [27]. By this means, ideas of masculinity became closely associated with the concept of power over meat. Fiddes describes the relationship between gender, meat and power as follows: "Men are meat in the sense that meat is full of power. Women, on the other hand, are meat in the sense that it is an expression of power to consume their meat" [22: 184].

Ever since meat has become available to large sections of the population, meats have differentiated themselves gender-wise as red (male) and white (female) meat, with different respective values. Yet not only the quality but also the quantity counts as an expression of gender difference. According to western culinary taxonomy, and with respect to gender role expectations, fruit and vegetables are the weak foods, and are therefore for females. Meat and alcohol are strong foodstuffs, and are therefore masculine [23]. These stereotypical differences are constantly being renewed and reproduced in different social interactions. Prominent examples of this can be found in mass media productions such as food commercials or magazines (e.g. the German *Beef!*, whose headline declares: "For men with taste"). Differences are found not only as regards meat consumption: meat production and processing, as well as slaughtering and butchering, remain traditionally male domains [23]. The process of slaughter is a symbol of nature's submission to human beings—namely, to men.

---

[1]The archeologist Linda Owen points out that ideas of a strict role division during the early Paleolithic era between male hunters and female gatherers is probably based on a 'Stone Age cliché'. First, there is no archeological proof and secondly, ethnological observations show that the hunters and gatherers still existing today have females that go on the hunt, even if for smaller animals.

Because of its value, meat is still regarded as an expression of a satisfying, proper meal [28, 29]. Sunday and holiday meals without meat are generally unthinkable. According to a German study from Hayn [30], intensive 'cheap and cheap meat eaters' make up about 13% of the country's total population. In this group, meat is considered the ideal food, because it is easy to prepare in creative ways. The need for simplification also influences lifestyle orientations. The menu of this group is characterized by its pronounced penchant for meat and sausage: one in ten people in Germany eats beef at least every other day. The primary focus of cheap and cheap meat eaters lies with the 'middle-aged' group, with an average age of 38. Nonetheless, this style has spread to the 46–60 year-olds as well as to the under 25 year-olds. Middle to lower incomes are the norm for this style, which is also associated with an above-average unemployment rate (15%).

8.3.2 The Structure of a Meat-Based Diet

The symbolic meaning of meat is closely related to the structure of a meat-based diet. An important prerequisite of this structure is the meat industry, because social practices acquire structure in the form of arrangements which provide the basis for their execution and reproduction [31].[2] This means that the permanent and inexpensive availability of meat in modern industrial society has made a meat-based diet possible. At the same time, this availability made the social values linked with meat viable for an increasing number of people. Thus the steadily sinking private household spend on groceries and meat (44% in 1960; 15% in 2013) can be interpreted as an indicator of prosperity.

Today's meat-based diet has been substantially shaped by developments in the meat industry that occurred in the 1960s. The meat industry had in fact already begun to boom by the end of the 19th century [34: ff.]. To describe this phenomenon, the UN Food and Agriculture Organization plays on the term 'green revolution' by coining the neologism 'livestock revolution' [35]. This term makes reference to the 'ultra-efficient, maximum performance and highest possible yield' credo that is the hallmark of conventional agriculture today. On the one hand, the increasing use of fertilizer, pesticides, irrigation systems and machines has greatly enhanced farming yields. The rise in meat production has also been tied to many other interrelated factors. The widespread globalization and liberalization of the agricultural market took on a new quality and set the tone for the 1980s and 1990s. Massive national and European subsidies led to a substantial reduction in prices. Along with this came new technologies for breeding, animal husbandry, slaughtering, freezing, transportation—and also cheap oil for fertilizer and diesel fuel. The

---

[2]This has been also discussed as 'systems of provision' [32], adapted for consumption by Brand [33].

development continued, with increasing concentration of production on fewer but larger farm operations (in terms of their livestock levels). Today, industrial animal husbandry is restricted to a few countries, a small number of animal species, and a limited number of companies. The USA, Brazil and China belong to the largest producers of pork, beef and poultry meat worldwide. This trio of countries contributes to between 43 and 59% of worldwide production with these three animal species [17].

The international meat trade continues to grow—and in the last decade alone, it has risen by about 40%. This development is driven by increasing demand from many developing and emerging economies. Between 1990 and 2003 alone, the annual import and export rate of poultry meat rose by 10%. At the same time, pork saw an increase of 6%. Ever since the poultry industry in the EU banned milling slaughterhouse waste into animal feed, this waste has been sold to poor countries at low prices. As a result, the local markets in these countries have been destroyed. This doubled concentration in the meat industry—corporate expansion, intensive production—can be attributed to a couple of factors in particular—for example, today's low marginal gain in the meat industry due to increased production costs (e.g. through pressure on land), as well as a stagnation in meat consumption in industrial countries [17].

Industrial meat production in Europe is supported by the EU by means of annual financial assistance. EU financial aid includes, among other things, regional subsidies and the provision of transportation infrastructure, and is especially important for the animal feed industry. For investments in animal stalls, the EU offers support covering up to 50% of total costs. This provides a strong incentive to produce more pork, beef and poultry. In addition, the EU's household budget directly apportions over EUR 240 million to the meat processing industry every year. Meat remains inexpensive partly thanks to the low remuneration rates paid by slaughter houses in countries such as Germany, where a minimum wage for slaughter house workers was only just recently introduced [17].

8.4   How Is a Modification in a Meat-Based Diet Conceivable?

Bearing the powerful symbolic and structural attributes of a meat-based diet in mind, the question must be asked as to how a shift in the habit of eating large amounts of meat might nevertheless be possible. Though meat-eating practices have proven to be (at present) relatively stable, they could nonetheless collapse at some point. The need for interpreting the complex environmental conditions of meat production – as shown in Sects. 8.3.1 and 8.3.2—could in itself initiate a change in dietary practices (see [19, 20]). If the production conditions for meat-based diets change, this could cause dietary practices to experience a crisis. For example, the

BSE crisis and other meat production scandals were linked to a massive loss of consumer confidence. Such events often stimulate consumers to reflect on their own nutritional habits and modify their meat-based diets. Changes in dietary practices might involve, for example, consuming less meat or selecting more organic meats from smaller, regional farms. In such cases, a crisis can lead to demands for incremental change. However, meat-based dietary practices may turn out to be completely unnecessary if meat is completely cut out from the diet (vegetarianism).

As this example shows, dietary practices involving meat can be transformed. Changes in dietary practices can only be initiated by significant disturbances, irritations or surprises. A multitude of opportunities exist for addressing dietary practices that have become untenable. This could involve, for example (along with the structural changes in meat production and consumption mentioned above), events in people's lives such as childbirth, relocation or illness, poignant impressions (e.g. environmental disasters, movies) and even information and knowledge (e.g. the health impacts of heavy meat consumption) [36].

Long-term changes in daily practices however, occur only rarely. Much more commonly observed is a short-term change in dietary practices. As soon as disturbances lose their novelty, whether it is the switch to organic baby food or the latest dioxin scandal, they are quickly forgotten, and the old practices will take over again. This shows the generally short-term nature of the ongoing debates.

For long-term changes in dietary practices to occur, approaches resulting from the disruptions must meet the relevant structural conditions. These approaches must be able to easily conform to daily routines. Alternative practices may reproduce their structures. However, when implemented, the corresponding functional and social relationships must already be present. This is only conceivable as a co-evolutionary change, which in current political discussions is referred to as transformation. In the non-trivial sense, transformation as a contemporary change is more different; it can be understood as mutually referential structures.

If dietary practices fail in certain situations, the question arises as to how well needs can be met through alternatives, or which alternatives are available to meet those needs. Here the next immediate issue is the appropriate infrastructural offers. For modified meat or vegetarian dietary practices, other supply options are necessary (e.g. organic supermarkets) and a different investment (in terms of financial and time costs).

For the transformation of daily practices, four 'reframing' strategies are suggested for political management on the structural level [37]. These can also be applied to daily diet practices. In this way, those elements that are considered problematic can be exchanged (1) This includes for example, supporting organic products. A good example of this in Germany is how, through the federal program, organic agriculture and other forms of sustainable agriculture emerged after the BSE scandal. In this case, this will mean the communication of alternative semantic content. Organic products and supermarkets today should be presented as modern and disassociated from the 'tree-hugger' image. The price image of organic goods would thereby be reinterpreted; no longer would they be perceived as 'too expensive', but conventional products would instead seem cheap. New infrastructural offers (like, for example, organic or vegan supermarkets, as well as a thoroughly different approach to livestock farming[3]) make it possible for not only individual elements but also entire existing (meat-based) dietary practices to be replaced by alternatives (2) Another strategy could involve a network of cross-references and relationships between practices. This means that multiple practices could be changed (e.g. individual dietary practices and practices for school catering). When for example, functional and temporal sequences of routine practices are interrupted, this can lead to their being modified (e.g. extending the eating break times at school) (3) If the relationships between several practices are examined, this leads to a broad perspective where different but relevant actors are taken into account (4) By this means, for example, a new catering concept for a university or company could be initiated. This could be done under the premise of sustainability and health with a nutritional and organizational analysis of practices, which would lead to change. The four strategies clearly refer to each other. However, this also means that only when preferred alternative practices are given the corresponding structural conditions can they have a chance for stabilization through comprehensive diffusion.

8.5 Conclusions

This chapter demonstrates that current patterns of meat production and consumption have multiple negative consequences from a sustainability perspective. These impacts call for a more responsible stewardship of resources and a more humane treatment of livestock. Moreover, this perspective envisages reduced consumption of meat as a possible way of minimizing these consequences. On the one hand, it is clear that meat is a substantial element with deep historical roots in dietary practices, and that it is structurally enabled by economic and political arrangements. These arrangements became increasingly widespread during the process of civilization and are imbued with ancient symbolic meaning. It is not so easy to simply stop eating meat and change dietary behaviors. Looking at social practices more closely allows a necessary understanding of meat-based diets and their dietary practices. Only then can modifying approaches be identified which do not merely

---

[3]The recent report on farming emphasized the importance of reducing livestock numbers and seriously taking animal rights into account. However, farmers only fear increasing costs that would cause a weakened position on the global food market [38].

superficially emphasize preventative behavior, but also directly aim at preventative measures.

8.6 Summary: Key Messages

- Current patterns of meat production and consumption have multiple negative consequences from a sustainability perspective.
- Nutrition and sustainability are closely linked, and meat production and consumption are widely recognized as environmentally harmful.
- The adoption of healthy nutritional habits could lead to a more sustainable nutrition system, but this requires a change of practices in the food system for the production as well as for the consumption side.
- Only by understanding the nature of meat-based diets and their associated dietary practices will it be possible to bring about significant change in people's dietary habits.

References

1. Statista   (2015):   http://de.statista.com/statistik/daten/studie/36573/umfrage/pro-kopf-verbrauch-von-fleisch-in-deutschland-seit-2000/ (31.3.2015).
2. Steinfeld, H.; Gerber, P.; Wassenaar, T.; Castel, V.; Rosales, M.; Haande, C. (2006): Livestock's Long Shadow. Environmental Issues and Options. Food and Agriculture Organization of the United States.
3. Schaffnit-Chatterjee, C. (2011): Mitigating climate change through agriculture: An untapped potential, Deutsche Bank Research.
4. Tukker, A.; Eder, P.; Suh, S. (2006): Environmental impacts of products: Policy relevant information and data challenges. Journal of Industrial Ecology 10(3): 183–198.
5. Fritsche, U. R., Eberle, U., Wiegmann, K. und Schmidt, K. (2007): Treibhausgasemissionen durch Erzeugung und Verarbeitung von Lebensmitteln – Arbeitspapier. Öko-Institut e.V., Darmstadt/Hamburg, www.oeko.de.
6. Nieberg, H. (2009): Auf den Nahrungskonsum zurückzuführende THG-Emissionen. In: Osterburg, B.; Nieberg, H.; Rüter, S.; Isermeyer, V.; Haenel, H.D.; Hahne, J.; Krentler, J.G.; Paulsen, H.M.; Schuchardt, F.; Schweinle, J.; Weiland, P. (Hrsg.): Erfassung, Bewertung und Minderung von Treibhausgasemissionen des deutschen Agrar- und Ernährungssektors. Arbeitsberichte aus der vTI-Agrarökonomie 03/2009. Braunschweig: vTI.
7. UNESCO (2014): http://www.unesco.de/wissenschaft/2014/weltwasserbericht2014.html (31.3.2015).
8. Statistisches Bundesamt (2012): Wasserfussabdruck von Ernährungsgütern in Deutschland. http://www.wasserfussabdruck.org/Reports/Flachmann%20et%20al%202012.%20Wasserfussabdruck%20von%20Ernahrungsgutern%20in%20Deutschland.pdf (31.3.2015).
9. Doyle, U. (2011): Wie wir überleben? Ernährung in Zeiten des Klimawandels – Fokus Fleisch. Berlin: Sachverständigenrat für Umweltfragen.
10. UBA (Umweltbundesamt) (2009): Nachhaltige Flächennutzung und nachwachsende Rohstoffe. Dessau-Roßlau. UBA.

11. WWF (2012): Klimawandel auf dem Teller. http://www.wwf.de/fileadmin/fm-wwf/ Publikationen-PDF/Klimawandel_auf_dem_Teller.pdf (31.3.2015).
12. Alison J. McAfee, Emeir M. McSorley, Geraldine J. Cuskelly, Bruce W. Moss, Julie M.W. Wallace, Maxine P. Bonham, Anna M. Fearon (2010): Red meat consumption: An overview of the risks and benefits. Meat Science 84 (2010) 1–13.
13. Berndsen, M., & van der Pligt, J. (2005). Risks of meat. The relative impact of cognitive, affective, and moral concerns. Appetite, 44, 195–205.
14. MRI (2008): Nationale Verzehrsstudie II. Herausgeber. Max Rubner-Institut. Bundesforschungsinstitut für Ernährung und Lebensmittel.
15. Dickau, K. (2009): Deutsche Gesellschaft für Ernährung e. V. (Hrsg.): Die Nährstoffe – Bausteine für Ihre Gesundheit, 2. Aufl., Bonn (aid).
16. WCRF (World Cancer Research Fund International) (2007): Zusammenfassung: Ernährung, körperliche Aktivität und Krebsprävention – Eine globale Perspektive. London: WCRF.
17. Heinrich Böll Stiftung (2013): Fleischatlas. Daten und Fakten über Tiere als Nahrungsmittel. http://www.bund.net/fileadmin/bundnet/publikationen/landwirtschaft/140328_bund_ landwirtschaft_fleischatlas_2013.pdf (31.3.2015).
18. Schatzki, T. (2002): The Site of the Social: A Philosophical Account of the Constitution of Social Life and Change. Pennsylvania State: University Press.
19. Shove, E.; Pantzar, M.; Watson, M. (2012): The Dynamics of Social Practice. Los Angeles et al.: Sage.
20. Reckwitz, Andreas (2003): Grundelemente einer Theorie sozialer Praktiken. Zeitschrift für Soziologie 32: 282–301.
21. Brand, K.-W. (2013): Umweltsoziologie. Entwicklungslinien, Basiskonzepte und Erklärungsmodelle. Reihe Grundlagentexte Soziologie. Weinheim: Beltz-Juventa.
22. Fiddes, N. (2001): Fleisch. Symbol der Macht. 3. Auflage. Frankfurt (Main). Zweitausendeins.
23. Setzwein, M. (2004): Ernährung-Körper-Geschlecht. Zur sozialen Konstruktion von Geschlecht im kulinarischen Kontext. Wiesbaden: VS Verlag für Sozialwissenschaften.
24. Mellinger, N. (2000): Fleisch. Ursprung und Wandel einer Lust. Frankfurt (Main): Campus.
25. Owen, L. R. (2005): Distorting the Past: Gender and the Division of Labor in the European Upper Paleolithic. Tübingen Publications in Prehistory. Kern Verlag Tübingen.
26. Röder, Brigitte (2013): Urmenschliche Bürger - bürgerliche Urmenschen. Zur Archaisierung des bürgerlichen Geschlechter- und Familienmodells über die Urgeschichte. In: Dominique Grisard, Ulle Jäger und Tomke König (Hg.): Verschieden sein. Nachdenken über Geschlecht und Differenz. Sulzbach: Helmer, S. 243–256.
27. Diamond, J. (1991): Der dritte Schimpanse: Evolution und Zukunft des Menschen. Fischer Taschenbuch Verlag.
28. Douglas, M. (1972): Deciphering a Meal. Daedalus 101 (1), Myth, symbol and Culture, 61–81.
29. Charles, N.; Kerr, M. (1988): Women, Food, and Families, Manchester: Manchester.
30. Hayn, D. (2005): Ernährungsstile. Über die Vielfalt des Ernährungshandelns im Alltag. In: Kritischer Agrarbericht. 284–288.
31. Schatzki, T. (2010): Materiality and Social Life. Nature and Culture 5: 123–149, doi:10.3167/ nc.2010.050202.
32. Fine, B. (2002): The World of Consumption. The material and cultural revisited. London: Routledge.
33. Brand, Karl-Werner (2009). 'Systems of Provision' und nachhaltiger Konsum – Erklärungskraft eines systemischen Ansatzes. Diskutiert am Beispiel des Ernährungssystems. In: Weller, I. (Hrsg.). Systems of Provision & Industrial Ecology: Neue Perspektiven für die Forschung zu nachhaltigem Konsum? Universität Bremen, artec-paper (September 2009). http://www.uni-bremen.de/fileadmin/user_upload/single_sites/ artec/artec_Dokumente/artec-paper/162_paper.pdf (30.8.2016).
34. Osterhammel, J. (2009): Die Verwandlung der Welt. Eine Geschichte des 19. Jahrhunderts. Beck: München.

35. Delgado, C.; Rosegrant, M.; Steinfeld, H.; Ehui, S.; Courboi, C. (1999): Livestock to 2020 – The Next Food Revolution. Food, Agriculture and the Environment Discussion Paper 28. IFPRI, Washington D.C.
36. Schäfer, M.; Jaeger-Erben, M. (2012): Life events as windows of opportunity for changing towards sustainable consumption pattern? The change in everyday routines in life course transitions. In: Defila R, Di Giulio A, Kaufmann-Hayoz R (eds): The nature of sustainable consumption and how to achieve it Oekom: München, pp 195–210.
37. Spurling, N.; McMeekin, A.; Shove, E.; Southerton, D.; Welch, D. (2013): Interventions in practice: Reframing policy approaches to consumer behaviour. Sustainable Practices Research Group Report. www.sprg.ac.uk/uploads/sprg-report-sept-2013.pdf [20.12.2014].
38. Bundesministerium für Ernährung und Landwirtschaft (BMEL) (2015): Wege zu einer gesellschaftlich akzeptierten Nutztierhaltung. Gutachten. Wissenschaftlicher Beirat für Agrarpolitik beim BMEL. http://www.bmel.de/SharedDocs/Downloads/Ministerium/Beiraete/Agrarpolitik/GutachtenNutztierhaltung.pdf?__blob=publicationFile (31.3.2015).

Chapter 9
Food Insecurity: Determinants and Impacts

Nicole Darmon and France Caillavet

Abstract This chapter reviews studies examining food security on a household level in developed countries. It focuses on two issues: the individual determinants of food insecurity, and the impact of food insecurity on health. On the first issue, reflecting a wide variety of situations depending on the country and the population sample under consideration, this chapter examines the relevant socio-demographic and socio-economic variables, as well as the cultural factors associated with food insecurity. Despite their great heterogeneity, the studies examined show that the group of factors significantly linked to food insecurity generally overlap with poverty indicators such as income and standard-of-living indicators or the determinants of poverty. One very robust finding concerns the link between a lack of academic or professional qualifications and food insecurity. Despite this, poverty and food insecurity cannot be equated. Concerning the issue of the relationship between food insecurity and health, most studies are cross-sectional studies of the general population in English-speaking countries. Reviewing the impact on children's health, adult health, diet and nutritional intake, and weight status, findings converge to show that food insecurity is associated with poor health at all ages. They show the importance of taking action to improve the situation of homes suffering from this multifaceted trend.

Keywords Food insecurity · Food security · Household · Poverty · Diet · Health · Nutritional intake

N. Darmon (✉)
Human Nutrition Division, INRA 1110, CIRAD, SupAgro, CIHEAM-IAMM, Montpellier, France
e-mail: nicole.darmon@inra.fr

F. Caillavet
ALISS, INRA 1303, 65 Boulevard de Brandebourg, 94205 Ivry-Sur-Seine, France
e-mail: france.caillavet@inra.fr

9.1 Introduction

From the 1990s onwards, many studies have been published on food insecurity assessed on different scales: households, sub-populations, countries or the whole planet. This chapter reviews studies examining food security on a household level in developed countries. They reflect a wide variety of situations depending on the country and the population sample under consideration, not always representative at a national level. Most often, food insecurity is assessed with the U.S. Household Food Security Survey Module (HFSS, see the chapter by K. Castetbon for definitions of food insecurity and a review of existing tools to measure it). The studies analyze individual social factors such as the characteristics of members of households associated with food insecurity, and in particular socioeconomic parameters, which, to a great extent, overlap with the indicators or determinants of poverty. Studies examining the impact of food insecurity on health at different stages of life show the importance of taking action to improve the situation of homes suffering from this multifaceted trend.

9.2 Individual Social Factors Associated with Food Insecurity

One of the factors of food insecurity studies concerns research into the individual social factors (socio-demographic, socio-economic, cultural, etc.) associated with this situation. Most studies on this subject were conducted in North America (United States and Canada) and, to a lesser extent, in France and Australia. Some of them deal with specific populations characterized by low-income or ethnic minorities.

9.2.1 Socio-demographic Variables

Gender is taken into account in most analyses: being a woman is often, but not systematically, associated with increased risk of food insecurity [26, 32, 38]. Interestingly, one study found that among married households, women respondents reported higher household food insecurity than did men in similar Canadian households, independently of individual or socioeconomic characteristics [53]. It may reflect the gendered social responsibility of food putting more pressure on women.

Frequently, gender and age interact: in France, according to the national dietary INCA 2 survey, food insecurity (assessed using an adapted version of the US Department of Agriculture's Food Insufficiency Indicator) more often affects young women [7]. In the United States, on the other hand, this positive association between being young and food-insecure is found for men only [17, 21]. In Australia, the influence of age varies depending on the study, with the 18–49 years [60] or 0–49 years [26] age groups preferentially associated with food insecurity. In the United States, food insecurity concerns above all the youngest members of the over-60s population [21]. However, these individual characteristics may also be insignificant, as shown in the study by Martin et al. [51] in the United States and by Martin-Fernandez et al. [52] in France.

The association between food insecurity and the structure of the household (single-parent, single-member, etc.) overlaps with the association observed with marital status. A representative study of the greater Paris region [52] highlights the larger proportion of food-insecure people among single-parent and single-member households compared with two-parent households. This result is also found in North-American samples for single-parent households [32, 69]. Furthermore, the presence of children appears to be associated with greater food vulnerability in Texas [36], and in Australia [26]. In France (Greater Paris), this association is found with the presence of children below the age of three [52].

Lastly, in the North American context, a relationship between food insecurity and African-American origins has been identified but is not always substantiated [17, 46]. A high proportion of food-insecure people is also found in Hispanic groups [17, 33, 56, 72] and those using Spanish during the interview [56]. A high prevalence is also observed in Native American Indians in the United States [62] and in Canada [80]. However, this association was not observed for Asian populations [68]. Birth outside the country is positively associated with food insecurity in the US [33, 68]. In Australia, on the other hand, children with one parent born outside the country have a lower probability of finding themselves in a situation of food insecurity [66]. This difference is probably explained by the disparities in migrants' origins and their level of education. Recent immigration may be a factor for higher risk of food insecurity in Canada [77].

9.2.2 Socio-economic Variables

The question of the existence of a link between food insecurity and poverty is a recurring debate in studies [7, 14, 31]. Food insecurity is associated with lower household incomes in North American samples [42, 56] or in Australian ones [26, 66], but it also partly coincides with average incomes. This observation is also made in the French representative study based on INCA 2: the average income per unit of consumption (controlling the effects of household size, according to the INSEE scale) is higher for food-insecure people than for those in the 1st quartile of income among food-secure individuals [7] (Fig. 9.1).

On a dynamic point of view, a Canadian study found that improvements in income or in employment status during the year were associated with a decrease in the severity of food insecurity [49].

Fig. 9.1 Income of adults living in a food-insecure household for financial reasons (FI) or in a food-secure household (FS) depending on income quartile (FS1 to FS4), according to Bocquier et al. [7]. EUR/month. UC: EUR per month and per unit of consumption; FS1, 2, 3, 4: 1st, 2nd, 3rd and 4th income quartile respectively

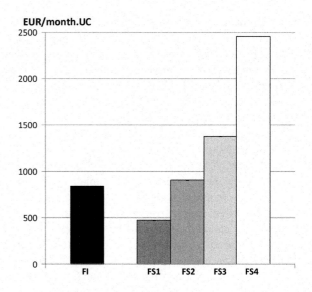

In both France and the United States, households headed by an individual with a higher education level are less likely to experience food insecurity (France: [7]), (United States: [20, 32, 73]). Depending on the studies and the variables used, being unemployed [56], inactive [26] on United States samples or dedicated to house-keeping in an Australian study is positively associated with food insecurity [66]. In France, data from INCA 2 show that the head of the family's belonging to a low socio-professional category (unemployed or working class) is associated with individuals' food insecurity [7].

Some studies validate the hypothesis of a protective effect of the household's assets on food security. In the United States, Guo [32] finds an association between possessing assets and food security including after adjustment for income levels: homeowners are thus less likely to suffer from food insecurity, and the same is true for those who own a car, a savings account or securities (stocks/bonds). The importance of these assets is confirmed in other countries. The impossibility of saving also appears to be a situation linked to food insecurity [26]. In France, a link has also been found between food insecurity and lower rates of car ownership, or under-equipped kitchens. Food insecurity also appears to be associated with housing conditions (when expressed in terms of the share of the budget devoted to housing) on a Canadian sample [42], and with living in social housing or rented accommodation in Australian studies [26, 60], in the US [18] and in France [7] where we found a negative association with being a homeowner and possessing a garden.

The issue of budgetary priorities is at the heart of the phenomenon of food insecurity: one American study found an association between the seasonal variation of food insecurity and the household's heating and air-conditioning expenses [61]. Several studies (e.g. [5, 17, 41]), including some in France [7], showed a positive association between food insecurity and smoking. They suggest that smokers are confronted with difficult budgetary choices between food or tobacco expenditure, and the decision is often made in favor of tobacco.

9.2.3   Cultural Factors

North American studies indicate that acculturation increases the risk of food insecurity [54], while being integrated in a social network limits this risk even in a situation of poverty [51]. However, these studies on the impact of social capital are based on very localized samples.

In the US, among children aged 3–19 years (n = 11,247) participating in the *National Health and Nutrition Examination Survey* 1999–2004, positive associations were found between children's food insecurity and eating more meals at school or not recently having benefited from a nutritional supplement [22]. In France, we observed an increased proportion of snacking between means and time spent watching television in adults from food-insecure households compared with those not experiencing food insecurity [7].

An Australian article notes a positive relationship between procurement constraints (problems accessing food stores because of lack of transport and/or lack of time to procure or prepare food) and food insecurity [60]. Some studies introduce the impact of neighborhood-level factors: low social cohesion in Canada [10] and low neighborhood walkability in United States [8, 13] were shown to be positively related to food insecurity.

Cooking patterns may be a factor associated with food insecurity. In particular, a positive association is observed between food security and making complex culinary preparations [4, 25, 55].

Individual social factors connected with food insecurity and financial poverty are often closely linked. However, poverty and food insecurity should not be confused —although households suffering food insecurity are far more likely to be low-income households or experiencing significant financial or social difficulties, these notions cannot strictly be superimposed: households with few financial resources do not necessarily claim to be in a situation of food insecurity, and other, more wealthy households could be classed in this category. Scales to measure food insecurity take into account means of adapting to difficulties in accessing food and we can therefore surmise that people have variable adaptive resources (connected with their past, their social support, their perception of the future, etc.).

9.3   The Health and Food Consumption
of Food-Insecure People

Most studies that analyze the relationship between food insecurity and health are cross-sectional studies of the general population in Anglo-Saxon countries. Findings converge to show that food insecurity is associated with poor health at all ages. Being cross-sectional, these studies do not enable us to establish causal relationships. However, the associations observed generally persist after adjusting for risk factors, which in turn are associated with food insecurity (low income, tobacco consumption, excess weight, etc.). Moreover, recent longitudinal studies provide evidence of causal relationships, with both food insecurity contributing to poor health [70] and diseases increasing the risk or the severity of food insecurity [16, 27, 75].

9.3.1   Food Insecurity and Children's Health

Health problems from an early age are associated with food insecurity. A case-control study conducted in the United States shows an association between food insecurity (assessed by means of five questions during pregnancy) and an increased risk of malformation at birth [9]. Food insecurity also appears to constitute a risk factor for poor health in infants. A link between food insecurity and the risk of iron deficiency anemia is recorded in children under 36 months examined in city health centers in Minneapolis [64] and Boston [74]. Another study, also conducted in city health centers in Boston (n = 17,158), shows more frequent hospitalizations from birth in infants under 36 months from food-insecure homes compared with those living in food-secure homes after adjusting for many factors [15].

In children of pre-school and school age, the association between poor health and food insecurity has been known for a long time. An analysis of data from NHANES III (the *National Health and Nutrition Examination Survey*) (1988–1994) showed that, even after taking into account numerous confounding factors including poverty levels, children from food-insecure households were at greater risk of suffering from headaches and stomach aches, and younger children (pre-school age) suffered more frequently from influenza [3]. According to data from the 1999–2004 NHANES, food insecurity increased the risk of iron deficiency anemia by a factor of 2.95 in pre-teens (12–15 years) [22]. Lower bone mineralization was also observed in boys aged between 8 and 11 from food-insecure households, but not in other age and gender categories [23]. The *Early Childhood Longitudinal Study—Kindergarten Cohort*, that followed a nationally representative sample of US children from kindergarten entry in 1998–1999 through eighth grade found that food insecurity was generally a transient rather than a persistent condition in children, but when it was persistent over the nine-year period, food insecurity was associated with lower health status [70].

Several studies report that food insecurity impairs children's normal development at each age, from infancy [68] through childhood and adolescence [12]. Children aged three through eight years in food-insecure households were reported by parents to have lower physical function, while children aged 12 through 17 years reported lower psychosocial function [12]. Behavioral, social and emotional problems at school were noted in children from food-insecure households aged between five and 12, with learning difficulties, psychological counseling, retaking the year and expulsions or suspensions being more frequent [1]. A prospective longitudinal study of 1,116 United Kingdom families with twins (1999–2000) found that food-insecure children have lower IQs and higher levels of behavioral and emotional problems relative to their peers [6]. In the US, data from the *Early Childhood Longitudinal Study—Kindergarten* study indicate that food insecurity experiences predict children's social skill scores with detrimental developmental consequences for several years [37].

In adolescence (15–16 years), depressive and suicidal symptoms have been observed more frequently in young people living in food-insecure homes than in those from food-secure homes (NHANES III), with disparities according to gender and ethnic background [2].

9.3.2 Food Insecurity and Adult Health

In Canada, the *National Population Health Survey* (1996–1997) showed that food insecurity in adults was linked to perceived poor health and an increased risk of depression, heart disease, diabetes, hypertension and food allergies [78]. The prevalence of mental illness was reported to be alarmingly high in Canadian adults reporting food insecurity [59]. Another study, based on data from the *Canadian Community Health Survey* (CCHS, cycle 3.1, n = 132,947 people over the age of 12) conducted in 2005 highlighted the link between diabetes and food insecurity [30]: a higher rate of food insecurity was observed in diabetic versus non-diabetic Canadians (9.3 vs. 6.8%). After adjusting for several factors including income and education, compared with food-secure diabetics, food-insecure diabetics are proportionally more likely to smoke, take little physical exercise and eat fewer than five portions of fruit and vegetables per day. They are also more likely to have become diabetic (age when diagnosed) before the age of 40, to suffer from non-treated diseases, to have been hospitalized for over 24 h the previous year, to claim to be in poor health (general and mental) and to consider themselves dissatisfied with and stressed by life [30].

In the United States, the 1999–2006 *NHANES* showed, after adjusting for several factors, a higher risk of presenting a metabolic syndrome in adults in a marginally food-secure situation than those enjoying food security [65]. For severe food insecurity, an increased risk of diabetes has also been reported [72]. For pregnant women, data from the American prospective study *Pregnancy, Infection, and Nutrition* were used to analyze retrospectively food insecurity in 810 pregnant women with incomes four times below the poverty line. Findings showed a risk of pre-pregnancy obesity multiplied by three and more significant weight gains during pregnancy linked to food insecurity; marginal food insecurity is associated with an increase in gestational diabetes by a factor of 2.75 [45]. Based on *NHANES* 1999–2010 data, whereas income status is not associated with iron deficiency in pregnant women, odds of iron deficiency were 2.90 higher for food-insecure pregnant women compared with their food-secure counterparts, possibly contributing to cognitive impairment in the neonates [63].

Some longitudinal studies suggest that the causal relation between health status and food insecurity is going in the way that poor health contributes to household food insecurity. Thus, in the U.S., data from the *Early Childhood Longitudinal Study Birth Cohort* indicate that maternal depression—but not poor infant health [16]—is an independent risk factor for household food insecurity [27]. In Canada, data from the 2007–2008 *Canadian Community Health Survey* (n = 77,053 aged 18–64 years) showed that chronic physical and mental health conditions increase vulnerability to household food insecurity [75].

9.3.3 Food Insecurity, Diet and Nutritional Intake

Paradoxically, although we might expect the impact of food insecurity on diet to be well known, not only are there few studies available, but furthermore, the findings of these studies are often contradictory. The few studies that have analyzed the link between food insecurity and diet or nutritional intake in children in the general population in the United States [11, 43] and Canada [41], found no significant relationship. The hypothesis most frequently put forward to interpret this finding is food-insecure parents protecting their children from the harmful effects of food insecurity by sparing them from quantitative and qualitative food deprivation [34]. However, a relationship exists if household income is introduced into the analysis. In the study by Casey et al. [11] children aged between 0 and 17 years (n = 5569) from homes that were both poor and food-insecure consumed significantly fewer fruits and vegetables, spent more time in front of the television and took less exercise than children from wealthier, food-secure homes. In other studies carried out in the United States among poor populations, for both adults [40, 56] and children [19, 29], being food-insecure had little effect on diet including the consumption of fruit and vegetables, which was very low in these populations, whether or not they were food-insecure. In another study conducted among a low-income population of parents and caregivers (n = 2095) living with adolescents and participating in the F-EAT (Families and Eating and Activity Among Teens) project, food-insecure parents more often reported having fast food at family meals and serving sugar-sweetened beverages at family meals, and they reported serving green salad, vegetables, and fruit less often than did food-secure parents [8]. There were also large differences in perceived access to fruits and vegetables between food-secure and food-insecure parents (e.g. 40% vs. 14% of food-insecure parents vs. food-secure parents reported that fruits were too expensive).

On the subject of the energy intake of food-insecure adults, results are somewhat conflicting. One earlier study based on data from the *Continuing Survey of Food Intake by Individuals* conducted between 1989 and 1991 in the United States [67] and another based on data from the *Canadian Community Health Survey* in 2004 [41] observed lower energy intake and therefore lower essential nutrient intakes (particularly vitamins A and C, as well as calcium and iron in the Canadian study) in food-insecure people compared with others. However, an American study based on data from the *NHANES* 1999–2002 found no difference in energy intake but showed a lower number of meals per day for food-insecure people, with, for women, higher-calorie meals and for men, more snacking and higher-calorie snacks [81]. A more recent study of the diets of low-income adults (n = 8129 lower-income adults ≤ 300% of the federal poverty level) based on data from the *NHANES* 1999–2008 showed that, despite no differences for energy and macronutrient intakes between food-secure and food-insecure low-income adults, food insecurity was associated with lower dietary quality scores, mainly due to a lower consumption of vegetables and a higher consumption of some unhealthy foods, such as salty snacks, sugar-sweetened beverages, red/processed meat [47].

In France, data from the national food consumption INCA 2 survey did not show measurable differences in food-insecure people's energy intake, nor did they show differences in terms of the macronutrient contribution (proteins, fats and carbohydrates) of this energy intake [7]. This study confirms the association between low income and a diet of lower nutritional quality, on average denser in energy and less rich in nutrients, with, notably, lower consumption of fruit, vegetables and fish and a higher consumption of products containing sugar (Fig. 9.2).

9.3.4 Food Insecurity and Weight Status

Many studies, most of them North American, have analyzed the relationship between weight status and food insecurity in children and adolescents. In a review of studies published in 2011 based on 21 surveys conducted between 1995 and 2009, Eisenmann et al. [24] concluded that obesity and food insecurity often coexist, but the risk of developing excess weight is not significantly different for young people in situations of food insecurity and food-secure young people. In fact, recent studies conducted among under-privileged preschool children on the Women Infants and Children (WIC) program found a link between excess weight and food insecurity, but these associations depend on the gender of the child, the presence or absence of hunger, the level of household income [58] and maternal weight status [57]. Concern of food-insecure mothers about future overweight of their child and controlling feeding styles represent potential mechanisms by which food insecurity

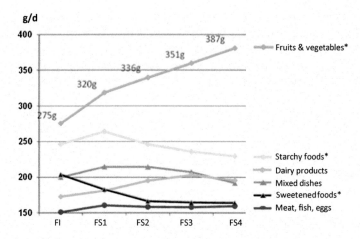

Fig. 9.2 Average consumption (adjusted for age, gender and energy intake) of the different food groups for adults living in food-insecure (FI) or food-secure (FS) households for financial reasons according to income quartile (FS1 to FS4), based on Bocquier et al. [7]. g/d: grams of food consumed per person per day; FS1, 2, 3, 4: respectively 1st, 2nd, 3rd and 4th income quartile. *Asterisk* significant difference between FI and FS4 at threshold limit of 5%

could be related to child obesity [28]. For adolescents, the survey of young people aged between 10 and 15 from low-income homes (Three-City Study) did not reveal a link between food insecurity and obesity [48]. Nevertheless, this study showed an association between the mother's state of stress (estimated by means of a score based on self-esteem, perceived health and employment situation) and food insecurity, with maternal stress increasing the probability of excess weight in food-insecure adolescents.

In surveys of the general population, a link between obesity and food insecurity is not systematically demonstrated in all age groups and according to gender, and at times this link disappears after adjusting for socio-economic factors such as income or education. Thus, in an American study based on data from the 1999 BRFSS (*Behavioral Risk Factor Surveillance System*) survey (n = 3945), worrying about one's diet (measured using a single question) was associated with morbid obesity (BMI $\geq$ 35), but this association became non-significant after adjusting for factors such as education, income, ethnic background, marital status and general health [44]. In the American *NHANES* (1999–2002), in which weight and height were measured and food insecurity was estimated with the HFSS questionnaire, the authors analyzed the role of gender and marital status in the relationship between weight status and food insecurity. Findings showed in women—but only married or widowed women—marginal food insecurity associated with a greater risk of obesity, and in men, marginal food insecurity associated with excess weight while severe food insecurity was associated with an increased risk of being underweight

[35, 79]. Using five questions focusing on the financial constraints affecting diet,[1] a Finnish study of a representative sample of 6,506 men and women aged between 25 and 64 showed that only the indicators 'buying cheaply' and 'fear of lack of money' were associated with an abnormal weight status, whether underweight or obese [71].

Some authors point out that the apparent contradictions between the studies concerning the link between food insecurity and obesity could be due to methodological aspects because findings are dependent on both the method of estimating BMI (height and weight declared or measured) [50] and also the method used to assess food insecurity [39]. Eventually, based on data from *NHANES* 2003–2006, food insecurity was found to be associated with less physical activity among both children and adults [76], probably a key factor to understand the link between food insecurity and obesity.

9.4   Conclusion

Despite their great heterogeneity, the studies examined show that the group of factors significantly linked to food insecurity overlap, for the majority, with poverty indicators such as income and standard-of-living indicators (housing conditions, owning a car, property or financial assets) or the determinants of poverty (ethnic characteristics, level of education, activity status and presence of children). One very robust finding concerns the link between a lack of qualifications and food insecurity, which continues after adjusting for income level, suggesting that education could have a protective effect with regard to food insecurity.

Despite this, poverty and food insecurity cannot be equated. Budgetary priorities depend strongly on the composition of the family and financial constraints. The studies examined demonstrate links between food insecurity and single-parent status, the presence of children and the interaction with other expenditure items such as accommodation, heating or tobacco. With regard to health, food insecurity is associated with poor health at all ages after adjusting for several risk factors, including low income. The diet of food-insecure people may be of a lower nutritional quality than the diet of low-income people, suggesting the existence of a specific effect of food insecurity on food choices.

In addition to its link with social inequalities, food insecurity emerges as a problem in its own right, improving our understanding of social gradients in terms of diet, nutritional status and nutrition-related health.

---

[1]1. Fear of shortage of money for food/ 2. Shortage of money for food/ 3. Shortage of food through lack of money/ 4. Buying cheap food/ 5. Shortage of food for at least 1 day.

9.5   Summary: Key Messages

- Studies examining the impact of food insecurity on health at different stages of life show the importance of taking action to improve the situation of homes suffering from this multifaceted trend.
- Most studies that analyze the relationship between food insecurity and health show that food insecurity is associated with poor health at all ages.
- Despite their great heterogeneity, the studies examined show that the group of factors significantly linked to food insecurity generally overlap with poverty indicators such as income and standard-of-living indicators or the determinants of poverty.
- One very robust finding concerns the link between a lack of qualifications and food insecurity.
- Several studies report an association between low income and a diet of lower nutritional quality, on average denser in energy and less rich in micronutrients, with, notably, lower consumption of fruit, vegetables and fish and a higher consumption of products containing sugar.
- Despite this, poverty and food insecurity cannot be equated.

References

1. Alaimo, K., Olson, C.M., & Frongillo, E.A., Jr. (2001a). Food insufficiency and American school-aged children's cognitive, academic, and psychosocial development. *Pediatrics*, **108**, 44–53.
2. Alaimo, K., Olson, C.M., & Frongillo, E.A. (2002). Family food insufficiency, but not low family income, is positively associated with dysthymia and suicide symptoms in adolescents. *J Nutr*, **132**, 719–25.
3. Alaimo, K., Olson, C.M., Frongillo, E.A., Jr., & Briefel, R.R. (2001b). Food insufficiency, family income, and health in US preschool and school-aged children. *Am J Public Health*, **91**, 781–6.
4. Appelhans, B.M., Waring, M.E., Schneider, K.L., & Pagoto, S.L. (2014). Food preparation supplies predict children's family meal and home-prepared dinner consumption in low-income households. *Appetite*, **76**, 1–8.
5. Armour, B.S., Pitts, M.M., & Lee, C.W. (2008). Cigarette smoking and food insecurity among low-income families in the United States, 2001. *Am J Health Promot*, **22**, 386–92.
6. Belsky, D.W., Moffitt, T.E., Arseneault, L., Melchior, M., & Caspi, A. (2010). Context and sequelae of food insecurity in children's development. *Am J Epidemiol*, **172**, 809–18.
7. Bocquier, A., Vieux, F., Lioret, S., Dubuisson, C., Caillavet, F., & Darmon, N. (2015). Socio-economic characteristics, living conditions and diet quality are associated with food insecurity in France. *Public Health Nutr*, **18**, 2952–2961.
8. Bruening, M., MacLehose, R., Loth, K., Story, M., & Neumark-Sztainer, D. (2012). Feeding a family in a recession: food insecurity among Minnesota parents. *Am J Public Health*, **102**, 520–6.
9. Carmichael, S.L., Yang, W., Herring, A., Abrams, B., & Shaw, G.M. (2007). Maternal food insecurity is associated with increased risk of certain birth defects. *J Nutr*, **137**, 2087–92.

10. Carter, M.A., Dubois, L., Tremblay, M.S., & Taljaard, M. (2012). Local social environmental factors are associated with household food insecurity in a longitudinal study of children. *BMC Public Health*, **12**, 1038.
11. Casey, P.H., Szeto, K., Lensing, S., Bogle, M., & Weber, J. (2001). Children in food-insufficient, low-income families: prevalence, health, and nutrition status. *Arch Pediatr Adolesc Med*, **155**, 508–14.
12. Casey, P.H., Szeto, K.L., Robbins, J.M., Stuff, J.E., Connell, C., Gossett, J.M., & Simpson, P. M. (2005). Child health-related quality of life and household food security. *Arch Pediatr Adolesc Med*, **159**, 51–6.
13. Chung, W.T., Gallo, W.T., Giunta, N., Canavan, M.E., Parikh, N.S., & Fahs, M.C. (2012). Linking neighborhood characteristics to food insecurity in older adults: the role of perceived safety, social cohesion, and walkability. *J Urban Health*, **89**, 407–18.
14. Cook, J.T. & Frank, D.A. (2008). Food security, poverty, and human development in the United States. *Ann N Y Acad Sci*, **1136**, 193–209.
15. Cook, J.T., Frank, D.A., Levenson, S.M., Neault, N.B., Heeren, T.C., Black, M.M., Berkowitz, C., Casey, P.H., Meyers, A.F., Cutts, D.B., & Chilton, M. (2006). Child food insecurity increases risks posed by household food insecurity to young children's health. *J Nutr*, **136**, 1073–6.
16. Corman, H., Noonan, K., & Reichman, N.E. (2014). Effects of infant health on family food insecurity: Evidence from two U.S. birth cohort studies. *Soc Sci Med*, **123C**, 18–25.
17. Cutler-Triggs, C., Fryer, G.E., Miyoshi, T.J., & Weitzman, M. (2008). Increased rates and severity of child and adult food insecurity in households with adult smokers. *Arch Pediatr Adolesc Med*, **162**, 1056–62.
18. Cutts, D.B., Meyers, A.F., Black, M.M., Casey, P.H., Chilton, M., Cook, J.T., Geppert, J., Ettinger, d.C., Heeren, T., Coleman, S., Rose-Jacobs, R., & Frank, D.A. (2011). US Housing insecurity and the health of very young children. *Am J Public Health*, **101**, 1508–14.
19. Dave, J.M., Evans, A.E., Saunders, R.P., Watkins, K.W., & Pfeiffer, K.A. (2009). Associations among food insecurity, acculturation, demographic factors, and fruit and vegetable intake at home in Hispanic children. *J Am Diet Assoc*, **109**, 697–701.
20. Dean, W.R., Sharkey, J.R., & Johnson, C.M. (2011). Food insecurity is associated with social capital, perceived personal disparity, and partnership status among older and senior adults in a largely rural area of central Texas. *J Nutr Gerontol Geriatr*, **30**, 169–86.
21. Duerr, L. (2006). Prevalence of food insecurity and comprehensiveness of its measurement for older adult congregate meals program participants. *J Nutr Elder*, **25**, 121–46.
22. Eicher-Miller, H.A., Mason, A.C., Weaver, C.M., McCabe, G.P., & Boushey, C.J. (2009). Food insecurity is associated with iron deficiency anemia in US adolescents. *Am J Clin Nutr*, **90**, 1358–71.
23. Eicher-Miller, H.A., Mason, A.C., Weaver, C.M., McCabe, G.P., & Boushey, C.J. (2011). Food insecurity is associated with diet and bone mass disparities in early adolescent males but not females in the United States. *J Nutr*, **141**, 1738–45.
24. Eisenmann, J.C., Gundersen, C., Lohman, B.J., Garasky, S., & Stewart, S.D. (2011). Is food insecurity related to overweight and obesity in children and adolescents? A summary of studies, 1995–2009. *Obes Rev*, **12**, e73-e83.
25. Engler-Stringer, R. & Berenbaum, S. (2006). Food and nutrition-related learning in collective kitchens in three Canadian cities. *Can J Diet Pract Res*, **67**, 178–83.
26. Foley, W., Ward, P., Carter, P., Coveney, J., Tsourtos, G., & Taylor, A. (2010). An ecological analysis of factors associated with food insecurity in South Australia, 2002–7. *Public Health Nutr*, **13**, 215-21.
27. Garg, A., Toy, S., Tripodis, Y., Cook, J., & Cordella, N. (2014). Influence of Maternal Depression on Household Food Insecurity for Low-Income Families. *Acad Pediatr*.
28. Gross, R.S., Mendelsohn, A.L., Fierman, A.H., Racine, A.D., & Messito, M.J. (2012). Food insecurity and obesogenic maternal infant feeding styles and practices in low-income families. *Pediatrics*, **130**, 254–61.

29. Grutzmacher, S. & Gross, S. (2011). Household food security and fruit and vegetable intake among low-income fourth-graders. *J Nutr Educ Behav*, **43**, 455–63.
30. Gucciardi, E., Vogt, J.A., DeMelo, M., & Stewart, D.E. (2009). Exploration of the relationship between household food insecurity and diabetes in Canada. *Diabetes Care*, **32**, 2218–24.
31. Gundersen, C., Kreuder, B., & Pepper, J. (2011). The economics of food insecurity in the United States. *Appl Econ Persp Policy*, **33**, 281–303.
32. Guo, B. (2011). Household assets and food security: evidence from the Survey of Program Dynamics. *J Fam Econ Iss*, **32**, 98–110.
33. Hager, E.R., Quigg, A.M., Black, M.M., Coleman, S.M., Heeren, T., Rose-Jacobs, R., Cook, J.T., de Cuba, S.A., Casey, P.H., Chilton, M., Cutts, D.B., Meyers, A.F., & Frank, D.A. (2010). Development and validity of a 2-item screen to identify families at risk for food insecurity. *Pediatrics*, **126**, e26-e32.
34. Hanson, K.L. & Connor, L.M. (2014). Food insecurity and dietary quality in US adults and children: a systematic review. *Am J Clin Nutr*, **100**, 684–92.
35. Hanson, K.L., Sobal, J., & Frongillo, E.A. (2007). Gender and marital status clarify associations between food insecurity and body weight. *J Nutr*, **137**, 1460–5.
36. Hilmers, A., Chen, T.A., & Cullen, K.W. (2014). Household food insecurity and dietary intake among Mexican-American women participating in federal food assistance programs. *Am J Health Promot*, **28**, e146-e154.
37. Howard, L.L. (2011). Transitions between food insecurity and food security predict children's social skill development during elementary school. *Br J Nutr*, **105**, 1852–60.
38. Jensen, H.H. (2002). Food insecurity and the food stamp program. *Am J Agric Econ*, **84**, 1215–28.
39. Kaiser, L.L., Townsend, M.S., Melgar-Quinonez, H.R., Fujii, M.L., & Crawford, P.B. (2004). Choice of instrument influences relations between food insecurity and obesity in Latino women. *Am J Clin Nutr*, **80**, 1372–8.
40. Kendall, A., Olson, C.M., & Frongillo, E.A., Jr. (1996). Relationship of hunger and food insecurity to food availability and consumption. *J Am Diet Assoc*, **96**, 1019–24.
41. Kirkpatrick, S.I. & Tarasuk, V. (2008). Food insecurity is associated with nutrient inadequacies among Canadian adults and adolescents. *J Nutr*, **138**, 604–12.
42. Kirkpatrick, S.I. & Tarasuk, V. (2011). Housing circumstances are associated with household food access among low-income urban families. *J Urban Health*, **88**, 284–96.
43. Knol, L.L., Haughton, B., & Fitzhugh, E.C. (2004). Food insufficiency is not related to the overall variety of foods consumed by young children in low-income families. *J Am Diet Assoc*, **104**, 640–4.
44. Laraia, B.A., Siega-Riz, A.M., & Evenson, K.R. (2004). Self-reported overweight and obesity are not associated with concern about enough food among adults in New York and Louisiana. *Prev Med*, **38**, 175–81.
45. Laraia, B.A., Siega-Riz, A.M., & Gundersen, C. (2010). Household food insecurity is associated with self-reported pregravid weight status, gestational weight gain, and pregnancy complications. *J Am Diet Assoc*, **110**, 692–701.
46. Laraia, B.A., Siega-Riz, A.M., Gundersen, C., & Dole, N. (2006). Psychosocial factors and socioeconomic indicators are associated with household food insecurity among pregnant women. *J Nutr*, **136**, 177–82.
47. Leung, C.W., Epel, E.S., Ritchie, L.D., Crawford, P.B., & Laraia, B.A. (2014). Food insecurity is inversely associated with diet quality of lower-income adults. *J Acad Nutr Diet*, **114**, 1943–53.
48. Lohman, B.J., Stewart, S., Gundersen, C., Garasky, S., & Eisenmann, J.C. (2009). Adolescent overweight and obesity: links to food insecurity and individual, maternal, and family stressors. *J Adolesc Health*, **45**, 230–7.
49. Loopstra, R. & Tarasuk, V. (2013). Severity of household food insecurity is sensitive to change in household income and employment status among low-income families. *J Nutr*, **143**, 1316–23.

50. Lyons, A.A., Park, J., & Nelson, C.H. (2008). Food insecurity and obesity: a comparison of self-reported and measured height and weight. *Am J Public Health*, **98**, 751–7.
51. Martin, K.S., Rogers, B.L., Cook, J.T., & Joseph, H.M. (2004). Social capital is associated with decreased risk of hunger. *Soc Sci Med*, **58**, 2645–54.
52. Martin-Fernandez, J., Grillo, F., Parizot, I., Caillavet, F., & Chauvin, P. (2013). Prevalence and socioeconomic and geographical inequalities of household food insecurity in the Paris region, France, 2010. *BMC Public Health*, **13**, 486.
53. Matheson, J., & McIntyre, L. (2014). Women respondents report higher household food insecurity than do men in similar Canadian households. *Public Health Nutr*, **17**, 40–8.
54. Mazur, R.E., Marquis, G.S., & Jensen, H.H. (2003). Diet and food insufficiency among Hispanic youths: acculturation and socioeconomic factors in the third National Health and Nutrition Examination Survey. *Am J Clin Nutr*, **78**, 1120–7.
55. McLaughlin, C., Tarasuk, V., & Kreiger, N. (2003). An examination of at-home food preparation activity among low-income, food-insecure women. *J Am Diet Assoc*, **103**, 1506–12.
56. Mello, J.A., Gans, K.M., Risica, P.M., Kirtania, U., Strolla, L.O., & Fournier, L. (2010). How is food insecurity associated with dietary behaviors? An analysis with low-income, ethnically diverse participants in a nutrition intervention study. *J Am Diet Assoc*, **110**, 1906–11.
57. Metallinos-Katsaras, E., Must, A., & Gorman, K. (2012). A longitudinal study of food insecurity on obesity in preschool children. *J Acad Nutr Diet*, **112**, 1949–58.
58. Metallinos-Katsaras, E., Sherry, B., & Kallio, J. (2009). Food insecurity is associated with overweight in children younger than 5 years of age. *J Am Diet Assoc*, **109**, 1790–4.
59. Muldoon, K.A., Duff, P.K., Fielden, S., & Anema, A. (2013). Food insufficiency is associated with psychiatric morbidity in a nationally representative study of mental illness among food insecure Canadians. *Soc Psychiatry Psychiatr Epidemiol*, **48**, 795–803.
60. Nolan, M., Williams, M., Rikard-Bell, G., & Mohsin, M. (2006). Food insecurity in three socially disadvantaged localities in Sydney, Australia. *Health Promot J Austr*, **17**, 247–54.
61. Nord, M. & Kantor, L.S. (2006). Seasonal variation in food insecurity is associated with heating and cooling costs among low-income elderly Americans. *J Nutr*, **136**, 2939–44.
62. Pardilla, M., Prasad, D., Suratkar, S., & Gittelsohn, J. (2014). High levels of household food insecurity on the Navajo Nation. *Public Health Nutr*, **17**, 58–65.
63. Park, C.Y. & Eicher-Miller, H.A. (2014). Iron deficiency is associated with food insecurity in pregnant females in the United States: National Health and Nutrition Examination Survey 1999–2010. *J Acad Nutr Diet*, **114**, 1967-73.
64. Park, K., Kersey, M., Geppert, J., Story, M., Cutts, D., & Himes, J.H. (2009). Household food insecurity is a risk factor for iron-deficiency anaemia in a multi-ethnic, low-income sample of infants and toddlers. *Public Health Nutr*, **12**, 2120–8.
65. Parker, E.D., Widome, R., Nettleton, J.A., & Pereira, M.A. (2010). Food security and metabolic syndrome in U.S. adults and adolescents: findings from the National Health and Nutrition Examination Survey, 1999–2006. *Ann Epidemiol*, **20**, 364-70.
66. Ramsey, R., Giskes, K., Turrell, G., & Gallegos, D. (2011). Food insecurity among Australian children: potential determinants, health and developmental consequences. *J Child Health Care*, **15**, 401–16.
67. Rose, D. & Oliveira, V. (1997). Nutrient intakes of individuals from food-insufficient households in the United States. *Am J Public Health*, **87**, 1956–61.
68. Rose-Jacobs, R., Black, M.M., Casey, P.H., Cook, J.T., Cutts, D.B., Chilton, M., Heeren, T., Levenson, S.M., Meyers, A.F., & Frank, D.A. (2008). Household food insecurity: associations with at-risk infant and toddler development. *Pediatrics*, **121**, 65–72.
69. Roustit, C., Hamelin, A.M., Grillo, F., Martin, J., & Chauvin, P. (2010). Food insecurity: could school food supplementation help break cycles of intergenerational transmission of social inequalities? *Pediatrics*, **126**, 1174–81.
70. Ryu, J.H. & Bartfeld, J.S. (2012). Household food insecurity during childhood and subsequent health status: the early childhood longitudinal study – kindergarten cohort. *Am J Public Health*, **102**, e50-e55.

71. Sarlio-Lahteenkorva, S. & Lahelma, E. (2001). Food insecurity is associated with past and present economic disadvantage and body mass index. *J Nutr*, **131**, 2880–4.

72. Seligman, H.K., Bindman, A.B., Vittinghoff, E., Kanaya, A.M., & Kushel, M.B. (2007). Food insecurity is associated with diabetes mellitus: results from the National Health Examination and Nutrition Examination Survey (NHANES) 1999–2002. *J Gen Intern Med*, **22**, 1018-23.

73. Sharkey, J.R., Dean, W.R., & Nalty, C.C. (2013). Child hunger and the protective effects of Supplemental Nutrition Assistance Program (SNAP) and alternative food sources among Mexican-origin families in Texas border colonias. *BMC Pediatr*, **13**, 143.

74. Skalicky, A., Meyers, A.F., Adams, W.G., Yang, Z., Cook, J.T., & Frank, D.A. (2006). Child food insecurity and iron deficiency anemia in low-income infants and toddlers in the United States. *Matern Child Health J*, **10**, 177–85.

75. Tarasuk, V., Mitchell, A., McLaren, L., & McIntyre, L. (2013). Chronic physical and mental health conditions among adults may increase vulnerability to household food insecurity. *J Nutr*, **143**, 1785–93.

76. To, Q.G., Frongillo, E.A., Gallegos, D., & Moore, J.B. (2014). Household food insecurity is associated with less physical activity among children and adults in the U.S. population. *J Nutr*, **144**, 1797–802.

77. Vahabi, M., Damba, C., Rocha, C., & Montoya, E.C. (2011). Food insecurity among Latin American recent immigrants in Toronto. *J Immigr Minor Health*, **13**, 929–39.

78. Vozoris, N.T. & Tarasuk, V.S. (2003). Household food insufficiency is associated with poorer health. *J Nutr*, **133**, 120–6.

79. Wilde, P.E. & Peterman, J.N. (2006). Individual weight change is associated with household food security status. *J Nutr*, **136**, 1395–400.

80. Willows, N.D., Veugelers, P., Raine, K., & Kuhle, S. (2009). Prevalence and sociodemographic risk factors related to household food security in Aboriginal peoples in Canada. *Public Health Nutr*, **12**, 1150–6.

81. Zizza, C.A., Duffy, P.A., & Gerrior, S.A. (2008). Food insecurity is not associated with lower energy intakes. *Obesity (Silver Spring)*, **16**, 1908–13.

Part III
Consequences of Nutrition Insecurity
(Hans Konrad Biesalski/JJ Strain)

Chapter 10
Sustainable Micronutrients in Europe: Is There Cause for Concern?

Hans Konrad Biesalski

Abstract Despite the fact that vitamin and mineral deficiencies seem to occur only in low-income countries, there are also numbers of individuals in high-income countries who are deficient in these essential micronutrients. Whether due to poverty, lack of nutrition education or poor health, significant sections of the population of Europe have been documented in a range of recent studies as being deficient in key micronutrients. Women of child-bearing age and especially women who are pregnant have heightened needs for the critical micronutrients vitamins B_2, B_6, B_{12}, niacin, folate, vitamins A, C and D, iron, magnesium, iodine and zinc. Micronutrient provision via the diet is a key factor in brain development, and an adequate micronutrient supply during the first 1,000 days of life is essential for long-term health and wellbeing. This chapter discusses the roles of the individual micronutrients on maternal and child health and proposes supplementation with multivitamin/mineral supplements during pregnancy as a safe approach to improving birth outcomes and reducing the risk of a range of diseases in later life. It concludes that to avoid effects of 'silent' micronutrient gaps, it is necessary to ensure a sufficient diet with adequate nutrients as proposed in the FAO/WHO statement on food security.

Keywords Vitamin and mineral deficiencies · Micronutrients · Hidden hunger · Pregnancy · The first 1,000 days · Brain development · Multivitamin/mineral supplement (MVM)

H.K. Biesalski (✉)
Nutrition medicine, Department of Biological Chemistry and Nutrition, Food Security Center, University Hohenheim, Garbenstraße 30, 70593 Stuttgart, Germany
e-mail: biesal@uni-hohenheim.de

© Springer International Publishing AG 2017   143
H.K. Biesalski et al. (eds.), *Sustainable Nutrition in a Changing World*,
DOI 10.1007/978-3-319-55942-1_10

10.1 Introduction

Vitamin and mineral deficiencies are a worldwide problem, but seem to occur only in low-income countries. The FAO and WHO estimate that more than a billion people suffer from iron deficiency, 0.5–1 billion from zinc deficiency, and 200 million from vitamin A deficiency. Most of these are women and children. In high-income countries, by contrast, vitamin and mineral deficiencies are widely thought to be no longer present due to the increasing availability of a varied and well-balanced diet.

> Food security exists when all people, at all times, have physical and economic access to sufficient, safe and nutritious food that meets their dietary needs and food preferences for an active and healthy life.
>
> World Food Summit, 1996

Consequently, food security as defined by FAO/WHO has been achieved in high-income countries, and any concern regarding adequate intake of essential micronutrients is apparently allayed. With food plentiful, varied and accessible, it seems unimaginable that the diet might not deliver all the important nutrients necessary for a healthy life. However, some individuals might not have access to an adequate diet due to low income, others due to their inadequate knowledge of nutrition essentials, and others again might have a diet which is not as nutritious as it should be in view of their body's increased need for essential micronutrients during a particular stage in their lives. Access to a diet that is quantitatively sufficient and diverse does not of itself guarantee adequate nutritional status. Depending on age and lifestyle, individuals may have need of higher levels of certain micronutrients. Moreover, inadequate supply might have harmful health effects above and beyond the signs of pure micronutrient deficiency.

10.2 Inadequate Supply: The Problem and Consequences of Hidden Hunger

Hidden hunger can be defined as an inadequate intake beyond deficiency or without typical clinical signs and symptoms.

Figure 10.1 is a schematic representation of hidden hunger. Supply of a micronutrient declines from left top to right bottom. As long as the supply of a micronutrient is not near zero, specific clinical signs will not develop (e.g. scurvy in the case of vitamin C deficiency, night blindness or blindness in the case of vitamin A deficiency). However, long before such signs appear, the inadequate supply results in more or less unspecific symptoms such as increased risk of infectious diseases (in the case of vitamin A and iron inadequacy) or chronic diarrhea (in the case of zinc deficiency).

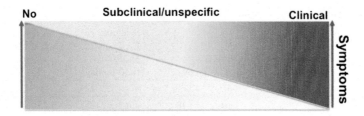

Fig. 10.1 A schematic representation of hidden hunger

There is ample evidence that inadequate micronutrient supply might have negative consequences for health and development. Especially in situations where demand increases—e.g. in cases of sudden or chronic disease, pregnancy or lactation—hidden hunger will significantly compromise reactivity of the immune system or the energy metabolism.

10.3 Is Hidden Hunger a Problem in European Countries?

In a recent Europe-wide study [1], the percentage of healthy people below the EAR (Estimated Average Requirement) was extracted from the various national surveys (Tables 10.1 and 10.2). However, below EAR means being at increased risk of deficiency. The EAR is the daily intake value that is estimated to meet the requirement in half of the apparently healthy individuals in a life stage or gender group. The other half by definition would not have its nutritional needs met.

Inadequate intake of calcium and vitamin D will have a strong impact on bone mineral density and subsequently on the development of early osteoporosis, with a significant impact on quality of life. However, a more serious condition is an inadequate intake of one or more micronutrients during pregnancy.

Table 10.1 Vitamins

Country	Vitamin C EAR: m: 60 mg f: 50 mg/day		Vitamin D EAR: m, f 10 µg/day		Folic acid EAR: m, f 200 µg/day		Vitamin B$_{12}$ EAR: m, f 1.4 µg/T day	
	m	f	m	f	m	f	m	f
GE	19	11	96	100	28	27	8	8
IR	40	37	100	100	10	20	14	23
SE	34	21	93	100	33	41	8	20
UK	36	34	97	100	18	26	13	10
DK	23	17	99	100	15	19	9	13
FI	22	17	96	100	28	38	21	18

Table 10.2 Minerals

Country	Calcium EAR: m/f 800 mg/day		Zinc EAR: m 6.4 mg f: 5.7 mg/day		Selenium EAR: m 35 μg f: 30 μg/day		Iodine EAR: m, f 100 μg/day	
	m	f	m	f	m	f	m	f
GE	25	26	10	10	n.d.*		43	49
IR	34	58	12	29	n.d.		n.d.	
SE	25	34	3	4	47	47	n.d.	
UK	35	61	16	31	n.d.		n.d.	
DK	28	31	5	6	31	36	6	10
FI	25	33	7	10	8	10	24	22

Data depicted in Table 10.3 show that iron, iodine, vitamin A, and zinc deficiencies in pregnant women and children below the age of five are present not only in low-income countries, but also to an extent in Europe, which is not a peripheral matter with respect to childhood development [2]. In some cases, the prevalence of a deficiency is similar between low- and high-income countries. A deficiency might result in different consequences of various severities; however, its cause is always the same. We need to understand that poor dietary quality and poor dietary diversity are some of the major reasons for micronutrient inadequacy. Iron deficiency or vitamin A inadequacy signal a diet that is low in food containing iron or vitamin A, or even both (e.g., meat, liver, eggs). A detected micronutrient deficiency can thus be taken as a biomarker for an inadequate diet that might result in more deficiencies than those in iron or vitamin A alone. Consequently, increasing diet diversity will close the known and unknown micronutrient gaps.

10.4 Pregnancy

A balanced diet with adequate energy intake usually provides an adequate supply of the essential micronutrients. Although a balanced diet is accessible for the European population as a whole, specific population groups are at risk of inadequate vitamin and mineral intakes, especially with regard to iron, folic acid, vitamin D and vitamin B_{12}. Micronutrient malnutrition represents an important challenge for public health worldwide, particularly in vulnerable population groups such as pregnant women. For example, a study in Hackney, London—the region with the highest incidence of low birth weight (LBW) infants in England and Wales [3]—showed that 78% of mothers had an inadequate diet that met fewer than four of 16 dietary reference intake values. On follow-up at nine months post-partum, over half of the unsupplemented, inadequate-diet group remained severely deficient in folate and had low serum ferritin levels. The risk of giving birth to a child with low birth weight for gestational age was fourfold for this group.

Table 10.3 Vitamin A deficiency

A

Region	Vitamin A deficiency			
	Children <5 years of age		Pregnant women	
	Night blindness	Serum retinol <0.70 μmol/L	Night blindness	Serum retinol <0.70 μmol/L
Global	0.9 (0.1–1.8)	33.3 (29.4–37.1)	7.8 (6.5–9.1)	15.3 (6.0–24.6)
Africa	2.1 (1.0–3.1)	41.6 (34.4–44.9)	9.4 (8.1–10.7)	14.3 (9.7–19.0)
Americas and the Caribbean	0.6 (0.0–1.3)	15.6 (6.6–24.5)	4.4 (2.7–6.2)	2.0 (0.4–3.6)
Asia	0.5 (0.0–1.3)	33.5 (30.7–36.3)	7.8 (6.6–9.0)	18.4 (5.4–31.4)
Europe	0.7 (0.0–1.5)	14.9 (0.1–29.7)	2.9 (1.1–4.6)	2.2 (0.0–4.3)
Oceania	0.5 (0.1–1.0)	12.6 (6.0–19.2)	9.2 (0.3–18.2)	1.4 (0.0–4.0)

B

Region	Iodine deficiency (UIC < 100 μg/L)	Zinc deficiency (weighted average of country means)	Iron-deficiency anemia (hemoglobin < 110 g/L)	
			Children <5 years of age	Pregnant women
Global	28.5 (28.2–28.9)	17.3 (15.9–18.8)	18.1 (15.6–20.8)	19.2 (17.1–21.5)
Africa	40.0 (39.4–40.6)	23.9 (21.1–26.8)	20.2 (18.6–21.7)	20.3 (18.3–22.4)
Americas and the Caribbean	13.7 (12.5–14.8)	9.6 (6.8–12.4)	12.7 (9.8–16.0)	15.2 (11.7–18.6)
Asia	31.6 (30.7–32.5)	19.4 (16.9–22.0)	19.0 (14.5–23.4)	19.8 (15.8–23.5)
Europe	44.2 (43.5–45.0)	7.6 (6.2–9.1)	12.1 (7.8–16.2)	16.2 (12.6–19.7)
Oceania	17.3 (16.6–18.1)	5.7 (1.0–10.3)	15.4 (7.0–25.2)	17.2 (9.7–25.6)

During the childbearing period, females are often not sufficiently supplied with all the water-soluble vitamins, especially folate. In both women of child-bearing age and pregnant women, micronutrient deficiencies or suboptimal/inadequate intakes may be associated with significantly elevated reproductive risks, ranging from infertility to fetal structural defects and long-term diseases (reviewed in Cetin et al. [4] and Berti et al. [5]). The reasons for inadequate intake are manifold: poor knowledge regarding adequate nutrition; special diets aimed at avoiding excessive weight gain; 'healthy' vegetarian or even vegan diets; problems with eating (nausea, vomiting); and misinformation regarding specific nutrients (e.g. vitamin A).

The adequacy of micronutrient intake during pregnancy seems to be influenced also by environmental, cultural and demographic variables, such as maternal age, clothing, geography, socioeconomic status (SES). The impact of SES on nutrient supply is discussed in Chaps. 1 and 3.

10.4.1 Critical Micronutrients During Pregnancy

Inadequate supply of several micronutrients has an impact on fetal development (Table 10.4).

Malnutrition during pregnancy, and in particular poor micronutrient intake, is a general risk for a small-for-gestational age (SGA) newborn.

The prevalence and consequences of inadequate micronutrient supply have been reviewed recently [6].

10.4.2 Folic Acid and Vitamin B_{12}

There is consistent scientific evidence that folic acid is of critical importance both pre- and periconceptionally in protecting against neural tube defects (NTDs) in the developing fetus [7]. Estimated folate requirements increase by 50% to 600 µg during pregnancy. Even though a small number of vegetables seem to be good sources of folate, the poor bioavailability of folate limits an adequate supply. Moreover, in most countries, females do not reach even the recommendations for non-pregnant women. For this reason, internationally, periconceptional supplementation of 400 µg/day of folic acid is recommended for the prevention of NTDs. A near 100% reduction of NTDs in addition to significant reductions of congenital heart defects was achieved by periconceptional supplementation of 800 µg/day of

Table 10.4 Critical micronutrients during pregnancy

Micronutrients	Developmental problems with low intake
Vitamin B_2, niacin	Risk of malformations of the urogenital tract
B-vitamins	Risk of malformations of the cardiovascular system
B_{12}, B_6	Low birth weight
Iron, magnesium, niacin	2.5 higher risk of neural tube defects (NTDs)
Zinc	Higher NTD risk
Iron, magnesium vitamin C	Lower risk of cleft formation
Folate	Four-fold higher risk of NTDs
Vitamin A	Risk of inadequate lung maturation, in particular in early born babies
Iodine	Low birth weight

folic acid combined with multivitamins [8]. Women with a low folate supply in combination with low vitamin B_{12} blood levels have a drastically increased risk of NTDs through the combined deficiency. These findings suggest that the most effective periconceptional prophylaxis to prevent NTDs may be the provision of both folic acid and vitamin B_{12}. Even though the relevance of periconceptional folic acid supplementation for the prevention of NTDs has been widely acknowledged and supported by expert bodies and governmental recommendations throughout the world, its practical application is still very inadequate.

10.4.3 Vitamin A

Vitamin A is obtained from the diet either as pre-formed vitamin A in the form of retinol or retinyl-esters, or as provitamin A-carotenoids. The highest content of preformed vitamin A is found in liver and liver oils of marine animals. Yellow and green leafy vegetables provide significant amounts of provitamin A-carotenoids [9]. However, high doses (<6 mg/day) of provitamin A are needed to substitute preformed retinol [10].

Fetal and neonatal vitamin A status depends on maternal vitamin A status. The fetal/neonatal synthesis of the retinol-binding protein is not sufficient to ensure continuous supply from stores in the liver. Therefore maternal vitamin A supply is of essential importance for adequate fetal supply, growth and development. An inadequate supply to the fetus during pregnancy is associated with malformations, preterm birth, low birth weight and low neonatal liver stores. Low vitamin A status of the newborn appears to contribute to the risk of bronchopulmonary dysplasia (lung disease in preterm).

The American Pediatrics Association [11] cites vitamin A as one of the most critical vitamins during pregnancy and the breastfeeding period, especially in terms of lung function and maturation. If the vitamin A supply of the mother is inadequate, her supply to the fetus will also be inadequate, as will later be her milk. These inadequacies cannot be compensated for by postnatal supplementation. Despite the fact that food rich in vitamin A and beta-carotene is generally available, risk groups for low vitamin A supply do exist in the western world.

10.4.4 Vitamin D

Over the past decade, interest in vitamin D status has been growing because of its potential links with a number of diseases and conditions. In fact, observational studies in non-pregnant individuals have associated low 25-OH-vitamin D levels in plasma with the risk of a wide range of common chronic diseases such as colon, breast and prostate cancer, metabolic syndrome, hypertension, multiple sclerosis, type I diabetes, and inflammatory bowel disease [12]. Given the evolving concept of vitamin D sufficiency, it is currently believed that sufficiency may be defined as serum 25(OH)D levels >75 nmol/L. The actual prevalence of vitamin D insufficiency during pregnancy is therefore not known with certainty, but it could be as high as 70% in western countries if insufficiency is defined as 25(OH)D concentrations below 75–80 nmol/L [13]. In light of the high incidence of non-sufficient vitamin D status in women of child-bearing age, the public health implications of these findings warrant attention.

With regard to fetal and infant outcomes, maternal vitamin D deficiency predisposes newborns to neonatal hypocalcemia, and subsequently to rickets. Observational studies also suggest that the bone mass of the newborn is related to the vitamin D status of the mother [14]. Low vitamin D concentrations during prenatal or early life development were proposed to affect functional characteristics of various body tissues, leading to a greater later risk of multiple sclerosis, cancer, insulin-dependent diabetes mellitus, and schizophrenia [15]. There is growing evidence that vitamin D deficiency during pregnancy disrupts brain development in the offspring and leads to changes which are persistent in the adult brain [16]. A recent meta-analysis shows that the risk of type 1 diabetes is significantly reduced in infants who were supplemented with vitamin D compared to those who were not supplemented, suggesting that vitamin D supplementation in early childhood may offer protection against the development of type 1 diabetes [2].

The data available to date suggest that vitamin D deficiency during pregnancy is not only linked to maternal skeletal preservation and fetal skeletal formation but may also affect maternal outcomes and fetal imprinting [17]. However, most of these findings are observational associations, and further evidence from controlled trials is required.

10.4.5 *Iron*

Neonates at term birth have a total body store of about 1 g of iron, and all this has been provided by the mother. The mother will, however, have to provide about 400 mg from her own hepatic stores. Extra iron is required for the growing fetus and for the formation of the placenta, as well as expansion of maternal red cell mass and blood loss during delivery [18]. Women often become pregnant without adequate iron reserves or are already iron-deficient. The most severe consequence of iron depletion is maternal iron deficiency anemia (IDA). IDA may be aggravated during pregnancy, as fetal iron metabolism depends completely on maternal metabolism [19]. Iron status seems to be implicated in some pregnancy disorders affecting mother and fetus such as preeclampsia and inappropriate catch-up growth [20, 21].

Iron deficiency anemia should be prevented and treated. Selective prophylaxis seems to be the most effective and appropriate approach: Screening of ferritin levels in early pregnancy may identify women who may benefit from iron supplementation. The increased iron absorption during pregnancy, coupled with the mobilization of iron stores, may be sufficient in women with high iron stores, who may not need iron supplements.

10.4.6   Iodine

Approximately half the European population still suffers from an inadequate iodine supply. Low urinary iodine excretion is especially common among pregnant women and school children. WHO recently increased its recommendation for iodine intake during pregnancy and lactation from 200 to 250 µg/day and suggested that a median urinary iodine concentration (UIC) of 150–250 µg/L indicates adequate iodine intake [22]. WHO recommends iodine supplementation in pregnancy only in countries where less than 90% of households use iodized salt or where the median UIC in schoolchildren is below 100 µg/L. However, different national surveys in the USA and Europe document that even when iodized salt is consumed, this might not be enough to cope with the increased iodine demand during pregnancy. Iodine supplementation (150 µg/day) has been recommended in the case of pregnancy [23].

Iodine is involved in nerve development, as well as thyroid follicle growth and the synthesis of thyroid hormones (THs), which are of essential importance for the development of the fetal central nervous system [24]. Pregnant women with UICs during the third trimester below 50 µg/L were significantly more likely to have an SGA infant, and mean birthweight was lower than among women, with the UICs between 100 and 149 µg/L. Higher TSH levels were also associated with a higher risk of having an SGA baby or a LBW newborn. The later mean intelligence quotient (IQ) of children born to women an UIC below 50 µ/L was found to be significantly lower compared to controls with adequate iodine supplementation [25]. Recent cross-sectional studies performed in several European countries revealed a median UIC in pregnant women in the range of 95–130 µg/L [22, 26]. Half the women were below 100 and about a quarter below 50 µg/L, indicating a maternal iodine status associated with moderate or severe iodine deficiency, respectively, in the offspring (see Chap. 14 for further discussion of this topic).

10.5   The First 1,000 Days: A Developmental Window Which Might Be Irreversibly Closed

During the first 1,000 days of a human life from conception until the end of the second year of life, the most important developmental steps occur. The nutrition status of the mother at the moment of conception is a critical condition influencing the development of the embryo.

Malnutrition during pregnancy and early childhood has a negative impact on physical growth and cognitive development. The magnitude depends on the severity of the malnutrition and on the micronutrients involved.

Malnutrition during pregnancy may result in Intra Uterine Growth Restriction (IUGR). The birth weight of the children is too low for gestational age. However, not only physical growth is restricted but also the growth and development of various internal organs—in particular, the kidneys, pancreas, and lungs. This increases the risk of IUGR children contracting non-communicable diseases such as obesity, high blood pressure, and diabetes (for review, see [27]).

There are two types of IUGR: symmetrical IUGR, in which all organs are affected by improper growth, and asymmetrical IUGR, in which the head and brain are normal. IUGR occurs as a result of lifestyle (alcohol, smoking, stress or malnutrition) during pregnancy.

The risk of low birth weight and preterm birth also increases with malnutrition. The most critical period for the development of the child is the 1,000-day window.

The phenotype of IUGR is low birth weight of the newborn. Newborns with low birth weight at term (<2.500 g) are four times more likely to die during their first 28 days of life than those weighing 2.500–2.999 g, and 10 times more likely to die than newborns weighing 3.000–3.499 g [28]. If malnutrition persists after birth, the children may not develop appropriately—a condition known as stunting. Stunting is defined as 2 Standard Deviations below the 95% percentile of height for age. This is independent of body weight. Improving the diet during childhood development after the 1,000 days of linear growth will in many cases not compensate, and the children remain stunted. The consequence is reduced physical strength.

Low birth weight is also the phenotype of intrauterine stunting and consequently also a visible marker for potentially impaired brain development. Indeed, it was documented that the effect of stunting on short-term memory was equivalent to the difference in short-term memory between children in US families that had experienced poverty for 13 years and children in families with incomes at least three times higher than the poverty levels [29]. Malnutrition is a frequent companion of poverty, not only in developing countries, and has a powerful impact on brain development.

10.6 Brain Development and Poverty: A Fateful Relationship

The human brain develops in different steps during embryogenesis. Interneuron connections develop during weeks 8–16 within the so-called cortical plate and are replaced by cortical neurons from week 24 until the perinatal period. The brain growth spurt begins in the last trimester of pregnancy and continues for the first two years after birth. During this time, the majority of dendritic growth, synaptogenesis and glial cell proliferation occurs [30, 31]. During the first two years of life—by the age of two, the brain has 80–90% of its future adult weight—this period is highly sensitive to micronutrient deficiencies [32, 33].

The structure of the brain at any time is a product of interactions between genetic, epigenetic and environmental factors [34]. Environmental factors include outside events and the internal physiological milieu. Consequently, poor nutrition or stress will have an impact on the brain structure and ultimately on its function. The connection between stress and poor nutrition is poverty. The developmental cognitive neuroscience dealing with poverty and social gradients is a new field of research which has only recently emerged. It has been shown that pregnancy and growing up with a low socio-economic-status (SES) will have neural and cognitive consequences [35, 36].

Children living in poverty have impaired cognitive outcome and school performance. Poor SES is related to reduced levels of attention, literacy and numeracy, which, together with other factors, may explain the poor educational level of children living in poverty [37]. Language and memory functions are related to brain regions sensitive to environmental and nutritional influences. Research in both animals and humans suggests that the experience of stress has important negative effects on the hippocampus and the amygdala, which are highly susceptible during the late fetal and early neonatal period.

The amygdala and hippocampus subserve emotion, language, and memory—functions that change markedly between the ages of four and 18 years. The volume of the amygdala and hippocampus increase with age. Both are involved in stress regulation and emotion processing and sensitive to environmental stimuli, including nutrition. Different studies report lower hippocampal volume in children and adolescents (age 5–17) from lower-income backgrounds compared to the same age group from higher SES [36,39,40].

Poor nutrition as a result of poor income is not the only reason for developmental changes of the brain. Poverty is strongly associated with other factors that have an impact on brain development, such as unsupportive parenting, poor education, lack of education of caregivers, and a high level of stressful events. In particular the income-to-need ratio, for example to ensure daily nutrition for others, might become a stressful event which influences brain development [41]. Income-to-need ratio—but not parental education—was positively associated with hippocampal size [19, 20]. Stressors more directly related to income, such as limited access to material resources (e.g., a variety of food), may have greater influence on hippocampal size than parental education related to cognitive stimulation and parenting style.

A study with healthy children from France showed a positive correlation between SES reading and verbal abilities and literacy [21]. The neural correlate was a significant correlation of SES and local gray matter volumes of bilateral hippocampi. Similar results were obtained from a study with US households, documenting a significant positive relationship between income and hippocampus gray matter volume. The authors suggest that differences in the hippocampus, perhaps due to stress tied to growing up in poverty, might partially explain differences in long-term memory, learning, control of neuroendocrine function, and modulation of emotional behavior. Lower family income may cause limited access to material resources, including food, which may be more important for predicting hippocampal size [42].

Two independent studies which might have used part of the same group of children in Brandenburg, Germany documented an impact of SES on physical and cognitive outcome. The first study [43] investigated children at admission into primary school (aged six years in the year 2000) and documented an impairment of literacy in 18.2% of the children from low SES compared to 8.2% mean SES and 4.3% in high SES, and an impairment of cognitive development of 13.2% versus 2.8% versus 0.9%.

In another study using anthropometric data from children living in Brandenburg, the effect of unemployment on childhood development was investigated [44].

Data from 253,050 preschool children during the period 1994–2006 were used and the authors stated that: *"After an initial substantial height increase of school starters in the Eastern German Land [federal state] of Brandenburg between the re-unification of 1990 and 1995, the upward trend stopped suddenly and even developed into a downturn in children's heights between 1997 and 2000. Since 2000, heights have been stagnating at a low level. This is all the more remarkable, as heights have never declined over longer time spans in Eastern German Laender [federal states] since 1880 – except for the most recent period 1997–2006."*

The authors further conclude: *"The interaction terms of unemployment and additional children are remarkably large. Above, it was already shown that households with four and more children fall behind smaller households with regard to children's height, the former's children being significantly shorter (−1.8 cm). The unemployment variable subtracts another height coefficient of −0.3 cm, in addition to the 'normal' sibling effect! In addition, if the parents are unemployed, the detriment is even larger."*

The height difference is around 1SD from the 95% percentile of the children within that area, so it cannot be defined as stunting, but it must be taken seriously. Together with the data from the other Brandenburg study showing a massive impact of SES on cognitive development in one of the richest countries of the world, the data are alarming because this has consequences for the later hopes of the children achieving a better education and income in order to escape from poverty. Accordingly, it was very recently reported in an analysis of 10 European countries that the economic conditions at the time of birth significantly influence cognitive function in later life [45]. The authors argue that birth during a time of recession may lead to a low quality and/or quantity of food, which impacts development during that time, with consequences for later life.

Poor nutrition is not only documented in low-income countries but also in families living in poverty in high-income countries [46]. Diet quality is affected not only by age, traditions and personal preferences but also by education, living conditions and income—important indices of SES and social class. If the income-to-need ratio is not sufficient to ensure an adequate food pattern, either other needs (e.g., education, medicine) are reduced or else the diet becomes poorer and poorer in quality. If food costs rise, food selection narrows to those items that provide the most energy at the lowest cost. When these conditions persist, essential nutrients disappear from the diet and malnutrition develops [47, 48]. Indeed, a recent study into the effect of poverty on children's living conditions showed that beside lack of cognitive stimulation, food insecurity also has a strong association with income [49]. There is clear evidence that SES has a strong impact on dietary quality because diet costs are positively related to food of higher quality [50].

The individual driving force for food selection is emphatically to reduce hunger with an appropriate quantity of food. Food quality is then the second choice. Indeed, when indicators of well-being in children living in poverty were compared in the US [51], the most obvious difference was related to the category *"Experienced hunger (food insecurity) at least once in past year."* This applied to 15.9% of poor children compared to 1.6% of non-poor—a nearly 10-fold difference—followed by child abuse and neglect (6.8-fold), lead poisoning (3.5-fold), and violent crimes, days of hospital stays, stunting, grade repetition or high school drop-out (all 2-fold).

Poverty and low income are often associated with poor dietary quality and consequently with more or less expressed malnutrition. Even when other factors (e.g., parental care, education) are involved, the impact of inadequate supply with essential nutrients on physical and in particular cerebral development should not be underestimated.

10.7   Micronutrients and Brain Development

We have scientific evidence that certain micronutrients—in particular iron, iodine, zinc, folate, vitamin A and vitamin D—are critically involved in pre- and postnatal brain development. These micronutrients are the major missing sources, whether isolated or in combination, in the diet of one-third of the world's population. Further micronutrients, protein and energy and n−3 fatty acids may also have an impact on brain development.

Table 10.4 summarizes the specific brain-related micronutrients and their impact on brain development during the late fetal and neonatal period. The magnitude of any impairment of brain development and at least effect on brain function depends on the severity of the micronutrient deficiency. In many cases, deficiencies do not exist in isolated form. Other micronutrients may also be involved, depending on the food pattern, and protein-energy malnutrition might be also present. The latter has also a negative impact on brain development [52], but will not be discussed further in this chapter.

Even though further vitamins are discussed as playing a role in brain development, studies investigating the effect within the 1,000-day window are not available. Studies (n = 6) investigating the effect of consuming fish containing n−3 fatty acids during pregnancy on cognitive outcome showed that higher intakes of fish in pregnant women are linked to higher scores on tests of cognitive function in their children at ages between 18 months and 14 years [53]. The n−3 fatty acids are not further discussed in this chapter, because they cannot be really attributed to hidden hunger.

Table 10.5 Impact of selected nutrients on brain development

Nutrient	Requirement	Brain area
Iron	Myelin formation	White matter
	Monoamine synthesis	Striatal frontal
	Neuronal and glial	Hippocampal-frontal
	Energy metabolism	
Iodine	Myelination, neuronal	Cortex, striatum
	proliferation	Hippocampus
Zinc	DNA synthesis	Autonomic nervous system
	Neurotransmitter	Hippocampus, cerebellum
Copper	Neurotransmitter	Cerebellum
	Synthesis, energy	
	Metabolism	
Vitamin A	Neurogenesis	Hippocampus
	Neurotrophic factors	
Vitamin D	Neurogenesis	Hippocampus
	Neurotrophic factors	White matter
LC-PUFA	Synaptogenesis	Eye
	Myelin	Cortex

A review discussing 14 different studies found associations between **iron deficiency** anemia and poor cognitive and motor development and behavioral problems in all studies. Longitudinal studies consistently indicate that children anemic in infancy continue to have poorer cognition, school achievement, and more behavior problems into middle childhood [54].

Severe **zinc deficiency** is rare, but moderate deficiency or inadequate supply affects up to 40% of the world's population [55]. Diets low in animal-derived food (the best source of zinc) or high in starchy food (which makes for low bioavailability of zinc) promote deficiency. Indeed, zinc deficiency during pregnancy as a consequence of a diet high in starchy food with high phytate (which lowers the bioavailability of zinc and iron) has been reported to be associated with lower scores on the psychomotor index of infants [56].

Various studies on zinc supplementation during pregnancy revealed controversial results on cognitive development. Zinc supplementation alone may unbalance the availability of other nutrients, or zinc deficiency may not occur on its own. Indeed, it has been documented that a combination of zinc and iron showed an improvement in cognition [57].

WHO considers **iodine deficiency** to be "the single most important preventable cause of brain damage" worldwide. Approximately one-third of the world's population is estimated to have insufficient iodine intake, in particular in Southeast Asia and Europe [58]. Adequate maternal iodine stores within the thyroid are important for normal fetal and infant neurodevelopment. Adequate thyroid iodine stores (in iodine-sufficient regions) ensure the increased demand for iodine during pregnancy if optimal intake is maintained. In iodine-deficient regions however, the potentially inadequate iodine stores are rapidly depleted during pregnancy, putting the fetus at risk of developmental impairment, especially of the brain.

The effect of mild to moderate iodine deficiency on fetal brain development is less clear, however. Observational studies from different countries in Europe and the USA document a significant association between mild maternal iodine deficiency and cognitive impairment in children. Depending on the severity and onset of iodine deficiency during pregnancy, the clinical signs are expressed to a greater or lesser extent. In particular the severity of cognitive impairment seems to be associated with the degree of iodine deficiency [59]. In early childhood, iodine deficiency impairs cognition, but in contrast to fetal iodine deficiency there is evidence of improvement with iodine treatment. Children from iodine-deficient areas had more cognitive impairments compared with children from areas with sufficient iodine [60]. Several European studies showed that isolated iodine deficiency during pregnancy is associated with impaired cognitive development in children (reviewed in [52]).

In a recent observational trial in the UK, the effect of inadequate iodine status in 14,551 pregnant women on the cognitive outcome of their children (13,988) was evaluated. The data support the hypothesis that inadequate iodine status during early pregnancy is adversely associated with child cognitive development. Low maternal iodine status was associated with an increased risk of suboptimum scores for verbal IQ at age eight, and reading accuracy, comprehension, and reading score at age nine. The authors have shown that risk of suboptimum cognitive scores in children is not confined to mothers with very low iodine status (i.e. <50 µg/g), but that iodine-to-creatinine ratios of 50–150 µg/g (which would suggest a more mild-to-moderate deficiency) are also associated with heightened risk [61].

Based on different intervention studies in children at different ages, it is argued that the developmental effects of iodine deficiency during early gestation are irreversible by later iodine repletion. Supplementation of pregnant women however, showed a clear benefit on cognitive outcome of the children. In iodine-insufficient areas of Spain, the effect of a supplementation during pregnancy on cognitive development of the offspring (aged three months to three years) was clearly documented in three out of four studies [62].

By contrast, supplementation after birth has no clear impact on cognitive development (reviewed in [63]). This underlines the importance of adequate nutrition of females, in particular at the onset of and during pregnancy [64, 65]. In addition, it has to be considered that the newborn depends on iodine from breast milk during lactation. In areas with inadequate iodine supply, breast milk iodine concentration is not sufficient to meet the needs of infants, even when their mothers were supplemented with 150 µg daily iodine during the first six months post-partum [66].

Vitamin D deficiency (VDD) is a worldwide problem with various health consequences in childhood and in adults. VDD is observed in 60% of Caucasian women and also in women with dark skin, where the rate is estimated to be even higher [67].

Maternal VDD during pregnancy has frequently been described as associated with adverse health outcome of the offspring, including intrauterine growth restriction and impaired bone mass. Vitamin D deficiency is also related to various cognitive and behavioral dysfunctions, e.g., schizophrenia [68]. Infants born to mothers with VDD had significantly lower birth weights and an increased risk of being too small for gestational age compared with infants born to mothers with adequate plasma levels as a sign of vitamin D sufficiency [69]. Low maternal serum vitamin D levels during pregnancy of 743 Caucasian women in Australia are significantly associated with offspring language impairment at five and 10 years of age [70]. Besides its well-known actions on bone and the immune system, vitamin D seems also important in the developing brain, controlling the gene expression of so-called neurotrophins, which are important for neurogenesis [62].

10.8   A Sustainable Approach to Improve Pregnancy Outcomes

Based on increasing data indicating that malnutrition during pregnancy also occurs in high-income countries, various meta-analyses have been performed to study the effect of supplementation on pregnancy and birth outcomes.

In a recent meta-analysis, the impact of a multivitamin/mineral supplement (MVM) on pregnancy outcome was evaluated.

Meta-analysis [71]

Malformation	Risk reduction	
	(OR/95% CI)[a]	
	MVM supplement	Study type
NTD	0.67 (0.58–0.77)	Case control
	0.52 (0.39–0.69)	Cohort and RCT
Cardiovascular	0.78 (0.67–0.92)	Case control
	0.61 (0.40–0.92)	Cohort and RCT
Limb	0.48 (0.30–0.76)	Case control
	0.57 (0.38–0.85)	Cohort and RCT
Cleft palate	0.76 (0.62–0.93)	Case Control
	0.42 (0.06–2.84)	Cohort and RCT
Cleft lip	0.63 (0.54–0.73)	Case control
	0.58 (0.28–1.19)	Cohort and RCT
Urogenital	0.48 (0.30–0.76)	Case control
	0.68 (0.35–1.31)	Cohort and RCT
Hydrocephalus	0.37 (0.24–0.56)	Case control
	1.54 (0.53–4.50)	Cohort and RCT

[a] $p < 0.01$

Prenatal supplementation with an MVM does indeed reduce malformations. It also increases birth weight and reduces the incidence of low for gestational age newborns [72]. Based on these findings, the Canadian Society of Gynaecology and Obstetrics makes the following recommendations:

- In cases of planned pregnancy, healthy females should take a folate-containing (0.4–1.0 mg) MVM on a daily basis.
- Females with specific risks (BMI > 35, diabetes, history of a child with NTDs) are advised to take folate (5.0 mg) together with an MVM 2–3 months prior to conception and up to 12 weeks after delivery.

10.9 Safety of MVM and Pregnancy

The rationale for MVM supplementation during pregnancy is the co-existence of multiple micronutrient deficiencies in pregnant women, especially in resource-poor settings [73]. Resources, however, are not only a question of availability but also of education and knowledge.

Trials of MVMs in pregnant women for primary prevention are carried out to improve either maternal health or birth outcome. Most trials did not specifically address AEs. Nevertheless, differences in birth outcome can be taken as harmful or as AEs. In a double-blind randomized, controlled trial (RCT) [74], the effect of MVM versus folic acid (400 µg) alone versus folic acid + iron (IFA) (30 mg) was tested in 18,775 nulliparous pregnant women. Prenatal MVM and IFA did not affect perinatal mortality (primary outcome) or preterm delivery, birth weight, birth length, or gestational duration (secondary outcomes). In a double-blind cluster-randomized trial, MVM ($n = 15,804$) or IFA (30 mg/400 µg) ($n = 15,486$) supplementation were used to study effect on early infant mortality (primary outcome) or neonatal mortality, fetal loss, or low birth weight (secondary outcomes) [75]. Compared with IFA supplementation, MVM reduced early infant mortality by a significant 18%. In addition, all secondary outcomes were significantly improved in the MVM group. Specific AEs were not reported. In different studies from the same group [76], the effect of MVM on pregnancy outcome was evaluated. MVM decreased the incidence of neural tube defects and other cleft formations. AEs were not reported. MVM versus IFA (60 mg/400 µg) during pregnancy showed a significant increase in birth weight in the MVM group. AEs were not reported.

A Danish cohort study [77] documented that regular use of MVM around the time of conception was associated with a decreased risk of preterm birth and small-for-gestational-age birth. Any AEs were not reported, but the authors concluded that "multivitamin use around the time of conception could be a safe and simple strategy." In an RCT with either MVM ($n = 600$) or IFA ($n = 600$) from

12 weeks gestation until delivery [78], morbidity during pregnancy was taken as an AE measure. Typical antenatal problems frequently occurring during pregnancy, such as nausea, dyspepsia, and abdominal pain, occurred in both groups without any significant difference. MVM supplementation was associated with increased birth weight when compared with IFA supplementation. In this study dealing with females from Nepal, nutrition status was not assessed, but might not have been optimal. In another study from Nepal [79], undernourished women were selected for MVM supplementation ($n = 99$) or placebo ($n = 101$). Both groups received IFA (60 mg/500 µg). AEs of supplementation (nausea, vomiting, diarrhea, abdominal pain, and anorexia) were documented in seven subjects receiving MVM and in 13 in the IFA control group. In a randomized double-blind RCT, the effect of MVM use ($n = 55$) versus placebo ($n = 59$) on subjective health and well-being was elucidated [30]. Those who supplemented with MVM experienced an increased energy level ($P = 0.022$) and enhanced mood ($P = 0.027$), both significant versus placebo. One participant in the MVM group reported minor gastrointestinal symptoms (nausea).

Taken together, in controlled clinical trials with MVM supplementation before and during pregnancy, AEs were not reported. The safety and improvement of pregnancy outcomes justify the recommendation to supplement MVM from early conception until delivery. The Genetics Committee of the Society of Obstetricians and Gynecologists of Canada made clear recommendations: Women in the reproductive age group should be advised of the benefits of folic acid in addition to a multivitamin supplement during wellness visits, especially if pregnancy is contemplated [80]. This recommendation is based on an extensive review of articles published between 1985 and 2007 and related to MVM supplementation and its impact on birth defects. Supplementation with MVMs including iron and folate significantly reduced congenital anomalies (anencephaly, myelomeningocele, meningocele, oral facial cleft, structural heart disease, limb defect, urinary tract anomaly, and hydrocephalus).

10.9.1 Conclusion

MVM supplements show clear benefits on pregnancy outcome and no harm. Recommendation of supplementation is indeed a sustainable approach and covers all inadequacy gaps due to new dietary behaviors or economic problems, achieving a sufficient dietary diversity and meeting the increased needs within the 1,000-day window.

Furthermore, an adequate micronutrient supply within the 1,000-day window will have a curbing impact on diseases in later life.

10.10   Impact of Maternal Malnutrition on Outcome of the Child in Later Life

It has long been speculated that a poor diet during pregnancy has an impact on diseases in later life. This so-called Barker Hypothesis (also known as intrauterine programming) is also related to poor intake of certain micronutrients during pregnancy. Figure 10.2 summarizes the present state of knowledge regarding the impact of micronutrient deficiencies on later disease development.

Inadequate micronutrient supply affects fetal development in different ways depending on the micronutrients in low supply. Hormonal adaptation may impact the growth hormone axis, low supply of methyl-donors will influence epigenetic changes, and inadequate vitamin A and D will influence the innate and acquired immune system and maturation of the lung.

Hormonal adaptations due to low supply of iron or zinc may have a long-term consequence on the growth hormone axis, including appetite regulation and at least body weight [82]. By contrast, prenatal zinc deficiency seems to reduce appetite [83]. Impact of deficiencies on kidney development may increase salt sensitivity

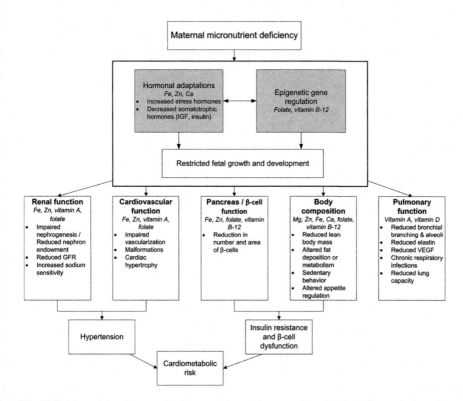

Fig. 10.2 The relation between inadequate micronutrient supply and risk of disease in later life (reproduced with permission from [81])

and subsequent risk of hypertension. Cardiovascular function, including blood vessel formation and endothelial function, is critically dependent on several micronutrients (vitamin A, folate, iron, zinc) [84]. The impact of vitamins D and A on the development of the immune system might explain the high incidence of type I diabetes in cases of low vitamin D levels during pregnancy. Indeed, a recent meta-analysis documented that vitamin D supplementation during early childhood significantly reduced type 1 diabetes compared to non-supplemented children [85].

10.10.1   Conclusion

Preventing nutrient gaps during pregnancy and early childhood may reduce the risk of diseases in later life. The major issue during pregnancy is sustainability of the micronutrient supply, because organ systems and hormonal axes develop and react differently from mother to child and within the fetus at different stages of gestation. In addition, the demand will vary in accordance with development and is controlled via supply from maternal or fetal stores. In many cases, micronutrient gaps are not detected and the consequences may occur years later and will not be correlated to a specific gap, which might have produced a 'genetic' imprinting on hormonal axis or organ function. To avoid effects of 'silent' micronutrient gaps, it is necessary to ensure a sufficient diet with adequate nutrients, as proposed in the FAO/WHO statement on food security.

10.11   Summary: Key Messages

- The problem of micronutrient deficiency (hidden hunger) is not confined to the developing world.
- Significant sections of the population of Europe have been documented in a number of recent studies as being deficient in key micronutrients.
- Women of child-bearing age and especially women who are pregnant have heightened needs for key micronutrients.
- Micronutrient provision via the diet is a key factor in brain development, and an adequate micronutrient supply during the first 1,000 days of life is essential for long-term health and wellbeing.
- Supplementation with multivitamin/mineral supplements during pregnancy is a safe approach to improving birth outcomes and reducing the risk of a range of diseases in later life.
- To avoid effects of 'silent' micronutrient gaps, it is necessary to ensure a sufficient diet with adequate nutrients, as proposed in the FAO/WHO statement on food security.

References

1. Vinas BR et al (2011) Projected prevalence of indaquate nutrient intake in Europe. Ann. Nutr. Metab. 59:84–95
2. Zipitis CS, Akobeng AK. Vitamin D supplementation in early childhood and risk of type 1 diabetes: a systematic review and meta-analysis. Arch Dis Child 2008;93:512e7.
3. Doyle W, Srivastava A, Crawford MA, Bhatti R, Brooke Z, Costeloe KL. Interpregnancy folate and iron status of women in an inner-city population. Brit J Nutr 2001;86:81e7.
4. Cetin I, Berti C, Calabrese S. Role of micronutrients in the periconceptional period. Hum Reprod Update 2010;16:80e95.
5. Berti C, Decsi T, Dykes F, Hermoso M, Koletzko B, Massari M, et al. Critical issues in setting micronutrient recommendations for pregnant women: an insight. Matern Child Nutr 2010;6:5Se22S.
6. Berti et al (2011) Micronutrients in pregnancy: Current knowledge and unresolved questions. Clin Nutr 30:689–701.
7. MRC Vitamin Study Research Group. Prevention of neural tube defects: results of the Medical research Council vitamin study. Lancet 1991;338:131e7.
8. Czeizel AE, Dobó M, Vargha P. Hungarian cohort-controlled trial of periconceptional multivitamin supplementation shows a reduction in certain congenital abnormalities. Birth Def Res (Part A) 2004;70:853e61.
9. Ross AC. Vitamin A and carotenoids. In: Shils ME, Shike M, Ross AC, editors. Modern nutrition in health and disease. 10th ed. USA: Lippincott Williams & Wilkins; 2006. p. 351e75.
10. Grune T, Lietz G, Palou A, Ross AC, Stahl W, Tang G, et al. b-Carotene is an important vitamin A source for humans. J Nutr 2010;140:2268Se85S.
11. American Academy of Pediatrics Committee on Nutrition. Nutritional needs of preterm infants. In: Kleinman RE, editor. Pediatric Nutrition Handbook. 4th ed. Elk Grove Village, IL: American Academy of Pediatrics; 1998. p. 55e87.
12. Almeras L, Eyles D, Benech P, Laffite D, Villard C, Patatian A, et al. Developmental vitamin D deficiency alters brain protein expression in the adult rat: implications for neuropsychiatric disorders. Proteomics 2007;7:769e80.
13. Yetley EA. Assessing the vitamin D status of the US population. Am J Clin Nutr 2008;88:558Se64S.
14. Salle BL, Delvin EE, Lapillonne A, Bishop NJ, Glorieux FH. Perinatal metabolism of vitamin D. Am J Clin Nutr 2000;71:1317Se24S.
15. Kovacs CS. Vitamin D in pregnancy and lactation: maternal, fetal, and neonatal outcomes from human and animal studies. Am J Clin Nutr 2008;88:520Se8S.
16. Feron F, Burne TH, Brown J, Smith E, McGrath JJ, Mackay-Sim A, et al. Developmental Vitamin D3 deficiency alters the adult rat brain. Brain Res Bull 2005;65:141e8.
17. Lapillonne A. Vitamin D deficiency during pregnancy may impair maternal and fetal outcomes. Med Hypotheses 2010;74:71e5.
18. Milman N. Iron and pregnancy-a delicate balance. Ann Hematol 2006;85:559e65.
19. Breymann C. Iron supplementation during pregnancy. Fet Mat Med Rev 2002;13:1e29.
20. Scholl TO. Iron status during pregnancy: setting the stage for mother and infant. Am J Clin Nutr 2005;81:1218Se22S.
21. Lao TT, Tham K-F, Chan LY. Third trimester iron status and pregnancy outcome in non-anemic women; pregnancy unfavourably affected by maternal iron excess. Hum Reprod 2000;15:1843e8.
22. Zimmermann MB. Iodine deficiency. Endocr Rev 2009;30:376e408.
23. Becker DV, Braverman LE, Delange F, Dunn JT, Franklyn JA, Hollowell JG, et al. Iodine supplementation for pregnancy and lactation e United States and Canada: recommendations of the American thyroid association. Thyroid 2006;16:949e51.

24. Morreale de Escobar G, Obregon MJ, Escobar del Rey F. Role of thyroid hormone during early brain development. Eur J Endocrinol 2004;151(Suppl.3):U25e37.
25. Santiago-Fernandez et al (2004) Intelligence qoutient and iodine intake: a cross sectional study in children. J Clin. Endocr. Metab. 89:3851e7
26. Gärtner R. Thyroid disease in pregnancy. Curr Opin Obstet Gynecol 2009;21:501e7.
27. Hanson MA, Gluckman PD (2014) Early developmental conditioning of later health and disease: physiology or pathphysiology. Physiol Rev. 94:1027–1076.
28. United nations subcommittee on nutrition. (2000) Nutrition policy paper 18.
29. Korenman, S., Miller, J.E., and Sjaastad, J.E. (1995) Long-term poverty and child development in the United States: Results from the National Longitudinal Survey of Youth. Children and Youth Services Review 17,1/2:127–51.
30. Gogtay N, Nugent TF, Herman DH, et al. (2006) Dynamic mapping of normal human hippocampal development. Hippocampus. 16:664–72.
31. Levitt P. (2003) Structural and functional maturation of the developing primate brain. J. Pediatr. 143, 35–45.
32. Lenroot RK, Giedd JN (2006) Brain development in children and adolescents: Insight from anatomical magnetic resonance imaging. Neurosci Behav Rev. 30, 718–729.
33. Georgieff MK (2007) Nutrition and the developing brain: nutrient priorities and measurement. Am. J. Clin. Nutr. 85, 614–620.
34. Lenroot, R., Giedd JN. (2006) Brain development in children and adolescents: Insights from anatomical magnetic resonance imaging. Neurosci & Behav Sci. 30:718–729.
35. Raizada R., Kishiyama M. (2010) Effects of socioeconomic status on brain development, and how cognitive neuroscience may contribute to levelling the playing field. Front hum neurosci 4, 1–11.
36. D'Angiulli A., Lipina JS., Olesinska A. (2012) Explicit and implicit issues in the developmental cognitive neuroscience of social inequality. Front Hum Neurosci 6, 1–17.
37. Lipina SJ., Posner MI. (2012) The impact of poverty on the development of brain networks. Front Hum Neurosci. 6, 1–12.
38. Noble KG., Houston SM., Kan E., Sowell ER. (2012) Neural correlates of socio-economic status in the developing human brain. Dev. Sci. 15, 516–527.
39. Houston JL., Chandra A., Wolfe B., Pollak SD (2011) Association between income and the hippocampus. PLoS One 6, 19712.
40. Jednorog K., Altarelli I., Monzalvo K. et al. (2012) The influence of socio-economic status on children's brain structure. PLoS One 7, 42486.
41. Luby J., Belden A., Botteron K. et al. (2013) The effects of poverty on childhood brain development. The mediating effects of caregiving and stressful life events. JAMA Pediatr. online doi:10.1001/jamapediatrics.2013.3139.
42. Hanson, J.L., Chandra, A., Wolfe, B.L., & Pollak, S.D. (2011). Association between income and the hippocampus. PLoS ONE, 6 (5), e18712.
43. Böhm A, Ellsäßer G, Kuhn J et al. (2003) Soziale Lage und Gesundheit von jungen Menschen im Land Brandenburg. Das Gesundheitswesen 65: 219–225.
44. Jörg Baten u. Andreas Böhm, (2010). Trends of Children's Height and Parental Unemployment: A Large-Scale Anthropometric Study on Eastern Germany, 1994–2006., German Economic Review 11: 1–24.
45. Doblhammer G., van den Berg GJ., Fritze T. (2013) Economic conditions at the tie of birth and cognitive abilities in late lief: evidence from ten European countries. PlosOne 8: e74915.
46. Mabli J., Castner L., Ohls J (2010) Food expenditure and diet quality among low income-households and individuals. Mathematica Policy research Ref. No. 06408.600.
47. Karp RJ. (2005) Malnutrition among children in the United States. The impact of poverty. In: Shils ME., Shike M., Ross AC et al. Modern nutrition in health and disease. 10ed. Baltimore Williams Willkins Lippincott 860–874.
48. Darmon N, Drewnowski A. (2008) Does social class predict diet quality? Am J Clin Nutr.; 87 (5):1107–17.

49. Berger LM., Paxson C., Waldfogel J. Income and child development (2005) Center for Research on Child Wellbeing Working Paper# 05-16-FF.
50. Aggarwal A, Monsivais P, Cook AJ, Drewnowski A. (2011) Does diet cost mediate the relation between socioeconomic position and diet quality? Eur J Clin Nutr; 65: 1059–66.
51. Brooks Gunn J., Duncan GJ (1997) The effects of poverty on children. In: Children and Poverty 7/2.
52. Laus MF., Vales LD., Costa TM., Almeida SS. Early postnatal protein-calorie malnutrition and cognition: A review of human and animal studies. Int J Env Res Pub Health (2011), 8: 590–612.
53. Ryan AS., Astwood JD., Gautier S. et al. (2010) Effects of long chain polyunsaturated fatty acids supplementation on neurodevelopment in childhood: a review of human studies. Prostaglandins Leukot Essent Fatty Acids 82:305–314.
54. Grantham-McGregor S., Ani C. (2001) A review o studies on the effect of iron deficiency on cognitive development in children. J Nutr. 131:649–668.
55. Ahmed T., Hossain M., Sanin K. (2012) Global burden of maternal and child undernutrition and micronutrient deficiencies. Ann. Nutr Metab. 61:8–17.
56. Fuglestad A., Ramel SE., Georgieff MK. (2010) In: Micronutrients and Brain Health Packer et al. (Eds.) Taylor and Francis Publ. UK.
57. Black MM, Baqui AH, Zaman K. et al. (2004) Iron and zinc supplementation promote motor development and exploratory behavior among Bangladeshi infants. Am J Clin Nutr. 80: 903–10.
58. WHO, UNICEF, ICCIDD. Assessment of iodine deficiency disorders and monitoring their elimination. (2007). Geneva World Health Organization. 3rd. Ed.
59. Azizi, F., Sarshar A., Nafarabadi M.et al., (1993) Impairment of neuromotor and cognitive development in iodine-deficient schoolchildren with normal physical growth, Acta Endocrinol 129, 497.
60. Vermiglio, F., Sidoti M., Finocchiaro MD. et al., (1990) Defective neuromotor and cognitive ability in iodine-deficient schoolchildren of an endemic goiter region in Sicily, J Clin Endocrinol Metab 70, 379.
61. Barth S., Steer C., Golding J. et al. (2013) Effect of inadequate iodine status in UK pregnant women on cognitive outcomes in their children: results from the Avon Longitudinal Study of Parents and Children (ALSPAC). Lancet 60436–60445.
62. Trumpff C., Schepper JD., Tafforeau J. et al (2013) Mild iodine deficiency in pregnancy in Europe and its consequences for cognitive and psychomotor development of children: a review. J Trace Elem Biol Med 27:174–183.
63. Melse-Boonstra A., Jaiswal N. (2010) Iodine deficiency in pregnancy, infancy and childhood and ist consequences for brain development. Best Pract & Res Clin Endocrinol & Metab 24:29–38.
64. Cao, X.-Y. Xin-Min J., Zhi-Hong Det al., (1994) Timing of vulnerability of the brain to iodine deficiency in endemic cretinism, N Engl J Med 331, 1739, 1994.
65. O'Donnell, K. Rakeman M., Xue-Yi C. et al., (2002) Effects of iodine supplementation during pregnancy on child growth and development at school age, Dev Med Child Neurol 44, 76.
66. Mulrine HM., Skeaff SA., Ferguson EL. et al. (2010) Breast milk iodine concentration declines over the first 6 mo post-partum in iodine deficient women. Am J Clin Nutr 92:849–856.
67. Bodnar LM, Simhan HN, Powers RW, et al. (2007) High prevalence of vitamin D insufficiency in black and white pregnant women residing in the northern United States and their neonates. J Nutr. 2007 Feb; 137(2):447–52.
68. McCann J., Ames BN. (2008) Is there convincing biological and behavioral evidence linking vitamin D to brain function. FASEB J. 22:982–1001.
69. Leffelaar ER, Vrijkotte TG, van Eijsden M. (2010) Maternal early pregnancy vitamin D status in relation to fetal and neonatal growth: results of the multi-ethnic Amsterdam Born Children and their Development cohort. Br J Nutr.; 104:108–17.

70. Whitehouse A., Holt B., Serralha M. et al (2012) Maternal serum vitamin D levels during pregnancy and offspring neurocognitive development. Ped. 129:485–93.

71. Goh Y et al (2006) Prenatal multivitamin supplementation and rates of congenital anomalies: A meta-analysis. JOGC 28: 680–689.

72. Wilson RD et al (2007) Pre-conceptional vitamin/folic acid supplementation 2007: the use of folic acid in combination with multivitamin supplements for the prevention of neural tube defects and the congenital anomalies. J Obstet Gynaecol Can 29:1003–1026.

73. Torheim LE, Ferguson EL, Penrose K, Arimond M. Women in resource-poor settings are at risk of inadequate intakes of multiple micronutrients. J Nutr. 2010;140(11):2051S–8S.

74. Liu JM, Mei Z, Ye R, Serdula MK, Ren A, Cogswell ME. Micronutrient supplementation and pregnancy outcomes: double-blind randomized controlled trial in China. JAMA Intern Med. 2013;173(4):276–82.

75. Shankar AH, Jahari AB, Sebayang SK, Aditiawarman, Apriatni M, Harefa B, Muadz H, Soesbandoro SD, Tjiong R, Fachry A, et al. Effect of maternal multiple micronutrient supplementation on fetal loss and infant death in Indonesia: a double-blind cluster-randomised trial. Lancet. 2008;371(9608):215–27.

76. Czeizel AE, Dudas I. Prevention of the first occurrence of neural-tube defects by periconceptional vitamin supplementation. N Engl J Med. 1992;327(26):1832–5. Czeizel AE. Prevention of congenital abnormalities by periconceptional multivitamin supplementation. BMJ. 1993;306(6893):1645-8. Czeizel AE. Reduction of urinary tract and cardiovascular defects by periconceptional multivitamin supplementation. Am J Med Genet. 1996;62(2):179-83.

77. Catov JM, Bodnar LM, Olsen J, Olsen S, Nohr EA. Periconceptional multivitamin use and risk of preterm or small-for-gestational-age births in the Danish National Birth Cohort. Am J Clin Nutr. 2011;94(3):906–12.

78. Osrin D, Vaidya A, Shrestha Y, et al. Effects of antenatal multiple micronutrient supplementation on birthweight and gestational duration in Nepal: double-blind, randomised controlled trial. Lancet. 2005;365(9463):955–62.

79. Gupta P, Ray M, Dua T, Radhakrishnan G, Kumar R, Sachdev HP. Multimicronutrient supplementation for undernourished pregnant women and the birth size of their offspring: a double-blind, randomized, placebo-controlled trial. Arch Pediatr Adolesc Med. 2007;161 (1):58–64.

80. Wilson RD, Johnson JA, Wyatt P, Allen V, Gagnon A, Langlois S, Blight C, Audibert F, Desilets V, Brock JA, et al. Pre-conceptional vitamin/folic acid supplementation 2007: the use of folic acid in combination with a multivitamin supplement for the prevention of neural tube defects and other congenital anomalies. J Obstet Gynaecol Can. 2007;29(12):1003–26.

81. Christian P, Stewart CP Maternal micronutrient deficiency, fetal development, and risk of chronic disease. J Nutr 140:437–445.

82. Taylor PD, Poston L Developmental programming of obesity in mammals. Exp Physiol 2007; 92:287–298.

83. Shay NF, Mangian HF Neurobiology of zinc influenced eating behavior. J Nutr. 2000; 130:1493–1499.

84. Singh RB et al (2015) Can prevention of low birth weight in newborn may be associated with primordial prevention of cardiovascular diseases and type 2 diabetes in adult life? J Cardiol Ther 5:1–15.

85. Zipitis CS, Akobeng AK Vitamin D supplementation in early childhood and risk of type 1 diabetes: a systematic review and meta-analysis Arch Dis Child 2008; 93:512–517.

Chapter 11
Micronutrient Status in Affluent Societies

Barbara Troesch

Abstract Hidden hunger, referring to micronutrient deficiencies often not apparent through distinct clinical symptoms, is known to be highly prevalent in many developing countries: The prevalence of such inadequacies in developed countries has been less discussed, even though it is worryingly high for some micronutrients even in affluent countries such as the U.S. Therefore the aim of this chapter is to review and discuss the available data on micronutrient intakes and status in affluent societies in general and in sub populations that are particularly at risk. As discussing all nutrients systematically would exceed the scope of this article, this chapter concentrates on nutrients of particular concern for the general population or during specific periods in the life cycle. It concludes that in affluent countries, micronutrient inadequacies are widespread, and that intakes of vitamins E, D and A and folate are particularly critical, pointing out that improving nutrition could help alleviate the social and financial burden of nutrition deficiency diseases. Better knowledge concerning their nutritional status might encourage people to improve their diet and consequently their long-term health.

Keywords Hidden hunger · Nutrition deficiency diseases · Micronutrient intakes · Micronutrient status · Micronutrient deficiency · Developed countries · Affluent societies

11.1 Is the Developed World Micronutrient-Secure?

Hidden hunger, referring to micronutrient deficiencies often not apparent through distinct clinical symptoms, is known to be highly prevalent in many developing countries: The recent *Lancet* series on maternal and child nutrition reports on the

B. Troesch (✉)
DSM Nutritional Products, Wurmisweg 576, 4303 Kaiseraugst, Switzerland
e-mail: barbara.troesch@dsm.com

© Springer International Publishing AG 2017   167
H.K. Biesalski et al. (eds.), *Sustainable Nutrition in a Changing World*,
DOI 10.1007/978-3-319-55942-1_11

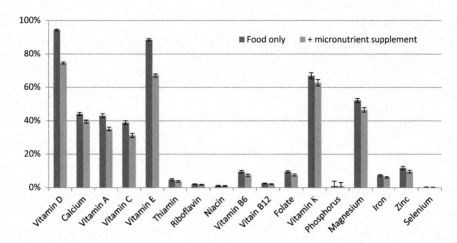

Fig. 11.1 Proportion of U.S. population aged ≥ 4 years with intakes below the *Estimated Average Requirement* or *Adequate Intake* (Food only [*dark blue*] or food and multiple micronutrient supplements [*light blue*], % ± standard error of the mean) (Adapted from Wallace et al. [3])

widespread occurrence of insufficient supply with a range of micronutrients in low- and middle-income countries (LMIC) [1]. For example, around 30% of school-aged children and 15% of pregnant women were reported to be vitamin A-deficient in countries with GDP < US$15,000 [2]. The prevalence of such inadequacies in developed countries has been less discussed, even though it is worryingly high for some micronutrients even in affluent countries such as the U.S. (Fig. 11.1) [3].

11.2   Vitamin D Status

A review of studies assessing serum 25-hydroxyvitamin D levels globally found that nearly 40% of the population had inadequate (<50 nmol/L) and approximately 7% deficient (<25 nmol/L) levels [4]. A similar picture is shown by the map of 25-hydroxyvitamin D levels in adults compiled by Wahl et al. [5] (Figure 11.2). The most recent European Nutrition and Health Report showed that average vitamin D intakes for women were below recommendations in all countries surveyed, and for men, in around two thirds of them [6]. In line with this, it was reported that between 50 and 100% of adults in various European countries had inadequate intakes of this vitamin [7]. Also in the U.S., more than 90% of adults were reported to have intakes of vitamin D below the *Estimated Average Requirement* in 2007–2010 [3]. Prevalence of 25-hydroxvitamin D levels below 30 nmol/L was ~18% in Europeans assessed between October and March, but only ~9% for those studied in April to September, reflecting the body's capacity for endogenous production during the summer months, and dark-skinned persons had a significantly higher risk

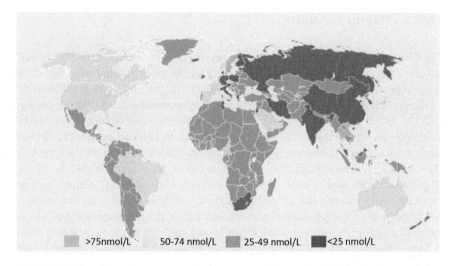

Fig. 11.2 Vitamin D status in adults (>18 years) around the world (Wahl et al. [5])

of inadequate levels [8]. The high prevalence of low vitamin D levels is thought to be highly relevant for public health, as it has been estimated that the risk ratio for all-cause mortality in the lowest compared with the highest quintiles of serum 25-hydroxyvitamin D is around 1.6 (95% confidence interval from 1.36 to 1.81) [9]. Unsurprisingly, it has been suggested that doubling serum levels could reduce all-cause mortality rates by about 17% in Europe, resulting in an increase in life expectancy of approximately two years [10].

At the same time, calcium intakes were found to be low for around 20% of adults in a range of European countries [7] and for more than 40% in the U.S. [3] (Fig. 11.1). Vitamin D plays an important role in calcium absorption and bone re-modelling, and insufficiency can accelerate age-related loss of bone and increase the risk of fracture [11]. The elderly seem to be particularly at risk of vitamin D inadequacy or even deficiency [4], and it has been proposed that nutritional supplements with 700–1000 IU or more per day should ideally be taken by this age group to prevent fractures resulting from falls [12], combined with regular intakes of dairy products to assure adequate intakes of calcium and protein [13]. Intakes of vitamin K, an additional key player for bone health, have also been reported as inadequate for large segments of the population [3, 14] (Fig. 11.1). Bone health seems to be further affected by lack of other micronutrients such as vitamins C and E, highlighting the important role that nutrition as a whole plays in reducing the risk of osteoporosis [15]. Worryingly, these are also frequently reported to be low in a significant proportion of the population (see below).

11.3 Vitamin C Status

The European Nutrition and Health Survey [6] reports mean vitamin C intakes ranging from ~ 60 to ~ 153 mg. However, despite the comparatively high mean intake reported for Germany (153 mg/d for adults) [6], half the adult population has a vitamin C intake below the current German recommendation of 100 mg per day [16, 17]. Using lower cut-off of 60 and 50 mg/d for men and women, respectively, the European survey reports 8–40% of adults with inadequate intakes [7]. Similar rates of inadequate intakes relative to recommendations were reported from the U.S. [3] (Fig. 11.1), even though the cut-offs used there are slightly higher at 75 and 60 mg/d for men and women, respectively [18]. Unfortunately, dietary surveys frequently only report mean or median intakes, which do not give an indication of the proportion of the population with intakes below the recommendations. Given the similarities of the mean intakes, it can be assumed that the same problem exists in many, also affluent, parts of the world: In Japan, median intakes increase from around 60 mg in the age group of 15–49 to above 100 mg in people aged ≥ 50 years [19], and mean intakes in South Korea were 116 mg in men and 105 mg in women [20].

11.4 Vitamin E Status

Vitamin E seems to be another nutrient of concern even in affluent countries, as high proportions of inadequate intakes have been reported from the U.S., some European countries, and also some countries in the Asia Pacific region [3, 21] (Fig. 11.1). A recent review showed that, globally, 82 and 61% of adults aged 14 years had intakes below 15 and 12 mg/day, respectively (Fig. 11.3), [22]. The former level corresponds to the *Recommended Daily Allowance* and the latter to the *Estimated Average Requirement* defined by the Institute of Medicine [18]. Even more worryingly, recent evidence, as yet mostly from epidemiologic studies, on cardiovascular health and immune function indicates that optimal plasma alpha-tocopherol levels might be higher than previously assumed [23].

11.5 Vitamin A Status

Vitamin A intakes from food are also low for more than 40% of Americans above the age of 13 years [3], while this is the case for $\sim 15\%$ of men and $\sim 10\%$ of women in Germany [17]. The differences are partially due to the conversion factor of 1:12 used in the U.S. [24], whereas 1:6 is used in Germany [16]. This is due to different interpretations of the evidence for the relative absorption of pro-vitamin A

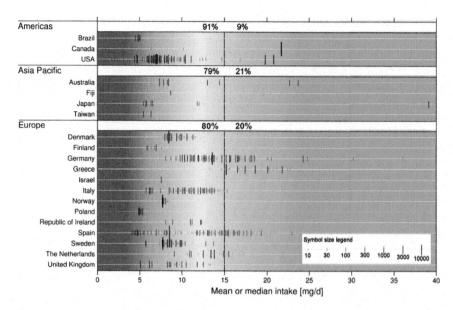

Fig. 11.3 Vitamin E intakes (total of all 8 isomers) reported as mean (*black*) or median (*blue*) by region and country from studies with persons aged ≥ 14 years. *Red* low intake (≤ 5 mg/d); *yellow* moderate intake (6–14 mg/d); *green* recommended intake or above (≥ 15 mg/d) (n = 128 studies); for more details, see Péter et al. [22]

and its conversion by the β-carotene monooxygenase by the Institute of Medicine [25] and DACH [16]. As beta-carotene contributes significantly to total vitamin A intakes [26], using the same conversion factor as in the U.S. would considerably increase the proportion of Germans with total vitamin A intakes below the recommendations. The accuracy of the conversion and the assessment of adequacy of vitamin A intakes is further complicated by the existence of various common polymorphisms for genes encoding enzymes involved in the conversion of beta-carotene to vitamin A: Carriers of these polymorphism can have an up to 50% reduction in enzyme activity, and therefore have an impaired ability to convert beta-carotene to vitamin A [27]. Consequently, such polymorphisms make it more difficult to achieve adequate intakes, and specific recommendations might be needed for these at-risk groups [28].

11.6   B-Vitamins Status

B-vitamins appear at first glance to be less of an issue in developed countries such as the U.S. [3] (Fig. 11.1). However, the proportion of adults with inadequate intakes of vitamin B_{12} reached 20% and 40% in Finland and Greece, respectively

[7]. In Canada, it has been reported that between 3 and 9% of non-pregnant women had deficient or marginal serum concentrations for vitamin B_{12}, respectively, which increased to 10 and 21% at week 16 and 23 and 35% at week 36 of gestation [29]. This is in line with a meta-analysis of global prevalence of vitamin B_{12} insufficiency during pregnancy, which found 21, 19 and 29% in the first, second and third trimester, respectively [30]. Moreover, comparison of intakes from 2005 to 2007 and 2012 to 2013 showed a small but significant downward trend for some of the B-vitamins in Germany, which might be linked to decreased intakes of fruits and fruit products [31].

For folate, the situation is even more critical, with proportions of intakes below recommendations ranging from 20 to 40% in some European countries [7]. In German women, folate intakes remained stable, albeit at a relatively low median with intakes of 200 µg/d [31], and only 8 and 3% of women aged 19–45 years and 15–19 years, respectively, reporting that they take folate-containing supplements [17]. A review of nutritional intakes in pregnant women in other affluent countries showed folate intakes of 75, 64 and 37% of *Estimated Average Requirements* for pregnant women in Japan, the U.S. and Australia, respectively [32]. Periconceptual folate use is generally low in Europe, with only the Netherlands and Denmark achieving levels around 40 and 30% of periconceptual folate use, respectively, while the other countries monitored (Belgium, Croatia, Germany, Ireland Italy, Portugal, Spain and Switzerland) had levels below 10%—in some cases, considerably so [33]. This is despite the fact that a clear dose response has been shown for maternal folate status and the risk of developing neural tube defects in the offspring [34]. Moreover, perinatal folic acid supplementation can significantly reduce the risk and poses no risk to the mother or the baby [35]. Each year, ~300,000 children are born with neural tube defects globally, and in Europe, more than 4,500 pregnancies are affected [36]. Moreover, low folate status during early pregnancy was found to be associated with smaller total brain volume, poorer language performance, reduction in memory and learning, and a decrease in visuo-spatial domains in Dutch children [37].

In addition, the availability of B-vitamins and other nutrients implicated in the one-carbon metabolism and consequently DNA methylation due to maternal nutrition during pregnancy seems to play an important role in epigenetic changes in the offspring [38]. Even though the mechanisms are not well understood, processes such as DNA methylation in the offspring as a result of maternal or even paternal diet have been shown in a range of studies in animals and humans [39]. A recent study in the Gambia, for example, showed different DNA methylation pattern in the blood of infants whose mothers had received periconceptional micronutrient supplements compared with those whose mothers received a placebo [40]. It has been suggested that these epigenetic alterations might have long-lasting consequences for cognition and health [41].

11.7 The Vitamin Status of Pregnant Women

While it was reported that the prevalence of low iron intakes was around or below 10% in European countries, these figures only include male adults, as data on woman were excluded for methodological reasons [7]. A study of the nutritional of pregnant women in affluent countries reports intakes to be 49, 55, 60, 72 and 107% of the *Estimated Average Requirement* in Japan, Australia and New Zealand, Europe, the U.S. and Canada and the UK, respectively [32]. In the U.S., 18% of pregnant women were classified as iron-deficient, and the prevalence increased as gestation progressed [42].

A review of vitamin D intakes in pregnant women in affluent countries reported intakes at 24, 43, 74 and 78% of the *Estimated Average Requirement* or *Adequate Intake* for Japan, U.S. and Canada, Australia and the UK, respectively [32]. Comparison of pregnant and non-pregnant age-matched controls showed significantly lower level in the former [43]. Even though pregnancy-related adaptations such as hemodilution raise some questions regarding optimal levels [44], this is still worrying, given the importance of vitamin D for early development [45]. A recent meta-analysis concluded that supplementation with vitamin D was effective in raising serum 25-hydroxy levels during pregnancy and might have a beneficial effect on the risk of pre-eclampsia, low birth weight and preterm birth—even though some questions remain to be resolved, particularly with respect to co-supplementation with calcium [46]. Currently, even recently revised recommendations contain no additional provision for vitamin D during pregnancy and lactation [47, 48]. However, it has been proposed that significantly higher amounts, in the range of 1500–2000 IU per day, are necessary to avoid deficiency during this highly demanding period [49]. Adequate maternal vitamin D levels are particularly important, as neonates were identified as a further group that is particularly at risk of vitamin D deficiency, [4] and low levels at birth are thought to have long-lasting consequences: low levels in cord blood were, for example, linked to increased risk of respiratory infection and wheezing five years later [50]. In addition to increasing vitamin D levels in maternal and cord blood, supplementation during pregnancy also led to an increase in birth weight and length [51]. It has been shown that achieving adequate maternal levels of vitamin D via supplements had a beneficial effect on neonatal status [52].

11.8 The Vitamin Status of Infants

During lactation, adequate intakes are also crucial, as the nutrient content of breast milk—particularly for iodine, specific fatty acids including DHA, thiamine, riboflavin, as well as vitamins A, B_6, B_{12}, C and D—are influenced by maternal diet and reserves [53]. In Germany, a significant proportion of infants was reported to have intakes below recommendations, those for vitamin D, E, C and folate being particularly low [54]. However, even with a balanced, nutrient-dense diet, it is difficult to meet the requirements for some nutrients during this crucial period: Even though the vitamin D content of breast milk can be increased by maternal supplementation, it has been shown that breast milk only covered around one fifth of the recommended daily dose for this age group [55], unless daily high-dose supplements were taken [56]. A study in Swedish infants showed that without the addition of vitamin D drops to the diet, many of these healthy-term infants would have had intakes associated with the risk of developing rickets [57]. Consequently, daily supplementation with drops of 400 IU/d are recommended for infants, starting at birth [58]. However, compliance with this supplementation was found to be low, and exclusively breast-fed infants in particular had difficulties meeting the recommended intakes in the U.S. due to the relatively low levels in human milk [59].

A study evaluating the nutritional adequacy of children aged one to three years in Brazil, Germany, Russia and the United States reported vitamins A, D, calcium, and folate only in Germany as nutrients of concern in this age group [60]. Moreover, nearly 60% of young children (12–24 months) in a study in the U.S. were found to have vitamin E intakes below the recommendations [61]. Swiss school children were reported to have inadequate intakes of various vitamins [62]. Intakes of calcium, as well as of vitamins D and E, were identified as critical in U.S. children who did not take supplements, while inadequate intakes of magnesium and vitamin A were found in a lower, but still substantial, proportion [63].

In addition to vitamins and minerals, intakes of other essential nutrients appear to be still rather low: Even though polyunsaturated fat intake has increased globally compared to the 1990s, it is still lower than what is generally regarded as optimal (Fig. 11.4) [64]. Only limited information on docosahexaenoic acid (DHA) and eicosaenoic acid (EPA) intakes is available, but a study in the U.S. found that on average, adults had intakes of 63 and 23 mg/d respectively, which slightly

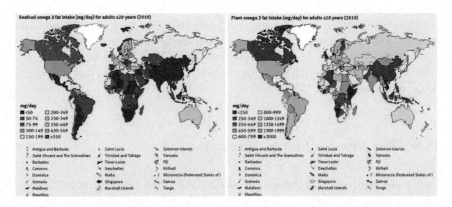

Fig. 11.4 Global and regional mean consumption levels of dietary seafood and plant omega-3 fat in 2010 for adults ≥ 20 years of age [64]

increased to 72 and 41 mg/day if supplements were included [65]. This is well below the >250 mg DHA and EPA that were proposed as optimal for healthy individuals [66].

11.9 The Vitamin Status of the Elderly

Malnutrition among the elderly is a significant and somewhat neglected public health problem that is thought to affect approximately 10% of people over the age of 65 years in the UK [67]. Even though frequently only protein-energy malnutrition is assessed, a study in the US showed that intakes below the *Estimated Average Requirements* were widespread for a range of micronutrients [68]. A review of the available data in Europe, Canada and the U.S. showed that vitamin D, thiamine, riboflavin, calcium, magnesium and selenium were identified as micronutrients of concern in the elderly [69]. Data from Germany shows that the situation is even more critical for elderly people living in care homes due to their physical or mental impairments [70] (Fig. 11.5). The situation is similar in Canada, where intakes of folate (before mandatory fortification was implemented), magnesium, zinc, vitamin E and B_6 were low for $\geq 70\%$ of elderly inhabitants of various care centers [71].

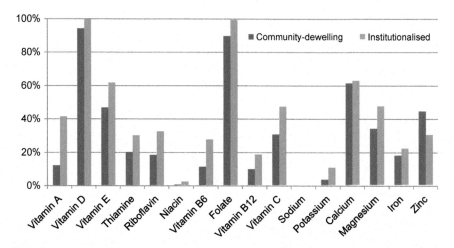

Fig. 11.5 Proportion of community-dwelling (*dark blue*) and institutionalized (*light blue*) German men aged ≥ 65 years with micronutrient intakes below the national recommendations (Adapted from [17, 26])

11.10   Dietary Supplements

The situation is somewhat improved by the use of dietary supplements: In one study, >80% of adults aged >50 years met the *Estimated Average Requirements* for vitamins A, B_6, B_{12}, C and E, folate, iron and zinc, thanks to supplementation [72]. In general, the use of dietary supplements in the elderly in Europe and Northern America seems to be gaining impetus and contributes significant amounts to their habitual intakes for a range of micronutrients (as reviewed by ter Borg et al. [69]). It has been suggested that regular use of dietary supplements is a promising way to improve micronutrient intakes in the elderly [73]. The same applies to the population as a whole: Data on dietary intake between 2007 and 2010 shows that around 50% of persons aged ≥ 4 years consumed dietary supplements with at least three vitamins and one mineral, which was an increase from the approximately 30% reported in previous surveys [3]. Figure 11.1 shows that, thanks to such supplements, the proportion of the population with intakes below recommendations decreases somewhat, but remains critically high for some nutrients [3]. In Europe, their use is somewhat less common, and a strong north-to-south gradient, with 40 and 5% users, respectively, was reported [7]. This gradient was observed in dietary patterns in general in Europe, as the diets of southern countries were found to provide adequate intakes of vitamin E, but were poor in vitamin A and D, while Nordic countries showed a near-opposite trend [74].

11.11   Food Fortification

Another commonly used approach to improve nutrient intakes is food fortification: In the case of vitamin D, for example, it has been shown that the fortification of products such as yoghurt, orange juice and bread had a significant effect on 25-hydroxyvitamin D levels [75]. Vitamin D-fortified foods were consumed by around three quarters of Irish children assessed in one study, and they made a significant contribution to their diet, which was otherwise fairly low in vitamin D [76]. The fortification of milk and margarine led to a significant improvement in vitamin D status in preschool children in Finland [77]. Fortified milk was also the main source of vitamin D in Finnish schoolchildren, and milk consumption was consequently the main determinant of vitamin D status in that population [78]. It has been shown that pregnant woman who consumed fortified cereals regularly had significantly higher intakes of folate, iron, zinc and calcium, as well as of vitamins A, C, D and E, and this reduced the risk of inadequate nutrient intakes by 60–90% [79].

11.12   Micronutrient Deficiency and Obesity

The problem of inadequate nutrient intakes is aggravated by the fact that the micronutrient status of the obese is frequently lower. This is not just due to lower intakes, but also because for some nutrients, such as iron, the low-level inflammation that accompanies obesity seems to reduce absorption [80]. The lower serum levels of 25-hydroxyvitamin D found in overweight and obese subjects compared to their normal-weight counterparts [81] might at least partially be due to increased sequestration of the vitamin in adipose tissue [82]. This effect is increasingly relevant, as obesity rates have doubled globally since 1980, resulting in 1.4 billion overweight adults in 2008 and more than 40 million overweight children under the age of five in 2011 [83]. It has been suggested that the recent increase in the prevalence of inadequate vitamin D status in the U.S. is predominantly attributable to the parallel increase in obesity [84]. While the development of obesity is complex and facilitated by a range of lifestyle and environmental factors, it appears that energy density is crucial [85]. There is mounting evidence that food insecurity contributes to the development of, or at least coexists with, obesity, particularly in situations where food insecurity leads to a disruption of normal eating patterns [86]. This is especially worrying as in 2012 in the U.S. alone, nearly 18 million and 7 million households were classified as food-insecure or even very food-insecure, respectively [87]. According to the authors, these figures had been relatively stable since the marked increase in 2008 following the global economic crisis of that year [87]. Economic constraints were frequently identified as a main driver encouraging consumption of an energy-dense, micronutrient-poor diet [88].

11.13   Micronutrient Deficiency and Non-communicable Diseases

It is widely accepted that inadequate nutrition during early life increases the risk of developing non-communicable diseases [89]. However, inadequate nutrition affects health at all stages of the life-course, and needs to be addressed accordingly [90]. Prolonged illness frequently dominates the final decade of life [91], which has a detrimental effect on the quality of life [92] and places a heavy burden on the economy due to its chronic nature [93]. This becomes even more important in light of the increasing prevalence of non-communicable diseases in low- and middle-income countries whose health budgets are even more limited than those of more affluent countries [93]. In times of increased financial austerity, the cost of health care is increasingly transferred from the state to the individual [94], further reducing the household budget available for food.

Consequently, affordable diets rich in essential nutrients, whether due to their natural composition or to fortification, have the potential to improve health and quality of life, and to help alleviate some of the pressure on the ever-increasing cost of health care. However, this will only improve nutrition if the general population understands the importance of eating such a diet, and adherence to dietary guidelines is notoriously poor [95]. If individuals were aware of their nutritional status in general or in respect of specific nutrients, they might see the relevance of adjusting their diets: A recent study found that giving people dietary guidance based on information about their genetic profile led to an improvement in nutritional habits [96]. For this to work, reliable, minimally invasive, cheap and quick methods to measure the nutrients level are needed. One example of such a method is the measurement of 25-hydroxyvitamin D levels via dried blood spots: For this, two drops of blood obtained by a finger prick are collected on a special card, dried and sent to a laboratory for analysis. The method has been validated according to the guidelines of the US FDA guidance for Industry and the EMA guidance on bioanalytical method validation. This method was used at a charity event in Heerlen, the Netherlands, and showed that of the people volunteering to participate, 8 and 29% had deficient (<30 nmol/L) or inadequate (31–50 nmol/L) vitamin D levels, respectively (unpublished data).

Another option is that the status of specific nutrients should be routinely assessed by general practitioners, pediatricians and gynecologists, as is the case for hemoglobin for women of reproductive age in some countries. Voluntary testing could also be offered by companies for their employees: Such an initiative, as an example, showed prevalence of inadequate (25–49 nMol/L) and even deficient (<24 nMol/L) levels of 25-hydroxyvitamin D in just below 50 and 21%, respectively. In addition, less than 6% had an omega-3 index in the desirable range (>8%), while 72 and 12% had intermediate (4–8%) or even undesirable (<4%) levels, respectively. The omega-3 index is a measure of docosahexaenoic and eicosapentaenoic acid as percentage of total fatty acids in the membranes of red blood cells and gives an indication of long-term intakes of these [97]. Widespread availability of such services could improve people's understanding of their own nutritional status and thereby empower them to improve their diet and simultaneously their long-term health.

11.14   Summary: Key Messages

- In affluent countries, micronutrient inadequacies are widespread, and intakes of vitamins E, D and A and folate are particularly critical.
- Vulnerable periods along the life-course, such as pregnancy, infancy or old age, require special attention.
- Obesity, inadequate micronutrient intake and food insecurity are interrelated, and often co-exist.
- Poor diet throughout the life-course is a risk factor for the development of non-communicable diseases.

- Given the difficulties of achieving adequate intakes through diet alone, fortification or supplementation should be considered for specific nutrients for the whole population or groups at increased risk.
- Improving nutrition could help alleviate the social and financial burden of such diseases.
- Better knowledge concerning their nutritional status might encourage people to improve their diet and consequently their long-term health.

References

1. Black, R.E., et al., *Maternal and child undernutrition and overweight in low-income and middle-income countries.* The Lancet, 2013.
2. World Health Organization, *Global prevalence of vitamin A deficiency in populations at risk 1995–2005,* in *WHO Global Database on Vitamin A Deficiency.* 2009: Geneva.
3. Wallace, T.C., M. McBurney, and V.L. Fulgoni, *Multivitamin/Mineral Supplement Contribution to Micronutrient Intakes in the United States, 2007–2010.* Journal of the American College of Nutrition, 2014. **33**(2): p. 94–102.
4. Hilger, J., et al., *A systematic review of vitamin D status in populations worldwide.* British Journal of Nutrition, 2014. **111**(01): p. 23–45.
5. Wahl, D.A., et al., *A global representation of vitamin D status in healthy populations.* Archives of Osteoporosis, 2012. **7**: p. 155–72.
6. Elmadfa, I., et al., *European nutrition and health report 2009.* 2010/02/06 ed. Forum of Nutrition, ed. I. Elmadfa. Vol. 62. 2009, Basel: Karger.
7. Roman Vinas, B., et al., *Projected prevalence of inadequate nutrient intakes in Europe.* Ann Nutr Metab, 2011. **59**(2–4): p. 84-95.
8. Cashman, K.D., et al., *Vitamin D deficiency in Europe: pandemic?* The American Journal of Clinical Nutrition, 2016. **103**(4): p. 1033–1044.
9. Schöttker, B., et al., *Vitamin D and mortality: meta-analysis of individual participant data from a large consortium of cohort studies from Europe and the United States.* British Medical Journal, 2014. **348**: p. g3656.
10. Grant, W.B., *An estimate of the global reduction in mortality rates through doubling vitamin D levels.* European Journal of Clinical Nutrition, 2011. **65**(9): p. 1016–1026.
11. Sahota, O., *Osteoporosis and the role of vitamin D and calcium-vitamin D deficiency, vitamin D insufficiency and vitamin D sufficiency.* Age Ageing, 2000. **29**(4): p. 301–4.
12. Bischoff-Ferrari, H., *Vitamin D: What is an adequate vitamin D level and how much supplementation is necessary?* Best Practice & Research Clinical Rheumatology, 2009. **23**(6): p. 789–795.
13. Bischoff-Ferrari and Staehelin, *Importance of Vitamin D and Calcium at Older Age.* International Journal for Vitamin and Nutrition Research, 2008. **78**(6): p. 286–292.
14. Maresz, K., *Proper Calcium Use: Vitamin K(2) as a Promoter of Bone and Cardiovascular Health.* Integrative Medicine: A Clinician's Journal, 2015. **14**(1): p. 34–39.
15. Ahmadieh, H. and A. Arabi, *Vitamins and bone health: beyond calcium and vitamin D.* Nutrition Reviews, 2011. **69**(10): p. 584–598.
16. Deutsche Gesellschaft für Ernährung, et al., *Referenzwerte für die Nährstoffzufuhr.* 2008, Frankfurt/ Main: Umschau Verlag.
17. Deutsche Gesellschaft für Ernährung e. V., *12. Ernährungsbericht 2012.* 2012, Bonn: Deutsche Gesellschaft für Ernährung e. V.
18. Institute of Medicine, *Dietary reference intakes of vitamin C, vitamin E, selenium, and carotenoids.* 2000, Washington, DC: National Academic Press.

19. Ministry of Health Labour and Welfare (Japan), *The Japan National Health and Nutrition Survey 2008*. 2008.
20. Kim, J. and Y.-H. Choi, *Physical activity, dietary vitamin C, and metabolic syndrome in the Korean adults: the Korea National Health and Nutrition Examination Survey 2008 to 2012*. Public Health, 2016.
21. Troesch, B., et al., *Dietary surveys indicate vitamin intakes below recommendations are common in representative Western countries*. British Journal of Nutrition, 2012. **108**(4): p. 692–698.
22. Péter, S., et al., *A systematic review of global alpha-tocopherol status as assessed by nutritional intake levels and blood serum concentrations*. International Journal for Vitamin and Nutrition Research, 2016. **14**: p. 1–21.
23. Péter, S., et al., *The Challenge of Setting Appropriate Intake Recommendations for Vitamin E: Considerations on Status and Functionality to Define Nutrient Requirements*. International Journal for Vitamin and Nutrition Research, 2013. **83**(2): p. 129–136.
24. Food and Nutrition Board and Institute of Medicine, *Dietary reference intakes of vitamin A, vitamin K, arsenic, boron, chromium, copper, iodine, iron, manganese, molybdenum, nickel, silicon, vanadium, and zinc*. 2001, Washington, DC: National Academic Press.
25. Institute of Medicine, *Dietary reference intakes of vitamin A, vitamin K, arsenic, boron, chromium, copper, iodine, iron, manganese, molybdenum, nickel, silicon, vanadium, and zinc*. 2001, Washington, DC: National Academic Press.
26. Max Rubner-Institut, *Nationale Verzehrsstudie II. Ergebnisbericht Teil 2. Die bundesweite Befragung zur Ernährung von Jugendlichen und Erwachsenen*. 2008 (http://www.was-esse-ich.de/uploads/media/NVSII_Abschlussbericht_Teil_2.pdf) (Accessed 02.07.2011): Karlsruhe.
27. Lietz, G., et al., *Single Nucleotide Polymorphisms Upstream from the β-Carotene 15,15'-Monoxygenase Gene Influence Provitamin A Conversion Efficiency in Female Volunteers*. The Journal of Nutrition, 2012. **142**: p. 161S-165S.
28. Grune, T., et al., *Beta-carotene is an important vitamin A source for humans*. J Nutr, 2010. **140**(12): p. 2268S–2285S.
29. Wu, B.T., et al., *Low plasma vitamin B-12 is associated with a lower pregnancy-associated rise in plasma free choline in Canadian pregnant women and lower postnatal growth rates in their male infants*. The American Journal of Clinical Nutrition, 2013. **98**(5): p. 1209–1217.
30. Sukumar, N., et al., *Prevalence of vitamin B-12 insufficiency during pregnancy and its effect on offspring birth weight: a systematic review and meta-analysis*. The American Journal of Clinical Nutrition, 2016.
31. Gose, M., et al., *Trends in food consumption and nutrient intake in Germany between 2006 and 2012: results of the German National Nutrition Monitoring (NEMONIT)*. British Journal of Nutrition, 2016. **115**(Supplement 08): p. 1498–1507.
32. Blumfield, M.L., et al., *Micronutrient intakes during pregnancy in developed countries: Systematic Review and Meta-Analysis*. Nutrition Reviews, 2013. **71**(2): p. 118–132.
33. EUROCAT, *Special Report: Prevention of Neural Tube Defects by Periconceptual Folic Acid Supplementation in Europe—December 2009*. 2009 (http://www.eurocat-network.eu/pagecontent.aspx?pageid=115) (Accessed 04.07.2011), EUROCAT Central Registry, University of Ulster.
34. Daly, L.E., et al., *Folate levels and neural tube defects: Implications for prevention*. JAMA, 1995. **274**(21): p. 1698–1702.
35. De-Regil, L.M., et al., *Effects and safety of periconceptional folate supplementation for preventing birth defects*. The Cochrane database of systematic reviews, 2010(10): p. CD007950-CD007950.
36. Holzgreve, W., et al., *Adding folate to the contraceptive pill: a new concept for the prevention of neural tube defects*. The Journal of Maternal-Fetal & Neonatal Medicine, 2012. **25**(9): p. 1529–1536.

37. Ars, C.L., et al., *Prenatal folate, homocysteine and vitamin B12 levels and child brain volumes, cognitive development and psychological functioning: the Generation R Study.* British Journal of Nutrition, 2016. **FirstView**: p. 1–9.
38. Dominguez-Salas, P., et al., *Maternal nutrition at conception modulates DNA methylation of human metastable epialleles.* Nature Communications, 2014. **5**: p. 3746.
39. Lillycrop, K.A. and G.C. Burdge, *Epigenetic mechanisms linking early nutrition to long term health.* Best Practice & Research Clinical Endocrinology & Metabolism, 2012. **26**(5): p. 667–676.
40. Khulan, B., et al., *Periconceptional maternal micronutrient supplementation is associated with widespread gender related changes in the epigenome: a study of a unique resource in the Gambia.* Human Molecular Genetics, 2012. **21**(9): p. 2086–2101.
41. McGarel, C., et al., *Emerging roles for folate and related B-vitamins in brain health across the lifecycle.* Proceedings of the Nutrition Society, 2015. **74**(01): p. 46–55.
42. Mei, Z., et al., *Assessment of iron status in US pregnant women from the National Health and Nutrition Examination Survey (NHANES), 1999–2006.* The American Journal of Clinical Nutrition, 2011. **93**(6): p. 1312–1320.
43. Holmes, V.A., et al., *Vitamin D deficiency and insufficiency in pregnant women: a longitudinal study.* British Journal of Nutrition, 2009. **102**(06): p. 876–881.
44. Gernand, A.D., et al., *Micronutrient deficiencies in pregnancy worldwide: health effects and prevention.* Nat Rev Endocrinol, 2016. **advance online publication**.
45. Hart, P.H., et al., *Vitamin D in Fetal Development: Findings From a Birth Cohort Study.* Pediatrics, 2015. **135**(1): p. e167–e173.
46. Brough, L., et al., *Effect of multiple-micronutrient supplementation on maternal nutrient status, infant birth weight and gestational age at birth in a low-income, multi-ethnic population.* British Journal of Nutrition, 2010. **104**(03): p. 437–445.
47. Institute of Medicine, *Dietary reference intakes for calcium and vitamin D.* DRI—Dietary Reference Intakes, ed. A.C. Ross, et al. 2011, Washington: The National Academies Press.
48. Deutsche Gesellschaft für Ernährung. *Referenzwerte für die Nährstoffzufuhr- Vitamin D (Calciferole).* 2012 17. Jan. 2012 17. Jan. 2012]; Available from: http://www.dge.de/modules. php?name=Content&pa=showpage&pid=4&page=12.
49. Bischoff-Ferrari, H.A., *Vitamin D – Role in Pregnancy and Early Childhood.* Annals of Nutrition and Metabolism, 2011. **59**(1): p. 17–21.
50. Camargo, C.A., Jr., et al., *Cord-blood 25-hydroxyvitamin D levels and risk of respiratory infection, wheezing, and asthma.* Pediatrics, 2011. **127**(1): p. e180–7.
51. Nandal, R., et al., *Comparison of cord blood vitamin D levels in newborns of vitamin D supplemented and unsupplemented pregnant women: a prospective, comparative study.* The Journal of Maternal-Fetal & Neonatal Medicine, 2016. **29**(11): p. 1812–1816.
52. Kovacs, C.S., *Vitamin D in pregnancy and lactation: maternal, fetal, and neonatal outcomes from human and animal studies.* The American Journal of Clinical Nutrition, 2008. **88**(2): p. 520S–528S.
53. Valentine, C.J. and C.L. Wagner, *Nutritional Management of the Breastfeeding Dyad.* Pediatric Clinics of North America, 2013. **60**(1): p. 261–274.
54. Deutsche Gesellschaft für Ernährung e. V., *Verzehrsstudie zur Ermittlung der Lebensmittelaufnahme von Säuglingen und Kleinkindern (VELS), in Ernährungsbericht 2008.* 2008, Deutsche Gesellschaft für Ernährung e. V.: Bonn. p. 53–60.
55. Streym, S.v., et al., *Vitamin D content in human breast milk: a 9-mo follow-up study.* 2016, American Society for Clinical Nutrition, Inc. p. 107.
56. Thiele, D.K., J.L. Senti, and C.M. Anderson, *Maternal Vitamin D Supplementation to Meet the Needs of the Breastfed Infant: A Systematic Review.* Journal of Human Lactation, 2013. **29**(2): p. 163–170.
57. Blomquist, H.K., et al., *Dietary intake of vitamin D during the second half of infancy in Swedish infants.* Scandinavian Journal of Nutrition, 2004. **48**(4): p. 173–177.
58. Ziegler, E.E., S.E. Nelson, and J.M. Jeter, *Vitamin D supplementation of breastfed infants: a randomized dose-response trial.* Pediatr Res, 2014. **76**(2): p. 177–83.

59. Perrine, C.G., et al., *Adherence to vitamin D recommendations among US infants*. Pediatrics, 2010. **125**(4): p. 627–32.
60. Hilger, J., et al., *Micronutrient Intake in Healthy Toddlers: A Multinational Perspective*. Nutrients, 2015. **7**(8): p. 6938–6955.
61. Devaney, B., et al., *Nutrient intakes of infants and toddlers*. J Am Diet Assoc, 2004. **104**(1 Suppl 1): p. s14–21.
62. Decarli, B., C. Cavadini, and P.A. Michaud, *Habitudes alimentaires et ingestats de nutriments d'un groupe d'adolescents vaudois de 9 à 19 ans*, in *Fünfter Schweizer Ernährungsbericht*, M. Eichholzer, et al., Editors. 2005, Bundesamt für Gesundheit: Bern. p. 133–150.
63. Bailey, R.L., et al., *Do Dietary Supplements Improve Micronutrient Sufficiency in Children and Adolescents?* The Journal of Pediatrics, 2012. **161**(5): p. 837–842.e3.
64. Micha, R., et al., *Global, regional, and national consumption levels of dietary fats and oils in 1990 and 2010: a systematic analysis including 266 country-specific nutrition surveys*. BMJ, 2014. **348**.
65. Papanikolaou, Y., et al., *U.S. adults are not meeting recommended levels for fish and omega-3 fatty acid intake: results of an analysis using observational data from NHANES 2003–2008*. Nutrition Journal, 2014. **13**(1): p. 31.
66. Aranceta, J. and C. Pérez-Rodrigo, *Recommended dietary reference intakes, nutritional goals and dietary guidelines for fat and fatty acids: a systematic review*. British Journal of Nutrition, 2012. **107**(SupplementS2): p. S8-S22.
67. Elia, M., et al., *The cost of disease-related malnutrition in the UK and economic considerations for the use of oral nutritional supplements (ONS) in adults*, M. Elia, Editor. 2006, British Association for Parenteral and Enteral Nutrition: Redditch, UK.
68. Marriott, B.P., et al., *Intake of Added Sugars and Selected Nutrients in the United States, National Health and Nutrition Examination Survey (NHANES) 2003—2006*. Critical Reviews in Food Science and Nutrition, 2010. **50**(3): p. 228–258.
69. ter Borg, S., et al., *Micronutrient intakes and potential inadequacies of community-dwelling older adults: a systematic review*. British Journal of Nutrition, 2015. **113**(08): p. 1195–1206.
70. Deutsche Gesellschaft für Ernährung e. V., *Ernährung älterer Menschen in stationären Einrichtungen (ErnSTES-Studies)*, in *Ernährungsbericht 2008*. 2008, Deutsche Gesellschaft für Ernährung e. V.: Bonn. p. 157–204.
71. Lengyel, C.O., S.J. Whiting, and G.A. Zello, *Nutrient inadequacies among elderly residents of long-term care facilities*. Can J Diet Pract Res, 2008. **69**(2): p. 82–8.
72. Sebastian, R.S., et al., *Older adults who use vitamin/mineral supplements differ from nonusers in nutrient intake adequacy and dietary attitudes*. Journal of the American Dietetic Association, 2007. **107**(8): p. 1322–32.
73. Fabian, E., et al., *Vitamin status in elderly people in relation to the use of nutritional supplements*. The Journal of Nutrition, Health & Aging, 2012. **16**: p. 206–212.
74. Freisling, H., et al., *Region-specific nutrient intake patterns exhibit a geographical gradient within and between European countries*. J Nutr, 2010. **140**(7): p. 1280–6.
75. Black, L.J., et al., *An Updated Systematic Review and Meta-Analysis of the Efficacy of Vitamin D Food Fortification*. The Journal of Nutrition, 2012. **142**(6): p. 1102–1108.
76. Hennessy, Á., et al., *The role of fortified foods and nutritional supplements in increasing vitamin D intake in Irish preschool children*. European Journal of Nutrition, 2016: p. 1–13.
77. Piirainen, T., K. Laitinen, and E. Isolauri, *Impact of national fortification of fluid milks and margarines with vitamin D on dietary intake and serum 25-hydroxyvitamin D concentration in 4-year-old children*. Eur J Clin Nutr, 2007. **61**(1): p. 123–128.
78. Soininen, S., et al., *Determinants of serum 25-hydroxyvitamin D concentration in Finnish children: the Physical Activity and Nutrition in Children (PANIC) study*. British Journal of Nutrition, 2016. **115**(06): p. 1080–1091.
79. Snook Parrott, M., et al., *Maternal cereal consumption and adequacy of micronutrient intake in the periconceptional period*. Public Health Nutrition, 2009. **12**(08): p. 1276–1283.

80. Cepeda-Lopez, A.C., I. Aeberli, and M.B. Zimmermann, *Does obesity increase risk for iron deficiency? A review of the literature and the potential mechanisms.* International Journal for Vitamin and Nutrition Research, 2010. **80**(4–5): p. 263–70.
81. Samuel, L. and L.N. Borrell, *The effect of body mass index on optimal vitamin D status in U.S. adults: the National Health and Nutrition Examination Survey 2001–2006.* Ann Epidemiol, 2013. **23**(7): p. 409–14.
82. Wortsman, J., et al., *Decreased bioavailability of vitamin D in obesity.* The American Journal of Clinical Nutrition, 2000. **72**(3): p. 690–693.
83. World Health Organization. *Fact sheet N° 311: Obesity and overweight.* 2014 March 2014 May 02, 2014]; Available from: http://www.who.int/mediacentre/factsheets/fs311/en/.
84. Ganji, V., X. Zhang, and V. Tangpricha, *Serum 25-Hydroxyvitamin D Concentrations and Prevalence Estimates of Hypovitaminosis D in the U.S. Population Based on Assay-Adjusted Data.* The Journal of Nutrition, 2012. **142**(3): p. 498–507.
85. Prentice, A.M. and S.A. Jebb, *Fast foods, energy density and obesity: a possible mechanistic link.* Obesity Reviews, 2003. **4**(4): p. 187–194.
86. Martin-Fernandez, J., et al., *Food insecurity, a determinant of obesity?—An analysis from a population-based survey in the paris metropolitan area, 2010.* Obesity Facts, 2014. **7**(2): p. 120–129.
87. Coleman-Jensen, A., M. Nord, and A. Singh, *Household Food Security in the United States in 2012.* 2013, U.S. Department of Agriculture, Economic Research Service.
88. Drewnowski, A. and N. Darmon, *The economics of obesity: dietary energy density and energy cost.* Am J Clin Nutr, 2005. **82**(1 Suppl): p. 265S–273S.
89. Plagemann, A., et al., *Early postnatal life as a critical time window for determination of long-term metabolic health.* Best Practice & Research Clinical Endocrinology & Metabolism, 2012. **26**(5): p. 641–653.
90. World Health Organization, *WHO global status report on noncommunicable diseases 2010*, W. Press, Editor. 2010: Geneva, Switzerland.
91. Lunenfeld, B., *An aging world – demographics and challenges.* Gynecological Endocrinology, 2008. **24**(1): p. 1–3.
92. Beaglehole, R., et al., *Priority actions for the non-communicable disease crisis.* The Lancet, 2011. **377**(9775): p. 1438–1447.
93. Adeyi, O., O. Smith, and S. Robles, *Public policy and the challenge of chronic noncommunicable diseases,* ed. W. Bank. 2007, Washington, DC.
94. Burke, S., et al., *Indicators of health system coverage and activity in Ireland during the economic crisis 2008–2014—From 'more with less' to 'less with less'.* Health Policy, 2014 epub(0).
95. Krebs-Smith, S.M., et al., *Americans Do Not Meet Federal Dietary Recommendations.* The Journal of Nutrition, 2010. **140**(10): p. 1832–1838.
96. Nielsen, D.E. and A. El-Sohemy, *Disclosure of Genetic Information and Change in Dietary Intake: A Randomized Controlled Trial.* PLoS ONE, 2014. **9**(11): p. e112665.
97. Harris, W.S. and C. von Schacky, *The Omega-3 Index: a new risk factor for death from coronary heart disease?* Preventive Medicine, 2004. **39**(1): p. 212–220.

Chapter 12
The B-Vitamins

**JJ Strain, Catherine Hughes, Kristina Pentieva, Mary Ward,
Leane Hoey and Helene McNulty**

Abstract It is likely that future scenarios will see trends toward a reduced consumption of animal-based foods and increased consumption of fruit and vegetables. This chapter reviews the metabolic roles, essentiality, deficiency symptoms and food sources of each of the B-vitamins and identifies how trends towards improving environmental sustainability could impact on B-vitamin status.

Keywords Thiamine (vitamin B_1) $\cdot$ Riboflavin (vitamin B_2) $\cdot$ Niacin $\cdot$ Vitamin B_6 $\cdot$ Folate $\cdot$ Folic acid $\cdot$ Vitamin B_{12} $\cdot$ Choline $\cdot$ Biotin $\cdot$ Pantothenic acid $\cdot$ Metabolic roles $\cdot$ Essentiality $\cdot$ Deficiency symptoms $\cdot$ Food sources $\cdot$ Environmental sustainability

12.1 Introduction

There is increasing interest in nutrition and sustainability and how food policy and dietary guidelines might be modified to take into account issues related to environmental sustainability [36, 45, 47] as well as promoting healthy eating to prevent chronic disease. There is much debate on what constitutes a healthy diet, and many different dietary approaches could be taken to decrease environmental impact and improve sustainability. One approach is to concentrate on reducing consumption of animal-based foods and increasing the consumption of fruit and vegetables [77]. This approach is supported by the environmental impact literature indicating the sustainability of plant-based diets [81] and the need to increase the efficiency of land-based production of animal protein [103] and to control fish supplies [30]. Improvements in environmental sustainability by increased uptake of the Mediterranean Diet have also received attention [33]. Although there will be problems with meeting dietary guidelines attuned to a more sustainable agenda and there is continuing debate as to

JJ Strain (✉) · C. Hughes · K. Pentieva · M. Ward · L. Hoey · H. McNulty
Northern Ireland Centre for Food and Health (NICHE), Biomedical Sciences Research
Institute, University of Ulster, Coleraine BT52 1SA, Northern Ireland, UK
e-mail: jj.strain@ulster.ac.uk

© Springer International Publishing AG 2017   185
H.K. Biesalski et al. (eds.), *Sustainable Nutrition in a Changing World*,
DOI 10.1007/978-3-319-55942-1_12

the optimum approach, it is likely that future scenarios will see trends towards a reduced consumption of animal-based foods and increased consumption of fruit and vegetables. This chapter will review the metabolic roles, essentiality, deficiency symptoms and food sources of each of the B vitamins, and will identify how trends towards improving environmental sustainability could impact on B-vitamin status.

12.2   Thiamin

Vitamin B_1 or thiamin, was the first of the B-vitamins to be identified, and occurs in the body as free thiamin or in one of its phosphorylated forms thiamin monophosphate (TMP), thiamin triphosphate (TTP) or thiamin pyrophosphate (TPP), also known as thiamin diphosphate (TDP) [7]. The majority—approximately 80% of ingested thiamin—occurs in humans as TDP, which plays a central role in the energy production from food. TDP acts as a co-enzyme for three key oxidative decarboxylation reactions: pyruvate dehydrogenase in carbohydrate metabolism, α-keto glutarate dehydrogenase in the citric acid cycle and α–keto-acid dehydrogenase in the metabolism of the branched-chain amino acids leucine, isoleucine and valine. Each dehydrogenase complex also requires a niacin and riboflavin containing co-enzyme. TDP is also required by the enzyme transketolase in the pentose phosphate pathway, an important alternative pathway of carbohydrate metabolism which generates the building blocks of nucleic acids, DNA and RNA and the niacin containing co-enzyme NADPH, essential for fatty acid synthesis [13]. Severe thiamin deficiency, rarely seen in developed countries, results in a disease called beriberi. Beriberi can occur as either dry or wet, with dry beriberi manifesting as neuropathy and muscle wasting while wet beriberi is characterized by congestive cardiac failure and edema in the lower limbs. It is of most concern in infancy due to the rapid growth and development that occurs in the early stages of the lifecycle. Wernicke-Korsakoff syndrome, which also occurs as a result of thiamin deficiency, is much more commonly reported in developed countries. The condition, which presents initially as a confused state, mainly affects chronic alcoholics but can also occur in those with gastrointestinal disorders, and if left untreated can lead to irreversible neurological damage and psychosis [53]. Supplemental thiamin is an effective treatment in most cases, if commenced in time.

Thiamin requirements are strongly associated with carbohydrate intake, given the role of the B-vitamin in carbohydrate metabolism. Requirements range from 1.0 to 1.4 mg/day and can usually be met by consuming a mixed or varied diet. Colonic microflora also produce thiamin, and while their contribution towards human thiamin requirements is currently not clear [51] it is undoubtedly an area of future interest in terms of sustainability. Rich sources of thiamin include wholegrain cereals, bread, lentils, beans, nuts, yeast and pork. Significant losses of thiamin occur during the milling process and during the processing of white rice, which has led to thiamin enrichment or fortification policies in many western countries [91];

such strategies are, however, not common in Asian countries. Heating foods can also reduce their thiamin content to some extent, and an enzyme known as thiaminase, present in raw fish, shellfish, tea and coffee, decreases thiamin absorption. Inadequate intakes of the vitamin have been observed in institutionalized older adults [102], in those with an alcohol dependency, and in countries where dietary sources of carbohydrate are high and thiamin intakes are low e.g. Southeast Asian countries such as Cambodia, where reported intakes are as low as 0.58 mg/day [100]. In terms of sustaining thiamin intake, fortification offers an effective model, However, strategies will need to be tailored to different populations on the basis of the relevant staple foods consumed [91].

12.3   Riboflavin

Riboflavin, also known as vitamin B_2, is a water-soluble vitamin and is the precursor of the coenzymes flavin mononucleotide (FMN) and flavin adenine dinucleotide (FAD), collectively known as flavin coenzymes. FAD and FMN participate in intermediary metabolism catalyzing numerous oxidation-reduction reactions involved in the metabolism of protein, fat and carbohydrates [55]. Flavin coenzymes are also required for the metabolism of iron and a number of B-vitamins—namely B_6, folate and niacin. FMN acts as a cofactor for the enzyme pyridoxine phosphate oxidase in the conversion of pyridoxine phosphate to its coenzyme form pyridoxal-5 phosphate (PLP) in vitamin B_6 metabolism. FAD meanwhile acts as a cofactor for the enzyme methylenetetrahydrofolate reductase (MTHFR) in the production of 5-methyltetrahydrofolate, essential for the remethylation of homocysteine to methionine [52]. Niacin synthesis is also reliant on the FAD-dependent enzyme kynurenine mono-oxygenase, which is required for the synthesis of the coenzymes nicotinamide adenine dinucleotide (NAD) and nicotinamide adenine dinucleotide phosphate (NADP) from tryptophan. Riboflavin deficiency decreases the conversion of tryptophan to NAD and NADP, resulting in a deficiency of niacin. In relation to iron metabolism, evidence from animal studies suggests that riboflavin deficiency can impair iron absorption and utilization for the synthesis of hemoglobin [74].

Clinical riboflavin deficiency (typically presenting as angular stomatitis, cheilosis and glossitis) is common in developing populations [4, 11] but rarely reported in Western societies, as intakes in the West are generally higher than dietary recommendations. What is less well recognized, however, is the emerging evidence indicating that sub-optimal riboflavin status may be much more wide spread in both developed and developing counties than previously considered [52]. The majority of population-based studies report dietary intake data, with only a limited number reporting biomarker riboflavin status. It appears, however, that despite apparently adequate riboflavin intakes, suboptimal status—as determined by the functional marker erythrocyte glutathione reductase activation coefficient

(EGRac)—may be quite common in many populations. Younger women, including pregnant and lactating women, and those who do not consume meat or dairy, appear to be most vulnerable. The significance of these findings is not clear; however, it is possible that marginal riboflavin status in the absence of clinical deficiency may have adverse functional effects and long-term consequences for health. Sub-optimal riboflavin status has been associated with preeclampsia in pregnant women [96]. More recently, a polymorphism in the riboflavin-dependent enzyme MTHFR, prevalent in 10% of adults worldwide but occurring in up to 30% of some populations, has been associated with hypertension [104, 105]. Furthermore, intervention with riboflavin has been shown to significantly decrease blood pressure in these genetically at-risk adults [41] and thus maintaining an adequate riboflavin status in these individuals could potentially delay the onset of hypertension [60].

Worldwide dietary recommendations for riboflavin range from 1.1 to 1.6 mg/day, with clinical deficiency signs appearing at intakes of between 0.5 and 0.6 mg/day [26]. The majority of riboflavin in food occurs in the form of FAD, with lesser amounts as FMN and free riboflavin. It is estimated that about 95% of riboflavin in the form of FAD or FMN is bioavailable, with absorption limited to approximately 30 mg of riboflavin at any one time [54]. The main dietary sources of riboflavin are milk and dairy products, while meat and fortified foods such as breakfast cereals also contribute significantly [29]. Yeast extracts are also a good source of riboflavin but are not consumed in large enough quantities to make a significant contribution to intake. Riboflavin intakes are thus likely to be low in populations consuming diets low in dairy and meat and could be limited in those consuming a vegetarian diet. In terms of maintaining a sustainable source of riboflavin, food fortification is likely to offer the most promising solution, although consideration would need to be given to the level of fortification introduced [1]. Riboflavin enrichment policies are currently in place in the US and Canada, to replace the riboflavin lost during milling in those countries; however, despite this practice, suboptimal status has been reported in certain subgroups [99].

12.4 Niacin

Niacin is a generic term for nicotinic acid and nicotinamide, which are substrates for the synthesis of the coenzymes nicotinamide adenine dinucleotide (NAD) and its phosphorylated derivative nicotinamide adenine dinucleotide phosphate (NADP). Both NAD and NADP are involved in oxidation and reduction reactions, which explains the crucial importance of niacin for energy metabolism. In addition, NAD also has non-redox functions and it is a key factor for various ADP-ribose transfer reactions which maintain genomic stability, DNA repair, gene expression, apoptosis, cellular signaling and insulin sensitivity [8, 46]. Deficiency of niacin results in pellagra, the clinical features of which include photosensitive dermatitis with skin lesions, inflammation of gastrointestinal mucosa with diarrhea, depression and dementia. Diarrhea further worsens niacin status and worsens the condition by affecting also the absorption and status of other nutrients. Untreated pellagra can lead to death from multi-organ failure [95]. In the past, when the cause of pellagra was still unknown, the spread of the disease in Europe and the US led to epidemics, especially among poor communities with limited food availability where maize or millet were the dietary staples. In order to combat the widespread niacin deficiency, mandatory niacin flour fortification programs have been introduced in many countries of the world since the 1940s. Recent epidemiological surveys from developed countries have shown that the average intake of niacin is much above the dietary requirements [6, 69, 85], which explains the fact that pellagra is virtually unknown there and is only occasionally found in malnourished alcoholic patients. However, outbreaks of pellagra still occur nowadays in people with restricted normal movements and activities, e.g. in refugee camps or jails, where food intake may be limited [61].

Meat, poultry and fish have high content of niacin. In addition, animal foods are also important as they are rich in the amino acid tryptophan, which can be used for synthesis of niacin in the body. However, some plant foods such as nuts, legumes and cereals are also a very good source of preformed niacin as well as tryptophan. Significant contributors to dietary intake of niacin are fortified flour and breakfast cereals; however, niacin food fortification is not in place in some countries. The bioavailability of niacin from foods is generally high but in some cereals, notably maize, niacin is in esterified forms (niacytin) which are unavailable for absorption after conventional cooking [16]. However, the bioavailability of niacin from its bound forms can be considerably improved by pre-treatment of the food with alkaline solutions (lime water) before cooking. Analysis of the composition of so called 'pellagragenic' diets (containing mainly cereals) by applying an alkaline pre-treatment has found that their niacin content was well in excess of the dietary requirements for intake [15]. This finding suggests that environmentally sustained diets based on foods predominantly from plant origin have the potential to provide sufficient amounts of niacin for maintaining an adequate status.

12.5   Vitamin B$_6$

The term vitamin B$_6$ refers to a group of several water-soluble compounds with the biological activity of pyridoxine which are converted to each other in the body. The metabolically active vitamin B$_6$ derivatives, pyridoxal phosphate and pyridoxamine phosphate, act as cofactors for more than 100 enzymes involved predominantly in the metabolism of amino acids but also in one-carbon metabolism, glycogenolysis and gluconeogenesis, regulation of the function of the nervous system through synthesis of neurotransmitters, immune function, formation of niacin from trypto-phan, hemoglobin synthesis, and modulation of steroid hormone activity. Severe deficiency of vitamin B$_6$ is uncommon. In the early 1950s, seizures were observed in infants who consumed low vitamin B$_6$-containing milk formula as a result of an error in the manufacturing process [12]. Abnormal electroencephalogram patterns have also been reported in some studies of experimental vitamin B_6 deficiency [49]. Other symptoms associated with severe vitamin B_6 deficiency include hyperirritability, depression, and confusion, hypochromic microcytic anemia, seborrheic dermatitis, cheilosis, glossitis and stomatitis [82]. Nationally representative surveys have shown that the mean intakes of vitamin B_6 of the adult population are between 1.5 and 4.9 mg/day [34, 66, 97], which are well above the intake recommendations set up in various countries. Despite the fact that in general the average dietary intake of vitamin B_6 is high, cross-sectional studies have reported that 16–24% of older adults have poor biochemical vitamin B_6 status [5, 66, 93]. These findings suggest that older adults might have increased requirements for vitamin B_6 intake.

Vitamin B_6 can be found in a variety of animal and plant foods. Particularly rich sources of vitamin B_6 are meat, poultry, fish, legumes and cereals. In contrast to other B vitamins, the absorption of vitamin B_6 in the intestine is through unsaturable passive diffusion. Compared to the bioavailability of the synthetic form of the vitamin, pyridoxine hydrochloride (assumed to be almost 100%), the average bioavailability of vitamin B_6 from a mixed diet was found to be around 75% [88]. However, a considerable proportion of vitamin B_6 in some plant foods (grains, legumes, potatoes, vegetables, oranges) is in the form of pyridoxine glucosides (PNG), which has been reported to have incomplete bioavailability [48]. Studies using stable isotopes in young adults reported that the bioavailability of PNG was around 50% of that of the synthetic vitamin [31, 67]. These results were also in agreement with the findings of a strictly controlled metabolic study which showed that vitamin B_6 status biomarkers were significantly lower in women maintained for 18 days on a diet containing 27% PNG compared with those in women receiving the same amount of vitamin B_6 but through a diet containing only 9% PNG [32]. Therefore, a more sustainable diet which would be based primarily on plant foods would be expected to affect vitamin B_6 status unfavorably, especially in some vulnerable groups of the population (e.g. older adults). However, this problem could be avoided by a proper selection and combination of a variety of plant food choices from different food groups, which would provide sufficient amounts of available vitamin B_6. In support of this view are the results from a cross-sectional study which showed that there was no significant difference in the vitamin B_6 status of vegans, vegetarians and the omnivorous who have followed their diets for more than a year [61].

12.6 Folate

12.6.1 Folate and Folic Acid

Elsewhere, Chap. 29 has considered the role of fortified foods in providing a sustainable source of this important B-vitamin and contributing to optimal nutritional status and better health outcomes for populations worldwide.

The terms folic acid and folate are often used interchangeably by scientists, health professionals and others to describe this B-vitamin. There are, however, important differences. Folic acid refers to the synthetic form of the B-vitamin known as folate as found in fortified foods and supplements, whereas 'folates' are the natural vitamin forms found in plant and animal and human tissues. There are structural differences between the two forms which have important consequences for the bioavailability of folates in the human diet. Folic acid is inherently more stable and bioavailable compared with an equivalent amount of the vitamin eaten as naturally occurring food folates. As described below from a global health point of view, folic acid can provide a sustainable form of the vitamin; this is not achievable through natural food folates.

Metabolically, folate is required for one-carbon metabolism [84]. This metabolism refers to reactions in which folate functions to donate or accept a one-carbon unit in essential pathways involving DNA and RNA biosynthesis, amino acid metabolism and numerous methylation reactions, including DNA methylation. Folate is therefore essential for cell division and tissue growth, and plays a particularly important role in early fetal development. To be metabolically active, folate needs to be in the reduced form of tetrahydrofolate (THF). Biologically active folates exist in various THF forms, but the most predominant form in cells and circulating in plasma is 5 methylTHF.

Other B-vitamins are required to sustain normal folate recycling and thus are also involved in one-carbon metabolism, namely vitamins B_{12}, B_6 and B_2 (i.e. riboflavin) [3]. Deficiency or low status of one of more of the related B-vitamins, or genetic polymorphisms in folate genes, can impair folate metabolism and cause adverse health outcomes (including hypertension owing to a novel folate-riboflavin interaction [89]. Such adverse effects can arise even if folate intakes are deemed to be adequate for a general population. In this way, sustaining optimal status of the related B-vitamins is essential for normal folate metabolism.

Folate deficiency leads to megaloblastic anemia, characterized by larger than normal red cell precursors (megaloblasts) in bone marrow, macrocytes in the peripheral blood and giantism in the morphology of proliferating cells. Biomarker status of folate is routinely assessed by measurement of folate concentrations in serum/plasma or in red blood cells [3]. Red blood cell (RBC) folate is considered the best index of longer-term status (i.e. over the previous months), while serum folate reflects more recent dietary intake. The measurement of plasma total homocysteine concentration provides a reliable functional marker of folate status, on the basis that normal homocysteine metabolism requires an adequate supply of folate. When folate status is low or deficient, plasma homocysteine is invariably found to be elevated.

Dietary folate intakes can be considered suboptimal in the diets of many people in that, although they may be adequate in preventing clinical deficiency (i.e. megaloblastic anemia), they are often insufficient to achieve a biomarker status of folate that is associated with optimal health [3]. This widespread under-provision of folate is generally attributed to the poor stability and incomplete bioavailability of natural food folates when compared with the synthetic vitamin folic acid (see below).

Other causes of folate depletion relate to higher requirements [3]. Pregnancy is a time when folate requirement is greatly increased in order to sustain the demand for rapid cell replication and growth of fetal, placental and maternal tissue. Likewise, folate requirement is increased during lactation in order to meet maternal and neonatal folate needs. Folate deficiency is also commonly reported in children with sickle cell disease. Folate deficiency is common in chronic alcoholism, which causes intestinal folate malabsorption, decreased hepatic uptake and increased urinary folate excretion. Several commonly used drugs are linked with folate deficiency through various mechanisms. These include: anticonvulsant drugs e.g. phenytoin, primidone; sulfasalazine (for treating inflammatory bowel disease); pyrimethamine (an antimalarial); triamterene (a diuretic); and metformin (used in type 2 diabetes). Methotrexate is a folate antagonist used in the treatment of cancer, rheumatoid arthritis and psoriasis; supplementation with folic acid (or folinic acid) can reduce antifolate toxicity and severe folate deficiency in treated patients.

The richest sources of naturally occurring food folates are green leafy vegetables, asparagus, beans, legumes, liver and yeast [3]. Folic acid, on the other hand, is found in the human diet only in fortified foods and supplements. It is a yellow-orange crystalline solid, tasteless, odorless and moderately soluble in pure water. Folic acid is readily converted to metabolically active folates after it is ingested. Folic acid is fully oxidized and is a monoglutamate, whereas natural food folates are a mixture of reduced folate forms and are typically found in the polyglutamate form. These structural differences between natural folates and folic acid have important consequences for the bioavailability of folates in the human diet.

The intestinal absorption of food folates is a two-step process which involves the hydrolysis of folate polyglutamates to the corresponding monoglutamyl derivatives, followed by their transport through the intestinal membranes into the enterocyte [58]. For various reasons, however, the bioavailability of naturally occurring folates is inherently limited and variable. Apart from their poor bioavailability, natural folates in foods can undergo significant losses before ingestion. Food folates (particularly green vegetables) can be unstable under certain conditions of cooking, and this can substantially reduce the folate content of the food before it is even ingested [57]. The instability and poor bioavailability of natural food folates greatly limits the extent to which optimal folate status can be achieved through intervention with food folate sources alone [20].

Folic acid is inherently more stable and bioavailable compared with an equivalent amount of the vitamin eaten as naturally occurring food folates. The bioavailability of folic acid is assumed to be 100% when ingested as a supplement, while folic acid in fortified food is estimated to have about 85% the bioavailability of supplemental folic acid [44].

In the US and certain other countries, folate recommendations are expressed as Dietary Folate Equivalents (DFEs), which takes into account differences in bioavailability between synthetic folic acid in fortified foods and naturally occurring dietary folate [44]. DFEs are defined as the micrograms of naturally occurring food folate plus 1.7 times the micrograms of folic acid from fortified food. The IOM [44] recommends 400 µg/day as DFE for adult females and males. To cover increased needs during pregnancy and lactation, it recommends 600 and 500 µg/day respectively.

Although a recent EFSA report has for the first time expressed folate recommendations as DFEs [24], in most European countries this conversion factor is not applied and the differences in bioavailability between the natural food forms and folic acid are disregarded: folate intakes and recommendations are expressed simply as total folate in µg/day rather than as DFEs [37]. Folate recommendations (total folate in µg/day) vary between 200 and 400 µg/day for adults in different European countries. Generally, those countries with more recently generated recommendations based on newer evidence estimate higher folate requirements than those countries (including the UK) with older recommendations still in place.

The UL refers only to folic acid intakes (the synthetic vitamin). No adverse effects have been associated with the consumption of excess folate from foods; therefore, there is no UL for naturally occurring food folates. ULs for folic acid have been set for the US [44], Australia/New Zealand, Europe [24], and for a number of specific European countries: the Nordic and DACH countries, France and The Netherlands. In the US, the IOM [44], estimated a UL for adults (≥ 19 years) for folic acid at 1000 µg/day.

Folate has important impacts on health. Conclusive evidence shows that folic acid supplementation in early pregnancy protects against neural tube defects (NTD) —major malformations in which there is a failure of the neural tube to close properly between the third and fourth week post conception. Although the preventive effect of folate in NTD is the major focus of public health efforts worldwide, folate has other roles in human health which extend throughout the lifecycle from conception to old age, including potential preventative effects against cardiovascular disease, cancer, cognitive dysfunction and osteoporosis [59].

Low and deficient folate status is a global problem which is not confined to developing countries [3]. One extensive review of folate deficiency worldwide assessed population-based surveys of folate status published between 1995 and 2005, including those which included biomarker data [56]. Folate deficiency was identified in specific age-groups in six out of eight countries for which biomarker data existed, most notably in pregnant women in Costa Rica (48.8%) and Venezuela (25.5%), preschool children in Venezuela (33.8%), and the elderly in the United Kingdom (15.0%).

The widespread under-provision of folate that exists in the diets of many people worldwide needs to be addressed. Because of the instability and relatively poor bioavailability of folates from natural sources, enhancing folate intake through plant or animal food sources will not lead to increased status. Folic acid is inherently more stable and bioavailable compared to an equivalent amount of the vitamin eaten as naturally occurring food folates. It is also cheap to produce. As reviewed elsewhere (Chap. 29), folic acid fortified foods can provide a sustainable form of this important B-vitamin and contribute greatly to achieving optimal folate status in populations globally. Folate's role in human health extends throughout the lifecycle from conception to old age, and fortification of food with folic acid is associated not only with better health outcomes for women of reproductive age but also for other sub-groups. Achieving optimal folate status should be an important public health goal for populations worldwide.

12.7 Vitamin B_{12}

Vitamin B_{12} is the generic term for a group of cobalt-containing compounds known as cobalamins. There are a number of different forms of the vitamin: methylcobalamin and deoxyadenosylcobalamin are the two metabolically active forms, while cyanocobalamin is the synthetic form of the vitamin used in supplements and fortified foods. Vitamin B_{12} is required as a cofactor for two mammalian enzymes, methionine synthase and methylmalonyl CoA mutase. Adenosylcobalamin acts as a co-factor for the latter enzyme which converts methylmalonyl CoA to succinyl CoA, a metabolite in the tricarboxylic acid cycle. This is an important reaction in the metabolism of branched-chain amino acids and odd-chain length fatty acids [83]. Methylcobalamin acts as a co-factor for the enzyme methionine synthase, which catalyzes the re-methylation of homocysteine to methionine, the precursor of S-adenosylmethionine. S-adenosylmethionine is a universal methyl donor essential for the methylation of phospholipids, neurotransmitters, amines, DNA, RNA and myelin basic protein [83]. Clinical signs of vitamin B_{12} deficiency include megaloblastic anemia (as a result of impaired DNA synthesis) and irreversible neurological dysfunction such as sub-acute combined degeneration of the spinal cord [87]. Sub-optimal vitamin B_{12} status characterized by metabolic evidence of deficiency—such as low serum total B_{12} and serum holotranscobalamin and elevated serum methymalonic acid and plasma homocysteine, but without overt signs of clinical deficiency—has also been associated with a number of age-related diseases, including cardiovascular disease [76], cognitive dysfunction [21], dementia [39] and osteoporosis [89].

Vitamin B_{12} is synthesized by microorganisms and is predominately found in foods of an animal origin such as meat, poultry and dairy products or in foods fortified with B_{12} [86]. Currently, inadequate dietary intake of vitamin B_{12} is not a major concern as intakes greatly exceed recommendations (which range between 1.0 and 2.8 µg/day worldwide), except among those that have very low intakes of animal-based foods [43]. There is a high prevalence of vitamin B_{12} deficiency among strict vegetarians and vegans [72], and low vitamin B_{12} is also more common in lower-income countries, where the consumption of animal foods is limited [2]. Therefore, the adoption of a more sustainable plant-based diet would have an unfavorable impact on vitamin B_{12} status, leading to an increase in the prevalence of vitamin B_{12} deficiency among the general population, a problem that at present is largely confined to older adults with malabsorption [43]. A few plant sources of vitamin B_{12} have been identified; however, they do not offer a viable alternative to animal-based foods, especially in the long term. Certain wild mushrooms contain vitamin B_{12} but would need to be ingested in such large quantities that they do not represent a feasible replacement food source [98]. Furthermore, two forms of edible algae (*Enteromorpha* sp. and *Porphyria* sp.) have been identified as sources of vitamin B_{12}; however, consumption of these products is not widespread within the Western diet [98]. Fortification of foods with vitamin B_{12} offers a viable alternative, but the effectiveness of this strategy will depend on the level of fortification introduced: levels of vitamin B_{12} currently used by the food industry in voluntary fortification are too low to improve status in the general population and need be increased [40]. Vitamin B_{12} food fortification would not only reduce the risk of inadequate intake but also address the issue of food-bound malabsorption, the most common cause of vitamin B_{12} deficiency [43].

12.8   Choline

Choline is involved in various biological reactions including one-carbon metabolism through its metabolite betaine, and the synthesis of the neurotransmitter acetylcholine and phospholipids such as phosphatidylcholine [107]. Deficiency of choline is rare, as it is found in both animal and plant-based foods, but manifests predominantly as fatty liver and impaired liver and muscle function [14, 26, 107]. More recently, studies have focused on the role of choline in pregnancy for neurodevelopment and prevention of neural tube defects, and in later life for reducing the risk of chronic diseases such as cancer, CVD and dementia [37, 91, 107]. Choline can be synthesized endogenously, but intake from food is required to meet current recommendations. An adequate intake (AI) level of 550 mg/day for men and 425 mg/day for women was set, with higher intakes of 450 and 550 mg/day established for pregnancy and lactation respectively [44].

Choline is found in food predominantly as phosphatidylcholine, a lipid-soluble compound, although-water soluble compounds (i.e. free choline, glycerophosphocholine and phosphocholine) are also present [17]. The choline content of many foods, however, only became available in the last decade [42, 71], enabling choline intake to be estimated. Observational cohort studies from the US [10, 17, 106] and from elsewhere [19, 22, 60] consistently report that median intakes are below recommendations, with only a small proportion of people having intakes that meet the AI. The contribution to total choline intake of different food sources varies between studies, but the main food sources reported tend to be foods of animal origin such as eggs, meat and milk, as choline is predominantly present in food as a lipid-soluble compound [9, 17, 18, 22, 68, 106]. Non-animal-based foods such as broccoli and other vegetables, fruit, legumes and bread make a smaller contribution to total intakes, with values of up to 10% reported [17, 18, 68, 106]. A study by

Mygind et al. [68] found, however, that combining foods such as fruit and bread led to a similar contribution to total choline intake as found for red meat. The Attica study in Greece reported that those people who had higher choline intakes consumed more red meat, fruit, vegetables and legumes [22]. In Taiwanese populations, soybean and soy products are found to be an important source of choline, contributing 6% to total intakes [19]. Lewis et al. [50] found that a daily serving of pulses can provide more choline than foods of animal origin, the richest sources typically reported in studies. A daily serving was calculated to provide 15% of the dietary recommendation for choline [50].

As choline is widely present in foods, achieving recommendations should not be an issue as long as a varied diet is consumed. The emergence of further food composition data for choline will enable intake from non-animal food sources to be more accurately calculated. These food sources, however, may differ in pathways of absorption and metabolism to animal sources [17, 18]; therefore, further research is required to determine whether the various forms of choline present in food differ in bioavailability in order to fully understand whether requirements for choline can be met through non-meat food sources.

12.9 Biotin

The water-soluble B-vitamin, biotin, is a bicyclic compound, which acts as a cofactor for five carboxylase enzymes which are important in fatty acid metabolism and in mitochondrial carbohydrate, lipid and amino acid metabolism. Biotin also has a role in gene regulation and genome stability [85]. Although biotin plays a central role in metabolic processes, frank, symptomatic biotin deficiency is a rare occurrence and has been observed only in intravenous feeding without biotin supplementation, and after raw egg-white feeding [64]. Deficiency symptoms include skin rashes, hair loss and neurological symptoms such as depression, lethargy and paresthesia [62]. Recent work, however, indicates that sub-optimal biotin status might be a problem in pregnancy [73]. Perry and co-workers found significant alterations in biomarkers of biotin metabolism in pregnant women and suggested that biotin intakes greatly exceeding current recommendations (Adequate Intake, AI: 30 µg biotin/day) are needed during pregnancy.

Biotin seems to be widely distributed in foods, and particularly rich sources include nuts, egg yolk, liver, dairy products, and some fruit and vegetables (e.g. bananas, avocados, raspberries, cabbage). The biotin content, however, of most foods has not been determined, nor has bioavailability [70]. A specific biotinidase appears to cleave protein-bound biotin in the intestine. 'Egg-white injury' is caused by tight binding of biotin by ovidin in raw egg-white. Dietary ovidin can prevent the absorption of dietary biotin and any biotin synthesized by intestinal bacteria.

The effect toward improving sustainability on biotin intakes and status will remain unclear until more is known on the biotin content of foods and dietary requirements, especially during pregnancy.

12.10   Pantothenic Acid

Pantothenic acid has an important role in energy-yielding metabolism as a vital component in the synthesis and maintenance of the cofactor coenzyme A and acyl carrier protein in the fatty acid synthase complex. Clinical symptoms of deficiency have only been observed in people who were fed diets low in, or devoid of, pantothenic acid [27] or fed w-methyl pantothenic acid, an antagonist of the vitamin [35]. The clinical symptoms observed in these experiments were wide-ranging, and included neuromotor disorders, mental depression, gastrointestinal effects, and various metabolic disturbances.

Pantothenic acid is widely distributed in all foodstuffs, and there is little information on bioavailability. Non-nutritional, pharmacological uses of pantothenic acid at doses much higher than the usual 3–7 mg/day (AI) have been proposed, and some efficacy has been demonstrated for acne [104, 105]. Problems with pantothenic acid status are unlikely, whether or not sustainability scenarios are implemented.

12.11   Summary: Key Messages

- It is likely that future scenarios will see trends toward a reduced consumption of animal-based foods and increased consumption of fruit and vegetables.
- Trends towards improving environmental sustainability could impact on B-vitamin status.

References

1. Allen L, de Benoist B, Dary O, Hurrell R, eds. Guidelines on Food Fortification with Micronutrientsexternal link disclaimer. Geneva: World Health Organization and Food and Agricultural Organization of the United Nations; 2006.
2. Allen LH (2010). Bioavailability of vitamin B_{12}. *International Journal for Vitamin and Nutrition Research*, 80, 330–335.
3. Bailey LB, Stover PJ, McNulty H, Fenech MF, Gregory JF, Mills JL, Pfeiffer CM, Fazili Z, Zhang M, Ueland PM, Molloy AM, Caudill MA, Shane B, Berry RJ, Bailey LR, Hausman D, Raghavan R & Raiten DJ (2015). Biomarkers of Nutrition for Development—Folate Review. *Journal of Nutrition*,145: 1636S-1680S.
4. Bates CJ, Powers HJ. (1985) A simple fluorimetric assay for pyridoxamine phosphate oxidase in erythrocyte haemolysates: effects of riboflavin supplementation and of glucose 6-phosphate dehydrogenase deficiency. *Hum Nutr: Clin Nutr,* 39,107–15.
5. Bates CJ, Pentieva KD, Prentice A, Mansoor MA, Finch S (1999). Plasma pyridoxal phosphate and pyridoxic acid and their relationship to plasma homocysteine in a representative sample of British men and women aged 65 years and over. *British Journal of Nutrition,* 81, 191–201.
6. Bates B, Lennox A, Prentice A, Bates C, Page P, Nicholson S and Swan G (2014). National Diet and 2026 Nutrition Survey. Results from Years 1, 2, 3 and 4 (combined) of the Rolling

Programme 2027 (2008/2009 – 2011/2012). A survey carried out on behalf of Public Health England and the Food 2028 Standards Agency.

7. Bemeur C, Butterworth RF (2014). Thiamin. In: Ross AC, Caballero B, Cousins RJ, Tucker KL, Ziegler TR, eds. *Modern Nutrition in Health and Disease.* 11th ed. Baltimore, MD: Lippincott Williams & Wilkins; 317–24.

8. Bogan KL and Brenner C (2008). Nicotinic acid, nicotinamide, and nicotinamide riboside: a molecular evaluation of NAD + precursor vitamins in human nutrition. *Annual Review of Nutrition,* 28, 115–130.

9. Bidulescu A, Chambless LE, Siega-Riz AM, Zeisel SH, Heiss G (2007). Usual choline and betaine dietary intake and incident coronary heart disease: the Atherosclerosis Risk in Communities (ARIC) Study. *BMC Cardiovascular Disorders* 7, 20.

10. Bidulescu A, Chambless LE, Siega-Riz AM, Zeisel SH, Heiss G (2009). Repeatability and measurement error in the assessment of choline and betaine dietary intake: the Atherosclerosis Risk in Communities (ARIC) Study. *BMC Cardiovascular Disorders* 8, 14.

11. Boisvert WA, Castaneda C, Mendoza I et al. (1993) Prevalence of riboflavin deficiency among Guatemalan elderly people and its relationship to milk intake. *Am J Clin Nutr* 58, 85.

12. Borschel MW (1995). Vitamin B6 in infancy: requirements and current feeding practices. In: *Vitamin B-6 metabolism in pregnancy, lactation and infancy.* Ed Raiten DJ. CRC Press, Boca Raton, FL, USA, 109–124.

13. Brody T (1999). *Nutritional Biochemistry.* 2nd ed. San Diego: Academic Press.

14. Buchman AL, Dubin MD, Moukarzel AA, Jenden DJ, Roch M, Rice KM, Gornbein J, Ament ME (1995). Choline deficiency: a cause of hepatic steatosis during parenteral nutrition that can be reversed with intravenous choline supplementation. *Hepatology* 22, 1399–1403.

15. Carpenter KJ and Lewin WJ (1985). A reexamination of the composition of diets associated with pellagra. *Journal of Nutrition,* 115, 543–552.

16. Carter EG and Carpenter KJ. The bioavailability for humans of bound niacin from wheat bran (1982). *American Journal of Clinical Nutrition,* 36, 855–861.

17. Chiuve SE, Giovannucci EL, Hankinson SE, Zeisel SH, Dougherty LW, Willett WC, Rimm EB (2007). The association between betaine and choline intakes and the plasma concentrations of homocysteine in women. *American Journal of Clinical Nutrition* 86, 1073–1081.

18. Cho E, Zeisel SH, Jacques P, Selhub J, Dougherty L, Colditz GA, Willett WC (2006). Dietary choline and betaine assessed by food-frequency questionnaire in relation to plasma total homocysteine concentration in the Framingham Offspring Study. *American Journal of Clinical Nutrition,* 83, 905–911.

19. Chu D-M, Wahlqvist ML, Chang H-Y, Yeh N-H, Lee M-S (2012). Choline and betaine food sources and intakes in Taiwanese. *Asia Pacific Journal of Clinical Nutrition,* 21(4), 547–557.

20. Cuskelly GJ, McNulty H, Scott JM (1996). Effect of increasing dietary folate on red-cell folate: implications for prevention of neural tube defects. *Lancet,* 347: 657–59.

21. de Jager CA, Oulhaj A, Jacoby R, Refsum H, Smith AD (2012). Cognitive and clinical outcomes of homocysteine-lowering B-vitamin treatment in mild cognitive impairment: a randomized controlled trial. *International Journal of Geriatric Psychiatry,* 27(6), 592–600.

22. Detopoulou P, Panagiotakos DB, Antonopoulou S, Pitsavos C, Stefanadis C (2008). Dietary choline and betaine intakes in relation to concentrations of inflammatory markers in healthy adults: the ATTICA study. *American Journal of Clinical Nutrition,* 87, 424–430.

23. Dietary Reference Intakes for Thiamin, Riboflavin, Niacin, Vitamin B$_6$, Folate, Vitamin B$_{12}$, Pantothenic Acid, Biotin and Choline. Report of the Standing Committee on the Scientific Evaluation of Dietary Reference Intakes and its Panel on Folate, Other B Vitamins and Choline and Subcommittee on Upper Reference Levels of Nutrients Food and Nutrition Board Institute of Medicine, *National Academy Press.*

24. EFSA. European Food Safety Authority Panel on Dietetic Products, Nutrition and Allergies (NDA). Scientific Opinion on Dietary Reference Values for Folate. EFSA Journal 2014; 12 (11):3893.(revised Feb 2015). Accessed at: http://www.efsa.europa.eu/en/efsajournal/pub/3893.

25. Fischer LM, daCosta KA, Kwock L, Stewart PW, Lu TS, Stabler SP, Allen RH, Zeisel SH (2007). Sex and menopausal status influence human dietary requirements for the nutrient choline. *American Journal of Clinical Nutrition*, 85, 1275–1285.
26. Food and Nutrition Board, Institute of Medicine (1998). Riboflavin. In *Dietary Reference Intakes: Thiamin, Riboflavin, Niacin, Vitamin B_6, Vitamin B_{12}, Pantothenic Acid, Biotin, and Choline*, 87–122 [RM Pitkin, editor]. Washington, DC: National Academy Press.
27. Fry PC, Fox HM, Tao HG (1976). Metabolic response to a pantothenic acid deficient diet in humans. *Journal of Nutritional Science & Vitaminology (Tokyo)*, 22, 339–346.
28. Galvin MA, Kiely M, Flynn A (2003). Impact of ready-to-eat breakfast cereal (RTEBC) consumption on adequacy of micronutrient intakes and compliance with dietary recommendations in Irish adults. *Public Health Nutr*, 6, 351–363.
29. Garcia SM and Rosenberg A (2010). Food security and marine capture fisheries: characteristics, trends, drivers and future perspectives. *Philosophical Transactions of the Royal Society*, 365, 2869–2880.
30. Germani A, Vitiello V, Guisti AM, Pinto A, Donini LM, del Balzo V (2014). Environmental and economic sustainability of the Mediterranean Diet. *International Journal of Food Sciences & Nutrition*, 65(8), 1008–1012.
31. Gregory JF, 3rd, Trumbo PR, Bailey LB, Toth JP, Baumgartner TG and Cerda JJ (1991). Bioavailability of pyridoxine-5'-beta-D-glucoside determined in humans by stable-isotopic methods. *Journal of Nutrition*, 121, 177–186.
32. Hansen CM, Leklem JE and Miller LT (1996). Vitamin B-6 status indicators decrease in women consuming a diet high in pyridoxine glucoside. *Journal of Nutrition*, 126, 2512–2518.
33. Henderson L, Irving K, Gregory J, Bates CJ, Prentice A, Perks J, Swan G, Farron M (2003). *The National Diet & Nutrition Survey: adults aged 19 to 64 years. Volume 3. Vitamin and mineral intake and urinary analytes*. London, Her Majesty's Stationery Office.
34. Herforth A, Frongillo EA, Sassi F, McLean MS, Arabi M, Tirado C, Remans R, Mantilla G, Thomson M, Pingali P (2014). Toward an integrated approach nutritional quality, environmental sustainability and economic viability: research and measurement gaps. *Annals of the New York Academy of Sciences*, 1–21.
35. Hodges RE, Bean WB, Ohlson MA, Bleiler R (1959). Human pantothenic acid deficiency produced by omega-methyl pantothenic acid. *Journal of Clinical Investigation*, 38, 1421–1425.
36. Hoey L, McNulty H, Duffy ME, Hughes CF, Strain JJ (2013). EURRECA—Estimating Folate Requirements for Deriving Dietary Reference Values. *Critical Reviews in Food Science and Nutrition*, 53: 1041–1050.
37. Hollenbeck CB (2012). An introduction to the nutrition and metabolism of choline. *Central nervous system agents in medicinal chemistry*, 12(2), 100–113.
38. Hooshmand B, Solomon A, Kåreholt I, Winblad B, Kivipelto M, Rusanen M, Hänninen T, Soininen H, Leiviskä J, Laatikainen T (2012). Associations between serum homocysteine, holotranscobalamin, folate and cognition in the elderly: A longitudinal study. *Journal of internal medicine*, 271(2), 204–212.
39. Hopkins SM, Gibney MJ, Nugent AP, McNulty H, Molloy AM, Scott JM, Flynn A, Strain JJ, Ward M, Walton J, McNulty BA (2015). Impact of voluntary fortification and supplement use on dietary intakes and biomarker status of folate and vitamin B-12 in Irish adults. *American Journal of Clinical Nutrition*, 101(6), 1163–72.
40. Horigan G, McNulty H, Ward M et al. (2010) Riboflavin lowers blood pressure in cardiovascular disease patients homozygous for the 677C → T polymorphism in MTHFR. *J Hypertens* 28, 478–486.
41. Howe JC, Williams JR, Holden JM, Zeisel SH, Mar MH (2004). USDA Database for the Choline Content of Common Foods, Release One. *Washington; Agricultural Research Service*.
42. Hughes CF, Ward M, Hoey L, McNulty H (2013). Vitamin B_{12} and ageing: current issues and interaction with folate. *Annals of Clinical Biochemistry*, 50, 315–29.

43. Institute of Medicine (1998). Dietary Reference Intakes: Thiamin, Riboflavin, Niacin, Vitamin B-6, Vitamin B-12, Pantothenic Acid, Biotin, and Choline. *Washington DC: National Academic Press*, 390–422.

44. Johnston JL, Fanzo JC and Cogill B (2014). Understanding sustainable diets: a descriptive analysis of the determinants and processes that influence diets and their impact on health, food security and environmental sustainability. *American Society for Nutrition*, 5, 418–429.

45. Kirkland JB (2009). Niacin status, NAD distribution and ADP-ribose metabolism. *Current Pharmaceutical Design*, 15, 3–11.

46. Kretsch MJ, Sauberlich HE and Newbrun E (1991). Electroencephalographic changes and periodontal status during short-term vitamin B-6 depletion of young, nonpregnant women. *American Journal of Clinical Nutrition*, 53, 1266–1274.

47. Lang T, Barling D (2013). Nutrition and sustainability: an emerging food policy discourse. *Proceedings of the Nutrition Society*, 72, 1–12.

48. Leklem, JE (1990). Vitamin B-6: a status report.*Journal of Nutrition*, 120 Suppl 11, 1503–1507.

49. Lewis ED, Kosik SJ, Zhao Y-Y, Jacobs RL, Curtis JM, Field CJ (2014). Total Choline and Choline-Containing Moieties of Commercially Available Pulses. *Plant Food Human Nutrition* 69, 115–121.

50. LeBlanc JG, Milani C, de Giori GS, Sesma F, van Sinderen D, Ventura M (2013). Bacteria as vitamin suppliers to their host: a gut microbiota perspective. *Curr Opin Biotechnol*, 24,160–168.

51. McAuley E, McNulty H, Hughes C, Strain JJ, Ward M (2016). Riboflavin status, MTHFR genotype and blood pressure: current evidence and implications for personalised nutrition. *Proc Nutr Soc*, 75, 405–14.

52. McCandless D (2009). Thiamine deficiency and associated clinical disorders. *Humana Press*.

53. McCormick DB (1989) Two interconnected B vitamins:riboflavin and pyridoxine. Physiol Rev 69, 1170–1198.

54. McCormick DB (1999) Riboflavin. In Modern Nutrition in Health and Disease, 9th ed., pp. 391–399 [Baltimore: Williams & Wilkins] Lang T and Barling D (2012). Conference on 'Future of Food and Health', Nutrition and sustainability: an emerging food policy discourse. *Proceedings of the Nutrition Society*, 72, 1–12.

55. McLean E, de Benoist B, Allen LH (2008). Review of the magnitude of folate deficiencies worldwide. *Food and Nutrition Bulletin*, 29 (suppl): S38-S51.

56. McKillop D, Pentieva K, Daly D, McPartlin J, Hughes J, Strain JJ, Scott JM, McNulty H (2002). The effect of different cooking methods on folate retention in various foods which are amongst the major contributors to folate intake in the UK diet. *British Journal of Nutrition*, 88: 681–688.

57. McNulty H and Pentieva K (2010). Folate bioavailability. In: Bailey L.B, editor. Folate in *Health and Disease*, 2nd ed. Boca Raton (FL): CRC Press, Taylor and Francis Group; pp. 25–47.

58. McNulty H, Pentieva K, Hoey L, Strain JJ, Ward M (2012). Nutrition throughout life: Folate. *International Journal for Vitamin and Nutrition Research*, 82:348–354.

59. McNulty H, Strain JJ, Hughes CF, Ward M (2017). Riboflavin, MTHFR genotype and blood pressure: a personalized approach to prevention and treatment of hypertension. *Molecular Aspects of Medicine*, 53,2–9.

60. Majchrzak D, Singer I, Männer M, Rust P, Genser D, Wagner KH, Elmadfa I (2006). B-vitamin status and concentrations of homocysteine in Austrian omnivores, vegetarians and vegans. *Annals of Nutrition and Metabolism*, 50, 485–91.

61. Malfait P, Moren A, Dillon JC, Brodel A, Begkoyian G, Etchegorry MG, Malenga G, Hakewill P (1993). An outbreak of pellagra related to changes in dietary niacin among Mozambican refugees in Malawi. *International Journal of Epidemiology*, 22, 504–11.

62. Mock DM (1999). Biotin status: which are valid indicators and how do we know? *Journal of Nutrition*, 129, (2S Suppl), 494S–497S

63. Mock DM (2013). Biotin. In: Zempleni JS, Suttie JW, Gregory JF, Stover PJ, editors. *Handbook of vitamins*. 5th ed. Boca Raton (FL): CRC press, 397–420.

64. Mock DM (2014). Adequate intake of biotin in pregnancy: why bother? *The Journal of Nutrition*, 1885.

65. Morris MS, Picciano MF, Jacques PF and Selhub J (2008). Plasma pyridoxal 5'-phosphate in the US population: the National Health and Nutrition Examination Survey, 2003–2004. *American Journal of Clinical Nutrition*, 87, 1446–1454.

66. Mygind VL, Evans SE, Peddie MC, Miller JC, Houghton LA (2013). Estimation of usual intake and food sources of choline and betaine in New Zealand reproductive age women. *Asia Pacific Journal of Clinical Nutrition*, 22(2), 319–324.

67. Nakano H, McMahon LG and Gregory JF, 3rd (1997). Pyridoxine-5'-beta-D-glucoside exhibits incomplete bioavailability as a source of vitamin B-6 and partially inhibits the utilization of co-ingested pyridoxine in humans. *Journal of Nutrition*, 127, 1508–1513.

68. National Center for Health Statistics (2008). National Health and Nutrition Examination Survey, 2005–2006 Data Files. Hyattsville, MD: Centers for Disease Control and Prevention; available at: http://wwwn.cdc.gov/nchs/nhanes/search/nhanes05_06.aspx.

69. Otten J, Pitzi H, Meyers L (2006). National Research Council. Dietary reference intakes: the essential guide to nutrient requirements. *Washington: The National Academic Press*, 196–201.

70. Patterson KY, Bhagwat SA, Williams JR, Howe JC, Holden JM (2008). USDA Database for the Choline Content of Common Foods: Release Two. *Washington; Agricultural Research Service*.

71. Pawlak R, Lester SE, Babatunde T (2014). The prevalence of cobalamin deficiency among vegetarians assessed by serum vitamin B_{12}: a review of literature. *European Journal of Clinical Nutrition*, 68(5), 541–8.

72. Perry CA, West AA, Gayle A, Lucas LK, Yan J, Jiang X, Malysheva O, Caudill MA (2014). Pregnancy and lactation alter biomarkers of biotin metabolism in women consuming a controlled diet. *The Journal of Nutrition*, 144, 1977–1983.

73. Powers HJ, Weaver LT, Austin S, Beresford JK (1993). A proposed intestinal mechanism for the effect of riboflavin deficiency on iron loss in the rat. *Br J Nutr*, 69, 553–561.

74. Prichards C (2014). Common Food Sources of Biotin. www.ezinearticles.com/?Common-Food-Sources-of-Biotin&id=6376085.

75. Rafnsson S, Saravanan P, Bhopal R, Yajnik C (2011). Is a low blood level of vitamin B_{12} a cardiovascular and diabetes risk factor? A systematic review of cohort studies. *European Journal of Nutrition*, 50, 97–106.

76. Reynold CJ, Buckley JD, Weinstein P, Boland J (2014). Are the dietary guidelines for meat, fat, fruit and vegetable consumption appropriate for environmental sustainability? A review of the literature. *Nutrients*, 2251–2265.

77. Rivers A (2014). What Food Contain Biotin? eHow www.ehow.com/facts_4910664_what-foods-contain-biotin-html.

78. Rich Foods in Biotin (2014). www.fitday.com/fitness-articles/nutrition/vitamins-minerals/8-foods-rich-in-bio.

79. Sadler MJ, Strain JJ, Caballero B (1999). Encyclopedia of Human Nutrition. *Academic Press*, Volume 1.

80. Sabaté J and Soret S (2014). Sustainability of plant-based diets: back to the future. *American Journal of Clinical Nutrition*, 100 (suppl), 476S-4782S.

81. Sauberlich HE (1981). Vitamin B6 status assessment: past and present. In: *Methods in Vitamin B6 Nutrition: Analysis and Status Assessment*. Eds Leklem JE and Reynolds RD. Plenum Press, New York - London, 203–239.

82. Scott J (2003). Folate (folic acid) and vitamin B_{12}. In:. *Human Nutrition and Dietetics*: Garrow JS, James WPT, Ralph A, editors. Churchill Livingstone; p. 271–80.

83. Shane, B (2010). Folate chemistry and metabolism. In: Bailey L.B, editor. Folate in Health and Disease, 2nd ed. Boca Raton (FL): CRC Press, Taylor and Francis Group, pp. 1–24.

84. Singh MP, Wijeratne SSK, Zempleni J (2013). Biotinylation of lysine 16 in histone H4 contributes toward nucleosome condensation. *Archives of Biochemistry Biophysics*, 529, 105–111.

85. Stabler SP, Allen RH (2004). Vitamin B$_{12}$ deficiency as a worldwide problem. *Annual Review of Nutrition*, 24, 299–326.

86. Stabler SP (2013). Vitamin B$_{12}$deficiency. *New England Journal of Medicine*, 368, 149–160.

87. Strain JJ, Hughes CF, McNulty H, Ward M (2015). Riboflavin Lowers Blood Pressure: A Review of a Novel Gene-nutrient Interaction. *Nutrition and Food Sciences Research*, 2: 3–6.

88. Tarr JB, Tamura T, Stokstad EL (1981). Availability of vitamin B6 and pantothenate in an average American diet in man. *American Journal of Clinical Nutrition*, 34, 1328–1337

89. Tucker KL, Hannan MT, Qiao N, Jacques PF, Selhub J, Cupples LA, Kiel DP (2005). Low plasma B$_{12}$ is associated with lower BMD: the Framingham Osteoporosis Study. *Journal of Bone and Mineral Research*, 20, 152–158.

90. Ueland PM (2010). Choline and betaine in health and disease. *Journal of Inherited Metabolic Disease*, 34, 3–15.

91. U.S. Department of Agriculture, Agricultural Research Service (2014). USDA National Nutrient Database for Standard Reference, Release 27. Nutrient Data Laboratory home page.

92. van der Wielen RP, Lowik MR, Haller J, van den Berg H, Ferry M and van Staveren WA (1996). Vitamin B-6 malnutrition among elderly Europeans: the SENECA study. *Journals of Gerontology. Series A, Biological Sciences and Medical Sciences*, 51, B417–424.

93. van der Kruk JJ, Jager-Wittenaar H, Nieweg RM, van der Schans CP (2014). Do Dutch nutrition and dietetics students meet nutritional requirements during education? *Public Health Nutrition*, 17(6), 1237–44.

94. Wan P, Moat S and Anstey A (2011). Pellagra: a review with emphasis on photosensitivity. *British Journal of Dermatology*, 164, 1188–1200.

95. Wacker J, Fruhauf J, Schulz M et al (2000). Riboflavin deficiency and preeclampsia. *Obstet Gynecol*, 96, 38–44.

96. Watanabe T, Suemura K, Taniguchi A, Ebara S, Kimura S, Fukui T (2010). Dietary intake of seven B vitamins based on a total diet study in Japan. *Journal of Nutritional Science and Vitaminology* (Tokyo), 56, 279–86.

97. Watanabe F, Yabuta Y, Tanioka Y, Bito T (2013). Biologically active vitamin B$_{12}$ compounds in foods for preventing deficiency among vegetarians and elderly subjects. *Journal of Agricultural and Food Chemistry*, 61, 6769–75.

98. Whitfield KC, McCann A, Karakochuk C et al. (2015) High rates of riboflavin deficiency in women of childbearing age in Cambodia and Canada. *J Nutr* 145, 628–633.

99. Whitfield KC, Karakochuk CD, Kroeun H, et al (2016). Perinatal Consumption of Thiamine-Fortified Fish Sauce in Rural Cambodia: A Randomized Clinical Trial. *JAMA Pediatr.* Aug 8:e162065.

100. Whitfield KC, Karakochuk CD, Liu Y, McCann A, Talukder A, Kroeun H, Ward M, McNulty H, Lynd LD, Kitts DD, Li-Chan EC, McLean J, Green TJ (2015). Poor thiamin and riboflavin status is common among women of childbearing age in rural and urban Cambodia. *Journal of Nutrition*, 145, 628–633.

101. Wilkinson TJ, Hanger HC, George PM, Sainsbury R (2000). Is thiamine deficiency in elderly people related to age or co-morbidity? *Age and Ageing*, 29, 111–6.

102. Wu G, Bazer FW, Cross HR (2014). Land-based production of animal protein: impacts, efficiency and sustainability. *Annals of the New York Academy of Sciences*, 1328, 18–28.

103. Yang B, Fan S, Zhi X et al. (2014) Associations of MTHFR gene polymorphisms with hypertension and hypertension in pregnancy: a meta-analysis from 114 studies with 15411 cases and 21970 controls. *PLoS ONE* 9, e87497.

104. Yang M, Moclair B, Hatcher V, Kaminetsky J, Mekas M, Chapas A, Capodice J (2014). A randomized, double-blind, placebo-controlled study of a novel pantothenic Acid-based

dietary supplement in subjects with mild to moderate facial acne. *Dermatology and Therapy (Heidelb)*, 4(1), 93–101.

105. Yonemori KM, Lim U, Koga KR, Wilkens LR, Au D, Boushey CJ, Le Marchand L, Kolonel LN, Murphy SP (2013). Dietary Choline and Betaine Intakes Vary in an Adult Multiethnic Population. *Journal of Nutrition,* 143(6), 894–899.
106. Zeisel SH, da Costa KA, Franklin PD, Alexander EA, Lamont JT, Sheard NF, Beiser A (1991). Choline, an essential nutrient for humans. *FASEB Journal* 5, 2093–2098.
107. Zeisel SH & da Costa KA (2009). Choline an essential nutrient for public health. *Nutrition Reviews* 67(11), 615–623.

Chapter 13
Iron and Zinc: Two Principal Trace Element Nutrients in the Context of Food Security Transitions

Noel W. Solomons and Klaus Schümann

Abstract The underlying premise of this series is that food insecurity and food scarcity will continue to emerge due to underlying environmental, agricultural and demographic imperatives. For iron and zinc, which represent the two most abundant trace elements in the human body, decreased food availability and declining caloric requirements have predictive consequences. Overt deficiency of both produces public health consequences. Iron deficiency affects stamina and cognitive and immune function, evolving in its extreme form to iron deficiency anemia. Zinc deficiency is associated with poor growth and decreased disease resistance. In a food-security context, these two nutrients are most abundant and most biologically available in animal-source foods. From plant sources, the absorption efficiency is low due to intrinsic inhibitors such as phytic acid. Actions to improve nutritional status and mitigate the effects of food insecurity need to be conceptualized, evaluated for efficacy, and integrated into public policy. Dietary diversification toward greater contribution of animal-source food is problematic in the face of environmental issues and agriculture trends. Periodic, weekly or daily iron supplementation is used situationally, but presents challenges in terms of acceptability and safety. Zinc supplementation is restricted to specific indications in selected sub-populations. Food fortification and the newer approach of biofortification offer the greatest theoretical promise for both nutrients.

Keywords Iron · Zinc · Deficiency · Excess and overload · Uptake · Bioavailability · Daily requirements · Public health · Food security

N.W. Solomons (✉)
Center for Studies of Sensory Impairment Aging and Metabolism (CeSSIAM),
Guatemala City, Guatemala
e-mail: cessiam@cessiam.org.gt

K. Schümann
Research Center for Nutrition and Food Science, Technische Universität München,
Freising, Germany
e-mail: kschuemann@hgrunowfoundation.org

© Springer International Publishing AG 2017　　　　　　　　　　　　　　　205
H.K. Biesalski et al. (eds.), *Sustainable Nutrition in a Changing World*,
DOI 10.1007/978-3-319-55942-1_13

13.1   Introduction

Iron and zinc are essential nutrients from lower one-celled organisms through the Plant Kingdom and into the highest order of mammalians, including *Homo sapiens*. Unlike vitamins or essential fatty acids, they are elemental and indestructible. Nutritional status is dependent upon how much iron and zinc is consumed, how efficiently these nutrients are absorbed, how avidly they are retained in the body, and how efficiently they can be utilized in their functional roles in physiology and structure. Both nutrients are on the radar screen of the World Health Organization (WHO): iron in the context of nutritional anemia, and, more recently, due to its involvement in the pathomechanisms of infections and inflammation; and zinc with respect to growth and child survival, and more recently, with respect to its beneficial effects in diarrhea.

13.2   The Chemistry and Physiology of Iron and Zinc

Iron (atomic no. 26; atomic mass, 55.8) is the fourth most abundant element in the earth's crust, following oxygen, silicon and aluminum. Zinc (atomic no. 30; atomic mass, 66.4) by contrast is twenty-fifth in abundance. Both metals have extensive chemical similarities, being part of the transition metals family on the Periodic Table of Elements. This means they possess an incompletely filled inner electron shell. However, they have one prominent dissimilarity: Whereas iron can transition from a divalent (reduced) *ferrous* oxidation state to a trivalent (oxidized) *ferric* state, with this latter being a potent oxidizing agent and generator of free radicals, zinc has only one, stable (divalent) status with negligible redox potential.

Iron and zinc are the two most abundant trace elements in the human body. An adult man has 4 g of iron in his body and a woman of reproductive age has 2.5 g of iron. Adults of both sexes have about 2–3 g of zinc in their bodies. Both metals are essential nutrients for humans, functioning in a host of metallo-proteins and metallo-enzymes.

13.3   Iron as a Public Health Problem in Relation to Food Insecurity

The WHO has created a series of world maps, assessing the geographic distribution of estimated deficiency conditions; these are available for anemia, iodine, and vitamin A. The WHO map for relative severity of anemia for preschool children is shown in Fig. 13.1 [1]. Although nutritional anemias can be caused by deficits other than iron deficiency, the extent of the world's population affected by anemia as public health problem is far more extensive than that for either iodine or vitamin A. Within countries, moreover, there is no more "egalitarian" nutrient deficiency

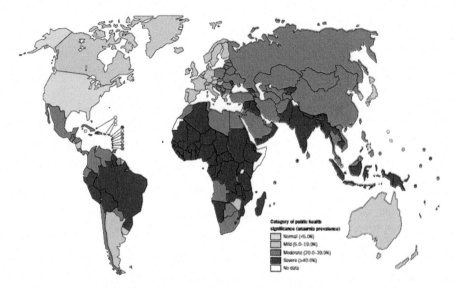

Fig. 13.1 Distribution of categories of public health significance of nutritional anemia among pre-school children worldwide. Reproduced with permission from Ref. [1]

than that of iron, which affects the middle and upper classes around the world more than any other. Population risk factors vary across the life course and are related to dietary characteristics and changing requirements, e.g. growth and during pregnancy, and due to blood-feeding parasites, among others.

Thus, anemia is not an exclusive indicator of iron deficiency. There are multiple biochemical approaches to assessing iron status at the individual level. A low serum ferritin or an elevated transferrin receptor value signifies iron deficiency (absent reserves), whereas an elevated level of zinc protoporphyrin (ZPP) reflects depleted iron stores; various biomarkers in combination can provide an estimation of total body iron [2].

13.3.1 The Consequences of Iron Deficiency

At the individual level, iron deficiency can reduce muscle function, attentiveness and alertness, even before the onset of anemia. The manifestations of iron deficiency anemia (IDA) include subjective symptoms ranging from weakness, distraction, moodiness and headache to exercise fatigue and sore tongue; physical signs include pallor of the skin and conjunctiva and brittle nails.

At the population level, widespread reduction in work efficiency and capacity can be seen with endemic iron deficiency anemia, as illustrated by hookworm-infested sugar-cane cutters in Guatemala and Venezuela. Serial follow-ups of children in Costa Rica and Chile have demonstrated an association of IDA in infancy, and delayed cognitive capacity into the teenage years. Finally, there is suggestive evidence that a background anemia is a risk factor for maternal and infant mortality at childbirth.

13.3.2   The Consequences of Iron Excess and Overload

Iron poisoning occurs when iron salts are ingested—accidentally or purposely—in large amounts; an excess of 60 mg/kg (equivalent to 4 g of iron in an average-sized adult male) can be reached, which represents the threshold for a fatal outcome. The cause is corrosive damage to the lining of the intestinal tract, resulting in profuse bleeding and shock due to acute fluid loss. Before safety measures in the packaging of iron supplements were instituted (blister packaging), this was the leading cause of poisoning deaths in US children.

Chronic excessive intakes of iron at lower dosage can have adverse cellular and tissue effects, predisposing to malignant, metabolic, neurodegenerative and cardiovascular disease. As stated by Basuli et al. [3]: "Most evidence supports the hypothesis that excess iron contributes to chronic disease by fostering excess production of free radicals. Overall, epidemiological studies, reinforced by basic science experiments, provide a strong line of evidence supporting the association between iron and elevated risk of cardiovascular disease and diabetes."

13.3.3   Issues of Biological Availability of Dietary Iron

13.3.3.1   Intrinsic Regulation of Iron Uptake

Because of its essentiality, the intestine has evolved the capacity to increase the efficiency of capture and transport of iron from the diet to the body. Due to its inherent abundance in the environment and the aforementioned potential for free-radical induction, there is a biological need to regulate its uptake. Ferrous iron is captured from the intestinal lumen by 'divalent metal transporter 1' (DMT-1), a protein that is involved in the transport of many essential and non-essential divalent metals. It is located on the duodenal brushborder membrane. It is not so much how many iron atoms get *into* the intestinal cell, but how many get *across* the basolateral side into the circulation that matters. This exit is governed by the transport protein, ferroportin, acting as the key point of regulatory control along with ferritin, which is indispensable to sequester and retain excessive iron in the mucosa [4]. The stock of ferroportin is, in turn, controlled by a hepatic protein, hepcidin, which binds and degrades it [5]. Iron status is sensed within the liver, and a cascade of signaling upregulates hepcidin expression when the iron stores are normal or elevated.

13.3.3.2 Endogenous and Extrinsic Factors in Bioavailability of Iron

Other host factors and components of the diet affect the efficiency of iron uptake. Low gastric acid secretion and environmentally-induced small intestinal damage are common in unhygienic settings, and can impair iron absorption. Dietary factors, including ascorbic acid and an elusive factor from animal protein foods (meat; fish and poultry), enhance iron absorption, whereas phytic acid, soy protein, calcium and polyphenols inhibit iron availability.

13.3.3.3 Iron Uptake from Human Milk

The WHO recommends exclusive breast feeding (EBF) from birth to six months. The concentration of iron in milk, the amount of milk consumed and the efficiency of absorption constitute the factors affecting net iron transfer to the infant. A typical iron concentration in early human lactation is 0.23 μg/mL; with a 600 mL intake, the infant would receive 0.13 mg of iron daily [6]. It declines even further with the progression of lactation, and maternal supplementation has no effect on breast-milk iron. The intrinsic bioavailability of human milk iron, however, can exceed 90%. The observed reality is that up to half of exclusively breast-fed infants can emerge from the first semester of infancy with iron deficiency anemia. The way to interpret and respond to this reality is a challenge.

13.3.3.4 Daily Requirements for Iron Consumption and Absorption

In a conceptual manner, daily requirements would be equivalent to the amount of iron needed by an adult to replace the amount lost in a day. In the absence of bleeding, iron is lost primarily in the turnover of intestinal cells, and to a lesser extent from the desquamation of skin. The average loss of iron by these routes is ~ 1 mg Fe/d. Between menarche and menopause, women have an additional monthly loss of blood via menstruation. The quantity is highly variable across fertile-aged women, but a median daily value of ~ 1.8 mg Fe has been derived from prorating across the 28-day cycle; this represents three times as much net loss of iron as men, and requires a threefold higher intake to remain in iron balance. From infancy to adolescence, a lesser intestinal and skin loss is seen, while growth of tissues and the red cell mass imposes an additional component of iron accretion to the iron uptake requirement.

How much iron needs to be ingested to allow for the respective uptakes depends on assumptions of its absorption efficiency (biological availability) from the food and beverage sources in the diet. For a discussion of population issues for both nutrients of this chapter, we are presented with a conundrum. On the one hand, the scope of this discussion is on a worldwide basis, making the FAO-WHO recommendations [7] more relevant and all-encompassing than those for the US and Canada [8]. On the other hand, the Estimated Average Intake (EAR) is a more

Table 13.1 WHO-FAO recommended iron intakes by population group and dietary bioavailability

Group	Age (years)	Mean body weight (kg)	Recommended nutrient intake[a] (mg day)			
			% Dietary iron bio-availability			
			15	12	10	5
Children	0.5–1	9	[6.2][b]	[7.7][b]	[9.3][b]	[18.6][b]
	1–3	13.3	3.9	4.8	5.8	11.6
	4–6	19.2	4.2	5.3	6.3	12.6
	7–10	28.1	5.9	7.4	8.9	17.8
Males	11–14	45	9.7	12.2	14.6	29.7
	15–17	64.4	12.5	15.7	18.8	37.6
	18+	75	9.1	11.4	13.7	27.4
Females	11–14[c]	46.1	9.3	11.7	14	28
	11–14	46.1	21.8	27.7	32.7	65.4
	15–17	56.4	20.7	25.8	31	62
	18+	62	19.6	24.5	29.4	58.8
		62	7.5	9.4	11.3	22.6
Post-menopausal Lactating		62	10	12.5	15	30

Reproduced with permission from Ref. [7]
[a]Based in part on a 1998 report from the FAO/WHO and is part of new calculations of the distribution of iron requirements in menstruating women. Because of the very skewed distribution of iron requirements in these women, dietary iron requirements are calculated for four levels of dietary iron bio-availability
[b]Bio-availability of dietary iron during this period varies greatly
[c]Non-menstruating

relevant reference value than the Recommended Nutrient Intake (RNI), which pertains more to the individual. However, it is intrinsically difficult to apply an EAR to iron, and there is no official EAR for the United Nations system [7]. To its credit, the WHO-FAO recommendations for both nutrients provide a range of assumptions for efficiency of absorption, based the intrinsic nutrient bioavailability from the typical local fare. Table 13.1 provides the RNI values for iron across age categories in relation to assumptions about the dietary fractional iron absorption from diets with different content of inhibitory or enhancing factors.

13.3.3.5 Dietary Sources of Iron

Iron is ubiquitous in both plant- and animal-source foods. In plants, the concentrations in the top soil and the soil pH are determinants of uptake. The iron content in eggs and milk is relatively uniform. Organ meats and red meat (beef, lamb) have between 6 and 2 mg/100 g, whereas white meats (poultry, pork) offer about 2 mg/100 g. This is primarily iron in the form of hemoglobin in blood or myoglobin in muscle, which is inherently more bioavailable than inorganic iron [9]. Bran, soybeans, pumpkin seeds and common beans are high in iron in an inorganic form, incorporated into the seed coat; this iron is poorly absorbed, however. Some commercially fortified foods, such as certain brands of cornflakes, can contain between 60 and 12 mg of iron per 100 g of dry cereal. As a consequence of the aforementioned factors in iron bioavailability, the concentration of iron in a food is a poor correlate of the content of biologically-available iron. One universal fact, however, is that all forms of mammalian milk, including human, are very poor sources of iron (<1 mg/L).

13.3.3.6   Typical Dietary Iron Consumption and Projected Effects of Food Insecurity

It is of little practical value to catalogue estimated intakes of iron in mg/day, given the variation in age-specific requirements and dietary bioavailability. The published literature from developing societies tends to support the conclusion that intakes of biologically available iron are consistently below recommended levels in many, if not most, sites of survey reconnaissance. This includes findings from Bangladesh, Chile, China, Costa Rica, India, Indonesia, Jordan, Kenya, Malaysia, Mexico, Morocco, Nepal, Pakistan, and Vietnam, among other nations. The interpretation and policy implications of these reports is not straight forward, however, as the assortment of age-groups, dietary-assessment approaches and reference criteria for adequate iron intakes vary widely. Taken together, however, the panorama inclines more toward individual requirements, adjusted for assumed bioavailability, falling below the standard for average population needs. What emerges, however, are two patterns of insufficient available iron. Bangladesh is the prototype for one variety [10], in which there is insufficient total food along with low iron density within the food supply. Chile and Costa Rica represent another pattern, in which total food availability is sufficient to satisfy energy and protein, but not enough biologically available iron accompanies those macronutrients in the diet [11, 12].

13.3.3.7   Consequences of Food Insecurity for Population Iron Status

The modeling of, and prognostication about, the future directions of food insecurity are the purview of other chapters in this volume. With respect the supply of the biologically available nutrient to meet the needs of the world's population, there is situation of 'dietary iron insecurity', which probably affects majority of the planet's inhabitants. One would need the models of predicted food supply shifts, however (see elsewhere in this volume), to provide a sophisticated prediction of the future drift for bioavailable dietary iron.

Refined from its bulk calorie definition, the existing pattern of insufficient bioavailable iron of diets around the world represents "iron insecurity". To the extent that much of the world currently suffers from iron deficiency, any worsening of food availability would portend an exacerbation of the situation. Logically, lower consumption of the same foods could only make the situation worse. Lesser quantities of foods with even lower iron quality would make the situation much worse. One of the caveats within these generalities has to do with the within-household distribution of a scarcer food supply. As infants and toddlers and fertile-aged women represent the most vulnerable groups for iron deficiency, any cultural or policy factors that would prioritize their food acquisition within the family would somewhat mitigate the decline. Conversely, unfavorable discrimination regarding access to these most susceptible segments would exacerbate the risk for disproportionately poorer iron status going forward.

13.4   Zinc as a Public Health Problem in Relation to Food Insecurity

Iron can be considered the principal micronutrient concern of the WHO and most nutrition-assistance agencies for six decades; by contrast, the concern for zinc has emerged only recently and, although recognized, it is not so firmly embraced by official policy entities. In fact, the International Zinc Nutrition Consultative Group (IZiNCG), founded in 2000, has been the lead entity and advocate for a concern for zinc as a problem in public health [13]. The world-map distribution estimate for stunting in children under the age of five years comes from IZiNCG [13] (Fig. 13.2).

As compared to iron, assessment of individual zinc status is elusive, and estimating the zinc status of a population is even more complex and challenging. Four approaches to the population estimate of zinc deficiency as a public health problem

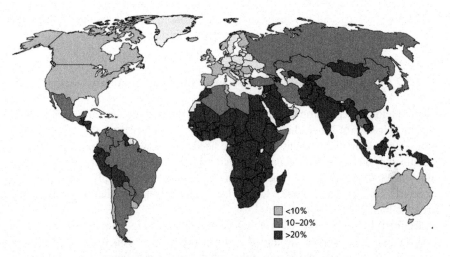

Fig. 13.2 Estimated prevalence of stunting (<−2 Z-score) among children under 5 years of age, by nation. Reproduced with permission from Hotz and Brown [13]

from IZiNCG [13] are listed in Box 13.1. Figure 13.2 is based on the combined application of the first two approaches aligned with national survey.

Box 13.1 Four approaches to estimation of population status of zinc

---

1. The presence or prevalence of clinical outcomes of zinc deficiency (e.g., stunting, diarrhea), or other ecologic factors associated with risk of zinc deficiency or risk of inadequate zinc intakes

2. Assessment of the adequacy of dietary zinc intakes in relation to theoretical requirements for absorbed zinc

3. Biochemical measures of zinc concentration, activity of zinc-dependent enzymes, or other zinc-responsive biocomponents in biologic fluids or tissues, assessed in comparison to reference values or established cutoffs

4. Measurement of functional responses following the intake of adequate supplemental zinc

Reproduced with permission from Hotz and Brown (IZiNCG) 2004, Ref. 13, p S131

13.4.1 The Consequences of Zinc Deficiency

The syndrome of severe zinc deficiency has been defined based on experience with the hereditary zinc-malabsorption disease, acrodermatitis enteropathica, and unsupplemented total parenteral alimentation. The manifestations include mental lethargy, thymic atrophy, scaly-flaky skin rash, diarrhea and gonadal hypofunction. Having earlier established an association between low zinc levels and low stature, Walravens et al. [14] documented a linear growth response to oral zinc supplementation in short-stature children in Denver, Colorado, in an important public health paradigm-extension. Hambidge [15] typifies mild human zinc deficiency as a condition primarily affecting linear and ponderal growth.

13.4.2 The Consequences of Zinc Excess and Overload

By contrast to iron, zinc is relatively safe and non-toxic. This is attributable to the fact that zinc has emetic effects at doses of 400 mg or more such that single doses above this would likely be vomited; moreover, the body is able to increase excretion of the element in the face of excessive intakes. The rodent LD50 (i.e. the chronic ingestion level that kills half of the animals) extrapolates to 27 g per day for a human adult [16]. The aforementioned emetic properties would make it impossible to ingest this amount in a single day without extensive fractionation of the dose.

13.4.3   Issues of Biological Availability of Dietary Zinc

13.4.3.1   Intrinsic Regulation of Zinc Uptake

Unlike iron, in which the status of the host tightly regulates the absorption of the metal, there is no down-regulation at the point of uptake for zinc. At intraluminal concentrations of zinc above 2 mM, corresponding to a dietary intake of over 10 mg across the day's meals, the intestine is permissive to the absorption of zinc presented on the intestinal surface. However, the relationship is not linear; the greater the amount of zinc presented from the intestinal lumen, the lower the fractional absorption of the mineral across the intestine into the body. Four mg of zinc will be absorbed from 9 mg of intake in a high-bioavailability diet (44%), but only 5 mg will be absorbed from 15 mg of intake from a similar diet (33%) [17]. At lower concentrations, i.e. below 2 mM, the intestine actively adapts, engaging molecular mechanisms of active uptake; this involved Zrt- and Irt-related protein 4 (ZIP4), a metal transport protein located at the luminal surface of the enterocyte, and zinc transporter protein 1 (ZnT1) at the basolateral surface of the cell, which combine to internalize luminal zinc and export it into the body, respectively, by an energy-dependent uptake mechanism [18].

Rather than at the point of absorption, total body equilibrium is maintained by adjustments made to the endogenous losses, which are primarily secreted in pancreatic juice, bile and in the serosal to mucosal direction across the cells of the intestinal mucosa [17]. This mechanism, however, has little capacity for conservation, such that insufficient dietary provision of zinc or its excessive gastrointestinal losses will result in deficiency of the nutrient.

13.4.3.2   Extrinsic Factors in Bioavailability of Zinc

The major extrinsic inhibitor to zinc absorption is phytic acid, a phosphorus-rich ringed compound in the structural components of plants, particularly seed grains [19]. The less refined the cereals and legumes in a diet, the richer it is in phytates, and the less accessible is zinc for absorption. Less important in a dietary context is a reduction in zinc absorption efficiency in the face of high concentrations of iron and calcium, but these competitors can become important in the context of supplementation.

13.4.3.3   Zinc Uptake from Human Milk

In the context of the WHO recommendations for six months of exclusive breast feeding, the aforementioned factors of milk concentration, volume consumed and fractional absorption determine zinc transfer to the breast-fed infant. As with iron, zinc concentrations vary through the course of lactation: a daily delivery of 1.6 mg in early lactation declines to 0.4 mg by the 6th month [20]. Similar to iron, the zinc levels in milk cannot be driven by increasing the delivery to the mother. Given the limitations in individual status assessment, the prevalence of zinc deficiency in infancy is not well established.

13.4.3.4 Daily Requirements for Zinc Consumption and Absorption

It is estimated that between 4 and 6 mg of zinc needs to be absorbed by a normal adult daily to replace the losses of endogenous zinc; this depends, in a non-linear manner on the amount of zinc ingested [17]. The variation in anti-nutritional inhibitors of zinc absorption characterize the efficiency of absorption from different cuisines. This is reflected in the Recommended Nutrient Intakes illustrated in Table 13.1 [7], presenting assumptions about fractional absorption of the nutrient.

13.4.3.5 Dietary Sources of Zinc

The richest known source of zinc is Atlantic oysters, with about 100 mg of zinc per 100 g of oyster flesh. North Atlantic herring is another rich source, with a third of that concentration. Other fish and seafood have up to 5 mg/100 g, and organ meats, muscle meats and poultry between 6 and 2 mg/100 g. Seeds and nuts have zinc concentrations of up to 8 mg/100 g, but this is accompanied by 5–2 g of phytic acid that reduces zinc bioavailability drastically. Whole grains and legumes have 3–1 g/100 g, but have up to 600 mg/100 g of phytic acid [21].

13.4.3.6 Typical Consumption and Projected Effects of Food Insecurity

As with iron, the recommendations for daily consumption of zinc involve assumptions about the intrinsic bioavailability of the nutrient in the diet, applying the scheme from Table 13.2. Low-income societies with unrefined grains as staples (e.g. Middle-Eastern flat breads, Meso-American maize *tortillas*, and Indian sub-Continent *chipattis*) would be assigned the low bioavailability assumption. Tuber-based (e.g. Andean) or polished-rice-based (e.g. East and Southeast Asian) cuisines would have the moderate or high bioavailability assumption. Interestingly, in terms of absolute zinc intake, a Chinese national survey revealed a 10.6 mg median daily zinc intake [22]; the corresponding mean value for toddlers in a convenience sample in Yun-Nan Province was 1.9 mg [23]. It has long been recognized that zinc is one of the most problematic nutrients for achieving adequate intakes from complementary feeding diets [24].

Table 13.2 WHO-FAO Recommended zinc intakes by population group and dietary bioavailability, expressed in μg/kg body weight/day

Group	High bioavailability[b]	Moderate bioavailability[c]	Low bioavailability[d]
Infants and children			
Females, 0–3 months	175[e]	457[f]	1067[g]
Males, 0–3 months	200[e]	514[f]	1200[g]
3–6 months	79[e]	204[f]	477[g]
6–12 months	66[e], 186	311	621
1–3 years	138	230	459
3–6 years	114	190	380
6–10 years	90	149	299
Adolescents			
Females, 10–12 years	68	113	227
Males, 10–12 years	80	133	267
Females, 12–15 years	64	107	215
Males, 12–15 years	76	126	253
Females, 15–16 years	56	93	187
Males, 15–18 years	61	102	205
Adults			
Females, 18–60+ years	36	59	119
Males, 16–60+ years	43	72	144

Reproduced with permission from Ref. [7]

[a]For information on diets, see Table 12.2

[b]Assume bioavailability of dietary zinc, 50%

[c]Assume bioavailability of dietary zinc, 30%

[d]Assume bioavailability of dietary zinc, 15%

[e]Applicable to infants fed maternal milk alone for which the bioavailability of zinc is assumed to be 80% and infant endogenous losses to be 20 μg/kg (0.31 μmol/kg). Corresponds to basal requirements with no allowance for storage

[f]Applicable to infants partly human-milk-fed or fed whey-adjusted cow milk formula or milk plus low-phytate solids. Corresponds to basal requirements with no allowance for storage

[g]Applicable to infants receiving phytate-rich vegetable-protein-based infant formula with or without whole-grain cereals. Corresponds to basal requirements with no allowance for storage

13.4.3.7 Consequences for Population Zinc Status

Iron can be stored in reserves, whereas there are no zinc stores or metabolically exchangeable deposits of zinc in the human body. Moreover, in contrast to iron, zinc is continuously excreted. As a consequence, individuals are dependent on a constant and steady supply of dietary zinc to satisfy the zinc-dependent functions of the body. Any seasonality in the dietary zinc supply would make us vulnerable to rapid negative balance in the scarcity seasons of a year.

Regarding future directions, the same principles hold for zinc as for iron. Bioavailable zinc is currently being widely under-consumed in the current food supply. Therefore, having less is bad and having more poorly-absorbed zinc within the lower amounts of food would predictably make matters worse. Current opinions would view growing children as the relatively more vulnerable segment for zinc deficiency; how children are favored or disfavored by the intra-family distribution of food resources would therefore impact on the severity of juvenile zinc deficiency going forward.

13.5 Implications for Public Policy and Future in Research

This book is predicated on a somewhat Malthusian premise, rooted in assumptions about exhaustion of the earth's capacity to sustain food production for an expanding human population; these have been proven false—or at least premature—in the past. Ironically, operating hand in hand with an increasing food insecurity hypothesis is concern for a worldwide pandemic of overweight and obesity, which presumes an excess of calorie availability on an individual basis. In fact, these two tendencies could be mutually compatible within an assumption of massive increase in sedentarism, inactivity even out of proportion to a falling dietary energy supply. Such a scenario as total caloric intakes decline would argue, therefore, for a concern about iron and zinc quality in the food supply, in terms of increased density per gram of food and enhanced bioavailability.

13.5.1 Bases for Policy Guidelines

Clearly, emerging policy should maintain a steady focus on food insecurity as a potential calamity. Both trace elements of interest illustrate a nutritional situation in which the density of a biologically available nutrient in common staple foods of grain or root and tuber origin is insufficient to satisfy the needs for daily uptake to keep the human body in balance. Thus, more pertinent to this chapter should be the imperative to address the satisfaction of human iron and zinc needs with any agricultural and health policy strategies implemented in future.

Box 13.2 provides an annotated outline of the conventional elements of the strategy to improve nutritional status. Within a context of increasing food insecurity, the luxury of dietary diversification would seem, at face value, to be the most remote and antithetical to the future projections. For both iron and zinc, supplementation is the most studied format. In that context, the limitations of compliance represent an unresolved challenge, and will probably exist for zinc as well. Two indications for zinc supplementation—namely, with oral rehydration for diarrhea and to prevent recurrent infectious episodes—are probably pharmacological and would not occur with the most adequate of dietary zinc offerings. Iron fortification of staple foods is well studied, with international recent guidelines emitted [25, 26]; biological impact is heavily dependent on the contribution of the staples to total dietary energy. Zinc fortification is still in diapers as a public policy, and insufficient evaluation of its beneficial effects has been conducted and published to guide policy. However, in the final analysis, a dynamic and ongoing assessment of the role for the available options in Box 13.2 will be needed to protect human nutritional well-being.

Box 13.2 Four modes of improving micronutrient intake or status

---

Dietary Diversification

Overall: This consists of modifying the selection of foods consumed in the diet to increase intake of nutrient-dense sources for specific problem micronutrients, to decrease anti-nutritional factors, to increase absorption enhancers, or any or all of the above

Specific Considerations: This involves changes in usual culinary and consumption patterns, and generally requires nutrition education reinforcements. Often the nutrient-dense sources were not part of the diet for reasons of scarcity, low affordability and/or cultural or personal unacceptability. Foods naturally rich in both iron and zinc are generally of animal (e.g. meat, seafood) origin, and their availability in the food supply often has environmental costs

---

Nutrient Supplementation

Overall definition: This consists of providing nutrients in amounts usually equal to or superior to the daily recommended intakes, taken in medicinal formats such as tablets, capsules or syrups, generally consumed away from meals

Specific considerations: Because supplements require a specific repetitive behavior and often have a strong or unpleasant taste (and in the case of zinc and iron in concentrated dosing, some untoward gastric side-effects), compliance can be sporadic and incomplete

Indefinite consumption of dosages in excess of the daily requirement can result in nutrient-excess conditions for both iron and zinc. Moreover, unless care is taken, supplements (more for iron than for zinc) can pose a poisoning hazard for young children in the household

The observed effects on health and/or nutrition in supplementation trials may—or may not—be replicable with a fortification format

---

Nutrient Fortification

Overall definition: This consists of specific addition of a nutrient to foods to increase their density per serving. In the past decade, the approach of *biofortification* agronomic methods to enrich the nutrient content of growing plants, including with iron and zinc, has been explored in crops and human feeding trials

Specific considerations: Consuming fortificant nutrients is part of the essential habit of eating and is more unconscious and sustainable. Fortification can add cost (usually modest) to a product, and not all varieties of a given product in the marketplace are fortified unless mandated by law. Conversely, an abundant number of processed foods may fortify with the same nutrient, and inadvertent overconsumption can result for the consumer

Experience has shown that the choice of the iron compound is important in terms of cost, reactivity and absorbability. Iron fortificants with the lowest cost and the least reactivity with the food or beverage tend to be the least acceptable and effective; conversely, the more bioavailable (chelated) iron compounds add substantially more cost to the fortified product

Zinc fortification of both staple foods and commercial processed products is in its infancy; the efficacy for improving status and mimicking the effects of zinc supplementation is incompletely documented at present

---

General Health Measures

Overall definition: This is to control endemic conditions that would lead to decreased absorption and would increase losses of the nutrient in question

Specific considerations: In the case of iron, elimination of blood-feeding protozoa and parasites such as amoebas, whipworm, hookworm and schistosomes through hygienic and anti-parasite prophylaxis programs

Zinc loss occurs with bouts of diarrhea (intestinal) and fever episodes (urinary). Hygiene and immunization interventions to limit infections together favor zinc retention

---

13.5.1.1   Investigational Needs

In the context of the unknowns of the food supply and food security going forward, one can project investigational needs in three domains: (1) population evaluation and monitoring; (2) technological innovation; and (3) nutrition science research.

13.5.1.2   Evaluation and Monitoring

In conjunction with iron status assessment of populations, which is becoming increasingly available from routine periodic surveys, initial and serial assessment of the nature of iron in the food supply and its dietary intake is essential. Going forward into the unknowns of food insecurity, it provides a threshold for action and offers a perspective on the effectiveness of the interventions. Hotz and Brown [13] provide guidelines for dietary assessment that probably would serve both nutrients well. Reliability in assessment of population zinc status, however, remains subject to numerous caveats associated with the approaches outlined in Box 13.1.

13.5.1.3   Technology for Fortification

Iron fortification is a mature technology with well-founded action guidelines [25, 26]; by contrast, guidance for zinc is in a most preliminary and evolving state [27]. A systematic review of zinc fortification trials shows the approach, on balance, to be efficacious in improving zinc status [28], within the constraints of interpreting status indices. Evaluation of zinc fortificant compounds from the technology laboratory to human field trials demands further investment. Biofortification technology and plant improvement could provide a substantial advance, as evidenced by studies with iron- and zinc-enriched pearl millet in Karnataka, India [29].

13.5.1.4   Nutrient Status Assessment

Although it involves the extraction of blood, biochemical assessment of the individual's iron status is reliably developed. An advance would be a blood-extraction-free and non-invasive approach, as is being explored with transcutaneous estimation of ZPP in several laboratories [30]. The development of a valid, field-friendly and inexpensive biomarker for zinc status remains elusive. For excess status for zinc, i.e. above and beyond adequacy, the options for simple detection are even more elusive. Improved zinc-status assessment for the individual is a priority.

13.6   Conclusions

These summary considerations point toward the conclusion that the maintenance of universal adequacy of iron and zinc status depends more directly on the *quality* of the diet than on satisfaction of caloric requirements, per se. Thus, to the extent that food security is gauged primarily by available dietary energy, the issues related to zinc and iron will be obscured. Both increased consumption of animal-source foods and fortification have their limitations and dangers. The animal-source route has environmental consequences and runs contrary to the hypothesis' premise of an impending contraction in food-production capacity. Fortification is a two-edged sword: it has the potential of falling short of full efficacy in the absence of an appropriate balance of bioavailable compounds and a receptive background diet, but uncontrolled duplication of fortification efforts throughout both staple and commercial food sectors could pose a risk of excessive consumption. Awareness of the potential for problems and the embrace of monitoring and evaluation, technical innovation and appropriate applied research are clearly keys to protecting the population from whatever panorama of food insecurity might emerge in the coming decades.

13.7   Summary: Key Messages

- Overt deficiency of iron and zinc produces public health consequences. Iron deficiency affects stamina and cognitive and immune function, evolving in its extreme form to iron deficiency anemia. Zinc deficiency is associated with poor growth and decreased disease resistance.
- In a food-security context, these two nutrients are most abundant and most biologically available in animal-source foods. Dietary diversification toward greater contribution of animal-source food is, however, problematic in the face of environmental issues and agriculture trends.
- Actions to improve nutritional status and mitigate the effects of food insecurity need to be conceptualized, evaluated for efficacy, and integrated into public policy.
- Food fortification and the newer approach of biofortification offer the greatest theoretical promise for both nutrients.
- Awareness of the potential for problems and the embrace of monitoring and evaluation, technical innovation and appropriate applied research are keys to protecting the population from whatever panorama of food insecurity might emerge in the coming decades.

References

1. World Health Organization/Centers for Disease Control and Prevention. The worldwide prevalence of anemia. WHO global database on anemia. Geneva: WHO, 2008.
2. Yang Z, Dewey KG, Lönnerdal B, Hernell O, Chaparro C, Adu-Afarwuah S, McLean ED, Cohen RJ, Domellöf M, Allen LH, Brown KH. Comparison of plasma ferritin concentration with the ratio of plasma transferrin receptor to ferritin in estimating body iron stores: results of 4 intervention trials. Am J Clin Nutr. 2008;87:1892–8.
3. Basuli D, Stevens RG, Torti FM, Torti SV. Epidemiological associations between iron and cardiovascular disease and diabetes. Front Pharmacol. 2014;5:117.
4. Vanoaica L, Darshan D, Richman L, Schümann K, Kühn LC. Intestinal ferritin H is required for an accurate control of iron absorption. Cell Metabol 2010;12:273–282.
5. Hentze MW, Muckenthaler MU, Galy B, Camaschella C. Two to tango: regulation of mammalian iron metabolism. Cell 2010;142:24–38.
6. Picciano MF, Guthrie HA. Copper, iron, and zinc contents of mature human milk. Am J Clin Nutr. 1976;29:242–54.
7. World Health Organization/Food and Nutrition Organization. Vitamin and mineral requirements in human nutrition, Second Edition. Geneva: WHO, 2004.
8. Food and Nutrition Board, Institute of Medicine. Dietary Reference Intakes of vitamin A, vitamin K, arsenic, boron, chromium, copper, iodine, iron, manganese, molybdenum, nickel, silicon, vanadium and zinc. Washington, DC: National Academy Press, 2001.
9. Hallberg L, Hulthén L. Perspectives on iron absorption. Blood Cells Mol Dis. 2002;29:562–73.
10. Arsenault JE, Yakes EA, Islam MM, Hossain MB, Ahmed T, Hotz C, Lewis B, Rahman AS, Jamil KM, Brown KH. Very low adequacy of micronutrient intakes by young children and women in rural Bangladesh is primarily explained by low food intake and limited diversity. J Nutr. 2013;143:197–203.
11. Olivares M, Walter T, Hertrampf E, Pizarro F. Anaemia and iron deficiency disease in children. Br Med Bull. 1999;55:534–543.
12. Monge-Rojas R. Marginal vitamin and mineral intake of Costa Rican adolescents. Arch Med Res. 2001;32:70–8.
13. Hotz C, Brown KH, eds. International Zinc Consultative Group (IZiNCG) Technical Document #1. Assessment of Risk of Zinc Deficiency in Populations and Options for its Control. Food Nutr Bull 2004:25 (Suppl 2):94–204.
14. Walravens PA, Krebs NF, Hambidge KM. Linear growth of low income preschool children receiving a zinc supplement. Am J Clin Nutr. 1983;38:195–201.
15. Hambidge KM. Mild zind deficiency in human subjects, in Mills CF (ed.). Zinc in human biology. London: Springer Verlag 1989: 281–296.
16. Plum LM, Rink L, Haase H. The essential toxin: impact of zinc on human health. Int J Environ Res Public Health. 2010;7:1342–1365.
17. Hambidge KM, Miller LV, Krebs NF. Physiological requirements for zinc. Int Vitam Nutr Res. 2011;81:72–8.
18. Cousins RJ: Gastrointestinal factors influencing zinc absorption and homeostasis. Int J Vitam Nutr Res. 2010;80:244–48.
19. Gibson RS, Heath AL, Szymlek-Gay EA. Is iron and zinc nutrition a concern for vegetarian infants and young children in industrialized countries? Am J Clin Nutr. 2014;100(Supplement 1):459S-468S.
20. Krebs NF, Hambidge KM, Jacobs MA, Rasbach JO. The effects of a dietary zinc supplement during lactation on longitudinal changes in maternal zinc status and milk zinc concentrations. Am J Clin Nutr. 1985;41:560–70.
21. Ma G, Li Y, Jin Y, Zhai F, Kok FJ, Yang X. Phytate intake and molar ratios of phytate to zinc, iron and calcium in the diets of people in China. Eur J Clin Nutr. 2007;61:368–74.

22. Sheng XY, Hambidge KM, Zhu XX, Ni JX, Bailey KB, Gibson RS, Krebs NF. Major variables of zinc homeostasis in Chinese toddlers. Am J Clin Nutr. 2006;84:389–94.
23. Brown KH, Dewey KG, Allen LH. Comlementary feeding of young children in developing countries: a review current of scientific knowledge. Geneva: WHO, 1998.
24. King JC, Cousins RJ. Zinc. In: Shils ME, Shike M, Ross AC, Caballero B, Cousins RJ. (eds). Modern Nutrition in Health and Disease, 10th edition. Philadelpia: Lippincott Williams & Wilkins 2006:271–285.
25. World Health Organization. Recommendations on Wheat and Maize Flour Fortification Meeting Report: Interim Consensus Statement. Geneva: WHO, 2009.
26. Hurrell R, Ranum P, de Pee S, Biebinger R, Hulthen L, Johnson Q, Lynch S. Revised recommendations for iron fortification of wheat flour and an evaluation of the expected impact of current national wheat flour fortification programs. Food Nutr Bull. 2010;31(1 Suppl): S7–21.
27. Brown KH, Hambidge KM, Ranum P; Zinc Fortification Working Group. Zinc fortification of cereal flours: current recommendations and research needs. Food Nutr Bull. 2010;31(1 Suppl):S62–74.
28. Das JK, Kumar R, Salam RA, Bhutta ZA. Systematic review of zinc fortification trials. Ann Nestle 2013;71:44–56.
29. Kodkany BS, Bellad RM, Mahantshetti NS, Westcott JE, Krebs NF, Kemp JF, Hambidge KM. Biofortification of pearl millet with iron and zinc in a randomized controlled trial increases absorption of these minerals above physiologic requirements in young children. J Nutr. 2013;143:1489–93.
30. Crowley CR, Solomons NW, Schümann K. Targeted provision of oral iron: the evolution of a practical screening option. Adv Nutr. 2012;3:560–9.

Chapter 14
Iodine Deficiency: Achievements and Challenges for the 21st Century

Alida Melse-Boonstra

Abstract Iodine deficiency impairs the production of thyroid hormones, which has severe health consequences for child growth and development. Iodine deficiency is the most common cause of preventable mental impairment (Walker et al. in Lancet 369:145–57, [44], Zimmermann in Clin Endocrinol (Oxf.) 75:287–8, [50]). Mass iodization of salt provides a cost-effective way to improve iodine intake, with annual costs estimated at US$0.02–0.05 per child (UNICEF in The State of the World's Children 2012: Children in an urban world, United Nations Children's Fund, New York [40]), and over time has tremendously reduced the prevalence of severe iodine deficiency disorders across the globe. It is not certain, however, whether the iodine requirements of pregnant and lactating women are sufficiently covered by salt iodization programs. Although in many industrialized countries iodine deficiency has been addressed for centuries, the problem is currently recurring in some countries. New WHO recommendations on reducing sodium intake may also contribute to this. In contrast, several countries are now struggling with excessive intake of iodine. In this chapter, the following issues are discussed:

- What is the current global iodine status?
- Should additional measures be taken to cover iodine requirements during pregnancy and lactation?
- What are the causes of recurring iodine deficiency in industrialized countries, and what can we learn from this?
- Will reduction of salt intake influence the effectiveness of salt iodization programs?
- What measures should be taken to prevent excessive iodine intake?
- How can iodization programs be monitored better?

Keywords Iodine deficiency · Iodine deficiency disorders · Iodine requirements · Iodine status · Iodine intake · Salt intake · Sodium · Salt iodization · Iodization program

A. Melse-Boonstra (✉)
Division of Human Nutrition, Wageningen University and Research,
Stippeneng 4, 6708 WE Wageningen, The Netherlands
e-mail: alida.melse@wur.nl

© Springer International Publishing AG 2017   223
H.K. Biesalski et al. (eds.), *Sustainable Nutrition in a Changing World*,
DOI 10.1007/978-3-319-55942-1_14

14.1 Iodine Status: Data and Implications

14.1.1 Global Iodine Status

Iodine deficiency was first acknowledged in the late 19th century as the cause of goiter and cretinism in mountainous areas. In the mid-20th century, iodization programs were started in several countries, such as Switzerland, the Netherlands, Sweden, Australia, the USA and Canada. Around 1990, many other countries followed suit and rolled out salt iodization programs, supported and stimulated by a coalition of international organizations, led by what is now the Iodine Global Network (IGN). Adequacy of population iodine status is monitored by a median urinary iodine concentration (UIC) between 100 and 299 µg/L in spot samples of school children aged 6–12 years [48]. Based on this, 67 countries could be regarded as having sufficient iodine status on the national level by the end of the second millennium. Since then, progress has slowed, but steady improvement has still been made (Fig. 14.1). In 2007, no countries were reported to be severely iodine-deficient anymore.

Despite this positive trend, it was estimated that the iodine intake of 30% of the world's school-aged children was insufficient in 2011, with 5.2% in the severely deficient range [4]. It should be noted that 75% of the children having low iodine intake are living in countries that are classified as iodine-sufficient [51]. The other 25% live in the 25 countries remaining with moderate-to-mild iodine deficiency (Fig. 14.2). Over the past 10 years, most progress has been made in Europe, the eastern Mediterranean, south-east Asia and the western Pacific regions, whereas progress has stagnated in Africa [31]. Moderate and mild iodine deficiency continue to threaten the full cognitive capacity of two billion people worldwide [4]. On the other hand, excessive iodine status has begun to appear and has recently been reported for 12 countries, mostly located in Latin America.

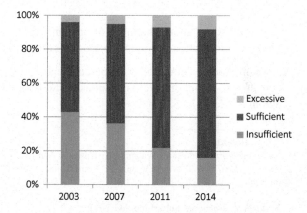

Fig. 14.1 WHO countries (percentage) by iodine status of school-aged children (SAC) over the period 2003–2014. Based on: IDD Newsletter, February 2015

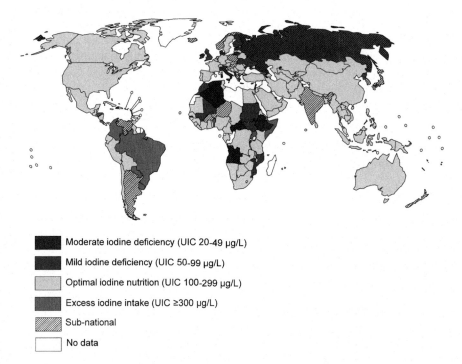

Moderate iodine deficiency (UIC 20-49 µg/L)

Mild iodine deficiency (UIC 50-99 µg/L)

Optimal iodine nutrition (UIC 100-299 µg/L)

Excess iodine intake (UIC ≥300 µg/L)

Sub-national

No data

Fig. 14.2 Global map of iodine nutrition 2014–2015. *Source* http://ign.org/p142000429.html, accessed October 2016

14.1.2 The Health Consequences and Economic Cost of Iodine Deficiency

Although severe iodine deficiency has disappeared from the global map as a public health problem (Fig. 14.2), it has not been eradicated. Cretinism, as the extreme end of the continuum of the spectrum of iodine deficiency disorders, is still found in some areas, leading to lifelong mental and physical handicaps [12]. The health consequences of moderate and mild iodine deficiency are less pronounced, but affect a far larger number of individuals and should therefore not be underestimated. The hypothyroidism resulting from moderate and mild iodine deficiency has been shown to be responsible for a 13.5 drop in IQ points (Bleichrodt and Born 1994). There is some paucity in the evidence that relates iodine deficiency to growth and developmental outcomes, which will need to be addressed [16]. Thyroid cancer is as yet an understudied consequence of iodine deficiency, and requires more investigation [52].

The health consequences of iodine deficiency result in both societal and economic costs. Age-standardized disability adjusted life years (DALYs) induced by iodine deficiency worldwide declined by 36% over the period 1990–2013, as estimated by the Global Burden of Disease study [17]; this can confidently be attributed to the worldwide iodization of salt. Furthermore, savings on health expenditure can still easily be achieved in areas with low iodized salt coverage. It was recently estimated, for example, that iodine supplementation during pregnancy in the UK can save €6,672 per woman on societal and health service costs, with a gain of 1.22 IQ points for the child [26, 30].

14.1.3 Salt Iodization, Iodine Supplementation, or Something Else?

In many countries, adequate salt iodization has been achieved relatively easy, but it can be an endless struggle in others. Especially in countries with a high number of small-scale salt producers, it is very difficult to achieve universal salt iodization [51]. Supplementation with iodized oil or tablets has been recommended as an alternative strategy when salt iodization cannot be implemented nationwide [48]. However, iodine supplementation poses its own challenges, since it requires political commitment, logistical support, education and communication. It was concluded that it is unlikely that iodine supplementation programs can be implemented rapidly and effectively when salt iodization fails [41].

Therefore, in situations where iodine deficiency remains persistent, alternative strategies are still required. The addition of iodine to irrigation water has proven successful in increasing iodine status, growth and development of children in China [38]. The biofortification of crops is another possible strategy, either through agronomic and breeding techniques [43], or through genetic engineering [27]. Consumption of 100 g of biofortified vegetables for two weeks by a group of 50 healthy volunteers was shown to increase their UIC significantly [39]. More studies are required in vulnerable areas to provide evidence of the effectiveness of this strategy, as well as its acceptance [14].

14.1.4 Iodine Nutrition in Vulnerable Groups: Pregnant and Lactating Women

Pregnant and lactating women are particularly vulnerable to iodine deficiency because of their higher iodine requirement as compared with non-pregnant women (Table 14.1). Iodine requirements increase during pregnancy due to heightened maternal thyroid hormone production; transfer of iodine and thyroid hormones to the fetus; and an increase in renal iodine clearance [53]. During lactation, requirements rise because the mammary gland concentrates iodine and secretes it into breastmilk to provide for the newborn infant. Because iodine requirements increase more than energy needs during pregnancy and lactation, this can easily lead to insufficient dietary iodine intake. Iodine deficiency, especially in early pregnancy, can lead to fetal hypothyroidism, which puts the offspring at risk of irreversibly impaired brain development [25].

It has recently been estimated that pregnant women in approximately two-thirds of European countries have an inadequate iodine intake (UIC < 150 μg/L), including those living in countries that have sufficient iodine status on the national level, as for example Turkey and Sweden [22, 55]. Low UIC (<100 μg/L) in lactating women has been reported from countries with mandatory and voluntary iodine fortification programs, including India, Denmark, Mali, New Zealand, Australia, Slovakia, Sudan, Turkey, Ireland and Germany [28]. Even in Switzerland, with its long-standing iodine prophylaxis program, lactating mothers and breastfed weaning infants appeared to have low UIC [3]. This indicates the necessity of supplementing lactating mothers [9] and fortifying infant foods and formula. It should be noted, however, that iodine requirements in infants are not firmly grounded on experimental data and that further studies are necessary [37]. The European Thyroid Association advises pregnant and lactating women, or those planning a pregnancy, to take an iodine supplement of 150 μg/d [23], but current practices have not yet been surveyed.

14.1.5 The Recurrence of Iodine Deficiency in Industrialized Countries

In the UK, iodine has been added to cattle feed since the 1930s to improve milk production. This resulted in an unplanned but welcome increase in iodine intake of the UK population through milk consumption, despite low coverage of salt iodization [33]. However, recent decline in milk consumption, and maybe also replacement of conventional by organic milk with lower iodine concentration, has led to recurrence of iodine deficiency in the UK, with a median UIC of 80 μg/L in 14–15 year old girls (n = 810) [5, 42]. In addition, the median UIC in pregnant

Table 14.1 Dietary iodine intake and median UIC cut-offs for iodine deficiency as recommended by WHO

	Iodine intake, μg/d	Median UIC cut-off, μg/L				
		Severe	Moderate	Mild	Adequate	Excessive
Children						
2–5 years	90					
6–12 years	120	<20	20–49	50–99	100–300	≥300
≥12 years	150					
Adults	150					
Pregnancy	250	<150			150–500	≥500
Lactation	250	<100			≥100	

Based on: WHO [48]

women (n = 1040) from the ALSPAC cohort in the Bristol area was 91.1 μg/L, indicating mild-to-moderate deficiency. Low UIC (<150 μg/L) during pregnancy was significantly associated with lower IQ of their offspring at 8 years of age [6]. Despite this, school-aged children from selected areas (n = 168) were reported to have adequate iodine status, which is attributed to a relatively higher milk intake in this age group [7]. So far, no policy measures have been taken in the UK to redress the situation.

Likewise, in Australia and New Zealand, iodine intake has very much depended on the use of iodophor udder cleansers in the dairy industry. When this was replaced with non-iodine containing antiseptics in the 1990s, these countries became iodine-deficient again. The Australian National Iodine Nutrition Survey conducted in 2004 showed that children in southeastern and midland Australia and in New Zealand were mild-to-borderline iodine-deficient, with median UIC ranging from 73.5 to 104 μg/L [24]. In New Zealand, pregnant women (n = 170) were found to have median UIC concentration of 38 μg/L, which is in the moderately deficient range, and 7% of the women had goiter [32]. Since 2009, Australia and New Zealand have mandated the iodization of salt in commercially-baked bread. Since then, iodine status is improving, but not yet sufficiently (Skaeff and Lonsdale-Cooper 2013) [11, 13, 15].

In the US, iodine intake has fallen, with pregnant women being only marginally sufficient [31, 50]. This has been ascribed to a number of reasons: reduction in the iodine content of dairy products; replacement of iodine-containing bread conditioners; reduced salt consumption; and declining use of iodized salt in processed foods [31].

These examples of recurring iodine deficiency in countries that used to be iodine-sufficient show the need to strengthen iodine control programs in industrialized countries, thereby avoiding reliance on accidental iodine sources. Since discretionary salt use in industrialized countries is very low, processed foods form an important target for fortification. Inclusion of iodized salt in the production of processed foods is therefore an important means to control iodine deficiency in industrialized countries.

14.1.6   Salt Restriction and Salt Iodization: A Contradiction in Terms?

In 2006, WHO instigated recommendations to restrict sodium intake by reducing salt consumption to <5 g per day in order to decrease hypertension and cardiovascular mortality [45]. This has led to the initiation of salt-reduction programs in many countries, which can potentially lead to a decrease in iodine intake if no measures are taken. To counteract this, iodine concentrations should be adjusted in accordance with declining salt intake [46, 47]. More iodine can be safely added to salt, even if salt intake drops <5 g/day [50].

14.1.7 Monitoring of Iodization Programs

The success of salt iodization programs is the result of the tireless efforts and goodwill of numerous individuals, organizations and salt producers around the world. These programs cannot be sustained, however, without monitoring and quality control. Challenges are often found at the factory level: inconsistent production, poor packaging, and ineffective transport channels. Problems can also occur at the governmental level, with establishing and enforcing legislation [36]. An effective monitoring system, comprising quality control at the production, retail and household level as well as regular surveys of population iodine status, form an essential part of salt iodization programs everywhere.

For surveying the iodine status of a nation, household salt samples and UIC in spot urine samples from a representative sample of school-aged children is the recommended method [48]. For salt, new methods are available for the rapid assessment of iodine content [34]. Collection of spot urine samples from school-aged children is easy, but its analysis requires a reliable laboratory to analyze iodine concentrations. Although it has been thought that iodine status in school-aged children would be representative for all population groups [48], there is clearly a mismatch between the iodine status of school children and that of pregnant women [10, 18, 19]. Nevertheless, survey data are mostly based on the iodine status of school-aged children, and nationwide data from pregnant women are scarce. This powerfully calls for the inclusion of pregnant women in iodine nutrition surveys, using an adequate UIC range of 150–499 µg/L.

Unfortunately, there is no biological indicator available for assessing the iodine status of an individual. As a consequence, it is difficult to discriminate the risk of iodine deficiency to the individual or even at sub-group level [4]. To provide a reliable estimate of individual status, at least 10 repeat spot urine collections or repeated 24-h urine collections are needed [1, 20]. This omission leads to the misclassification of individuals in epidemiologic studies, which may prevent important associations with health outcomes from being uncovered. Serum thyroglobulin (Tg) concentration is closest to what can be considered as an alternative to UIC. Tg is negatively correlated with UIC and positively correlated with thyroid-stimulating hormone (TSH) and thyroid volume in adults cross-sectionally, and its concentration responds to changes in iodine intake. The use of dried blood spots facilitates field-friendliness of the indicator as opposed to serum samples [54], but is more invasive than collection of a spot urine sample. More studies are required to evaluate the merits of Tg for identifying individuals or groups at risk of iodine deficiency.

14.1.8   The Emerging Issue of Excessive Iodine Intake

The recommended fortification level of salt is 20–40 ppm. Excessive iodine intake can occur when the level of iodine added to salt is too high; but also high iodine in groundwater can be the cause, as reported for regions in China [2]. Currently, 12 countries worldwide are reported to have excessive iodine status (Fig. 14.2). The human body protects against the overproduction of thyroid hormone during acute iodine excess by a transient decrease in thyroid hormone synthesis, a phenomenon known as the Wolff–Chaikoff effect [49]. This effect diminishes after several days to prevent the occurrence of hypothyroidism. In young infants, immaturity of the thyroid may still lead to hypothyroidism when exposed to excessive iodine [29]. Chronic iodine excess in children, adolescents and adults has been associated with increased thyroid volume and thyroid autoimmunity [21]. When not reverted, this may well lead to thyroid diseases at a later stage in life. Iodine fortification levels should therefore be regularly monitored and adjusted.

14.1.9   Summary

- At the global level, major progress has been made in correcting iodine deficiency, with 25 countries currently left with insufficient iodine status.
- Mild-to-moderate iodine deficiency is still estimated to affect two billion people worldwide.
- The iodine requirements of pregnant and lactating women are not fully covered by current iodine prophylaxis programs.
- Iodine deficiency has recurred in several industrialized countries that were chiefly relying on accidental iodine sources in the food supply.
- The number of countries with excessive iodine status is increasing, which can negatively affect health if not corrected.
- Sodium restriction through reduced salt intake requires adjustment of the iodine level in salt.

Lack of a simple biological indicator that reflects individual iodine status hampers diagnosis and epidemiology of iodine deficiency.

14.1.10   Conclusion

It can be concluded that the global burden of iodine deficiency disorders has declined significantly over the past few decades. Salt iodization has been shown to be a very effective public health measure for many individuals. However, the iodine requirements of pregnant and lactating women, as well as of young infants, appear not to be fully covered by the current iodine prophylaxis programs. Also, in some areas of the world, universal salt iodization is hard to achieve. Several industrialized countries with a long-standing tradition of iodine sufficiency have recently experienced declines in iodine intake. Recommendations for reducing salt intake also play a role in this, as well as some cases where iodine concentration in salt is set too high, or where salt intake is underestimated.

14.2 Concepts and Way Forward

It is apparent that iodine control programs need continuous monitoring and evaluation in response to changing dietary behavior, whether this involves salt reduction, reduced milk consumption, or increased inclusion of processed foods in diets. This holds true both for industrialized and for developing countries. The focus of iodine control programs should also be directed at pregnant and lactating women and young infants. This is because these are the population groups most vulnerable to the long-lasting consequences of iodine deficiency, and also because it is especially difficult to achieve adequate iodine status in these groups through measures targeted at the population as a whole. Specific measures, such as supplementation and fortification of specialized products, may be necessary. Better assessment of the iodine requirements of infants is needed. Finally, a biological indicator that better reflects individual status would greatly advance the diagnosis and epidemiology of iodine deficiency.

14.3 Future Development

There are a few challenges that stand out in the control of iodine deficiency in the coming decades. One of these is to find alternative solutions for areas where salt iodization is not an option. Biofortification is a promising strategy and needs to be developed further. Another challenge is to convince public health institutions in both developing and industrialized countries of the moral obligation to advance the health and cognitive capacity of the next generation by guaranteeing adequate iodine intake during the most vulnerable stages of existence—those of pregnancy and early life. This will significantly help to counter the social inequity and difference in productivity between nations at a very low cost.

14.4   Take-Home Message

There should be short measures in the monitoring and evaluation of iodine control programs. Regular iodine nutrition surveys should be carried out in all nations of the world, to both prevent iodine deficiency and iodine excess.

14.5   Summary: Key Messages

- Continued monitoring and evaluation of iodine control programs is necessary to adapt these programs to reflect changing dietary behaviors, i.e., salt reduction, decreased milk consumption, excessive intake;
- Specific monitoring of pregnant and lactating women is needed, since current iodine prophylaxis programs do not fully cover their requirements;
- For areas where salt iodization is not achievable, alternative strategies—such as water fortification or biofortification—should be developed;
- The absence of a biological indicator that reflects individual iodine status currently hampers diagnosis and epidemiology of iodine deficiency disorders.

References

1. Andersen S, Karmisholt J, Pedersen KM, Laurberg P (2008). Reliability of studies of iodine intake and recommendations for number of samples in groups and in individuals. Br J Nutr 2008;99:813–818.
2. Andersen S, Guan H, Teng W, Laurberg P (2009). Speciation of iodine in high iodine groundwater in china associated with goitre and hypothyroidism. Biol Trace Elem Res 2009;128:95–103.
3. Andersson M, Aeberli I, Wüst N, Piacenza AM, Bucher T, Henschen I, Haldimann M, Zimmermann MB (2010). The Swiss iodized salt program provides adequate iodine for school children and pregnant women, but weaning infants not receiving iodine-containing complementary foods as well as their mothers are iodine deficient. J Clin Endocrinol Metab 2010;95(12):5217–24.
4. Andersson M, Karumbunathan V, Zimmermann MB (2012). Global iodine status in 2011 and trends over the past decade. J Nutr 2012 Apr;142(4):744–50.
5. Bath SC, Button S, Rayman MP (2012). Iodine concentration of organic and conventional milk: implications for iodine intake. Br J Nutr 2012 Apr;107(7):935–40.
6. Bath SC, Steer CD, Golding J, Emmett P, Rayman MP (2013). Effect of inadequate iodine status in UK pregnant women on cognitive outcomes in their children: results from the Avon Longitudinal Study of Parents and Children (ALSPAC). Lancet 2013;27;382(9889):331–7.
7. Bath SC, Combet E, Scully P, Zimmermann MB, Hampshire-Jones KH, Rayman MP (2015). A multi-centre pilot study of iodine status in UK schoolchildren, aged 8–10 years. Eur J Nutr 2015 (in press).

8. Bleichrodt N & Born MP (1994). A metaanalysis of research on iodine and its relationship to cognitive development. In: Stanbury JB (editor). The damaged brain of iodine deficiency. Cognizant Communications: New York 1994:195–200.
9. Bouhouch RR, Bouhouch S, Cherkaoui M, Aboussad A, Stinca S, Haldimann M, Andersson M, Zimmermann MB (2014). Direct iodine supplementation of infants versus supplementation of their breastfeeding mothers: a double-blind, randomised, placebo-controlled trial. Lancet Diabetes Endocrinol 2014;2(3):197–209.
10. Caldwell KL, Pan Y, Mortinsen ME, Makhmudov A, Merrill L, Moye J. Iodine (2013), status in pregnant women in the National Children's Study and in U.S. women (15–44 years), NHANES 2005-2010. Thyroid 2013;23(8):927–37.
11. Charlton KE, Yeatman H, Brock E, Lucas C, Gemming L, Goodfellow A, Ma G (2013). Improvement in iodine status of pregnant Australian women 3 years after introduction of a mandatory iodine fortification programme. Prev Med 2013;57(1):26–30.
12. Chen ZP, Hetzel BS (2010). Cretinism revisited. Best Pract Res Clin Endocrinol Metab 2010;24:39–50.
13. Clifton VL, Hodyl NA, Fogarty PA, Torpy DJ, Roberts R, Nettelbeck T, Ma G, Hetzel B (2013). The impact of iodine supplementation and bread fortification on urinary iodine concentrations in a mildly iodine deficient population of pregnant women in South Australia. Nutr J 2013;12:32.
14. De Steur H, Mogendi JB, Wesana J, Makokha A, Gellynck X (2015). Stakeholder reactions toward iodine biofortified foods. An application of protection motivation theory. Appetite 2015;92:295–302.
15. Edmonds JC, McLean RM, Williams SM, Skeaff SA (2015). Urinary iodine concentration of New Zealand adults improves with mandatory fortification of bread with iodised salt but not to predicted levels. Eur J Nutr 2015 (in press).
16. Farebrother J, Naude CE, Nicol L, Andersson M, Zimmermann MB (2015). Iodised salt and iodine supplements for prenatal and postnatal growth: a rapid scoping of existing systematic reviews. Nutr J 2015;14:89.
17. GBD 2013 (2013) Risk Factors Collaborators. Global, regional, and national comparative risk assessment of 79 behavioural, environmental and occupational, and metabolic risks or clusters of risks in 188 countries, 1990–2013: a systematic analysis for the Global Burden of Disease Study 2013. Lancet 2015;pii: S0140-6736(15)00128-2.
18. Gowachirapant S, Winichagoon P, Wyss L, Tong B, Baumgartner J, Melse-Boonstra A, Zimmermann MB (2009). Urinary iodine concentrations indicate iodine deficiency in pregnant Thai women but iodine sufficiency in their school-aged children. J Nutr 2009;139 (6):1169–72.
19. Jaiswal N, Melse-Boonstra A, Sharma SK, Srinivasan K, Zimmermann MB (2015). The iodized salt programme in Bangalore, India provides adequate iodine intakes in pregnant women and more-than-adequate iodine intakes in their children. Public Health Nutr 2015;18 (3):403–13.
20. König F, Andersson M, Hotz K, Aeberli I, Zimmermann MB (2011). Ten repeat collections for urinary iodine from spot samples or 24-hour samples are needed to reliably estimate individual iodine status in women. J Nutr 2011;141:2049–2054.
21. Laurberg P, Cerqueira C, Ovesen L, Rasmussen LB, Perrild H, Andersen S, Pedersen IB, Carlé A (2010). Iodine intake as a determinant of thyroid disorders in populations. Best Pract Res Clin Endocrinol Metab 2010;24(1):13–27.
22. Lazarus JH (2014). Iodine status in Europe in 2014. Eur Thyroid J 2014;3(1):3–6.
23. Lazarus J, Brown RS, Daumerie C, Hubalewska-Dydejczyk A, Negro R, Vaidya B (2014). Europen thyroid association guidelines for the management of subclinical hypothyroidism in pregnancy and in children. Eur Thyroid J 2014;3:76–94.
24. Li, M., Eastman, C.J., Waite, K.V. et al (2006). Are Australian children iodine deficient? Results of the Australian National Iodine Nutrition Study. Medical Journal of Australia 2006;184:165–169.

25. Melse-Boonstra A, Jaiswal N (2010). Iodine deficiency in pregnancy, infancy and childhood and its consequences for brain development. Best Pract Res Clin Endocrinol Metab 2010;24 (1):29–38.
26. Monahan M, Boelaert K, Jolly K, Chan S, Barton P, Roberts TE (2015). Costs and benefits of iodine supplementation for pregnant women in a mildly to moderately iodine-deficient population: a modelling analysis. Lancet Diabetes Endocrinol 2015;3(9):715–22.
27. Mottiar Y (2013). Iodine biofortification through plant biotechnology. Nutrition 2013;29(11–12):1431.
28. Nazeri P, Mirmiran P, Shiva N, Mehrabi Y, Mojarrad M, Azizi F (2015). Iodine nutrition status in lactating mothers residing in countries with mandatory and voluntary iodine fortification programs: an updated systematic review. Thyroid 2015;25(6):611–20.
29. Nepal AK, Suwal R, Gautam S, Shah GS, Baral N, Andersson M, Zimmermann MB (2015). Subclinical Hypothyroidism and Elevated Thyroglobulin in Infants with Chronic Excess Iodine Intake. Thyroid 2015;25(7):851–9.
30. Pearce EN (2015). Iodine deficiency in pregnant women in the UK: the costs of inaction. Lancet Diabetes Endocrinol 2015;3(9):671–2.
31. Pearce EN1, Andersson M, Zimmermann MB (2013). Global iodine nutrition: Where do we stand in 2013? Thyroid 2013;23(5):523–8.
32. Pettigrew-Porter A, Skeaff S, Gray A, Thomson C, Croxson M (2011). Are pregnant women in New Zealand iodine deficient? A cross-sectional survey. Aust N Z J Obstet Gynaecol 2011;51(5):464–7.
33. Phillips DI (1997). Iodine, milk, and the elimination of endemic goitre in Britain: the story of an accidental public health triumph. J Epidemiol Community Health 1997;51:391–393.
34. Rohner F, Kangambèga MO, Khan N, Kargougou R, Garnier D, Sanou I, Ouaro BD, Petry N, Wirth JP, Jooste P (2015). Comparative Validation of Five Quantitative Rapid Test Kits for the Analysis of Salt Iodine Content: Laboratory Performance, User- and Field-Friendliness. PLoS One. 2015;10(9):e0138530.
35. Skeaff SA, Lonsdale-Cooper E (2013). Mandatory fortification of bread with iodised salt modestly improves iodine status in schoolchildren. Br J Nutr 2013;109(6):1109–13.
36. Sullivan KM (2010). The challenges of implementing and monitoring of salt iodisation programmes. Best Pract Res Clin Endocrinol Metab 2010;24(1):101–6.
37. Swanson CA, Zimmermann MB, Skeaff S, Pearce EN, Dwyer JT, Trumbo PR, Zehaluk C, Andrews KW, Carriquiry A, Caldwell KL, Egan SK, Long SE, Bailey RL, Sullivan KM, Holden JM, Betz JM, Phinney KW, Brooks SP, Johnson CL, Haggans CJ (2012). Summary of an NIH workshop to identify research needs to improve the monitoring of iodine status in the United States and to inform the DRI. J Nutr 2012;142(6):1175S-85S.
38. Syed S (2015). Iodine and the "near" eradication of cretinism. Pediatrics 2015;135(4):594–6.
39. Tonacchera M, Dimida A, De Servi M, Frigeri M, Ferrarini E, De Marco G, Grasso L, Agretti P, Piaggi P, Aghini-Lombardi F, Perata P, Pinchera A, Vitti P (2013). Iodine fortification of vegetables improves human iodine nutrition: in vivo evidence for a new model of iodine prophylaxis. J Clin Endocrinol Metab 2013;98(4):E694–7.
40. UNICEF (2012). The State of the World's Children 2012: Children in an urban world. New York, NY: United Nations Children's Fund; 2012.
41. Untoro J, Timmer A, Schultink W (2010). The challenges of iodine supplementation: a public health programme perspective. Best Pract Res Clin Endocrinol Metab 2010;24(1):89–99.
42. Vanderpump MP, Lazarus JH, Smyth PP, Laurberg P, Holder RL, Boelaert K, Franklyn JA (2011); British Thyroid Association UK Iodine Survey Group. Iodine status of UK schoolgirls: a cross-sectional survey. Lancet; 377:2007–2012.
43. Voogt W, Holwerda HT, Khodabaks R (2010). Biofortification of lettuce (Lactuca sativa L.) with iodine: the effect of iodine form and concentration in the nutrient solution on growth, development and iodine uptake of lettuce grown in water culture. J Sci Food Agric 2010;90 (5):906–13.

44. Walker SP, Wachs TD, Gardner JM, Lozoff B, Wasserman GA, Pollitt E, Carter JA (2007); International Child Development Steering Group. Child development: risk factors for adverse outcomes in developing countries. Lancet 2007;369(9556):145–57.
45. WHO (2006). Reducing salt intake in populations. WHO Forum and Technical Meeting, Paris. WHO, Geneva, Switzerland, 2006.
46. WHO (2008). Salt as a vehicle for fortification: report of a WHO Expert Consultation. World Health Organization, Geneva, Switzerland, 2008.
47. WHO/PAHO (2011) Regional Expert Group for Cardiovascular Disease Prevention Through Population-Wide Dietary Salt Reduction. Final report, 2011. http://new.paho.org/hq/index. php?option=com_content&view=article&id=2015&Itemid=1757&lang=en.
48. WHO/UNICEF/ ICCIDD (2007). Assessment of iodine deficiency disorders and monitoring their elimination. A guide for programme managers, 3rd edition. Geneva, WHO, 2007.
49. Wolff J, Chaikoff IL, Goldberg RC, Meier JR (1949). The temporary nature of the inhibitory action of excess iodine on organic iodine synthesis in the normal thyroid. Endocrinol 1949;45:504–513.
50. Zimmermann MB (2011). Iodine deficiency in industrialized countries. Clin Endocrinol (Oxf). 2011;75(3):287–8.
51. Zimmermann MB1, Andersson M (2012). Update on iodine status worldwide. Curr Opin Endocrinol Diabetes Obes 2012;19(5):382–7.
52. Zimmermann MB, Galetti V (2015). Iodine intake as a risk factor for thyroid cancer: a comprehensive review of animal and human studies. Thyroid Res 2015;8:8.
53. Zimmermann MB, Jooste PL, Pandav CS (2008). Iodine-deficiency disorders. Lancet 2008;372(9645):1251–62.
54. Zimmermann MB, Aeberli I, Andersson M, Assey V, Yorg JA, Jooste P, Jukic T, Kartono D, Kusic Z, Pretell E, San Luis TO Jr, Untoro J, Timmer A (2013). Thyroglobulin is a sensitive measure of both deficient and excess iodine intakes in children and indicates no adverse effects on thyroid function in the UIC range of 100–299 mug/L: a UNICEF/ICCIDD study group report. J Clin Endocrinol Metab 2013;98:1271–1280.
55. Zimmermann MB, Gizak M, Abbott K, Andersson M, Lazarus JH (2015). Iodine deficiency in pregnant women in Europe. Lancet Diabetes Endocrinol 2015;3(9):672–4.

Chapter 15
Adequate Protein in Nutrition: Arguments for More or Less?

Andreas F.H. Pfeiffer

Abstract The question as to how much protein is ideal in our nutrient intakes is highly controversial. Caloric intakes have increased in recent times, and the macronutrients are therefore being reevaluated in terms of their contribution to the epidemic of obesity. From a biochemical perspective, it appears logical to recommend increased protein intake from sources such as milk, eggs, fish and plant protein to replace carbohydrates and/or fat in the diet. Arguments exist both for and against increased protein intake, however. On the basis of experiments conducted with flies and mice, it would appear that elevated protein intake may increase the risk of certain types of tumor and consequently shorten life expectancy. At the same time, investigations into protein deficiency in mice would seem to indicate that lower protein intake may reduce metabolic diseases and increase life span in mammalians. High protein intake can help preserve muscle and bone mass in the elderly, but a diet high in red and processed meat can increase the risk of type 2 diabetes and may also increase the risk of cardiovascular disease. The question as to what level of protein intake is best for our health is not clearly established and appears to be age-dependent. The current major advances in understanding the biochemical mechanisms mediating the responses to protein deficiency and excess will help identify individual response patterns and may facilitate the identification of nutrigenetic phenotypes profiting from either dietary strategy.

Keywords Macronutrient requirements · Nutrient intake · Protein deficiency · Protein excess · Insulin · Metabolic response · GCN2 · FGF21 · mTOR · Klotho

A.F.H. Pfeiffer (✉)
Abteilung für Endokrinologie, Diabetes und Ernährungsmedizin, Charité—Universitätsmedizin Berlin (CBF), Hindenburgdamm 30, 12200 Berlin, Germany
e-mail: Andreas.Pfeiffer@charite.de

© Springer International Publishing AG 2017   237
H.K. Biesalski et al. (eds.), *Sustainable Nutrition in a Changing World*,
DOI 10.1007/978-3-319-55942-1_15

15.1 The Re-evaluation of Macronutrient Requirements

The question as to how much protein is ideal in our nutrient intakes is highly controversial. Protein requirements were traditionally calculated on the basis of nitrogen balance, and thus referred to minimal requirements. However, with the advent of obesity and metabolic syndrome as a frequent and major disease of industrial societies, other aspects of protein intake have come into focus. Caloric intakes have increased, and food availability is ubiquitous in an appetizing and attractive manner, making it difficult to control our hedonistic drives to excessively indulge in the pleasure of eating. The macronutrients are therefore currently being reevaluated from the perspective of their contribution to the epidemic of obesity. Carbohydrates, particularly sugar but also highly refined starch, are enticing foods which are easily overconsumed since they cause only moderate satiety, a rapid and large increase in insulin, leading to a lipogenesis and fatty liver, and an early reoccurrence of hunger due to falling blood sugar or even hypoglycemia. Fat has a high caloric density and is easily overconsumed, particularly in combination with carbohydrates such as cookies, nutrient bars and cakes, or in the form of fatty spreads and sausages with bread.

Protein intake has excellent satiating properties and causes postprandial thermogenesis and thus increased energy expenditure. Protein cannot be directly converted to fat in the intermediary metabolism such that lipogenesis from protein is not efficient—all attributes which may be considered protective against obesity. In addition, high protein intake may increase muscle mass, at least if combined with some exercise, and may thus increase basal metabolic rate [1]. Protein requires little insulin for postprandial metabolism and therefore helps prevent postprandial hyperinsulinemia and prolonged phases of increased blood glucose in subjects with impaired glucose tolerance, elevated fasting glucose or manifest diabetes mellitus type 2. The energy density of low-fat protein is usually rather low, with the result that fairly large portions may be consumed without excessive energy intake. Therefore, from a biochemical perspective, it appears logical to recommend increased protein intake to replace carbohydrates and/or fat. Protein sources may be meat, milk protein, eggs, fish or plant protein.

15.2 Arguments Against Elevated Protein Intake

Would such an elevated protein intake be safe, or perhaps even prevent obesity and its associated comorbidities? There are actually several arguments against elevated protein intake. Protein has numerous and quite diverse biochemical properties in addition to those associated with sugar metabolism. Among them are the stimulatory effects of branched chain amino acids on mTOR-complex 1 (mTORC1), which is a central component of the tyrosine kinase growth factor receptor signaling pathway including insulin and insulin-like growth factor 1-receptors. mTORC1 plays a pivotal role in protein synthesis, development, cellular hypertrophy and proliferation. Increased activation of mTORC1 leads to shortened life spans in simple eukaryotic organisms such as yeast or *caenorhabditis elegans*, but also in flies and mammals such as mice [2, 3]. The branched chain amino acids leucine, isoleucine and valine cooperate with growth factors in the activation of mTOR by inducing the migration of mTOR to lysosomal membranes, where it interacts with its activating G-protein Rheb [4]. The proliferative properties of mTOR enhance muscle formation but also tumor formation and growth. Indeed, some types of tumors have been associated with increased protein intake in humans [5, 6].

Protein intake increases, while protein restriction decreases, levels of IGF-1 in humans [7], which is a major growth factor that has been related to cancer, especially in younger adults [8]. The activity of IGF-1, which circulates in high concentrations, is determined by six binding proteins which mostly neutralize the bioactivity of the free IGF-1. These binding proteins are in part regulated by food intake and insulin [9]. Thus, IGF-binding protein 1 (IGFBP1) decreases within 60 min of food intake by about 50%, while IGFBP2 increases by about 20% in humans. Both responses are triggered by insulin, which is an important regulator of IGF-1 bioactivity apart from growth hormone [9]. In the case of prolonged fasting, IGFBP1 is upregulated severalfold by the counter player of insulin, FOXO1, which is inactivated by insulin-mediated phosphorylation through the AKT pathway. FOXO1 activity increases in the presence of low levels of insulin to regulate the fasting state, which comprises downregulation of IGF1 bioactivity [10]. In fact phylogenetically, the IGF and the insulin system separate only after the flies which still rely on a single hormone receptor for both systems, which may explain the important role of insulin in determining the bioactivity of IGF-1.

15.3 The Consequences of Low Protein Intake

Protein deficiency is finely sensed by the organism, which mounts a protective response in the event that a selective deficiency of essential amino acids occurs. Indeed, it was noted many years ago that moderate methionine deficiency protects the organism against obesity, insulin resistance and cancer by increasing anti-oxidative defense mechanisms, in particular the glutathione system, and resetting metabolic control, although the details remained elusive [11, 12]. This protective response was recently linked to a metabolic growth factor, fibroblast growth factor 21 (FGF21), which coordinates a multifaceted metabolic response to a deficiency of essential amino acids [13, 14]. FGF21 interacts with classical FGF1c-tyrosine kinase receptors, but requires an additional transmembrane protein component for eliciting its action, termed Klotho, which determines organ selectivity and confers specificity to the FGF21 responses. Klotho was named after the figure in Greek mythology *Moirai* or Fate, who was the spinner of the thread of life, because mouse Klotho knockouts had a greatly shortened lifespan, reduced body size and reduced fertility [15]. Notably, Klotho potently downregulates the insulin-

and IGF-1 signaling pathway. The expression of FGF21 is driven by a transcription factor sensing the amino acid deficiency by specific recognition of uncharged tRNAs termed 'general control non-derepressible 2' (GCN2) [16], which phosphorylates the transcriptional control factor eIF2alpha and thereby determines the transcription of a specific set of genes among which the activating transcription factor 4 (ATF4) plays a key role. This response to the restriction of amino acid intake is also observed in humans [14]. Notably, FGF21 agonists improve insulin sensitivity, lower LDL-cholesterol, increase HDL-cholesterol and increase energy expenditure in humans, and thus display a highly desirable profile of activities [17]. Therefore, lower protein intake is likely to trigger a metabolically favorable state which may well reduce metabolic diseases and increase life span in mammalians. Whether this also applies to humans is evidently an interesting question.

15.4   The Consequences of High Protein Intake

In mice, life span is decreased by high intakes of protein at the expense of carbohydrates, and this response was associated with elevated levels of branched chain amino acids in blood and the activation of mTORC1 in a study feeding mice 10 different ratios of protein to carbohydrates [18]. Higher intake of protein was clearly unfavorable in mice. Fat intake notably played a minor role in determining life span and morbidity in mice. This raises the question as to whether there is evidence that mTOR pathways are also activated in humans by higher protein intakes. Indeed, we observed increased expression of the mTOR target protein p70S6-kinase in human adipose tissue at the protein level upon increased consumption of protein at about 28% of isocaloric total energy intake (%E) compared to 15% E protein. This supports the notion that the mTOR pathway is affected by higher protein intake in humans.

Recent evidence from observational data of an NHANES survey associated higher protein intakes with increased cancer mortality in humans below 65 years of age, while this relation became inversed at ages above 65 years [8]. In the older population, cancer mortality was quite dramatically decreased with higher as compared to lower protein intakes. This difference was ascribed to the increases of IGF-1 and IGFBP1 in younger people on high-protein diets. This report certainly requires confirmation from other studies, as the models calculated by Levine et al. [8] did not provide numbers of cancer mortality and did not report cancer incidence in the younger people, which might be expected to parallel cancer mortality to some extent. Moreover, IGF-1 is bound to 6 IGFBPs which determine its biological activity such that total IGF-1 is a rather imprecise measure of IGF-1 bioactivity. IGFBP-1 is a minor IGFBP binding only a few percent of total IGF-1 in serum, but its regulation by insulin and the FOXO1-pathway is most pronounced. In fact, the clinical studies usually associated IGFBP3 with anti-neoplastic effects, which accounts for about 50% of the serum IGF-1 binding capacity [19, 20]. Other observational studies did not report such an age-dependent association and should be able to test this hypothesis. Controversial data have also been published regarding a possible association of cardiovascular disease with high protein intake with an American study seeing no association [21] and a Swedish study observing an association [22], although the latter was heavily criticized [23]. Nevertheless, there remain some concerns regarding health risks associated with high protein intake.

What are the major benefits of high protein intake? The putative benefits with regard to metabolic syndrome or diabetes have been listed at the beginning of this article. Meta-analyses of higher protein intake in people with type 2 diabetes indeed showed some moderate benefits of higher protein intakes in short-term studies compared to the lower protein intake groups, such as a slightly better weight loss on weight-loss diets, lower HbA1c and lower blood pressure [24]. However, increased protein and especially red meat and processed meat intake was a risk factor for type 2 diabetes in a meta-analysis of several prospective epidemiological studies [25], although consumption of low-fat dairy protein was protective [26]. A further major argument is the preservation of muscle and bone mass and of intact immunity in aging people who may be at elevated risk of sarcopenia, frailty and poor health due to insufficient protein intake [27]. Protein requirements are also increased in phases of recovery from diseases creating catabolic conditions. High protein intake has been shown to preserve or augment muscle mass in a long-term study of older people [28]. These arguments led to the suggestion of higher than currently recommended protein intakes of 1.0–1.2 g/kg body weight per day for older people by a consortium of geriatric experts, named the PROT-AGE group [27]. Indeed, the protective effects of low protein intake on cancer risk may be age-dependent [8] and did not consider the risks of osteoporosis, frailty, muscle loss and impaired immunity.

15.5   Establishing the Best Level of Protein Intake for Health

On balance, the question as to what level of protein intake is indeed best for our health is not clearly established and appears to be age-dependent. A possible conclusion might be that younger people may require lower protein intakes or less high-quality protein than older people. Clearly, sarcopenic individuals without kidney disease would be likely to benefit from higher consumption of high-quality protein. Whether younger people would benefit from lower intakes of high-quality protein by experiencing less malignant, metabolic and cardiovascular disease appears to be little established. On the other hand, the same applies to the putative benefits of higher protein intakes for the prevention of obesity, type 2 diabetes, dyslipidemia and hypertension. It appears questionable that epidemiological studies will be able to provide satisfactory answers. The current major advances in understanding the biochemical mechanisms mediating the responses to protein deficiency and excess regarding GCN2, FGF21, mTOR and others will help to identify individual response patterns and may permit the identification of nutrigenetic phenotypes profiting from either dietary strategy.

15.6 Summary: Key Messages

- The question as to how much protein is ideal in our nutrient intakes is highly controversial.
- From a biochemical perspective, it appears logical to recommend increased protein intake in the diet, but arguments exist both for and against this.
- Elevated protein intake may increase the risk of certain types of tumor and consequently shorten life expectancy. A diet high in red and processed meat can also increase the risk of type 2 diabetes and may additionally increase the risk of cardiovascular disease.
- Lower protein intake may reduce metabolic diseases and increase life span in mammalians, although this is yet to be proved for humans.
- The question as to what level of protein intake is best for our health is not clearly established and appears to be age-dependent.
- Current major advances in understanding will help identify individual response patterns and may permit the identification of nutrigenetic phenotypes profiting from either dietary strategy.

References

1. Westerterp-Plantenga MS, Lemmens SG, and Westerterp KR. Dietary protein - its role in satiety, energetics, weight loss and health. *Br J Nutr.* 2012;108 Suppl 2:S105–12.
2. Partridge L, Alic N, Bjedov I, and Piper MD. Ageing in Drosophila: the role of the insulin/Igf and TOR signalling network. *Exp Gerontol.* 2011;46(5):376–81.
3. Lopez-Otin C, Blasco MA, Partridge L, Serrano M, and Kroemer G. The hallmarks of aging. *Cell.* 2013;153(6):1194–217.
4. Han JM, Jeong SJ, Park MC, Kim G, Kwon NH, Kim HK, Ha SH, Ryu SH, and Kim S. Leucyl-tRNA synthetase is an intracellular leucine sensor for the mTORC1-signaling pathway. *Cell.* 2012;149(2):410–24.
5. Williams CD, Satia JA, Adair LS, Stevens J, Galanko J, Keku TO, and Sandler RS. Associations of red meat, fat, and protein intake with distal colorectal cancer risk. *Nutr Cancer.* 2010;62(6):701–9.
6. Kim MK, Kim JH, Nam SJ, Ryu S, and Kong G. Dietary intake of soy protein and tofu in association with breast cancer risk based on a case-control study. *Nutr Cancer.* 2008;60 (5):568–76.
7. Fontana L, Weiss EP, Villareal DT, Klein S, and Holloszy JO. Long-term effects of calorie or protein restriction on serum IGF-1 and IGFBP-3 concentration in humans. *Aging Cell.* 2008;7 (5):681–7.
8. Levine ME, Suarez JA, Brandhorst S, Balasubramanian P, Cheng CW, Madia F, Fontana L, Mirisola MG, Guevara-Aguirre J, Wan J, et al. Low Protein Intake Is Associated with a Major

Reduction in IGF-1, Cancer, and Overall Mortality in the 65 and Younger but Not Older Population. *Cell Metab.* 2014;19(3):407–17.

9. Arafat AM, Weickert MO, Frystyk J, Spranger J, Schofl C, Mohlig M, and Pfeiffer AF. The Role of Insulin-Like Growth Factor (IGF) Binding Protein-2 in the Insulin-Mediated Decrease in IGF-I Bioactivity. *J Clin Endocrinol Metab.* 2009;94(12):5093–101.

10. van der Vos KE, and Coffer PJ. The extending network of FOXO transcriptional target genes. *Antioxid Redox Signal.* 2011;14(4):579–92.

11. Malloy VL, Krajcik RA, Bailey SJ, Hristopoulos G, Plummer JD, and Orentreich N. Methionine restriction decreases visceral fat mass and preserves insulin action in aging male Fischer 344 rats independent of energy restriction. *Aging Cell.* 2006;5(4):305–14.

12. Richie JP, Jr., Leutzinger Y, Parthasarathy S, Malloy V, Orentreich N, and Zimmerman JA. Methionine restriction increases blood glutathione and longevity in F344 rats. *FASEB J.* 1994;8(15):1302–7.

13. Stone KP, Wanders D, Orgeron M, Cortez CC, and Gettys TW. Mechanisms of increased in vivo insulin sensitivity by dietary methionine restriction in mice. *Diabetes.* 2014;63 (11):3721–33.

14. Laeger T, Henagan TM, Albarado DC, Redman LM, Bray GA, Noland RC, Munzberg H, Hutson SM, Gettys TW, Schwartz MW, et al. FGF21 is an endocrine signal of protein restriction. *J Clin Invest.* 2014;124(9):3913–22.

15. Kuro-o M, Matsumura Y, Aizawa H, Kawaguchi H, Suga T, Utsugi T, Ohyama Y, Kurabayashi M, Kaname T, Kume E, et al. Mutation of the mouse klotho gene leads to a syndrome resembling ageing. *Nature.* 1997;390(6655):45–51.

16. Gallinetti J, Harputlugil E, and Mitchell JR. Amino acid sensing in dietary-restriction-mediated longevity: roles of signal-transducing kinases GCN2 and TOR. *Biochem J.* 2013;449(1):1–10.

17. Gaich G, Chien JY, Fu H, Glass LC, Deeg MA, Holland WL, Kharitonenkov A, Bumol T, Schilske HK, and Moller DE. The effects of LY2405319, an FGF21 analog, in obese human subjects with type 2 diabetes. *Cell Metab.* 2013;18(3):333–40.

18. Solon-Biet SM, McMahon AC, Ballard JW, Ruohonen K, Wu LE, Cogger VC, Warren A, Huang X, Pichaud N, Melvin RG, et al. The ratio of macronutrients, not caloric intake, dictates cardiometabolic health, aging, and longevity in ad libitum-fed mice. *Cell Metab.* 2014;19(3):418–30.

19. Cao H, Wang G, Meng L, Shen H, Feng Z, Liu Q, and Du J. Association between circulating levels of IGF-1 and IGFBP-3 and lung cancer risk: a meta-analysis. *PLoS One.* 2012;7(11): e49884.

20. Rinaldi S, Cleveland R, Norat T, Biessy C, Rohrmann S, Linseisen J, Boeing H, Pischon T, Panico S, Agnoli C, et al. Serum levels of IGF-I, IGFBP-3 and colorectal cancer risk: results from the EPIC cohort, plus a meta-analysis of prospective studies. *Int J Cancer.* 2010;126 (7):1702–15.

21. Halton TL, Willett WC, Liu S, Manson JE, Albert CM, Rexrode K, and Hu FB. Low-carbohydrate-diet score and the risk of coronary heart disease in women. *N Engl J Med.* 2006;355(19):1991–2002.

22. Lagiou P, Sandin S, Lof M, Trichopoulos D, Adami HO, and Weiderpass E. Low carbohydrate-high protein diet and incidence of cardiovascular diseases in Swedish women: prospective cohort study. *BMJ.* 2012;344:e4026.

23. Rolland C, and Rolland-Harris E. Increased incidence of cardiovascular disease: are low-carbohydrate-high-protein diets truly to blame? *Evid Based Med.* 2013;18(4):e37.

24. Dong JY, Zhang ZL, Wang PY, and Qin LQ. Effects of high-protein diets on body weight, glycaemic control, blood lipids and blood pressure in type 2 diabetes: meta-analysis of randomised controlled trials. *Br J Nutr.* 2013;110(5):781–9.

25. Aune D, Ursin G, and Veierod MB. Meat consumption and the risk of type 2 diabetes: a systematic review and meta-analysis of cohort studies. *Diabetologia.* 2009;52(11):2277–87.

26. Aune D, Norat T, Romundstad P, and Vatten LJ. Dairy products and the risk of type 2 diabetes: a systematic review and dose-response meta-analysis of cohort studies. *Am J Clin Nutr.* 2013;98(4):1066–83.
27. Bauer J, Biolo G, Cederholm T, Cesari M, Cruz-Jentoft AJ, Morley JE, Phillips S, Sieber C, Stehle P, Teta D, et al. Evidence-based Recommendations for Optimal Dietary Protein Intake in Older People: A Position Paper From the PROT-AGE Study Group. *J Am Med Dir Assoc.* 2013.
28. Houston DK, Nicklas BJ, Ding J, Harris TB, Tylavsky FA, Newman AB, Lee JS, Sahyoun NR, Visser M, and Kritchevsky SB. Dietary protein intake is associated with lean mass change in older, community-dwelling adults: the Health, Aging, and Body Composition (Health ABC) Study. *Am J Clin Nutr.* 2008;87(1):150–5.

Chapter 16
Malnutrition: Consequences for Clinical Outcomes in the Context of German Hospitals

Carl Meißner

Abstract Some 70–75% of diseases are primarily caused by diet and lifestyle-induced problems. Undernutrition and malnutrition affect all relevant clinical factors: mortality, length of hospital stay, morbidity, and thus the quality of life. Undernutrition and malnutrition are common in hospitals, and are a growing problem. They are costly and have clinical consequences. Europe-wide studies and meta-analyses testify to the significance of the therapeutic provision of nutrition for patients admitted to hospital, and also demonstrate its cost-effectiveness. For the therapy to be successful, early, targeted assessment of the patient's status is necessary in order to ensure the guideline-based implementation of recognized dietary concepts. This requires a qualified nutrition support team consisting of medical nutritionists, general nutritionists, dietitians and other qualified nutrition professionals. Every patient admitted to hospital should be examined and documented in accordance with the established parameters for undernutrition and malnutrition, and a diet plan developed for his or her specific needs. Undernutrition and malnutrition cost €9 billion per year in Germany alone. These costs could be reduced by the application of medical nutrition therapy in hospitals. Individuals can also protect themselves by adopting a healthy lifestyle. This begins with the consumption of healthy foods.

Keywords Undernutrition · Malnutrition · Dietary concept · Staging system · ERAS · DGEM · Cancer · Hospital · Patient · Supplementary drinks and foods · Artificial feeding

C. Meißner (✉)
Klinikum Magdeburg Gemeinnützige GmbH, Klinik Für Allgemein- Und Viszeralchirurgie, Birkenallee 34, 39130 Magdeburg, Germany
e-mail: Carl.Meissner@gmx.de

© Springer International Publishing AG 2017   245
H.K. Biesalski et al. (eds.), *Sustainable Nutrition in a Changing World*,
DOI 10.1007/978-3-319-55942-1_16

16.1 The Vital Role of Nutrition in Medicine

Nutrition plays a central role in the prevention and prophylaxis of diseases in patients of all ages [1]. The relationship between 'food' and 'wellbeing' has been known for thousands of years. All previous cultures had to look for food, and they used certain of these foods to heal the sick and the infirm. Unfortunately, the nutritional medicine that is practiced in the day-to-day life of German hospitals does not reflect its true potential for offering promising cures.

Three out of four cases of disease requiring medical treatment are essentially nutrition- and lifestyle-related [2]. Only 20% of patients who are admitted to hospital for treatment present with a normal nutritional status. They form the smallest group. Approximately 55% of patients admitted are overweight, and another 25% suffer from undernutrition or malnutrition. On top of this comes the fact that approximately 75% of all hospitalized patients experience significant weight loss during their time in hospital [2, 3]. Thus the aim must be not only to identify as quickly as possible patients with increased nutritional and metabolic risk, but also to immediately initiate a nutrition-based medical treatment.

No standard definition for the terms 'undernutrition' and 'malnutrition' exists worldwide. The DGEM (German Society for Nutritional Medicine) has created guidelines on the topic, and explains malnutrition as a reduction of energy storage (resulting in a reduction in fat mass). Malnutrition can be defined as a disease-associated weight loss or loss of protein (resulting in a reduction in muscle mass) or else as a lack of specific essential nutrients [4].

16.2 The Importance of Early Detection and Treatment

The early detection and treatment of malnutrition in hospital patients affects the entire course of the conditions from which they suffer. An early intervention can have a significant impact on morbidity, the treatment chosen, the length of hospital stay, mortality, and—a point not be underestimated—the patient's quality of life [5–8]. Early intervention also reduces the cost of treatment for the individual patient, and well as having a broader impact on healthcare budgets. The cost of treating malnutrition, including the costs of the associated complications, approximates to €9 billion annually. Clinical studies show that treatment by means of nutritional medicine generates considerable savings [2]. This means that the diet must be an integral part of the preoperative and postoperative therapeutic treatments.

Over 200 studies demonstrate the presence of undernutrition or malnutrition since the 1970s. Patients were recorded before admission to the hospital, during treatment or after surgery.

16.3   The Causes of Undernutrition and Malnutrition

The causes of undernutrition and malnutrition are very varied and complex in our industrialized countries. They include low socio-economic status, social isolation, depression, alcoholism, poor dental status, ill-fitting false teeth, badly fitted dentures, other addictions, poverty, and lack of money. Last but not least, the inability to obtain adequate food or to prepare it properly presents problems that should not be underestimated.

It is essential to recognize early malnutrition and its causes and to initiate appropriate treatment measures. This is one of the tasks of the physician, besides the physical examination of the patient and the creation of a targeted medical history. This history should include documented nutrition-related factors, such as weight change, appetite pattern, food intake and gastrointestinal symptoms.

16.4   Determining the Patient's Nutritional Status

Various options exist for determining the patient's nutritional status. In recent years, the Subjective Assessment (SGA), the Nutritional Risk Score (NRS 2002) and the Mini Nutritional Assessment score (MNA) have all come to the fore. The latter is used in the context of elderly patients. The use of this score and the determination of BMI (Body Mass Index) should be a routine part of the hospital admissions procedure, so that targeted nutritional medicine measures can be applied as soon as possible [9].

Especially in the surgical disciplines, new challenges are presenting themselves because demographic change in Germany is producing more and more elderly and geriatric patients. Not just the responsible physician but an entire team is required to meet these requirements with regard to undernourishment and malnutrition. In German hospitals, such 'nutrition teams' are already achieving good results. These teams are essential for the implementation of nutritional and medical knowledge in the hospital. They consist of nutritional doctors, care staff with qualifications in nutrition, specialists in nutritional and domestic science, and dieticians. Their structure, tasks and organization are defined in guidelines and are entirely practicable [9]. The cost-efficiency and clinical effectiveness of these teams have also been proven in studies [10–15]. The provision of supplementary artificial nutrition is one of the most important preparations for surgery, so that the patient can be operated on in a good nutritional state.

16.5   ERAS (Enhanced Recovery After Surgery)

ERAS (Enhanced Recovery After Surgery)—a program to improve rehabilitation after operations—aims to reduce the time patients spend in hospital. Nutritional medicine has an important contribution to make here. It must be fully integrated into the overall therapeutic concept. On admission, the patient is screened, and the metabolic risk is assessed. Periods of fasting should be avoided if possible, and the intake of food should be resumed as quickly as possible following surgery [16].

Nutrition is a component of the ERAS program, with a metabolic concept. It involves early build-up of food intake, and no long-term reduction in calorie provision: major operations especially can lead to post-operative complications. There is no rigid program for the procedure. In the case of patients who are at risk, a flexible approach is required. This means that the use of enteral or parenteral nutrition should be considered. For the ERAS program, this means that a nutritional risk screening takes place when a patient is admitted to hospital.

16.6   The Staged Therapeutic Approach

The staged therapeutic approach has proved its value in the case of patients who, on admission to hospital, have difficulty ingesting food or are incapable of doing so.

After the patient's medical history has been drawn up, detailing nutritionally relevant content and analysis of underlying causes, an individual nutritional anamnesis must be carried out. This should include a description of a diet that is both high in energy and easily digestible. It is also worth providing training in nutrition to the family and friends who have the patient in their care. This includes the provision of small snacks such as finger food, energy drinks, and savory morsels throughout the day, as well as modest physical activity between meals.

The meals are enriched with cost-effective, high-energy, flavorless food additives such as maltodextrin, as well as protein concentrates. Studies on drinking high-calorie beverages and consuming supplementary foods have shown that the administration of these nutritional supplements clearly reduces the incidence of complications and mortality in patients with undernutrition and malnutrition. This also holds true for patients who stay in hospital for only a short time. Especially in this group, in fact, a reduction in the incidence of complications and mortality has been shown [17]. These supplementary drinks and foods should be offered between meals and in the evening as well. If there is a medical indication, supplementary foods may be prescribed for the patient. Medical insurance companies are duty-bound to cover the associated costs.

Artificial feeding of the patient should only be a course of last resort, when all the other measures described have failed. Both medical and ethical considerations need to be taken into account here. These include the disease(s) from which the patient is suffering, the current condition of the patient, the psychosomatic situation, comorbidity, the patient's personal wishes, and the expected prognosis. The option of tube feeding has shown its value in such cases. It improves the patient's nutritional status, reduces complications, has a positive effect on the individual prognosis, and thus improves the patient's quality of life [4, 9]. The PEG-probe is the method of choice for artificial-enteral nutrition of more than two weeks' duration. It may be broken off at any time and normal feeding procedures resumed.

16.7 The Costs of Undernutrition and Malnutrition

Undernutrition and malnutrition always drive up morbidity and mortality rates, and the associated costs in the Federal Republic of Germany run into the millions annually (see above). Numerous studies demonstrate and, indeed, emphasize the fact that the results are even more relevant from a health budget perspective. The provision of supplementary beverages and food to patients suffering from undernutrition and malnutrition is highly cost-effective, and above all relieves the pressure on hospital budgets [18, 19]. Early nutritional intervention in the case of malnourished patients shortens hospital stays: a reduction of 2.5 days [20] vis-à-vis patients without this additional food has been demonstrated. Also proven is the saving of €1,000 per patient when liquid nutrition is administered preparatory to operations. In the light of the results of these studies and meta-analyses, the earliest possible treatment of malnutrition should be prioritized within the framework of cost-saving measures in the German health care system. The EU has criticized the high number of malnourished patients in European hospitals, describing the situation as totally unacceptable, and fully endorses the clearly documented medical consequences for the health system. Unintentional weight loss is often the first indication of cancer. As the disease progresses, this can develop into irreversible malnutrition (cachexia). It is impossible to determine at what point in the disease process malnutrition occurs. It leads to loss of strength on the part of the patient, longer hospital stays, poor response to therapies, and increased morbidity and mortality. Following the DEGEM guideline 'Enteral Nutrition', an overview of basic medical nutritional considerations in operational disciplines has been drawn up [13]. Organ insufficiency and tumor diseases lead to poor nutritional intake and malnutrition in patients. Empirical observations show that the prevalence of malnutrition depends on the type of tumor involved [21]. Above all, patients suffering from colonic and gastrointestinal tumors, as well as head and neck tumors, are more likely to present with malnutrition than patients with breast carcinomas.

The risk factors that this malnutrition encourages have already been described. If the malnutrition continues, it is not possible for the patient's body to build back healthy muscle and organ tissue. Generally, any delay in food intake following surgery is not recommended. The type of food supply will depend on the general condition of the patient. Operations on the upper digestive tract permit the administration of food enterally, e.g., via a probe, while patients undergoing operations on the lower digestive tract can usually take in food orally immediately after the surgical intervention.

16.8   The Causes of Malnutrition in Hospital Patients

The DGEM guidelines (2013 update) [22] describe the various forms of deficiency and malnutrition. They are:

1. Disease-specific nutritional deficiencies (malignant tumors);
2. Disease-specific malnutrition (dementia, anorexia nervosa);
3. Chronic disease-specific nutritional deficiencies (organ disease, CED); and
4. Acute disease-specific malnutrition (severe infections).

The causes of malnutrition vary widely from patient to patient. Tumor patients have difficulty ingesting food, have an insufficient digestive capacity and often suffer from diarrhea. They have loss of appetite due to nausea and vomiting, suffer pain when eating, and experience malabsorption and diarrhea. The tumor changes the metabolism of the patient, increasing his or her requirement for energy and nutrients. Patients with tumors suffer from weight loss. They lose not just body fat but also muscle and organ mass. Significant investigations have shown that muscle strength diminishes even before the loss of muscle mass can be measured, and that weight loss leads to a reduction in the muscular strength of the hand [23]. As cancer patients also suffer from edema and/or ascites, the weight loss is often not immediately noticed. Only when volumes of liquid are excreted does it become apparent. A loss of more than 15% bodyweight affects the physique, and a loss of more than 30% leads to death.

16.9   Immunonutrition

The need for additional nutrition before surgery exists even in the case of patients who do not suffer from malnutrition. Mortality rates are higher in patients who are unable to meet their energy requirements via an adequate diet for approximately 14 days, and also in the case of patients who are unable to take in food orally for approximately seven days [24, 26]. Patients who receive supplementary food (orally, in the form of fortified beverages) have better operative outcomes. This has been shown by over 30 studies in the fields of digestive surgery and traumatology [23, 26]. For interventions of this type, the preoperative intake of additional liquid food for 5–7 days is recommended: this strengthens the immune system. Both morbidity and time spent in hospital are reduced [25, 26]. These nutrition-medical 'interventions'—immunonutrition—strengthen the body and positively influence the patient's physical capability, mobility, and quality of life. These days one speaks of comprehensive nutrition, which means that not only sufficient energy is supplied to the body, but also sufficient proteins and/or amino acids. This is especially important for oncology patients. A lack of requisite protein in the diet also has a negative impact on muscle mass, connective tissue, the synthesis of neurotransmitters, and the immune system. Protein intake controls the work of the digestive enzymes and influences the formation of edema, susceptibility to infections, insulin resistance, pain regulation, and stress states such as anxiety, depression and moods [21]. All cancer patients are at risk of malnutrition or inadequate nutrition. Therefore a diet concept should be created for each patient individually, depending on the specific parameters of his or her condition. The DGEM has created criteria for such a concept in its guidelines [22].

For disease-specific malnutrition:

- BMI <18.5 or
- Unintentional weight loss >10% in the last three to six months, or
- BMI <20 and unintentional weight loss >5% in the last three to six months.

For adults >65% years:

- BMI <20, >5% weight loss in three months
- Fasting period/fasting for more than seven days.

In surgical patients:

- Serum albumin concentration <30 g/l—independent risk of complications.

Weight loss in cancer patients is not a new phenomenon (Table 16.1).

Studies and works by Dewys, Ballmer et al. as well as by Arends have demonstrated this. Immediately after diagnosis, the majority of patients experience a significant weight loss. All cancer patients are exposed to the risk of cancer cachexia. This occurs when the weight loss caused by the disease is at least 5% over a period of up to 12 months or is detected in cancer patients between three and six months after diagnosis, and when three of the following criteria are met:

- Reduced muscle strength
- Fatigue
- Anorexia
- Low fat-free body mass

Table 16.1 Oncology weight loss and tumor entity weight loss [31–33]

Oncology weight loss	Tumor entity weight loss (in %, before diagnosis)
Breast cancer	36
Colon cancer	54
Bronchial cancer	61
Esophageal cancer	69
Pancreatic cancer	83
Gastric cancer	85

- Abnormal laboratory parameters: increased inflammatory markers—CRP >5 mg/dl, IL-6 <4 pg/ml, anemia (Hb <12 g/dl), serum albumin (<3.2 g/dl).

A BMI under 20 also points to cachexia, even if no weight loss is measured. If malnutrition is either diagnosed or else expected in a patient, a diet plan must immediately be created. The food helps to maintain or improve the patient's nutritional status, quality of life, and clinical outcome. The means by which the food is administered (orally, enterally, or parenterally) should be adapted to the circumstances of the patient. Particularly in need are patients receiving chemotherapy or undergoing other onerous therapies. They require special care.

The patient's nutritional needs are not covered when:

- the energy deficit is >10 kcal/kg of body weight;
- 500 kcal/day for seven days;
- a deterioration of nutritional status and a weight loss of 5–10% is present;
- oral food intake is <75% of requirements (low);
- oral food intake is <50% of requirements (moderate); and
- oral food intake is <25% of demand (strongly) [27].

Comprehensive nutrition regulates the energy flow and nutrient supply. The attempt to optimize it must be made in the case of each patient, taking into account the above-mentioned parameters and criteria. The DGEM has created a staging system and makes recommendations for the selection of the necessary nutritional and medical measures [22]. Oral food intake (drinking high-calorie food) is most important of all. If this not possible, artificial feeding must be initiated at once, regardless of whether the patient is an inpatient or an outpatient.

The nutrition team decides what level of nutrition therapy is used (Table 16.2). Tumor patients who have no difficulty swallowing or chewing and have no digestive disturbances are fed orally with liquid food.

Additional parenteral nutrition must be initiated if the patient's condition worsens and weight loss occurs (cancer patients). Artificial feeding should be continued for as long as it serves to improve the patient's nutritional status and quality of life. Periodic monitoring is required.

Table 16.2 Stage scheme of diet after DGEM [22]

Stage	Form of diet or nutrition support
I	Normal diet Special diet form Food enrichment (macro, micro nutrients) Diet counseling
II	I + oral balanced diets (OBD)
III	(I, II) + supplementary enteral/parenteral nutrition
IV	Total enteral nutrition
V	Enteral nutrition + parenteral nutrition
VI	Parenteral nutrition + minimal enteral nutrition
VII	Total parenteral nutrition

Cancer cachexia arises from a combination of malnutrition and its underlying causes, such as permanent loss of appetite or insulin resistance. From a nutritional therapy perspective, this has the following consequences.

At the latest in the event of a weight loss of 5% or more vis-à-vis an original healthy starting weight, a nutrition diagnosis with a diet history and individual nutrition counseling must take place. Regular follow-up appointments for further nutritional support must be set up. Routine nutritional support is necessary. Changes may be made to the food intake, ultimately using parenteral nutrition if this is necessary.

16.10   The Treatment of Patients at Greatest Risk

The diet administered must be high in fat and protein in order to strengthen the organism. Particular attention is necessary in the case of chemotherapy patients. The side effects of chemotherapy reinforce the action of malnutrition. Chemotherapy always affects the patient's nutritional status. Here it is important to restore or maintain by means of a diet plan the patient's ability to undergo therapy. Patients at greatest risk are found in the contexts of surgery, oncology, geriatric care and intensive care. The risk factors for complications are the severity of the disease, age >70 years, the presence of a tumor, and the surgery itself [27]. Screening for malnutrition on first contact with the patient is essential. If there is a weight loss >10–15% within six months, a BMI <18.5% kg/m^2, the Subjective Global Assessment (SGA)—Grade C or NRS >3, the serum albumin <30 g/l (liver and kidney disorder excluded), a 'severe metabolic risk' exists [27]. The oral intake of food must be strictly observed, and the patient's weight BMI constantly monitored. In most cases, oral intake of food is not sufficient to stabilize the metabolism of tumor patients, despite the provision of additional energy and protein-rich liquid food. Here, artificial feeding must be considered. The artificial diet is also necessary in the case of patients who are not suffering from disease-related malnutrition, but who are judged unlikely to be able to take food orally for a long time after the operation. The nutritional therapy should always start early, and only after the presence of malnutrition has been ascertained. It is used in the case of high-risk patients, major surgical operations, and severe complications that arise following surgical intervention or other treatment despite good care.

16.11   Nutrition: A Discipline in its Own Right

Nutrition is not a paramedicine but a discipline in its own right. What we achieve with nutritional medicine cannot be achieved by administering a single drug.

Some 70–75% of diseases are primarily caused by diet and lifestyle-induced problems. Undernutrition and malnutrition are common in hospitals, and are a growing problem. They are costly and have clinical consequences. Each patient admitted to hospital must be examined and documented in accordance with the established parameters for undernutrition and malnutrition. A nutritional medical intervention is necessary at the outset in the case of patients with cancer. The object is the maintenance of healthy cell mass, stabilization of the metabolism, the improvement of the patient's general condition, and thus a good preparation for all oncological measures.

Undernutrition and malnutrition affect all relevant clinical factors: mortality, length of hospital stay, morbidity, and thus the quality of life.

Drinking high-calorie food, food additives and artificial nutrition via probe have a high therapeutic benefit [28]. Dozens of studies testify to the significance of therapeutic provision of nutrition and demonstrate its cost-effectiveness for hospitals. For the therapy to be successful, the early, targeted assessment of the patient's status is necessary in order to ensure the guideline-based implementation of the dietary concepts based on the staging system. This requires a qualified team consisting of medical nutritionists, general nutritionists, dietitians and other qualified nutrition professionals. This team is responsible for the implementation of the guidelines [23]. The evaluation scores are a reliable basis for the detection of undernutrition and malnutrition (Table 16.2) [29, 30].

Europe-wide studies and meta-analyses powerfully confirm the importance of medical nutritional analysis for patients admitted for hospital treatment [8].

Malnutrition is a risk factor for hospitals and clinics that affects all clinical factors—above all, mortality, morbidity, length of hospital stay, complications, the therapeutic outcome, and, last but not least, the patient's quality of life. Only the thoroughgoing implementation of established nutritional concepts designed to maintain and improve the patient's energy and protein balance will guarantee success. Undernutrition and malnutrition cost €9 billion per year in Germany alone. Politicians and health care providers agree that it is possible to reduce these costs. Individuals can also protect themselves by adopting a healthy lifestyle. This begins with the consumption of healthy foods.

16.12   Summary: Key Messages

- Undernutrition and malnutrition affect all relevant clinical factors.
- Undernutrition and malnutrition are common in hospitals, and are a growing problem.
- Studies and meta-analyses testify to the significance of the therapeutic provision of nutrition for patients admitted to hospital, and also demonstrate its cost-effectiveness.
- For the therapy to be successful, early, targeted assessment of the patient's status is necessary in order to ensure the guideline-based implementation of recognized dietary concepts.
- This requires a qualified nutrition support team.

- Every patient admitted to hospital should be examined, and a diet plan developed for his or her specific needs.
- Undernutrition and malnutrition cost €9 billion per year in Germany alone. These costs could be reduced by the application of medical nutrition therapy in hospitals.

References

1. Löser Ch.: Ernährung- Herausforderung und Geißel des 21. Jh. Hessisches Ärztebl. 8; 481–484 (2007).
2. Meissner C. et al: Routinemäßige Ernährungsevaluation und nachfolgende Initiierung einer fall- und befundadaptierten Ernährungstherapie im klinisch-chirurgischen Alltag "STANDARD OPERATING PROCEDURE" (SOP). Ärzteblatt Sachsen-Anhalt 26 (2015) 6: 53–58.
3. Weimann A, Jauch KW, Kernen M, Hiesmayr JM, Horbach T, Kuse ER, Vestweber KH, DEGEM- Leitlinien Enterale Ernährung: Chirurgie und Transplantation. Aktuel Ernaehr Med 2003; 28, Supplement 1: S 51–S 60.
4. Stratton RJ, Green CJ, Elia M: Disease-related malnutrition: an evidence-based approach to treatment. Oxon: CABI Publishing 2003.
5. Hiesmayr M et al The Nutrition Day Audit Team. Decreased food intake is a risk factor for mortality in hospitalised patients: The Nutrition Day survey. 2006. Clin. Nutr. 2009; 28; 484–91.
6. Pirlich M et al. The German hospital malnutrition study. Clin. Nutr. 2006; 25: 563–74.
7. Rittler P et al. Krankheitsbedingte Mangelernährung - eine Herausforderung für unser Gesundheitssystem. Pabst Lengerich, 2010, p 49–59.
8. Svensen J et al. Euro OOPS study group. Euro OOPS: an international, multicentre study to implement nutritional risk screening and evaluate clinical outcome, Clin. Nutr. 2008; 27: 340–9.
9. Löser Ch. Unter- und Mangelernährung im Krankenhaus, Übersichtsarbeit, DÄBL, Jg 107, Hft 51–52, 911–9.
10. Senkal M, Dormann A, Stehle P, et al.: Survey on structure and performance of nutrition support teams in Germany. Clin Nutr 2002; 21: 329–35.
11. Rasmussen HH, Kondrup J, Staun M, et al.: A method for implementation of nutritional therapy in hospitals. Clin Nutr 2006; 25: 515–23.
12. Kennedy JF, Nightingale JM: Cost savings of an adult hospital nutrition support team. Nutrition 2005; 21: 1127–33.
13. Scott F, Beech R, Smedley F, et al.: Prospective, randomized, controlled, single-blind trial of the costs and consequences of septemate nutrition team follow-up over 12 months after percutaneous endoscopie gastrostomy. Nutrition 2006; 21: 1071–7.
14. Bozzetti F, Perioperative nutritional support in the ERAS approach. Clin Nutr 32: 872–873.
15. Milne AC, Avenell A, Potter J: Meta-analysis: protein and energy supplementation in older people. A. Inter Med 2006; 114: 37–48.
16. Russel CA: The impact of malnutrition on health care costs and economic considerations for the use of oral nutritional supplements. Clin Nutr 2007; Suppl 1: 25–32.
17. Löser Chr: Mangelernährung im Krankenhaus - Prävalent, klinische Folgen, Budgetrelevanz. Dtsch Med Wschr 2001; 126: 729–34.
18. Kruizenga HM, Van Tulder MW, Seidell JC, et al.: Effectiveness and cost- effectiveness of early screening and treatment of malnourished patients. Am J Clin Nutr 2005; 82: 1082–9.

19. Stute A, Tumorpatienten: Mangelernährung und Kachexie verhindern, ECM- Ernährung und Medizin 2014; 29: 70–73.

20. Valentini L, Volk D, Schütz T et al: Leitlinien der Deutschen Gesellschaft für Ernährungsmedizin (DGEM): DGEM-Terminologie in der Klinischen Ernährung. Aktuel Ernährungsmed 2013; 38: 97–111.

21. Norman K, Schütz T, Kemps M et al. The Subjective Global Assessment reliably identifies malnutrition- related muscle dysfunction. Clin Nutr 2005; 24: 143–150.

22. Sanddröm R, Drott C, Hyltander A, Arfridsson B, Schersten T, Wickström I, Lundholm K. The effect of postoperative intravenous feeding (TPN) on outcome following major surgery evaluated in a randomized study. Ann Surg 1993 Feb; 217 (2): 185–95.

23. ASPEN Board of Directors and the Clinical Guidelines Task Force. Guidelines for the use of parenteral and enteral nutrition in adult and pediatric patients. JPEN J Parenter Enteral Nutr 2002 Jan–Feb; 26 (1 Suppl.): 1 SA–138 SA. No abstract available. JPEN J Parenter Enteral Nutr 2002 Mär–Apr; 26 (2): 144.

24. Braga M, Gianotti L, Radaelli G, Vignali A, Mari G, Gentilini O, Di Carlo V. Perioperative immunonutrition in patients undergoing cancer surgery: results of a randomized double- blend phase 3 trial. Arch Surg. 199 April; 134 (4): 428–33.

25. Braga M, Gianotti L, Nespoli L, Radaelli G, Di Carlo V. Nutritional approach in malnourished surgical patients: a prospective randomized study. Arch Surg. 2002 Feb; 137 (2): 174–80.

26. Erans WJ, Morley JE, Argile's J et al. Cachexia: a new definition. Clin Nutr 2008; 27: 793–799.

27. Weimann A, Breitenstein S, Breuer JP et al (2013) S3 - Leitlinie der Deutschen Gesellschaft für Ernährungsmedizin Klinische Ernährung in der Chirurgie. Aktuel Ernährungsmed 38: 399–16.

28. Löser Chr, Aschl G, He'butema X, et al.: ESPEN Guidelines on artificial enteral nutrition - Percutaneous endoscopic gastrostomy PEG. Clin Nutr 2005; 24: 848–61.

29. Volkert D, Berner YN, Berry E et al.: ESPEN Guidelines on enteral nutrition: geriatrics Clin Nutr 2006; 25: 330–60.

30. Löser Ch, Lübbers H, Mahlke R, et al.: Der ungewollte Gewichtsverlust des alten Menschen. Dtsch Ärzteblatt 2007; 49: 3411–20.

31. Dewys WD, Begg C, Lavin PT, et al.: Prognostic effect of weight loss prior to chemotherapy in cancer patients. Eastern Cooperative Oncology Group. Am J Med. 1980 Oct;69(4):491–7.

32. Andreyev HJ, Norman AR, Oates J, et al.: Why do patients with weight loss have a worse outcome when undergoing chemotherapy for gastrointestinal malignancies? Eur J Cancer. 1998 Mar;34(4):503–9.

33. Ross P J, Ashley S, Norton A et al. Do patients with weight loss have a worse outcome when undergoing chemotherapy for lung cancers?. Br J Cancer. 2004; 90 1905–1911.

Part IV
Solutions and Future Challenges (Manfred Eggersdorfer/Peter Weber)

Chapter 17
Ensuring Food and Nutrition Security in Affluent Societies

Peter Weber

Keywords Food and nutrition security (FNS) · Affluent societies · Global food trade · Stakeholder interaction and alignment · Innovative products · Regulatory framework · Consumer protection

Addressing Food and Nutrition Security (FNS) in affluent societies is a challenge in itself, as there is a common belief that the plentiful availability of food in supermarkets and food shops automatically guarantees that individuals will actually receive the intakes of macro- and micronutrients appropriate to their nutritional needs. The evidence collected in the previous chapters of this book proves this belief to be quite false, and it also clearly demonstrates the possible implications for individual and public health, including the high attendant healthcare costs

We also need to recognize that the problems affecting affluent societies are not limited to the western world. Asian countries such as China and India, or countries in Latin America, may mirror the same FNS problems as their economies grow and affluence spreads to significant parts of their populations. The situation has changed from one of food scarcity to one of sufficient food energy, but this is sometimes accompanied by low nutrient density. This state of affairs is even further aggravated by the sharp increase of global trade in food, which greatly influences what we eat.

Given these problems of FNS in affluent societies, the following part of this book aims to discuss possible solutions and the challenges involved in implementing them. To bring about positive change in the field of food and nutrition will require engagement of the key stakeholders. The relevant science, which has been addressed extensively in the previous chapters of this book, provides the insights and understanding necessary for the development of appropriate solutions. In addition, to provide nutritional solutions—whether delivered as food or as food supplements—the food industry needs to engage with the challenge and develop appropriate food products. Meanwhile governments, for their part, must provide the

P. Weber (✉)
DSM Nutritional Products Europe Ltd, Wurmisweg 576,
4303 Kaiseraugst, Switzerland
e-mail: peter.weber@dsm.com

© Springer International Publishing AG 2017
H.K. Biesalski et al. (eds.), *Sustainable Nutrition in a Changing World*,
DOI 10.1007/978-3-319-55942-1_17

Fig. 17.1 Stakeholders in food and nutrition security

appropriate regulatory framework to allow for appropriate innovative products while simultaneously making sure that the required standards are met so as to protect consumers. Finally, consumers will play an important role in bringing about the necessary changes. They need be prepared for novel product solutions and also educated as to appropriate dietary choices.

These key stakeholders in the food and nutrition market need to interact and align (Fig. 17.1), otherwise this will not happen. We must also bear in mind that even though for some nutritional problems apparently obvious solutions exist, these are often not implemented even in developed countries where it would clearly be possible to do so. One such example is improving folate status via mandatory flour fortification: Even though the proof of this concept has been demonstrated in countries such as the US (1), there is reluctance to implement similar programs in various European countries (2). For other nutritional adequacies, promising interventions or policies still need to be developed.

This part critically evaluates the options to improve FNS, address the existing hurdles, and generate possible solutions now and in the future to the general benefit of public health.

References

1. Jacques PF, Selhub J, Bostom AG, Wilson PW, Rosenberg IH. The effect of folic acid fortification on plasma folate and total homocysteine concentrations. N Engl J Med. 1999 May 13;340:1449–54.
2. Herrmann W, Obeid R. The Mandatory Fortification of Staple Foods With Folic Acid: A Current Controversy in Germany. Dtsch Arztebl Int. 2011;108:249–54.

Chapter 18
The Food Industry as a Partner for Public Health?

Jörg Spieldenner and Janet H. Matope

Abstract The incessant global challenge of malnutrition, coupled with increases in non-communicable diseases (NCDs) worldwide, calls for action on the part of the food industry. As the world shifts towards the implementation of the Sustainable Development Goals (SDGs), there is growing momentum for the elimination of malnutrition to be embedded more firmly, as this will shape the nutrition public health agenda for the next 15 years. Given the food industry's extensive reach, besides its manufacturing capabilities and direct interaction with consumers, it has a major role to play in tackling malnutrition. The food industry has a unique opportunity to leverage its resources and expertise to contribute to the global public health agenda of healthier and more sustainable diets for all. There are several ways in which the food industry can take action to meet internal and external nutrition commitments. These include mapping nutritional gaps through nutrition landscaping activities, the formulation of healthier products, and impact research. The reformulation of commonly consumed food and beverage products to reduce nutrients associated with adverse health effects while incorporating essential nutrients can make a critical contribution to addressing chronic diseases and achieving global nutrition goals. Preconditions for successful public-private partnerships, however, are the exchange of information and transparency regarding the methodology of reformulation and the methods for measuring impact.

Keywords Food industry · Public health · Micronutrient deficiencies (MNDs) · Malnutrition · Nutrition landscaping · Product formulation · Impact research

J. Spieldenner (✉) · J.H. Matope
Nestlé Research Center, 1000 Lausanne 25, Vers Chez Les Blancs, Switzerland
e-mail: jorg.spieldenner@rdls.nestle.com

© Springer International Publishing AG 2017
H.K. Biesalski et al. (eds.), *Sustainable Nutrition in a Changing World*,
DOI 10.1007/978-3-319-55942-1_18

18.1   The Challenge: Malnutrition

The incessant global challenge of malnutrition, coupled with increases in non-communicable diseases (NCDs) worldwide, calls for concerted action—including action on the part of the food industry.

According to the World Food Programme [1], malnutrition includes undernutrition, micronutrient deficiencies (MNDs) and 'overnutrition' (overweight and obesity). Nearly every country in the world experiences some form of malnutrition, with one of the major challenges being MNDs. The World Health Organization (WHO) [2] estimates that approximately one third of the world's population suffers from micronutrient deficiencies, meaning that their diets are deficient in essential vitamins and minerals such as iron, vitamin A, iodine and zinc. The most vulnerable groups are children under the age of five and pregnant women, especially in developing countries, where nutritious foods are often not accessible to the poor. MNDs (also termed 'Hidden Hunger,' as there are no visible warning signs of this condition) have detrimental effects on maternal health and early childhood development, and may result in irreversible damage, such as blindness, brain damage and premature death.

In addition to MNDs, many countries face the increasing burden of overweight, obesity and NCDs. The WHO has stated that mortality rates due to non-communicable diseases such as hypertension and type 2 diabetes will increase by 15% globally between 2010 and 2020 if 'business as usual' continues [3]. A major contributory factor to NCDs worldwide is diet. For example, high blood pressure—which is linked to high sodium intake—affects more than 22% of adults globally [4].

18.2   Global Efforts to Prevent Malnutrition

Globally, there have been efforts to prevent and control all forms of malnutrition, as nutrition has been recognized as a basic pillar for social and economic development. In 2000, when the UN Millennium Development Goals (MDGs) [5] were established, several of them were related to reducing malnutrition by 2015. However, as the deadline has now expired, the 2015 targets were not reached in some countries, although significant gains were made globally. Therefore, as the world shifts towards the Sustainable Development Goals (SDGs) [6]—which build on the MDGs—there is growing momentum for the elimination of malnutrition to be embedded more firmly, as this will shape the nutrition public health agenda for the next 15 years.

Furthermore, over 170 countries adopted the Rome Declaration on Nutrition [7] (Fig. 18.1) and the Framework for Action in 2014, which acknowledged that the elimination of all forms of malnutrition is imperative for public health as well as for social and economic reasons. The Declaration stressed that special attention must be given to maternal and child nutrition, especially during the first 1,000 days of life (from conception to the age of two). This crucial period, as was made clear in the 2008 *Lancet* series on maternal health and child nutrition [8], represents a critical 'window of opportunity' to prevent malnutrition. The Declaration also highlighted the need for the public and private sectors to work together toward ending all forms of malnutrition globally, including obesity and diet-related NCDs.

The Rome Declaration for Nutrition and its Framework for Action were further reinforced in April 2016, when the United Nations General Assembly proclaimed the years 2016–2025 as the UN Decade of Action on Nutrition [9]. The objective of the Decade is to provide an voluntary umbrella under which governments, non-governmental organizations (NGOs), academia, the private sector and other relevant stakeholders can come together to eradicate malnutrition. Their collective efforts are aimed at increasing nutrition investments and implementing nutrition policies and programs, allowing for a healthier, more sustainable future for all.

Given the food industry's extensive reach, besides its manufacturing capabilities and direct interaction with consumers, it has a major role to play in tackling malnutrition. This chapter discusses the food industry as a key stakeholder and how it has a unique opportunity to leverage its resources and expertise to contribute to the global public health agenda of healthier and more sustainable diets for all.

18.3   The Food Industry as a Stakeholder via Its Commitments

Some multinational food companies have already taken action to respond to the public health agenda of improved global nutrition through the implementation of internal company commitments and policies. The 2016 Access to Nutrition Index Report [10] (ATNI)—an independent benchmarking tool which rates major food companies on their nutrition-related policies, practices and performance on a reoccurring basis—found that of the 25 companies assessed, Danone, Nestlé, and Unilever were the top three performers when it came to improving consumer access to better nutrition. According to the index, these three companies performed rather well because they were found to have incorporated explicit commitments to improving nutrition into their core business strategies, which included considerations such as reformulating products and innovating them to make them healthier [10].

Food industry companies have also shown their commitment to improving public health by addressing nutrition issues jointly. One of the most noticeable actions that shows the industry's collective commitment is the establishment of the International Food and Beverage Alliance [11] (IFBA) in 2008—a joint partnership between the world's leading food and beverage companies which was set up to answer a call to action in support of the 2004 WHO Global Strategy on Diet, Physical Activity and Health [12]. Part of the strategy emphasized the need to limit

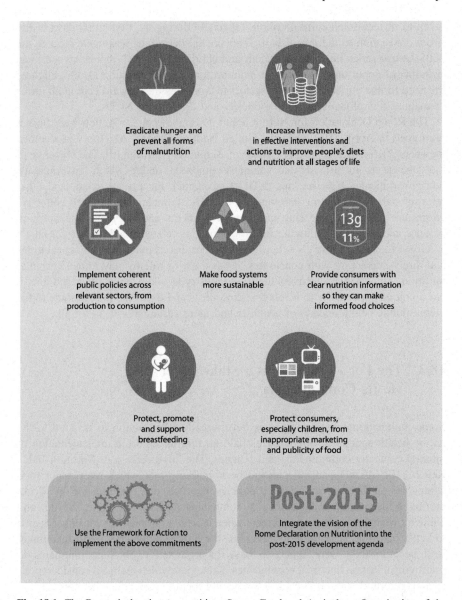

Fig. 18.1 The Rome declaration on nutrition. *Source* Food and Agriculture Organization of the United Nations (2014). Second International Conference on Nutrition. Rome Declaration on Nutrition. Available at: http://www.fao.org/resources/infographics/infographics-details/en/c/266118/. Reproduced with permission

the intake of sugars, fats and salt in foods, while encouraging the consumption of fruits, vegetables, whole grains and nuts. It was determined that this required a multi-sectoral approach that included joint action with the food industry.

There are various ways in which the food industry takes action to meet internal and external nutrition commitments, including nutrition landscaping activities, the formulation of healthier products, and impact research.

18.4   The Food Industry's Contribution via Nutrition Landscaping

According to the WHO [13], Nutrition Landscaping is a systematic approach commonly used to determine how and where to best invest resources in order to yield maximum benefits (Fig. 18.2). Landscaping can help not only policy makers, but also food companies, to identify possible actions that need to be prioritized geographically in order to accelerate the scaling-up of effective nutrition intervention programs and the reformulation of food products.

The food industry uses landscaping to map nutrient gaps scientifically, and the methodologies employed aim to consider different aspects such as dietary intakes, socio-cultural factors and the economic environment. Landscaping activities involve collating and analyzing health data from local governments and international health authorities. These data help food companies to understand consumer barriers to good nutrition by identifying the key nutrient gaps and excesses in the diet, including poor dietary patterns attributable to inadequate intake of nutrients from different food groups such as fruits and vegetables.

The data also helps food companies gain insight into the connection between relevant lifestyle variables and health-related parameters. Companies can apply this knowledge in various countries, and can utilize it as a roadmap for innovation and renovation of product portfolios and for the implementation of nutritional solutions that best meet the needs of consumers geographically, and within a specific population group. Once nutrition gaps in various populations have been identified, companies can also put measures in place to meet consumers' dietary needs. These measures include the formulation of more nutritious products.

Fig. 18.2 The scientific approach to nutrition landscaping. *Source* Made by the authors for this publication

18.5   The Food Industry's Contribution
via the Formulation of Healthier Foods

Public health nutrition experts such as Winkler [14] have stressed that improving nutrition in the 21st century depends partly on innovation and renewal within the food industry. In addition, an 'Overcoming Obesity' cost-effectiveness study conducted by McKinsey Global Institute [15] in the UK determined that portion control and product reformulation had the highest impact in reducing obesity, and concluded that food and beverage companies had a major role to play (see Fig. 18.3).

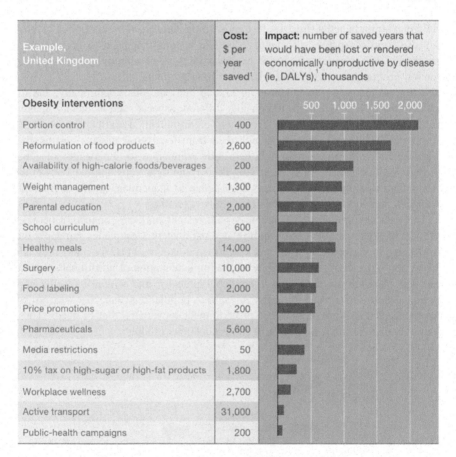

Example, United Kingdom	Cost: $ per year saved[1]	Impact: number of saved years that would have been lost or rendered economically unproductive by disease (ie, DALYs),[3] thousands
Obesity interventions		500 1,000 1,500 2,000
Portion control	400	
Reformulation of food products	2,600	
Availability of high-calorie foods/beverages	200	
Weight management	1,300	
Parental education	2,000	
School curriculum	600	
Healthy meals	14,000	
Surgery	10,000	
Food labeling	2,000	
Price promotions	200	
Pharmaceuticals	5,600	
Media restrictions	50	
10% tax on high-sugar or high-fat products	1,800	
Workplace wellness	2,700	
Active transport	31,000	
Public-health campaigns	200	

[1]Impact and costs are estimated and measured in disability-adjusted life years (DALYs) across full 2014 population in the United Kingdom. For full methodology, download the McKinsey Global Institute (MGI) discussion paper *Overcoming obesity: An initial economic analysis*, on mckinsey.com.

Fig. 18.3 Cost-effective interventions to reduce obesity in the United Kingdom. *Source* Exhibit from *How the world could better fight obesity*, November 2014, McKinsey Global Institute, www.mckinsey.com.

Currently, food companies are reformulating products by improving their nutritional composition through reducing saturated fats, added sugars, and sodium while incorporating whole grains, protein and fibers, in addition to micronutrient fortification.

While product reformulation is inherently in the domain of individual company action, food companies have collaborated on various efforts that have provided a framework for industry advancement. According to Yach et al., [16] since the launch of the WHO Global Strategy on Diet, Physical Activity and Health in 2004, IFBA members have reformulated or developed over 28,000 nutritionally enhanced products. Companies have also ramped up their efforts to develop products fortified with iron, vitamin A and iodine to compensate for chronic micronutrient shortages, particularly in developing nations. This is key, as during the 2008 Copenhagen Consensus [17] project, economic experts ranked micronutrient interventions, including fortification, as top priorities out of 40 global development interventions reviewed. They determined that micronutrient interventions were not only vital to improve health status but also cost-effective, thus making this approach one of the best available investments.

In addition to enhancing the nutritional composition of products, companies have taken action to improve portion control, primarily by providing consumers with more options regarding portion sizes. It is reported that increases in portion sizes since the 1970s for a wide range of foods and beverages have resulted in increased energy intake of about 150–200 more calories per day for both adults and children [18]. Additionally, there appears to be confusion from the consumer perspective regarding the recommended daily portion size of many common foods such as pastas, breads, cereals and juices. This may be caused by a number of factors, including the type and size of the container and the type of food being consumed (for example, amorphous foods such a portion of mashed potatoes [19] are harder to quantify than solid, countable foods such as an apple).

Currently, food companies are working to reduce portion sizes by reformulating products into single-portion packs, or simply by dividing packages into separate units that can be opened individually. Another approach includes the use of re-sealable food packages, signaling to the consumer that the product can be consumed in multiple sittings.

Although portion sizes are a relatively new area of exploration, going forward, it is vital for the food industry to generate evidence regarding portion size interventions and how these may affect the eating behaviors of the consumer. Companies should aim to study consumer habits that reflect real-life consumption and dietary intake that is influenced by portion sizes, in addition to continuing to improve the nutritional quality of their products.

18.5.1   Nutrient Profiling: A Prerequisite for Product Formulation

One of the tools available to guide reformulation efforts is nutrient profiling as identified by The European Union (EU) [20]. Nutrient profiling is a scientific method for assessing the nutritional composition of food and beverages [21]. The food industry uses nutrient profiling to understand the nutritional contribution of its products to a consumer's overall diet in relation to local dietary guidelines, in an effort to prevent disease.

There are several published nutrient profiling systems, some of which focus on nutrients to limit (total fat, saturated fat, trans fatty acids, added sugar and sodium), nutrients to encourage (whole grains, fiber, calcium, protein), or nutrients to both limit *and* encourage. An important consideration when reformulating products is that the nutrients to limit should not be compensated for by the addition of nutrients to encourage.

Examples of peer-reviewed published food industry nutrient profiling systems include those of Nestlé [22] and Unilever [23]. Both these systems incorporate rigorous methodology based on nutrition science and dietary recommendations from organizations such as the WHO and other regulatory authorities.

Nestlé's system is known as the Nestlé Nutritional Profiling System or NNPS, and was set up in 2004 with the objective of driving nutritional innovation and renovation in the Nestlé product portfolio. The system works by profiling each individual food and beverage product against specific criteria. It takes into consideration the product's role in a consumer's diet, the ingredients (including fat, added sugar, calcium and wholegrain), and the serving size usually consumed, whether by adults or by children. The system also considers nutritional factors to limit and those to encourage as being pertinent to public health. This system is one of the few that considers both nutrients to limit and to encourage with specific thresholds for both children and adults [24]. It is also the first nutrient profiling system in the industry that covers a wide range of product categories.

18.5.2   Challenges in Product Formulation

Overall, product reformulation is a complex process, and there are some challenges and limitations that food manufactures have to take into consideration. For example, food manufacturers face the challenge of making products more nutritious while taking into account consumer preferences such as perception of quality, taste, appearance and affordability. In this case, progressive, incremental change seems to be the best approach to shifting consumer tastes and encouraging acceptance of a reformulated product. Research shows that a consumer's preference for sodium can be altered and lowered without the consumer noticing, following reductions in sodium content of the diet over a period of time [24]. Manufacturers must also consider the technical or functional role of some nutrients. For example, salt is generally used as a natural preservative in many products, controls water activity, and helps minimize food spoilage. Its reduction may therefore result in a shorter product shelf life [25]. Salt also contributes to the sensory and textural properties of many products. Another example is sugars that may contribute more than just sweetness, as they can also play a role in the texture, flavor and stability of a food product. Food manufacturers therefore face the challenge of finding cost-effective alternatives to reduce public-health-sensitive nutrients while attempting to retain the characteristics of the product accepted by the consumer.

In addition, the food industry also faces the challenge of determining whether or not reformulated products positively influence the long-term health status of a consumer, which is the ultimate goal.

18.6   The Food Industry's Contribution via Impact Research

The food industry as a key stakeholder is expected to provide evidence about how product reformulation and other interventions aimed at improving nutrition ultimately affect public health issues such as malnutrition and health-related quality of life (HRQoL). In other words, like the other stakeholders, the food industry will also have to substantiate the translation of its public health efforts into tangible results. This is becoming even more important as limited resources in the field of nutrition are demanding an even higher level of evidence-based, cost-effective solutions that address global health issues. Currently the WHO, other UN bodies, governments and NGOs are placing greater emphasis on outcome measures such as the reduction of population mortality rates and the incidence of chronic disease.

It appears that the best approach for the food industry to assess the potential economic benefit and sustainability of nutrition interventions is via the field of Health Economics in Nutrition—a rather new research field using methods of health economics that is dedicated to researching the interdependency between dietary habits, nutrition interventions, health, and costs (e.g. public expenditure). This field has only recently emerged and can be defined as a "discipline dedicated to researching and characterizing health and economic outcomes in nutrition for the benefit of society" [26].

Health Economics in Nutrition can be useful in trying to determine the most cost-effective nutrition interventions. However, as the science behind it is relatively new, the discipline lacks a specific methodology, and the research community and regulatory authorities have yet to establish clear criteria and guidelines for how best to evaluate the economic impact of nutrition interventions. In the absence of a specific methodology, directives are typically developed based around the classical health economics model, which includes principles of evidence-based medicine, with its strong reliance on randomized controlled trials (RCTs). However, nutrition researchers have expressed concerns that the design of these trials is more suited to assess the efficacy and safety of drugs, not that of nutrients or foods [27]. According to Lenoir-Wijnkoop et al., [26] "the complexity of food and its interactions with multiple interdependent genetic, physiological, metabolic and psychological processes that have an impact on human physical functioning and psycho-social well-being" requires a modified approach that is different from that used in the pharmaceutical field.

This comes as no surprise, as the use of health economics was initially developed to aid decision-making in healthcare when attempting to determine how best to allocate resources between two or more available treatment strategies or options, and is therefore simply not practical for use in nutrition interventions. Nutrition interventions are often dedicated to prevention rather than treatment, and are frequently influenced by a multitude of factors, unlike a classical pharmaceutical dose-effect response in controlled therapeutic settings. This adds complexity to the process of establishing a correlation between food consumption and downstream consequences such as future health status. The difference is that pharmaceutical products need a thorough risk: benefit analysis, whereas food regulatory processes make risk of any kind unacceptable [28]. Other differences include the fact that food is available to all populations regardless of health status, while pharmaceutical products are restricted to a specific group of subjects. Lastly, consumer food choices are influenced by habits, personal preferences, and cultural socio-economic status, and patterns of food consumption are consequently more random than is the case with products which are medically recommended or prescribed.

One possible approach to assess the effectiveness of nutrition interventions may be studies that allow for a high 'external validity', which is the extent to which research studies can be applied within the general population. External validity is generally low in RCTs, but high in observational trials—meaning that although a treatment may be effective in an RCT, the treatment will not be valid if it is not reflective of real-life conditions.

18.6.1 A Pragmatic Way to Determine Impact

Accordingly, there are a variety of metrics that exist for measuring the health economic impact of nutrition [29]. One important field is to determine the cost-saving potential of preventing diseases by means of nutrition interventions. One example is a series of studies published by Wieser et al. to determine a cost-effective, commercially-based nutrition intervention addressing micronutrient deficiencies in Filipino children aged 6 to 59 months. The authors first assessed the efficacy of food product categories delivering micronutrients in the diet with a systematic literature review [30]. This was followed by a burden-of-disease study that computed the cost of MNDs by using data from a 2008 dietary intake survey conducted by the Philippines Food and Nutrition Research Institute (FNRI) [31].

Learning Questions	Approach to Measurement
Making the Case	
1. Is food fortification effective?*	✓ **Systematic review** of food fortification literature
2. What are the health and economic consequences of deficiencies?	✓ **Health economic model** simulating the consequences of MNDs in childhood
Measuring the Innovation	
3. What are the patterns of awareness and demand among Filipino households?	✓ **Household survey** of 1800 households, across socio-economic groups
4. What is their sensitivity to price?	✓ **Hypothetical marketing experiment** to assess reactions to price discounts
5. How cost-effective are price-based interventions?	✓ **Cost-effectiveness estimations** of tiered pricing schemes
Measuring the Impact	
6. Do the predicted health and economic benefits happen?	❑ **Field study** on real-life impact on anemia, morbidity and finances

* Nestlé fully understands that food fortification is one of several ways to address micronutrient deficiencies, with a varied diet being the most highly recommended approach

Fig. 18.4 Example of how Nestlé is helping to address micronutrient deficiencies in developing countries through impact research. *Source* Shared Value Initiative. Measuring Shared Value Innovation and Impact in Health (2012). Available at: http://www.sharedvalue.org/resources/measuring-shared-value-innovation-and-impact-health

For the cost-effectiveness study, a health economic model was created that predicted the health outlook for children, given that they had sufficient micronutrient intake. This health economic model was complemented by a Willingness to Pay [32] survey of 1,600 households to determine price points and other barriers for the consumption of a commercially distributed existing product. The study found that a commercially available product is a cost-effective way to reduce the burden of MNDs in the Philippines. Such an approach may constitute a potential blueprint for similar studies in the field of preventing diseases through nutrition interventions. This type of framework has already been adopted by the FSG (an international consulting firm that supports leaders in creating large-scale, lasting social change) [33] in an effort to help the private sector determine the cost-effectiveness of health-related business interventions and their applicability in the real world (Fig. 18.4).

18.7   Conclusion

Public-private partnerships have a pivotal role to play in addressing public health via nutrition. In this regard, the food industry can be a partner not only to develop practical solutions to address global health, but also to provide the necessary scientific substantiation, proof of effectiveness, and measuring or modeling of health outcomes.

Consequently, the reformulation of commonly consumed food and beverage products in order to reduce nutrients associated with adverse health effects while incorporating essential nutrients can make a critical contribution to addressing chronic disease and achieving global nutrition goals. Preconditions for successful public-private partnerships, however, are the exchange of information and transparency regarding the methodology of reformulation and the methods for measuring impact. These are needed to build confidence and to create trust based upon common objectives among all the stakeholders involved.

18.8 Summary: Key Messages

- The incessant global challenge of malnutrition, coupled with increases in non-communicable diseases (NCDs) worldwide, calls for action on the part of the food industry.
- As the world shifts towards the Sustainable Development Goals (SDGs), there is growing momentum for malnutrition to be embedded more firmly, as this will shape the nutrition public health agenda for the next 15 years.
- Given the food industry's extensive reach, besides its manufacturing capabilities and direct interaction with consumers, it has a major role to play in tackling malnutrition.
- There are several ways in which the food industry can take action to meet internal and external nutrition commitments in this regard. These include nutrition landscaping activities, formulation of healthier products, and impact research.
- The reformulation of commonly consumed food and beverage products in order to reduce nutrients associated with adverse health effects while incorporating essential nutrients can make a critical contribution to addressing chronic disease and achieving global nutrition goals.
- Preconditions for successful public-private partnerships are exchange of information and transparency regarding the methodology of product reformulation and the methods for measuring impact.

References

1. World Food Programme (2015). Available at: https://www.wfp.org/hunger/glossary.
2. World Health Organization. The World Health Report (2002). Available at: http://www.who.int/whr/2002/chapter4/en/index3.html.
3. World Health Organization. (2013) Available at: http://www.who.int/nmh/publications/ncd_report_chapter1.pdf.
4. World Health Organization. Global action plan for the prevention and control of NCDs 2013–2020.

5. United Nations, The Millennium Development Goals Report (2013).
6. United Nations. Indicators for Sustainability Development Goals. Available at: https://sustainabledevelopment.un.org/topics/sustainabledevelopmentgoals.
7. Food and Agriculture Organization of the United Nations (2014). Second International Conference on Nutrition. Rome Declaration on Nutrition. Available at: http://www.fao.org/resources/infographics/infographics-details/en/c/266118/. Reproduced with permission.
8. The Lancet. Maternal and Child Nutrition (2013). Available at: http://www.thelancet.com/series/maternal-and-child-nutrition.
9. Food and Agriculture Organization of the United Nations. United Nations Decade of Action on Nutrition 2016–2025. (2016). Available at http://www.fao.org/3/a-i6137e.pdf.
10. Access to Nutrition Index (2016). 2016 Global Index. Available at https://www.accesstonutrition.org/.
11. International Food & Beverage Alliance (2015). Available at: https://ifballiance.org/.
12. Waxman A, World Health A. WHO global strategy on diet, physical activity and health (2004). Food and Nutrition bulletin. 25(3):292–302.
13. World Health Organization. Nutritional Landscape Information System (2015). Available at: http://www.who.int/nutrition/nlis/en/.
14. Winkler JT. Nutritional reformulation: the unobtrusive strategy. (2014) The Journal of the Institute of Food Science and Technology.
15. Exhibit from "How the world could better fight obesity", November 2014, McKinsey Global Institute, www.mckinsey.com. Copyright (c), 2014 McKinsey & Company All rights reserved Reprinted by permission.
16. Yach D, Khan M, Bradley D, Hargrove R, Kehoe S & Mensah G (2010).The Role and Challenges of the Food Industry in Addressing Chronic Disease, 6 Globalization and Health 1–8, 1.
17. Sue Horton, France Begin, Alison Greig & Anand Lakshman. Micronutrient Supplements for Child Survival (Vitamin and Zinc). http://www.copenhagenconsensus.com/sites/default/files/bpp_micronutrient_vitamina_zinc.pdf.
18. Piernas, Carmen, & Popkin, Barry M. (2011). Food Portion Patterns and Trends among U.S. Children and the Relationship to Total Eating Occasion Size, 1977–2006. The Journal of Nutrition, 141(6), 1159–1164.
19. Institute of Grocery Distribution (2009). Portion size communication in therapeutic practice: a survey of dietitians and nutritionists.
20. European Commission (EC). (2009). Reformulating food products for health: context and key issues for moving forward in Europe.
21. World Health Organization (2010). Nutrient Profiling Report of a WHO/IASO Technical Meeting London, United Kingdom 4–6.
22. Vlassopoulos A, Masset G, Rheiner Charles V, Hoover C, Chesneau-Guillemont C, Leroy F, et al. (2016). A nutrient profiling system for the (re)formulation of a global food and beverage portfolio Eur J Nutr. doi:10.1007/s00394-016-1161-9.
23. Nijman, C. A., et al. (2007). 'A method to improve the nutritional quality of foods and beverages based on dietary recommendations.' Eur J Clin Nutr 61(4): 461–471.
24. U.S Institute of Medicine (2010) Strategies to Reduce Sodium Intake in the United States. National Academies Press.
25. Buttriss JL. (2013)Food reformulation: the challenges to the food industry. Proceedings of the Nutrition Society. 72 (01):61–69.
26. Lenoir-Wijnkoop I, Dapoigny M, Dubois D, et al. (2011) Nutrition economics – characterising the economic and health impact of nutrition. Br J Nutr 105, 157–166.
27. Andrew Shao, PhD, and Douglas MacKay, ND (2010). A Commentary on the Nutrient-Chronic Disease Relationship and the New Paradigm of Evidence-Based Nutrition.
28. Freijer K (2014), Health Economics-An introduction. ISPOR CONNECTIONS. Vol 20:4.
29. Gyles CL, Lenoir-Wijnkoop I, Carlberg JG, Senanayake V, Gutierrez-Ibarluzea I, Poley MJ, Dubois D, Jones PJ (2012). Health economics and nutrition: a review of published evidence. Nutr Rev. 70(12):693–708.

30. Eichler K1, Wieser S, Rüthemann I, Brügger U. (2012). Effects of micronutrient fortified milk and cereal food for infants and children: a systematic review. BMC Public Health. Jul 6;12:506. doi:10.1186/1471-2458-12-506.
31. Wieser S, Plessow R, Eichler K, Malek O, Capanzana MV, Agdeppa I, et al. (2013). Burden of micronutrient deficiencies by socio-economic strata in children aged 6 months to 5 years in the Philippines. BMC Public Health. Dec 11;13:1167. doi:10.1186/1471-2458-13-1167.
32. Wieser S, Brunner B, Plessow R, Eichler K, Solomons N, Malek O, Spieldenner J, Bruegger U. (2015) Cost-Effectiveness of Price Reductions in Fortified Powdered Milk for the Reduction of Micronutrient Deficiencies in 6–23 Month Old Children in the Philippines. European Journal of Nutrition & Food Safety. Special issue; 5(5): 436-437.
33. Shared Value Initiative. Measuring Shared Value Innovation and Impact in Health (2012). Available at: http://www.sharedvalue.org/resources/measuring-shared-value-innovation-and-impact-health.

Chapter 19
Improving Food and Nutrition Security in Affluent Societies: The View of a Food Ingredients Manufacturer

Marcel Wubbolts

Abstract One approach to ensuring Food and Nutrition Security is to fortify foods with nutrients whose intakes are considered critical for good health. This can be done either by replacing what has been lost during food processing or by adding additional amounts of certain nutrients. In either instance, it is the responsibility of the ingredients supplier to provide products that comply with the physical-chemical properties of the food to which they are added. Moreover, along with the desired nutritional value, the final product has to offer the authentic taste demanded by the consumer. Another option besides food fortification is the provision of dietary supplements. These can be designed to meet basic nutritional needs, as in the case of multivitamin preparations, or to deliver individual nutrients to fill gaps in the diet. The challenge for the food ingredients supplier is to have not only the prerequisite technical capabilities but also the necessary expertise to develop, in close collaboration with the private and public sectors, solutions that the consumer will accept.

Keywords Nutrients · Nutritional ingredients · Nutritional ingredients manufacturer · Bioavailability · Efficacy · Taste · Fortification · Dietary supplements · Consumer

DSM is the world's leading supplier of vitamins, polyunsaturated fatty acids (PUFA) and carotenoids besides enzymes and other food ingredients. All these nutrients are an integral part of our diet and are necessary for good health. DSM's ingredients portfolio comprises many essential nutrients which are insufficiently present in the diets of people suffering from Food and Nutrition Insecurity. Suppliers such as DSM produce these ingredients and formulate them in such ways that they may be added to a range of foods, dietary supplements and animal feeds by the respective manufacturers without compromising their efficacy or bioavailability.

M. Wubbolts (✉)
Royal DSM, Poststraat 1, 6135 KR Sittard, The Netherlands
e-mail: marcel.wubbolts@dsm.com

© Springer International Publishing AG 2017   275
H.K. Biesalski et al. (eds.), *Sustainable Nutrition in a Changing World*,
DOI 10.1007/978-3-319-55942-1_19

19.1 Ensuring Bioavailability, Efficacy and Taste

One obvious option for addressing Food and Nutrition Security (FNS) is to fortify foods with nutrients whose intakes are considered critical. This can be done either by replacing what has been lost during food processing or by adding additional quantities of certain nutrients. Both approaches present a challenge for the food ingredient provider, however. Some of the ingredients (such as vitamins A, D, E and K and carotenoids) are fat-soluble, but might be used in water-based matrices, while others (such as PUFA) may be accompanied by an unwanted taste. In addition, the half-life of water-soluble compounds tends to be rather short. All these factors can reduce bioavailability in the final product and the bioefficacy of these compounds in the human organism, and can even impact palatability in such a way that consumers will not accept the final product. In addition, the food matrices may further complicate matters by interacting with the ingredients. So it is an important responsibility of the ingredients supplier to provide products that comply with the physical–chemical properties of the food to which they are added. Moreover, besides the desired nutritional value, the final product has to provide the authentic taste the consumer demands.

19.2 Dietary Supplements

Besides enriching or fortifying foods to improve FNS, another option is to provide dietary supplements. These can be designed to meet basic nutritional needs, as in the case of multivitamin preparations, or to provide individual nutrients—for example, vitamin D supplements can be taken to reduce the risk of bone fractures or of falls and to improve bone health in postmenopausal women (1). Moreover, supplements can compensate for shortages which may have occurred because of a life event such as a severe illness that may have reduced appetite, compromised the absorption of nutrients in the gastrointestinal system, or required a longer stay in hospital (2). Once again, the food ingredients supplier needs to provide specific compounds that meet the requirements of individual dietary supplement preparations.

19.3 Meeting the Needs of Consumers—Rich and Poor

When designing solutions to ensure Food and Nutrition Security, the experience and capabilities of the food ingredients supplier are essential for translating scientific insights and know-how into practical and effective products, whether these are destined for inclusion in food products or for provision in the form of dietary supplements. The challenge for the food ingredients supplier is not only to have the

Fig. 19.1 Routes between the food ingredient supplier and the consumer. Reproduced by permission of Royal DSM

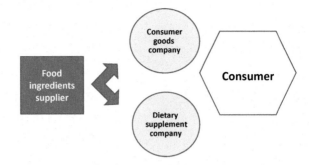

technical capabilities for producing the nutritional ingredients so that they meet the relevant criteria but also to have the necessary expertise in nutrition, human health and biochemistry to be able to develop solutions in close collaboration with the respective consumer goods and dietary supplement companies and public health bodies. Last but not least, the food ingredients supplier requires an understanding of what the consumer will accept (Fig. 19.1).

In addition to these considerations, the food industry also has a social responsibility to provide solutions that are not only nutritious but also affordable. The approximately 4 billion people living at the economic Base of the Pyramid (BoP), for example, need nutritional solutions that combine quality and safety with accessible pricing. DSM is exploring ways of meeting the needs of this highly vulnerable part of the world's population in an extensive collaboration with the United Nations World Food Programme (WFP).

Whether in affluent societies or in those with severe economic constraints, Food and Nutrition Security can only be delivered through the very active interplay of science, the food industry, public health policy-makers, and the consumer.

References

1. Bischoff-Ferrari, Staehelin. Importance of Vitamin D and Calcium at Older Age. International Journal for Vitamin and Nutrition Research. 2008 November 30, 2008;78:286–92.
2. Medical Nutrition International Industry. Tackling Malnutrition: Oral nutritional supplements as an integrated part of patient and disease management in hospital and in the community; 2010.

Chapter 20
Food and Nutrition Security: A Consumer Perspective

Klaus G. Grunert

Abstract Having access to nutritious food will have a positive impact on people's nutritional status only when these nutritious products are actually bought, transformed into meals, and eaten. Food has multiple functions for the consumer: it is at one and the same time a source of pleasure, a platform for socializing, a tool for strengthening family life, and an avenue for personal growth. People's dietary intake is the result of a *complex range of decisions*, and all these decisions have an impact on dietary intake and consequently nutritional status. One of the most important *environments* in which consumers make decisions is the supermarket. Both the food industry and retailers have in recent years adapted the shopping environment so as to encourage the selection of healthier products. The *ability* of consumers to make nutritionally sound choices is related to the level of their own nutritional knowledge. Investigations into nutritional knowledge have revealed considerable differences, and these can be linked both to a range of demographic factors and to distinctions between nations. The biggest bottleneck when it comes to turning a supply of nutritious food into a nutritious diet is *motivation*, or the lack of it. In addition, there is a deeply ingrained conviction that health and pleasure do not go hand in hand, and that food-based indulgence is by necessity unhealthy.

Keywords Consumer · Dietary intake · Nutritional status · Nutritional content · Choice · Pleasure · Health

K.G. Grunert (✉)
Department of Management, MAPP Centre, Aarhus University,
Bartholins Allé 10, 8000 Aarhus C, Denmark
e-mail: klg@mgmt.au.dk

© Springer International Publishing AG 2017
H.K. Biesalski et al. (eds.), *Sustainable Nutrition in a Changing World*,
DOI 10.1007/978-3-319-55942-1_20

20.1 The Multiple Functions of Food

Food and nutrition security is about having access to sufficient, affordable and nutritious food. But from a consumer perspective, having access to food is only the beginning of the story. Having access to nutritious food will have a positive impact on people's nutritional status only when these nutritious products are actually bought, transformed into meals, and eaten.

For consumers, food is not just a source of nutrients: is has multiple functions [2]. In addition to providing nutrition, food is also a source of pleasure, a platform for socializing, a tool for strengthening family life, and an avenue for personal growth. Hence the way consumers relate to food is complex, and purely nutritional considerations are not always at the forefront of their minds.

People's dietary intake is the result of a *complex range of decisions*. The type of decision that has received most attention from a nutritional perspective has been the decision regarding which food products to buy. However, purchasing decisions are only the start of the matter. People also make decisions about how to prepare products; how to combine various ingredients into a meal; when, where and how often to eat; and—last but not least—how much to eat in a given mealtime situation. All these decisions have an impact on their dietary intake and hence their nutritional status. While certain aspects of consumers' decision-making processes when buying food are relatively well researched, much less is known about the processes that occur subsequently within the household. There is some evidence, however, to suggest that the frequency of cooking meals in the household is related to considerations of healthy eating [5].

How these decisions are made—and whether or not they result in nutritionally desirable outcomes—will depend on the ability and motivation of consumers to make the right decisions, and on the environments in which such decisions are made (see Fig. 20.1).

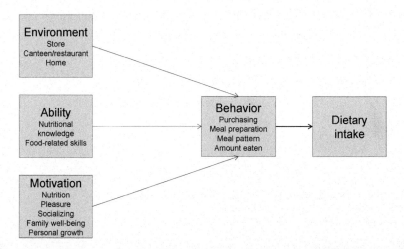

Fig. 20.1 The determinants of behavior that lead to dietary intake. *Source* Developed by author

20.2   The Supermarket Environment

One of the most important *environments* in which consumers make decisions is the supermarket. A supermarket is an information-rich environment with lots of stimuli that influence consumer choice—not necessarily in a nutritionally desirable manner. Still, both the food industry and retailers have in recent years adapted the shopping environment in such a way as to encourage the selection of healthier products by shoppers. Nutrition labeling has become widespread, and health claims and symbols emphasize specific aspects of nutritional content and their implications for health benefits. These measures do not seem to exercise a major effect on consumer choices (e.g., [6]), but over time they can result in small but steady changes in the direction of better diets [7]. The limited effect of these informational measures has led to a widespread discussion of the non-informational nudging of choices in a healthier direction—for example, by means of shelf placement and store layout.

20.3   Consumer Choices

The *ability* of consumers to make nutritionally sound choices is related to their own nutritional knowledge. This includes knowledge concerning dietary guidelines, desirable levels of intake of various nutrients and food product categories, and the extent to which certain nutrients are present in different product categories. Investigations into the nutritional knowledge of consumers have revealed considerable differences, and these can be linked both to a range of demographic factors and to distinctions between nations [3]. With regard to desirable levels of intake of the key macronutrients, there is reason to believe that many consumers are reasonably aware of these, and the same is true for desirable levels of intake of the major food categories. The situation is different for micronutrients, however, where consumer knowledge and even awareness is probably lower [4].

The biggest bottleneck when it comes to turning a supply of nutritious food into a nutritious diet is *motivation*, or the lack of it. Of course, all people are interested in their health. But, as noted above, food is linked to multiple motives, of which health is only one. In addition, many food choices are made habitually, and when they are not habit-based, they usually involve simple choice heuristics, whereby decisions are based on key cues such as brand, price, looks and provenance. In addition, there is a deeply ingrained conviction that health and pleasure do not go hand in hand, that food-based indulgence is by necessity unhealthy, and that healthy food is a source of nutrients but not a source of pleasure [1]. Consumers handle this in different ways—some by not making any compromises one way or another, but most by trying to find some kind of balance across product categories and eating occasions.

20.4   Summary: Key Messages

- Having access to nutritious food will have a positive impact on people's nutritional status only when these nutritious products are actually bought, transformed into meals, and eaten.
- Food has multiple functions for the consumer: it is at one and the same time a source of pleasure, a platform for socializing, a tool to strengthen family life, and an avenue for personal growth.
- People's dietary intake is the result of a *complex range of decisions*, and these all have an impact on dietary intake and consequently nutritional status.
- Both the food industry and retailers have in recent years adapted the shopping environment in such a way as to encourage the selection of healthier products.
- The *ability* of consumers to make nutritionally sound choices is related to their own nutritional knowledge.
- The biggest bottleneck when it comes to turning a supply of nutritious food into a nutritious diet is *motivation*. In addition, there is a deeply ingrained conviction that health and pleasure do not go hand in hand, and that food-based indulgence is by necessity unhealthy.

References

1. Chrysochou, P., Askegaard, S., Grunert, K. G., & Kristensen, D. B. (2010). Social discourses of healthy eating. A market segmentation approach. *Appetite, 55*(2), 288–297.
2. Furst, T., Connors, M., Bisogni, C. A., Sobal, J., & Falk, L. W. (1996). Food choice: a conceptual model of the process. *Appetite, 26*(3), 247–266.
3. Grunert, K. G., Wills, J., Celemín, L. F., Lähteenmäki, L., Shouldered, J., & Genannt Bonsmann, S. S. (2012). Socio-demographic and attitudinal determinants of nutrition knowledge of food shoppers in six European countries. *Food Quality and Preference, 26*(2), 166–177.
4. Jensen, B. B., Lähteenmäki, L., Grunert, K. G., Brown, K. A., Timotijevic, L., Barnett, J., ... & Raats, M. M. (2012). Changing micronutrient intake through (voluntary) behavior change. The case of folate. *Appetite, 58*(3), 1014–1022.
5. Larson, N. I., Perry, C. L., Story, M., & Neumark-Sztainer, D. (2006). Food preparation by young adults is associated with better diet quality. *Journal of the American Dietetic Association, 106*(12), 2001–2007.
6. Sacks, G., Rayner, M., & Swinburn, B. (2009). Impact of front-of-pack 'traffic-light' nutrition labelling on consumer food purchases in the UK. *Health promotion international, 24*(4), 344–352.
7. Sutherland, L. A., Kaley, L. A., & Fischer, L. (2010). Guiding stars: the effect of a nutrition navigation program on consumer purchases at the supermarket. *The American journal of clinical nutrition, 91*(4), 1090S–1094S.

Chapter 21
Food Chain Processes and Food Quality

M.A.J.S. (Tiny) van Boekel

Abstract This chapter examines the relationship between the quality of foods and the processes in the food chains that deliver those foods. Food quality is ultimately a question of consumer perception. Actors in the food chain should have the common goal of delivering high-quality food to consumers. Using quality analysis critical control points (QACCP) might help improve the management of quality in the food chain. The food chain will have to innovate in order to improve sustainability, but this presents challenges. A key problem is that the timescale for innovation may be completely different for different actors within the food chain. The ultimate aim is to offer the customer a final product that has the desired quality at the lowest cost, not only for the consumer but also for the environment. This requires combined action on the part of the various actors in the food chain in order to effectively apply the concept of people, planet and profit, and will call for new approaches.

Keywords Food production · Food chain · Food quality · Food chain actor · Consumer · Quality analysis critical control points (QACCP) · Innovation · Sustainability

21.1   Introduction

When addressing the topic of Sustainable Nutrition Security in a changing world, it is pertinent to study how food is currently produced. In modern society, food production has developed into what we now call food chains [1]. A food chain can ideally be described as an integrated process of acquiring raw materials from agriculture, horticulture, fisheries and animal husbandry, converting these into products, and delivering them to the consumer. A chain is characterized by a flow of goods downstream, a flow of money upstream, and a flow of information up- and

M.A.J.S. (Tiny) van Boekel (✉)
Wageningen University, P.O. Box 9101, 6700 HB Wageningen, The Netherlands
e-mail: Tiny.vanBoekel@wur.nl

© Springer International Publishing AG 2017   283
H.K. Biesalski et al. (eds.), *Sustainable Nutrition in a Changing World*,
DOI 10.1007/978-3-319-55942-1_21

downstream. Traditionally, such a chain has been product-driven, and geared to delivering a limited range of products of average quality in a cost-efficient way.

The question may be asked as to whether the food chain really is linear, or whether it is perhaps a non-linear network of actors. Whatever the description, the target is to produce and deliver foods to the consumer in an efficient and effective way. Diverse players are active in such a chain or network, each with their own goals and optimization problems. However, there should be one common goal—namely, to deliver high-quality food to the end-user. This begs the question as to what constitutes food quality. This question is not easily answered, because food quality is an elusive concept.

21.2   Food Quality

A very broad definition of food quality is that a food is of high quality if it satisfies the expectations of the consumer. It is important to realize that food quality is thus a result of an interplay between a consumer and the food that he or she consumes.

Intrinsic properties are part of the food, due to its composition and structure. Extrinsic properties, by contrast, are not direct properties of the food itself but result instead from the environment in which the food is produced. For instance, the price at which a food item is offered for sale is not a property of the food itself and is therefore considered extrinsic. An organically grown apple may have the same intrinsic properties as a conventionally produced one, but the fact that it was organically grown may make a big difference to the person who eats it. This example shows that quality is a concept constructed within the consumer rather than a property of the product itself. Nevertheless, it is also clear that the properties of the food influence the perception of consumers. Quality is a multidimensional concept: it contains both subjective and objective elements, and is situation-specific and dynamic in time. A consumer, however, does not analyze all the elements of food quality consciously; rather, he or she gives an integrated response based on a range of complex mental judgements. While all these aspects (and several more, indeed) play a role, it is not an easy task for food technologists to determine which are the most important. Consumer studies remain essential in this respect. In any case, it may help actors in the food chain if intrinsic and extrinsic quality attributes are disentangled from one another so as to make clear which factors are controllable by a specific actor.

Another substantial problem in the food chain is that the quality perception of various actors can be quite different, and sometimes mutually contradictory. A farmer, for instance, may be more concerned with the yield or disease resistance of a crop than with its eating quality. A consumer may be against the use of agrochemicals but at the same time demand that there should be no signs of disease on the produce that he or she buys. The food industry wants to deliver a safe food that does not spoil, while the consumer wants a product that is minimally processed but is also safe to eat and has a long shelf life. Actors in the food chain should focus on these matters, in order to make bridges between seemingly conflicting wishes. In any case, the consumer should be the starting-point for action in the food chain. Supply chain management is therefore an important consideration [1].

A possible way to get a grip on food quality in the chain is a concept analogous to the well-known HACCP concept, quality analysis critical control points (QACCP, [2, 3]). The idea is to first define quality attributes and then investigate the behavior of each of these attributes in each element of the food chain. The factors (such as temperature, relative humidity, etc.) that have a major impact on the behavior of the quality attribute are considered critical control points.

Food quality obviously also pertains to nutrition, and improvement of nutritional quality should be a goal of actors in the food chain. However, when it comes to sustainable nutrition, the problem lies less in the quality of individual products than in the combination of products within a diet, as this is the major factor influencing the health of a consumer. In view of diet-related health problems such as obesity, this should be a major concern for actors in the food chain. It is not so clear, however, what actions should be taken, since obesity is a multi-faceted problem and is more related to the diet in general than to individual products, although some authors advocate that the food industry should take action [4, 5].

21.3 Sustainability

From a technology point of view, sustainability can be improved by reducing water and energy use, and by avoiding losses and re-using side streams where losses cannot be avoided. If we picture the food chain as the 'technosphere', it becomes essential to take the ecosphere into account as well (Fig. 21.1). By optimizing the use of energy, water and raw materials, a circular economy can be established. This may have an effect on intrinsic as well as extrinsic food quality. The question then arises as to how these aspects can be brought into balance. Again, consumers play an important role here, because it is ultimately they who decide about quality.

The food chain will have to innovate in order to improve sustainability. Cooperation between actors becomes even more essential here [6]. Innovation in the food industry cannot be isolated from the other actors in the chain, and institutional governance then becomes a major issue. A key problem in innovation from a food-chain perspective is, however, that the timescale for innovation may be completely different for different actors.

As for market dynamics, it is relatively easy to put something new on the market by launching so-called 'me-too' products, introducing line extensions, or repositioning existing products. These kinds of 'innovation' do not require investments in technology, so new products can be launched in a matter of months. The question is, of course, whether or not this can be considered innovation. Moreover, it is

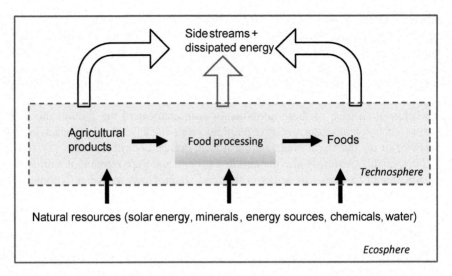

Fig. 21.1 Schematic representation of the relation between the technosphere (where food chain actors are busy) and the ecosphere (the environment). *Source* Produced by the author

doubtful that improvements in sustainability can be achieved by this level of intervention.

Real innovation is more demanding in the food technology domain in the case where new technologies have to be introduced: this requires a considerable investment in terms of money, time and skills in order to master new technologies and design new processes and products. Consequently, innovation in this domain typically requires several years. In terms of primary production, it may take a decade in cases where raw materials need to be changed by means of selective breeding. Genetic modification techniques may considerably speed up such developments, but nevertheless it may still be some years before production is possible. At the same time, consumer acceptance also presents a major issue. This huge difference in timescales is a perennial problem for the food chain and has obvious implications for innovation. There are also huge differences in spatial scales, running from the molecular scale (involving the composition of foods) to the global scale (involving logistics, governance and food politics). Each of these worlds has its own dynamics.

All in all, innovation in the perspective of the food chain is challenging. The ultimate aim is to offer the customer a final product that has the desired quality at the lowest cost, not only for the consumer but also for the environment (Fig. 21.2). This requires combined action on the part of the various actors in the food chain in order to effectively apply the concept of people, planet and profit. It will require new approaches [7–11].

Fig. 21.2 Broader picture of food quality in relation to a sustainable diet. *Source* Produced by the author

21.4 Summary: Key Messages

- Food quality is ultimately a question of consumer perception.
- Actors in the food chain should have the common goal of delivering high-quality food to consumers.
- The food chain will have to innovate in order to improve sustainability, but this will present challenges.
- The ultimate aim is to offer the customer a final product that has the desired quality at the lowest cost, not only for the consumer but also for the environment.
- This requires combined action on the part of the various actors in the food chain in order to effectively apply the concept of people, planet and profit. New approaches will be called for.

References

1. W.M.F. Jongen, M.T.G. Meulenberg, Editors. (2005). Innovation in Agri-Food Systems. Product quality and consumer acceptance. Wageningen Academic Publishers.
2. M.A.J.S. van Boekel (2005). Technological Innovation in the food industry: product design. In: Innovation in Agri-Food Systems. Product quality and consumer acceptance, W.M.F. Jongen & M.T.G. Meulenberg (Eds). Wageningen Academic Publishers.
3. R. Verkerk, A.R. Linnemann & M.A.J.S. van Boekel (2007). Quality Analysis Critical Control Points in consumer-oriented agro-food chains. In: R. Ruben, M.A.J.S. van Boekel, A. van Tilburg, J. Trienekens (Eds.). Tropical Food Chains. Governance regimes for quality management. Wageningen Academic Publishers.
4. J.C. Seidell (1999). Prevention of obesity: the role of the food industry. Nutrition, Metabolism, and Cardiovascular Diseases 9: 45–50.
5. D. Stuckler, MN. Nestle (2012). Big Food, Food Systems, and Global Health. PLOS Medicine 9: 1–4.
6. J. G.A.J. van der Vorst, S.-O. Tromp & D.-J. van der Zee (2009). Simulation modelling for food supply chain redesign; integrated decision making on product quality, sustainability and logistics. International Journal of Production Research 47: 6611–6631.

7. N. Perrot, I.C. Trelea, C. Baudrit, G. Trystram, P. Bourgine (2011). Modeling and analysis of complex food systems: state of the art and new trends. Trends in Food Science & Technology 22: 304–314.

8. A. Surana, S. Kumara, M. Greaves, C. Nandini, U. Raghavan (2013). Supply chain networks: a complex adaptive systems perspective. International Journal of Production Research 43: 4235–4265.

9. R. Akkerman, P. Farahani, M. Grunow (2010). Quality, safety and sustainability in food distribution: a review of quantitative operations management approaches and challenges OR Spectrum 32:863–904.

10. M. Pullman, M.J. Maloni, C.R. Carter (2009). Food for thought: social versus environmental Sustainability practices and performance outcomes. Journal of Supply Chain Management 45: 38–45.

11. P.M. Wognum, H. Bremmers, J.H. Trienekens, J.G.A.J. van der Vorst, J.M. Bloemhof (2011). Systems for sustainability and transparency of food supply chains - Current status and challenges. Advanced Engineering Informatics 25: 65–76.

Chapter 22
The Bioavailability of Carotenoid Forms

Loni Schweikert

Abstract Ingestion of carotenoids from foods can vary remarkably and is dependent on numerous factors, such as the composition of the food in question. What is valid for foods also holds true for carotenoid forms offered for addition to foods, beverages and nutritional supplements. Successful commercialization of carotenoids depends on appropriate forms being tailored to their intended use. The fortification of many foods and nutritional supplements requires water-dispersible delivery systems such as emulsions, micelles or hydro-colloidal suspensions. This chapter discusses in detail the various formulation technologies available. Major forms marketed nowadays are oily suspensions, oil-in-water emulsions and water-dispersible powders. Nutritional supplements contain micronutrients in dense concentrations and therefore require high-potency forms. The extent to which the composition of the form has a crucial influence on bioavailability is not easy to judge, since in many cases the formulation excipients and applied technologies are linked. Nevertheless, the fact that forms comprising the same potency of carotenoid can vary dramatically in bioavailability has been proven once more.

Keywords Carotenoid · Bioavailability · Commercial form · Active ingredient · Delivery system · Dietary fortification

22.1 The Bioavailability of Carotenoids

It is well known that ingestion of carotenoids from foods can vary remarkably and that it is dependent on numerous factors such as the composition of the food in question, e.g. its oil content, as well as on the way the food is processed, as studied in the case of beta-carotene during processing of carrot puree [1].

L. Schweikert (✉)
DSM Nutritional Products Ltd., Wurmisweg 576, 4303 Kaiseraugst, Switzerland
e-mail: loni.schweikert@dsm.com

© Springer International Publishing AG 2017   289
H.K. Biesalski et al. (eds.), *Sustainable Nutrition in a Changing World*,
DOI 10.1007/978-3-319-55942-1_22

Taking the physico-chemical properties of carotenoids into account, this should not come as a surprise. Abundant carotenoids in nature such as beta-carotene, lycopene, lutein and zeaxanthin are not soluble in water. Although claimed to be oil-soluble, their solubility in vegetable oil at ambient temperature is limited, and thus their dissolution rate and kinetics as a first step of making them bioaccessible can be decisive for their further fate during ingestion. Bioaccessibility is defined as the amount of a nutrient which has been released out of the food matrix and is ready for uptake from the gastrointestinal tract [2], whereas bioavailability generally refers to the fraction of a nutrient or biologically active ingredient that is absorbed [3, 4]. Ultimately, the biological functions of carotenoids as potent antioxidants or the pro-vitamin A activity of some of them depend on the amount being absorbed by the body.

What is valid for foods also holds true for carotenoid forms offered for addition to foods, beverages and nutritional supplements. Moreover, the chemical structures containing conjugated systems of double bonds make them highly prone to oxidative degradation, which is another reason to formulate them in protective matrices and to combine them with antioxidants. A survey of carotenoid degradation paths triggered by stress factors such as oxygen exposure in combination with heat, light, acids and oxidation catalysts (e.g. iron) is summarized by Boon et al. [5] and has to be taken into consideration for the design of functioning and bioavailable carotenoid forms. Last but not least, a significant application is the use of carotenoids such as beta-carotene or apocarotenal for coloration, which requires a physical transformation of the insoluble crystals into water-dispersible forms. It is worth mentioning that not only the color strength but also the color shade of carotenoids can to a certain extent be modulated by formulation. Auweter et al. [6] prepared different water-dispersible beta-carotene precipitates by varying the process conditions, and found remarkable differences in color shade. The investigation of the supramolecular structures revealed that the coloring properties of beta-carotene are related to different aggregation types. All in all, a successful commercialization of carotenoids depends on appropriate forms tailored to their intended use as a color or as a biologically active ingredient.

22.2 Dietary Fortification with Carotenoids

Fortification of many foods and nutritional supplements requires water-dispersible delivery systems such as emulsions, micelles or hydro-colloidal suspensions. Which type of form to choose is to a large extent driven by the requirements of the target application. In the early 'sixties of the last century, the first water-dispersible carotenoid forms based on an emulsifier and optionally hydrocolloids were described in a patent from Hoffmann-La Roche [7]. Nowadays, numerous forms and technologies have been developed for this purpose and have facilitated successful marketing of these products. Simple emulsions carry the carotenoid dissolved in oily droplets surrounded with a colloidal system and are expected to enable easy absorption by the gastro-intestinal system. By designing the interfacial structure between oil droplet and the aqueous phase with appropriate surface-active ingredients, physical and electrostatic barriers can be created, minimizing exposure to harmful pro-oxidants from the environment, whereas lipophilic antioxidants in the oil phase provide additional protection. Special forms of emulsions are layer-by-layer emulsions, made by adding a polyelectrolyte—e.g. a protein, a carbohydrate—of the opposite charge of the emulsion droplets. By repeating the process, additional layers can be deposited [8]. Other form types contain carotenoids as small solid particles embedded in a protective matrix. Liquid forms based on water as a carrier can be dried. By applying and combining different technologies, various formulations can be prepared. A survey of form types is provided in Table 22.1.

22.3 Commercial Carotenoid Forms

The composition and characteristics of commercial carotenoid forms depend not only on their intended use but also on the underlying regulations governing their deployment. Since the European Commission has passed a regulation on the provision of food information to consumers that "All ingredients present in the form of engineered nanomaterials shall be clearly indicated ..." [10], nano-preparations such as micelles, nano-emulsions and solid lipid nano-particles in general are not the preferred choices in consumer products, although their potential as carriers for lipophilic bio-actives are considered promising for various food applications [11].

Major forms marketed nowadays are oily suspensions, oil-in-water emulsions, and water-dispersible powders, in which the carotenoid is finely embedded in a colloidal system or a carrier oil. For beverage coloration, a water-dispersible powder or emulsion will enable convenient and reliable application, whereas an oily suspension is used for fat-based foods such as margarines or fatty spreads.

Nutritional supplements, e.g. tablets and capsules, contain micronutrients in dense concentrations and therefore require high-potency forms, ideally carrying up to 20–30% of the carotenoid. A recent study compared the bioavailability of different micronutrients, including beta-carotene, out of tablets and soft gel capsules [12], determining the area-under-the-curve (AUCs) in the plasma over 168 h and found a significantly higher bioavailability of beta-carotene out of tablets. Various reasons for this finding were discussed: the vegetable oil serving as carrier for beta-carotene and present in excess in the soft gel could compete for emulsification by chylomicrons—this is an integral part of absorption for both oil and beta-carotene—or the use as a water-dispersible form could facilitate absorption because no in vivo emulsification is required.

Table 22.1 Formulation technologies for vitamins and carotenoids

Technology	Particle morphology	Size (μm)	Active	Processing aids raw materials	Solubility
Layer by layer coating		100–1000	Hydro- and lipophilic actives	Hydrocolloids with opposite charges	Hydrophilic
Beadlets		200–800	Lipophilic actives	Matrix: hydrocolloid, outer layer: starch	Hydrophilic
Solid-lipid nanoparticles		0.1–100	Carotenoids Lipophilic vitamins	Triglycerides Fatty acids Waxes	Lipophilic
Precipitation		0.1–100	Carotenoids	Supercritical fluids Organic solvents	Hydrophilic Lipophilic
Spray drying		10–200	PUFA Oily extracts	Maltodextrin Starch Gum Arabic	Hydrophilic
Spray chilling		10–1000	Hydrophilic vitamins Carotenoids	Waxes	Lipophilic
Complex coacervation		10–1000	Carotenoids Lipophilic actives	Gelatin Gum Arabic	(Hydrophilic)
Microbeads		10–5000	Polyphenols Lipophilic actives	Alginates	Hydrophilic
Extrusion		500–5000	Hydro- and lipophilic actives	Maltodextrin Starch Waxes	Hydrophilic Lipophilic

●	Lipophilic active	●	Hydrophilic active	
●	Hydrophilic matrix	●	Hydrophilic gel	●
	Lipophilic matrix			

Source Teleki et al. [9], modified for publication here

22.4   Commercial Form and Bioavailability

There is evidence that different isomers exhibit different bioavailabilities. In the case of lycopene, higher cis-levels in human serum than in the ingested food indicate a preferred uptake of cis-lycopene isomers [13]. Whether thermal processing in general increases bioavailability because of isomerization or because of other parameters such as morphological changes during heat processing is not completely clear, and is probably different for different carotenoids. For beta-carotene as a potent pro-vitamin A—according to FDA 1 mg corresponds to 1667 IU vitamin A—the current official US American Pharmacopeia USP 38-NF33 requires an all-trans content of >95% for beta-carotene capsules. However, clarification as to whether all-trans carotene is really higher in bioavailability and bioconversion will need further research.

As to the extent to which the composition of the form as such plays a crucial role for bioavailability, it is not easy to judge, since in many cases the formulation excipients and applied technologies are linked, thus adding further complexity to this question. Nevertheless, the fact that forms comprising the same potency of carotenoid can vary dramatically in bioavailability has been once more proven in a human study in which healthy volunteers were supplemented with two different forms of lutein—one based on starch and the other on alginate. 14 h post-dose measurement of total plasma lutein increased by 7% with the alginate-based form only, whereas the starch-based form led to an increase of 126% [14].

22.5   Conclusions

As a conclusion, it can be stated that bioavailability of carotenoids can depend on many factors, such as processing conditions, isomeric composition and excipients used for formulation or preparation of the delivery system.

22.6   Summary: Key Messages

- Ingestion of carotenoids from foods can vary remarkably and is dependent on numerous factors.
- Successful commercialization of carotenoids depends on appropriate forms being tailored to their intended use.
- Major forms marketed nowadays are oily suspensions, oil-in-water emulsions and water-dispersible powders, in which the carotenoid is finely embedded in a colloidal system or a carrier oil.

- The extent to which the composition of the form as such plays a crucial role for bioavailability is not easy to judge, since in many cases the formulation excipients and applied technologies are linked.
- The bioavailability of carotenoids can depend on many factors, such as processing conditions, isomeric composition and excipients used for formulation or preparation of the delivery system.

References

1. Knockaert, Griet; Lemmens, Lien; Van Buggenhout, Sandy; Hendricks, Marc; van Loey, Ann; Food Chemistry (2012) 60–67.
2. Hedrien, E.; Diaz, V.; Svanberg, U.; European Journal of Clinical Nutrition, (2002) 56 (5), 425–423.
3. Heaney, R. P.; The Journal of Nutrition (2001) 131 (4), 1344S–8S.
4. Castenmiller, J.J.M.; West, C.E.; Annual Review of Nutrition (1998) 18, 18–38.
5. Boon, Caitlins S.; McClements, Julian D.; Weiss, Jochen, Decker, Eric A.; Critical Review in Food Science and Nutrition (2010) 50, 515–532.
6. Auweter, H.; Haberkorn, H.; Heckmann, W.; Horn, D.; Lüddecke, E., Rieger, J.; Weiss, H.; Angew. Chem. Int. Ed. (1999) 38(15), 2188–2191.
7. Application made in Switzerland (no. 11603), Oct. 17th, 1960.
8. Guzey, D.; Kim, H.J.; McClements, D. J.; Food Hydrocolloids (2004) 18(6), 967–975.
9. Teleki, A.; Hitzfeld, A.; Eggersdorfer, M.; KONA Powder and Particle Journal (2013) 30, 144–163.
10. Regulation (EU) No 1169/2011 of the European Parliament and of the Council of 25 October 2011.
11. McClements, D. J.; Journal of Food Science (2015) 80 (7), N 1602–N 1611.
12. Johnson, E.; Vishwanathan, R.; Rasmussen, H. M.; Lang, J.C.; Molecular Vision (2014) 20, 1228–1242.
13. Boileau, T. W.; Boileau, A. C.; Erdman, J. W.; Exp. Biol. Med. (2002) 227, 914–919.
14. Evans, M.; Beck, M.; Elliott, J.; Etheve, S.; Roberts, R.; Schalch, W.; European Journal of Nutrition (2013) 52 (4), 1381–1391.

Chapter 23
The Stability of Vitamins A and E in Edible Oils

Marc Pignitter and Veronika Somoza

Abstract Vegetable oils are in themselves a major source of vitamin E and are also used for fortification with vitamin A. Approximately 90% of Americans are facing insufficient dietary intake of vitamin E. Hypovitaminosis A is a major public health problem in many developing countries. Both vitamin deficiencies can be overcome by an adequate intake of fortified plant oils. Many fortification programs have been initiated to reduce the prevalence of vitamin A deficiency in developing countries. Studies evaluating the stability of vitamins in fortified oil were performed to improve the efficiency in supplying vitamins A and E to people. The stability of vitamins was shown to depend on storage conditions, such as duration of storage, material of container, oxygen tension, temperature, oxidative status of the plant oil and, most importantly, exposure to light. Storage of fortified soybean oil in polyethylene terephthalate bottles under household-representative conditions for 56 days was shown to induce a substantial loss of vitamins A and E. The oxidative degradation of vitamins A and E leads to the formation of not yet fully known decomposition products whose biological effects still need to be investigated. The low stability of vitamins A and E and the formation of yet unknown oxidized vitamin products require a re-evaluation of the amounts of vitamins added to the edible oils and an optimization of the storage conditions for these products to ensure adequate intake of vitamins A and E.

Keywords Vitamin A · Vitamin E · Vegetable oil · Dietary intake · Storage · Status · Oxidation · Degradation · Fortification

M. Pignitter (✉) · V. Somoza
Department of Nutritional and Physiological Chemistry, Faculty of Chemistry, University of Vienna, 1090 Vienna, Austria
e-mail: marc.pignitter@univie.ac.at

© Springer International Publishing AG 2017   295
H.K. Biesalski et al. (eds.), *Sustainable Nutrition in a Changing World*,
DOI 10.1007/978-3-319-55942-1_23

23.1   Introduction

An estimated 190 million pre-school-age children are affected by a low serum vitamin A level (<0.70 μmol/L) [1]. Oil fortification with vitamin A is a sustainable and cost-efficient strategy to mitigate low levels of vitamin A in humans in countries with high prevalence of vitamin A deficiency. The oil-soluble vitamin A is homogenously distributed in a vegetable oil. It could be demonstrated that the oil matrix protects the vitamin A from oxidative degradation and thus facilitates absorption of the vitamin [2]. The most common market forms used for the fortification of oil with vitamin A are vitamin A acetate and palmitate. Both forms showed higher stability compared to retinol [3]. However, retinyl palmitate may have higher stability than retinyl acetate. Gopal et al. [3] showed that heating a premix of retinyl palmitate and retinyl acetate at 180 °C for 25 min led to a retention of 56% of the retinyl acetate, while 80% of the retinyl palmitate was retained. Thus, retinyl palmitate is commonly used for the fortification of edible oil with vitamin A.

Soybean oil is commonly used as food vehicle for vitamin A, as it constitutes about half of total edible vegetable oil production worldwide. A total of 33 million tons of soybean oil is produced annually worldwide [4]. Conditions of storage of fortified oils have been reported to determine the stability of vitamin A [5–7]. In African countries, fortified soybean oil is exposed to sunlight, elevated temperatures and oxygen during distribution among the population. In developed countries, soybean oil is usually packaged in transparent polyethylene terephthalate (PET) bottles and offered in retail stores. Very often, soybean oil is also exposed to visible light in the supermarket. In the kitchen, soybean oil is exposed to visible light and increasing oxygen volume over time in the headspace of the bottle due to consumer handling.

The stability of vitamin A in vegetable oil needs to be ensured in order to successfully deliver vitamin A to people deficient in vitamin A. It can be hypothesized that the storage conditions of fortified edible oil affects the efficiency of fortification programs.

Besides being a suitable vehicle for vitamin A, vegetable oils are also known to be the major source of vitamin E. Very recently, Maret Traber published a review [8] drawing attention to the fact that more than 90% of Americans do not consume sufficient dietary vitamin E. Among the vitamin E congeners, α-tocopherol is the most physiologically active homologue, while the gamma- and delta-tocopherol are associated with higher antioxidant activity [9–12]. There is a huge variation in the distribution of vitamin E between and within vegetable oil types. The vitamin E content in soybean oil was reported to be between 9 and 360 mg/kg for α-tocopherol, 90–2400 mg/kg for γ-tocopherol, 154–932 mg/kg for δ-tocopherol and up to 50 mg/kg for β-tocopherol [13]. Thus, the question arises whether the vitamin E content of vegetable oils is sufficient to protect the oil from oxidative degradation and to deliver appropriate amounts of physiologically relevant vitamin

E to humans. Sufficient amounts of vitamin E can only be delivered when vitamin E stability in edible oils is ensured.

23.2 Loss of Vitamins A and E During Storage of Vegetable Oils Under Household Conditions

Recently, it could be demonstrated that storage of soybean oil which was filled in transparent PET bottles and exposed to cold fluorescent light under household- and retail-representative conditions at 22 °C for two months led to a huge loss of approximately 60 and 80% of α- and γ-tocopherol, respectively [6, 14]. The consumer-representative storage of soybean oil fortified with retinyl palmitate for two months also induced a decrease of $55.3 \pm 0.29\%$ α-tocopherol and $67.7 \pm 0.59\%$ γ-tocopherol [6]. It could be shown that the vitamin E stability correlates well with the peroxide value of the vegetable oil ($r = 0.979$; $p < 0.001$). The stability of vitamin E was also shown to depend on the oxidative status of the oil. While storage of mildly oxidized soybean oil, characterized by a peroxide value of 1.30 ± 0.38 meq O_2/kg, for 28 days led to a slight decrease of total tocopherols of approximately 15%, the storage of highly oxidized soybean oil, characterized by a peroxide value of 12.2 ± 0.23 meq O_2/kg, for the same period resulted in an approximately 56% reduction of total tocopherols. Player et al. [15] could even demonstrate a complete loss of α-tocopherol after storage of soybean oil for 16 days at 50 °C. The total loss of α-tocopherol could be confirmed by another study after storing soybean oil at 95 °C for one day [16].

Similar findings were reported for vitamin A. Puysuwan et al. [17] demonstrated a vitamin A loss of 89% in fortified soybean oil stored with intermittent openings in closed polyethylene terephthalate bottles at room temperature in Thailand in the presence of sunlight for four weeks. Another study also showed a high degradation of vitamin A of 79% in soybean oil stored at 25 °C in the presence of light for four weeks [7]. The stability of retinyl palmitate was shown to depend on the oxidative quality of soybean oil at the time of fortification with retinyl palmitate [5, 6]. After 56 days of storage, the concentration of retinyl palmitate was significantly reduced by $84.8 \pm 5.76\%$, independent of temperature and light exposure [6]. When retinyl palmitate was added to already oxidized soybean oil, characterized by a peroxide value of 17.3 meq O_2/kg, a retinyl palmitate reduction by $80.3 \pm 13.6\%$ was determined already after 28 days of storage. Thus, storage of the mildly oxidized soybean oil fortified with retinyl palmitate induced an average daily decrease of retinol concentration of $1.52 \pm 0.10\%$, whereas storage of highly oxidized soybean oil fortified with retinyl palmitate caused an average decrease of retinol concentration of $2.57 \pm 0.06\%$ per day. Addition of retinyl palmitate to soybean oil also increased its antioxidant capacity by exhibiting a tocopherol-saving effect, which was completely inhibited when highly oxidized soybean oil was used for fortification. Thus, fortification of low-oxidized soybean oil with retinyl palmitate increased its oxidative stability, although a significant loss of retinyl palmitate during household storage and handling was demonstrated over time. When retinyl palmitate was added to highly oxidized soybean oil, this storage-associated loss was accelerated and its antioxidative activity was completely abrogated.

23.3 Vitamin A- and E-Derived Degradation Products

The storage-induced loss of vitamins in vegetable oils raises the question as to which kinds of products are formed by oxidation of vitamins A and E.

Vitamin E is known to be a prominent antioxidant in lipophilic environments due to its electron-donating ability. Its electron donor activity strongly depends on the bond dissociation energy of the O–H bond on the chromanol ring of tocopherols. The bond dissociation energy, ranging between 75.8 and 79.8 kcal/mol, was reported to decrease with the number of methyl groups in the order of α- < β- < γ- < δ-tocopherol [18]. Compared to phenol, with a bond dissociation energy of 87.0 kcal/mol [19], the tocopherols have a low bond dissociation energy, resulting in prominent antioxidative activities. Lipid peroxyl radicals are supposed to be converted to non-radical lipid hydroperoxides by a hydrogen atom transfer from tocopherols rather than an electron transfer with subsequent proton transfer [20]. The strong antioxidant potential is also evident from the low standard reduction potentials of 270–405 mV for tocopherols necessary to provide a hydrogen atom to lipid alkyl, peroxyl and alkoxyl radicals with a higher standard one-electron reduction potential of 600–1600 mV [21]. The products of the hydrogen transfer reaction are non-radical lipid products and tocopheroxyl radicals (Fig. 23.1). The resonance-stabilized tocopheroxyl radical undergoes a disproportionate reaction with a second tocopheroxyl radical or other lipid peroxyl radicals to yield tocopheryl quinone and tocopheryl hydroquinone via intermediates, such as tocopherone cation and hydroxy tocopherone [22–25]. Tocopheroxyl radicals might also be converted to isomeric epoxy tocopheryl chinones. Some studies reported the formation of tocopherol dimers and trimers from oxygen-centered tocopheroxyl radical [21, 26]. The tocopheroxyl radical might also undergo an addition reaction leading to the production of 8α-alkylperoxy-tocopherone [27]. In addition, tocopherol(quinone) hydroperoxides were proposed to be formed from tocopheroxyl radicals [28]. Tocopherols were shown not only to act as antioxidants, but also as pro-oxidants, depending on concentration, temperature, pH and the presence of other compounds. Pro-oxidative reactions might be initiated by the cleavage of the O–O bond in the peroxide by tocopherol leading to alkoxyl radical and tocopheroxyl radical, thereby propagating lipid oxidation. The oxidized tocopherols were shown to have pro-oxidative activities by lowering the oxidative stability of soybean oil after addition of oxidized tocopherols [29]. The formation of the main tocopherol oxidation products, such as tocopherolquinone and tocopherolquinone epoxides, could be demonstrated in maize germ oil enriched with α-tocopherol to a concentration of 1420 mg/kg after heating the oil in the dark for two to 11 h at 90,

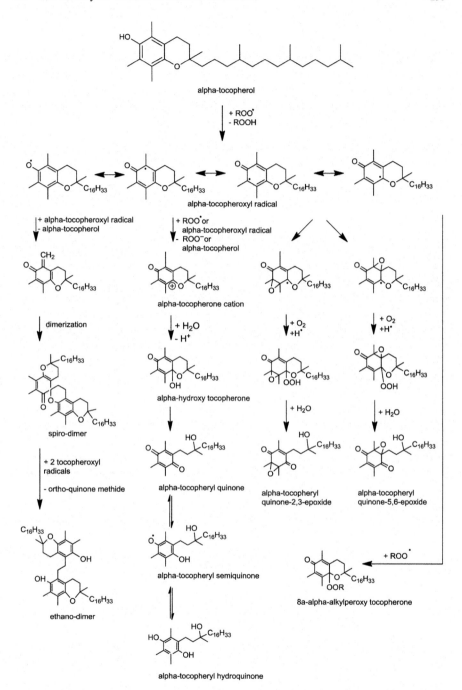

Fig. 23.1 Lipid radical-induced oxidation of alpha-tocopherol

180 or 220 °C [30]. The generation of tocopherol oxidation products in edible oils stored under household and retail conditions has not yet been investigated.

For vitamin A, three ways of oxidative degradation were proposed [31]. In accordance with the proposed mechanisms for carotenoid reactions with radicals, retinol might also initiate a peroxyl radical scavenging reaction by donating an electron (1), a hydrogen atom (2) or by addition of peroxyl radicals to the poly-conjugated backbone of retinol (3).

1. Retinol + ROO$^\cdot$ → Retinol$^{\cdot+}$ + ROO$^-$ (e$^-$-transfer).
2. Retinol + ROO$^\cdot$ → Retinol$^\cdot$ + ROOH (H-abstraction).
3. Retinol + ROO$^\cdot$ → Retinol$^\cdot$-OOR (addition).

It was suggested that the addition reaction is the most likely mechanism in a non-polar environment, as the product of the electron transfer reaction is a radical cation and the hydrogen transfer reaction was reported to be kinetically unfavored [32, 33]. The radical addition reaction might result in the formation of carbon-centered radicals at the polyene chain but also at the cyclohexenyl ring [33, 34]. Martin et al. [35] showed that the carbon-centered radicals could react with molecular oxygen to form a peroxyl radical at high oxygen tension (1 atm), leading to the loss of the antioxidant activity and a predominant pro-oxidative activity of carotenoids (Fig. 23.2a). At low oxygen pressure, the formation of a non-radical bis-peroxyl adduct might be favored by reaction of the carbon-centered radical with a lipid peroxyl radical [34]. However, others could not confirm any reactions of the carotenoid carbon-centered radical with molecular oxygen [36]. The carbon-centered radical was also suggested to decompose to epoxides. Cherng et al. [37] studied the photodecomposition of retinyl palmitate in ethanol. The UVA light-induced degradation of retinyl palmitate was explained by three mechanistic pathways. (1) Retinyl palmitate can be decomposed to carbon-centered peroxyl radicals, leading to the formation of 5,6-epoxy-retinyl palmitate and 4-keto-retinyl palmitate through a free radical mechanism. (2) *All-trans* anhydroretinol and three cis-isomers (6Z-, 8Z- and 12Z-anhydroretinol) were generated through an ionic photodissociation mechanism. (3) Photosensitization of retinyl palmitate by UVA light was shown to form singlet oxygen (Fig. 23.2b). In lipid environments, singlet oxygen favors peroxidation of lipids. In vegetable oils, the formation of any decomposition products of retinol or retinyl palmitate has not yet been addressed in the literature.

23.4 The Impact of Low Vitamin A and E Stability in Vegetable Oils on Delivery of Vitamins to Humans

As a storage-induced loss of vitamin A was obtained in fortified plant oils, the health-related impact of the decomposition products of retinol is of utmost interest. While fortification programs aim at delivering vitamin A to populations with high

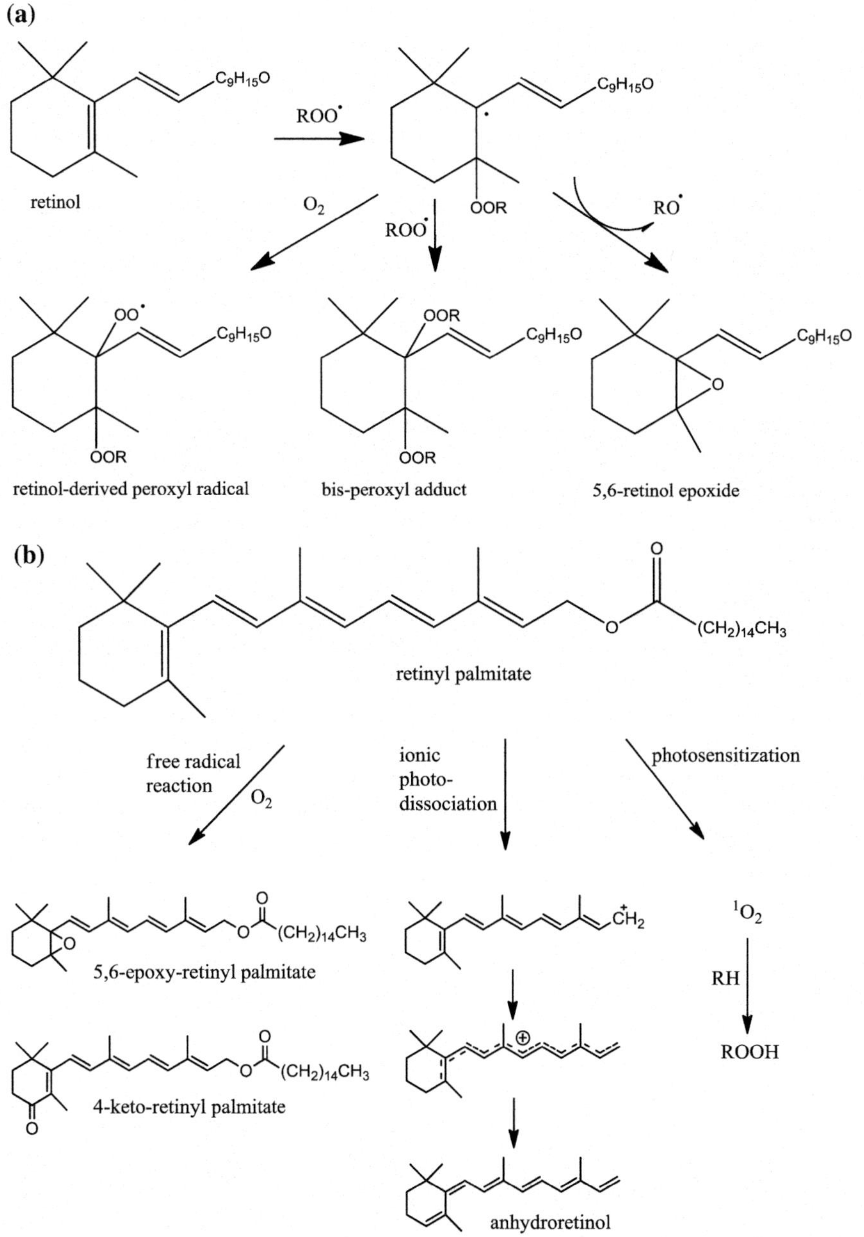

(a)

(b)

Fig. 23.2 Proposed pathways of lipid radical-induced oxidation of retinol (**a**) and photodecomposition of retinyl palmitate (**b**) adapted from [34, 37]

prevalence of vitamin A deficiency, there is an urgent need to investigate the bioactivity of vitamin A-derived degradation products. So far, there are no studies dealing with the pharmacokinetic behavior of oxidized retinol and the effects of these retinol-derived compounds in vivo. Cherng et al. [37] demonstrated that the decomposition products of retinyl palmitate were not genotoxic. However, UVA light-induced sensitization of retinyl palmitate resulted in the formation of reactive oxygen species which are known to propagate lipid radical chain reactions.

Independent of the unknown effects of oxidized retinol, the primary aim of fortification programs to reduce micronutrient malnutrition might not be reached when the stability of vitamin A is not ensured or considered. Re-evaluation of storage conditions of fortified oils and the amounts of added vitamin A palmitate to edible oils might be a necessary measure to ensure delivery of proper amounts of vitamin A to people who lack access to sufficient amounts of micronutrients.

In contrast to vitamin A, the major oxidation products of tocopherols, tocopheryl quinones, were shown to exert biological effects [38]. Tocopheryl quinone was suggested to act by its redox properties or by binding to biomolecules. A more pronounced inhibitory effect on the mitochondrial electron transfer complexes was attributed to tocopheryl quinones compared to the unoxidized tocopherols. Tocopheryl quinones were also shown to interfere in mitochondrial superoxide radical release [39], mitochondrial membrane potential and trigger apoptosis [40]. By arylating biomolecules, such as glutathione, the oxidized tocopherols were shown to induce endoplasmic reticulum stress [41].

Due to the so far demonstrated differential bioactivity of tocopherols and their oxidation products, the storage-induced loss of tocopherols in plant oils and the insufficient consumption of vitamin E by more than 90% of Americans, optimized storage conditions of plant oils as well as a standardization of the vitamin E content of different edible oils might be necessary to provide adequate amounts of vitamin E to the Western world.

23.4.1   Conclusion and Outlook

The limited stability of vitamins A and E in soybean oil might be a hidden factor behind a low vitamin A/E status. The initial vitamin E content (α-tocopherol + 0.25 $\times$ γ-tocopherol [42]) in soybean oil per serving (20 g) amounts to approximately 4 mg. Storage-induced loss of vitamin E might result in an intake of solely 1.6 mg vitamin E per serving, making an adequate intake [43] of 12 mg vitamin E per day difficult to achieve. Thus, a re-evaluation of legislation and fortification programs to allow higher levels of fortification that take into account vitamin A/E loss during storage to reach optimum target plasma levels with one portion size needs to be performed. It might also be worth considering the oxidative quality of the edible oil to be fortified and the use of a light-protecting container to ensure maximum stability and delivery of vitamins A and E.

23.5 Summary: Key Messages

- Vegetable oils are in themselves a major source of vitamin E and are also used for fortification with vitamin A.
- Approximately 90% of Americans are facing insufficient dietary intake of vitamin E, while hypovitaminosis A is a major public health problem in many developing countries.
- Both vitamin deficiencies can be overcome by an adequate intake of fortified plant oils.
- Studies evaluating the stability of vitamins in fortified oil were performed to improve the efficiency in supplying vitamins A and E to people.
- The stability of vitamins was shown to depend on storage conditions
- The oxidative degradation of vitamins A and E leads to the formation of not yet fully known decomposition products whose biological effects still need to be investigated.
- The low stability of vitamins A and E and the formation of yet unknown oxidized vitamin products require a re-evaluation of the amounts of vitamins added to the edible oils and an optimization of the storage conditions for these products in order to ensure adequate intake of vitamins A and E.

References

1. World Health Organization. Global prevalence of vitamin A deficiency in populations at risk 1995–2005. WHO Global Database on Vitamin A Deficiency. 2009.
2. Bagriansky J, Ranum P. Vitamin A Fortification of P.L. 480 Vegetable Oil. SUSTAIN, wwwsustaintechorg, Washington DC. 1998.
3. Gopal S, Ketyum F. Vitamin A and D in Ghee and Vanaspati. Journal of Scientific and Industrial Research. 1956; 15c: 48–51.
4. Gunstone FD, Harwood JL. Occurrence and characterisation of oils and fats. In: Gunstone FD, Harwood JL, Dijkstra AJ, editors. The Lipid Handbook. Boca Raton: CRC Press; 2007.
5. Laillou A, Hafez SA, Mahmoud AH, Mansour M, Rohner F, Fortin S, et al. Vegetable oil of poor quality is limiting the success of fortification with vitamin A in Egypt. Food Nutr Bull. 2012; 33: 186–193.
6. Pignitter M, Dumhart B, Gartner S, Jirsa F, Steiger G, Kraemer K, et al. Vitamin A is rapidly degraded in retinyl palmitate-fortified soybean oil stored under household conditions. J Agric Food Chem. 2014; 62: 7559–7566.
7. Viana M, Boy E, Boutilieir Z, Furr HC, Craft NE. Stability of vitamin A in Bolivian fortified cooking oil. Faseb J. 2007; 21: A682-A682.
8. Traber MG. Vitamin E inadequacy in humans: causes and consequences. Adv Nutr. 2014; 5: 503–514.
9. Saldeen T, Li DY, Mehta JL. Differential effects of alpha- and gamma-tocopherol on low-density lipoprotein oxidation, superoxide activity, platelet aggregation and arterial thrombogenesis. J Am Coll Cardiol. 1999; 34: 1208–1215.
10. Tomasch R, Wagner KH, Elmadfa I. Antioxidative power of plant oils in humans: The influence of alpha- and gamma-tocopherol. Ann Nutr Metab. 2001; 45: 110–115.

11. Wagner KH, Isnardy B, Elmadfa I. Gamma- and delta-tocopherols are more effective than alpha-tocopherol on the autoxidation of a 10% rapeseed oil triacylglycerol-in-water emulsion with and without a radical initiator. Eur J Lipid Sci Tech. 2004; 106: 44–51.

12. Winkler-Moser JK, Logan A, Bakota EL. Antioxidant activities and interactions of a- and g-tocopherols within canola and soybean oil emulsions. Eur J Lipid Sci Tech. 2014; 116: 606–617.

13. Sayago A, Marin MI, Aparicio R, Morales MT. Vitamin E and vegetable oils. Grasas Aceites. 2007; 58: 74–86.

14. Pignitter M, Stolze K, Gartner S, Dumhart B, Stoll C, Steiger G, et al. Cold fluorescent light as major inducer of lipid oxidation in soybean oil stored at household conditions for eight weeks. J Agric Food Chem. 2014; 62: 2297–2305.

15. Player ME, Kim HJ, Lee HO, Min DB. Stability of alpha-, gamma-, or delta-tocopherol during soybean oil oxidation. J Food Sci. 2006; 71: C456–C460.

16. Elisia I, Young JW, Yuan YV, Kitts DD. Association between tocopherol isoform composition and lipid oxidation in selected multiple edible oils. Food Res Int. 2013; 52: 508–514.

17. Puysuwan L, Chavasit V, Sungpuag P, Hediger D, Punvichai T. Feasibility and use of vitamin A-fortified vegetable oils among consumers of different socioeconomic status in Thailand. Food Nutr Bull. 2007; 28: 181–188.

18. Wright JS, Johnson ER, DiLabio GA. Predicting the activity of phenolic antioxidants: Theoretical method, analysis of substituent effects, and application to major families of antioxidants. J Am Chem Soc. 2001; 123: 1173–1183.

19. Bordwell FG, Liu WZ. Solvent effects on homolytic bond dissociation energies of hydroxylic acids. J Am Chem Soc. 1996; 118: 10819–10823.

20. Njus D, Kelley PM. Vitamin-C and Vitamin-E Donate Single Hydrogen-Atoms In vivo. Febs Lett. 1991; 284: 147–151.

21. Kamal-Eldin A, Appelqvist LA. The chemistry and antioxidant properties of tocopherols and tocotrienols. Lipids. 1996; 31: 671–701.

22. Verleyen T, Kamal-Eldin A, Dobarganes C, Verhe R, Dewettinck K, Huyghebaert A. Modeling of alpha-tocopherol loss and oxidation products formed during thermoxidation in triolein and tripalmitin mixtures. Lipids. 2001; 36: 719–726.

23. Liebler DC, Burr JA, Philips L, Ham AJ. Gas chromatography-mass spectrometry analysis of vitamin E and its oxidation products. Anal Biochem. 1996; 236: 27–34.

24. Faustman C, Liebler DC, Burr JA. alpha-tocopherol oxidation in beef and in bovine muscle microsomes. J Agric Food Chem. 1999; 47: 1396–1399.

25. Liebler DC, Burr JA. Oxidation of vitamin E during iron-catalyzed lipid peroxidation: evidence for electron-transfer reactions of the tocopheroxyl radical. Biochemistry. 1992; 31: 8278–8284.

26. Rosenau T, Kloser E, Gille L, Mazzini F, Netscher T. Vitamin E chemistry. Studies into initial oxidation intermediates of alpha-tocopherol: disproving the involvement of 5a-C-centered "chromanol methide" radicals. J Org Chem. 2007; 72: 3268–3281.

27. Liebler DC, Baker PF, Kaysen KL. Oxidation of Vitamin-E—Evidence for Competing Autoxidation and Peroxyl Radical Trapping Reactions of the Tocopheroxyl Radical. J Am Chem Soc. 1990; 112: 6995–7000.

28. Pazos M, Sanchez L, Medina I. Alpha-tocopherol oxidation in fish muscle during chilling and frozen storage. J Agric Food Chem. 2005; 53: 4000–4005.

29. Jung MY, Min DB. Effects of Oxidized Alpha-Tocopherol, Gamma-Tocopherol and Delta-Tocopherols on the Oxidative Stability of Purified Soybean Oil. Food Chem. 1992; 45: 183–187.

30. Murkovic M, Wiltschko B, Pfannhauser W. Formation of alpha-tocopherolquinone and alpha-tocopherolquinone epoxides in plant oil. Fett-Lipid. 1997; 99: 165–169.

31. El-Agamey A, Lowe GM, McGarvey DJ, Mortensen A, Phillip DM, Truscott TG, et al. Carotenoid radical chemistry and antioxidant/pro-oxidant properties. Arch Biochem Biophys. 2004; 430: 37–48.

32. Everett SA, Dennis MF, Patel KB, Maddix S, Kundu SC, Willson RL. Scavenging of nitrogen dioxide, thiyl, and sulfonyl free radicals by the nutritional antioxidant beta-carotene. J Biol Chem. 1996; 271: 3988–3994.
33. Burton GW, Ingold KU. Beta-Carotene—an Unusual Type of Lipid Antioxidant. Science. 1984; 224: 569–573.
34. Tesoriere L, DArpa D, Re R, Livrea MA. Antioxidant reactions of all-trans retinol in phospholipid bilayers: Effect of oxygen partial pressure, radical fluxes, and retinol concentration. Arch Biochem Biophys. 1997; 343: 13–18.
35. Martin HD, Ruck C, Schmidt M, Sell S, Beutner S, Mayer B, et al. Chemistry of carotenoid oxidation and free radical reactions. Pure Appl Chem. 1999; 71: 2253–2262.
36. El-Agamey A, McGarvey DJ. Carotenoid addition radicals do not react with molecular oxygen: Aspects of carotenoid reactions with acylperoxyl radicals in polar and non-polar media. Free Radical Res. 2002; 36: 97–100.
37. Cherng SH, Xia QS, Blankenship LR, Freeman JP, Wamer WG, Howard PC, et al. Photodecomposition of retinyl palmitate in ethanol by UVA light-formation of photodecom-position products, reactive oxygen species, and lipid peroxides. Chem Res Toxicol. 2005; 18: 129–138.
38. Gille L, Staniek K, Rosenau T, Duvigneau JC, Kozlov AV. Tocopheryl quinones and mitochondria. Mol Nutr Food Res. 2010; 54: 601–615.
39. Gille L, Staniek K, Nohl H. Effects of tocopheryl quinone on the heart: Model experiments with xanthine oxidase, heart mitochondria, and isolated perfused rat hearts. Free Radical Bio Med. 2001; 30: 865–876.
40. Calviello G, Di Nicuolo F, Piccioni E, Marcocci ME, Serini S, Maggiano N, et al. gamma-Tocopheryl quinone induces apoptosis in cancer cells via caspase-9 activation and cytochrome c release. Carcinogenesis. 2003; 24: 427–433.
41. Wang X, Thomas B, Sachdeva R, Arterburn L, Frye L, Hatcher PG, et al. Mechanism of arylating quinone toxicity involving Michael adduct formation and induction of endoplasmic reticulum stress. Proc Natl Acad Sci U S A. 2006; 103: 3604–3609.
42. Elmadfa I, Bosse W. Vitamin E: Eigenschaften, Wirkungsweise und therapeutische Bedeutung. Stuttgart: Wissenschaftliche Verlagsgesellschaft; 1985.
43. European Commission. Commission Directive 2008/100/EC. Official Journal of the European Union. 2008: http://eur-lex.europa.eu/LexUriServ/LexUriServ.do?uri=OJ:L:2008:2285:0009: 0012:EN:PDF.

Chapter 24
The Search for Optimal Macronutrient Recommendations

Wim H.M. Saris

Abstract RDAs are essential for evaluating the quality of food intake as well as for planning food supply. Commenced in the 1950s, the 'Seven Countries Study' conducted by Ancel Keys gave rise to the general RDA to reduce the proportion of saturated fat in the daily diet. As a consequence, for at least two decades, all RDA committees reduced their fat recommendations from about 40 En% to levels as low as 25 En%, emphasizing in particular the reduction of saturated fat. With some time lag, the food industry followed the advice of nutritional scientists and created in nearly all product sectors low-fat alternatives with similar taste patterns to the products they replaced. However, these changes failed to influence the increasing rise of obesity worldwide. The so-called 'American Paradox' was born: A decrease in fat intake and a simultaneous increase in sugar intake were observed, but the increase in the prevalence of obesity was not arrested. This chapter examines the roles of the macronutrients fat, carbohydrate and protein in the diet and their respective and combined influences on weight change. It concludes that only RCTs under ad libitum conditions are valid for making judgements about the importance of the macronutrient composition of the diet in relation to energy intake and weight change, and that the world must rise to the challenge of increasing the nutrient quality of existing diets while simultaneously reducing their energy density at reasonable cost.

Keywords Macronutrients · Fat · Carbohydrate · Protein · RDAs · Sugar · Bodyweight · Obesity · Diet

W.H.M. Saris (✉)
Department of Human Biology, NUTRIM School for Nutrition
and Translational Research in Metabolism, Maastricht University
Medical Center, Maastricht 6200 MD, The Netherlands
e-mail: w.saris@maastrichtuniversity.nl

© Springer International Publishing AG 2017   307
H.K. Biesalski et al. (eds.), *Sustainable Nutrition in a Changing World*,
DOI 10.1007/978-3-319-55942-1_24

24.1 Introduction

Studying the intake of nutrients in relation to health involves first discussing how much of a specific nutrient is required for optimal health. Recommended Daily Allowances, or RDAs, have been part of the daily work of nutritional scientists for over 75 years. RDAs are essential for evaluating the quality of food intake as well as for planning food supply. In fact, the need for planning actually gave rise to the RDA concept during the Second World War, when the U.S. Army asked the American physiologist Ancel Keys to study the energy and nutrient needs of soldiers who would have to land on the beaches of Normandy and subsist there without being provisioned with food for at least a week. This resulted in the so-called K-rations that were used by U.S. troops during the D-Day landings. Later, Keys was asked to study how to revive subjects after severe starvation, since the Allies were already aware of the situation in the Nazi concentration camps in Poland. The two-volume, 1,385-page *Biology of Human Starvation* that Keys published in 1950 became a classic in the field of energy requirement studies, achieving enormous impact [1].

Ancel Keys continued his studies of the body's nutritional needs and in the 1950s initiated the so-called 'Seven Countries Study'—an epidemiological ecological study into the relationship between diet and cardiovascular health which identified the health benefits of the so-called Mediterranean diet, which is today considered arguably the healthiest diet in the world on account of the fact that it reduces susceptibility to cardiovascular disease and supports the prevention and/or treatment of a variety of non-communicable diseases (NCDs). The Seven Countries Study also gave rise to the general RDA to reduce the proportion of saturated fat in the diet.

The origin of the Mediterranean diet as a concept coined by Keys lay in a rural area of Crete which was one of the seven study sites, and whose inhabitants enjoyed a traditional diet low in red meat and with a high intake of olive oil. Recently in the same region where Ancel Keys collected the data for this ground-breaking research, a similar study was conducted to examine the changes in dietary habits and lifestyle that had taken place since Keys first commenced his investigations in the 1950s. The study found that nowadays farmers in the area have a much higher bodyweight. They move around their fields on quad bikes and consume a diet that does not differ from what is generally eaten throughout the western world, except for the use of olive oil in place of butter and various vegetable oils [2].

Ancel Keys' studies into different types of dietary fat and their relationships with cardiovascular disease triggered the debate about the optimal RDA for fat, carbohydrates and, to a lesser extent, protein. However, investigating the effects of just one of the energy-related macronutrients has its impact on the others. High fat means low carbohydrates, and vice versa. That makes this part of the establishment of RDAs difficult, if not impossible. In the 1960s, the cholesterol-raising effect of saturated fat became clear. Besides the replacement of saturated fat in the diet by unsaturated fat, the drive to encourage the consumption of less fat and consequently more carbohydrate was a logical step. This sounded not only reasonable in relation to cardiovascular disease but, with the increasing prevalence of obesity in particular in the U.S. in the 1970s and early 1980s, it would help maintain energy balance, given the difference in energy density, and thus keep body weight down to acceptable levels—in theory, at least.

24.2   Fat or Carbohydrate?

Over the years, three types of evidence have been advanced to support the theory that the energy percentage from dietary fat is the major nutrition-related factor in the increase in the prevalence of obesity. First, population studies showed an association between the estimated percentage of fat in the national diet and the prevalence of obesity [3]. Second, the dietary trend in fat intake at national level showed a parallel between increasing fat consumption and weight gain. Third, it became clear from animal studies and human ad libitum trials that high-fat diets lead to overfeeding and bodyweight gain. More convincing was the observation from randomized controlled trials (RCTs) that ad libitum reduction in total fat intake leads to bodyweight loss (minus 10 En% Fat intake results in approximately 2.8 kg weight loss) [4].

As a consequence, for at least two decades, all RDA committees reduced their fat recommendations from about 40 En% to levels as low as 25 En%, emphasizing in particular the reduction of saturated fat in the diet. With some time lag, the food industry followed the advice of the nutrition scientists and created in nearly all product sectors low-fat alternatives with similar taste patterns to the products they replaced. However, these changes failed to influence the increasing rise of obesity worldwide. For the cardiovascular health outcomes, this emphasis on low fat instead of low saturated fat turned out not to be the best recommendation. Low-fat/high-carbohydrate diets lower not only the LDL cholesterol but also HDL cholesterol (Fig. 24.1) [5].

However, the advice to increase fat intake with, of course, a better ratio between saturated and unsaturated fat was in contrast to the recommendations for body weight control. The so called 'American Paradox' was born: A clear decrease in fat intake was observed based on the NHANES food surveillance studies in the U.S. and later also in Europe, but on the other hand the rise in obesity was not arrested. On the contrary, it was sharper than ever before. Here we face another inherent weakness of nutritional science. We are completely dependent on the reliability of the subject's food intake records. It is well known from the Doubly Labeled Water technique that with higher BMI, energy intake—and in particular fat and sugar intake—is under-reported. Consumers know that fatty and sugary foods are not the healthiest ones to eat, because they have been educated to this understanding for decades now. As a consequence, most probably, they unconsciously omit to note them in their food diaries. This led to the recent publication from the Energy Balance Working Group with the title, 'Energy balance measurement: when something is not better than nothing' [6]. Moreover, if one calculates—on the basis of the WHO food production balance sheets in the U.S. and Europe—the production of edible oils from 1965 to 1998 per capita, there is a considerable increase of about 25% over the same period during which consumers reported lower fat

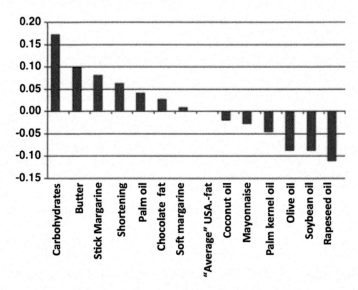

Fig. 24.1 Predicted change in total/HDL-cholesterol ratio if 10 En% of the mixed fat in the 'average' U.S. diet were to be replaced with a particular fat or with carbohydrates. *Source* Mensink et al. [5], American Society for Nutrition

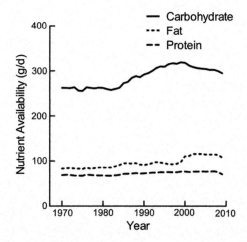

Fig. 24.2 Macronutrient availability per capita in the U.S. Data were derived from the USDA food availability database. Beltsville (MD); Economic research service; 2011 (www.ers.usda.gov/data/foodconsumption). *Source* Carden and Carr [7]

intakes. The food availability figures published recently by Carden and Carr show a similarly contrasting pattern (Fig. 24.2) [7].

Of course, one can argue that with the decreasing cost of food, consumers are simply binning more of it. It is difficult, however, to explain the American Paradox completely on the basis of the increase in food waste. Fat intake has therefore most probably not decreased over the past decades, and a moderate recommendation for fat intake in relation to body weight control is still valid.

Nevertheless the role of dietary fat provoked a lively debate around 1997–98, with various articles, rebuttals, editorials and letters to editors. The position taken by the cardiovascular-oriented epidemiologists was that the relation between dietary fat and obesity was unconvincing. By contrast, that of the experimental-oriented experts based on physiological evidence was clearly in favor of the role of dietary fat under ad libitum conditions. However, neither camp was able to provide sufficient evidence for a causal relationship. At last they agreed that there was no evidence that under iso-energetic conditions dietary fat promotes weight gains more than carbohydrate intake, or vice versa.

24.3 The Sugar Debate

Besides the steady increase in fat intake, another trend became clear in the 1990s— namely, the increase in the intake of refined carbohydrates, in particular through increased consumption of sugar-sweetened beverages. These trends led to the hypothesis that dietary sugar is an important factor in determining bodyweight. In fact Yudkin had, since the late 1950s, proposed that sugar might be more important than fat in causing obesity and CHD. In the course of the years, it became evident that the global increase in sugar consumption is indeed an important factor for a positive energy balance, and thus weight gain. Refined carbohydrates do not contribute much to the sensation of satiety due to their lack of fiber and rapid insulin release. In addition, the greater portion of these refined carbohydrates is consumed in the form of liquid energy from sugar-sweetened drinks. These drinks are much less satiating compared with equal amounts of energy obtained from sugar in solid foods [8]. Thus, beverage calories can be viewed as 'add-on' calories that enhance the risk of weight gain. A recent review concluded that there was convincing evidence that sugar-sweetened beverages exacerbated the risk of becoming obese in individuals with a genetic predisposition toward increased body weight [9]. The meta-analysis of RCT under ad libitum conditions from Malik et al. showed a +0.9 kg body weight gain with a consumption of 0.6–1.0 l of sugar-sweetened beverages per day versus control [10]. The impact on blood glucose, and consequently insulin levels, might also play an important role [11]. Therefore an association has been proposed between sugar intake, in particular from sugar-sweetened beverages, and type 2 diabetes based on a meta-analysis of six studies [12].

Physiological mechanisms focused on glycemic index and fructose metabolism, in particular on the intake of High Fructose Corn Syrup (HFCS) and body weight gain. In the US, HFCS is used for sugar-sweetened beverages rather than the beet sugar, which is used in Europe. Since fructose has a higher sweetening capacity than glucose, HFCSs are frequently used. Next to the 'add-on' calorie effect, fructose is also linked to an increase in lipid accumulation due to de novo-lipogenesis seen by increased post-prandial triglyceride levels, liver fat and visceral fat, and consequently the risk of metabolic syndrome [13]. Therefore over the past two decades there has been a strong message in the scientific literature to reduce sugar intake, and in particular the intake of fructose, so as to reduce the risk of obesity and metabolic consequences [14].

However, this view is challenged by others such as Kahn and Sievenpiper, who argue that there is no clear evidence that any dietary or added sugar or HFCS has an unique or detrimental impact on the development of obesity relative to any other source of calories [15]. The prevalence of overweight and obesity in the U.S. has no link to the increase in the estimated increase in the consumption of dietary sugar. Starting from around 2000, sugar consumption appears to have declined considerably, while the prevalence of obesity has still continued to rise. Such data are intriguing but certainly not convincing—although in the same period, the consumption of mineral water was increasing. But probably more important is the fact that these figures are mostly based on food intake data, which are notoriously unreliable, especially when the population is aware of the health issues related to soft drinks and added sugar. Therefore RCTs on the effects of sugar are more important, and in particular meta-analysis on the outcome of these trials might offer some more insight.

Recently, four meta-analyses were published, and although they are partly based on the same RCTs, the inclusion and exclusion, as well as the grouping, was different in each instance. All based the outcome on weight change. With iso-caloric exchange of added sugar or purified fructose with other macronutrients (mostly carbohydrates), no significant change in bodyweight was shown in RCTs where sugar was reduced relative to the other macronutrients in the control group [16, 17]. Te Morenga et al. and Kaiser et al. found no differences in five trials in children and eight trials in children and adults respectively [16, 18]. However, Malik et al. did find an effect in two out of five trials [10]. Interestingly, in all individual trials in which the subjects consumed fewer calories from sugar, they also consumed less total energy. It shows again that total energy consumption is the factor determining whether body weight is affected. This is confirmed in those trials in which an increased amount of calories from sugar were given as a supplement to the normal diet. A modest but significant weight gain was observed. In other words, many of the arguments made in support of the link between sugar consumption and obesity have been made before—with similar arguments and even sometimes by the same researchers—to show the link between dietary fat and obesity. It shows that there is nothing special about calories coming from sugar compared with other ingredients or food items such as French fries or potato chips. It is all about energy intake. This effect was best demonstrated in the NUGENOB RCT trial, in which subjects were put on a −600 kcal deficit diet with either a high-carbohydrate or a high-fat diet [19]. The deficit was individually measured and very well controlled.

Over a 12-week period, the weight loss was absolutely identical in both groups, showing again that in metabolic terms, a calorie is a calorie, independent of whether fat or carbohydrate is used to reach a certain energy intake.

24.4   The Move to Low-Glycemic Food

Jenkins and colleagues developed the concept of the glycemic index in 1981 for the management of glycemic control of type 2 diabetic patients. The GI ranks the carbohydrate content of food according to the post-prandial glycemic response of an equivalent carbohydrate portion of a reference food such as 50 g of glucose. Later, in 1997, the glycemic load (GL) was introduced to quantify the overall glycemic effect of food with respect to its specific carbohydrate content in typically consumed quantities. Low-glycemic diets have been associated with lower weight gain. The number of long-term ad libitum RCTs is, however, limited. The multi-center, well-controlled CARMEN study using a supermarket system to get a better controlled selection of food with low fat and low or high GI (defined in this study as simple vs. complex carbohydrate) showed a significant effect on weight loss (−1.8 and −0.9 kg respectively), with a 10 En% fat reduction in the diet over a six-month period compared to the control group [20]. However, body weight change did not attain significance between the groups with either high-GI or low-GI foods in the diet. There was a tendency for a greater weight loss in the low-GI group. Recently, a meta-analysis on the long-term effects showed some evidence for beneficial effects of low-GI/GL diets with respect to fasting insulin and C-reactive protein [21]. But also fat-free mass decreased significantly, while weight and waist circumference did not change. These results indicate that the indirect effects of low GI on metabolism are more important, and that most probably in the long term it also has a beneficial effect on energy balance and weight control.

24.5   The Role of Protein in the Diet

The search for a diet that is more effective for weight control has shifted in the past decade to the role of protein. The mechanisms by which higher protein intake may promote a negative fat balance and the reduction of body fat stores are well established in short-term human studies. One of the physiological explanations is the well-documented thermic effect of protein compared to carbohydrate and fat. In that respect, protein differs clearly in terms of energetic efficiency, leading to a lower energy yield per gram. Moreover, protein generally exerts a greater satiety effect per calorie than the other macronutrients, whether it is consumed in drinks or solid food [22]. In addition, protein intake stimulates gain in lean body mass—the major determinant of resting and 24-h energy expenditure. These physiological effects are of importance during weight loss to preserve lean body mass.

The pan-European randomized, controlled multi-center trial DioGenes investigated dietary means of preventing weight regain following weight loss in free-living conditions [23]. In this trial, a 6-month dietary intervention tested the effect of ad libitum diets varying in protein and glycemic index on weight maintenance, after an initial eight-week low-calorie diet (LCD) to induce a major weight loss ($-\sim 11$ kg) before the subjects were randomized to one of the diets (Fig. 24.3).

The results at six months showed a clear weight maintenance advantage of the high protein/low glycemic index group compared to the low protein/high glycemic index groups or the control group consuming a diet based on the national dietary recommendations. In two of the centers using the more controlled supermarket system, the results after one year still showed a significant effect of the high-protein diet [24]. No consistent effect of glycemic index on weight regain was found any longer, indicating that in particular the level of protein intake has a more powerful effect on body weight maintenance compared to type of carbohydrate. Interestingly, also in this study the low GI groups showed a significant drop in C-reactive protein, indicating the beneficial effects of low GI/GL on glucose metabolism and inflammation. Since the study was executed in families, the effects of the diet on the weight of the children was also followed, showing the remarkable effect that obese children started to lose weight spontaneously [25]. A recent meta-analysis on long-term weight maintenance confirmed that even a small change in the ratio of protein to carbohydrate makes a difference for weight control [26].

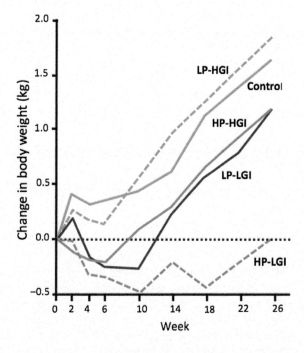

Fig. 24.3 Change in body weight for each of the dietary groups (high/low protein (HP/LP) and high/low glycemic index (HGI/LGI) during the weight maintenance intervention (26 weeks) after randomization, for participants who lost >8 kg bodyweight during the low-calorie-diet phase (8 weeks). *Source* Larsen et al. [23]. Reprinted with permission from Massachusetts Medical Society

24.6 It's Energy Intake that Counts

The obesity epidemic has fostered increasing interest among consumers in dietary treatment strategies for losing weight and avoiding weight regain. This has led to a multi-billion-dollar industry with named or branded weight-loss programs providing structured dietary and lifestyle recommendations via popular books or commercial organizations. It has yielded diets with the complete range of macronutrient composition from high to extreme low fat, carbohydrate and protein composition. Recently Johnston et al. [27] published a network meta-analysis of 48 randomized trials of popular diets based on the macronutrient composition with 6–12 months weight loss outcome compared to no diet. The weight loss differences between any of the individual low-carbohydrate or low-fat diets were minimal, leading to the conclusion that popular diets are equally effective and that evidence is lacking to recommend any particular diet. The greatest weight loss was found with the Atkins diet (low carbohydrate) and the Ornish diet (low fat). This led to an editorial with the title 'A diet by any other name is still about energy' [28]. It underscores the importance of the energy deficit for losing weight whatever the macronutrient composition may be, as indicated earlier with the NUGENOB study. However, we have to be cautious about concluding that the macronutrient composition is of no relevance, since these popular diets are characterized by energy-restricted intake. In a free-living ad libitum situation, the availability, palatability and macronutrient composition of the food is much more influential in determining the total energy intake. Therefore only RCTs under ad libitum conditions are valid for making judgements about the importance of the macronutrient composition of the diet in relation to weight change.

Some scientists proposed going back in history to see what our ancestors were eating when we were not surrounded by cheap and appetizing food at every street corner. Eaton has called this "Stone-Agers in the Fast Lane," though it may be reasonable to assume that nutritional requirements, which are relatively universal across human populations, were established in pre-historic times [29]. Although the emerging science of genomics has raised some questions, one can still assume that our current gene pool is adapted to foods consumed during the Stone Age. Paleo-anthropological research into the evolution of the human diet, drawing on the analysis of preserved remains and materials and using today's isotope technologies, gave a fairly good picture of the diet of Stone Age people about 50,000 years ago. Such diets were based chiefly on wild game, fish and uncultivated plant foods. They provided abundant protein; a fat profile significantly different from that of our affluent Western nations today; high fiber; carbohydrate from fruits and vegetables (and some honey) but not from cereals, refined sugars and dairy products; and high levels of most micronutrients. Calculation of the average macronutrient intake reveals an interesting picture of a relatively high protein intake of about 30 En%, low in fat of around 20 En% with a high level of unsaturated fatty acids and 50 En% unrefined carbohydrates. These figures correspond with the ones presented earlier in this chapter. Low fat intake and increased protein intake, leaving about 50 En% for mostly unrefined carbohydrates.

24.7   The Economics of the Choice of Macronutrients

In the past 50 years, developments in agriculture and food technology have made the production of raw materials for our industrially manufactured food products very efficient. In particular the production costs of sugars and vegetable oils have become extremely low. Therefore foods produced from these refined raw materials are low in price. Drewnowski presented the hypothesis that simple economic laws have most probably dictated macronutrient composition changes of our diet in recent decades [30]. Several studies have shown the contribution of fast food, caloric beverages and snacks to the obesity epidemic. In all cases, there is a strong relation between energy density of the food and the food price per kcal. Drewnowski reviewed the evidence in different food groups to show the link between the price and energy density of products such as fast food products versus full-service restaurant food; soft drinks versus milk or mineral water; and refined grains versus fiber-rich wholegrain products. In general, one can say that the 'Western' eating patterns are more energy-dense and lower in cost then a more 'prudent', nutrient-dense diet. In addition, epidemiological studies have shown over the past decades that obesity is related to the consumption of these mostly energy-dense, low-cost foods. Moreover, socio-economic status is an important determinant of obesity worldwide.

This brings a completely different dimension to the search for the key factors causing the obesity epidemic worldwide and, what is more important, for the best means of tackling them. So far, most attention has been given to the physiological factors involved in the energy intake from foods, such as satiation capacity of macronutrients and energy efficiency, the psychological factors such as craving, and the solid/liquid physical status of the food. Meanwhile the cost of food in association with energy density and portion size probably dictates the direction of food patterns to a situation of overfeeding in terms of energy, with a relatively poor quality in terms of micronutrient composition [31]. Income has been identified as an important factor determining the reduced intake of fruit and vegetables, meat, fish and eggs, leading to a lower nutrient density and a higher energy density of the daily food intake.

From the perspective of nutrition security, it is reasonable to expect for the coming decades that food energy will not be a problem even for the growing population worldwide. More challenging both for the food and nutritional scientific community, as well as for the food industry, is the need to increase the nutrient quality of the existing diets and at the same time decrease their energy density at reasonable cost. Fruit, vegetables and less refined food products that contribute to higher diversity of the diet are important determinants. Research suggests that we have perhaps concentrated too much on the foods whose consumption we should reduce and neglected to encourage people to eat more of the foods that protect against obesity.

However, consumer acceptance is crucial in this matter. Is it possible to get cooked potatoes and beans onto the daily menu once more instead of French fries and pizza? The alternative is to design and produce less refined and energy-dense, affordable, tasty foods. In addition to this, the means of producing sustainable and healthy food will become a central theme for all stakeholders involved. These will be the important challenges for the food industry in the coming decades.

24.8   Summary: Key Messages

- RDAs are essential for evaluating the quality of food intake as well as for planning food supply.
- In the recent past, RDA committees reduced the fat recommendations from about 40 En% to levels as low as 25 En%, emphasizing the reduction of saturated fat in particular.
- Data about macronutrient intake from food questionnaires are increasingly unreliable, given consumers' understanding of what is healthy or unhealthy to eat.
- Next to the increase in fat intake, and despite an abundance of low-fat food alternatives, there has been a considerable increase in refined sugar intake over the past 40 years.
- The roles of the macronutrients fat, carbohydrate and protein in the diet and their respective and combined influences on energy intake and weight change are still the subject of scientific debate.
- Only RCTs under ad libitum conditions are valid for making judgements about the importance of the macronutrient composition of the diet in relation to energy intake and weight control.
- The world must rise to the challenge of increasing the nutrient quality of existing diets while simultaneously reducing their energy density at a reasonable cost.
- This can only be achieved if nutritional solutions are made available that are acceptable to consumers.

References

1. Keys A, Brozek J, Henschel A, Mickelsen O, Longstreet Taylor H, The biology of human starvation, Volume 1 and 2, The University of Minnesota Press, Minneapolis 1950.
2. Vardavas CI, Linarkis M, Hatzis C, Saris WHM, Kafatos A, Cardiovascular disease risk factors and dietary habits of farmers from Crete 45 years after the first description of the Mediterranean diet. Eur. J. Card. Prev. and Rehab. 2010: 17; 440–446.
3. Bray GA, Popkin BM. Dietary fat intake does affect obesity! Amer. J. Clin. Nutr. 1998: 68; 1157–1173.
4. Astrup A, Grunwald GK, Melanson EL, Saris WHM, Hill JO. The role of low-fat diets in body weight control: a meta-analysis of ad libitum dietary intervention studies. Int. J. Obes. 2000: 24; 1545–1552.

5. Mensink RP, Zock PL, Kester ADM, Katan MB. Effects of dietary lipids and carbohydrates on the ratio of serum total to HDL cholesterol and on serum lipids and apolipoproteins: a meta-analysis of 60 controlled trials Amer. J. Clin. Nutr. 2003: 77; 1146–1155.

6. Dhurandhar NV, Schoeller D, Brown AW, Heymsfield SB, Thomas D, Sorensen TIA, Speakman JR, Allison DB and the energy balance measurement working group. Energy balance measurement: when something is not better than nothing. Int. J. Obes. 2014:38; 1–5.

7. Carden TJ and Carr TP. Food availability of glucose and fat, but not fructose, increased in the US between 1970 and 2009 Analysis of the USDA food availability data system. Nutr. J. 2013: 12; 130–138.

8. Mattes RD. Fluid energy—where's the problem? J. Amer. Diet. Ass. 2006: 106; 1965–1961.

9. Hu FB. Resolved: there is sufficient scientific evidence that decreasing sugar sweetened beverage consumption will reduce the prevalence and risk of obesity. Obesity reviews 2013: 14; 606–619.

10. Malik VS, Pan A, Willett WC, Hu FB. Sugar—sweetened beverages and weight gain in children and adults: a systematic review and meta-analysis Amer. J. Clin. Nutr. 2013: 98; 1084–1102.

11. Fung TT, Malik V, Rexrode KM, Manson JE, Willett WC, Hu FB. Sweetened beverage consumption and risk of coronary heart disease in women. Amer. J. Clin. Nutr. 2009: 89; 1037–1042.

12. Greenwood DC, Threapleton DE, Evans CE, Cleghorn CL, Nykjear C, Woodhead C. Association between sugar-sweetened and artificially sweetened soft drinks and type 2 diabetes; systematic review and dose-response meta-analysis of prospective studies Brit. J. Nutr. 2014: 112; 725–796.

13. Stanhope KL, Schwarz JM, Keim NL, Griffen SC, Bremer AA, et al. Consuming fructose – sweetened, not glucose sweetened, beverages increase visceral adiposity and lipids and decreases insulin sensitivity in overweight/obese humans J. Clin. Invest. 2009: 119; 1322–1334.

14. Bray GA, Popkins BM. Calorie-sweetened beverages and fructose: what have we learned 10 years later Pediatr. Obes. 2013: 8; 242–248.

15. Kahn R, Sievenpiper JL. Dietary sugar and body weight: have we reached a crisis in the epidemic of obesity and diabetes. We have, but the pox on sugar is overwrought and overworked—Diabetes Care 2014: 37; 957–962.

16. Te Morenga L, Mallard S, Mann J. Dietary sugars and body weight: systematic review and meta-analysis of randomized controlled trials and cohort studies. BMJ. 2013: 346; e 7492.

17. Sievenpieper JL, de Souza RJ, Mirrahimi A, Carleton AJ, Beyene J, et al. Effect of fructose on body weight in controlled feeding trial: a systematic review and meta-analysis Ann. Intern. Med. 2012: 156; 291–304.

18. Kaiser KA, Shikany JM, Keating KD, Allison DB. Will reducing sugar-sweetened beverage consumption reduce obesity? Evidence supporting conjecture id strong but evidence when testing is weak Obes. Rev. 2013: 14; 620–633.

19. Petersen M, Taylor MA, Saris WHM, Verdich C, Toubro S, et al. Randomized, multi-center trial of two hypo-energetic diets in obese subjects: high- versus low-fat content. Int. J Obes. 2006: 30; 552–560.

20. Saris WH, A Astrup, AM Prentice, HJF Zunft, X Formiguera, et al. Randomized controlled trial of changes in dietary carbohydrate/fat ratio and simple vs. complex carbohydrates on body weight and blood lipids: the CARMEN study. Int. J. Obes. 2000: 24; 1310–1318.

21. Schwingshackl L, Hoffmann G. Long-term effects of low glycemic index/load vs. high glycemic index/load diets on parameters of obesity and obesity-associated risks: a systematic review and meta-analysis. Nutr. Metab. Cardiovasc. Dis. 2013: 23; 699–706.

22. Maersk M, Belza A, Holst JJ, Fenger-Gron M, Pedersen SB et al. Satiety scores and satiety hormones response after sucrose-sweetened soft drink compared with iso-caloric semi-skimmed milk and with non-caloric soft drink: a controlled trial. Eur. J. Clin. Nutr. 2012: 66; 523–529.

23. Larsen TM, Dalskov SM, van Baak MA, Jebb SA, Papadaki A, et al. for the Diet, Obesity, and Genes (Diogenes) Project. Diets with High or Low Protein Content and Glycemic Index for Weight-Loss Maintenance. New Eng. J. Med. 2010: 363; 2102–2013.
24. Aller EE, Larsen TM, Claus H, Lindroos AK, Kafatos A, et al. Weight loss maintenance in overweight subjects on ad libitum diets with high or low protein content and glycemic index: the Diogenes trial. Int. J. Obes. 2014: 38; 1511–1517.
25. Papadaki A, Linardakis M, Larsen TM, van baak MA, Lindroos AK, et al and on behalf of the DiOGenes Study Group. The Effect of Protein and Glycemic Index on Children's Body Composition: The DiOGenes Randomized Study Pediatrics 2010: 126; e1143–52.
26. Clifton PM, Condo D, Keogh JB. Long-term weight maintenance after advice to consume low carbohydrate, higher protein diets—a systematic review and meta-analysis Nutr. Metab. Cardiovasc. Dis. 2014: 24; 224–235.
27. Johnston BC, Kanters S, Bandayrel K, Wu P, Faysal F, et al. Comparison of weight loss among named diet programs in overweight and obese adults; a meta-analysis. J.A.M.A. 2014: 312; 923–933.
28. Van Horn L. A diet by any other name is still about energy J.A.M.A. 2014; 312: 900–901.
29. Eaton SB, Shostak M, Konner M. The Paleolithic prescription. A program of diet & exercise and a design for living. Harper & Row Publ. New York 1988.
30. Drewnowski A. The real contribution of added sugar and fats to obesity. Epidemiological Reviews 29: 29; 160–171.
31. Aggarwal A, Monsivais P, Drewnowski A. Nutrient intakes linked to better health outcomes are associated with higher diet costs in the US. Plos One 2012: 7; e 37533.

Chapter 25
Producing Sufficient Animal-Source Protein for the Growing World Population

Gilbert M. Weber and Wilhelm Windisch

Abstract The recommendation for macronutrient intakes by humans suggests obtaining 45–65% of the daily caloric intake from carbohydrates, 10–45% from fat, and 10–35% from protein. According to the Dietary Reference Intakes (RDI) issued by the Institute of Medicine of the US Food and Nutrition Board [8], adults need to eat about 60 g of protein per day. Protein that comes from animal sources is in general nutritionally more complete than protein that comes from plant sources, because it contains the essential amino acids in a more adequate pattern. Average meat consumption varies greatly between the developed and the developing world. Although levels of meat consumption are tending to stagnate in highly developed societies, a strong upturn is expected in emerging economies due to increasing urbanization and growing affluence. This chapter discusses the specifics of the current production of animal-derived protein, focusing on poultry meat and eggs, pork, beef, dairy, and aquaculture. The growing demand for animal-sourced protein is analyzed and possible means of meeting it presented, including improved breeding programs and various approaches to means of enhancing the nutritional intake and consequent performance of livestock. The chapter concludes with a consideration of the environmental concerns that must be addressed if the world's livestock population grows significantly in response to increased global demand for animal-source protein.

Keywords Nutrients · Protein · Meat · Poultry · Swine · Ruminants · Aquaculture · Feed additives · Feed utilization · Alternative feed ingredients · Environmental impact

G.M. Weber (✉)
DSM Nutritional Products, Nutrition Innovation Center, Wurmisweg 576,
4303 Kaiseraugst, Switzerland
e-mail: gilbert.weber@dsm.com; familie_weber@bluewin.ch

W. Windisch
TUWZA8Q Institute for Animal Nutrition, Technical University of Munich,
85354 Freising Liesel-Beckmann-Str. 2/II, Germany
e-mail: wilhelm.windisch@mytum.de

© Springer International Publishing AG 2017
H.K. Biesalski et al. (eds.), *Sustainable Nutrition in a Changing World*,
DOI 10.1007/978-3-319-55942-1_25

25.1 Introduction

Nutrients are needed for growth, metabolism and other body functions. Among these, *macronutrients* are elements that provide mainly 'calories' and protein, while *micronutrients* have a variety of physiological functions related to development, disease prevention and wellbeing.

The recommendation for macronutrient intakes by humans suggests obtaining 45–65% of the daily caloric intake from carbohydrates, 10–45% from fat, and 10–35% from protein. Protein is the major constituent of most cells, making up more than 50% of their dry weight. Besides providing energy to the body, dietary protein is also required for growth, tissue repair, immune system function, and hormone and enzyme production, as well as for the development and maintenance of the muscles. According to the Dietary Reference Intakes (RDI) issued by the Institute of Medicine of the US Food and Nutrition Board [8], adults need to eat about 60 g of protein per day. If more protein is consumed than is needed, the body converts it into fat, which can be broken down and used for energy as the need arises. The typical diet of the Western world contains more protein than is strictly necessary, which could be one of the factors contributing to the problem of obesity.

Protein is mainly found in meats from poultry, swine and cattle, as well as in fish, eggs and dairy products (cheese and milk). It is also present in plant sources such as legumes (soya), grains, nuts, seeds and certain vegetables. Protein that comes from animal sources is in general nutritionally more complete, because it contains the essential amino acids in a more adequate pattern, which is not the case for plant proteins.

Global average meat consumption is 41.9 kg per person per year (data from 2009; [3]). However, there is a large variance between the developed and the developing world. The highest consumption figures are found in Kuwait (119 kg), Australia (112 kg), the Bahamas (110 kg), Luxembourg (108 kg), New Zealand (106 kg) and Austria (102 kg), while the lowest consumption levels are recorded in Bangladesh (4.0 kg), India (4.4 kg), Burundi (5.2 kg), Sri Lanka (6.3 kg) and Rwanda (6.5 kg). Although meat consumption is tending to stagnate in highly developed societies, a strong lift is expected in emerging economies due to increasing urbanization and growing affluence.

25.2 Current Production of Animal-Derived Protein

25.2.1 Poultry Meat and Eggs

Several avian species have been domesticated for the production of food, the most important being broiler chickens and laying hens, which are both derived from *Gallus gallus domesticus* and are currently kept all over the globe for the production of high-quality meat and eggs. A second species, whose occurrence is more regional, is the turkey, which can be grown to higher weights, but overall is less efficient than the broiler. Of lesser importance are species such as ducks and geese, partridges, quails and pheasants, as well as ostriches and emus. The farming of such species is usually restricted to specific geographies, and the products are consumed on special occasions only.

Due to rising demand, broiler production has developed from family-based backyard flock systems to a highly integrated industry. Poultry houses with a capacity of up to 100,000 birds are used, which are ventilated for a good climate and have the floor littered with an absorptive material such as wood shavings for taking the birds' excreta. Sometimes several of these houses are combined in large complexes with production capacities for several million broilers.

In these poultry houses, day-old chicks with a size of 40–50 g are brought to market weight of 2.5–3.5 kg, depending on the preferences of the end-consumer. Genetic progress by primary breeding companies has yielded a small number of hybrid strains with an exceptional growing capacity, allowing these birds to achieve slaughter weight in just 35–49 days. During the fattening period, they are supplied with a usually pelleted compound feed which contains all macronutrients as well as the necessary micronutrients, minerals and trace elements in an equilibrated manner. Energy is predominantly provided by cereals (corn and wheat), and protein by soybean meal. In order to adapt the nutrient supply of broilers most accurately to their requirements, the feed compositions are different in the various fattening periods: the starter (1–10 days), grower (11–24 days), and finisher phases (25 days —market). The feed is efficiently transformed into chicken body mass with a feed conversion ratio of 1 to 1.5–2.0 (for 1 kg of live weight gain, 1.5–2.0 kg of feed are required), making broilers the most efficient land-based farm animal. Consumption of broilers as whole birds is losing importance, and carcasses are usually cut into parts and sold as breasts, legs and wings. Less attractive parts of the carcass and small pieces of meat can also be further processed into nuggets, chicken patties, sausages and other products.

Turkeys are produced under similar conditions as broilers. However, they can be grown for longer periods (15–25 weeks), and thus achieve a much higher weight (up to 25 kg). In some countries, turkeys are still considered a holiday product and are therefore produced only during certain seasons. By contrast, in other markets the meat from continuous turkey production is processed into a variety of specialties such as ham, sausages and patties, which are leaner than pork products and thus considered healthier by consumers. The fastest-growing birds are ducks: in 6 weeks they can get to over 3 kg of live weight. Several different husbandry conditions are possible for ducks, but intensive farming is performed, as with broilers. In Asian countries, duck meat represents a common dish for every day, while in the Western world it is still restricted to certain seasons.

Poultry meat is relatively cheap, is considered a healthy food, and is well accepted around the globe, as there are no restrictions on its consumption by major religions or local traditions. Poultry meat production is therefore constantly increasing, and poultry will soon become the most popular animal-derived food.

Laying hens have first to be raised as replacement pullets for 18 weeks until they start the production of eggs for approximately 45 weeks. Peak production after 4–6 weeks can reach 95%+, but over the whole period, laying performance is at approximately 85%—i.e., a hen can produce more than 280 eggs, equating to approximately 15 kg of egg mass, in its lifetime. In the most advanced markets, layers are replaced by young pullets after the first production period, but under certain conditions the hens are molted and thus can be utilized for a second cycle, although laying performance drops to a lower level.

The husbandry of laying hens is rather variable; the most economic production system is to keep them in groups of up to 10 birds in wire-floored cages. This system prevents the birds from coming into contact with their droppings and consequently limits the spread of infectious diseases, both from bacteria and from parasites. As cages are not considered welfare-friendly, however, these have been replaced in many regions by floor-pen or larger aviary systems under the influence of pressure from end-consumers. Eggs are considered among the most nutritious foods, since a whole egg contains all the nutrients required for the embryonic development of chickens. As such, they can be used for various dishes, but they are also contained in many other food items, such as pasta, mayonnaise and cakes, to give just a few examples.

The output of waste from poultry production is a challenge for the environment, as it can potentially cause soil, water and air pollution. Litter and excreta are rather dry and thus can easily be transported to be utilized as fertilizer on farmland. Recently, the phosphorous (P) load in poultry manure has been considerably reduced by the increasing utilization of phytases as feed additives. Such products can release plant-bound P from the feed raw materials and make it available to the bird. Accordingly, less mineral P has to be added to the feed and less P leaks into the environment via the excreta. A similar effect for reducing nitrogen output can be achieved by supplementing poultry feed with proteases, which increase the digestibility of protein. A concern remains the release of ammonia from poultry operations, which have a bad smell and contribute to the overall pollution of the air.

25.2.2 Pork Production

Today's swine industry is still less concentrated and less integrated than the poultry industry. The majority of swine farms have around 100 head of animals, and only rarely does this number rise to 1,000 or above. Different systems exist, but the most common is Farrow-to-Feeder, which is based on a herd of breeding sows for the production of weaner piglets, combined with feeding them to a weight of approximately 15–30 kg. At this young age, the piglets are kept in groups of up to 20 individuals on a deep-litter system. Subsequently these piglets are sold to Feeder-to-Finish farms, which fatten the pigs to slaughter weight in groups of 5–10 animals in pens with slatted floors.

These farmers are sometimes grain producers, who can use home-grown feeds to finish the pigs and also can utilize the manure as fertilizer on their fields. There are, however, an increasing number of large farms which source weaned piglets and keep them up to slaughter weight. These operations typically have no independent feed supply, but instead buy a complete compound feed from specialized feed mills. As with poultry, swine undergo different feeding phases. After birth, piglets start by drinking milk from their dams, but already during the suckling phase they are offered a so-called creep feed in order to get used to solid feed. Weaning usually occurs at four weeks of age, but there is a trend for reducing the suckling period to three weeks or even less. Thereafter, piglets are given a pre-starter for two weeks and then a starter feed for another four to six weeks. During the fattening phase, one or two grower diets are supplied, followed by the finisher for the last phase prior to slaughter. Swine feed is based on similar raw materials as poultry diets (corn, cereals, soybean), and therefore this industry competes somewhat with the use of those raw materials for direct human consumption.

Pig production is less efficient than that of broilers: it takes roughly three months from weaning (approximately 7–8 kg) to the finishing stage of 90–100 kg, and the overall feed conversion ratio is around 1:3. Dressing yield (the ratio of hot carcass weight to live weight) is close to 80% [11]. Pig meat is not accepted by certain religious communities such as Muslims and Jews, and accordingly this industry is not present in several large countries of the Middle East, or in Asia. Nevertheless, pork is the most widely consumed meat in the world. Various parts of the carcass offer high-quality meat, such as fillet, pork chops or ham, which can easily form the basis of a variety of dishes, supporting a modern lifestyle. The remaining parts can be further processed into specialties such as bacon, ground patties and sausages.

The environmental impact of swine production is similar to that of poultry. The slurry, however, is usually fluid and thus should preferentially be used as fertilizer on cropland close to the farm, since transport or drying is not economical. Feed enzymes such as phytase reduce the leakage of undesirable compounds into the water. Yet the problem of strong smell from swine fatting farms is more acute than that of poultry operations; such barns are therefore usually positioned well distant from populous agglomerations.

25.2.3 Ruminants: Beef Cattle and Dairy Cows

Although production of meat via beef cattle is the least efficient of all animal protein types, it is ecologically important as it represents the utilization of a vegetable biomass which otherwise would be wasted to yield high-quality protein for human consumption. Ruminants can digest ligno-cellulosic material in their rumen with the help of a complex microflora from bacteria, fungi and protozoa: this process results in protein (bacterial biomass) and volatile fatty acids as energy source for the host animal. Beef production makes it possible to take advantage of land that for various reasons cannot support crop production, but can sustain the growth of grass and forage. In fact, the vast majority of global agricultural areas consist of non-arable grassland which may be utilized only by domestic herbivores. Calves are produced in cow-calf systems and after weaning are kept on such farms until the age of about six to eight months and a weight of 350–400 kg. Thereafter, they are finished under various production conditions, which range from extensive or semi-intensive pasture systems to intensive fattening in feedlots. Beef cattle are slaughtered at a weight of 550–600 kg, which they reach after approximately one year.

In most countries, the dairy industry uses cattle breeds that were genetically selected for milk production over many generations. After weaning, female calves are reared either on pastureland or else in confined systems until they reach sexual maturity as heifers within 15 months of age. Male calves are further fattened or slaughtered after weaning to deliver meat. Following artificial insemination, heifers deliver their first calf at an age of two years and start their lactation cycle with a duration of around 305 days. Cows are fed with a TMR (total mixed ration) which is composed of roughage (hay or straw), corn or grass silage, and a mineral mixture; this feed is produced fresh on the farm.

In order to sustain the high milk production, particularly at peak lactation, cows additionally receive a compound feed, based on corn or other cereals plus soybean meal. Dairy cows are usually kept indoors in tie stall or free stall barns. Cows are inseminated again during their lactation cycle so that they can deliver approximately one calf per year and continuously produce milk, except during the dry period of four to eight weeks prior to the next calving. A challenge for the profitability of dairy farmers is to keep a dairy cow in production over several cycles in order to compensate for the investment in rearing the heifer to first calving. On average, dairy cows in highly developed production systems deliver only 2.5 lactation cycles. Frequent health problems in dairy cattle, which result in the culling of cows, are fertility problems, lameness due to serious hoof disorders, and chronic mastitis.

Ruminant manure is used for the fertilization of grassland and cropland, if possible on the same farm. More recently, this manure has begun also to be used to produce biogas as an energy source in on-farm fermenters. An unresolved problem remains the emission of methane by ruminants. Methane is a more potent greenhouse gas than carbon dioxide, and the emissions from agriculture contribute substantially to global warming.

25.2.4 Aquaculture

Since the capture of wild fish is stagnating due to the overfishing of the oceans, aquaculture has developed exponentially worldwide in order to satisfy the growing demand for this type of food. The farming of aquatic species represents the most diverse food-producing industry, ranging from invertebrates such a mollusks (e.g. mussels) or crustaceans (shrimp), through a large variety of fish, to reptiles such as crocodiles.

The animals belong either to freshwater or marine species, and rearing is performed in different types of water environment such as tanks, ponds, rivers, lakes and the ocean. Cultured freshwater species are dominated by catfish, trout, tilapia and bass. This type of aquaculture requires extensive water resources, but recently efforts have been geared toward running such operations more sustainably within recirculating systems. Marine fish farming primarily uses salmon and cod, but yellowtail, barramundi, seabass and seabream are also favored species. This type of aquaculture usually takes place in the ocean and keeps the fish in nets or cages at rather high density. Since infectious diseases and parasitic attacks can easily spread through a whole stock under such conditions, treatment with antibiotics or other therapeutics is unavoidable. As a consequence, such products are unintentionally released into the nearby water environment and cause certain undesirable side-effects on the ecosystem. Recently vaccines against an increasing number of pathogens have become available, the use of which has considerably diminished the pollution problem caused by veterinary drugs.

A special requirement of carnivorous fish species such as salmonids is fishmeal for fast growth. This is produced in enormous quantities by processing wild-caught fish. As such farming conditions might not be sustainable in the future with the increasing demand for fish-derived food, research efforts are currently directed towards diet compositions which would allow the use of more vegetable protein, e.g., soya. Moreover, there are indications that aquaculture could make use of insect protein, whose amino acid composition is largely similar to that of fishmeal. Fish excreta can also cause environmental issues. As decomposition of this organic material consumes oxygen, this process can negatively impact on the variety of wildlife on the ocean floor close to fish farms.

25.3 Global Demand and Future Requirements

According to FAO [4], total global meat production in 2010 reached 296.1 million tons (mT), of which pork had the largest share with 109.4 mT, followed by poultry with 99.1 mT and beef with 67.8 mT (Table 25.1). The highest per-annum growth rate between 2000 and 2010 was observed in poultry (4.3%), followed by pork (2.2%). It can therefore be expected that in a few years' time, poultry meat production will overtake that of pork.

The largest regional meat production was recorded in China (80.9 mT), which represented 27.3% of the global output (Table 25.1). China also produced the highest quantity of pork, accounting for close to 50% of global production. For poultry meat, Latin America was the leading region, with 21.3 mT, closely followed by North America, with an output of 20.8 mT. For beef, too, Latin America is the leading region, with 17.4 mT and still positive growth rates (2.4%), while in North America (13.3 mT) and Europe (11.0 mT), production is decreasing (−0.2 and −0.4%, respectively). Although overall still relatively small, Africa

Table 25.1 Global production of meat in 2010 (overall and various categories) and annual growth rates (2000–2010) in different geographic regions

Geographic region	Total meat production		Poultry		Pork		Beef and buffalo		Sheep and goat	
	Million tons	p.a. growth (%)	Million tons	p.a. growth (%)	Million tons	p.a. growth (%)	Million tons	p.a. growth (%)	Million tons	p.a. growth (%)
World	296.1	2.6	99.1	4.3	109.4	2.2	67.8	1.8	13.5	2.1
Europe	56.6	1.3	16.2	4.8	26.9	1.1	11.0	−0.4	1.3	−1.2
North America	46.6	1.1	20.8	1.8	12.1	1.7	13.3	−0.2	0.1	−2.3
Central and Latin America	46.3	3.7	21.3	5.6	6.6	2.6	17.4	2.4	0.4	0.8
Africa	17.3	4.4	4.8	5.2	1.2	6.0	6.9	5.6	2.9	3.2
Asia (excl. China)	42.6		17.6		10.6		10.1		3.7	
China	80.9	2.7	17.3	3.3	51.5	2.4	6.5	2.5	4.0	4.0
Oceania	5.8	0.7	1.1	3.6	0.5	−0.3	2.8	0.7	1.1	−1.5

Source FAO [4]

Total egg production reached 69.1 mT in 2010, with a growth rate of 2.5% over the last 10 years (Table 25.2). With 28.0 mT, China was by far the largest producer, followed by the rest of Asia (14.6 mT) and Europe (10.5 mT). The highest growth rates were recorded in Latin America (3.6%) and Africa (3.5%), although the latter continent had rather low production levels (2.7 mT). Milk production is comparatively low at 0.72 mT on a global scale. The most productive regions were Asia (excluding China: 0.22 mT), with the largest production in India (0.12 mT) and Europe (0.21 mT), but the highest growth rate was observed in China (+12.9%)

There is still more fish coming from capture (88.6 mT) than from aquaculture (59.9 mT), but fish sourced via fishing is on the decline in most regions of the world. By contrast, farmed fish is growing, particularly in Asia, which, including China, produced 53.3 mT, with a growth rate of 7.1%. Strongly growing regions are Africa (+16.4%) and Latin America (+10.1%)

Table 25.2 Global production of eggs and milk as well as fish in 2010 and annual growth rates (2000–2010) in different geographic regions

Geographic region	Total egg production		Total milk production		Fish production (capture)		Fish production (aquaculture)	
	Million tons	p.a. growth (%)	Million tons	p.a. growth (%)	Million tons	p.a. growth (%)	Million tons	p.a. growth (%)
World	69.1	2.5	0.72	2.7	88.6	0.4	59.9	7.2
Europe	10.5	1.4	0.21	0	13.8	−1.2	2.5	3.1
North America	5.8	0.9	0.10	1.3	5.5	−0.6	0.7	1.2
Central and Latin America	7.2	3.6	0.08	3.4	11.7	−4.1	1.9	10.1
Africa	2.7	3.5	0.04	4.9	7.6	2.0	1.3	16.4
Asia (excl. China)	14.6		0.22		32.4		16.3	
China	28.0	2.4	0.04	12.9	16.3	0.4	37.0	5.5
Oceania	0.3	2.2	0.03	1.6	1.2	2.8	0.2	4.8

Source FAO [3, 4]

According to OECD [10], global meat production will increase by 19% between 2014 and 2023, with the highest share of this increase in poultry (34.0%), which will become the most common meat type in 2020, and in swine (23.5%). This strong additional demand results from the growing world population, but also from the increasing affluence of people in emerging economies, as there is a close relationship between income level and meat consumption. If this strong growth were to persist or even accelerate, meat production might have to be doubled by the year 2050, when the world's population is predicted to reach 9 billion people

showed the highest growth rates in meat production in 2010 (+4.4%), particularly in poultry (+5.2%) and pork (+6.0%).

25.3.1 Opportunities to Expand Meat Production

Doubling animal-derived protein production in a sustainable way represents an enormous challenge for this industry. It means finding the land for situating the farms for the additional animals (both those which are fattened and those which produce offspring), but also increasing the production of the feed raw materials, particularly the main ingredients such as corn, cereals and soybean. For the transport of both feed and animals, appropriate carriage capacity and infrastructure would be needed, and new processing plants would have to be constructed. Furthermore, the additional waste (manure, slurry, gases, slaughter offal) should be handled in a way that optimally protects the environment (soil, water, air).

25.3.2 Breeding

An increase in the efficiency of meat production needs to accompany the overall rise in livestock production. In poultry, growth rates and feed conversion rates have already been massively improved. While a common hybrid broiler from 1957 took more than 100 days to reach a body weight of 1.8 kg with a feed conversion ratio (FCR) of 4.42, a fast-growing modern breed reached the same weight in 32 days with an FCR of 1.47 [5]. From 1971 to 2003, genetic progress in breeding broilers has linearly increased growth rates and improved feed conversion by 1% per year [9]. This development must be pursued. For swine, there seems to be considerable potential for better performance, but due to the lower level of integration of this industry and higher variability of the production systems than in the poultry sector, progress is slower. Similar developments are occurring in beef cattle. In dairy cows, milk production has been impressively increased, and there are breeds which can produce 12,000 kg or more in one lactation, which represents around 40 kg per day. Such high-yielding cows are rather demanding in terms of feeding and husbandry, and often have to be culled after one or two lactations due to health problems. It is therefore questionable whether this productivity can be still further improved. Although already rather efficient, aquaculture could still increase overall performance by improving the flesh yield in fish.

25.3.3 Nutrition

For maximum efficiency of meat production, nutrition—in terms both of macronutrients and of micronutrients, and particularly as regards vitamin supply—needs to be optimized. High-yielding hybrids are delicate animals, and their nutrition must be carefully balanced in order to exploit their full genetic potential and obtain end-products with a high nutritional value. An equilibrated diet allows strong performance in farm animals, coupled with good health and welfare. Adequate vitamin supplementation avoids clinical or subclinical deficiency symptoms and reduces various production issues such as leg problems and lameness due to skeletal disorders (vitamin D_3 deficiency), infectious diseases due to insufficient immune responses (deficiency in vitamins E and C), footpad dermatitis in poultry, and hoof problems in swine and ruminants (biotin deficiency). Furthermore, supplemental vitamins and other micronutrients which are not instantly utilized by the metabolism are deposited in meat and eggs or else transferred into the milk and by this route eventually improve the nutritional value of these products for the consumer.

A variety of specific feed additives are available that can improve performance and reduce growth depression or even death due to diseases of various origins. Until recently, antibiotic growth promotors (AGPs) were added to the feed of livestock for the prevention of infections involving harmful pathogens. Since certain of these products are structurally related to antibiotics used in human medicine, the considerable risk of inducing cross-resistance in life-threatening infectious microorganisms has been recognized. Consequently, the prophylactic use of AGPs has been banned in Europe and in all countries that export meat to Europe. In the rest of the world, AGPs are still allowed, but their prophylactic use is also under scrutiny in North America, as well as other regions. Yet the therapeutic use of antibiotics for treating animal diseases is not being questioned at present, although the approval for certain products derived from human medicine has been revoked. As alternatives to AGPs, so-called 'Eubiotics', which have the ability to beneficially modulate the gut microflora, are being developed. Pre- and probiotics, organic acids and plant extracts (largely, essential oils), have the potential to foster adequate gut health. They modulate the microflora and the digestive functionality in the intestine in a positive way, i.e., they stimulate the growth of beneficial bacteria such as *Lactobacilli* or *Bifidobacteria*, and they inhibit the growth of pathogens such as *Clostridium perfringens* (which causes necrotic enteritis in poultry) or *E. coli* (which causes post-weaning diarrhea in piglets). Furthermore, they stimulate the secretion of endogenous digestive enzymes.

25.3.4 Feed Utilization

To improve the sustainability of animal-derived protein production, the limited resources of feedstocks must be exploited to the maximum. For this reason, feed enzymes are commonly used in monogastric animals (poultry, swine), and first products are also applied to fish and ruminants to improve the digestibility of nutrients. Carbohydrases with different specific activities can degrade fibrous material in cereals and thereby make energy available to the host which otherwise would be wasted. Proteases improve the digestibility of protein, which is the most expensive feed ingredient and of which the supply might become limited in the future. Finally, phytases release phosphorous (P) from plant-bound phytate, which could not be utilized by monogastric animals in former times. By using such products, less P needs to be mixed into the feeds, which represents a considerable saving for the farmer, but has also an environmental benefit. The non-digested P is excreted by the animal, and, via fertilization of grass- and cropland with farm animal manure, contributes to the critical eutrophication of rivers and lakes.

25.3.5 Alternative Feed Ingredients

Another precondition for keeping the higher production rate sustainable is to find alternative feed ingredients, as the production of common crops might not be increased to the extent that would be needed, and since the main feedstuffs (corn, cereals, soybean) compete directly with human requirements for food. Furthermore, the biofuel industry consumes an increasing amount of potential feed ingredients, although the waste from fermentation processes can often be used for feeding livestock again. There are tropical raw materials available that could serve this purpose. A recent meta-analysis of studies with sorghum and millet to replace corn as an energy source, and cottonseed meal as alternative to soybean meal as a protein source, revealed that to a certain extent, such tropical feed ingredients could be used [1]. As some of these plant materials contain anti-nutritional factors such as tannins, the use of such material could be increased by the availability of feed enzymes, which would neutralize these anti-nutritional factors.

Beside vegetable sources of protein, insects have recently come into consideration as potential feed ingredients for livestock and aquaculture production. The larvae of insects in particular contain up to 60% of high-quality protein, and the indigestible chitin content is lower than in the adult stage. Insects could be considered as a normal component of the food chain for monogastric species and carnivorous fish in nature, and therefore this protein source should be acceptable both to regulatory authorities and to consumers of the respective end-product. Insects can be grown on bio-waste from the food processing industry or from households, and certain species could even utilize ligno-cellulosic biomass, which otherwise would be lost if not fed to ruminants. Insects have a more efficient feed conversion capacity than any other farmed animal, and the requirements for management and husbandry are rather low. What currently still makes insect material expensive as a feed raw material is the necessary, but energy-intensive, drying process, as it can only be mixed into compound feed in meal form. Furthermore, the separation of the protein from the lipid fraction, which eventually results in a higher value material, is not trivial, and is therefore costly.

25.3.6 Longevity of High-Yielding Livestock Animals

Under production conditions, livestock animals are prone to fatal diseases, due to stress and the infectious pressure of pathogens of various origins. Furthermore, high productivity rapidly exhausts the metabolic resources of long-lived animal categories (laying/breeder hens, breeding sows, dairy cows) and reduces their life expectancy. Since a substantial investment of time and resources is required to bring these animals to sexual maturity, a prolongation of their lifespan and accordingly additional breeding cycles would contribute substantially to an improvement of the production efficacy with more eggs or day-old chicks, more piglets and more milk.

25.4 Environmental Considerations

Facing the massive increase in demand for animal-derived food and consequently the enormous expansion of animal husbandry, the emissions from this industry must be given special attention [2]. The first concern should be the sustainable disposal of manure. Although animal excreta and slurry are convenient fertilizers, care must be taken that grass- and croplands are not oversupplied with nutrients which cannot be bound by the soil matrix and therefore would leak out into rivers and lakes, causing eutrophication of the water resources. Furthermore, trace elements such as zinc, copper and cobalt, which are essential for animal performance, can accumulate in the soil and thereby create damage to growing crops. Making animal-derived protein production more efficient should result in less excreta per unit of edible product. But considering the expected expansion of production, novel concepts for processing the manure and potentially extracting valuable fractions from this material for re-use are urgently required.

Gas emissions of carbon dioxide, ammonia and methane, which contribute to the greenhouse effect and thus aggravate the global warming problem, should not be allowed to increase [6]. For this environmental issue, a few feed additives are available on the market, but none of them currently seems sufficiently efficacious to allow anticipated levels of production growth in poultry and swine with neutral or shrinking emissions. Methane from enteric fermentation in ruminants represents the single largest source of anthropogenic origin. For this segment, a feed additive is under development which has the potential to reduce methane emissions by at least 30% [7]. Nevertheless, more research and development in this field is urgently needed.

25.5 Summary: Key Messages

- According to the Dietary Reference Intakes (RDI) issued by the Institute of Medicine of the US Food and Nutrition Board [8], adults need to eat about 60 g of protein per day.
- Protein that comes from animal sources is in general nutritionally more complete than protein that comes from plant sources, because it contains the essential amino acids in a more adequate pattern.
- Average meat consumption varies greatly between the developed and the developing world. A strong increase is expected in emerging economies due to increasing urbanization and growing affluence.
- Poultry meat is relatively cheap, is considered a healthy food, and is well accepted around the globe, as there are no restrictions by major religions or local traditions. Poultry meat production is therefore constantly increasing, and poultry will soon become the most popular animal-derived food, although global pork production still currently exceeds poultry production.

- The growing demand for animal-sourced protein may be met by improving breeding programs and enhancing the performance of livestock via improved nutrition, but the environmental impact of a greatly increased livestock population will have to be carefully managed.

References

1. Batonon-Alavo, D.I., M. Umar Faruk, P. Lescoat, G.M. Weber and D. Bastianelli (2015): Inclusion of sorghum, millet and cottonseed meal in broiler diets: A meta-analysis of effects on performance. Animal, open access, page 1–11.
2. FAO (2006): Livestock's long shadow. FAO report.
3. FAO (2013a): Current Worldwide Annual Meat Consumption per capita, Livestock and Fish Primary Equivalent, Food and Agriculture Organization of the United Nations Available at www.faostat.fao.org.
4. FAO (2013b): Statistical Yearbook 2013. Food and Agriculture Organization of the United Nations, Rome.
5. Havenstein, G.B., P.R. Ferket and M.A. Qureshi (2003): Growth, livability, and feed conversion of 1957 versus 2001 broilers when fed representative 1957 and 2001 broiler diets. Poult. Sci. 82:1500–1508.
6. Herrero M, Henderson B, Havlík P, Thornton P, Conant R, Smith P, Wirsenius S, Hristov A, Gerber PJ, Gill M, Butterbach-bahl K, Valin H, Garnett T and Stehfest E (2016): Greenhouse gas mitigation potentials in the livestock sector. Nature Climate Change; published online: 21 March 2016| Doi:10.1038/nclimate2925.
7. Hristov AN, Oh J, Giallongo F, Frederick TW, Harper MT, Weeks HL, Branco AF, Moate PJ, Deighton MH, Williams SRO, Kindermann M and Duval S (2015): An inhibitor persistently decreased enteric methane emission from dairy cows with no negative effect on milk production. PNAS I Doi/10.1073/pnas.1504124112.
8. IOM (2006): Dietary Reference Intakes: The Essential Guide to Nutrient Requirements. Available at www.iom.edu.
9. Laughlin, K. (2007): The evolution of genetics, breeding and production. Harper Adams University College, Report No.15.
10. OECD (2014): Agricultural Outlook 2013–2023. Organisation for Economic Co-operation and Development, Paris, France. Available at www.oecd.org.
11. Yang, Y., J. Guo, J.-S. Kim, M.-H. Wang and B.-J. Chae (2012): Effects of growth rate on carcass and meat quality traits and their association with metabolism-related gene expression in finishing pigs. Anim. Sci. J., 83: 169–177.

Chapter 26
Nutrient Density: An Important Concept to Ensure Food and Nutrition Security in Modern Societies

Barbara Troesch, Peter Weber and Adam Drewnowski

Abstract Dietary habits, particularly in affluent societies, increasingly rely on foods prepared and consumed away from home. Foods eaten away from home tend to be higher in energy and fat than are foods sourced in grocery stores and prepared and consumed in the household. This article explores the effect this change in dietary habit has on nutritional intake, and discusses the role that nutrient density—defined here as the ratio of essential nutrients to energy—can play in improving nutrition in line with modern lifestyles. In affluent societies and increasingly in low-and middle-income countries too, large numbers of people depend more and more on food that has not been prepared by themselves. At the same time, an imbalance exists between elevated energy intakes and inadequate micronutrient intakes. Increasing the nutrient density of diets is a promising approach to improving nutrition in our modern world. Changed dietary habits come with new responsibilities for food providers, who need to make sure that their products provide adequate amounts of nutrients. Acceptability, transparency, labeling and costs will have a key role to play in convincing consumers to integrate such products into their diets.

Keywords Nutrient density · Energy density · Foods eaten away from home · Nutritional intake · Restaurant · Street food · Convenience food · Food producer · Consumer

B. Troesch (✉) · P. Weber
DSM Nutritional Products Ltd, Wurmisweg 576, 4303 Kaiseraugst, Switzerland
e-mail: barbara.troesch@dsm.com

P. Weber
e-mail: peter.weber@dsm.com

A. Drewnowski
Center for Public Health Nutrition, University of Washington,
305 Raitt Hall #353410, Seattle WA 98195-3410, USA
e-mail: adamdrew@u.washington.edu

© Springer International Publishing AG 2017
H.K. Biesalski et al. (eds.), *Sustainable Nutrition in a Changing World*,
DOI 10.1007/978-3-319-55942-1_26

26.1   The Growth in Foods Eaten Away from Home

Dietary habits, particularly in affluent societies, increasingly rely on foods prepared and consumed away from home (Fig. 26.1). While this category is rather heterogeneous, foods eaten away from home tend to be higher in saturated fats and sodium than foods sourced in grocery stores and prepared and consumed in the household. In the frame of this article, 'foods eaten away from home' refers to commercially produced foods that are consumed in restaurants, as take-away meals or street foods, in canteens and so on, as opposed to meals prepared and consumed at home or at someone else's private dwelling. The aim of this article is to show the effect this change in dietary habit has on nutritional intake and to discuss the role that nutrient density—defined here as the ratio of essential nutrients to energy—can play in improving nutrition in line with these modern lifestyles.

Data from national intake surveys show that over a period of 30 years, Americans aged ≥ 18 years became 40% more likely to eat three or more meals per week away from home [1]. They also found that the frequency of eating out positively correlated with intake of energy as well as total energy from fat, particularly saturated fat [1]. The authors conclude that this trend, with the accompanying increase in calorie and fat intake, is likely to contribute to the increased prevalence of obesity [1].

The increased caloric intake away from home was confirmed by another study in the U.S.: Guthrie and colleagues [2] found that between 1977–1978 and 1994–1996, the contribution to the total diet of food consumed away from home at

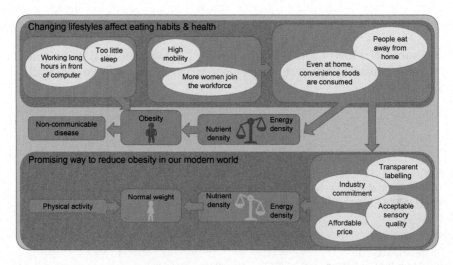

Fig. 26.1 Changing lifestyles affect our eating habits as well as the composition of our diets and consequently obesity prevalence and public health. Initiatives targeted at increasing nutrient density and decreasing energy density can counter these negative developments. *Source* Developed by the authors for this publication

locations such as restaurants, fast food establishments, schools and day care centers increased from ~20 to 30% of calories. This trend was most pronounced in young adults aged 18–39 years, who showed a near doubling of calories eaten away from home. Similarly, in a study in 10 European countries, eating out was a phenomenon found to be more common in younger than in older adults [3]. For children as well as adults, the main contributors to this shift were fast food restaurants [2]. In children, this category even caught up with meals at schools and daycare centers at the expense of meals eaten at home, resulting in an increase in calories from fast food from 2 to 10% [2]. With the exception of school meals, which had more calcium and dietary fiber than food eaten at home, meals consumed away from home tended to have a higher energy density and a lower nutrient density. A recent study showed that cooking at home was more frequently associated with a higher dietary quality in regard to intakes of energy, fat, sugar and carbohydrates than fast food, frozen and ready-to-eat meals [4].

A recent review confirmed that meals eaten away from home tended to be higher in energy and fat and lower in micronutrients [5]. Lachat and colleagues [5] showed that eating a considerable proportion of food outside the home was a global phenomenon, even though there were differences in the importance of the various categories: While in the U.S. fast food made up a higher proportion, in Spain restaurants and in Kenya street foods were the predominant source of calories besides what was consumed at home. Still, with one exception, the study showed a clear correlation between eating out and energy density of the diet. A systematic review investigating the link between eating away from home and body weight concluded—even though the definitions of eating away from home varied greatly—that the evidence suggested a positive correlation between eating out and obesity [6].

26.2 Convenience Foods, Eating Out and Low Micronutrient Intake

Even when eating at home, however, commercially produced convenience foods are a popular alternative to preparing meals from basic ingredients. Ready-to-eat processed foods were also found to be a very heterogeneous category, with fortified cereals providing significant amounts of specific micronutrients, while for example sugar-sweetened beverages had a high impact on sugar consumption, with no significant nutritional value [7]. Consequently, concerns have been raised that increased intakes of such convenience foods, as well as the energy-dense products frequently consumed when eating away from home, are at least partially to blame for the increase in obesity: Rates have doubled globally since 1980, resulting in 1.4 billion overweight adults in 2008 and more than 40 million overweight children under the age of five in 2011 [8]. Energy-dense diets appear to play an important part in the obesity epidemic: A series of experiments in humans showed that energy density rather than fat content determined overeating [9]. The authors reason that humans have a weak innate ability to adapt food intake to its energy density, as this had not been important with the meager diets of our ancestors [9].

Low access to supermarkets where fresh foods could be bought and the ready availability of take-out meals were found to contribute to a obesogenic environment [10].

Sleep deprivation, often a result of our hectic lifestyles, appears to affect appetite regulation and thereby contributes to weight gain [11]; increased energy intake was also caused by cognitively demanding, typically computerized, work combined with the pressure to excel which has become an integral part of modern society [12]. Some of these lifestyles favoring the development of obesity are unlikely to disappear anytime soon, as they are thought to increase competitiveness in the modern world [12].

At the same time, intakes of a number of vitamins seem to be low in a significant proportion of the population, even in affluent Western countries, with vitamins A, D, E and folic acid appearing to be the most critical [13]. There is some evidence that inadequate micronutrient intakes are even more pronounced in obese persons, even though some of this might be at least partially due to underreporting of food consumption [14]. However, not only low intakes, but also impaired bioavailability and utilization of micronutrients may be involved in the inadequate micronutrient status in obesity. For some nutrients, such as iron, the low level inflammation that accompanies obesity probably decreases its absorption [15]. The lower levels of serum 25-hydroxy vitamin D found in overweight and obese subjects compared to their normal weight counterparts [16] might at least partially be due to increased sequestration of the fat-soluble vitamin in adipose tissue [17].

It is well accepted that adequate nutrition is important for short- as well as long-term development. Moreover, good health and nutrition are thought to be important factors for a child's ability to rise out of poverty [18], which is particularly important, as low socio-economic status is in itself a risk factor for inadequate nutrition, obesity and consequently the development of diseases later in life [19]. It is neither realistic nor necessarily desirable to encourage people to go back to preparing all their meals from unprocessed foods. As more women join the workforce and mobility is increasingly demanded by the labor market, it should not be expected that people will revert to extended lunch breaks at home. Consequently, it is crucial to find approaches that combine modern lifestyles with diets that reduce the risk of obesity while providing sufficient amounts of essential nutrients at reasonable prices. It is not an intrinsic characteristic of commercially produced foods that they are high in energy and low in micronutrients. According to the recently published scientific statement of the American Society of Nutrition, processed foods are important for food and nutrient security, and "*diets are more likely to meet food guidance recommendations if nutrient-dense foods, either processed or not, are selected* [20]".

By eating out, consumers delegate the food preparation to commercial entities and consequently rely on the availability of healthy, nutrient-dense choices. Therefore, ways need to be found to provide foods that allow the diet to be energy-neutral while providing sufficient amounts of essential nutrients and consequently forming the basis for optimal health. The nutrient-density approach is promising, as it has been shown that consuming nutrient-dense foods led to a decreased risk of cardiovascular disease, diabetes and all-cause mortality [21]. Various indicators to measure nutrient density have been proposed, and these were reviewed in detail elsewhere [22]. One example of an indicator of nutrient density is the Nutrient Rich Food Index (NRF), which can be used to rank foods, single meals or diets according to their nutritional value, and can help consumers improve their diet [23]. When applied to the diets of an elderly Dutch cohort, the Nutrient Rich Food Index showed a correlation with all-cause mortality, while no association with CVD incidence was found [24]. This latter finding might reflect the importance of past rather than present diet, as more attention might be paid to the quality of the diet once a disease is diagnosed: The authors report that participants with hypertension and diabetes actually had a higher NRF score than their peers [24].

26.3   The Nutrient Density Approach to Nutrition

While nutrient-dense foods are often more expensive than energy-dense options, a recent study identified around 30 fruits and vegetables which had a good nutrient-to-cost ratio, including, for example, fresh oranges and carrots, but also canned or frozen vegetables such as tomatoes and green peas [25]. It had also been suggested that certain processed foods such as canned fruits represent convenient, durable alternatives with a micronutrient content comparable to the fresh product [26]. Milk and milk products are good sources of calcium, but also of protein, and they represent, together with beans and eggs, further examples of high-quality foods available at affordable prices [27]. When consumer acceptance measured as frequency of use was included in the calculation, white potatoes emerged as a food that combined high nutritional quality with a relatively low energy density and high affordability and acceptance [28].

In a next step, efforts should be made to integrate the concept of nutrient density into the segment of foods eaten away from home, as this allows combining modern lifestyles with a balanced diet (Fig. 26.1). Traditional as well as emerging technologies exist that make it possible to produce affordable, acceptable and nutritionally valuable foods, meals and diets. However, the solutions have to take into account the changing needs and windows of opportunities over the life course. While a range of stakeholders such as industry, government and academia have a responsibility to educate the public via measures such as laws and labeling of foods, the responsibility of the individual as well as his or her right to freedom of choice cannot be neglected. Consumers need to understand and be able to easily identify which foods or diets in stores, restaurants or fast food outlets are good for them. However, they will also need to be motivated to eat, but not overeat these foods, which can only be achieved by the right balance between palatability and appetite control [29]. Therefore, it is not sufficient to maximize the micronutrient content of a food while reducing its energy content. However, high protein and dietary fiber were found to be useful components when developing diets that were tasty, but did not result in overconsumption [29].

Given the impact a nutrient-dense, low-energy diet can be expected to have on health [21], the nutrient density approach can be a valuable tool in nutrition education and dietary guidance. The opportunity is to understand how nutrition modulates health and to identify, develop and implement nutritional solutions promoting a healthy life. The complex relationship between nutrition, obesity, modern life styles, and non-communicable diseases, but also poverty or low socio-economic status, is not entirely understood. However, despite the wide range of factors affecting health, we feel that shifting diets from energy-dense to nutrient-dense can have a significant effect on the risk of developing chronic diseases along the life course and helping to keep not only life expectancy, but also quality of life, high. Demographic changes such as the increase in life expectancy, aging of population and urbanization pose further challenges for food and nutritional security: ever more food needs to be produced with fewer resources [30]. Consequently, it has been proposed to include sustainability as an additional factor in the equation for a desirable diet [31].

However, while the concept of nutrient density has been studied in depth and various indicators have been developed to measure it, no consensus has yet been reached as to which is the most appropriate of these for assessing overall dietary quality. A generally accepted, transparent system is needed that can classify individual foods as well as complete diets based on their quality. Moreover, this system needs to be communicated to consumers in easily understandable terms, allowing them to base their nutritional choices on it so as to achieve a more balanced diet.

26.4   The Shared Responsibility for Developing Better Nutrition

Scientists and the food industry should jointly develop options for affordable nutrient-enriched products that can cover nutritional deficits in consumers' diets. One of the challenges, but also opportunities, for food industry and gastronomy is to develop products and services which enable people to choose appealing, affordable diets which, in combination with physical activity, allow for optimal health throughout the life-course. Enabling them to make their low-priced market offerings healthier through nutrient fortification and by replacing or reducing amounts of unhealthy ingredients such as saturated fats, trans-fatty acids, sodium and sugar would be a major step forward along the road to good nutrition. In addition, transparent, well-accepted labeling of foods in stores and restaurants will be necessary to help consumers easily understand the positive influence that the consumption of nutrient-dense foods can have on their overall energy and nutrient balance. Consequently, a combined effort on the part of academia, governments, the food industry and the gastronomy sector is necessary to find ways of providing nutritious, convenient, affordable and acceptable products that are compatible with a modern lifestyle.

26.5 Summary: Key Messages

- In affluent societies, and increasingly in low-and middle-income countries too, large numbers of people depend on food not prepared by themselves.
- At the same time, an imbalance exists between elevated energy and inadequate micronutrient intakes.
- Increasing the nutrient density of diets is a promising approach to improving nutrition in our modern world.
- Changed dietary habits come with new responsibilities for food providers, who need to make sure that their products provide adequate amounts of nutrients.
- Acceptability, transparency, labeling and costs will play a key role in convincing consumers to integrate such products into their diets.

References

1. Kant, A.K. and B.I. Graubard, *Eating out in America, 1987–2000: trends and nutritional correlates.* Preventive Medicine, 2004. **38**(2): p. 243–249.
2. Guthrie, J.F., B.-H. Lin, and E. Frazao, *Role of Food Prepared Away from Home in the American Diet, 1977–78 versus 1994–96: Changes and Consequences.* Journal of Nutrition Education and Behavior, 2002. **34**(3): p. 140–150.
3. Orfanos, P., et al., *Eating out of home: energy, macro- and micronutrient intakes in 10 European countries. The European Prospective Investigation into Cancer and Nutrition.* European Journal of Clinical Nutrition, 2009. **63**(S4): p. S239–S262.
4. Wolfson, J.A. and S.N. Bleich, *Is cooking at home associated with better diet quality or weight-loss intention?* Public Health Nutrition, 2015. **18**(08): p. 1397–1406.
5. Lachat, C., et al., *Eating out of home and its association with dietary intake: a systematic review of the evidence.* Obesity Reviews, 2012. **13**(4): p. 329–346.
6. Bezerra, I.N., C. Curioni, and R. Sichieri, *Association between eating out of home and body weight.* Nutrition Reviews, 2012. **70**(2): p. 65–79.
7. Eicher-Miller, H.A., V.L. Fulgoni, and D.R. Keast, *Contributions of Processed Foods to Dietary Intake in the US from 2003–2008: A Report of the Food and Nutrition Science Solutions Joint Task Force of the Academy of Nutrition and Dietetics, American Society for Nutrition, Institute of Food Technologists, and International Food Information Council.* The Journal of Nutrition, 2012. **142**(11): p. 2065S–2072S.
8. World Health Organization. *Fact sheet N°311: Obesity and overweight.* 2014 March 2014 May 02, 2014]; Available from: http://www.who.int/mediacentre/factsheets/fs311/en/.
9. Prentice, A.M. and S.A. Jebb, *Fast foods, energy density and obesity: a possible mechanistic link.* Obesity Reviews, 2003. **4**(4): p. 187–194.

10. Giskes, K., et al., *A systematic review of environmental factors and obesogenic dietary intakes among adults: are we getting closer to understanding obesogenic environments?* Obesity Reviews, 2011. **12**(5): p. e95–e106.

11. Chaput, J.P., *Short sleep duration as a cause of obesity: myth or reality?* Obesity Reviews, 2011. **12**(5): p. e2–e3.

12. Tremblay, A. and H. Arguin, *Healthy Eating at School to Compensate for the Activity-Related Obesigenic Lifestyle in Children and Adolescents: The Quebec Experience.* Advances in Nutrition: An International Review Journal, 2011. **2**(2): p. 167S–170S.

13. Troesch, B., et al., *Dietary surveys indicate vitamin intakes below recommendations are common in representative Western countries.* British Journal of Nutrition, 2012. **108**(4): p. 692–698.

14. Agarwal, S., et al., *Comparison of Prevalence of Inadequate Nutrient Intake Based on Body Weight Status of Adults in the United States: An Analysis of NHANES 2001–2008.* Journal of the American College of Nutrition, 2015. **34**(2): p. 126–134.

15. Cepeda-Lopez, A.C., I. Aeberli, and M.B. Zimmermann, *Does obesity increase risk for iron deficiency? A review of the literature and the potential mechanisms.* International Journal for Vitamin and Nutrition Research, 2010. **80**(4–5): p. 263–70.

16. Samuel, L. and L.N. Borrell, *The effect of body mass index on optimal vitamin D status in U.S. adults: the National Health and Nutrition Examination Survey 2001–2006.* Ann Epidemiol, 2013. **23**(7): p. 409–14.

17. Wortsman, J., et al., *Decreased bioavailability of vitamin D in obesity.* The American Journal of Clinical Nutrition, 2000. **72**(3): p. 690–693.

18. UNICEF, *Improving child nutrition- The achievable imperative for global progress,* UNICEF, Editor. 2013: New York.

19. Pampel, F.C., J.T. Denney, and P.M. Krueger, *Obesity, SES, and economic development: A test of the reversal hypothesis.* Social Science & Medicine, 2012. **74**(7): p. 1073–1081.

20. Weaver, C.M., et al., *Processed foods: contributions to nutrition.* The American Journal of Clinical Nutrition, 2014. **99**(6): p. 1525–1542.

21. Chiuve, S.E., L. Sampson, and W.C. Willett, *The association between a nutritional quality index and risk of chronic disease.* Am J Prev Med, 2011. **40**(5): p. 505–13.

22. Drewnowski, A., *Concept of a nutritious food: toward a nutrient density score.* Am J Clin Nutr, 2005. **82**(4): p. 721–32.

23. Drewnowski, A., *Defining Nutrient Density: Development and Validation of the Nutrient Rich Foods Index.* Journal of the American College of Nutrition, 2009. **28**(4): p. 421S–426S.

24. Streppel, M.T., et al., *Nutrient-rich foods, cardiovascular diseases and all-cause mortality: the Rotterdam study.* Eur J Clin Nutr, 2014. **68**(6): p. 741–747.

25. Darmon, N., et al., *A Nutrient Density Standard for Vegetables and Fruits: Nutrients per Calorie and Nutrients per Unit Cost.* Journal of the American Dietetic Association, 2005. **105**(12): p. 1881–1887.

26. Durst, R.W. and G.W. Weaver, *Nutritional content of fresh and canned peaches.* Journal of the Science of Food and Agriculture, 2013. **93**(3): p. 593–603.

27. Drewnowski, A., *The contribution of milk and milk products to micronutrient density and affordability of the U.S. diet.* J Am Coll Nutr, 2011. **30**(5 Suppl 1): p. 422S–8S.

28. Drewnowski, A. and C.D. Rehm, *Vegetable Cost Metrics Show That Potatoes and Beans Provide Most Nutrients Per Penny.* PLoS ONE, 2013. **8**(5): p. e63277.

29. Poortvliet, P.C., et al., *Effects of a healthy meal course on spontaneous energy intake, satiety and palatability.* British Journal of Nutrition, 2007. **97**(03): p. 584–590.

30. Von Grebmer, K., et al., *Global Hunger Index. The challenge of hunger: ensuring sustainable food security under land, water and energy stress.* 2012, International Food Policy Research Institute: Washington, DC.

31. Drewnowski, A., *Healthy diets for a healthy planet.* The American Journal of Clinical Nutrition, 2014 epub.

Chapter 27
Does It Work? Is It Worth It? Evaluating the Costs and Benefits of Nutritional Interventions

Simon Wieser and Christina Tzogiou

Abstract This chapter attempts to demonstrate how economic evaluation can help maximize the cost-effectiveness of nutritional interventions. The main types of economic evaluation are outlined and the input parameters necessary to carry them out are described. The cost-effectiveness plane presented is as a way to synthesize all the information and to decide whether an intervention is worth the money spent on it. The importance and strength of this approach are discussed, along with its limitations. The process of economic evaluation can contribute substantially to the design and identification of cost-effective interventions and thus help achieve the maximum reduction of malnutrition with the limited funds available. The cost-effectiveness framework developed in health economics is a useful tool for the design and evaluation of nutritional interventions. It forces the evaluators to explore the various aspects affecting the effectiveness of the intervention in a real-world situation. It also takes account of the different cost dimensions affecting the health and wellbeing of the individual as well as overall economic development.

Keywords Economic evaluation · Economic development · Cost-effectiveness · Cost-effectiveness plane · Nutritional intervention · Malnutrition · DALYs · Public health

27.1 The Scale of Malnutrition in the Developing World

Malnutrition is still a massive problem in many parts of the developing world. Hunger and insufficient intake of macro- and micronutrients lead to immense human suffering and inhibit social and economic development. Malnutrition in

S. Wieser (✉) · C. Tzogiou
Winterthur Institute of Health Economics, Zurich University of Applied Sciences,
Gertrudstrasse 15, Postfach 958, 8401 Winterthur, Switzerland
e-mail: simon.wieser@zhaw.ch

C. Tzogiou
e-mail: christina.tzogiou@zhaw.ch

© Springer International Publishing AG 2017   343
H.K. Biesalski et al. (eds.), *Sustainable Nutrition in a Changing World*,
DOI 10.1007/978-3-319-55942-1_27

women of childbearing age and young children is particularly detrimental, due to its often irreversible consequences on physical and cognitive development [1, 2]. Many malnourished children are stuck in a poverty trap, as they will not be able to reach their full potential and thus will become poor parents in adult life [3].

Governments, international organizations and NGOs spend large amounts of money on interventions designed to reduce malnutrition and nutrient deficiencies. The Indian government, for example, is spending approximately 1% of Indian GDP on food programs [4], while donors at the global conference on Nutrition for Growth in 2013 pledged to commit over US$23 billion to the struggle against hunger and malnutrition in the developing world [5]. Interventions aiming to improve nutrition in general include price subsidies, the distribution of staple foods or food vouchers, cash transfers, and educational programs. Interventions aiming at micronutrient deficiencies include micronutrient supplementation and various forms of food fortification. Interventions may target the overall population, specific socio-economic groups, or individual age groups.

However, it is often unclear whether these interventions work and whether they represent good value for money. A number of studies have contributed substantially to the identification of cost-effective interventions in various populations [6–12], but the overall evidence is limited and often outdated. Some important tools are available for the assessment of new interventions, but these usually consider only part of the health and cost consequences of malnutrition. The *Lives Saved Tool (LiST)*, for example, considers only the life-years lost due to maternal and child malnutrition, but not the important lifetime consequences for the surviving children [13].

The main objective of this chapter is to show how economic evaluation can help maximize the cost-effectiveness of nutritional interventions. We lay out the main types of economic evaluation and describe the input parameters necessary to carry them out. We focus on the cost-effectiveness plane as a way of synthesizing all the information and deciding whether an intervention is worth the money spent on it. We will show the importance and strength of this approach, but also its limitations.

27.2 The Main Questions of Economic Evaluations

An economic evaluation of a nutritional intervention is concerned with two main questions: *Does the intervention work?* and, if yes, *Is the intervention worth it?* The first question is the question of *effectiveness,* and the answer should tell us the extent to which malnutrition and its consequences are reduced by the intervention. The second question is the question of *cost-effectiveness,* and the answer should tell us whether the money is well spent on this intervention or whether it would be better spent on other interventions.

27.3 Does It Work? and if Yes, to What Extent?

The first step in evaluating the cost-effectiveness of a nutritional intervention is to assess its effectiveness. This involves collecting all the available evidence on the effectiveness of the intervention in the context of the current nutritional situation and comparing it with suitable alternative interventions.

The effectiveness of an intervention has multiple dimensions:

1. The *clinical effectiveness* of the intervention in reducing nutritional deficiencies and their adverse health consequences. This may be measured by intermediary outcomes, such as changes in biomarkers (hemoglobin level, urinary iodine concentration, etc.) or in anthropometric measures (stunting rate, birth weight, etc.), or final outcomes, such as lower morbidity and mortality, and effects on the cognitive development of children (IQ scores, etc.).
2. The *effectiveness in the mode of delivery* of the intervention in reaching the targeted households with the designated quantity of additional nutrients. This effectiveness may be weakened if the intervention fails to reach the targeted socio-economic group, if resources are lost due to corruption and mismanagement, or if the distribution channels are not sustainable in the long run.
3. The *compliance of the household* with the intended use of the nutrients provided. The additional foods targeted at pre-school children or pregnant women may, for example, be consumed by other household members. Furthermore, micronutrient supplements provided to the household may not be consumed at all, or not in the intended quantity and frequency.
4. The degree of *substitution of other food sources* may substantially influence the effectiveness of the intervention. The households may buy less food and different types of food than they did before the intervention, and this may lead to unexpected changes in the overall nutrient intake. In an extreme case, the additional calories provided may be completely offset by a reduction in consumption of the foods previously purchased on the market.

Effectiveness in these four dimensions is well ensured in the case of iodized salt, for example: (1) The clinical effectiveness is well documented; (2) centralized salt iodization of commercially distributed salt allows all households to be reached (no targeting necessary, sustainability of distribution channel); (3) compliance is assured, as salt is universally consumed on a regular basis; and (4) substitution is not an issue, as consumption of other foods will not be reduced. Nevertheless, it is important to bear in mind the target population. For example, a six-month-old infant that is fed with non-fortified complementary foods and is no longer being breastfed may not have a sufficient iodine intake.

However, for many other nutritional interventions, effectiveness is much less clear in one or more of these dimensions. Researchers have the task of assessing the effectiveness in all these dimensions with all the methodological tools available (randomized trials, observational studies, project monitoring, etc.). Program leaders have the task of choosing, designing and implementing nutritional interventions in order to maximize their effectiveness.

Generating the evidence for the effectiveness of nutritional interventions is often difficult. It may, for instance, be unethical to carry out studies with severely malnourished children. Randomized trials of clinical effectiveness are often hard to conduct, and observational studies are hampered by the difficulty of monitoring what people are eating. Yet there has recently been substantial progress in the randomized evaluation of policies [3].

27.4 Is It Worth It?

Economic evaluations can help us choose the most cost-effective nutritional interventions and thus obtain the highest reduction of malnutrition that can be achieved with the financial resources available. These evaluations are based on a thorough comparison of all the costs and benefits of the interventions.

Figure 27.1 provides an overview of the most important cost categories considered in economic evaluations. The figure distinguishes three dimensions of these costs: (1) Whether they represent an expenditure of resources of other individuals in the society or a loss of resources for the individuals affected by malnutrition; (2) the

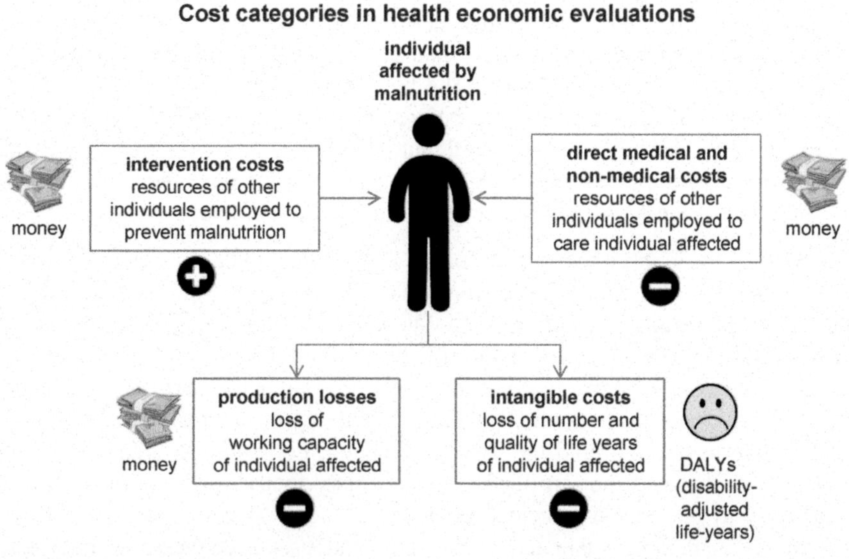

Cost categories in health economic evaluations

Fig. 27.1 The figure illustrates the cost categories which should be considered in a complete evaluation of a nutritional intervention. The *plus/minus* signs show whether these costs will increase or decrease in a typical intervention. Direct costs, production losses and intangible costs would disappear in the case of an ideal intervention or if malnutrition could be eradicated by economic development. *Source* Created by the authors for this publication

dimension employed to measure these costs (money, disability-adjusted life-years [DALYs]); and (3) whether these costs will increase or decrease in a typical intervention (plus/minus signs).

The *intervention costs* include the overall costs of the nutritional program. In the case of a price subsidy, these costs should thus not only include the amount of the subsidies paid but also the program administration costs (administration, field personnel).

The *direct medical and non-medical costs* include all the expenses incurred to treat the diseases and disabilities attributable to malnutrition. They correspond to the costs of medical services, medications, and transportation, for example, and are also quantified in monetary terms. These expenditures may be covered by the public healthcare system, by NGOs or—as is most often the case in developing countries—directly by the families of the individuals affected.

Production losses represent the loss of working capacity of the malnourished individuals due to lower productivity at work, absence from the workplace, disability, and premature death. They are a loss of current and future monetary incomes for the individuals affected, and lead to lower economic growth for the country as whole.

Intangible costs represent the quality of life and the years of life lost due to malnutrition. They are usually quantified in terms of DALYs, a metric developed by the WHO and the Word Bank in the context of the Global Burden of Disease, Injuries and Risk Factors Study [14]. DALYs express the total health burden of a disease in healthy life-years lost by combining the life-years lost due to premature mortality caused by the disease with a measure that quantifies the years lived in states of reduced health [15]. These health states are weighted with disability weights reflecting the magnitude of the reduced quality of life.[1] DALYs have important advantages over other outcome measures of nutritional interventions, such as the degree of coverage of the population reached with the intervention or other nutrition-specific outcomes. They are a direct measure of the final goal of the intervention, namely to improve health and thereby reduce mortality and increase the quality of life. Furthermore, the DALYs saved may be compared with interventions in other health-related domains besides nutrition, such as health care, sanitation, access to clean water, and so on.

Disability weights have recently been re-estimated using a new methodology which is based on large population surveys [18]. Nearly all disability weights for the health consequences of malnutrition have increased with the new methodology [19], and the discounting of future health and age-weights has been eliminated. Based on this new estimation, the burden of malnutrition thus appears substantially higher than previously estimated.

When estimating the cost consequences of malnutrition, we should also consider whether these consequences are permanent or not. The physical and cognitive

---

[1]Additional DALY weights for some malnutrition-related diseases have been proposed by Stein [16] as well as Zimmermann and Qaim [17].

development of children may be irreversibly affected by the malnutrition of the children during their first years of life and by the malnutrition of their mothers before and during pregnancy. The resulting irreversible long-term cost consequences are likely to dominate the overall costs of malnutrition in these particularly vulnerable populations [19, 20].

27.5 The Cost-Effectiveness Plane as a Key Analytic Tool

The evaluation of a nutritional intervention is usually carried out by means of a cost-effectiveness analysis or a cost-benefit analysis. Both types of economic evaluation are based on the costs presented in Fig. 27.1 and compare the costs and benefits of the interventions. However, the benefits are measured in terms of DALYs averted in the cost-effectiveness analysis[2] and in monetary terms in the cost-benefit analysis. We focus here on the cost-effectiveness analysis because it is better suited to the economic evaluation of nutritional interventions in developing countries. Furthermore, a cost-effectiveness analysis can be transformed relatively easily into a cost-benefit analysis.

Figure 27.2 compares the costs and benefits of a nutritional intervention in a simple diagram, the *cost-effectiveness plane*. The horizontal axis measures the DALYs averted by the intervention, while the vertical axis shows the monetary costs and savings of the intervention. The DALYs now appear as a benefit, as the DALYs prevented by a successful nutritional intervention express the effectiveness of the intervention. The vertical axis measures the costs of the intervention and simultaneously the monetary savings in terms of reduced direct costs and production losses. Figure 27.2 illustrates these monetary dimensions with an example: The upward-pointing arrow represents intervention costs of US$600, while the downward-pointing arrow represents the direct cost and production losses of US$400 averted by the intervention. The net social costs of the interventions thus amount to US$200. The cost-effectiveness is calculated by dividing the net social costs of the intervention of US$200 by the 40 DALYs averted. The resulting cost-effectiveness ratio of 5 US$/DALY can be interpreted as the net price the society has to pay to avert one DALY.

The answer to the question "*Is the intervention worth it?*" depends on how much society is willing to pay for averting 1 DALY. Five US$/DALY looks like a good buy, but what if the net cost per DALY is at 500, 5000, or 50,000 US$/DALY? Whether an intervention is cost-effective or not must be determined by comparing the net costs per DALY averted with a threshold value. The WHO

---

[2]Strictly speaking, it is not a cost-effectiveness but a cost-utility analysis, as DALYs are really a measure of health-related utility [21].

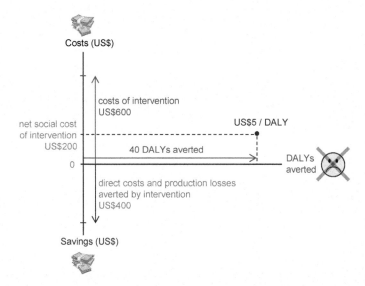

Fig. 27.2 The cost-effectiveness plane illustrates the different dimensions of the costs and benefits of an intervention. Monetary costs and savings are represented on the *vertical axis* and DALYs averted on the *horizontal axis*. The cost-effectiveness ratio (US$5/DALY) can be interpreted as the net social cost of averting one DALY. The numbers were chosen for the process of explanation and do not refer to a specific intervention. *Source* Created by the authors for this publication

recommendations on cost-effectiveness define an intervention as cost-effective if the cost per DALY is between one and three times the GDP per capita and as highly cost-effective if the cost per DALY is less than the GDP per capita [22]. From a social perspective, it would of course be best if the intervention were cost-saving. This is the case when the monetary costs saved by the intervention are greater than the costs of the intervention.

The results of a cost-effectiveness analysis can be translated into a cost-benefit analysis by assigning a monetary value to the DALYs averted. If we assume a value of US$50 per DALY in the example in Fig. 27.2, then the 40 DALYs averted correspond to savings of US$2,000. Adding these to the savings of US$400 in terms of direct costs and production losses averted, we obtain total savings of US$2,400. Having costs and benefits all in the same monetary dimension allows us to calculate the *return on investment* of the prevention program by dividing the total savings by the costs of the intervention, this figure equaling 3 ([US$2,400 − US$600]/US$600 = 3). For every dollar invested in the nutritional program, society would thus gain three additional dollars. Assigning a monetary value to DALYs is, however, often criticized as being ethically and methodologically questionable [23].

27.6   Strengths and Limitations of Cost-Effectiveness Evaluations

The cost-effectiveness analysis is an excellent framework for evaluating the overall impact of a nutritional intervention. The various dimensions determining the effectiveness of an intervention oblige the evaluator to identify and quantify the health consequences averted by it. The consequent estimation of the number of DALYs averted represents a crucial input for the cost-effectiveness estimation. This estimation is often the most difficult part of the evaluation—a difficulty common to evaluations of interventions in other public health fields [24].

Economic evaluations may be carried out with a view to identifying the most cost-effective interventions to be implemented or as policy evaluations when the intervention is already in place. Additionally, the evaluations may contribute to the design of new interventions by identifying populations in particular need or by detecting which features of existing interventions work and which do not.

However, the number of economic evaluations of nutritional interventions is still limited, and their quality could often be substantially improved. Higher standards in the evaluation design and in the reporting of results are needed. It may be useful to take a look at similar efforts in other public health fields [25] and at the approaches to the economic evaluations of nutritional interventions used by applied economists in the fields of agricultural economics (e.g. Vosti et al. [26] or Masters et al. [27]) and development economics (e.g. Banerjee et al. [28] or Luo et al. [29]).

Economic evaluations have a number of limitations.

First, they represent modeling exercises combining information from a multitude of sources in extended causal chains. These chains lead from policy measures, through changes in behavior, nutritional status and health, to economic and quality-of-life outcomes. The results of these models are thus only as good as the underlying scientific evidence and the accuracy of the model represented by the relevant causal links.

Second, it is often hard to acquire the evidence necessary to carry out the evaluation. Evidence as to the prevalence of nutritional deficiencies in specific populations is often missing or outdated, and studies on the effectiveness of nutritional interventions often only report the effects on short-term nutritional outcomes. Sometimes it may also be difficult to obtain the data required to calculate the necessary population-attributable fraction of a nutritional risk factor or the disability weights for specific health states. This is especially true for sub-clinical nutritional deficiencies which do not lead to immediately apparent health impairments.

Third, these evaluations require the combination of nutritional, clinical, economic and modelling knowledge. These different types of knowledge are seldom present in a single research group. Interdisciplinary research teams must thus be assembled, and must agree upon a common strategy for proceeding with the evaluation.

27.7 Conclusions

The economic evaluation of nutritional interventions can contribute substantially to the design and identification of cost-effective interventions and thus help achieve the maximum reduction of malnutrition with the limited funds available. The cost-effectiveness framework developed in health economics is a useful tool for the design and evaluation of nutritional interventions. It forces the evaluators to explore the various aspects affecting the effectiveness of the intervention in a real-world situation. It also takes account of the various cost dimensions affecting the health and wellbeing of the individual as well as overall economic development.

27.8 Summary: Key Messages

- Economic evaluation can help maximize the cost-effectiveness of nutritional interventions.
- The cost-effectiveness plane is as a way of synthesizing all the information and deciding whether an intervention is worth the money spent on it.
- The process of economic evaluation can contribute substantially to the design and identification of cost-effective interventions and thus help achieve the maximum reduction of malnutrition with the limited funds available.
- The cost-effectiveness framework developed in health economics is a useful tool for designing and evaluating nutritional interventions. It forces the evaluators to explore the various aspects affecting the effectiveness of the intervention in a real-world situation. It also takes account of the different cost dimensions affecting the health and wellbeing of the individual as well as overall economic development.

References

1. Black, R.E., et al., *Maternal and child undernutrition and overweight in low-income and middle-income countries.* Lancet, 2013. **382**(9890): p. 427–51.
2. Biesalski, H.K., *Hidden hunger.* 2013, Springer: Berlin; New York.
3. Banerjee, A. and E. Duflo, *Poor Economics: a radical thinking of the way to fight global poverty.* 2011, Philadelphia: PublicAffairs.
4. Shankar, S.T. and T. Sridhar, *Does food subsidy affect household nutrition?* Int J Sociol Soc Policy, 2014. **34**(1/2): p. 107–132.
5. SUN Movement, *Annual Progress Report.* 2014, Scaling Up Nutrition.
6. Bhutta, Z.A., et al., *Evidence-based interventions for improvement of maternal and child nutrition: what can be done and at what cost?* Lancet, 2013. **382**(9890): p. 452–77.
7. Horton, S. and R.H. Steckel, *Malnutrition,* in *How much have global problems cost the world?,* B. Lomborg, Editor. 2013, Cambridge University Press: Cambridge. p. 247–272.

8. Horton, S., et al., *Scaling up nutrition: What will it cost?* 2010, Washington, D.C.: World Bank.
9. Dewey, K.G. and S. Adu-Afarwuah, *Systematic review of the efficacy and effectiveness of complementary feeding interventions in developing countries.* Maternal & Child Nutrition, 2008. **4**: p. 24–85.
10. Horton, S., H. Alderman, and J.A. Rivera, *Hunger and malnutrition. Copenhagen consensus challenge paper.* 2008, Copenhagen Consensus Center.
11. Bhutta, Z.A., et al., *What works? Interventions for maternal and child undernutrition and survival.* Lancet, 2008. **371**(9610): p. 417–440.
12. Fiedler, J.L. and B. Macdonald, *A strategic approach to the unfinished fortification agenda: feasibility, costs, and cost-effectiveness analysis of fortification programs in 48 countries.* Food Nutr Bull, 2009. **30**(4): p. 283–316.
13. Walker, N., Y. Tam, and I. Friberg, *Overview of the Lives Saved Tool (LiST).* BMC Public Health, 2013. **13**(Suppl 3): p. S1.
14. Murray, C.J. and A.D. Lopez, *The Global Burden of Disease: A comprehensive assessment of mortality and disability from diseases, injuries and risk factors in 1990 and projected to 2020.* Global Burden of disease and injury Series, ed. C.J. Murray and A.D. Lopez. 1996, Cambridge: Harvard University Press. 1–1022.
15. Salomon, J.A., et al., *Healthy life expectancy for 187 countries, 1990–2010: a systematic analysis for the Global Burden Disease Study 2010.* Lancet, 2012. **380**(9859): p. 2144–62.
16. Stein, A.J., et al., *Analyzing the health benefits of biofortified staple crops by means of the disability-adjusted life years approach: a handbook focusing on iron, zinc and vitamin A.* HarvestPlus Technical Monograph. Vol. 4. 2005, Washington, DC: International Food Research Institute and International Center for Tropical Agriculture.
17. Zimmermann, R. and M. Qaim, *Potential health benefits of Golden Rice: a Philippine case study.* Food Policy, 2004. **29**(2): p. 147–168.
18. Vos, T., et al., *Years lived with disability (YLDs) for 1160 sequelae of 289 diseases and injuries 1990–2010: a systematic analysis for the Global Burden of Disease Study 2010.* Lancet, 2012. **380**(9859): p. 2163–96.
19. Plessow, R., et al., *Social costs of iron deficiency anemia in 6–59-month-old children in India.* PLoS One, 2015.
20. Wieser, S., et al., *Burden of micronutrient deficiencies by socio-economic strata in children aged 6 months to 5 years in the Philippines.* BMC Public Health, 2013. **13**(1): p. 1167.
21. Drummond, M., *Methods for the economic evaluation of health care programmes.* 1997, Oxford; New York: Oxford University Press.
22. WHO. *Cost effectiveness and strategic planning (WHO-CHOICE) - Cost-effectiveness thresholds.* [cited 2015 July 17, 2015]; Available from: http://www.who.int/choice/costs/CER_thresholds/en/.
23. Dolan, P. and R. Edlin, *Is it really possible to build a bridge between cost-benefit analysis and cost-effectiveness analysis?* J Health Econ, 2002. **21**(5): p. 827–43.
24. Weatherly, H., et al., *Methods for assessing the cost-effectiveness of public health interventions: Key challenges and recommendations.* Health Policy, 2009. **93**(2–3): p. 85–92.
25. Edwards, R.T., J.M. Charles, and H. Lloyd-Williams, *Public health economics: a systematic review of guidance for the economic evaluation of public health interventions and discussion of key methodological issues.* BMC Public Health, 2013. **13**(1): p. 1001.
26. Vosti, S.A., et al., *An Economic Optimization Model for Improving the Efficiency of Vitamin A Interventions: An Application to Young Children in Cameroon.* Food and Nutrition Bulletin, 2015. **36**(3 suppl): p. S193–S207.
27. Masters, W.A., et al., *Agriculture, nutrition, and health in global development: typology and metrics for integrated interventions and research.* Annals of the New York Academy of Sciences, 2014. **1331**(1): p. 258–269.

28. Banerjee, A., E. Duflo, and R. Glennerster, *Is Decentralized Iron Fortification a Feasible Option to Fight Anemia Among the Poorest?*, in *NBER Book Series - The Economics of Aging*, D.A. Wise, Editor. 2011, University of Chicago Press: Chicago. p. 317–344.
29. Luo, R., et al., *The Limits of Health and Nutrition Education: Evidence from Three Randomized-Controlled Trials in Rural China.* CESifo Economic Studies, 2012. **58**(2): p. 385–404.

Chapter 28
Approaches to Ensuring Food and Nutrition Security in the Elderly

M.H. Mohajeri, P. Weber and M. Eggersdorfer

Abstract Aging is not a single process, but an accumulation of modifications, affecting different parts of the body to varying degrees. An estimated 2 billion people aged 60 years and older will inhabit the planet in 2050. Advancing age increases the incidence of non-communicable diseases (NCDs). Epidemiologically, there is a direct link between nutritional status and several NCDs. There is compelling evidence that good nutrition is instrumental for maintaining good health among the elderly population, yet the value of high-quality dietary intake is often under-recognized. Vitamins B, D, E, polyunsaturated fatty acids and protein are especially important for maintaining health in older adults. Elderly individuals are particularly at risk of not receiving the nutrition required for maintaining their good physical and mental health status due to societal, familial, economical or medical reasons. The economic power of individuals, along with food prices, influences people's food choices. Accumulative evidence strongly suggests that food security is closely associated with demographic characteristics, food expenditure, variables and food supplement consumption. The focus of this article is on the parameters influencing nutrition (and malnutrition) within the elderly population, and this group's specific micronutrient needs.

Keywords Aging · Vitamin · NCD · Diet · Malnutrition · Policy guidelines

28.1 Introduction

The World Health Organization (WHO) Aging Report in 2014 indicated that the world's population of people aged 60 years and older will increase from 600 million in 2000 to 2 billion in 2050 [1]. Thus the percentage of people older than 60 years will increase from 11 to 22% by 2050.

M.H. Mohajeri (✉) · P. Weber · M. Eggersdorfer
DSM Nutritional Products Ltd., R&D Human Nutrition and Health,
P.O. Box 2676 Bldg. 205/216, CH-4002 Basel, Switzerland
e-mail: hasan.mohajeri@dsm.com

© Springer International Publishing AG 2017
H.K. Biesalski et al. (eds.), *Sustainable Nutrition in a Changing World*,
DOI 10.1007/978-3-319-55942-1_28

One of mankind's most remarkable achievements is increased life expectancy. Scientific breakthroughs and modern medicine have increased the average human lifespan by four years in just the past two decades [2]. Unfortunately, for many people this gain in years is not matched by gain in years of healthy life. Living longer brings many benefits but also confronts the aging population with age-specific needs. We face a continuous increase of NCDs such as osteoporosis, diabetes, Alzheimer's disease (AD), cardiovascular diseases (CVD) and cancer in the elderly population.

While the aging process itself is distinct from disease, it increases the vulnerability to becoming infirm (see [3]). The aging of the world's population is associated with a high burden of chronic diseases, of which many have a strong nutritional component. Aging and the linked pathologies are also accompanied by a multitude of social changes. Decreased income after retirement, lack of mobility and social contacts, as well as intakes of multiple medications, chronic alcoholism, depressive mood and loss of appetite often lead to a decrease in food intake [4].

There is growing evidence that lifestyle factors, including nutrition, have substantial effects on health and well-being. Yet over 70% of over 71-year olds do not meet the recommended intakes for fruits, vegetables and whole grains. Indeed, nutrition insufficiency is one of the major obstacles to human development, and economists see nutrition as an important input to economic growth [5]. Moreover, economic factors are also determinants of nutritional status. NCDs in later life may be prevented by good nutrition throughout the lifespan. Even improving nutrition later in life can delay the onset of certain NCDs [6]. Research needs to be intensified to understand how nutrition modulates health along the life course and to identify, develop and implement nutritional solutions which promote healthy aging.

Currently, government campaigns aim at promoting healthy lifestyles throughout life [7]. To be most effective, such educational programs should start as early as possible, ideally with the education of parents with regard to healthy nutrition for their children. However, education alone will not lead to better nutritional choices. Food pricing, sensory characteristics and food availability will also play an important role, as will the provision of food at nursing homes for the elderly.

The U.S. Department of Agriculture (USDA) defines household food security as "access by all members at all times to enough food for an active, healthy life". At a minimum, nutritionally adequate and safe foods should be readily available, and also capable of acquisition in socially acceptable ways (i.e. without stealing, accessing emergency food supplies, or relying on other coping strategies). By analogy, food insecurity implies a "limited or uncertain availability of nutritionally adequate and safe foods or limited or uncertain ability to acquire acceptable foods in socially acceptable ways" (see: [8]).

Kim et al. [9] examined the effect of food security and participation in food assistance programs on overweight and depression among elderly individuals and their spouses. The authors showed that elderly people affected by food insecurity at follow-up had significantly higher BMI. In addition, elderly people who were food-insecure at baseline experienced greater increases in BMI than their food-secure counterparts. Moreover, there was a link between increased BMI and the transition from food-secure to insecure living. In addition, significantly higher depression scores were found among the food-insecure elderly people than their food-secure counterparts. This study supports the notion that low-cost, poor-quality foods are consumed when finances are limited [8].

Lastly, genetics and disease have been shown to be an important factor in determining nutritional needs. New scientific insights provide fresh opportunities for a healthy life. Currently, scientific efforts are focusing on personalized nutrition as a new method for targeting optimal nutrient status. We aim here to outline how healthy aging may be affected by nutrition in the elderly (nutrient-energy density), socioeconomic factors, food pricing, and feeding in nursing homes. This will provide more insight into appropriate assessment of nutritional needs and open up opportunities to take action in favor of a healthily aging population.

28.2 External Factors Influence Nutritional Choices

Calorie needs decrease with age while nutrient needs remain the same, or even increase in the case of some nutrients [3]. This poses problems for individuals who are unable to shop and cook due to their physical or mental limitations, and for people living on a limited budget [10]. Lack of financial and other resources leads approximately 14% of American households to experience food insecurity at times during the year, which hinders their ability to maintain consistent access to nutritious food [8]. Several segments of the older adult population are particularly vulnerable to food insecurity, which puts them at high risk of developing chronic health problems that can be exacerbated by food insecurity, poor nutritional status, and low physical activity [11]. Moreover, the WHO asserts that the global increases in food prices threaten public health and jeopardize the health of the most disadvantaged groups, such as women, children, the elderly, and low-income families [5]. At present, economics is not integrated with mainstream nutrition science or practice, but its integration into nutrition science could facilitate greater understanding of how socioeconomic status may interact with human nutritional status and health.

People choose and consume food rather than nutrients. Hence, the appropriate and logical approach to eliminate the (risk of) malnutrition in the elderly is by producing nutritious and appealing but also affordable foodstuffs. To be successful, it was suggested that the dietary patterns and habits of the targeted population must be taken into consideration. Food consumption is affected by a whole range of drivers, including the availability, accessibility, and choice of foods. These factors may in turn be influenced by geography, demography, disposable income, socioeconomic status, urbanization, marketing, religion, culture, and consumer attitudes [12, 13].

Consumption of an energy-rich but nutrient-poor diet can potentially result in nutrient deficiencies, as observed even in developed countries such as the United States, among children, the elderly, and low-income populations [14]. Five dimensions of 'food access' (availability, accessibility, affordability, accommodation, and acceptability) are defined to capture important factors influencing the choice of food [15]. In order to establish the energy and nutrient intakes of major food groups, dietary guidance must identify foods that are nutrient-rich, affordable, and appealing. These assessments should determine the cost of nutrient-per-calorie so that foods that are affordable and appealing, as well as nutrient-rich, can be recommended in dietary guidelines [16].

28.3 Nutritional Status in the Elderly

Food insecurity and malnutrition are linked with health problems across the lifespan (Fig. 28.1). Micronutrients are essential to maintaining normal physical and cognitive functions in the aging body, and inadequate intakes will subsequently lead to deterioration of health and the development of certain diseases. Older adults are particularly susceptible to deficiencies in various micronutrients. The prevalence of deficiency and malnutrition is highest among the very old, women, and those in care homes and institutions [17]. In the elderly population, the risk of inadequate or

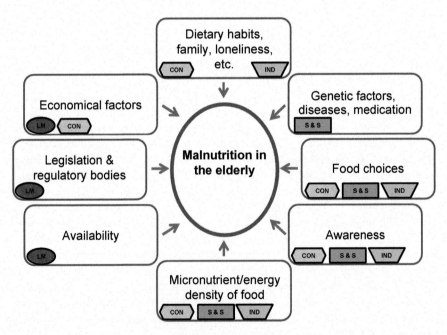

Fig. 28.1 The occurrence of malnutrition has multifactorial causes. Influencing its prevalence in society may therefore require the collaboration of many stakeholders (*LM* National and international law makers; *CON* Consumers; *S&S* Science and social media; *IND* Food and supplement industry)

insufficient coverage with nutritious food is associated with lower income, poor food and nutrient intake, and increased risk of several nutritional, physical and mental-health-related problems [3]. Home delivery of meals to food-insecure individuals was associated with better food security and with improved health, suggesting that food insecurity may be directly responsible for the incidence of diseases in the community [11]. While additional research is needed to document the health care costs associated with food insecurity, sufficient evidence exists to warrant providing food assistance as well as delivering the most needed micronutrients to individuals at risk, including the elderly [11].

28.4 Recommendations for the Elderly

28.4.1 Vitamin E

Epidemiological observations link increased vitamin E intake with protection against Alzheimer's Disease (AD). AD is a progressive, age-dependent neurode-generative disorder and the fourth leading cause of death in industrialized countries [3]. AD incidence is expected to increase significantly as the life expectancy of the population continues to increase. A study completed in 1997 demonstrated the effectiveness of vitamin E in functionally benefiting AD patients [18]. Recently, vitamin E's beneficial effects against AD progression was re-confirmed [19], showing that a daily dose of 2000 mg vitamin E for more than two years delayed the progression of mild or moderate AD and reduced elderly people's dependence on the help of caregivers. Importantly, the study showed that vitamin E treatment was safe, i.e. it induced no specific side-effects. This increased intake of vitamin E was therefore promoted by the authors for those who are at risk of AD, or who suffer from mild or moderate AD. This finding is not only of high relevance for the patients and their caregivers; it is also relevant for healthcare systems, as there are currently no pharmaceutical solutions for AD in place.

28.4.2 Vitamin D

The Institute of Medicine (IOM) recommends a plasma level of 50 nmol/L or higher vitamin D (15 µg [600 IU] from age 1 to 70 years, and 800 IU [20 µg/d] for those over age 70 years) for the general population [20]. Intakes fall far short of these recommendations, however. European authorities, the International Osteoporosis Foundation, and the Endocrine Society recommend a higher status of at least 75 nmol/L. Importantly, no European country reaches the desirable level of 75 nmol/L [21]. The general population of countries such as Germany, Switzerland, and Italy did not even reach 50 nmol/L [21]. Vitamin D status depends on exposure to sunlight, as this vitamin is produced naturally in the human skin by the agency of UV irradiation. Sun exposure, however, is usually not recommended because solar radiation increases the risk of skin cancer. The US Centers for Disease Control and Prevention (CDC) notes that "unprotected skin can be damaged by the sun's UV rays in as little as 15 min" [22].

Due to lack of sun exposure as well as to nutritional insufficiencies, deficiency status in nursing homes and hospitals may be more common in elderly populations. Poor vitamin D status is prevalent around the world and is associated with poor bone health, osteoporosis, and other age-dependent conditions [20]. Low vitamin D status was associated with an increased risk of mobility limitation and disability in community-dwelling, initially well-functioning older adults [23]. Observational studies show that the intake of vitamin D supplements [24, 25] and fortified foods [26] was associated with higher vitamin D status in elderly populations.

Mapping of vitamin D status in Europe has made it apparent that insufficient micronutrient intake is not confined to one single country [27]. It is a global issue [28] that requires collaboration on a global scale. Global policies are needed to ensure vitamin D adequacy across the lifespan. This involves ensuring the coordination of recommendations for vitamin D-fortified foods and supplements. Currently, evidence-based programs of fortification of foods with vitamin D for the general population are in place to target vitamin D deficiency [28].

28.4.3   Vitamins B_6, B_{12} and Folic Acid

Vitamins B_6, B_{12} and folic acid play a role in the etiology of age-related CVD because they are implicated in the homocysteine (Hcy) metabolism, which is—at elevated levels—a risk factor for vascular diseases. Epidemiological studies show that older people with increased blood Hcy levels tend to have lower B-vitamin status, as well as lower cognitive tests scores [29, 30] and were also more prone to vascular diseases, including dementia and AD [3]. The consequences of severe vitamin B_{12} deficiency, such as neurological disorders, are well recognized [31]. A number of randomized clinical trials (RCT) have examined the effectiveness of B-vitamin supplementation to lower Hcy levels and prevent the above-mentioned disorders, with primary measures focusing on cognitive and vascular outcomes. Poor vitamin B_{12}status is prevalent in the elderly (5–20%) [31]. This is even more dramatic among financially insecure older adults, such as recipients of home-delivered or congregate meals and those aged >98 years [32], or those with diseases of the gastro-intestinal tract [3]. Dietary supplements and fortified foods normally contain crystalline vitamin B_{12}, which is believed to be absorbed more readily in those with atrophic gastritis and is therefore recommended in the US for people aged over 51 years [31]. It is mentioned that, due to malabsorption, the elderly population in need of vitamin B_{12} is unlikely to benefit from typical levels of food fortification, which are usually set to provide the RDA. Cross-sectional and longitudinal studies found that lower plasma vitamin B_{12} was associated with AD and with mild cognitive impairment [33]. A two-year randomized controlled trial was undertaken (using a daily dose of 0.5 mg vitamin B_{12}, 0.8 mg folic acid and 20 mg vitamin B_6) to test the effect of vitamin B supplementation on brain-aging parameters. This supplementation regime was associated with lower rates of brain atrophy [30] and a better executive function relative to the placebo [29]. This line of research impressively demonstrates the great promise of B-vitamins to protect brain and cognitive health in the elderly.

28.4.4 Protein

A variety of approaches indicate that for achieving maximal muscle protein synthesis in older adults, about 30 g high-quality protein ought to be consumed with every meal [34, 35]. In the US in 2009–2010, total protein intake was 74.4 g/d in older men and 60.1 g/d in older women [36]. Emerging empiric data show that a high-protein diet during weight loss might help preserve muscle mass, promote fat loss and enhance muscle function in the elderly [37]. Moreover, in overweight and obese older individuals, high-protein diets were more effective in reducing percentage of body fat than diets higher in carbohydrate over a four-month period of weight loss (energy restriction and exercise) and eight months of weight maintenance [38].

Sufficient protein intake is important for maintaining lean body mass and slowing down, and possibly preventing, sarcopenia and osteoporosis [39]—both of which musculoskeletal conditions are linked to advanced age. Ingestion of amino acids is shown to promote muscle synthesis in both young and old healthy individuals [40], but this ability becomes less efficient with age, particularly when the level of essential amino acids (EAA) is limited [40]. By analogy, a similar degree of stimulation of muscle protein synthesis requires higher EEA ingestion in older than in young adults [40]. A Cochrane review summarized the effects of protein and energy supplementation in people at risk of malnutrition. The results showed that supplementation produced weight gain in older people in 42 trials (out of 62 clinical trials) [41]. Moreover, in older people who were already malnourished, the mortality rate was reduced when they were supplemented with protein- and energy-rich diets [41]. The above data suggest that protein metabolism is less efficient in older age. It has therefore been recommended that older people may need to increase their protein intake in order to prevent muscle loss and malnutrition. Currently, the protein intake recommendation for older adults in Europe is at the same level as for younger adults (0.8 g/kg per day) [40, 42]. Future research will clarify whether further recommendations can be made in respect of older adults concerning optimal/elevated protein intake during the day with a view to maintaining skeletal muscle mass as people age. Lastly, if dietary protein recommendations were to increase, this could also have cost implications for those older adults, many of whom are already on limited budgets.

28.4.5 Fats and Unsaturated Fatty Acids

Fats are important energy sources and also facilitate the absorption of fat-soluble vitamins. Moreover, fats have vital structural and regulatory functions in the human body. Fat is the most energy-dense nutrient, and because of its high energy density, overconsumption can lead to excessive total energy intake, which promotes overweight and obesity [43]. Moreover, trans fatty acids are associated with adverse effects on cardiovascular health [44]. By contrast, the consumption of monounsaturated (MUFA) and polyunsaturated fatty acids (PUFA) is linked to beneficial effects on metabolic health, including reduced insulin sensitivity [45, 46] and cardiovascular risk [45, 46]. In these respects, PUFAs seem to be more effective than MUFAs [45].

Long-chain poly polyunsaturated omega-3 fatty acids (LC-PUFAs) are proposed to be beneficial to brain function in aging adults by virtue of reducing oxidative stress and inflammation [47]. Most cross-sectional and longitudinal observational studies demonstrate encouraging effects of LC-PUFAs (from the diet or via dietary supplementation) on cognitive function in healthy older adults [48]. The evidence on supplementation from clinical trials is also emerging. LC-PUFAs, such as docosahexaenoic acid (DHA), are especially important for brain health as they are important building-blocks for neuronal cell membranes and are instrumental in brain development, neurotransmission, modulation of ion channels, and neuroprotection (see [3]). EFSA has set a reference intake range of 20–35% of daily total energy from fat for European adults [49], and recommends that the intake of saturated fatty acids and trans fatty acids should be as low as possible within the context of a nutritionally adequate diet [49]. Moreover, EFSA approved a health claim for DHA that it "contributes to the maintenance of normal brain function" [49].

28.4.6 Sodium Reduction

There is a link between high blood pressure and increased risk of stroke, left ventricular hypertrophy and proteinuria [50]. High sodium (Na) intake is associated with many age-related health conditions, including high blood pressure [50]. Decreased sodium intake reduces blood pressure, particularly in older people [50]. Reducing the sodium content of food is recognized as leading to lowering of Na intake in several countries, including the UK [51]. Of note, a variety of approaches, such as appropriate policies, cooperation on the part of the food industry and nutrition education are needed to achieve Na reduction across the lifespan, including in older people [52].

28.4.7 Calcium

Adequate intakes of calcium (in combination with adequate intakes of vitamin D) are essential for the prevention of osteoporosis. See Chap. 10, Table 10.2 for an overview of actual intake levels in selected countries.

28.5 Economic Impact

The Global Nutrition Report (http://www.ifpri.org/sites/default/files/publications/gnr14.pdf) calculates that malnutrition, visible as under- or over-nutrition (or both), was observed in all 193 countries assessed and that it affects two billion people around the globe. The Report estimates that malnutrition is costing the global economy US$3.5 trillion (€2.8 trillion) each year, and that it also reduces the quality of life of affected people (Fig. 28.2).

The United Nations World Food Programme estimates that poor nutrition is the cause of about three million deaths of children under five years old each year. There is a great deal of evidence demonstrating that supplementation of essential nutrients decreased the risk of disease. According to the Council for Responsible Nutrition, "There is ample evidence to suggest that the public will benefit from the adoption of healthy dietary patterns and healthy lifestyle habits, including the regular use of nutritional supplements."

28.5.1 Increased Political Commitment for Tackling Malnutrition in Recent Years

The World Health Organization (WHO) commented on the Global Nutrition Report with the observation that the fight for better nutrition needs to involve as many parties as possible. "Ending malnutrition throughout the world requires action on many fronts. The health sector cannot do it alone. But political commitment is

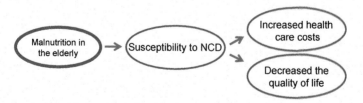

Fig. 28.2 Malnutrition, i.e. insufficient coverage with essential nutrients, increases susceptibility to developing NCDs. The increased NCD rate leads to a rise in health care costs for society and a reduction of the quality of life for those affected

growing. More and more countries know what they need to do to ensure access to healthy diets for all. This report will help us track progress toward global nutrition targets and understand where greater investments are needed."

28.5.2   Involvement of Many Partners Is Necessary to Combat Malnutrition

Product pricing and personal finances have a significant impact on nutritional options. Particularly for those who have less money to spend on food, healthy nutritional choices are currently limited. Current pricing is set in such a way that the lowest-cost nutritional options are the most energy-dense, containing high levels of fat and sugar [53]. It is known that price reductions of healthy nutritional options have a positive impact on consumer behaviors. French [54] reported two community-based intervention studies involving price reductions in secondary schools. An exponential increase was reported following price reductions of lower-fat snacks and fresh fruits: a price reduction of 50% resulted in an approximate doubling of consumers' choices in favor of healthy snacks and fresh fruit.

This begs the question as to who is responsible for product pricing and ensuring that even elderly people on low incomes can have access to healthy nutritional options. Also, what is the best way to ensure that the elderly are well informed about the possibilities for nutritious and affordable food available in their communities? The answer includes three parties: the nutrition industry, governments and legislators, and consumers.

The nutrition industry is a logical starting-point for optimizing energy/nutrient density and the product pricing of processed foods. Automatic harvesting and long-distance shipping, extensive processing, improper storage and soil deficiencies all play their part in reducing the nutritional value of today's food, making it virtually impossible to obtain adequate nutrition from our current food supply. This may be a reason why the supplement industry has experienced substantial growth over the last decades, indicating a real need for supplements on the part of consumers.

Nutrition companies are challenged to produce nutritious yet affordable food products. New technological tools, such as electronic applications for smart phones and computers, may be an efficient method for providing consumers with real-time and accurate information about each product. Such information may be customized to meet the specific needs of population subgroups, including the elderly.

The adequacy and quality of the food supply depends on several parameters, such as local production and trade, legislation of trade and production, and consumer awareness, among others (Fig. 28.1). In Poland, after the fall of the Berlin Wall in 1989, the food trade developed quickly, leading to an increase in fruit consumption (citrus fruits and bananas) and a change in the quality of edible fat. Coronary heart disease dramatically decreased against a history of progressively increasing rates of incidence, which had been among the highest globally [5].

In the current economic climate, dominated as it is by intense competition and mature markets, it is up to the government and legislators to support any initiative to market nutritious food for affordable prices. Not only should governments support access to healthy foods; they should also provide an infrastructure for the general public to be educated about nutrition (Fig. 28.1). Several activities have been initiated by the European Union authorities for educating consumers, but these efforts should also be continued at the legislative level.

We all want to pursue a healthy life. Therefore it is our responsibility to ensure that we live healthily. As described above, product pricing will impact nutritional choices, but a better understanding of healthy nutrition is primarily the consumer's own responsibility, and consumers ought to inform themselves and adapt their food choices accordingly. Although some individuals might need to buy cheap food on account of their economic limitations, they can still decide not to buy certain products that are neither nutritious nor essential. However, a completely free choice is not always possible. For example, in healthcare facilities, the meal choices are pre-selected by healthcare professionals and are often based on what the budget will allow. With increasing healthcare costs, good nutrition in healthcare facilities might be at stake. For hospital patients of any age, good nutrition has the potential to positively influence recovery time. For elderly people, whether in nursing homes or still living at home, good nutrition could affect hospitalization and disease development or progression (Fig. 28.2). Also here, health authorities must consider issuing a regulatory guideline to ensure high-quality nutrition, which will in turn help ease the recovery process, thus reducing healthcare costs.

Additional research and efforts on the part of society are needed to keep building the evidence base for appropriate/improved diet and health in older people. Longitudinal studies to distinguish acute and chronic food insecurity, along with greater inclusion of the nutrition industry and the legislature, are prerequisites for securing healthy and affordable nutrition for the elderly.

28.6 Discussion

28.6.1 Optimal Coverage with Essential Nutrients Is Indispensable for Healthy Aging

In a recent publication, we showed that the elderly population is especially prone to malnutrition and discussed several reasons for this increased risk [3]. Inadequate intake of several vitamins has been linked to chronic diseases, including coronary heart disease, cancer, and osteoporosis [55]. Moreover, technological advances— including genetic modification of plants, mechanized harvesting combined with extensive processing, storage, and shipping of food, in conjunction with faster-paced lifestyles—have altered our dietary patterns such that a majority of the population does not take in even the recommended daily allowance (RDA) of essential nutrients [56]. From the fact that RDA is the quantity of a nutrient necessary to prevent a deficiency syndrome it follows logically that an insufficient supply of the essential nutrients may be responsible for many of the chronic diseases, and that a deficiency status is not a precondition for the onset of a non-communicable disease.

Epidemiological findings suggest a causal relationship between nutrition, diet and chronic diseases [57]. According to the United States Department of Statistics (2004), five out of six major causes of death (cardiovascular disease, cancer, stroke, accidents, diabetes and AD) are common NCDs [58]. Chronic diseases not only shorten lives and cause death, but also have enormous economic impact (Fig. 28.2). Fortunately, many chronic diseases can be positively influenced by dietary and supplement choices. The performance of additional RCTs is essential to account for the individual confounders, but it is beyond doubt that many macro- and micronutrients are necessary to live, and to age, healthily. Supplying the (aging) population with these essential nutrients would probably help to prevent many NCDs.

28.6.2   Legislation and Research Needs to Reduce Malnutrition of Older Adults

Regulatory authorities and policy makers can play a fundamental role in ensuring healthy nutrition for the elderly population. In the US, the 'Dietary Guidelines for Americans' must, according to Federal law, be followed in the planning of meals for older adults residing in various health care facilities [59]. Very few age-specific recommendations are provided by this guideline. The few that are include reducing sodium, elevating vitamin D and consuming vitamin B_{12} from fortified foods or dietary supplements, as well food patterns for various energy levels. The trend in the United States is that an increasing number of older adults are interested in living at home as long as possible instead of opting for institutionalization [59]. Therefore a community-based delivery of nutrition services for older adults was suggested as a means to promote health and independent living in the community [59]. A successful transition from acute, sub-acute and chronic care to living at home urgently requires optimal coordination of nutrition services between medical and community settings [59]. These are good examples of legislation- and society-driven initiatives to improve nutrition security in the elderly.

28.6.3   The Need for Collaboration Between All Involved Parties

Intensive collaboration between experts in healthy aging—consisting of the food/supplement industry, scientific research, geriatric medicine, and regulatory bodies—has been put forward as a prerequisite for tackling malnutrition in the elderly population [59]. The development of nutritional solutions for the elderly should be led by daily needs. Ideally, the food and supplement industry should participate in the identification, design, testing and promotion of the products [60]. Multiple potential influences on dietary habits of the elderly population exist, such as taste, family and community characteristics, the offering of the food and supplement industry, public policy and—very importantly—the level of the individual personal awareness of the importance of healthy food (Fig. 28.1). To improve nutrition and ensure an adequate supply of all necessary micro- and macronutrients to the elderly population, additional research and liaison between the scientific community, industry, and policy-makers is essential: this should aim to increase our understanding of the subject and strengthen the relevant legislation so as to improve the diet and, with it, the health status of older people.

Food prices have surged in recent years, and have triggered serious concerns about food security around the world. Lo and coworkers showed that personal nutrition decisions—and thus the quality of nutritional intake and of an individual's health—are affected by economic factors [5]. Food price and low income, for example, are shown to be a barrier to making healthier food choices, and dietary costs are intrinsically linked with dietary quality the world over [5]. Therefore collaborative, multinational, cross-disciplinary nutritional efforts should be undertaken in the prevention and management of food crises. Resource scarcity lends additional momentum to nutritional policies in the context of a variety of public health programs. The Copenhagen Consensus of 2004, developed by a panel of world-leading economists, placed the fight against malnutrition second among the ten best globally available investments for improving human welfare; and this rose to first place in 2008 [5].

Intensified basic and applied research are needed to improve our understanding, dissemination, and application of food and nutrition guidelines for older adults. In modern societies, where many elderly people live on their own or are dependent on caregivers, enhanced measurement and continued investigation of food security are clearly warranted.

28.7 Summary: Key Messages

- The percentage of people older than 60 years will increase from 11 to 22% by 2050.
- Aging is an accumulation of modifications, affecting different parts of the body to varying degrees.
- Advancing age increases the incidence of non-communicable diseases (NCDs).
- Epidemiologically, there is a direct link between nutritional status and several NCDs.
- Good nutrition is instrumental for maintaining good health among the elderly population, yet the value of high-quality dietary intake is often under-recognized.

- Vitamins B, D, E, polyunsaturated fatty acids and protein are particularly important for maintaining health in older adults.
- Elderly individuals are particularly at risk of not receiving the nutrition required for maintaining good physical and mental health status.
- Collaboration between experts in healthy aging is a prerequisite for tackling malnutrition in the elderly population.
- Intensified research is needed to improve our understanding, dissemination, and application of food and nutrition guidelines for older adults.

References

1. WHO, *Aging*. http://www.who.int/topics/ageing/en/, 2012. (accessed August 2014).
2. Kirkwood, T.B., *A systematic look at an old problem*. Nature, 2008. **451**(7179): p. 644–7.
3. Mohajeri, M.H., B. Troesch, and P. Weber, *Inadequate supply of vitamins and DHA in the elderly: Implications for brain aging and Alzheimer-type dementia*. Nutrition, 2015. **31**(2): p. 261–275.
4. Johnson, K.A., M.A. Bernard, and K. Funderburg, *Vitamin nutrition in older adults*. Clin Geriatr Med, 2002. **18**(4): p. 773–99.
5. Lo, Y.T., et al., *Health and nutrition economics: diet costs are associated with diet quality*. Asia Pac J Clin Nutr, 2009. **18**(4): p. 598–604.
6. Dwyer, J., *Starting down the right path: nutrition connections with chronic diseases of later life*. Am J Clin Nutr, 2006. **83**(2): p. 415S–420S.
7. WHO, *Global Strategy on Diet, Physical Activity and Health* 2012.
8. Franklin, B., et al., *Exploring mediators of food insecurity and obesity: a review of recent literature*. J Community Health, 2012. **37**(1): p. 253–264.
9. Kim, K. and E.A. Frongillo, *Participation in food assistance programs modifies the relation of food insecurity with weight and depression in elders*. J Nutr, 2007. **137**(4): p. 1005–10.
10. Sahyoun, N.R. and A. Vaudin, *Home-Delivered Meals and Nutrition Status Among Older Adults*. Nutr Clin Pract, 2014. **29**(4): p. 459–465.
11. Lee, J.S., J.G. Fischer, and M.A. Johnson, *Food insecurity, food and nutrition programs, and aging: experiences from Georgia*. J Nutr Elder, 2010. **29**(2): p. 116–49.
12. Kearney, J., *Food consumption trends and drivers*. Philos Trans R Soc Lond B Biol Sci, 2010. **365**(1554): p. 2793–807.
13. Hawkesworth, S., et al., *Feeding the world healthily: the challenge of measuring the effects of agriculture on health*. Philos Trans R Soc Lond B Biol Sci, 2010. **365**(1554): p. 3083–97.
14. Wang, Y. and M.A. Beydoun, *The obesity epidemic in the United States–gender, age, socioeconomic, racial/ethnic, and geographic characteristics: a systematic review and meta-regression analysis*. Epidemiol Rev, 2007. **29**: p. 6–28.
15. Caspi, C.E., et al., *The local food environment and diet: a systematic review*. Health Place, 2012. **18**(5): p. 1172–87.
16. Drewnowski, A. and V. Fulgoni, 3rd, *Nutrient profiling of foods: creating a nutrient-rich food index*. Nutr Rev, 2008. **66**(1): p. 23–39.
17. Arvanitakis, M., et al., *Nutrition in care homes and home care: recommendations - a summary based on the report approved by the Council of Europe*. Clin Nutr, 2009. **28**(5): p. 492–6.
18. Sano, M., et al., *A controlled trial of selegiline, alpha-tocopherol, or both as treatment for Alzheimer's disease. The Alzheimer's Disease Cooperative Study*. N Engl J Med, 1997. **336** (17): p. 1216–22.

19. Dysken, M.W., et al., *Effect of vitamin E and memantine on functional decline in Alzheimer disease: the TEAM-AD VA cooperative randomized trial.* JAMA, 2014. **311**(1): p. 33–44.
20. IOM, *Institute of Medicine, Dietary Reference Intakes for Calcium and Vitamin D.* 2011. Washington, DC: National Academy of Sciences, National Academy Press.
21. Hilger, J., et al., *A systematic review of vitamin D status in populations worldwide.* Br J Nutr, 2014. **111**(1): p. 23–45.
22. Centers for Disease Control and Prevention (2012) *Skin cancer awareness: protect your skin.* http://www.cdc.gov/Features/SkinCancer/ 2012 (accessed October 2012).
23. Houston, D.K., et al., *Low 25-hydroxyvitamin D predicts the onset of mobility limitation and disability in community-dwelling older adults: the Health ABC Study.* J Gerontol A Biol Sci Med Sci, 2013. **68**(2): p. 181–7.
24. Johnson, M.A., et al., *Age, race and season predict vitamin D status in African American and white octogenarians and centenarians.* J Nutr Health Aging, 2008. **12**(10): p. 690–5.
25. Tripkovic, L., et al., *Comparison of vitamin D2 and vitamin D3 supplementation in raising serum 25-hydroxyvitamin D status: a systematic review and meta-analysis.* Am J Clin Nutr, 2012. **95**(6): p. 1357–64.
26. O'Mahony, L., et al., *The potential role of vitamin D enhanced foods in improving vitamin D status.* Nutrients, 2011. **3**(12): p. 1023–41.
27. Brouwer-Brolsma, E.M., et al., *Vitamin D: do we get enough? A discussion between vitamin D experts in order to make a step towards the harmonisation of dietary reference intakes for vitamin D across Europe.* Osteoporos Int, 2013. **24**(5): p. 1567–77.
28. Holick, M.F., et al., *Evaluation, treatment, and prevention of vitamin D deficiency: an Endocrine Society clinical practice guideline.* J Clin Endocrinol Metab, 2011. **96**(7): p. 1911–30.
29. de Jager, C.A., et al., *Cognitive and clinical outcomes of homocysteine-lowering B-vitamin treatment in mild cognitive impairment: a randomized controlled trial.* Int J Geriatr Psychiatry, 2012. **27**(6): p. 592–600.
30. Smith, A.D., et al., *Homocysteine-lowering by B vitamins slows the rate of accelerated brain atrophy in mild cognitive impairment: a randomized controlled trial.* PLoS One, 2010. **5**(9): p. e12244.
31. IOM, *Dietary Reference Intakes for Thiamin, Riboflavin, Niacin, Vitamin B6, Folate, Vitamin B12, Pantothenic Acid, Biotin, and Choline..* Washington, DC: National Academy of Sciences, National Academy Press, 1998.
32. Johnson, M.A., et al., *Vitamin B12 deficiency in African American and white octogenarians and centenarians in Georgia.* J Nutr Health Aging, 2010. **14**(5): p. 339–45.
33. Moore, E., et al., *Cognitive impairment and vitamin B12: a review.* Int Psychogeriatr, 2012. **24**(4): p. 541–56.
34. Symons, T.B., et al., *A moderate serving of high-quality protein maximally stimulates skeletal muscle protein synthesis in young and elderly subjects.* J Am Diet Assoc, 2009. **109**(9): p. 1582–6.
35. Symons, T.B., et al., *The anabolic response to resistance exercise and a protein-rich meal is not diminished by age.* J Nutr Health Aging, 2011. **15**(5): p. 376–81.
36. Agricultural Research Service, United States Department of Agriculture. *What we eat in America, NHANES 2009–2010.* http://www.ars.usda.gov/SP2UserFiles/Place/12355000/pdf/0910/tables_1-40_2009-2010.pdf 2012. (accessed August 2013).
37. Mojtahedi, M.C., et al., *The effects of a higher protein intake during energy restriction on changes in body composition and physical function in older women.* J Gerontol A Biol Sci Med Sci, 2011. **66**(11): p. 1218–25.
38. Evans, E.M., et al., *Effects of protein intake and gender on body composition changes: a randomized clinical weight loss trial.* Nutr Metab (Lond), 2012. **9**(1): p. 55.
39. Gaffney-Stomberg, E., et al., *Increasing dietary protein requirements in elderly people for optimal muscle and bone health.* J Am Geriatr Soc, 2009. **57**(6): p. 1073–9.
40. Paddon-Jones, D. and B.B. Rasmussen, *Dietary protein recommendations and the prevention of sarcopenia.* Curr Opin Clin Nutr Metab Care, 2009. **12**(1): p. 86–90.

41. Milne, A.C., et al., *Protein and energy supplementation in elderly people at risk from malnutrition.* Cochrane Database Syst Rev, 2009(2): p. CD003288.
42. EFSA, *Panel on Dietetic Products Nutrition and Allergies (NDA): 'Scientific Opinion on Dietary Reference Values forprotein.* EFSA Journal, 2012. **10**(2): p. 2557.
43. Swinburn, B.A., et al., *Diet, nutrition and the prevention of excess weight gain and obesity.* Public Health Nutr, 2004. **7**(1A): p. 123–46.
44. Brouwer, I.A., A.J. Wanders, and M.B. Katan, *Trans fatty acids and cardiovascular health: research completed?* Eur J Clin Nutr, 2013. **67**(5): p. 541–7.
45. Schwingshackl, L. and G. Hoffmann, *Monounsaturated fatty acids and risk of cardiovascular disease: synopsis of the evidence available from systematic reviews and meta-analyses.* Nutrients, 2012. **4**(12): p. 1989–2007.
46. Wallin, A., et al., *Fish consumption, dietary long-chain n-3 fatty acids, and risk of type 2 diabetes: systematic review and meta-analysis of prospective studies.* Diabetes Care, 2012. **35** (4): p. 918–29.
47. van de Rest, O., et al., *B vitamins and n-3 fatty acids for brain development and function: review of human studies.* Ann Nutr Metab, 2012. **60**(4): p. 272–92.
48. Ubeda, N., M. Achon, and G. Varela-Moreiras, *Omega 3 fatty acids in the elderly.* Br J Nutr, 2012. **107 Suppl 2**: p. S137–51.
49. EFSA, *Panel on Dietetic Products Nutrition and Allergies (NDA): 'Scientific Opinion on Dietary Reference Values for fats, including saturated fatty acids, polyunsaturated fatty acids, monounsaturated fatty acids, trans fatty acids, and cholesterol* EFSA Journal, 2010. **8**(3): p. 1461.
50. Frisoli, T.M., et al., *Salt and hypertension: is salt dietary reduction worth the effort?* Am J Med, 2012. **125**(5): p. 433–9.
51. Wyness, L.A., J.L. Butriss, and S.A. Stanner, *Reducing the population's sodium intake: the UK Food Standards Agency's salt reduction programme.* Public Health Nutr, 2012. **15**(2): p. 254–61.
52. WHO, *Strategies to Monitor and Evaluate Population Sodium Consumption and Sources of Sodium in the Diet, Report of a Joint Technical Meeting Convened by WHO and the Government of Canada, Canada* http://whqlibdoc.who.int/publications/2011/9789241501699_eng.pdf, 2010: p. 42.
53. Drewnowski, A. and N. Darmon, *The economics of obesity: dietary energy density and energy cost.* Am J Clin Nutr, 2005. **82**(1 Suppl): p. 265S–273S.
54. French, S.A., *Pricing effects on food choices.* J Nutr, 2003. **133**(3): p. 841S–843S.
55. Franz, M.J., et al., *Evidence-based nutrition principles and recommendations for the treatment and prevention of diabetes and related complications.* Diabetes Care, 2002. **25**(1): p. 148–98.
56. Mooradian, A.D., et al., *Selected vitamins and minerals in diabetes.* Diabetes Care, 1994. **17** (5): p. 464–79.
57. http://www.cdc.gov/diabetes/data/statistics/2014StatisticsReport.html, *Center for Disease Control and Prevention: CDC Publications and Products: National Diabetes Fact sheet* 2014.
58. NIH, *Consensus Statement Osteoporosis prevention, diagnosis, and therapy.* NIH Consensus Statement, 2000. **17**(1): p. 1–45.
59. Johnson, M.A., *Strategies to improve diet in older adults.* Proc Nutr Soc, 2013. **72**(1): p. 166–72.
60. Costa, A.I. and W.M. Jongen, *Designing new meals for an ageing population.* Crit Rev Food Sci Nutr, 2010. **50**(6): p. 489–502.

Chapter 29
The Role of Food Fortification: The Example of Folic Acid

Helene McNulty

Abstract Food fortification is the process of adding essential micronutrients to food. This chapter considers the role of folic acid-fortified foods in impacting folate status and in maintaining better health in populations worldwide. The evidence linking low, but not necessarily deficient, folate status with neural tube defects (NTDs) is conclusive and beyond debate: therefore achieving optimal folate status is an important public health goal for populations worldwide. However, despite the known and emerging health benefits of optimal folate status, achieving this at a population level presents significant challenges, particularly for countries that lack policies of mandatory folic acid fortification of food. This chapter explores whether fortified foods can provide a sustainable source of folic acid and deliver improved folate status and better health outcomes while presenting a minimal risk to health. It concludes that there is a very strong case for folic acid fortification and indicates that the proven benefits would more than outweigh any potential risks.

Keywords Food fortification · Folate · Folic acid · Folate status · Folate deficiency · Folate inadequacy · Neural tube defects (NTDs) · Health outcomes

29.1 Introduction

Food fortification is the process of adding essential micronutrients to food. Fortified foods can play an important role in helping individuals and populations worldwide to achieve more optimal nutritional status. There are over two billion people worldwide who suffer from various micronutrient deficiencies, and many others will have sub-optimal micronutrient status in the absence of clinical deficiency signs but with adverse consequences for health. The World Health Organization (WHO) and the Food and Agricultural Organization of the United Nations

H. McNulty (✉)
Northern Ireland Centre for Food and Health (NICHE), Ulster University, Coleraine BT52 1SA, Northern Ireland, UK
e-mail: h.mcnulty@ulster.ac.uk

© Springer International Publishing AG 2017
H.K. Biesalski et al. (eds.), *Sustainable Nutrition in a Changing World*,
DOI 10.1007/978-3-319-55942-1_29

(FAO) recognize that the purpose of food fortification is "to improve the nutritional quality of the food supply and to provide a public health benefit with minimal risk to health." Folate is an excellent example of a nutrient for which the role of food fortification can be fully appreciated.

The achievement of optimal folate status is an important public health goal for populations worldwide. In practice, however, it is challenging. Folic acid—the form of folate used for fortification—is cheap to produce, very stable once added to foods, and highly bioavailable when ingested. Thus, depending on local fortification policy, the folate status of populations can vary greatly from one country to the next, and this is reflected in differences in health outcomes, most notably in the case of neural tube defects which are causatively linked with low maternal folate.

This chapter will consider the role of folic acid-fortified foods in impacting folate status and in maintaining better health in populations worldwide. The key question to be addressed is: Can fortified foods provide a sustainable source of this vitamin to achieve more optimal folate status, better health outcomes, minimal health risk and therefore the public health benefit envisaged by WHO/FAO for populations worldwide?

29.2   Folate Terminology

The terms 'folic acid' and 'folate' are often used interchangeably. However, there are important differences which are relevant to this chapter. 'Folic acid' refers to the synthetic form of the B vitamin known as folate; it is the folate form used for food fortification. The major sources of naturally occurring folates in foods are green leafy vegetables, asparagus, beans, legumes, liver and yeast, whereas folic acid is found in the human diet only in fortified foods and supplements. Folic acid, however, is readily converted to the natural cofactor forms after ingestion.

Folic acid is a fully oxidized molecule and is a monoglutamate, meaning that it contains just one glutamate moiety in its structure. Naturally occurring food folates, on the other hand, are a mixture of reduced folate forms (predominantly 5-methyltetrahydrofolate) and are usually found as polyglutamates, containing a variable number of glutamate residues. These chemical differences mean that, at equivalent intake levels, folic acid is inherently more stable and more bioavailable compared with naturally occurring food folates [1].

29.3   Roles of Folate in Human Health

Biologically, folate is required for one-carbon metabolism. This involves the transfer and utilization of one-carbon units in essential pathways incorporating nucleotide biosynthesis, amino acid metabolism and the production of *S*-adenosylmethionine required for numerous methylation reactions [2]. Folate plays a particularly important role in pregnancy and fetal development as it is essential for cell division and tissue growth. Notably, conclusive evidence has existed for over 20 years that folic acid supplementation in early pregnancy protects against neural tube defects (NTDs).

Although the preventative role of folate in NTDs is the major focus of public health efforts worldwide, newer evidence supports several other roles for folate, from pregnancy, through childhood, to preventing chronic disease in ageing, including cardiovascular diseases, certain cancers, osteoporosis, and cognitive dysfunction. Thus folate's role in human health extends throughout the lifecycle from conception to old age [3]. Folate in early life is considered fundamental; indeed, recent interest is focused on the effects of maternal folate status during pregnancy on health outcomes in later life, such as cognition in childhood and beyond.

Optimal folate functioning and the health effects of folate involve not only important metabolic interrelationships with other B-vitamins, namely vitamins B_{12}, B_6 and B_2 (i.e. riboflavin), but also highly relevant gene-nutrient interactions [4]. Thus sub-optimal status of one of more of the related B-vitamins, or genetic polymorphisms in folate genes, can impair folate metabolism and cause adverse health outcomes, even if folate intakes are deemed to be adequate for a general population.

29.4 Folate Insufficiency—A Worldwide Concern

The public health benefit targeted by folic acid-fortified foods is first and foremost to prevent deficient folate status.

29.4.1 Folate Deficiency

Clinical folate deficiency leads to megaloblastic anemia. This condition is characterized by immature, enlarged blood cells (reflecting impaired DNA synthesis) and is reversible with folic acid treatment. Deficient status of folate is not uncommon even in otherwise well-nourished populations. It can arise in any situation where requirements are increased or availability is decreased, or both, with the clinical manifestation of folate deficiency (i.e. megaloblastic anemia) more likely to be present when both occur simultaneously [4].

Pregnancy is a time when folate requirement is greatly increased to sustain the demand for rapid cell replication and growth of fetal, placental and maternal tissue, and folate deficiency of pregnancy has been recognized for many years. In fact, the discovery of folate as an essential nutrient dates back to the 1930s, when a fatal anemia of pregnancy was first described in India which was subsequently proven to be responsive to folate treatment [3]. Certain gastrointestinal conditions, most notably coeliac disease, can also lead to deficient folate status through chronic malabsorption. In addition, heavy alcohol consumption and several commonly used drugs, e.g. phenytoin and primidone (anticonvulsants), pyrimethamine (an anti-malarial), and sulfasalazine (used in inflammatory bowel disease), are all associated with folate deficiency through various mechanisms.

Low dietary intake is, however, the most common cause of deficient/low folate status across several populations worldwide. As will be discussed below, dietary intakes are often found to be insufficient to maintain optimal folate status even in otherwise well-nourished populations and in the absence of malabsorption or other factors contributing to folate deficiency.

29.4.2   Identifying Folate Deficiency in Populations Worldwide

'Folate deficiency' in populations is typically identified in terms of establishing that there is a significant proportion of that population (e.g. >5%) with biomarker concentrations of folate falling below a cut-off point indicative of deficiency. Ideally this would be established using nationally representative data, but for many countries such data are not available. Even where population-based data exist, different analytical methods may have been used for determining folate biomarker concentrations, and/or different biomarker cut-off points applied to define the severity of deficiency. As a result of these factors, it is difficult to directly compare the assessment of folate status from one country to the next.

The most extensive review of folate deficiency worldwide assessed population-based surveys of folate status published between 1995 and 2005, including some which included biomarker data [5]. Folate deficiency (i.e. >5% of the population with serum folate concentrations below the normal range) was identified in specific age-groups in six out of eight countries for which biomarker data existed, most notably in pregnant women in Costa Rica (48.8%) and Venezuela (25.5%), preschool children in Venezuela (33.8%), and the elderly in the United Kingdom (15.0%). It is worth noting, however, that the national survey in Costa Rica was conducted in 1996 prior to the introduction of mandatory fortification of flour with folic acid, and it is very likely that folate deficiency is now much less of a problem as a result of this public health measure.

29.4.3   Folate Insufficiency in the Absence of Clinical Folate Deficiency

It is important to appreciate that the absence of folate deficiency does not necessarily mean that folate status is optimal in terms of maintaining health and preventing folate-related disease (e.g. NTDs or chronic disease in aging). Thus in many developed countries folate deficiency may be relatively rare, but sub-optimal folate status is commonly encountered. Establishing the extent of low (sub-optimal) folate status within or between different populations would ideally involve linking dietary intake data with folate biomarkers.

Policy makers and others, however, may sometimes rely only on reports of dietary intakes when assessing folate adequacy. Dietary data only without corresponding biomarkers will, however, provide an incomplete picture of folate status in a given population because no account can be taken of the amount of folate absorbed and available for metabolic processes (i.e. bioavailability) in the assessment of folate status. In addition, although nationally representative dietary surveys provide the most reliable means of evaluating intakes, such surveys are not always available, and even where they do exist, corresponding biomarker data are rarely also available. Moreover, comparison of dietary folate intakes between countries can be problematic because of different approaches used to express folate intakes from one country to the next (as discussed below).

29.5 Fortified Food as a Sustainable Source of Folate

In the absence of folic acid fortification, achieving optimal folate status in healthy populations is difficult. This is because foods fortified with folic acid provide a highly bioavailable vitamin form, whereas folates from natural food sources can be unstable (under normal conditions of cooking) and, moreover, have limited bioavailability once ingested.

29.5.1 Folate Bioavailability from Natural Food Sources and Fortified Foods

Bioavailability can be defined as the proportion of an ingested nutrient that is absorbed and becomes available for metabolic processes or storage. The intestinal absorption of food folates is a two-step process. The first step involves the hydrolysis of folate polyglutamates to the corresponding monoglutamate derivatives. This occurs in the proximal part of the jejunum with the involvement of a brush border enzyme and an optimal pH of 6.5 (the latter appears to be critical for the complete deconjugation of folate polyglutamates). Once hydrolyzed, the second step is the transport of monoglutamyl folates through the intestinal membranes into the enterocyte. Folic acid is a monoglutamate and thus does not require deconjugation before uptake by intestinal cells.

The bioavailability of naturally occurring food folates is limited for various reasons [1]. As reduced folate forms, they are inherently unstable outside living cells. Moreover, other dietary constituents can contribute to the instability of labile folates during digestion. In addition, the ease with which folates are released from different food matrices and the removal of the polyglutamyl 'tail' (de-conjugation) before uptake by intestinal cells can vary greatly. As a result, naturally occurring folates show incomplete bioavailability when compared with folic acid at equivalent levels of intake.

Apart from their limited bioavailability, natural folates in foods can undergo significant losses before ingestion. Food folates (particularly green vegetables) can be unstable under certain conditions of cooking, and this can substantially reduce the folate content of the food before it is even ingested [6]. This is an additional, and often overlooked, factor limiting the extent to which natural food folates can impact on folate status.

In contrast, folic acid (as used in fortified food and supplements) provides a highly stable and bioavailable vitamin form. The bioavailability of folic acid is assumed to be 100% when ingested as a supplement, while folic acid in fortified food is estimated to have 85% the bioavailability of supplemental folic acid [7]. By comparison, food folates have variable but generally much lower bioavailability, estimated from a mixed diet to be no more than 50% that of supplemental folic acid [7].

29.5.2   Implications of Folate Bioavailability for Dietary Recommendations

Folate intakes and recommendations in the United States and certain other countries are expressed as Dietary Folate Equivalents (DFEs), a calculation which was devised to take into account the greater bioavailability of folic acid from fortified foods compared to naturally occurring dietary folates. DFEs are defined as the micrograms of naturally occurring food folate plus 1.7 times the micrograms of folic acid from fortified food. The IOM [7] recommends 400 µg/d as DFEs for adult females and males. To cover increased needs during pregnancy and lactation, it recommends 600 and 500 µg/day respectively.

In most European countries however, this conversion factor is not applied and folate intakes are currently expressed simply as total folate in µg/d (rather than as DFEs), thus disregarding the differences in bioavailability between the natural food forms and folic acid [8]. Although a recent European Safety Authority (EFSA) report has for the first time expressed folate recommendations as DFEs [9], the practical limitations of adopting this approach will delay its full implementation. The EFSA panel acknowledged the challenge in replacing total folate intakes with DFEs within member states, recognizing that folate intake data for many countries have not been analyzed in a way that allows natural food folates and folic acid added to foods to be differentiated; indeed the EFSA panel called for more research in this regard [9].

29.6   Folic Acid Fortification and Folate Status in Populations Worldwide

As discussed above, folic acid (compared with natural food folates) provides a highly bioavailable source of folate. For this reason, biomarker folate status within and between populations can vary considerably depending primarily on the level of exposure to folic acid through fortified food. Biomarker status of folate is thus found to be lowest in those countries without access to folic acid-fortified foods and highest in countries with mandatory fortification. Within countries such as the UK and Ireland with voluntary fortification policies in place, folate status will vary depending on individual consumer practices.

Mandatory fortification of foods is governed by regulations that are country-specific and take into account food consumption patterns. Over 80 countries to date have passed regulations for the mandatory fortification of staple foods with folic acid (Fig. 29.1) [11].

Voluntary fortification of foods with folic acid is undertaken in many countries, whereas it is prohibited by the governments of others. In some cases, the foods that

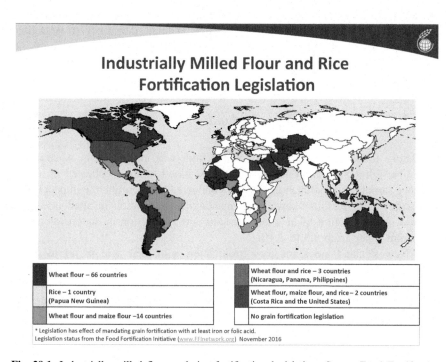

Fig. 29.1 Industrially milled flour and rice fortification legislation. *Source* Food Fortification Initiative (FFI). Reprinted with permission

can be fortified and the amounts of folic acid that can be added are controlled under government regulations, whereas in others no regulations apply and decisions concerning fortification are at the discretion of individual manufacturers. Although voluntary folic acid fortification (where permitted) will invariably increase mean dietary intakes and biomarker concentrations of folate, the benefit will only be achieved by those who choose to eat the fortified food product. Thus, compared with mandatory fortification, voluntary fortification can create more disparities in folate status (and thus in any related health outcomes).

29.6.1   North and South America

In the United States and Canada, cereal grain food products have been fortified with folic acid for the past 20 years under a mandatory policy at a level of 1.4 mg per kg flour or grain product [10]. In Chile, only bread is fortified with folic acid (220 µg folic acid per 100 g bread flour), aimed at providing an average of 400 µg/d folic acid to women 15–44 years of age [11]. Studies comparing folate status before and after the introduction of mandatory fortification in these countries show clear benefits on a population-wide basis, with marked increases in folate biomarker concentrations, and correspondingly, a decline in folate deficiency to negligible proportions. Correspondingly, as will be discussed below, significant impacts on health outcomes have been achieved.

29.6.2   Australia and New Zealand

Mandatory folic acid-fortification of wheat flour was introduced in Australia in September 2009. One analysis of over 20,000 blood samples collected in a convenience sample of Australian adults was conducted to determine the impact of the new policy [12]. Results showed that mandatory fortification resulted in a 31% increase in mean serum folate concentrations and a reduction in the prevalence of low serum folate from 9.3 to 2.1%.

In New Zealand, no mandatory fortification with folic acid is yet in place. Voluntary fortification is, however, permitted, typically involving the addition of folic acid to bread and breakfast cereals. Evidence from the 2008–09 population-based New Zealand Adult Nutrition Survey (NZANS) showed generally satisfactory folate status and a low prevalence of deficiency, based on folate biomarker analysis of over 3,000 blood samples from a total sample of 4,721 survey participants [13]. Usage of folic acid supplements and consumption of fortified foods were each associated with significantly higher folate status.

29.6.3   Europe

National fortification policy varies considerably throughout the European Union. Although many European countries, such as the UK and Ireland, permit the addition of folic acid and other nutrients to foods on a voluntary basis (i.e. at the manufacturer's discretion), others prohibit fortification of any foods (e.g. Denmark) or specifically limit fortification with folic acid (e.g. the Netherlands).

Nationally representative dietary surveys are available for several European countries [14]. However, such surveys are often conducted without the collection of blood samples, thereby preventing the examination of biomarker concentrations in relation to population intakes of folate. Where biomarker data are reported, much variability in folate status is found to exist across different European countries, and this is largely explained by differences in exposure to folic acid fortified foods.

29.6.3.1   Ireland (Liberal Fortification Policy)

In Ireland, as in the UK, a voluntary (and relatively liberal) fortification policy is in place which permits folic acid and other micronutrients to be added to various foods (e.g. breakfast cereals). This allows the consumer to have ready access to fortified foods. Studies show that nearly 80% of the Irish population consumes fortified foods on a regular basis [15].

The National Adult Nutrition Survey (NANS) of 1,500 adults aged 18+ years has provided recent population-based data on folate status for Irish adults. This is the first representative dietary survey in Ireland (and one of the very few in Europe) to also provide corresponding folate biomarker data and to do so in a way that enables the impact of fortification to be clearly examined. The highest folate concentrations, across all population subgroups of Irish adults, were found in those consuming folic acid [15]. Folic acid was predominantly provided through fortified foods, with 68% of the population consuming folic acid from fortified foods and a further 11% consuming folic acid from the combination of fortified foods and supplements [15]. Non-consumers of folic acid (from either fortified food or supplements) had the lowest concentrations of serum and RBC folate, while consumers of folic acid from both sources had the highest concentrations. Although mean folate concentrations were generally high in Irish adults, non-consumers of folic acid from fortified food or supplements (18% of the population) were at high risk of suboptimal folate status.

29.6.3.2   Denmark (Fortification Prohibited)

Danish legislation regarding food fortification is very restrictive compared to most other European countries. As a result, no food items fortified with folic acid are available to consumers on the retail market in Denmark. When folate status was evaluated in a random sample of 6,784 Danish adults aged 30–60 years, the overall prevalence of low serum folate (i.e. <6.8 nmol/L) was 31.4%, much greater than would be expected for an affluent population [16]. In addition to the fact that the study cohort was not population-based, a limitation of this study is that blood samples were assayed after eight years of storage at-20 °C—conditions generally considered inadequate to prevent folate loss during storage, which may have contributed to some extent to the high prevalence of deficient folate status reported. The overall findings remain meaningful, however, and generally reinforce the view that, in the absence of folic acid fortification, achievement of adequate biomarker status of folate is difficult even in well-nourished populations.

29.6.4   Effects of Fortification on Folate Status in Children

Folate status was reported in a nationally representative sample of British children aged 4–18 years based on survey data from 2,127 randomly sampled children, of which laboratory measures of folate were available for 840 [17]. Exposure to fortified food, permitted on the basis of voluntary policy, was predominantly provided by breakfast cereal. In the total sample (median age 12.2 years), both serum and RBC folate biomarkers were significantly higher in males compared to females. Of note, folate status decreased significantly with age from four to 18 years [17]. Fortified breakfast cereal intake and vitamin supplement use were each associated with significantly higher folate (and lower homocysteine) concentrations; however, these factors did not explain the differences in biomarkers with age. Similarly, in the United States, higher serum and RBC folate concentrations were reported in children aged 4–11 years compared with 12–19 year olds, whether this was based on pre-fortification (1988–1994) or post-fortification (1999–2010) folate values [18].

The decline in folate status biomarkers with age observed in British and American children, despite apparently adequate dietary intakes, may be an indication that folate requirements of older children are increased owing to higher metabolic demands for growth from childhood to adolescence. In any case, these findings may have implications for emerging dietary folate recommendations in children and adolescents.

29.7   The Role of Folic Acid Fortification in Achieving Better Health Outcomes

The variability in folate status arising through differences in fortification in different countries as discussed above is in turn reflected in differences in health outcomes. Public health efforts and related policy in relation to folate are focused on preventing spina bifida and related birth defects, collectively known as neural tube defects (NTDs). Although over 80 countries worldwide have passed regulations for the mandatory fortification of foods with folic acid, to date the practice remains virtually non-existent in Europe. Although under consideration for some time in the United Kingdom and Ireland, it has not yet been mandated in either country and continues to be debated. In the meantime, voluntary fortification with folic acid is permitted in some (but by no means all) European countries.

NTDs are major birth defects occurring as a result of failure of the neural tube to close properly in early pregnancy and leading to death or varying degrees of disability involving the spinal cord, the most common form of which is spina bifida. For almost 25 years, conclusive evidence has existed that folic acid in early pregnancy can prevent the occurrence of NTDs. This evidence has led to very clear folic acid recommendations for women of reproductive age which are in place worldwide. For the prevention of NTDs, women worldwide are advised to take 400 μg/day folic acid from preconception until the end of the first trimester of pregnancy.

29.7.1   Health Outcomes in Regions with and Without Mandatory Fortification

In the absence of mandatory fortification, folic acid supplementation has been the focus of health promotion for the prevention of NTDs in Europe. Over the years, health promotion campaigns have been introduced to encourage women to follow the recommendations correctly. Despite these efforts, however, it is evident that promoting folic acid supplementation has had little impact as a strategy to prevent NTDs.

Supplementation with folic acid, while undoubtedly highly effective as a means to optimize folate status in individual women who take the supplements, is not an effective population strategy. This is primarily because the neural tube closes in the first few weeks of pregnancy (by day 28 post-conception), and therefore the timing of folic acid usage by women is critical to preventing NTD-affected pregnancies. Thus the malformations of NTDs may have occurred before a woman even knows that she is pregnant. For this reason, supplementation will be ineffective for women with unplanned pregnancies, estimated to account for 50% of all pregnancies. Even in women who have planned their pregnancy, compliance with current folate recommendations is poor; globally, preconception use of folic acid as per current recommendations is only about 20–30% [19, 20]. Thus for many women the period from preconception until the 28th day of the pregnancy (when folic acid is protective against NTDs) may have passed before folic acid supplementation is started. One study of pregnant women attending an antenatal clinic in Northern Ireland showed that although over 80% of women were aware of folic acid and had taken it during the first trimester, the majority (i.e. 4 in every 5) were not meeting the specific recommendation to take 400 μg/day folic acid from before conception until the 12th week of pregnancy [20]. Moreover, women who did not start folic acid supplements as recommended were twice as likely as those that did to have sub-optimal folate status, as indicated by failure to achieve the RBC folate level of 400 μg/L (906 nmol/L) or above associated with lowest risk of a pregnancy affected by NTDs (Fig. 29.2) [20].

Thus in European countries, policy to prevent NTDs has been largely ineffective because women are generally not compliant with folic acid supplementation as recommended before and during early pregnancy, with serious consequences. Notably, over 10 years ago, powerful evidence was published from a large multi-center study examining 13 million birth records from nine European countries which showed that there was no detectable impact on incidence of NTDs in any country over the 10-year period from 1988 to 1998, covering the time before and after current folic acid recommendations were introduced and actively promoted [21]. A more recent report recorded 7,478 NTD cases in the period 2000–10, representing a 1.6 times higher prevalence of NTDs in Europe compared to regions with mandatory folic acid fortification [22]. The most comprehensive report to date showed trends in the prevalence of NTDs in Europe based on 12.5 million births from 19 European countries over a 20-year period from 1991 to 2011 [23]. During

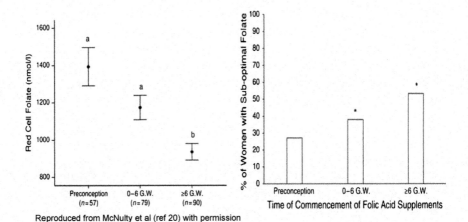

Reproduced from McNulty et al (ref 20) with permission

Fig. 29.2 Folate status at the 14th gestational week (GW) in pregnant women according to time of starting folic acid supplements. Depicts red blood cell folate concentrations (*left-hand plot*) and the proportion of pregnant women with suboptimal folate status (*right-hand plot*) at the 14th gestational week according to reported time of starting folic acid supplement use. The cut-off for optimal red blood cell folate was taken as ≥ 907 nmol/L (400 μg/l), the maternal concentration associated with lowest risk of having a pregnancy affected by NTDs [29]. Only 19% of this sample had started taking folic acid supplements before conception, as recommended. *Significantly greater proportions of women with suboptimal red cell folate status were detected in the two groups who started folic acid supplementation after conception (during 0–6 or after 6 gestational weeks) compared with the preconception group (Chi-square test: $X^2 = 11.03$; $P < 0.0001$). *Source* Reproduced from McNulty et al. [20] with permission

this time, there was no decrease in the prevalence of NTDs and 11,353 new cases of NTDs (5,776 spina bifida cases) were recorded. All three reports prove the ineffectiveness of current public health strategies (based primarily on folic acid supplementation) in preventing NTDs in Europe and have called for mandatory fortification to be implemented [21–23].

By contrast, the policy of mandatory fortification of foods with folic acid, by ensuring a better and even distribution of folate status in the general population, has proven itself in terms of lowering the risk of NTDs. Those countries worldwide (more than 80) where mandatory folic acid fortification has been introduced have experienced marked reductions in NTDs. Reported rates of NTDs have declined by between 27 and 50% in the USA, Canada and Chile in response to mandatory folic acid fortification of food [24–27]. Such evidence makes a strong case for adopting mandatory fortification in European countries. Of particular concern are reports that the incidence of NTDs in Ireland has been increasing in recent years [28].

The question often arises as to the impact of *voluntary* fortification on NTDs. The measurement of RBC folate in women of reproductive age is a useful way to assess NTD risk within populations on the basis of the known continuous dose-response inverse relationship between maternal RBC folate concentrations and NTDs [29]. Of note, the New Zealand Adult Nutrition Survey (NZANS) referred to above [13] identified that while mean folate concentrations appeared satisfactory in women aged 16–44 years under conditions of voluntary fortification, only 27% had RBC folate concentrations considered optimal in terms of reaching the level associated with lowest risk of an NTD-affected pregnancy (i.e. 906 nmol/L or higher). Likewise, the recent National Adult Nutrition Survey (NANS) in Ireland [15] showed generally high mean folate intakes and status in the Irish population, but non-consumers of folic acid from fortified food or supplements (18% of the population) were at greatest risk of suboptimal folate status. Of concern, among young women who were non-consumers of folic acid, only 16% had attained a folate biomarker concentration for optimal protection against NTDs (Fig. 29.3) [15]. What these studies show is that it is not enough to rely on mean dietary intake and biomarker data when assessing folate status within populations. At-risk groups (women of reproductive age) need to be specifically investigated with a focus on those with lower intakes and status (i.e. non-consumers of folic acid from fortified foods or supplements).

Thus the recent population-based evidence from Ireland and New Zealand shows that voluntary fortification is a poor substitute for mandatory fortification in terms of optimizing the folate status of women generally [13, 15]. In the absence of mandatory fortification, folate status in many populations is insufficient to protect against the occurrence of NTDs and possibly other folate-related diseases. On this basis, dietary folate intakes can be considered suboptimal in the diets of many Europeans in that, although they may be adequate in preventing clinical deficiency (megaloblastic anemia), they are typically insufficient in achieving a biomarker status of folate that is associated with the lowest risk of NTDs.

Public health policy in this area recognizes that, apart from preventing NTDs, there are other potential benefits of optimal folate metabolism throughout the

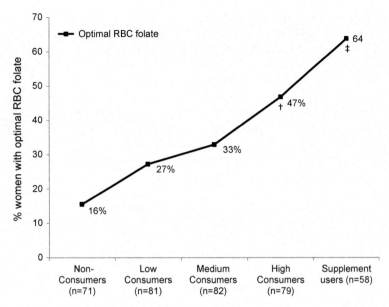

Fig. 29.3 Proportion of Irish women aged 18–50 years with optimal red blood cell (RBC) folate status for protection against NTDs according to folic acid intake from fortified foods and supplements. The cut-off for optimal red blood cell (RBC) folate was taken as ≥ 907 nmol/L (400 μg/l), the maternal concentration associated with the lowest risk of having a pregnancy affected by NTDs [29]. Non-consumers consumed no folic acid (via fortified food or supplements) during assessment by food diary. Those who consumed folic acid from fortified foods but not supplements were stratified into tertiles of folic acid intake; low consumers (1–33 μg/d), medium consumers (34–86 μg/d) and high consumers (≥ 87 μg/d). Supplement users consumed folic acid supplements (and 83% of supplement users also consumed fortified foods). Median RBC folate concentrations were 638, 705, 775, 859 and 1233 nmol/L across non-consumers, low, medium and high consumers of fortified food and supplements users respectively. The proportions of women with optimal folate status was compared across consumption groups using binary logistic regression controlling for smoking status and MTHFR genotype. *Double dagger* denotes significantly different from non-consumers, low and medium consumers; *Dagger* denotes significantly different from non-consumers (Bonferonni post hoc test) P < 0.05. *Source* Adapted from Hopkins et al. [15] with permission

lifecycle [3]. The evidence base at this time supports a number of such roles for folate, including preventing the development of cardiovascular disease and certain cancers, and maintaining better cognitive and bone health in aging. In this regard, there are important roles (and interactions) of vitamins B_2, B_6 and B_{12} which are required to maintain normal folate metabolism, and more recently the influence of common genetic variations and their interactions with folate and related B-vitamins is emerging, including a novel discovery in relation to preventing hypertension [3, 4]. Fortification can play a role in ensuring a more optimal status of not only folate but also related B-vitamins.

29.8 Are There Any Risks to Health?

As discussed, the United States, along with over 80 countries worldwide, has passed regulations for the mandatory fortification of food with folic acid with proven benefits in preventing NTDs. Many other counties have not introduced such polices or experienced reductions in NTD rates. Mandatory folic acid fortification remains controversial, however, with many opposed to introducing such a policy on safety grounds. Because of these concerns, European governments, including Ireland and the UK, have delayed decisions to implement population-based folic acid fortification.

Folic acid, the synthetic form of folate, is used widely for food fortification and supplementation purposes. Once ingested, folic acid is reduced by dihydrofolate reductase (DHFR), and after subsequent methylation, it is released in the systemic circulation as 5-methyltetrahydrofolate. However, the capacity of DHFR in humans to efficiently metabolize folic acid is limited and thus exposure to high oral doses of folic acid can result in the appearance of unmetabolized folic acid in the circulation. The latter is not a normal constituent of plasma or other tissues. On this basis, concerns have been raised regarding potential (though as yet unconfirmed) adverse health effects of unmetabolized folic acid in the circulation arising through high folic acid exposures from supplements and fortified foods.

Traditionally the concern related to the potential risk that long-term exposure to high-dose folic acid might mask the anemia of vitamin B_{12} deficiency in older people while allowing the associated irreversible neurological symptoms to progress [30], but this is no longer considered to be a public health concern—at least in relation to folic acid intakes from fortified foods. Also analysis of NHANES data in the US showed that among elderly participants with low vitamin B_{12} status, the presence of unmetabolized folic acid in serum was associated with worse cognitive performance compared to those with low B_{12} status and no detectable folic acid in the circulation [31]; subsequent studies have not confirmed such effects, so these findings remain somewhat controversial. Other evidence suggested that folic acid doses in excess of 1 mg/d may potentially promote the growth of undiagnosed colorectal adenomas in those with pre-existing lesions [32]; however, one recent meta-analysis (involving 50,000 individuals) concluded that folic acid supplementation neither increased nor decreased site-specific cancer within the first five years of treatment [33]. Observational studies conducted in countries with either mandatory or voluntary folic acid food fortification have reported detectable amounts of unmetabolized folic acid in the circulation in considerable proportions of adults and children, albeit at low concentrations. Whether or not the presence of unmetabolized folic acid arising from higher folic acid intakes is a cause for concern remains to be confirmed. However, the vast majority of studies published to date show no harmful effects. Given that there is some degree of uncertainty regarding the long-term effects of exposure to high dose folic acid, however, it is important to avoid population-wide chronic exposures to folic acid at levels higher than are necessary for beneficial effects.

The risk-benefit debate surrounding food fortification with folic acid continues among scientists and policymakers. It is, however, unlikely that there are any adverse effects associated with the presence of unmetabolized folic acid in the circulation at the generally low concentrations arising through food fortification. Indeed, an expert international panel tasked with reviewing all aspects of folate biology and biomarkers recently concluded that it was "not aware of any toxic or abnormal effects of circulating folic acid" even from much higher exposures than those obtained by food fortification [4].

29.9 Summary: Key Messages

- Foods fortified with folic acid can provide a sustainable form of this important B-vitamin and contribute greatly to achieving optimal folate status in populations worldwide. Apart from the public health benefit of achieving better folate status, there is also clear evidence that fortification of food with folic acid is associated with better health outcomes.
- Folate inadequacy exists in numerous countries, especially those with no or limited access to fortified food, including many European countries, and this has resulted in an increased risk of adverse health outcomes particularly in relation to NTDs. The evidence linking low, but not necessarily deficient, folate status with NTDs is conclusive and beyond debate.
- Despite the known and emerging health benefits, achieving optimal folate at a population level presents significant challenges for developed as well as developing countries. This is because natural food folates are inherently unstable and have limited bioavailability, and they can also undergo significant losses before they are even ingested; thus their ability to influence folate biomarker status is limited. Fortified foods can overcome these challenges because folic acid (the vitamin form used for fortification) is highly stable and bioavailable.
- As a sole health promotion measure to prevent NTDs in most European countries, the lack of success of folic acid supplementation is reflected in adverse health outcomes, with clear evidence that there has been no change in NTDs over the 20-year period during which this strategy has been in place.
- There are urgent public health implications for the countries worldwide without policies of mandatory folic acid fortification of food. Some countries have delayed decisions to introduce mandatory fortification with folic acid on the basis of concerns relating to possible risk. The balance of evidence at this time, however, shows a very strong case for fortification and indicates that the proven benefits would more than outweigh any potential risks.

References

1. McNulty, H. and Pentieva, K. Folate bioavailability. In: Bailey L.B, editor. Folate in Health and Disease, 2nd ed. Boca Raton (FL): CRC Press, Taylor and Francis Group; 2010. pp. 25–47.
2. Shane, B. Folate chemistry and metabolism. In: Bailey L.B, editor. Folate in Health and Disease, 2nd ed. Boca Raton (FL): CRC Press, Taylor and Francis Group; 2010. pp. 1–24,
3. McNulty H, Pentieva K, Hoey L, Strain JJ, Ward M. Nutrition throughout life: Folate. International Journal for Vitamin and Nutrition Research 2012; 82:348–354.
4. Bailey LB, Stover PJ, McNulty H, Fenech MF, Gregory JF, Mills JL, Pfeiffer CM, Fazili Z, Zhang M, Ueland PM, Molloy AM, Caudill MA, Shane B, Berry RJ, Bailey LR, Hausman D, Raghavan R & Raiten DJ. Biomarkers of Nutrition for Development—Folate Review. Journal of Nutrition 2015; 145: 1636S–1680S.
5. McLean E., de Benoist B., Allen L.H. Review of the magnitude of folate deficiencies worldwide. Food and Nutrition Bulletin 2008; 29 (suppl): S38–S51.
6. McKillop D, Pentieva K, Daly D, McPartlin J, Hughes J, Strain JJ, Scott JM, McNulty H. The effect of different cooking methods on folate retention in various foods which are amongst the major contributors to folate intake in the UK diet. British Journal of Nutrition 2002; 88: 681–688.
7. Institute of Medicine. Dietary Reference Intakes for thiamin, riboflavin, niacin, vitamin B6, folate, vitamin B12, pantothenic acid, biotin, and choline. Washington (DC): National Academy Press, 1998.
8. Hoey L, McNulty H, Duffy ME, Hughes CF, Strain JJ. EURRECA—Estimating Folate Requirements for Deriving Dietary Reference Values. Critical Reviews in Food Science and Nutrition 2013; 53: 1041–1050.
9. EFSA. European Food Safety Authority Panel on Dietetic Products, Nutrition and Allergies (NDA). Scientific Opinion on Dietary Reference Values for Folate. EFSA Journal 2014; 12 (11):3893 (revised Feb 2015). Accessed at:http://www.efsa.europa.eu/en/efsajournal/pub/3893.
10. Berry R, Mullinare J, Hamner HC. Folic acid fortification: neural tube defect risk reduction - a global perspective. In: Bailey L.B, editor. Folate in Health and Disease, 2nd ed. Boca Raton (FL): CRC Press, Taylor and Francis Group; 2010. pp. 179–204.
11. Food Fortification Initiative. Accessed at: http://ffinetwork.org.
12. Brown RD, Langshaw MR, Uhr EJ, Gibson JN, Joshua DE. The impact of mandatory fortification of flour with folic acid on the blood folate levels of an Australian population. Med J Aust 2011; 194: 65–67.
13. University of Otago and Ministry of Health. A Focus on Nutrition: Key findings of the 2008/09 New Zealand Adult Nutrition Survey. Wellington: Ministry of Health. 2011.
14. Flynn A, Hirvonen T, Mensink G B, Ocke MC, Serra-Majem L, Stos K, Wildemann T. Intake of selected nutrients from foods, from fortification and from supplements in various European countries. Food Nutr Res 2009 (Supplement 1); 1–53.
15. Hopkins SM, Gibney MJ, Nugent AP, McNulty H, Molloy AM, Scott JM, Flynn A, Strain JJ, Ward M, Walton J, McNulty BA. Impact of voluntary fortification and supplement use on dietary intakes and biomarker status of folate and vitamin B12 in Irish adults. American Journal of Clinical Nutrition 2015; 101: 1163–1172.
16. Thuesen BH, Husemoen LL, Ovesen L, Jorgensen T, Fenger M, Linneberg A. Lifestyle and genetic determinants of folate and vitamin B12 levels in a general adult population. British Journal Nutrition 2010; 103: 1195–1204.
17. Kerr MA, Livingstone B, Bates CJ, Bradbury I, Scott JM, Ward M, Pentieva K, Mansoor MA, McNulty HM. Folate, related B vitamins and homocysteine in childhood and adolescence: potential implications for disease risk in later life. Pediatrics 2009; 123: 627–635.
18. Pfeiffer CM, Hughes JP, Lacher DA, Bailey RL, Berry RJ, Zhang M, Johnson CL. Estimation of trends in serum and RBC folate in the U.S. population from pre- to postfortification using assay-adjusted data from the NHANES 1988–2010. J Nutr 2012; 142: 886–893.

19. Ray JG, Singh G, Burrows RF. Evidence for suboptimal use of periconceptional folic acid supplements globally. BJOG 2004;111:399–408.
20. McNulty B, McNulty B, Pentieva K, Marshall B, Ward M, Molloy AM, Scott JM, McNulty H. Women's compliance with current folic acid recommendations and achievement of optimal vitamin status for preventing neural tube defects. Human Reproduction 2011; 26: 1530–1536.
21. Botto LD, Lisi A, Robert-Gnansia E, et al. International retrospective cohort study of neural tube defects in relation to folic acid recommendations: are the recommendations working. Br Med J 2005; 330:571–573.
22. Obeid R, Pietrzik K, Oakley Jr GP, Kancherla V, Holzgreve W, Wieser S. Preventable spina bifida and anencephaly in Europe. Birth Defects Research (Part A) 2015; 103:763–771, 2015.
23. Khoshnood B, Loane M, Dolk H, et al. Long term trends in prevalence of neural tube defects in Europe: Population based study. *BMJ (Online)* 2015; 351: 1–5.
24. Honein MA, Paulozzi LJ, Mathews TJ, Erickson JD, Wong LYC. Impact of folic acid fortification of the US food supply on the occurrence of neural tube defects. J Am Med Assoc 2001; 285: 2981–2986.
25. Williams J, Mai CT, Mulinare J, Isenberg J, Flood TJ, Ethan M, Frohnert B, Kirby RS. Updated estimates of neural tube defects prevented by mandatory folic Acid fortification - United States, 1995–2011. MMWR Morb Mortal Wkly Rep 2015; 64:1–5.
26. De Wals P, Tairou F, Van Allen MI, Uh S-H, Lowry RB, Sibbald B, Evans JA, Van den Hof MC, Zimmer P, Crowley M, Fernandez B, Lee NS, Niyonsenga T. Reduction in neural-tube defects after folic acid fortification in Canada. New Engl. J. Med. 2007; 357: 135–142.
27. Cortés F, Mellado C, Pardo RA, Villarroel LA, Hertrampf E. Wheat flour fortification with folic acid: changes in neural tube defects rates in Chile. Am J Med Genet A 2012; 158A:1885–90.
28. McDonnell R, Delany V, O'Mahony MT, Mullaney C, Lee B, Turner MJ. Neural tube defects in the Republic of Ireland in 2009–11. Journal of Public Health 2014; 37:57–63.
29. Daly LE, Kirke PN, Molloy AM, Weir DC, Scott JM. Folate levels and Neural tube defects. Implications for prevention. J Am Med Assoc 1995; 274:1698–1702.
30. Savage JD, Lindenbaum J. Folate-cobalamin interactions. In: Bailey L.B, editor. Folate and Health and Disease. New York: Marcel Decker; 1995. pp. 237–86.
31. Morris MS, Jacques PF, Rosenberg IH, Selhub J. Circulating unmetabolized folic acid and 5-methyltetrahydrofolate in relation to anemia, macrocytosis, and cognitive test performance in American seniors. Am J Clin Nutr 2010;91:1733–44.
32. Cole BF, Baron JA, Sandler RS, Haile RW, Ahnen DJ, Bresalier RS, McKeown-Eyssen G, Summers RW, Rothstein RI, Burke CA, et al. Folic acid for the prevention of colorectal adenomas: a randomised clinical trial. JAMA 2007; 297: 2351–2359.
33. Vollset SE, Clarke R, Lewington S, Ebbing M, Halsey J, Lonn E, Armitage J, Manson JE, Hankey GJ, Spence JD, et al. Effects of folic acid supplementation on overall and site-specific cancer incidence during the randomised trials: meta-analyses of data on 50,000 individuals. Lancet 2013;381:1029–36.

Chapter 30
The Role of Fortification and Dietary Supplements in Affluent Countries: Challenges and Opportunities

Johanna T. Dwyer and Regan L. Bailey

Abstract This chapter asks whether there is a role for enrichment/fortification and/or dietary supplements in highly industrialized countries today, and what challenges and opportunities exist regarding their use. It considers fortification and supplementation together because both affect total nutrient exposures and both are popular in developed countries. Fortification increases the nutrient density of certain foods in specific ways. Dietary supplements of some types add nutrients in another, more concentrated, form. Other important determinants of dietary quality—such as variety in servings of food groups, moderation of nutrient or food intakes, balance of macronutrients, and variety of foods within and across food groups—must be achieved with other nutritional strategies. Dietary supplements that provide nutrients that are low or lacking in the diets of specific population subgroups have beneficial effects, but care should be taken to avoid over-promising the benefits of fortification and supplementation; a well-balanced diet is critical to optimal health. The public health rationale for non-nutrient supplements (plant food supplements) is unclear. Neither fortification nor supplementation can remedy all the diet-related problems of affluent countries, many of which also require dietary diversity, balance, and moderation in eating habits to achieve more healthful optimal food patterns.

Keywords Fortification · Supplementation · Dietary supplement · Nutrient · Nutritional strategies · Well-balanced diet · Healthful food patterns

J.T. Dwyer (✉)
Office of Dietary Supplements, National Institutes of Health,
6100 Executive Blvd, Bethesda, MD 20892, USA
e-mail: Dwyerj1@od.nih.gov; Jdwyer1@tuftsmedicalcenter.org

J.T. Dwyer
The Jean Mayer US Department of Agriculture Human Nutrition Research Center on Aging,
The School of Medicine, Friedman School of Nutrition Science and Policy, and the Frances
Stern Nutrition Center, Tufts Medical Center, Tufts University, Boston, MA 02111, USA

R.L. Bailey
Department of Nutrition Science, Purdue University, West Lafayette, IN, USA

R.L. Bailey
Office of Dietary Supplements, National Institutes of Health, Bethesda, USA

© Springer International Publishing AG 2017   389
H.K. Biesalski et al. (eds.), *Sustainable Nutrition in a Changing World*,
DOI 10.1007/978-3-319-55942-1_30

30.1   State of the Art

30.1.1   Goals

The rationale for the addition of nutrients to the diet is that most foods contain several naturally occurring nutrients at relatively low levels. The addition of nutrients by enrichment (replacing nutrients lost in processing), fortification (adding nutrients at higher levels than naturally occur in the food), or supplementation enhances intakes in foods that are widely consumed, raising them to more desirable levels.

30.1.2   Vision for the Future

Greater harmonization between countries in their regulatory approaches is desirable. Codex Alimentarius has made laudable progress in laying down specifications, and the European Union has begun to develop a common regulatory framework. However, there is little hope that the various industrialized countries with their different regulatory systems will agree on common regulations covering fortification and dietary supplements that will harmonize their regulatory approaches completely. Nevertheless, it may be possible in the near future to develop a common, agreed upon framework for evaluating the scientific issues involving safety and efficacy. This should include systematic, evidence-based reviews of the literature collected by an independent panel of experts. Countries can then use these findings to develop regulations that fit with their individual cultures, politics, and economics.

30.1.3   Challenges

The fortification of foods and the use of dietary supplements are valuable strategies for improving nutrition in developing countries. But is there a place for them in affluent countries? This section reviews the nutrition-related challenges existing in such countries today.

- **Industrialized countries all have nutritional environments of affluence, with pockets of deficiency, imbalance and excess**
  In most highly industrialized countries today, enriched and fortified foods and dietary supplements are all to some extent present in the eating environment. Dietary supplement use is high [1, 2]. Rather than the widespread micronutrient deficiencies that afflicted the 19th century, today excessive consumption of food energy, saturated and trans fats, sugars, salt, and alcohol by much of the population increases risks of diet-related disease, and it is these disorders that

constitute the major challenges to health. Nevertheless, some widespread problems and pockets of deficiencies and imbalances remain, often making fortification and nutrient supplementation necessary.

- **Definitions Differ**
  The terms and legal interpretations of *enrichment*, *fortification*, and *dietary supplement* differ from one country to another, and so it is important to define them precisely.
- **Affluent countries differ in their regulatory philosophies**
  While all industrialized countries share the goal of optimal nutritional status, their regulatory philosophies vary. These differences are strikingly apparent in their diverse approaches to regulations pertaining to fortification and dietary supplements [3].

  - **Fortification** Fortification philosophy in the U.S. is voluntary, but if the manufacturer chooses to do so, regulations govern what foods can be fortified and at what levels. Aside from ensuring food safety, manufacturers are free to fortify foods for which standards have not been developed, such as cereals, fruit drinks, and vitamin waters. In Canada, Australia, and New Zealand voluntary fortification done solely for marketing purposes is not permitted. The European Union (EU) has extensive regulations governing fortification [3], including European Regulation 1925/2006 rules that provide lists for the addition of vitamins, minerals, and other substances to foods and amounts that are allowed [4].
  - **Dietary supplements** In the U.S., the Dietary Supplement and Health and Education Act of 1994 (DSHEA) is the legislative framework that defines and regulates dietary supplements. A very basic difference from many other industrialized countries is that a variety of supplement products are defined as foods under DSHEA, some of which would be regarded not as foods but as herbal medicines, food supplements, or drugs in other countries. These include not only vitamins, minerals, and amino acids but also herbs and other botanicals, other dietary substances to supplement the diet by increasing total dietary intake, concentrates, metabolites, constituents, extracts, or combinations. Since U.S. law regards them as foods when they are sold as supplements, manufacturers do not need to seek pre-market regulatory approval from the Food and Drug Administration (FDA) before marketing these products, whereas they do for medications. DSHEA does not set a limit on the amount of vitamins, minerals, botanicals or other ingredients that can be put into supplements. Also, the FDA can remove a supplement from the marketplace only if it finds proof that the supplement is dangerous. This has led critics to claim that unsafe or ineffective supplements can be sold freely. While Good Manufacturing Practice (GMP) along with other guidance is promulgated by the Agency to protect the public health, it is true that regulators have a more limited capacity to monitor adverse reactions from supplements than from drugs. The EU system is quite different in that dietary supplements (termed by the EU 'food supplements'), are defined as additions

to a normal diet with concentrated sources of nutrients or other substances that have a nutritional or physiological effect. Rules governing these products are published in EU Directive 2002/46/EC to protect consumers against potential health risks. This directive also ensures that misleading information is not provided and gives a list of vitamins and minerals that may be added, permitted sources from which they may be manufactured, and maximum and minimum levels set for each nutrient that is added to supplements. Some botanical dietary supplements sold in the US are considered herbal medicines in the EU and are regulated more strictly. The Herbal Directive 2004/24/EC covers traditional herbal medicinal products in the EU market, and herbal medicinal products need a marketing authorization before they can be sold.

30.2 Fortification and Enrichment Contribute to Intakes: A U.S. Case Study

We recently described the contributions of micronutrients to usual intakes from all sources (naturally occurring and those added to food [both fortified and enriched] and dietary supplements) and compared intakes to Dietary Reference Intakes aged two years and over, using data from the U.S. National Health and Nutrition Examination Survey (NHANES) [5]. In evaluations of this sort for policy purposes, total nutrient intakes of supplement users and non-users are needed to assess dietary impacts. In foods, the major sources of most water-soluble vitamins were enrichment and fortification, whereas the major sources of most minerals (with the exception of iron) were naturally-occurring nutrients intrinsic to foods. Both fortification and supplement use lowered the risk of inadequacy across most nutrients. However, the need to increase several nutrients of concern, such as vitamin D, calcium, and potassium, was not completely met by any of these strategies. Supplements increased the likelihood of intakes exceeding the Upper Tolerable Intake Level (UL) for some nutrients.

30.2.1 Fortification

The World Health Organization (WHO) and the Food and Agricultural Organization (FAO) define fortification as the practice of deliberately increasing the content of an essential micronutrient (e.g. vitamins or minerals) in a food to restore or improve the nutritional quality of the food supply and to provide a public health benefit with minimal risk to health [6]. A century ago, fortification eliminated many common dietary deficiency diseases such as xerophthalmia, rickets, pellagra, and endemic goiter in many highly industrialized countries, and it remains a useful public health strategy in these countries when a public health need exists [7, 8]. The effectiveness of fortification in the case of a specific nutrient depends on the magnitude of the estimated prevalence of inadequacy, the reliability and validity of that prevalence estimate, the health risks associated with the specific inadequacy, and an indication that the particular nutrient inadequacy can be ameliorated by increasing the availability of the nutrient in the food supply [6]. Ideally, fortificants should not alter the appearance, taste, texture, or odor of the food, nor recipes or methods of cooking [6].

Food fortification presents many challenges to regulators [9]. The latest Codex Alimentarius document governing fortification (now referred to as the Codex General Principles for the Addition of Essential Nutrients to Foods) was recently updated [10]. Codex guidelines include a recommendation for a sound public health rationale for fortification. They emphasize examining population exposure to nutrients from all sources, an assessment of need for the nutrient, and the use of scientific risk analysis to ensure sufficiency while not exceeding the UL [10]. Codex also emphasizes that labeling and advertising of the fortified food should not mislead or deceive consumers as to the food's merits [10].

Mandatory fortification occurs when food manufacturers are required by law to add certain vitamins or minerals to a specified food or foods to fulfill a demonstrated public health need [8]. One advantage of mandatory fortification is that the scope and coverage estimates can be precisely determined, and health effects are easily followed. The 'playing field' is leveled between producers, since the law applies to all products in the category covered, and thus competition on the basis of the price of fortified vs. the price of unfortified products is less intense. When fortification is mandatory, the private sector or the government may find it easier to develop and provide premixes for distributing the nutrients to food processors, along with guidance for their proper use. In the U.S., mandatory fortification is sometimes called enrichment, and refers to adding or restoring nutrients to conform to a standard of identity for the enriched food. For example, there are standards of identity for the addition of folic acid, thiamine, riboflavin and iron to flour. Certain other nutrients—such as vitamin A and D in milk, and iodine in salt—can be added voluntarily, but when they are added, the levels are specified in regulations. In Australia, manufacturers are required by law to add vitamin D to edible oil spreads (e.g. margarine), and thiamin and folic acid to wheat flour for making bread. In Canada, the Food and Drug Regulations specify the foods to which micronutrients can be added and the levels to which they may be added.

Even in highly industrialized countries, simply legislating for mandatory fortification does not mean that the population will benefit from it. A clear need for the nutrient must be established, preferably from population-based surveys of diet and from biomarkers of nutritional status. There must be a supportive infrastructure and system to implement and enforce regulations. Regulatory authorities must promulgate and publish standards, and provide assistance in implementing quality control measures so that the fortified products contain neither insufficient nor grossly excessive amounts of the nutrient. Also, in order to evaluate the effects of

Table 30.1 Some guiding principles for discretionary fortification in the U.S.

1. Justification should be based on documented public health needs, particularly the prevalence of dietary inadequacy in the population, and surveys of high-risk groups. Fortification is usually based not only on diet but also on other indicators of nutritional status such as biomarkers and clinical observations
2. Food intake data should be used with the UL to provide evidence from modeling approaches to explain how current exposures would be altered by fortification. This should be followed by exposure analysis and evaluation of the severity of possible adverse effects seen with intakes of foods, fortified foods, dietary supplements or pharmacological doses of nutrients. If the fortification of the food poses a significant risk of adverse effects to the population, it should not be undertaken
3. Consider fortifying foods up to good (10–19% Daily Value) or excellent (>20% Daily Value) levels when the results of modeling call for it
4. Some special-use products should be fortified. These include infant formulas, meal replacements and oral nutritional supplements
5. Before changing fortification policy, consideration should be given to the benefits and risks [20]

Source Committee on Uses of the Dietary Reference Intakes in Nutrition Labeling [20]

fortification, a population-based monitoring and assessment system must be in place.

Voluntary or discretionary fortification occurs when food manufacturers can choose which vitamins and minerals they add to food. In the early 20th century in the U.S., manufacturers rapidly and voluntarily accomplished iodine fortification of table salt at no additional cost to the consumer once the health benefits became clear and the medical community endorsed this. Later in the century, the same phenomenon occurred with iron fortification of infant formulas. Regulatory philosophies differ among industrialized countries with respect to whether fortification should be mandatory or not. For example, in New Zealand, breakfast cereals are fortified with a range of vitamins and minerals, although the amounts that can be added are regulated, whereas in the U.S. the amounts are not. In the U.S., most fortification is discretionary, and not mandated by law. However, if the manufacturer decides to fortify, it must be at a particular level. For example, such strictures apply to the amounts of vitamin D added to milk and folic acid added to wheat flour for making bread. In some highly industrialized countries, with many branded and packaged foods, manufacturers may prefer to voluntarily add the fortificant and advertise its presence in the product to gain a marketing advantage.

Table 30.1 presents a brief description of guidelines for voluntary fortification in the U.S. that were developed by a committee of the National Academies of Science.

30.2.1.1   Safety

The safety of fortification depends on well designed and enforced policies formulated on the basis of population-based surveys of food consumption; knowledge of the dietary intakes of high-risk groups; biomarkers and clinical indictors of deficiency and nutritional status; and indicators to show that the program resulted in increases in nutritional status without causing harm [11]. If the addition of non-nutrients to foods is permitted, it depends upon the underlying safety of the substance and evidence that the levels being used are safe.

30.2.1.2 Benefits

Fortification is a relatively simple technology. Its beauty is that when it is properly designed and administered to a population or a target group that is demonstrably in need of the nutrient, it is a safe, efficient and inexpensive way to improve nutritional status without making people change their eating habits. If the food vehicle is widely consumed, it may reach a very large number of those otherwise at risk of dietary deficiency. In addition to foods fortified with a single nutrient, more highly fortified foods include fortified formulas that are complete foods for young infants, meal replacements for those on reducing diets, and oral nutritional supplements for those at nutritional risk due to disease. There are also substitute foods, such as soy beverages fortified with calcium, vitamin D, and vitamin B_{12} for those who are vegetarians. In addition to helping to meet nutrient requirements, some fortificants, such as vitamins C and E, have technical effects that are useful in food processing, and other fortificants increase the bioavailability of other nutrients (such as vitamin C on iron bioavailability).

30.2.1.3 Disadvantages

The major disadvantage of fortification is that everyone in the population is exposed to it, regardless of whether or not they will benefit from it or whether they actually wish to consume fortified foods [12]. There is the possibility that while there are beneficial effects from fortifying certain target groups who are at risk of deficiency, other subgroups may be harmed. For example, iron fortification of foods makes many foods inedible to individuals suffering from hemochromatosis, whose storage of iron is abnormal, especially if they consume large amounts of alcohol.

When fortifying, the doses delivered differ depending on the amounts of the fortified foods consumed by those in various age/sex groups. For some target subgroups, the level of fortification may be insufficient to bring nutrient intakes up to desired levels without causing excessive intakes in other groups. In such instances, other measures, such as nutrition education, or dietary supplements, or both, may also be needed. Cost is another consideration. The optimal forms of a nutrient from the standpoint of bioavailability may be very expensive (as is the case with iron gluconate vs. electrolytic iron, or calcium-citrate-malate vs. calcium carbonate). For other nutrients, such as iodine, an estimate of current consumption from various foods is difficult to ascertain. Food composition tables may not exist, or, as is the case with iodine, many of the food sources are adventitious or else by-products of processing rather than having been deliberately added, making estimates of exposure from food sources highly imprecise [13]. 'Overage' in adding the fortificant to food may be necessary to ensure that when the product is consumed, enough of the nutrient is left after degradation in storage to meet label claims regarding the amount present.

The potential for excessive intakes of nutrients is possible when fortified foods are consumed together with dietary supplements. For example, after World War II in the United Kingdom, in addition to fortifying margarine with vitamin D, baby milk products were fortified with vitamin D and mothers also gave infants large amounts of cod liver oil, which is high in vitamin D. Some infants developed vitamin D intoxication and metastatic calcification of soft tissues. The event engendered skepticism toward vitamin-D-fortified milks that lasted for many decades. For safety and targeting reasons, in countries such as the U.S. where use is high, nutrient intakes and the status of nutrients such as vitamin D and folate are closely monitored.

30.2.1.4 Knowledge Gaps

The degree to which government should control fortification, the uses to which fortification may be put, and the regulations governing its use differ from country to country. A major challenge involving fortification is whether, and under what circumstances, voluntary (discretionary) fortification should be allowed. In some countries where vitamin D deficiency is common, fortification is mandatory in fat spreads and cooking oils, but it is voluntary in other foods, and its use is not widespread, so that the overall impact is insufficient to render exposures to vitamin D in most of the population satisfactory.

Foods may be fortified when there is no demonstrable public health need. The Codex principles cover voluntary fortification, but only for when food manufacturers choose to add specified essential nutrients to particular foods or food categories and the purpose is a public health need [14]. However, in the U.S., where discretionary fortification is allowed, the rationale for discretionary fortification sometimes seems driven more by marketing considerations and hopes that it will help sell products than by public health considerations. Registration prior to the granting of permission for discretionary fortification may help avoid some of the abuses that might occur.

Foods for increasing micronutrient intakes must reach the high-risk target groups. The optimal vehicle or vehicles for fortification may vary across the population when sub-populations at risk vary greatly from the norm in their food consumption practices (e.g. non-milk consumers in countries where vitamin D fortification of milk is used, or decreased consumption of vitamin-D-fortified milk and iodized salt among teenaged girls). One strategy to overcome this is to simultaneously fortify several foods which reach different target groups and thereby to increase intakes among greater numbers of people. However, it is difficult to assess the potential impacts of such fortification approaches and to avoid excess when several foods are varied at the same time without very sophisticated modeling techniques. For these reasons, careful monitoring of all fortification practices is essential [15].

Monitoring gaps exist. Fortification policies may also fail to keep up with changes in the frequency of consumption of the staple food that is being fortified, resulting in under-consumption of the nutrient by the target group.

Food composition databases are often incomplete or out of date, especially in countries where the discretionary addition of nutrients is allowed. Food composition databases based on label declarations of nutrient content may not reflect overages, (e.g. the additional amounts of nutrients added to prevent the deterioration of products during storage). Nutrient databases that more clearly distinguish between naturally occurring nutrients and fortificants and nutrient databases for dietary supplements are lacking in most countries. Food composition tables also often lack values for 25OH D in meat products and in some eggs from animals that have been given feeds containing this hormone.

Gaps need to be filled with respect to the various nutritional qualities of fortified foods. Some decry discretionary fortification as 'promiscuous'. They claim that the fortification of foods high in sugar, fat, and other sources of calories and salt is like 'putting lipstick on a pig' [12]. U.S. regulators have acted to urge producers of some of the more egregious products—such as calcium-fortified chocolate syrup, or low-calorie soft drinks with added vitamins—to voluntarily withdraw their products from the market. Nevertheless, some products—such as vitamin waters, highly fortified sports bars, and some other highly fortified foods—do remain on sale. They may not be dangerous, but they have little merit from the standpoint of improving public health. The regulatory agencies use their limited resources to act first upon products that may pose clear health hazards, such as those with excessive or imbalanced nutrients coupled with high doses of caffeine and other botanical bioactives in high amounts.

30.2.2 Future Challenges

30.2.2.1 Regulatory Philosophy

- How do highly industrialized countries differ in their regulations with respect to fortification and supplementation? Are there historical, philosophical or legislative differences? Who is responsible, what is the process, and how might there be more harmonization between countries?
- Does the lack of an agreed public health need for fortification preclude its use?
- When, under what circumstances, and with what standards of evidence, should the precautionary principle be applied in permitting the fortification of foods with folic acid, iron, and vitamin D?

30.2.2.2 Regulatory Policy

- Regulations on novel uses of fortification are needed. These include omega 3 fatty acids fed to chickens so that the eggs and poultry meat are rich sources of these fatty acids. Vitamin-D-fortified feeds are also used in some animal production systems. Lately, irradiated mushrooms that are a good source of vitamin D, selenium-fortified mushrooms, and energy drinks fortified with many different nutrients have been sold in U.S. markets and elsewhere.
- What is the best strategy for increasing nutrition status among those who are most vulnerable in highly industrialized countries, without running risks of excess in other members of the population who have lesser requirements?
- What effects, if any, will changes in product labeling have on nutrient intakes? For example, in the U.S., changes in the Nutrition Facts labels are currently being revised with updated nutrient requirements, and so label declarations for the same amounts of fortificants as 'good' or 'excellent' sources may change.
- When a clear public health need ascertained by regulatory authorities does not exist, should voluntary (discretionary) fortification be permitted? When, other than for safety reasons, should such voluntary fortification be prohibited?
- Since recommendations are for sodium reduction in most industrialized countries, and the most popular vehicle for iodizing is a condiment, should other foods be fortified with iodine in lieu of salt?
- How should bio-fortification be regulated? Should regulations differ for products of biotechnology (such as 'golden rice' with carotenoids added) compared to selective plant breeding using traditional conventional methods?
- What evidence should be required to declare that a public health need exists for fortifying foods with nutrients that are not currently routinely used for this purpose—omega 3 fatty acids, choline, fiber, flavonoids, glucosinolates, caffeine, and others for which emerging science may be promising?
- Should fortification be extended to non-nutrient bioactive constituents such as caffeine, flavonoids, polyphenols and others? How should supplements containing these substances be regulated?

30.2.2.3 Nutrition and Epidemiology

- How can better models be developed to predict the impacts of fortification? For example, folic acid fortification in the US increased consumption of folic acid not by the predicted 100 µg, but by nearly twice that level.
- How can epidemiologists provide policy makers with better information about both the lower and the higher ends of the nutrient intake distributions in both dietary supplement users and non-users, and better assess risk?
- What proportions of sub-groups, such as children, who take micronutrient supplements and eat many fortified foods, exceed the ULs? If they do, what, if any, are the adverse health consequences? If adverse effects do exist, how should policy be altered to lessen exposure risks?

30.2.2.4 Food Science

- More and better technologies are needed to develop more highly bioavailable fortificants that are reasonably priced for calcium, fiber, magnesium, potassium, and iron.
- How can the technical and other obstacles that prevent fortification with some nutrients of public health concern (e.g. potassium, vitamin K) be overcome? If they cannot be overcome, what is the most desirable way to raise intakes?
- Can bio-fortification and recombinant technologies be effectively used to help ensure food security during this era of concerns over sustainability and climate change?

30.3 Dietary Supplements

The Codex Alimentarius suggests, and most national regulatory authorities agree, that since foods contain many substances in addition to nutrients that promote health, the consumption of such foods should be encouraged before vitamin and mineral supplements come into consideration [16, 17]. However, when diets are insufficient or consumers believe that their diets require supplementation, dietary supplements may be considered. That said, the fact remains that the definitions, legislation, and regulations governing dietary supplements differ dramatically from one industrialized country to another. However, in virtually all countries, the definition of dietary supplements includes vitamins, minerals, and most other essential nutrients. The complication is that nutrient supplements are only one of many types of products in the dietary supplement category in countries such as the U.S., whereas in other countries nutrient supplements are in a category of their own.

30.3.1 Safety

The safety of most nutrient supplements when used in doses near recommended levels is well established. Dietary supplements of vitamins and minerals or other nutrients can provide a specific nutrient in relatively high doses without providing food energy or other nutrients that may already be present in abundance. However, there is also a potential for high exposures, particularly among children whose requirements are low but who may be given high doses of some supplements.

Non-nutrient supplements, such as botanicals, present a broader array of safety concerns than do nutrient supplements. The botanical ingredients themselves are many and complex, and they may present safety hazards if they are sourced from the incorrect species. The bioactive compound or compounds may be unknown. Blends and extracts may be poorly characterized and of unknown safety in some instances. Products may be spiked with illegal drugs and adulterants such as contaminates, pesticides, and heavy metals that may pose risks unrelated to their stated ingredients. The risk is greater that some harmful or adulterated nutrient or non-nutrient supplement products will reach the market in countries that regulate them as foods with no premarket approval than it is in countries that require registration or regulate these supplements as medicines or pharmaceuticals.

30.3.2 Benefits

Dietary supplements fill nutrient gaps that are, or cannot be, met through food alone. Formulations of one, two, or more nutrients can be customized for the needs of specific population groups such as infants, pregnant women, or the elderly, and can be targeted to them. Examples include vitamin D supplements for breast-fed infants, folic acid and iron supplements for peri-conceptional and pregnant women, and omega 3 fatty acid supplements for premature infants. If use is restricted to groups most in need, supplements avoid the risk of wasting nutrients on groups not in need or who might even be harmed by them.

30.3.3 Disadvantages

Both the conditions of use and the products themselves must be considered. Absorption and bioavailability may vary when products are consumed on an empty stomach rather than with meals. The potential exists for some supplements to interact with prescription medications. Also some individuals may use dietary supplements as alternatives to conventional medicines, and/or delay conventional medical treatment that might otherwise have been beneficial.

The primary disadvantage to supplementation is the potential for very high exposures to nutrients or other bioactive constituents that they contain. In the U.S., the FDA is prohibited from limiting the composition of dietary supplements or levels except for clearly demonstrable safety reasons, and so products can legally exceed the UL. Because nutrient-containing supplements are concentrated sources of micronutrients, there is the potential for those who use them to exceed the UL if they consume such supplements in high doses, and this may pose safety risks. This is a particular problem in highly industrialized countries, since the background food supply is often already adequate in many nutrients, and fortified with others. Moreover, supplement users tend to be individuals who already have nutritionally adequate or superior diets [18, 19].

30.3.4 Knowledge Gaps

The largest gap in our knowledge of dietary supplements concerns their efficacy in preventing or reducing the risk of adverse health outcomes, especially that of non-nutrients. The safety of certain supplements, such as folic acid used in supplements and fortificants, needs continued monitoring in order to assure safety and efficacy.

Methods are needed for producing lower-cost, high-quality dietary supplements for individuals who are dependent on these sources of nutrients on account of rare disorders of amino acid, carbohydrate and fatty acid metabolism, as well as the vitamin dependency disorders. Policies to ensure that such patients receive them are also needed.

Technologies that improve the bioavailability of minerals, reduce bulk and control release (e.g. potassium supplements), improve shelf life (omega 3 fatty acids), and enhance the sensory characteristics of supplements would be welcome.

30.3.5 Future Challenges

30.3.5.1 Regulatory Philosophy

- Are there better ways to develop mechanisms and infrastructures to encourage voluntary compliance with standards, increase accountability, and decrease the political and economic risks of enforcement?
- How can governments ensure better monitoring and inspection so as to ensure high-quality products?
- How can the technical capabilities for production be enhanced in the private sector, particularly in cases where facilities are located in non-industrialized countries with weak regulatory infrastructures?

30.3.5.2 Nutrition and Epidemiology

- What roles do genetics and the microbiome have on the bioavailability and uptake of nutrients and other bioactives?
- Does the form in which a nutrient is consumed affect bioavailability, uptake, metabolism, or nutritional status, and if so, are there simple ways of measuring these effects?
- How can biomarkers be developed to better assess the nutritional status of several nutrients with respect to both intake and nutritional status (e.g. zinc)?
- How can national nutrition monitoring systems be encouraged to include nutrient-containing dietary supplements, rather than only intakes from food, in considering total nutrient exposures?

- How can better methods be developed for the modeling of population intakes, with sufficient samples at the extremes of the distribution (<5% and >95% intakes) to ensure better monitoring and to permit more scientific planning for fortification and supplementation?
- If nutrient fortification and supplementation give rise to excess, do they have the same effects on affluent populations in industrialized countries who suffer from obesity, diet-related non-communicable diseases and caloric excess as they do in populations in developing countries with more deficiencies?

30.3.5.3 Food Science

- How can formulations of multivitamin-mineral supplements, especially for those at the highest nutritional risk (i.e., children, pregnant women and the elderly) be tailored to better reflect the nutrient requirements and gaps that are present in those groups?
- How can more complete dietary supplement databases of ingredients and label claims be developed and disseminated?
- To what extent do label claims reflect analytical values for the bioactives in dietary supplement products?
- How can better and less costly methods be developed to detect the spiking, contamination and adulteration of dietary supplements so as to ensure product safety?
- Should nano-materials be permitted as dietary supplement ingredients, and if so, how should they be regulated?

30.4 The Way Forward

The urgent task going forward is for nutrition scientists to use all the tools available to ensure that total nutrient intakes of the population will be adequate but not excessive. Table 30.2 presents some of the many concepts that need further development in the future.

Population-based surveys will continue to be essential to monitor safety and to identify problems associated with deficits or excesses of nutrient intake, and in what subgroups these problems exist. Oversampling may be advisable in groups at risk of deficiency (e.g. the very old, the very young, or the chronically ill).

Models for predicting or assessing the effects of nutrients and other bioactives on chronic disease outcomes need refinement. For nutrient/chronic disease associations, there are existing models for a few nutrients, such as fluoride and dental caries. For non-nutrient bioactives with possibly beneficial health effects but which may also have adverse effects, little evidence is available, and models must be developed.

Table 30.2 Likely future developments in food fortification and dietary supplementation: issues and concepts

Regulatory philosophy and policy
Gain a better understanding of the philosophy and regulatory stances that lead to different regulations governing fortification and supplementation from country to country
Develop better systems for reporting adverse events from dietary supplement and fortificant use
Document and understand the potential unintended consequences of high nutrient exposures
Assess the comparative effectiveness and impact of fortification and supplementation on health care costs
Strengthen information and education provided to health professionals on the benefits and limitations of fortification and supplementation
Develop better payment schemes or other incentives to ensure the use of dietary supplements by those most at risk (e.g. prescription of prenatal supplements during pregnancy)
Develop improved fortification and supplementation targeted to reach those at greatest risk
Strengthen the evidence base for recommendations for non-nutrient bioactives such as phytosterols, and, if evidence of possible benefits exists, assess their suitability as fortificants in selected staples [21]
Nutrition and epidemiology
Assess the impact of the active form of vitamin D in meats on vitamin D nutritional status
Review the evidence for the effectiveness of existing programs, such as flour fortification programs and their effects on anemia [22]
Perform more rigorous evaluation of the effects of commonly used nutrient fortificants and supplements on disease risks and outcomes (examples: vitamin D and cancers; omega 3 and primary prevention of cardiovascular disease; selenium and prostate cancer)
Food science and technology
Develop better, more complete, databases for dietary supplement labels and analytical values
Characterize the safety and effects of extracts of commonly marketed botanicals (e.g. green tea extracts, capsaicin extracts)
Improve supplement quality in countries where standards are poor
Develop sophisticated methods for determining contaminants and adulterants in supplements
Develop methods to detect supplements spiked with illegal or prescription drugs
Develop better fortificants (e.g. develop more absorbable forms [such as ferrous gluconate in the case of iron] that cost less for zinc, magnesium and other nutrients)
Explore the costs and benefits of bio-fortification and where it has a place
Develop methods for identifying fortified products and supplements with inadequate or excessive amounts of nutrients
Study the risks and benefits of nanotechnology, and develop effective regulations for this technology
Revise food staple vehicles for fortification if dietary intakes change: iodine in salt, vitamin D in milk

Closer collaboration will be vital between nutrition scientists, toxicologists and policy makers in model development. Statistical modeling and risk assessment methods must be more highly developed and must better integrate nutritional and toxicological concepts. The study of nutrient requirements calls for the use of risk-risk models and the understanding of U-shaped risk curves, since consuming both too little and too much may have adverse effects on health. The association between nutrient intakes and later risks of chronic disease remains uncertain. Although methods for estimating nutrient requirements to avoid deficiency are well developed and are relatively easy to handle from the statistical standpoint, those for estimating upper safe or tolerable levels of nutrient intakes need further work. More data are needed to establish ULs with greater certainty, particularly in children. More uniformity is also needed in choosing the standards for the health outcomes that are used to define ULs of nutrient intakes. At present the ULs vary from one nutrient to another, and the criteria for assessing risk range from very mild to severe adverse events. The UL is difficult to handle statistically. With non-nutrient bioactives in fortificants and supplements, there may be no actual requirement, and it is unclear what dose-response relationships exist from the standpoint of safety. They are unlikely to be similar for all ingredients. There is little reason to think that the need for them, if in fact such a need exists, conforms to normal distributions.

More harmonization is desirable between research groups and countries in compiling, updating, and evaluating data on nutrient requirements, as well as on nutrient and non-nutrient ingredient safety and efficacy for ingredients used as fortificants and in dietary supplements. This approach may be particularly valuable for the myriad dietary supplements containing many poorly characterized ingredients that are not nutrients. Systematic evidence-based reviews resulting from these efforts can then be used as the basis for deliberations by scientific experts and by regulators to develop guidance based on sound science.

30.5 Summary: Key Messages

- Fortification and supplementation are two methods for improving nutritional status in highly industrialized countries where a diverse diet already exists. They have an important place when used judiciously in well-crafted programs to deliver nutrients to target groups at risk of insufficiency.
- Some nutrients are more amenable to fortification or supplementation than others.
- More comparative effectiveness studies of fortification and supplementation are needed.
- Marketing-driven fortification has little or no public health benefit and may have unintended risks.
- Care should be taken not to overpromise the benefits of fortification and supplementation; a well-balanced diet is critical to optimal health.
- Dietary supplements that provide nutrients that are low or lacking among specific population subgroups have beneficial effects. The public health rationale for non-nutrient supplements (plant food supplements) is unclear.

- Neither fortification nor supplementation can remedy all the diet-related problems of affluent countries, many of which also require dietary diversity, balance and moderation to achieve more healthful food patterns.

References

1. Bailey, R.L., Gahche JJ, Lentino CV, Dwyer JT, Engel JS, Thomas PR, Betz JM, Sempos CT, and Picciano MF, *Dietary supplement use in the United States, 2003–2006.* J Nutr, 2011. **141** (2): p. 261–6.
2. Bailey, R.L., Gahche JJ, Miller PE, Thomas PR, Dwyer JT., *Why US Adults Use Dietary Supplements.* JAMA Internal Medicine, 2013.
3. Schwitters B., Achanta G, van der Vlie D, Morisset H, Bost A, Hanekam JC, *The European regulation of food supplements and food fortification.* Environmental Law & Management, 2007. **19**(1): p. 19–29.
4. European Food Safety Authority, *European Union regulatory framework.* Available from: http://www.efsa.europa.eu/en/topics/topic/supplements.
5. Fulgoni, V.L., Keast DR, Bailey RL, DwyerJ., *Foods, fortificants, and supplements: Where do Americans get their nutrients?* J Nutr, 2011. **141**(10): p. 1847–54.
6. World Health Organization and Food and Agricultural Organization, *Guidelines on Food Fortification with Micronutrients*, L. Allen, de Benoist B, Dary O, Hurrell R., Editors. 2006, United Nations: Geneva.
7. West, K.P., Stewart, C.P., Caballero, B., Black, R.E., *Nutrition*, in *Global Health: Diseases, Programs, Systems, and Policies. Third Edition.*, M.H. Merson, Black, R.E., Mills, A.J., Editor. 2012, Jones & Bartlett Learning. p. 271–304.
8. Dwyer, J.T., Woteki C, Bailey R, Britten P, Carriquiry A, Miller D, Moshfegh A, Murphy M, Smith-Edge M., *Fortification: new findings and implications.* Nutr Rev, 2014. **72**(2): p. 127–41.
9. MacKerras D, Thomas D, March J, Hazelton J Chapter 24 Food fortification: a regulator's perspective. In Handbook of Food Fortification and Health: From Concepts to Public Health Applications volumes Preedy VR, Srirajaskantin R, Patel VB editors 2013 pg 305–318 Springer Science and Business, New York.
10. World Health Organization and Food and Agricultural Organization. *Codex Alimentarius: International Food Standards.* 2015; Available from: http://www.codexalimentarius.org/.
11. Crane, N.T., Wilson DB, Cook DA, Lewis CJ, Yetley EA and Rader JI, *Evaluating food fortification options: general principles revisited with folic acid.* Am J Public Health, 1995. **85**(5): p. 660–6.
12. Sacco, J.E., Dodd KW, Kirkpatrick SF, Tarasuk V, *Voluntary food fortification in the United States: potential for excessive intakes.* Eur J Clin Nutr, 2013. **67**(6): p. 592–7.
13. Swanson, C.A., Zimmerman MB, Skeaff S, Pearce EN, Dwyer JT, Trumbo PR, Zehaluk C, Andrews KW, Carriquiry A, Caldwell KL, Egan SK, Long SE, Bailey RL, Sullivan KM, Holden JM, Betz JM, Phinney KW, Brooks SPJ, Johnson CL, Haggans CJ., *Summary of an NIH workshop to identify research needs to improve the monitoring of iodine status in the United States and to inform the Dietary Reference Intakes.* J Nutr, 2012. **142**(6): p. 1175S–85S.
14. Codex Alimentarius Commission, *General Principles for the Addition of Essential Nutrients to Foods* (CAC/GL 9-1987) Revised 2015, 2015 World Health Organization. Available at www.codexalimentarius.org/input/download/…CXG_0093_2015.pdf.
15. Lewis, CJ., Crane NT, Wilson DB and Yetley EA., *Estimated folate intakes: data updated to reflect food fortification, increased bioavailability, and dietary supplement use.* Am J Clin Nutr, 1999. **70**(2): p. 198–207.

16. Dietary Guidelines Advisory Committee, *Report of the Dietary Guidelines Advisory Committee on the Dietary Guidelines for Americans, 2010, to the Secretary of Agriculture and the Secretary of Health and Human Services*. 2010, Agricultural Research Service US Department of Agriculture: Washington DC.

17. Codex Alimentarius Commission, *Guidelines for Vitamin and Mineral Food Supplements*. 2005, World Health Organization. Available at www.codexalimentarius.org/input/download/standards/…/cxg_055e.pdf.

18. Bailey, R.L., Fulgoni VL, Keast DR, Dwyer JT., *Examination of vitamin intakes among US adults by dietary supplement use*. J Acad Nutr Diet, 2012. **112**(5): p. 657–663 e4.

19. Bailey, R.L., Fulgoni VL, Keast DR, Lentino CV, Dwyer JT, *Do dietary supplements improve micronutrient sufficiency in children and adolescents?* J Pediatr, 2012. **161**(5): p. 837–42.

20. Committee on Uses of the Dietary Reference Intakes in Nutrition Labeling, Institute of Medicine, *Dietary Reference Intakes: Guiding Principles for Nutrition Labeling and Fortification*, in *Dietary Reference Intakes: Guiding Principles for Nutrition Labeling and Fortification*. 2003, National Academies Press: Washington, DC.

21. Bielsalski HK, Erdman JW, Hathcock J, Ellwood K, Betty S, Johnson E, Marcholi R, Launtsen L, Rice HB, Shao A, Griffiths JC *Nutrient reference values for bioactives: new approaches needed? A conference report* Eur J Nutr doi10.1007/500394-013-0503-0 published online on March 1, 2013.

22. Pachon H, Spohrer R, Mei Z, Serdula MK *Evidence of the effectiveness of flour fortification programs on iron status and anemia: a systematic review* Nutrition Reviews 2015 doi:10.1093/nutrit/nuv037 accessed October 7, 2015.

Printed by Printforce, the Netherlands